DESIGN MUSEUM

A–Z of Design & Designers

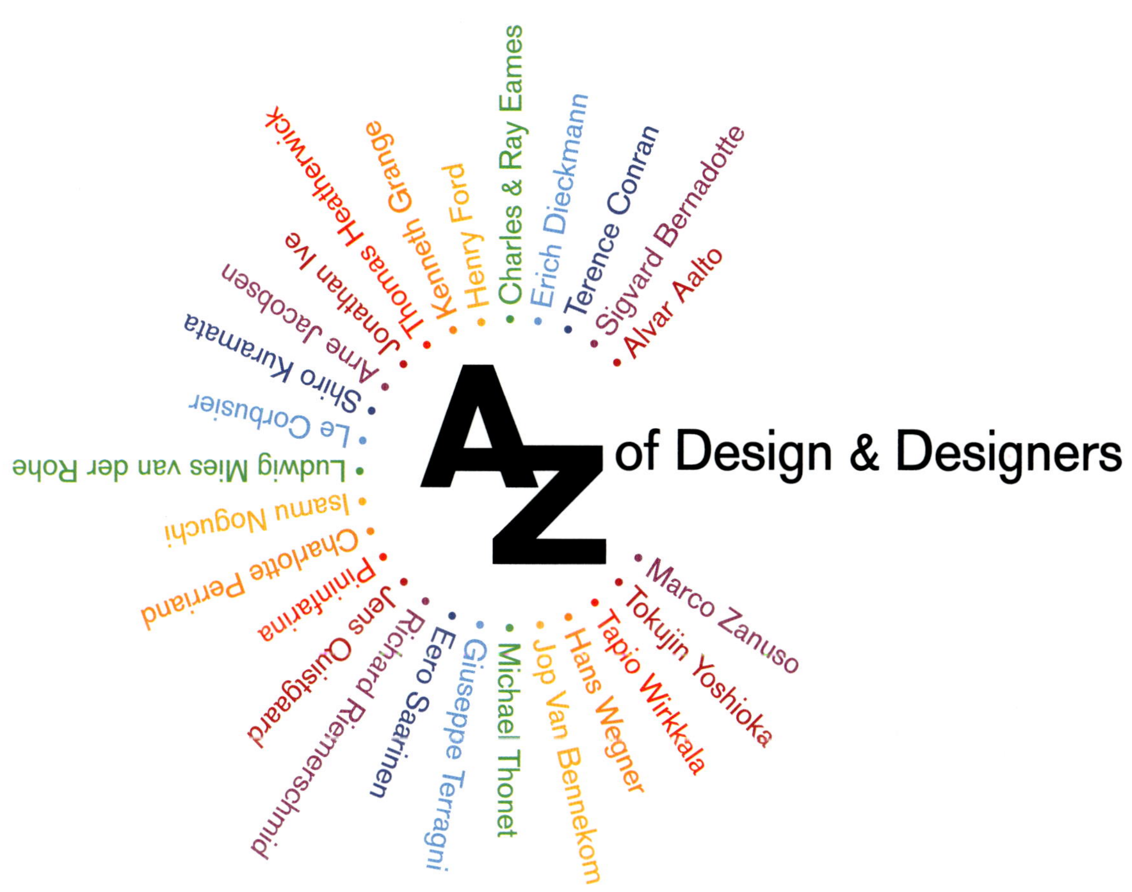

Published in 2016 by Goodman Fiell
An imprint of the Carlton Publishing Group
20 Mortimer Street
London W1T 3JW

10 9 8 7 6 5 4 3 2 1

A CIP catalogue record for this book is available from the British Library.

ISBN 978 1 78313 005 4

Printed in China

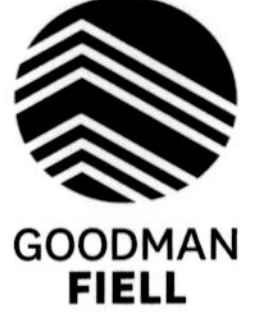

Jacket Picture Credits
Spine: Model 1227 task light designed by George Carwardine for Herbert Terry & Sons, c.1938 (Anglepoise). Back cover (clockwise from left): Kaivo textile for Marimekko, designed by Maija Isola, 1964 (Marimekko); Bibliothèque shelving unit for Ateliers Jean Prouvé and André Chetaille, designed by Charlotte Perriand, 1952 (Image courtesy of Wright, Chicago); Seagram Building in New York City, designed by Ludwig Mies van der Rohe, 1958 (Wikimedia Commons); BAT 5 concept car for Alfa Romeo designed by Bertone, 1953 (Wikimedia Commons).

DESIGN MUSEUM

A–Z of Design & Designers

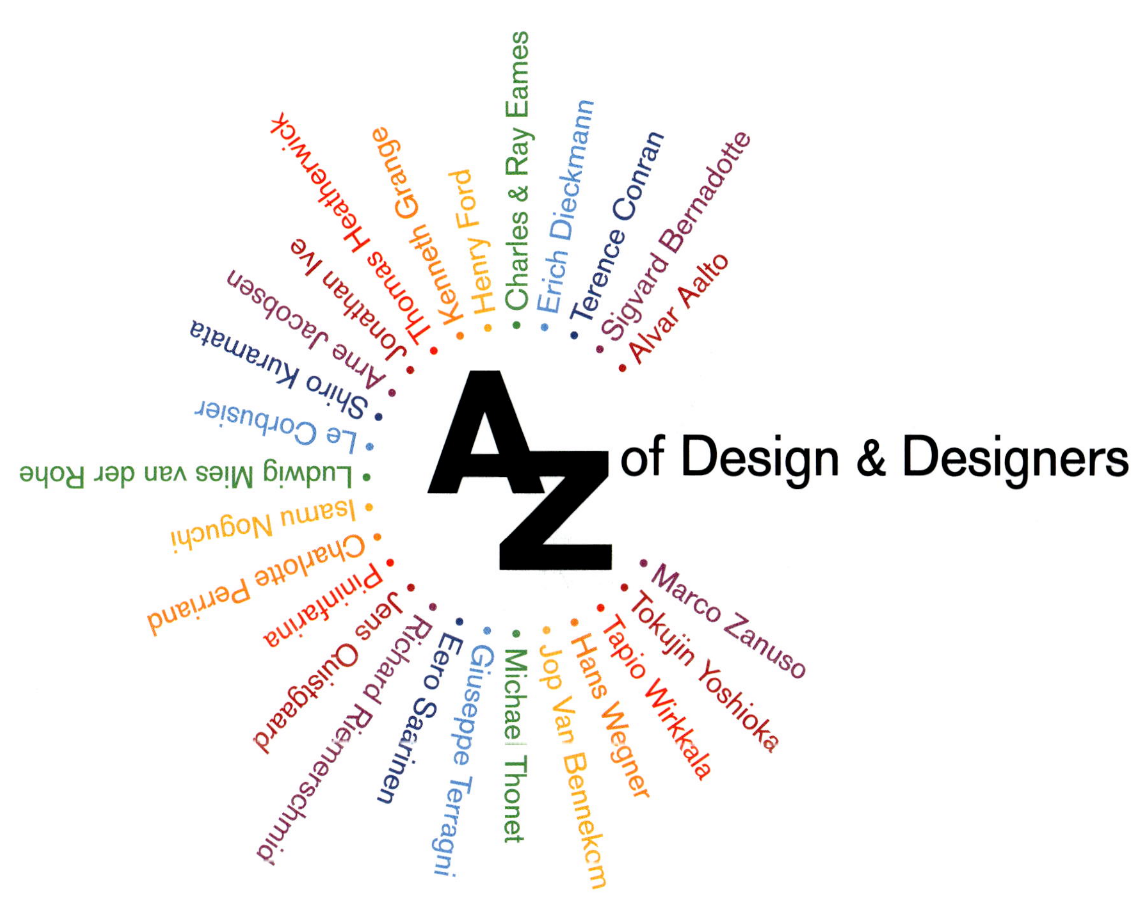

Charlotte &
Peter Fiell

Introduction by
Deyan Sudjic
Director of the Design Museum

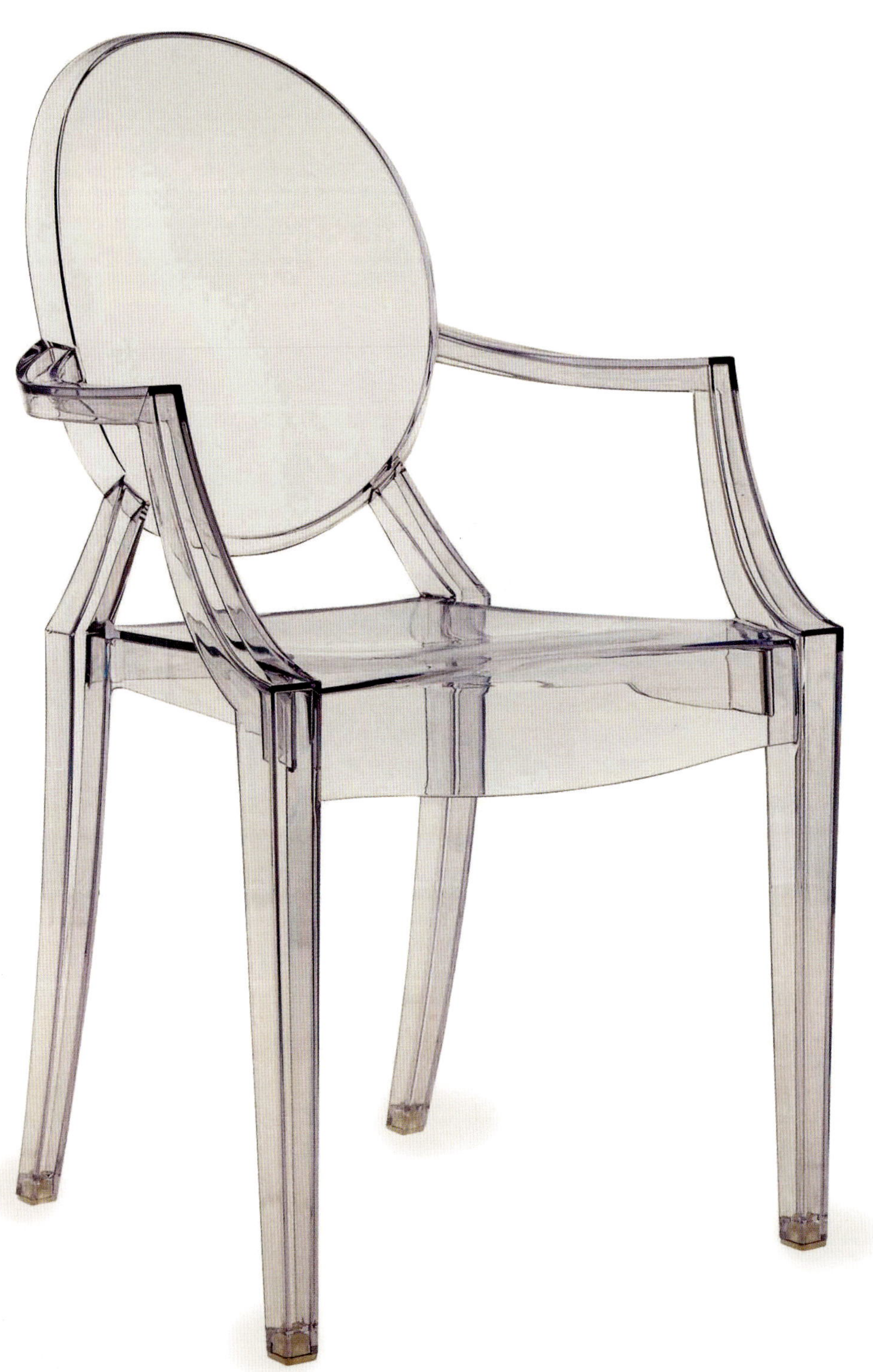

Contents

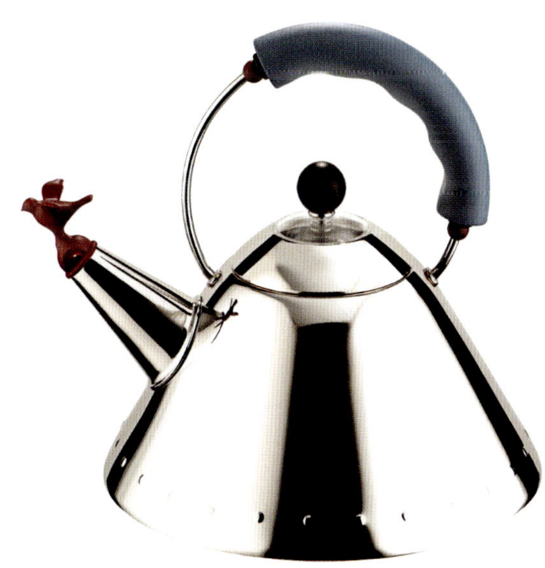

Introduction

The inspiration for this book is the Design Museum's online library of biographical reference, based on its exhibitions programme and built up over the years since it opened in 1989. In that time, the library has provided an introduction to the subject for the museum's visitors and a lasting resource for the curious everywhere.

This book goes further and deeper, and contains a wide range of entries that cover individual designers, manufacturers, schools and movements that have been selected, researched and written by Peter and Charlotte Fiell. They are not encyclopaedic in their scope, but focus primarily on architecture, industrial design, product design, transportation, communications and furniture, from the twentieth and twenty-first centuries. Taken as a whole, the book charts the roots of contemporary design in the Arts and Crafts tradition and the recent transition of design from the analogue to the digital world. The entries combine basic data with subjective opinion – subjective both in the detailed content of individual entries and in the balance of the overall selection. These choices reflect a particular perspective on the subject, as well as the evolution of the study of design since the museum was established and the particular circumstances around its beginnings.

In 1983 Terence Conran, perhaps the most successful design entrepreneur of his generation, and the critic Stephen Bayley established what was to become the Design Museum as a gallery within the Victoria and Albert Museum, known as the Boilerhouse Project. It was in part at least a polemical attempt to remind the V&A of its origins as an institution exploring new technologies and new thinking about mass production. The V&A had its roots in the Great Exhibition of 1851 and was conceived by Sir Henry Cole as a place that would inspire and educate consumers and offer manufacturers the chance to find new ways to overtake their international competitors. In its earliest incarnation, in Marlborough House, before the museum moved to South Kensington, Cole showed a variety of examples of textiles, ceramics, glass and metalware that he believed set a standard, alongside the so-called chamber of horrors – a gallery of what he regarded as "bad" design. His finger wagging earned him the mockery of Charles Dickens, in its attempt to prescribe taste for others. But Cole at least had the good grace and wit to concede that it was the most popular part of his display. It also set the template for the concept of "good" design; a term which came to take on a quasi-moral aspect that persists to this day. It may no longer be the application of applied decorative ornament in the form of a stencil-painted wheatsheaf motif to a pop-up toaster that attracts moral opprobrium as it once did. But good design is now seen to rest in the virtues of water pumps and sanitation systems devised for use in *favelas*, rather than in weapon systems, no matter how technologically advanced, or in the seduction of consumers with form, colour and material.

It was not long however before the V&A became something else – a museum of the decorative arts. It evolved from Cole's time into a treasure house of exquisite objects from every part of the world and from almost every period in history, going as far back as the fourth millennium BC. It became a place for the connoisseur of the exquisite, as represented by one of its directors in the 1970s, Sir John Pope-Hennessy, who knew a great deal about Italian Renaissance sculpture but, as Reyner Banham found to his dismay, had little interest in

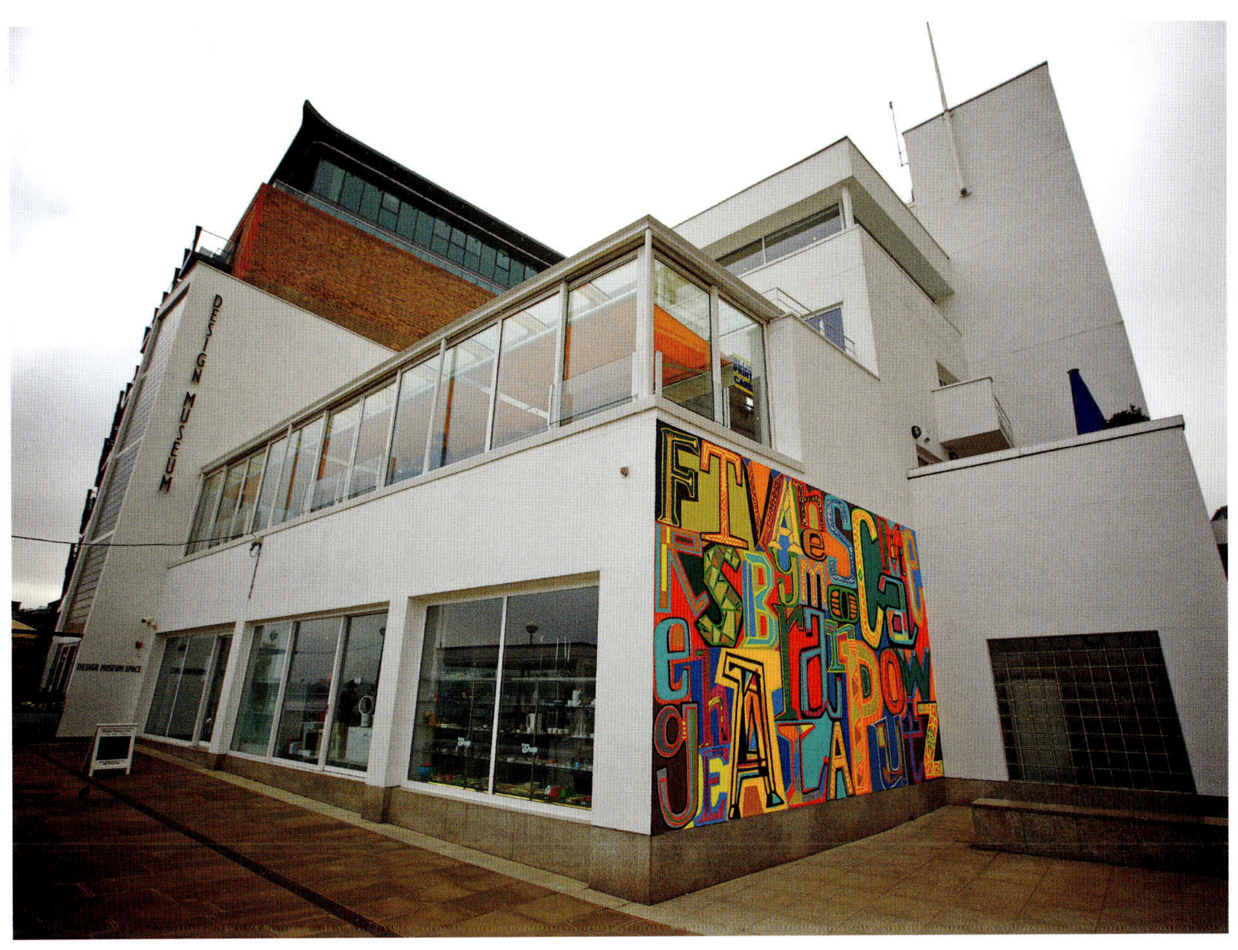

ABOVE:
Design Museum
Shad Thames, 1989–2016

the products of twentieth-century industrial design. If such things were allowed into the V&A at all, it was through the increasingly marginalized "circulating collections" condescended to by more academic keepers as they pursued what was regarded as the more elevated study of artefacts untainted by concerns of modern commerce. Mark Haworth-Booth recalls the day in 1972 when the critic and architectural historian Reyner Banham's plans for an exhibition entitled *Invention and Design* were rejected.

> We hoped that it would stimulate a broader appreciation of design. Banham briskly disposed of the idea of twentieth-century design classics. The century, he declared, had only produced one design classic in its first three score years and ten – the Barcelona chair, by Mies van der Rohe. And that, he added, "could have been made in any century at all since the forging of steel became possible". He wrote: "Designs for the technology and production processes of our time must be provisional, temporary – they illuminate their period rather than the eternal values of the human condition. If they don't date, they are in some senses suspect [...] there is no point in having high technology unless

> it improves the product in some sense, and each technological improvement erodes, or completely removes, the basic assumptions on which the designer based his conception. Thus the significant products of a culture are true only to their time, and their times may be very short."
>
> Banham's proposal for the show involved a study of chairs, bicycles, radios, typewriters, telephones and kitchen appliances. All that was required was the approval of the V&A's director, Sir John Pope-Hennessy [...] Sir John listened to the proposal and then told us of a visit he had recently made to the Moderna Museet in Stockholm. There he had seen, he said, a marvellous exhibition about kitchen design. This would surely be a far more interesting subject. There was an appalled silence, into which I inserted the question, "Yes, but how do you define what belongs in a kitchen?" The Pope's reply was unhesitating: "I don't know, I never go into my kitchen."

It was exactly such attitudes that the Design Museum attempted to overturn. Conran and Bayley went to Roy Strong, Pope-Hennessy's successor, and were given the space to set up the Boilerhouse and to use it for exhibitions of the kind that Banham had in mind.

Among other things, Conran and Bayley explored the history of Sony, the branding of Coca-Cola and the design of a new Ford car. It marked the acceptance in Britain of a new approach to the subject of design that had been many years in the making.

The V&A had been the first institution to set a model for collecting contemporary design when it took on the artefacts acquired from the Great Exhibition. It inspired a string of other museums of applied art, as they were called, across Europe, from Vienna to Frankfurt and Paris to Moscow. But once the energy of their initial founding impetus had petered out, they either moved towards art and history, with greater or lesser degrees of success, or else they faded into dusty and unvisited irrelevance. The V&A had its Raphael cartoons and its Canova sculpture. In Vienna at the Museum für Angewandte Kunst one reforming director brought in a selection of fashionable contemporary artists, from Donald Judd to Jenny Holzer, to rehang the collection in an attempt to attract a new audience.

It was only in the 1920s that the Museum of Modern Art in New York offered an alternative to the V&A's founding vision. At MoMA, which was essentially a museum dedicated to a particular cultural movement – Modernism, architecture and design, in so far as they reflected the values and visual essence of that movement, were allowed into the collection, provided that they were presented as if they were a variety of sculpture. In those early days of MoMA what an object looked like was considered of greater significance than what it did or how it was made or who used it.

An actual ball bearing was shown in MoMA at the same time as a Leger painting of a ball bearing. In the catalogue it is described exactly as if it were an artwork, with material, size, date, and artist's name.

The Boilerhouse and its evolution into the Design Museum made the development of a third model possible. In time it was able to move from focussing on the idea of "good" design, from understanding design as sculpture, towards an exploration of the many meanings of design, some of which are to be understood as concerned with utilitarian problem solving.

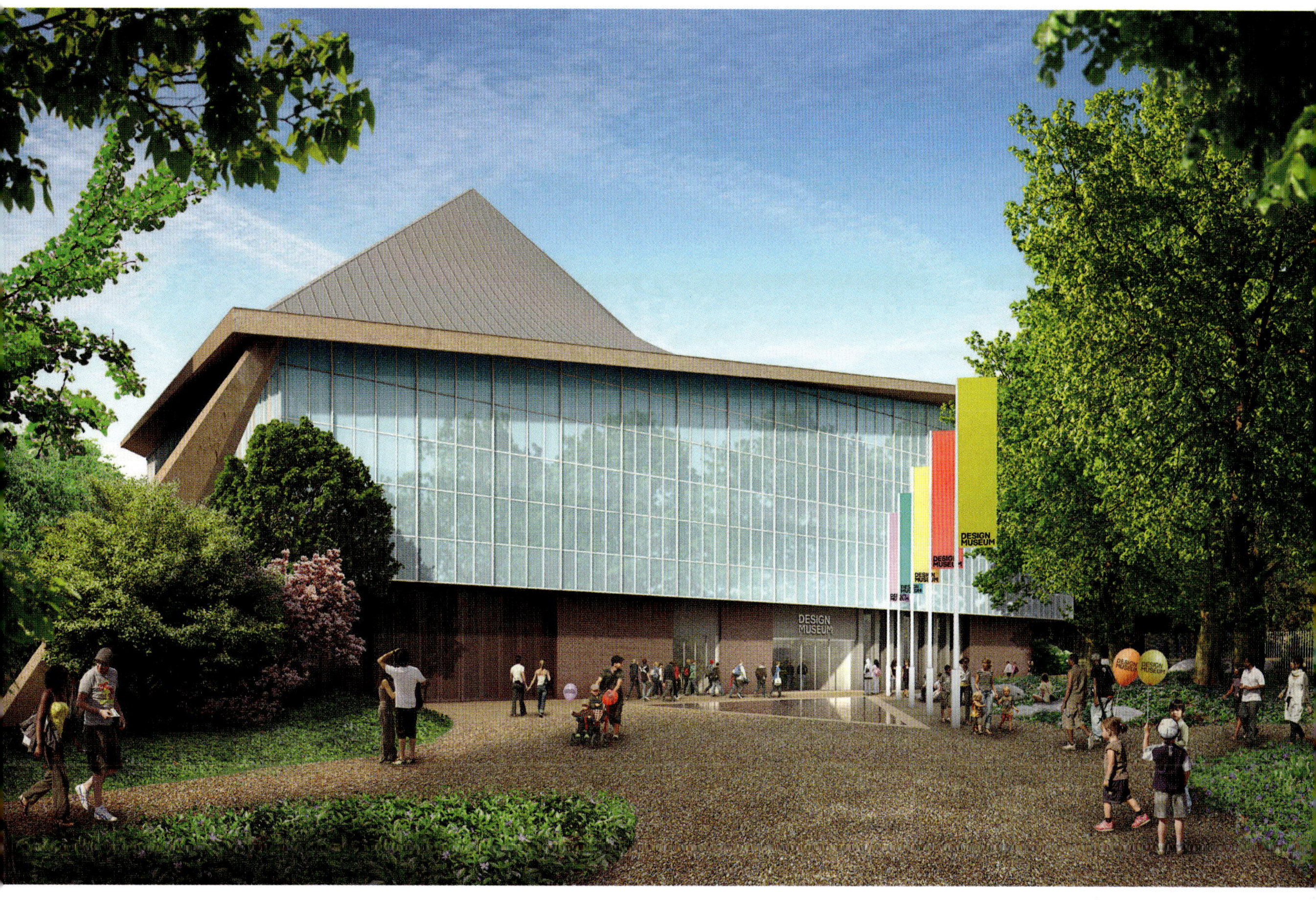

ABOVE:
Exterior view of new Design Museum
John Pawson, 2016

But equally it is also possible to use design as a critical tool to ask questions about the world, rather than to solve problems or to stimulate consumers to consume.

Ideas about museums do not take shape in an intellectual vacuum. In the English speaking world, Nikolaus Pevsner's book *Pioneers of Modern Design: From William Morris to Walter Gropius* was perhaps the first coherent narrative account of the emergence of design as a distinct discipline to gain a wide readership, even if Siegfried Gideon had a more layered view of the subject in *Mechanization Takes Command*. Pevsner approached design as an evangelist for Modernism. In his view the Bauhaus offered the final word on logic, reason and appropriateness. In attempting to connect his work to the anti-machine utopianism of William Morris he established a reassuring pedigree for attitudes that his English readers might otherwise find unnervingly disconcerting. Pevsner's survey approach was followed in the 1970s and 1980s by Stephen Bayley's *In Good Shape*, published by the Design Council, which formed a kind of manifesto for the Boilerhouse in its analysis of a chronological succession of objects. *Objects of Desire* by Adrian Forty went further and successfully injected semiotics and politics into the discussion.

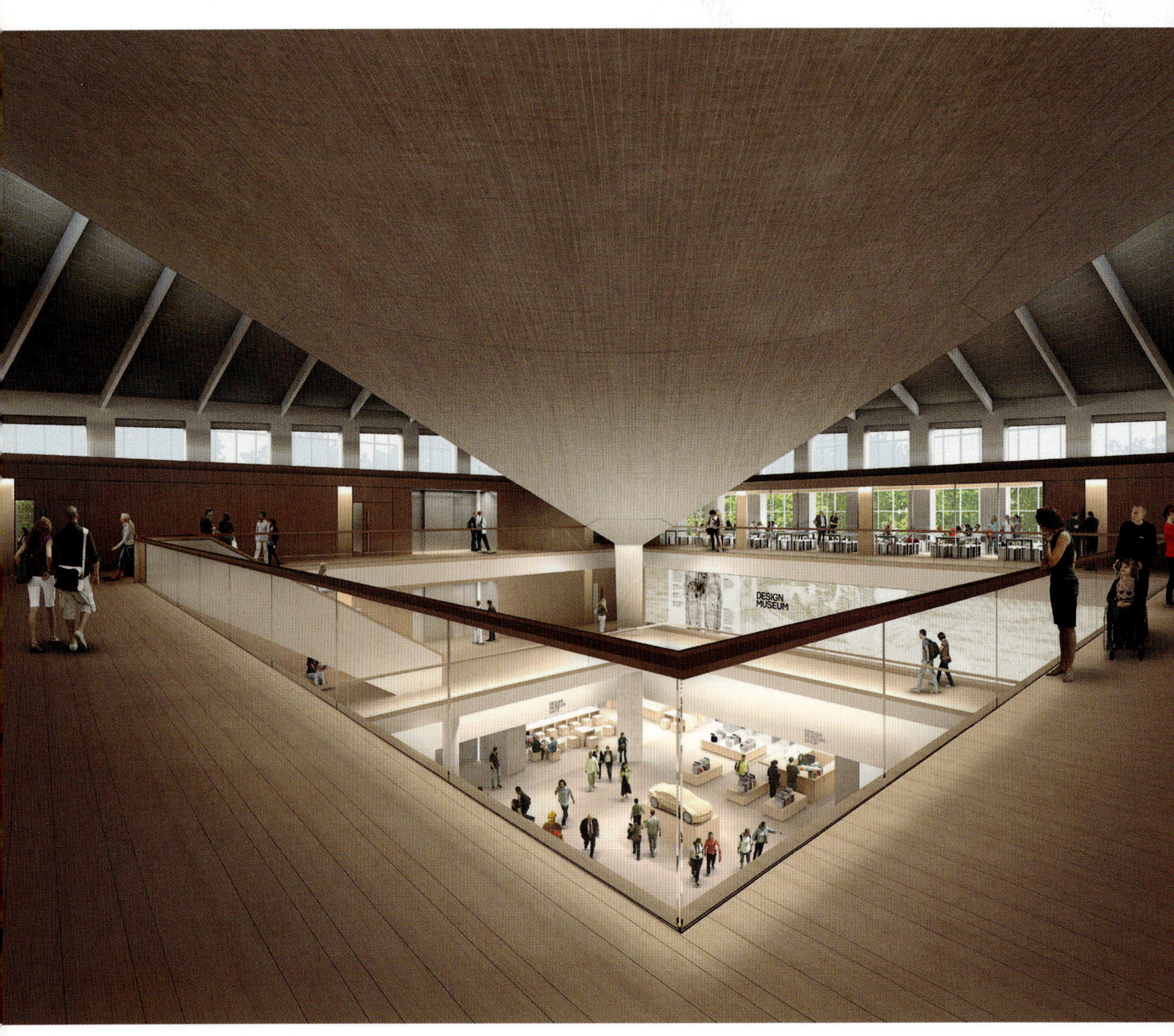

ABOVE:
Visualization of second floor of new Design Museum
John Pawson, 2016

What distinguishes design in general, as opposed to narrower definitions of the subject – furniture design for example, or typography – is that it does not remain static as a discipline. When the Boilerhouse metamorphosed into the Design Museum, in its own home in a converted banana-ripening warehouse at Shad Thames, it would have been possible to give a convincing account of design through a well-chosen selection of chairs. This selection would have traced the technological development from handcraft to mass production: from the bentwood of Michael Thonet, through the tubular steel cantilever, associated with Marcel Breuer and the Bauhaus, to the fibreglass of the Eames. It would have charted a technological and aesthetic shift; one that echoed a series of stylistic developments.

But design is now moving beyond the object. The very idea of good design, with its moral connotations, has come to seem something of a period piece, associated with a very particular moment. Design is now about methods and systems; it is about the intangible and the critical, as well as the utilitarian.

The range of entries in this book reflects this trajectory of the understanding of design and its emergence from its roots in the Arts and Crafts to the radicalism of critical design that first began to make itself felt in the 1960s. It is about consumer products and software, the Bauhaus and Charles and Ray Eames, about Apple and Jonathan Ive. It takes us from Alvar Aalto to the graphic design of Jonathan Barnbrook. It charts the shift from the Arts and Crafts to Post-Modernism and beyond. It looks at the significance of Margarete Schütte-Lihotzky's Frankfurt Kitchen and the kettle that Michael Graves designed for Alessi. It shows the impact of Ettore Sottsass's revolutionary red Valentine Typewriter for Olivetti as well as that of Sony's Walkman.

The entries provide an introduction to the architectural developments since the Bauhaus, recognizing the impact that architectural thinking has had on the wider range of design philosophies.

It looks at how Thonet introduced mass production to furniture making and transformed the relationship of the individual to their possessions. There are individual designers represented from every generation and attitude, from the elegant restraint of Massimo and Lella Vignelli, Italians who transplanted themselves to America after the Second World War, to Tokujin Yoshioka, one of the younger Japanese, who has experimented with form and challenging materials.

In 2016 the Design Museum moved into its new home, the former Commonwealth Institute – a Mid-Century Modern landmark, transformed for its new purpose by John Pawson. It will go on tracing the evolution of design and its continuing significance as a discipline through which to understand the world around us.

Deyan Sudjic, Director, Design Museum

Alvar Aalto

Finnish, 1898–1976

The most important Finnish architect of the twentieth century, Alvar Aalto was a central figure in international Modernism. His greatest buildings, like the Viipuri Library (1927–35) and Paimio Sanatorium (1928–33), fused the naturalism of Finnish National Romanticism with Modernist ideals – as did his influential furniture and glassware.

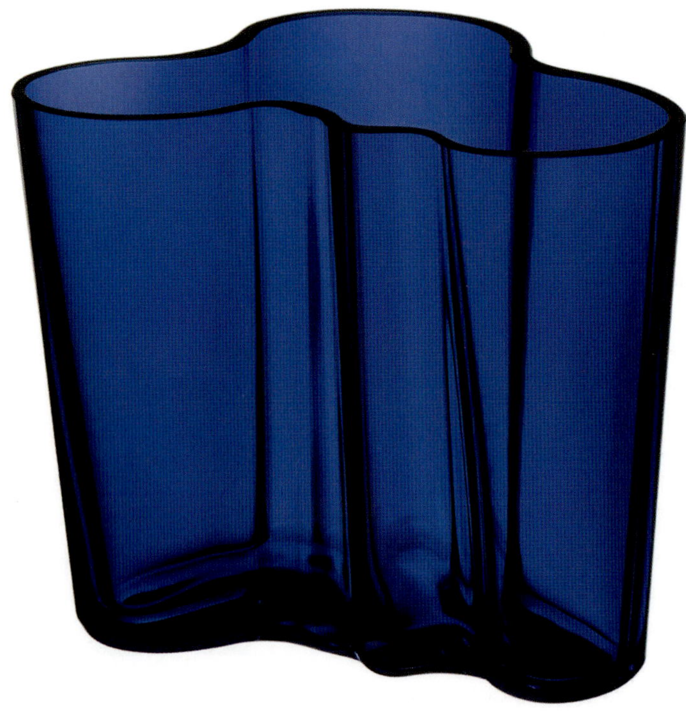

ABOVE:
Model No. 3031
Savoy Vase for Karhula (later Iittala), 1936

Having studied architecture at Helsinki Institute of Technology, Hugo Alvar Henrik Aalto initially worked for the Swedish architect Arvid Bjerke. He subsequently opened his own office in Jyväskylä in 1923. It could be said that Aalto's timing was flawless as Finland had won its independence in 1917 and by the mid-1920s there was no shortage of architectural commissions in the newly independent country, which was eager to forge its own distinctive national identity. Aalto was one of a group of young artists and intellectuals longing to play their part in Finland's cultural renaissance. They included the young architect Aino Marsio, whom he married in 1925. Initially, Aalto eked out a living as a journalist, while entering a series of architectural competitions. His early buildings were workers' housing and student clubs in Jyväskylä, but in 1927 Aalto won a commission for the Southwestern Finland Agricultural Cooperative Building in Turku. More liberal than Helsinki and closer to their growing circle of friends elsewhere in Europe, Turku so appealed to Alvar and Aino that they made it their home. By now Aalto was attracting attention from the Finnish media as much for his work as for his cosmopolitan intellectual sophistication.

Although having initially worked within the style of National Romanticism, Aalto's Turun Sanomat newspaper offices (1928–29), Viipuri Library and Paimio Sanatorium revealed the influence of the International Style, which he had admired on European trips. However, rather than simply replicating that style, he redefined it. In their scale, mastery of light and distinctive palettes, Aalto's buildings were characterized by a robust humanism. For instance, he designed the Paimio Sanatorium from the perspective of a patient and created a serene but cheering environment with an unerring attention to detail.

Aalto also designed all the sanatorium furniture, including the subsequently named Paimio chair (1931–32) which, although inspired by the tubular steel Marcel Breuer chairs in his own home, incorporated a combination of moulded laminated wood and plywood, which Aalto believed would be warmer and more comfortable for the patients using it than metal. On its completion in 1933, the Paimio Sanatorium was hailed by the influential critic Siegfried Giedion as a Modernist masterpiece, yet despite Aalto's growing prominence in international circles, he felt somewhat marginalized in Finland. After moving to Helsinki, he and Aino built a new home and studio in 1936. They also founded their own company, Artek, to manufacture their furniture designs.

Two years later, Aalto and Aino were asked to design the Savoy Restaurant in Helsinki. For this prestigious commission Aalto designed the gracefully curvaceous 1936 Savoy Vase – inspired, or so claimed Aalto, by "a young Eskimo [or Sami] girl's leather breeches" – which would presage the popularity of biomorphic forms during the post-war years. During the late 1930s, Aalto also designed the Villa Mairea for the industrialist and art collector Harry Gullichsen and his wife Maire, which in accord with the clients' wishes was both modern and Finnish with its masterful composition of logs, steel posts, concrete beams and grass roofs.

Around this period Aalto also designed his acclaimed pavilion for the 1937 Paris *Exposition Internationale des Arts et Techniques dans la Vie Moderne*, which ultimately led to an exhibition of his work at the Museum of Modern Art, New York, in 1938. The following year Aalto upped the ante in his design for the Finnish Pavilion at the New York World's Fair, which, like the earlier Villa Mairea, paid homage to the forms found in Finland's forests. Walking through it was like a magical forest stroll and led Frank Lloyd Wright to describe it as a work of genius. This landmark project solidified Aalto's reputation in the United States, where he was subsequently awarded visiting professorships and architectural commissions, including the Baker House Senior Dormitory (1946–49) at the Massachusetts Institute of Technology. By now firmly established as a world-class architect, Aalto went on to win a string of awards and constructed some notable buildings in Italy, Germany and France. He also received commissions from Iraq and Iran; however, these sadly remained unbuilt. Yet none of Aalto's post-war projects matched the lyrical quality of his pre-war work and as a result it is these early Finnish masterpieces for which he is now best remembered.

RIGHT:
Model No. 41
Paimio armchair for Artek, 1931–32

Apple

American, founded 1976

Becoming the world's most valuable company in 2012, Apple eloquently demonstrates the transformative power of good design. While many companies produce similarly well-made computers and other smart devices, Apple is arguably the only one that manufactures icons. The iMac, the iPhone, the iPad and the Apple Watch are devices revered by the company's many devotees for their excellent quality, born of designing not merely a product but a comprehensive product experience. As Apple's co-founder Steve Jobs so memorably noted, "Design is not just what it looks like and feels like. Design is how it works." And the reason that Apple products are so different from others on the market is that Apple's Chief Design Officer, Jonathan Ive, has the design wherewithal to translate the late tech guru's futuristic visions into beautiful easy-to-operate realities.

But in many ways this is not particularly surprising, since Apple was initially established in 1976 by Jobs and Steve Wozniak in order to make computer technology more user friendly. The pair's first computer, the Apple I, was released in 1976, but it was the follow-up Apple II,

BELOW:
Apple Macintosh 128K desktop computer,
1984

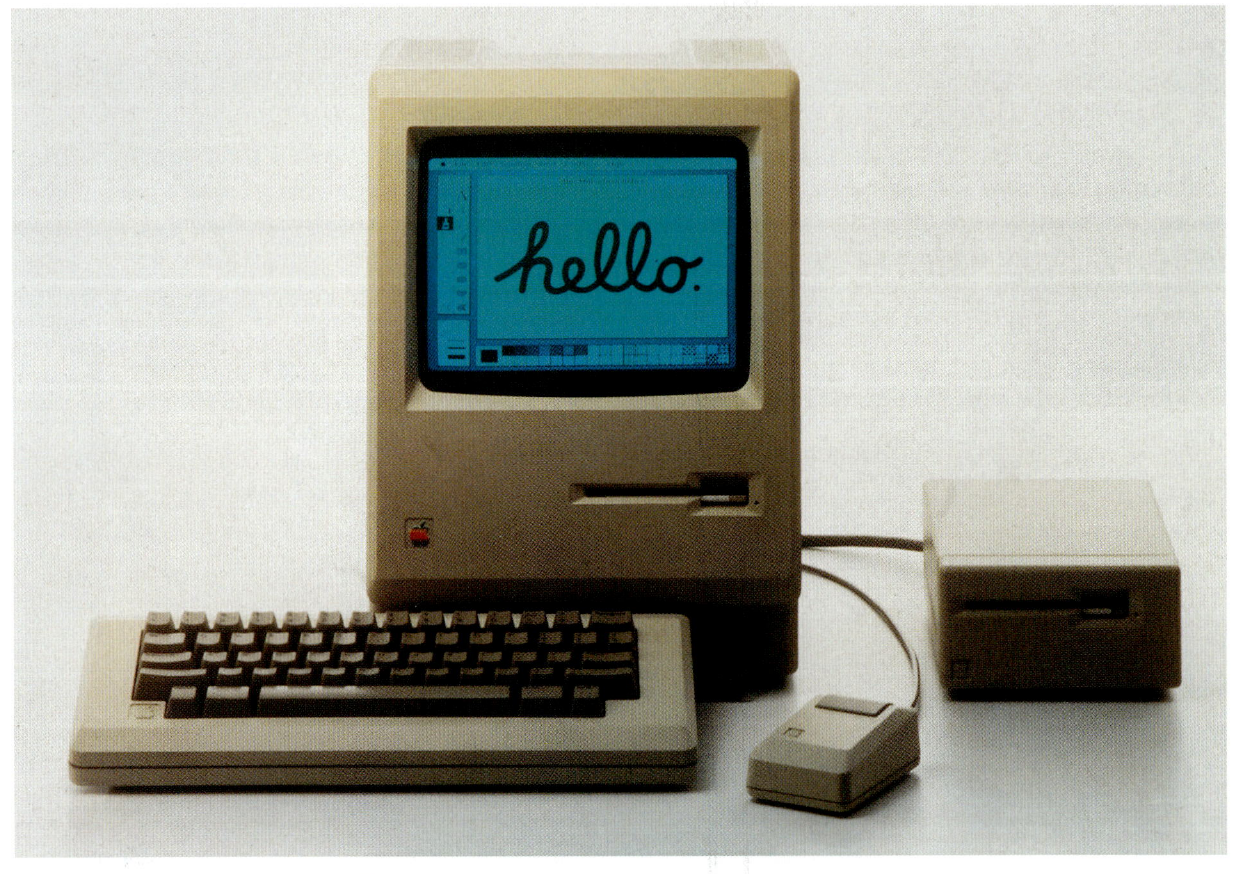

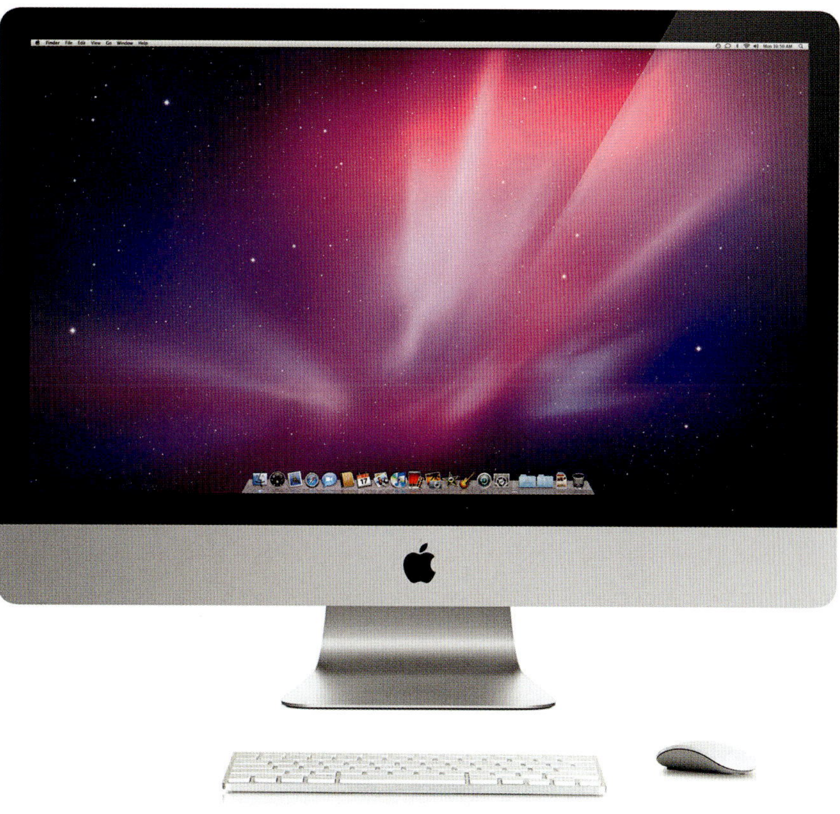

ABOVE:
iMac 27-inch desktop computer,
2015

launched the following year, that went on to revolutionize computing, becoming one of the very first commercially successful microcomputers. It was, however, the more refined Apple Macintosh launched in 1984 that marked a real breakthrough, not only for the company but also for personal computing in general. With its advanced GUI – graphic-user-interface – designed by Susan Kare, this desktop machine styled by frog design was much easier to understand and use than previous models. With its high-definition screen, integrated monitor, disk drive and handy mouse, it announced unequivocally the arrival of the home computer. Yet despite creating such a well-designed product, Jobs was ousted from Apple the year after its launch, and over the next decade Apple experienced what can only be described as a wilderness period. The company lost its exclusive rights to its icon-based interface and suffered from a surfeit of lower-priced PCs on the market. Although Apple's computers performed better, they were at this stage also far more expensive and as such functioned as somewhat niche products for the design and publishing industries, thanks to their superior graphics and publishing capabilities.

In 1996, however, Jobs returned to the fray and soon afterwards a crucial cross-licensing deal was agreed between Apple and long-term rival Microsoft. Two years later saw the launch of the revolutionary iMac. Designed by Ive, it redefined the personal computer with its visually unified gumdrop-shaped housing made of translucent polycarbonate. Not only did

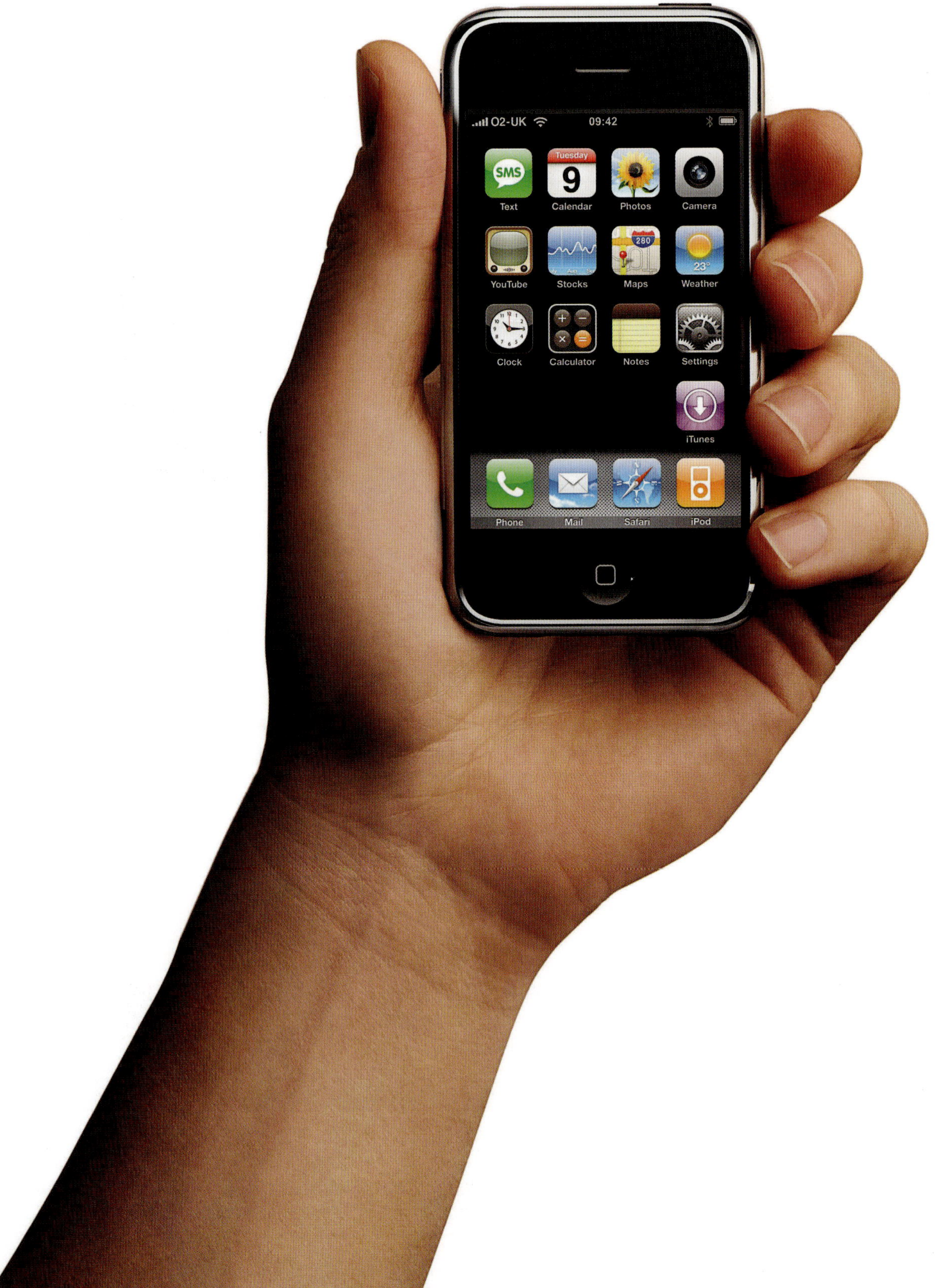

O2-UK
09:42
SMS
Text
Tuesday
9
Calendar
Photos
Camera
YouTube
Stocks
280
Maps
23°
Weather
Clock
Calculator
Notes
Settings
iTunes
Phone
Mail
Safari
iPod

OPPOSITE:
iPhone,
2007

BELOW:
Apple Watch,
2014

the iMac transform the look of the desktop computer into a stylish and emotionally engaging object of desire, but crucially it also reversed the declining fortunes of Apple. Even more importantly, Ive's radical new design managed powerfully to differentiate Macs from PCs, and people who bought into its seductive looks subsequently came to appreciate the company's superior user-friendly closed operating systems. Once the emotional connection had been forged between an iMac and its user, those users were far more likely to buy other Apple products too – and that is exactly what they did, with the first iPod introduced in 2001, the first iPhone in 2007 and the first iPad in 2010.

The number of Apple devices that has been subsequently sold is staggering, especially when one considers that they are all premium-priced products. This testifies to the belief that good design makes good business sense and that there is a ready market for products which have been carefully designed to make life easier. This is especially true in today's digitally connected world when the interface between modern users and the complex technology on which they increasingly rely needs to be made as intuitive as possible.

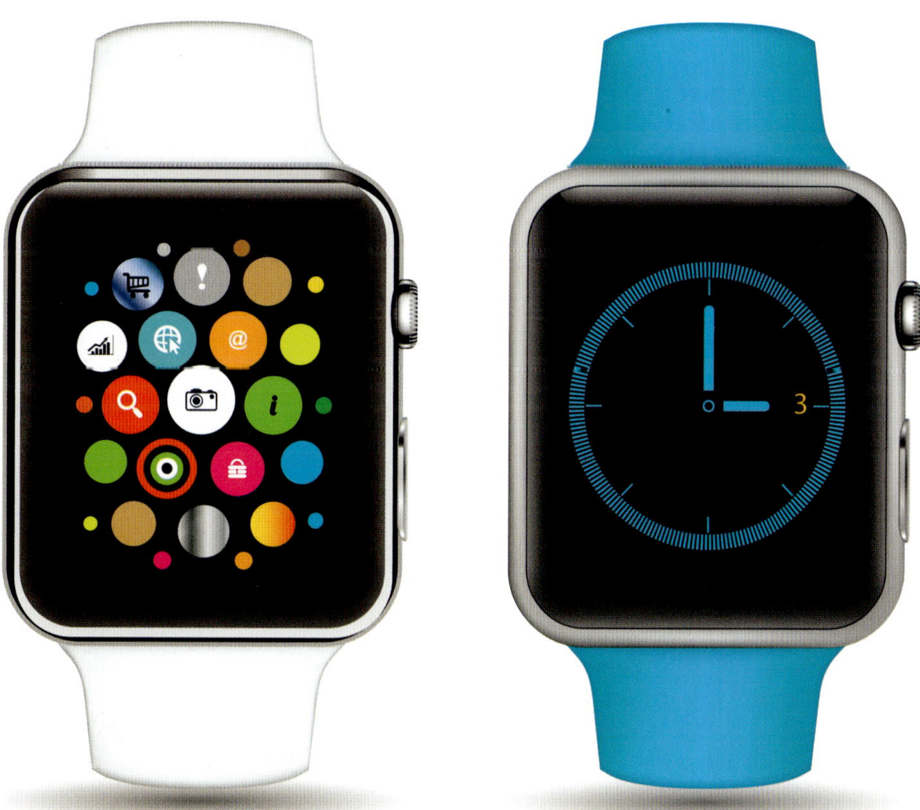

Ron Arad

Israeli/active Britain, 1951–

A celebrated and highly creative architect-designer, Ron Arad playfully subverts existing notions of design in order to create objects – from one-off pieces to mass-produced furnishings – that are not only sculptural accomplishments but also highly innovative in terms of function and the deployment of materials. Born in Tel Aviv to artistic parents, Arad initially studied at the Bezalel Academy of Art and Design in Jerusalem, before moving to London in 1973 in order to continue his training at the Architectural Association School of Architecture. The AA was then one of the most innovative and dynamic architectural teaching institutions in the world and, while there, Arad was extremely fortunate to study under Peter Cook (b.1936), the founder of the avant-garde and futuristic architectural group Archigram, and the Deconstructivist architect Bernard Tschumi (b.1944). Being taught to think outside the normal parameters of architectural practice by these two legendary educators held Arad in extremely good stead when he eventually graduated in 1979.

Newly qualified, he did a brief stint at an architecture practice, which convinced him to go it alone as a designer-maker. To this end, he set up his own company, One Off, with Caroline Thorman in 1981. This new venture created furniture pieces that bridged the gap between the late 1970s High-Tech style and the early 1980s Creative Salvage movement – using Kee-Klamp scaffolding and combining it with a reclaimed seat from a Rover 2000 car, Arad created one of his most iconic designs, the Rover chair of 1981. This was followed by his stereo of 1983 fashioned in concrete and which, with its rough-and-ready aesthetic, "captured London's early 1980s spirit of rugged individualism and post-punk nihilism set against a backdrop of urban blight" according to a press release for a Design Museum exhibition. Setting himself up as a designer-maker almost by necessity proved to be a fortuitous decision in the long run: Arad's one-off pieces, such as his Big Easy chair of 1988, became prized trophies for a new generation of "design-art" collectors emerging in the late 1980s and early 1990s. His work also attracted the attention of the Swiss manufacturer Vitra, for whom he created the Well-Tempered chair in 1986, as a limited-edition design. Following this, Moroso, the Italian furniture manufacturer, translated some of Arad's one-off metal designs into soft upholstered production pieces and subsequently launched them as the Spring Collection in 1991. More affordable

BELOW:
Rover chair
for One Off, 1981

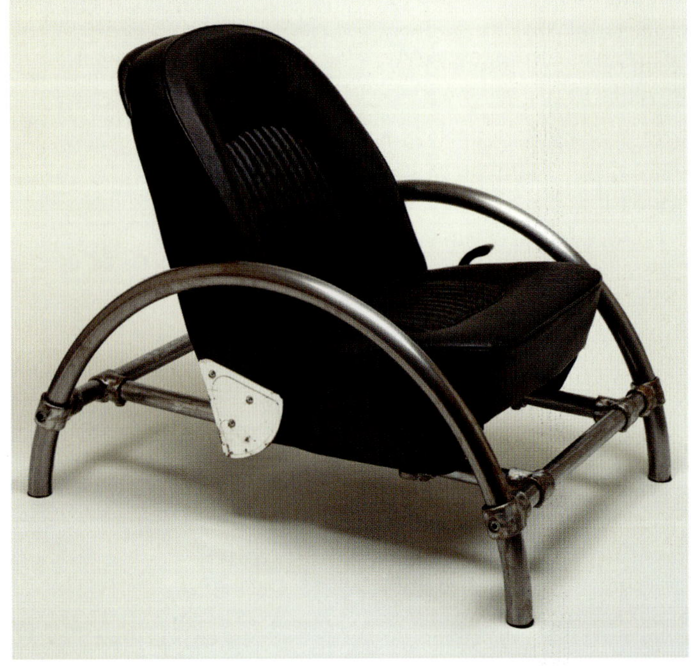

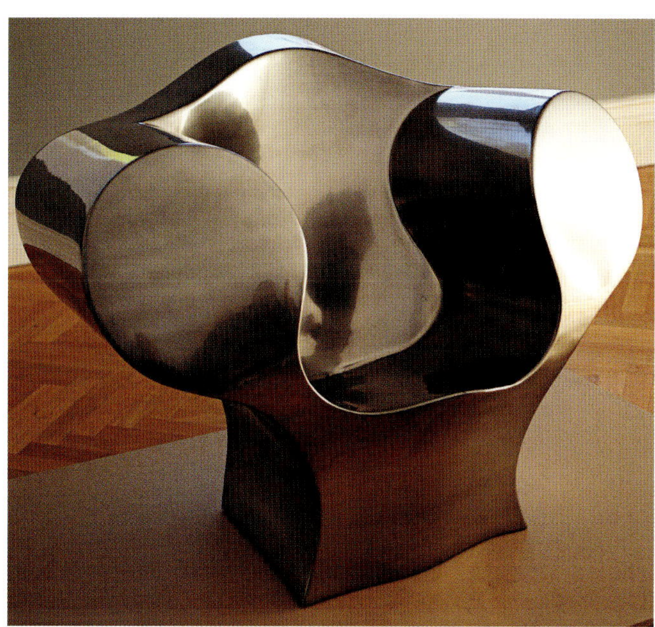

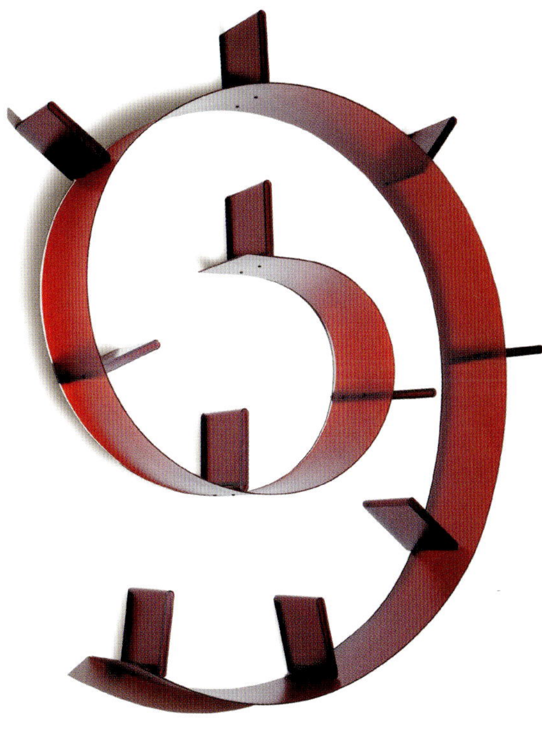

ABOVE LEFT:
Big Easy Volume II
armchair for One Off, 1988

ABOVE RIGHT:
Bookworm bookshelf
for Kartell, 1994

and more comfortable than his one-off pieces, Arad's Spring Collection had a cartoonish and characterful presence and helped to democratize progressive design by taking it out of the realm of limited editions.

Throughout the 1990s, Arad continued to create experimental one-off pieces alongside innovative and sculptural designs intended for mass-production, with his playful Bookworm shelving (1994) and his groundbreaking FPE (Fantastic Plastic Elastic) chair (1997), both for Kartell, being among his most commercially successful designs. In 1997, he was appointed professor of product design at the Royal College of Art, London, where he subsequently introduced the Design Products MA course in 1998. That same year, he began a fruitful collaboration with Galerie Mourmans in Belgium to produce limited editions of his hand-made pieces – which became lauded for their uniqueness. During the 2000s, Arad applied his formidable creative abilities not only to the design of products, such as chandeliers for Swarovski that incorporate LEDs operated by SMS text messages, but also to the design of buildings, including the Holon Design Museum (co-designed with Bruno Asa), Israel's first museum dedicated to design. In 2011, Arad was awarded the London Design Week Medal for design excellence and two years later was appointed a Royal Academician (Royal Academy of Arts) – both of which were acknowledgements of his tireless application of design experimentation and creative design thinking.

Archizoom Associati

Italian, 1966–1974

Founded in Florence in 1966, Archizoom Associati was a leading protagonist of the Italian Radical Design movement, with its name paying homage to the progressive British architecture group Archigram and the fourth issue of its journal, whose cover featured the word "ZOOM". Its original founders, Andrea Branzi, Gilberto Corretti, Paolo Deganello and Massimo Morozzi had all recently graduated from the University of Florence and it is no coincidence that in the year of the group's founding the historic centre of the Renaissance city had been submerged by a great flood, with the River Arno bursting its banks. As the Japanese architect Arata Isozaki later noted, this natural disaster "had a profound effect" on the members of Archizoom, being both a real and symbolic destruction of culture.

One of the first designs that Archizoom created was the Superonda seating unit (1966); its title, meaning "super wave", was of course directly inspired by the Florentine flood, as was its form, made from a single block of polyurethane foam cut into a rolling wave-like shape and then upholstered in gleaming vinyl. This early design was more a sculptural plaything than a truly functional piece of furniture, and yet it predicted the desire for more interactive and ephemeral products that was emerging among the younger Pop generation. In 1968, the group was joined by Dario and Lucia Bartolini, and also designed its famous Safari seating unit for Poltronova (1968), which, with its faux leopard-skin upholstery, intentionally mocked the pretentions of good design and good taste and instead celebrated the kitsch of popular culture. The same could also be said of the group's San Remo floor light (1968), which took the form of a luminous palm tree and was designed by Dario Bartolini as an engagement present for his future bride.

BELOW:
Safari seating unit
for Poltronova, 1968

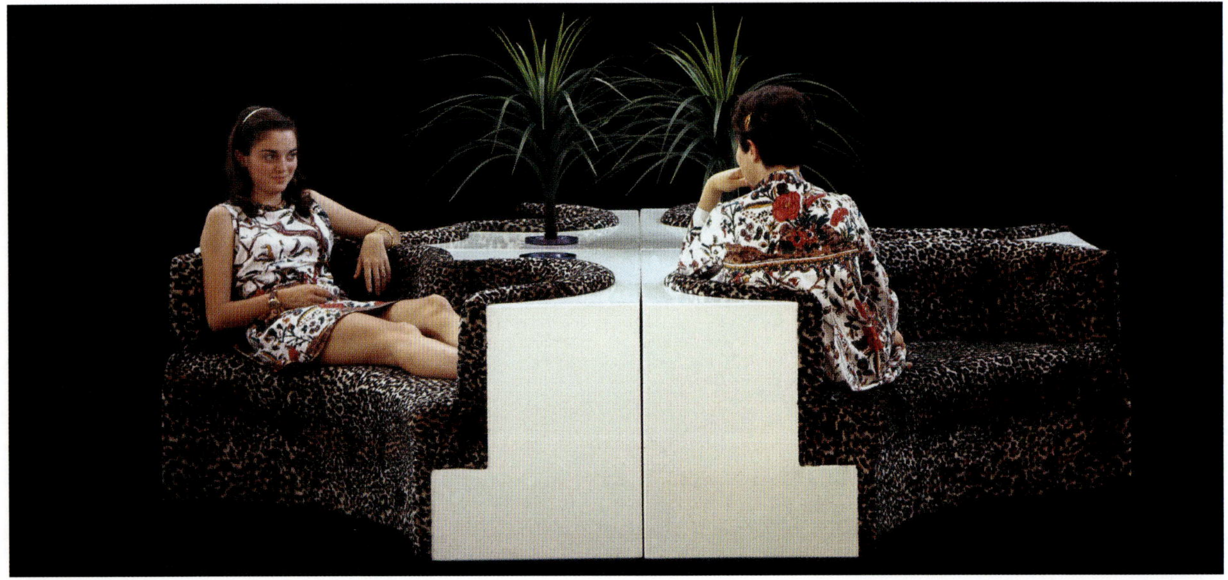

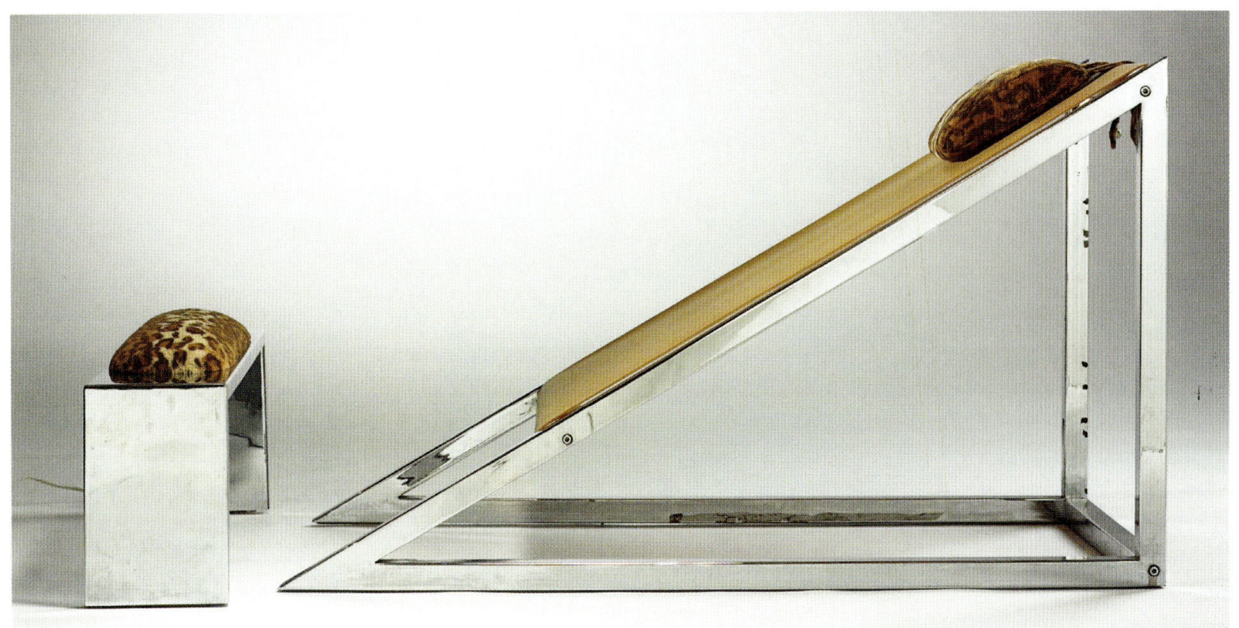

ABOVE:
Mies chair and ottoman
for Poltronova, 1969

Through playfully ironic designs, like Archizoom's Mies chair (1969) that mocked the architectural Neo-Rationalist tendencies of the time, the Radical Design movement aimed to subvert established socio-cultural meanings. Archizoom's early architectural visions such as No-Stop City (1969) were similarly motivated by a desire to counter the Modernist status quo, and sought to reveal that when Rationalism is pushed to an extreme it becomes an utter absurdity. As Branzi observed about this vast "*Superarchitettura*" proposal, "The real revolution in radical architecture is the revolution of kitsch: mass cultural consumption, pop art, an industrial-commercial language. There is the idea of radicalizing the industrial component of modern architecture to the extreme."

The projection of this type of so-called "negative utopia" was fuelled by a desire, as Branzi further explains, to "expose the underlying contradictions of the [Modern] movement, along with the fragile nature of its apparent unity of research". Countering the Modern Movement's doctrine of "less is more", Archizoom and other Radical Design groups in Italy such as Superstudio, UFO and Gruppo Strum argued that messy complexity offered far more potential for creative and intellectual engagement – and in so doing sowed the seeds for the later emergence of Post-Modernism. In 1972, Archizoom participated in the *Italy: The New Domestic Landscape – Achievements and Problems of Italian Design* exhibition at the Museum of Modern Art, New York and the following year developed the *Vestirisi è facile* (Dressing Is Easy) range of kit clothing. Eventually, however, the group disbanded in 1974 with its members each following their own separate career paths.

Despite only lasting eight years, Archizoom – inspired by Art Nouveau, Art Deco, Pop Art and kitsch – produced an impressive portfolio of challenging designs that pushed aesthetic and functional boundaries and created architectural projections that speculated on future utopias where technology had freed humans from the daily grind of manual labour. By irreverently questioning the function and good taste of Modernism, Archizoom stimulated widespread debate within both the architecture and design communities and ultimately changed the discourse of contemporary design practice.

Gunnar Erik Asplund

Swedish, 1885–1940

Gunnar Erik Asplund, once described by *Architectural Review* as the "high priest of functionalism in Sweden", was the country's leading architect during the first half of the twentieth century, and became one of the greatest advocates of Modernism throughout Scandinavia.

He studied at the KTH or Kungliga Tekniska Högskolan (Royal Institute of Technology) in Stockholm between 1905 and 1909, where the teaching was strongly influenced by Neo-Classicism. Asplund's early work, such as his chapel at the Woodlands Cemetery in Stockholm (1919), blended the Nordic vernacular with classical elements. His best-known furniture design, the Senna lounge chair, originally made for the Swedish Pavilion at the *Exposition Internationale des Arts Décoratifs et Industriels Modernes* held in Paris in 1925, exemplified this same synthesis of styles. Ultimately his work at this period was a Nordic version of National

BELOW:
Paradiset (Paradise) Restaurant
at the *Stockholmsutställningen* (Stockholm Exhibition), 1930

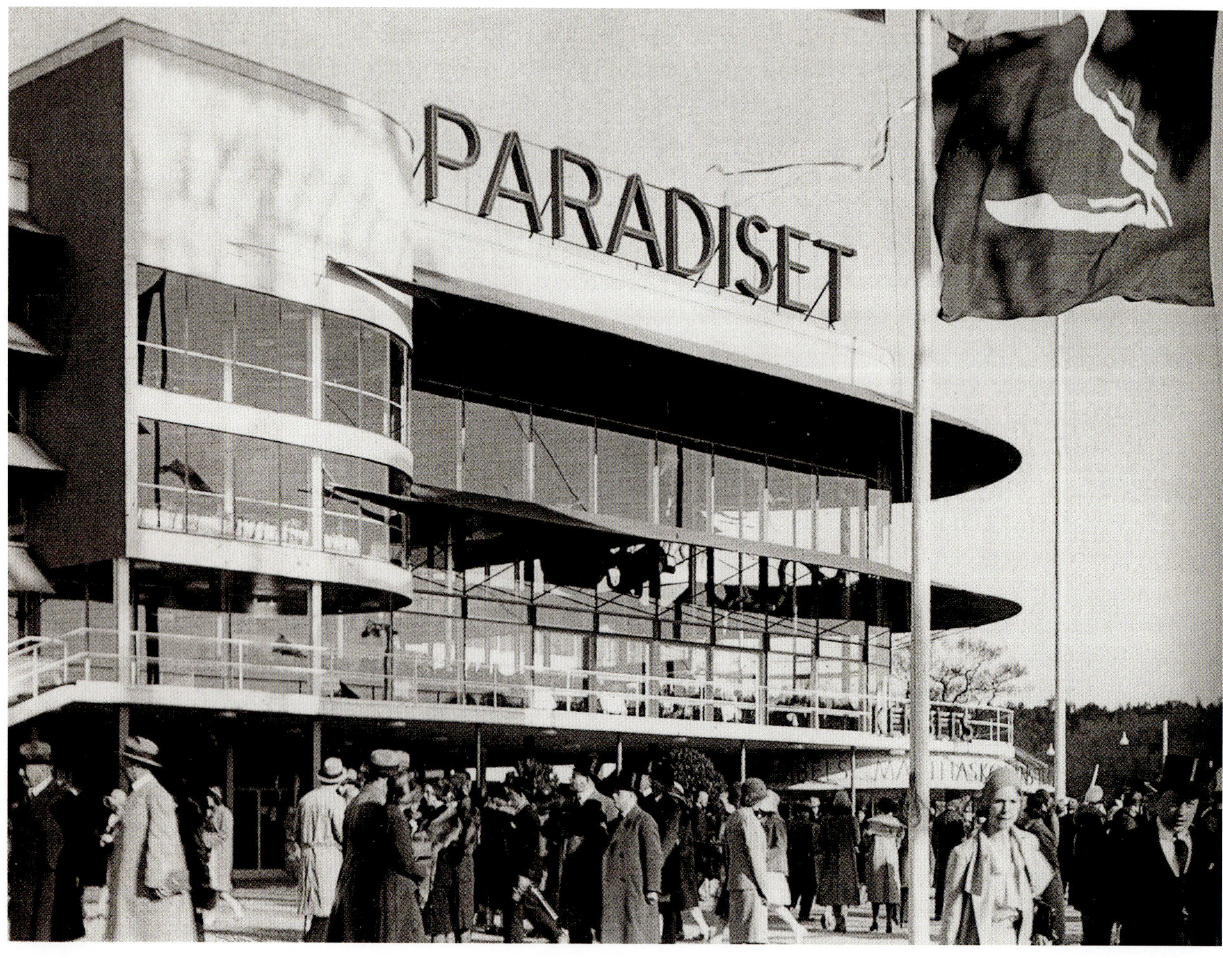

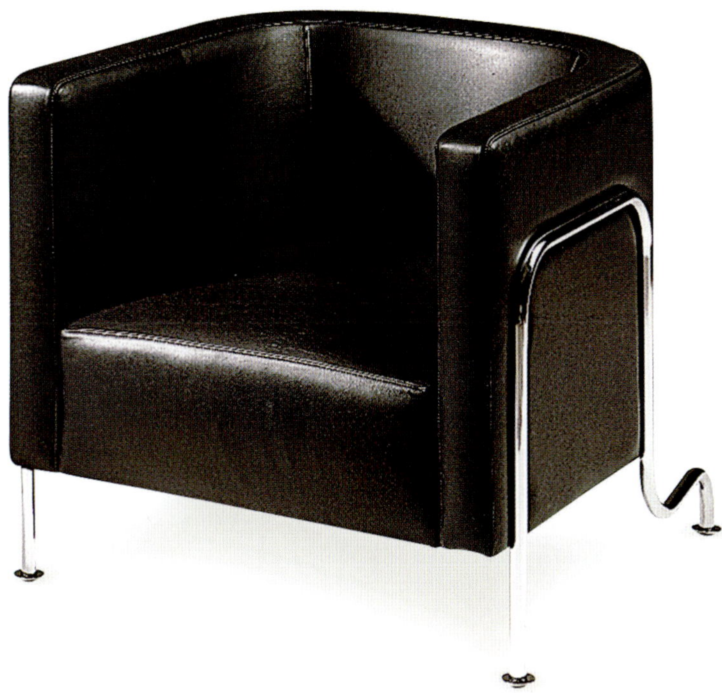

ABOVE:
GA2 club chair
(reissued by Källemo), 1932

Romanticism, or so-called "Swedish Grace". With its stripped-down elemental façade, his masterpiece, the Stockholm Public Library of 1922 (completed 1928), reflected a move from Neo-Classicism some way toward a kind of abstraction.

When Asplund was appointed chief architect for the Swedish Society of Craft's landmark *Stockholmsutstallningen* (Stockholm Exhibition) of 1930 (inspired by the Weissenhof-Siedlung built for the Deutscher Werkbund's exhibition in Stuttgart in 1927), he designed a series of pavilions that were thoroughly modern, exemplifying the new *Funktionalism* emerging in Sweden. The influence of the International Style was clear in Asplund's design for the Restaurant Paradiset at the exhibition, which incorporated modern industrial materials such as steel and glass yet retained an engagingly light-hearted Scandinavian sensibility through use of fabric awnings and curved forms that softened and humanized the composition.

Asplund was a co-author of the *Acceptera* (Accept) manifesto of 1931, which argued for the adoption of functionalist principles and was highly influential in the development of Swedish architecture. It was in this period that he designed two tubular metal and leather chairs that were three-dimensional manifestations of the new functionalist spirit. One was a radically Modern interpretation of the traditional club chair; the other, designed for the boardroom of the Swedish Society of Crafts, looked back to Classical forms. As Alvar Aalto noted in his obituary, Asplund can be seen as a Modern classicist, who attempted throughout his career "to tie the threads of a living future with those of the living past".

Edward Barber & Jay Osgerby

British, 1969– / British, 1969–

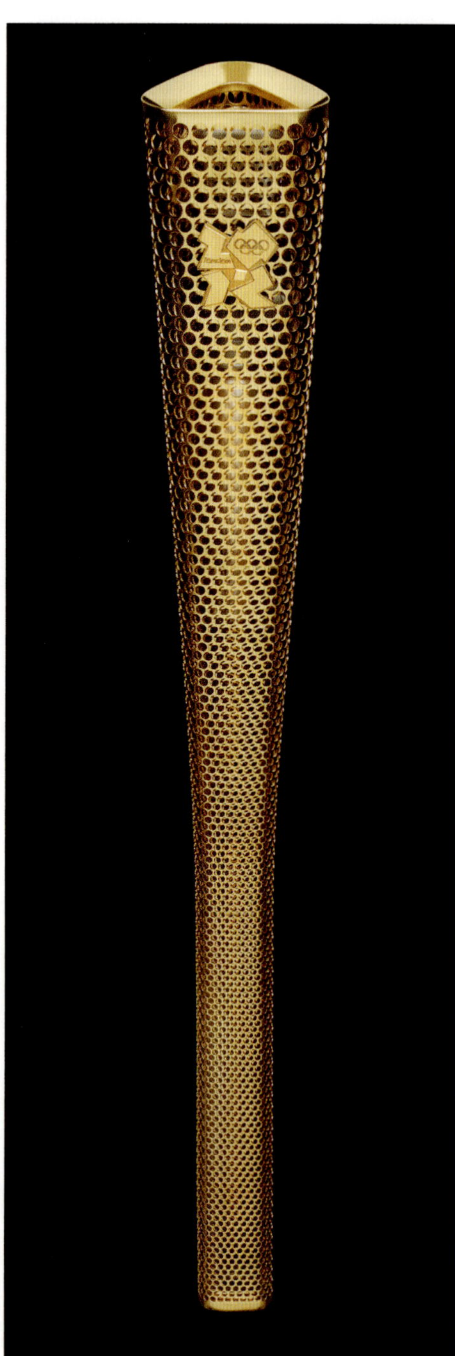

The London-based design duo Edward Barber and Jay Osgerby are well respected for their research-led approach to the design of furniture, lighting and home accessories as well as for their large-scale design installations. They are renowned for designing the London 2012 Olympic torch, which combined advanced laser-cutting technology with functional design principles.

They met while studying on the postgraduate MA architecture programme at the Royal College of Art in London, Barber having previously studied interior design at Leeds Polytechnic and Osgerby having studied product design at Ravensbourne College, London. After completing their course at the RCA, they set up their own design studio in London's Trellick Tower – a block of Brutalist flats designed by Ernö Goldfinger in the 1960s. The following year Barber and Osgerby designed their Loop table (1997), which was constructed of a continuous band of moulded plywood and was produced by the resurrected British manufacturing company Isokon. Like their later work, it revealed the strong influence of 1930s British Modernism, specifically the earlier plywood pieces that Isokon had manufactured during the inter-war period.

This design was followed by a number of projects that involved the folding and shaping of sheet material, such as plywood and Perspex, which were inspired by their experiments into form-making using the stiff white card employed for architectural model-making. In 2004, Barber and Osgerby were awarded the Jerwood Applied Arts Prize for their contribution to furniture design and this led to a commission the following year to create new furniture for the De La Warr Pavilion in Bexhill-on-Sea – a Modernist architectural masterpiece overlooking the Sussex coastline and designed in 1935 by Erich Mendelsohn and Serge Chermayeff. The resulting design, known as the De La Warr chair, employed a Y-shaped frame made of die-cast aluminium and tubular steel, while its seat and back sections were formed from pressed aluminium that had holes punched into it, not only to allow rain drainage and physical lightness but also to help reduce wind-drag – an important consideration for furniture intended for use on the exposed terraces of a British seaside pavilion. Widely publicized, this project helped launch the duo's profile still further and increasingly they began working with international clients, which led notably to their Tab light (2008) for Flos, the Poppins umbrella stand (2010) for Magis, the tilting Tip

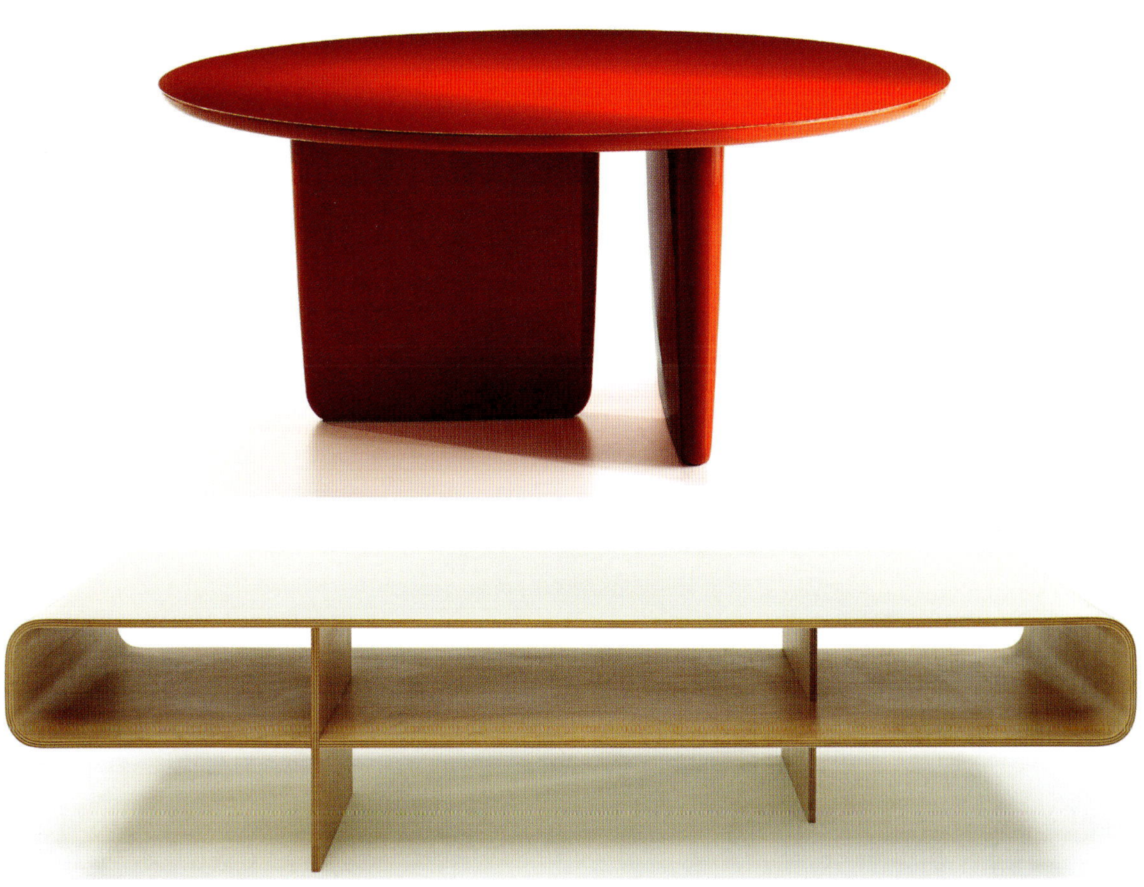

Ton chair (2011) and Zeb barstool (2014) for Vitra, the Tobi-Ishi table for B&B Italia (2012) and the Port vase for Venini (2014). In 2010, the two designers were commissioned to create an installation for Sony at the Milan Furniture Fair. They noted, "The Sony project was an incredibly exciting one for the studio. It was one of the first times [we] were able to show this [experimental] side of [our] work, and on such a grand scale."

Now regarded as at the forefront of British design and having an impressive track record of creating products with a very British ethos, it is unsurprising that Barber and Osgerby were selected by the London Organizing Committee of the Olympic Games (LOCOG) to design the London 2012 Olympic Torch. The result was not an exercise in stylistic bravado but rather a very British solution, thoughtfully conceived and beautifully engineered. Apart from their design work, Barber and Osgerby also have a dedicated architectural practice, Universal Design Studio, which designed the new Information Age gallery at London's Science Museum. What makes the pair's visually refined yet practical solutions so compelling is they infuse their work with a very British twist that builds on the nation's proud design heritage.

OPPOSITE:
Olympic torch
for 2012 London Olympic Games, 2012

TOP:
Tobi-Ishi table
for B&B Italia, 2012

ABOVE:
Loop table
for Isokon, 1997

Jonathan Barnbrook

British, 1966–

The British graphic designer and typographer Jonathan Barnbrook is well known for his highly politicized work. Even as a teenager he showed a propensity for graphic design, winning a competition to design the cover of his school's magazine. While growing up he was a music enthusiast, which he describes as "a form of rebellion and also a way to relate to the world". Because of this, one of his earliest influences was the artwork on record sleeves, which for him enhanced the enjoyment of music. Already disdaining the influence of American popular culture, he preferred homegrown creative talent which he found he could better relate to. After school he took a diploma in graphic design at Barnfield College in Luton, his hometown, and then moved to London in order to take a degree in graphic design at Saint Martin's School of Art (later to become Central Saint Martins). It was here that Barnbrook developed an interest in pure typography and, crucially, learnt how to use a traditional letterpress as well as analogue typesetting machines.

Between 1988 and 1990 he undertook a master's degree at the Royal College of Art in London and, while still a student, designed his first font – the gothic-inspired Bastard (1990). He subsequently set up on his own, and his first commercial font, Exocet (1991), was released by the progressive California-based font foundry Emigre under Rudy VanderLans and Zuzana Licko. 1992 saw the release of another font by Emigre, Manson (the name of which was altered to Mason after complaints), and the same year Barnbrook began working with the

BELOW LEFT:
Bastard font family
for VirusFonts, 1990

BELOW RIGHT:
Exocet font family
for VirusFonts, 1991

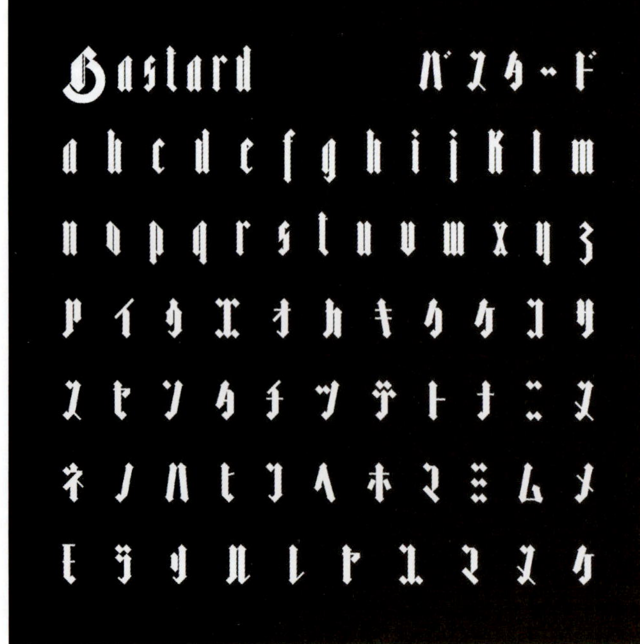

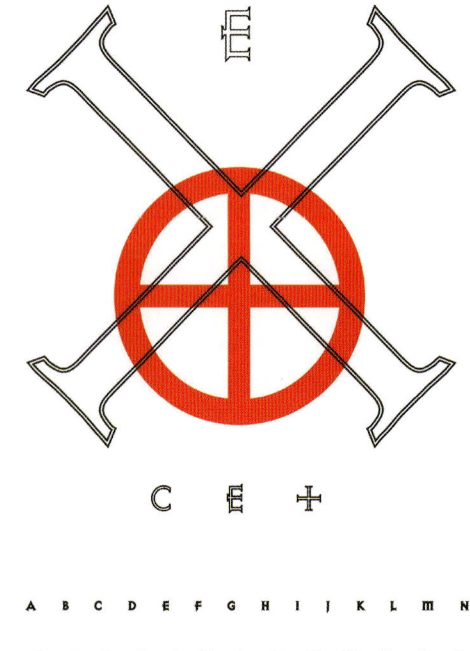

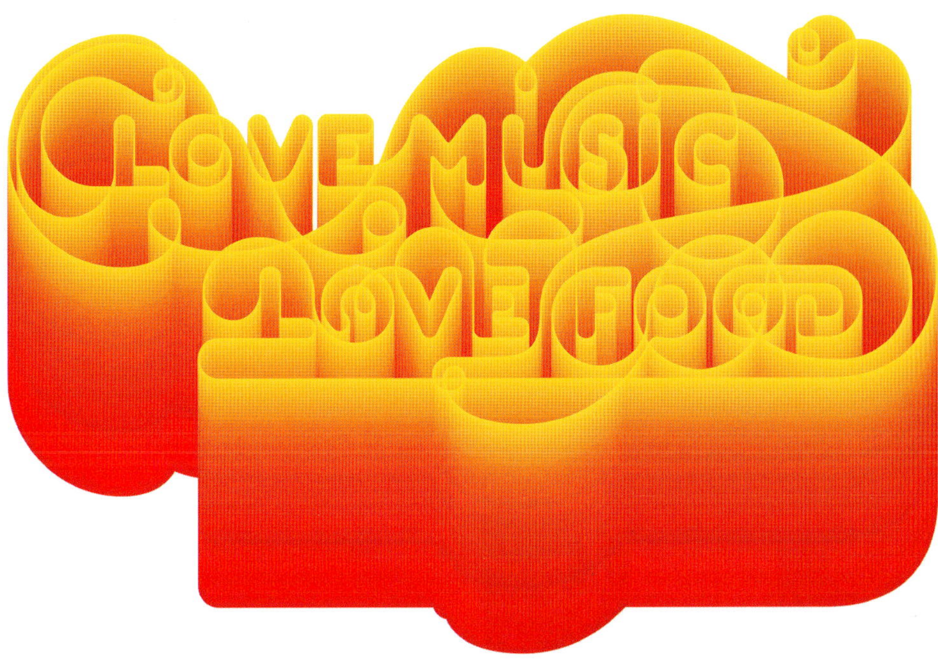

ABOVE:
Identity for Love Music Love Food, 2009
(UK-based music charity associated with Teenage Cancer Trust)

advertising director Tony Kaye, for whom he created a number of typographic-based motion sequences. Eventually, in 1997, Barnbrook set up his own font company, VirusFonts, which has subsequently released a large number of distinctive digital fonts with tongue-in-cheek titles, including False Idol (1997), Drone (1997), Moron (2001), Infidel (2003), Hopeless Diamond (2009) and Doctrine (2013), as well as various pictograms. Also in 1997, Barnbrook designed the first of several books for the artist Damien Hirst, entitled *I Want to Spend the Rest of my Life Everywhere, with Everyone, One to One, Always, Forever, Now*, which was a *tour-de-force* of graphic creativity incorporating innovative pop-ups, gatefolds and die-cuts that at a stroke redefined the concept of the artist's monograph. Two years later, he began collaborating with the Canadian not-for-profit magazine *Adbusters*, creating hard-hitting social-message artwork that was highly critical of the capitalist system and its profiteering corporations.

Certainly, Barnbrook's strong ethical beliefs have fundamentally shaped his career as a graphic designer, for – unlike many of his contemporaries in the graphic design world – he has doggedly refused to take on well-paid commercial work for companies that do not share his values. To this end, he was one of the main signatories of the "First Things First" Manifesto released in 2000, which called on the creative community to produce more meaningful work. In 2004 he released his anti-Olympics pictogram family known as Olympukes, which ridiculed the insidious corporate sponsorship of the event, then in 2007 published the *Barnbrook Bible* and had a major retrospective exhibition entitled *Friendly Fire* at the Design Museum, London. As Barnbrook observes, "graphic design has always been a method of social change. Throughout history leaders have facilitated social change through the distribution of the printed word. It really is that simple."

Saul Bass

American, 1920–1996

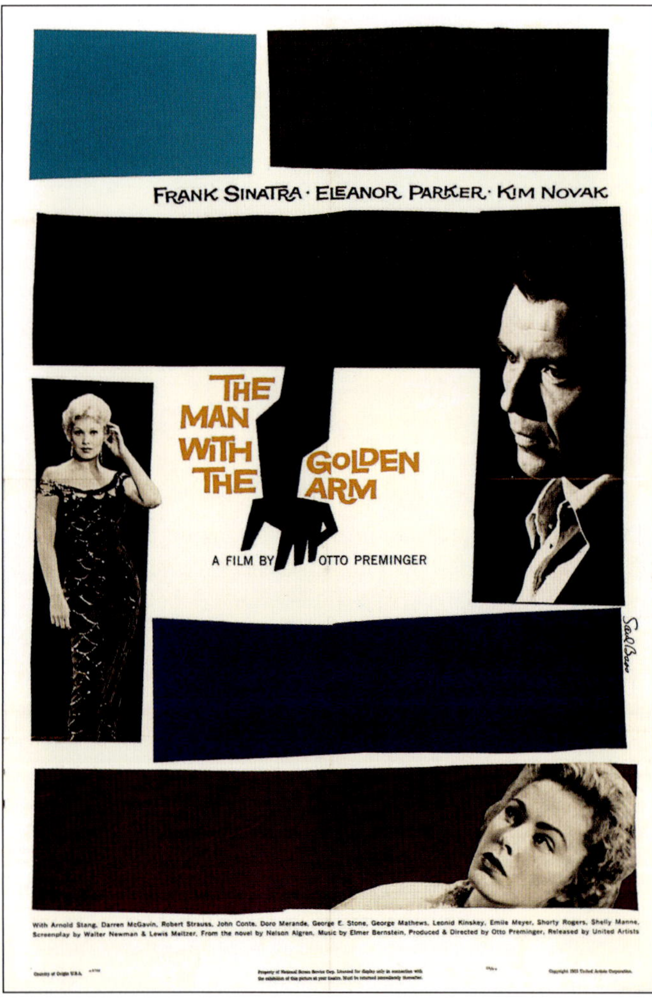

ABOVE:
Poster for *The Man with the Golden Arm*
1955

Saul Bass was among the most important graphic designers of the mid-twentieth century and the undisputed master of film title design and film posters.

When the reels of film for Otto Preminger's controversial drugs movie *The Man with the Golden Arm* arrived at US movie theatres in 1955, a note was stuck on the cans: "Projectionists – pull curtain before titles". Until then, the opening lists of cast and crew which passed for movie titles were so dull that projectionists often pulled back the curtains to reveal the screen only once they'd finished. But Bass's titles for *The Man with the Golden Arm* were intended be an integral part of the film, the theme of which was the struggle of its jazz-playing hero, performed by Frank Sinatra, to overcome his heroin addiction. Bass's innovative title sequence featured an animated black paper cut-out of a heroin addict's arm. Knowing that the arm was a powerful symbol of addiction, Bass also used it for the film's promotional poster. This simple yet sophisticated animation caused a sensation and ultimately transformed the movie title into an art form.

Even before this cinematic *tour-de-force*, however, Bass had already achieved a considerable reputation as a graphic designer. He had initially studied at the Art Students League, New York, and then at Brooklyn College under the Hungarian graphic designer György Kepes. It was Kepes who had been responsible for introducing Bass to the work of the Bauhaus and the Russian Constructivists. After working for various Manhattan design firms, Bass established himself as a freelance "commercial artist". Chafing at the creative constraints imposed on him in New York, he eventually moved to Los Angeles in 1946 and four years later opened his own studio. In 1954 Otto Preminger invited him to design the poster for his new movie, *Carmen Jones* and, impressed by the result, the director commissioned Bass to create the film's title sequence as well.

Bass subsequently devised titles for Robert Aldrich's *The Big Knife* and Billy Wilder's *The Seven Year Itch* – both in 1955. But it was his next Preminger project, *The Man with the Golden*

BELOW:
Poster for *Exodus*
1960

BOTTOM:
Poster for *Vertigo*
1958

Arm, which established Bass as the doyen of film title design. Blessed with the gift of identifying the one image that best symbolized the movie, Bass then re-created it in a strikingly modern style. Martin Scorsese once described his approach as shaping "an emblematic image, instantly recognizable and immediately tied to the film". For example, in his title sequence for Alfred Hitchcock's *Vertigo* (1958), Bass shot a close-up of a woman's face and then her eye before spinning it into a sinister spiral as a bloody red soaks the screen. For another Hitchcock film, *North by Northwest* (1959), the credits swoop up and down a grid of vertical and diagonal lines like passengers in elevators. It is only as the movie begins – with Cary Grant stepping out of an elevator – that the movie-goer realizes the grid is actually the façade of a skyscraper. Equally haunting are the vertical bars sweeping across the screen in a manic, mirrored helter-skelter motif at the beginning of Hitchcock's 1960 *Psycho*, this staccato sequence being symbolic of Norman Bates's fractured psyche.

During his career, Bass created over fifty title sequences, for Preminger, Alfred Hitchcock, Stanley Kubrick, John Frankenheimer and Martin Scorsese among others, from the animated alley cat in 1962's *Walk on the Wild Side* to the adrenalin-laced motor racing sequence in 1966's *Grand Prix*. He also directed a series of shorts, culminating in the Oscar-winning *Why Man Creates*, and finally realized his ambition to direct a feature with 1974's *Phase IV*. When this film unfortunately flopped, Bass returned to commercial graphic design, including corporate identities for United Airlines, AT&T, Minolta, Bell Telephone System and Warner Communications. He also designed the poster for the 1984 Los Angeles Olympic Games. In 1987, he returned to creating movie titles, namely for James Brooks's *Broadcast News* and then for Penny Marshall's 1988 *Big*. In 1990, Bass found a new long-term collaborator in Martin Scorsese who had grown up with – and idolized – his 1950s and 1960s titles. He went on to create sequences for Scorsese's *Goodfellas* (1990), *Cape Fear* (1991), *The Age of Innocence* (1993) and *Casino* (1995) – the latter showing Robert De Niro falling through the sinister neon lights of the Las Vegas Strip to symbolize his character's descent into hell. As his *New York Times* obituary noted in 1996, Saul Bass was "the minimalist auteur who put a jagged arm in motion in 1955 and created an entire film genre… and elevated it into an art".

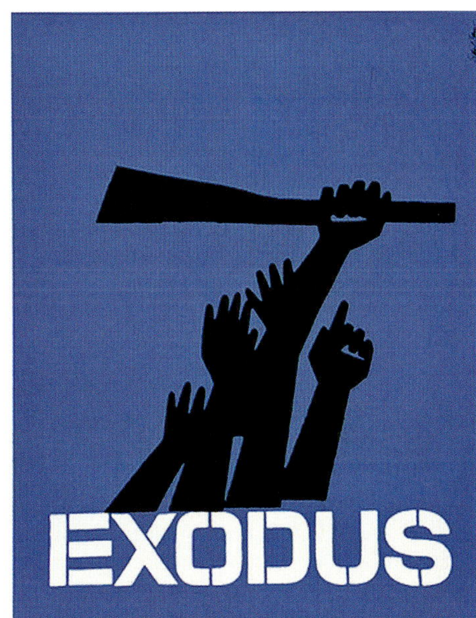

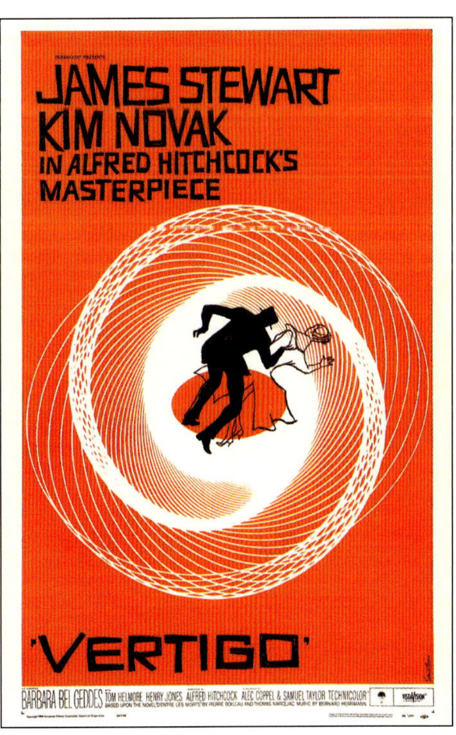

Bauhaus

Germany, 1919–1933

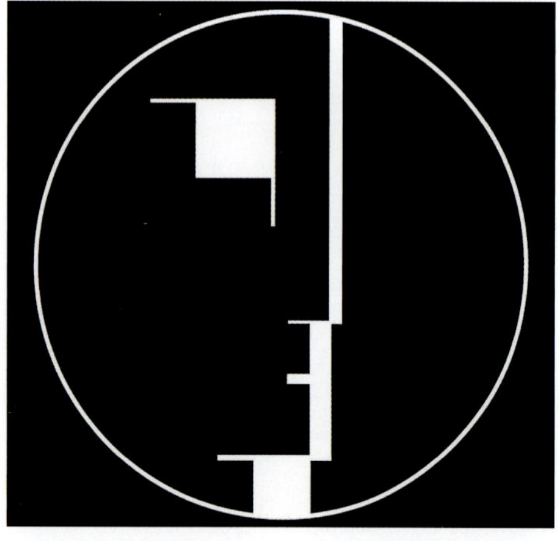

LEFT:
Bauhaus logo
by Oskar Schlemmer, 1922

Although the Bauhaus operated for just fourteen years – from 1919 to 1933 – over that time it became one of the most influential design schools ever and profoundly transformed both the teaching and practice of design. The origins of this remarkable institution can be traced back to a letter written to the German city of Weimar's regional state ministry by the architect Walter Gropius in 1916, in which he suggested creating a new interdisciplinary college of art and design through the merger of the city's Kunstgewerbeschule (School of Applied Arts) and its Hochschule für bildende Künste (College of Fine Arts). The central goal of this new school was to provide "artistic advisory services to industry, trade and craft".

In due course the two schools were amalgamated to form the new type of college that Gropius had envisioned, where the teaching of art and technical skill were completely unified. In 1919 Gropius was appointed director of the new Staatliches Bauhaus, and that same year the Bauhaus manifesto was published. The word *Bauhaus* means "building house" (*Staatliches* means "state") and the name reflected Gropius's belief that constructing was an important social, symbolic and intellectual endeavour.

The Bauhaus's curriculum consisted of a one-year preliminary course, which was initially obligatory, that provided students with a grounding in all the different creative disciplines – much like the foundation courses it inspired which were until quite recently an essential element to art and design education in Britain. After this one-year induction, students joined the school's various workshops with the stipulation that they had to train in at least one craft discipline. These workshops were run along guild-like lines with the tutors being referred to as "masters" and the students known as "apprentices" and having to pass journeyman's exams.

The Bauhaus had two very distinct phases – Expressionist and Rationalist – which reflected the power struggle between tutors, some of whom believed in the power of individual creative expression (such as the charismatic Johannes Itten who had devised the preliminary course) while others felt that a more rational approach allied to industrial production needed to be taken. While the school was based in Weimar, the Expressionists' ethos dominated the curriculum; after Itten's departure in 1922, however, his successors, Josef Albers and Lászlό Moholy-Nagy, began to instigate an increasingly industrial approach, which included students going on factory visits in order to learn about the design requirements of mechanized production. In 1923, the Bauhaus staged a major exhibition, which included not only designs by its students – such as Wilhelm Wagenfeld's famous ME1

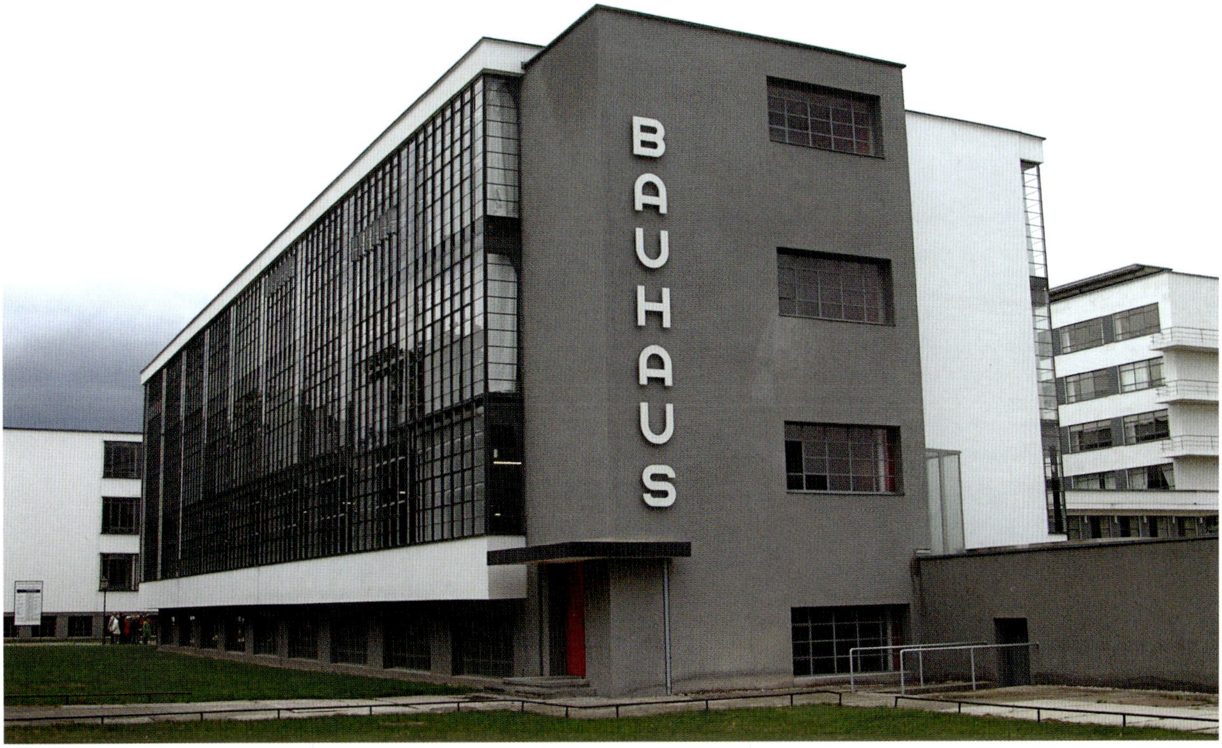

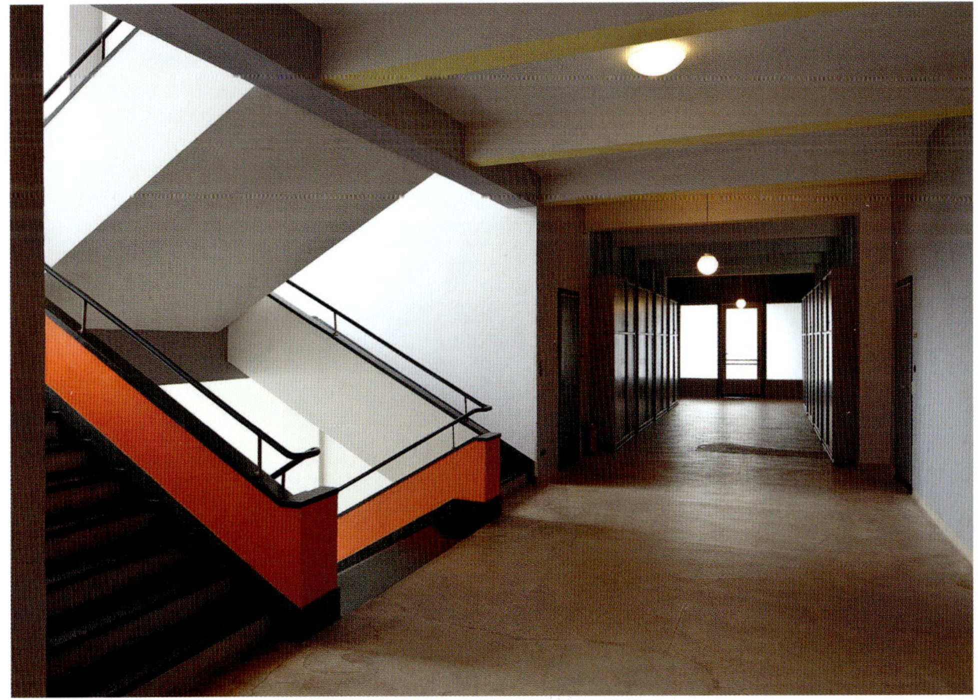

ABOVE:
Dessau Bauhaus building
by Walter Gropius, 1926

LEFT:
Interior of the Dessau Bauhaus building
by Walter Gropius, 1926

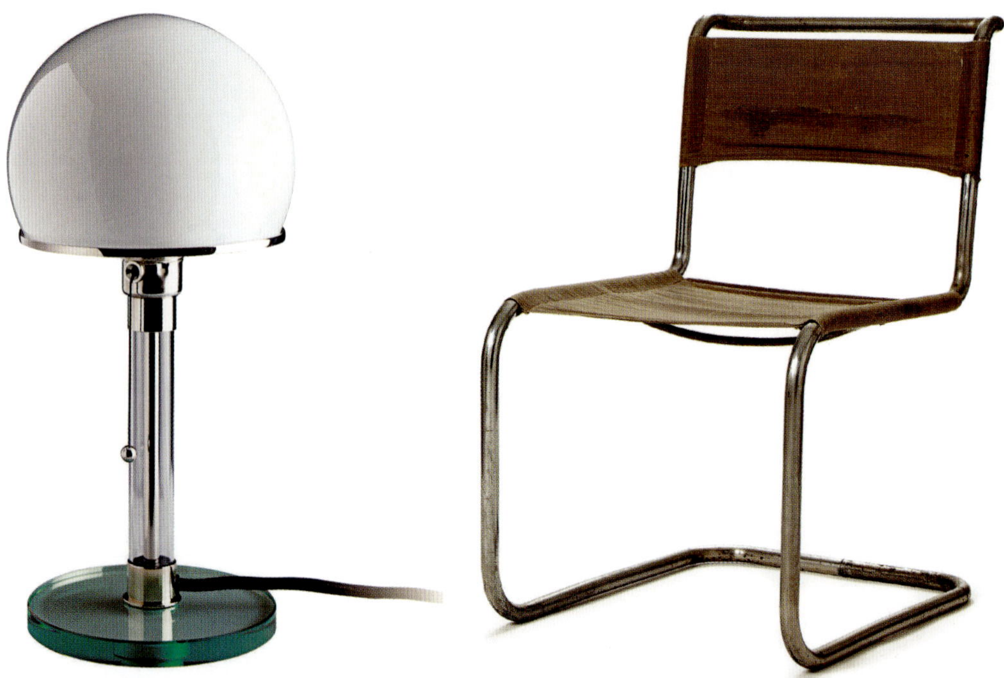

ABOVE LEFT:
ME1 table lamp
by Wilhelm Wagenfeld
1923–24

ABOVE RIGHT:
B33 chair
by Marcel Breuer for Gebrüder Thonet, 1927–28

table lamp (1923–24) – but also work by architect-designers aligned to the Dutch De Stijl movement. Importantly, the stridently Modern graphic artwork designed for the exhibition helped to promote a new, more Rational identity for the school with its incorporation of sans serif "New Typography". Despite the critical success of this exhibition, because of the Bauhaus's political alignment with the left, the school's state funding was halved when a new centre-right coalition swept to power in Weimar in 1924. As a result, the following year, Gropius was forced to relocate the Bauhaus to Dessau, where the ruling Social Democrats were more receptive to its aims.

Crucially, Dessau was a major industrial centre, and its local politicians had a better understanding of the need for good industrial-design teaching and therefore offered the Bauhaus much-needed funding to construct a new purpose-built school and staff accommodation. Completed in 1926, the new Bauhaus building, designed by Gropius, was a Modern statement in which form was driven by function, and ultimately marked a turning point in the school's movement away from craft-workshop ideals and towards full acceptance of industrialized production.

In order to further the Bauhaus's industrial-design credentials and to enable it to raise additional funding from the sale of its products, Gropius established Bauhaus GmbH to market the designs produced at the school. However, despite appearing machine-made, many of the designs created at the Bauhaus only speculated on true industrial manufacture and were in practice unsuitable for large-scale mechanized production. There were nonetheless some notable exceptions, including the furniture designed by Marcel Breuer that incorporated frames innovatively made out of tubular steel, such as the B33 chair (1927–28), which, although not the first chair he created from this modern industrial material, was one of his most significant furniture designs.

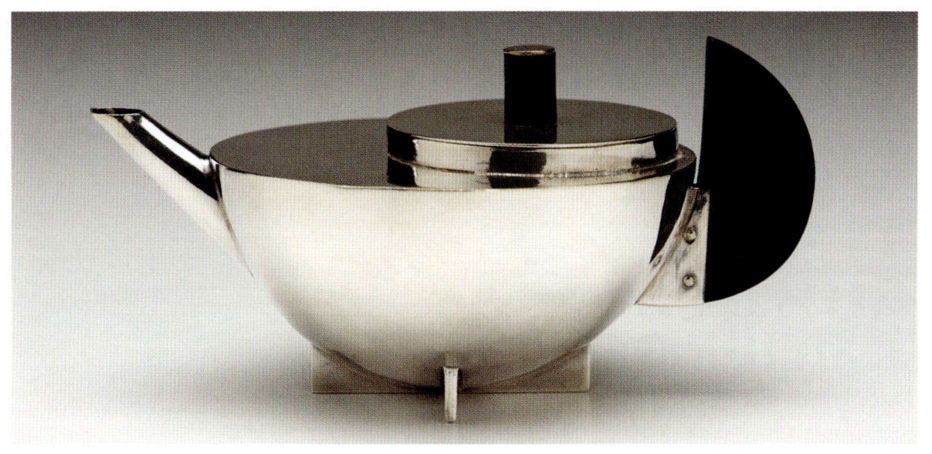

LEFT:
Model no. MT 49
teapot by Marianne Brandt, 1924–27

BELOW LEFT:
***Die Bühne im Bauhaus* (The Stage at the Bauhaus)**
Bauhaus Bücher (Book) 4 by Oskar Schlemmer, 1925

BELOW RIGHT:
***Grundbegriffe der neuen gestaltenden Kunst* (Basic Terms of New Formative Art)**
Bauhaus Bücher (Book) 6 by Theo van Doesburg, 1925

In 1928, Walter Gropius stepped down as the school's director. During the tenure of his successor, Hannes Meyer, the Bauhaus became increasingly politicized – so much so that in 1930 Ludwig Mies van der Rohe replaced Meyer, but to no avail since the Nazi political tide was sweeping Germany; when the National Socialists won power in Dessau in 1932 the school was forced yet again to relocate, this time to Berlin. There it was forcibly closed the following year, and although this marked the physical disappearance of the Bauhaus, its spirit lived on through the diaspora of Bauhaus designers who later emigrated to England and the United States.

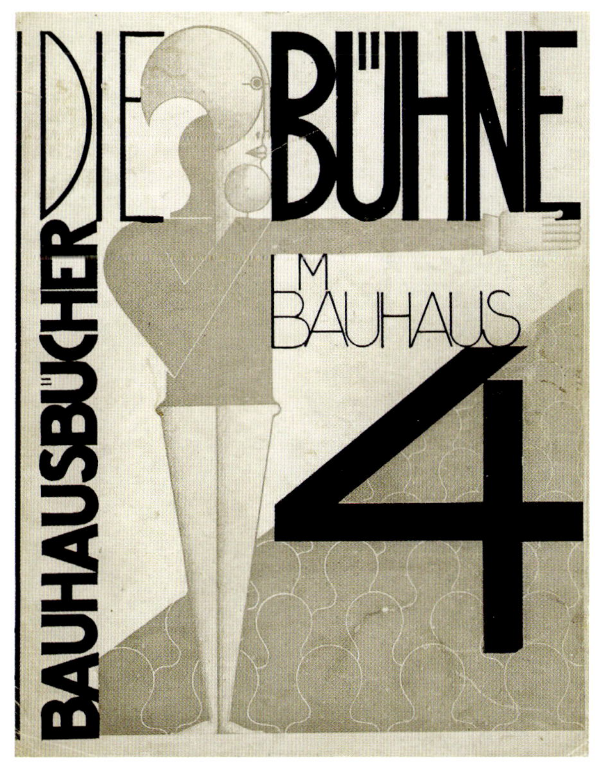

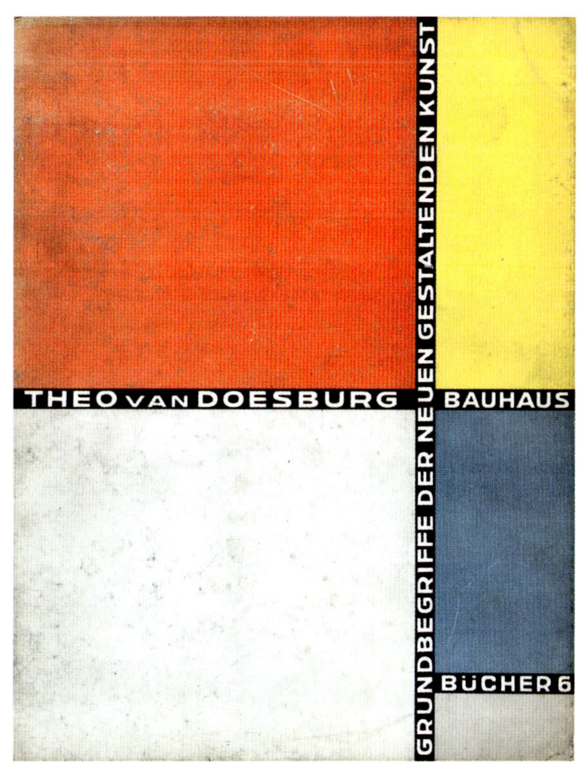

Herbert Bayer

Austrian/American, 1900–1985

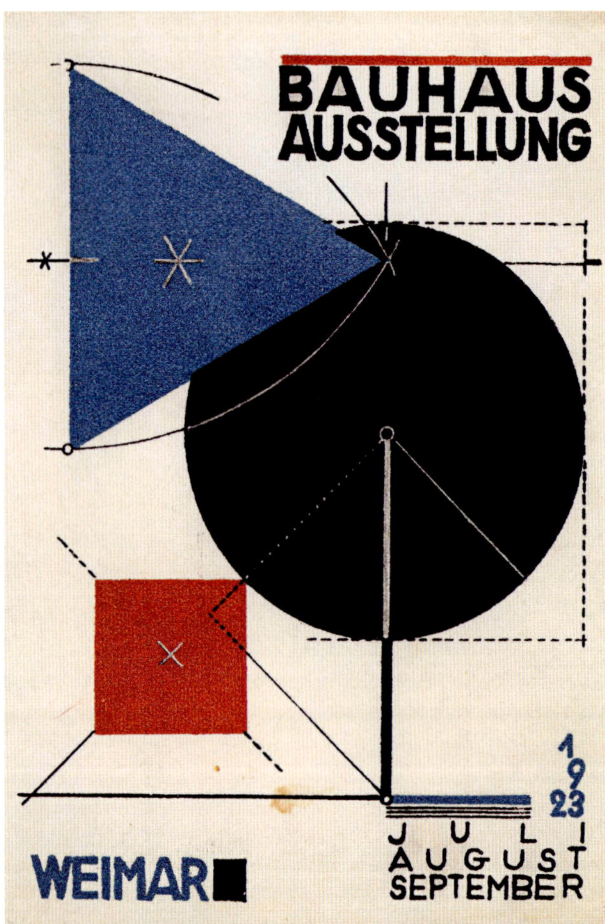

ABOVE:
***Bauhaus Ausstellung* poster**
for Bauhaus exhibition in
Weimar, 1923

One of the most influential graphic designers of the twentieth century, Austrian-born Herbert Bayer was highly instrumental in disseminating the goals of Bauhaus Modernism to a wider international audience, especially when he emigrated to the United States in the late 1930s.

Having apprenticed in the Linz-based architectural office of Georg Schmidthammer, where he produced his first typographical work, he later worked in the studio of Emanuel Josef Margold at the Darmstadt Artists' Colony. Margold had a formative influence on the young Bayer, for he not only designed textiles, wallpapers, ceramics, jewellery, and interiors but was also a pioneering commercial artist, designing posters, postcards and the like for the Wiener Werkstätte as well as advertising graphics and packaging for the biscuit manufacturer Bahlsen. Following his stint with Margold, from 1921 to 1923 Bayer studied at the Staatliches Bauhaus in Weimar, first attending Johannes Itten's preparatory course and then serving an apprenticeship with Oskar Schlemmer and Wassily Kandinsky in the school's wall-painting workshop. He subsequently studied in Italy and Berchtesgaden, Bavaria, and obtained his journeyman's certificate as a mural painter in 1925.

Between 1925 and 1928, Bayer was a lecturer at the Bauhaus Dessau, and during this period was appointed a "junior master" and headed the newly established *Drucke und Reklame* (printing and publicity) workshop, which was in 1927 renamed the *Werkstatt für Typographie und Werbsachengestaltung* (workshop for typography and advertisement design). In this position, he was responsible for all the Bauhaus publicity material and also the layout design of the series of books published by the Bauhaus.

Importantly, Bayer introduced lower-case sans serif typography to Bauhaus graphics, most notably his famous universal typeface designed in 1925 at the behest of Walter Gropius, with its streamlined and unadorned lower-case letters that were intended to promote better legibility. At the Bauhaus, Bayer also encouraged the use of photomontage in advertising design. In 1928, he left the Bauhaus and moved to Berlin, where he worked as art director for the German edition of *Vogue* magazine and also as creative director for the German branch of the international advertising agency Dorland studio, where he promoted the attributes of simplicity and clarity in what was then still known as "commercial art".

Along with Walter Gropius and László Moholy-Nagy, Bayer designed the Deutscher Werkbund exhibit for the 1930 Paris *Salon de la Société des Artistes Décorateurs*. With the rise of the Third Reich in Germany, however, Bayer's association with the Bauhaus, which was viewed by the Nazis as a hotbed of Communism, made it increasingly difficult to find employment and he was eventually forced to escape persecution, as were so many other members of the German avant-garde – indeed three of his de Chirico-esque Dunstlocher paintings (1935–37) were included in the Nazis' *Entartete Kunst* (Degenerate Art) exhibition held in Munich in 1937.

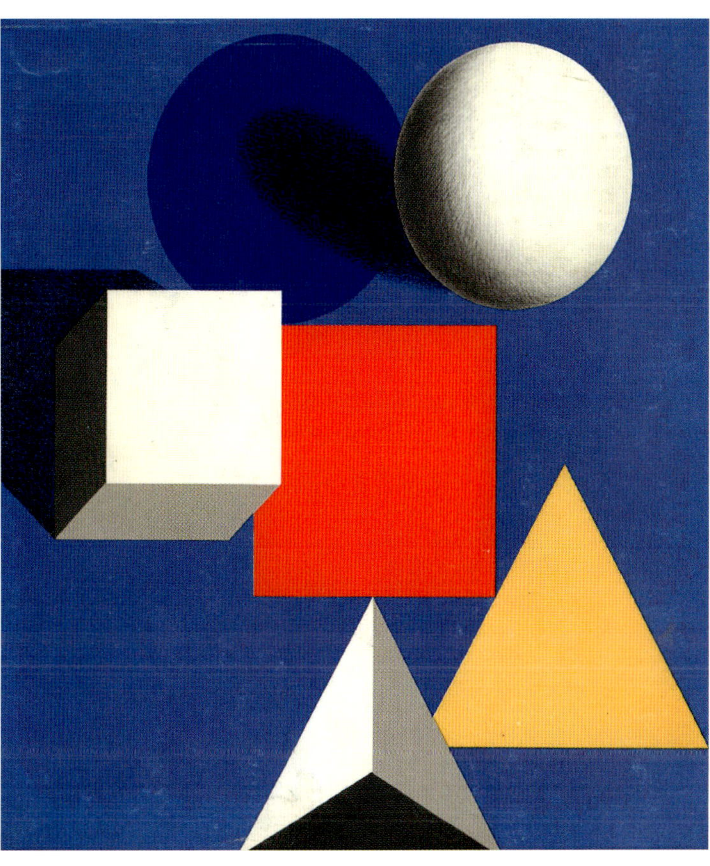

ABOVE:
***Bauhaus 50 Jahre* catalogue cover**
for fiftieth-anniversary exhibition held in Stuttgart, 1968

Bayer eventually emigrated to America in 1938 and the same year created the exhibition catalogue for the influential *Bauhaus 1919–1928* show held at the Museum of Modern Art, New York. He subsequently designed promotional brochures for the General Electric Company in 1942 that were notable for his dynamic visualizations of complex scientific principles. He was also a director of the Dorland International advertising agency until 1945 and from 1946 to 1956 he headed the design department of the Container Corporation of America, where he created a series of eye-catching and thought-provoking display advertisements that countered the American advertising industry's prevailing love of "hard-sell" ads. Bayer also worked as a consultant for many other American corporations and designed a number of *Fortune* magazine covers. From 1946, he mainly concentrated on architectural commissions, including the design of buildings for the Aspen Institute for Humanistic Studies, Colorado. In 1975, he moved to Montecito, California, where he dedicated himself primarily to painting.

Herbert Bayer was a member of that unique generation of European-born designers who transformed the cultural life of America by successfully managing to synthesize the principles of European Modernism with the demands of corporate America to create a fertile creative climate which enabled American design to flourish during the post-war years.

Yves Béhar

Swiss/active USA, 1967–

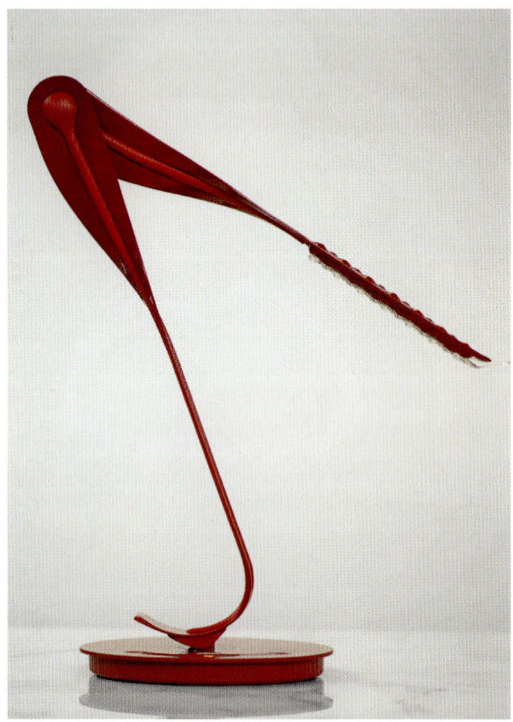

Swiss-born Yves Béhar has emerged in recent years as one of the world's most accomplished designers and a high-profile advocate of design responsibility. He is a firm adherent of process-led design and believes that designers need to take a far more holistic approach to problem solving. For every project, he attempts to deliver the optimum solution using the minimum means, so that it is as environmentally sustainable as possible.

Béhar initially studied industrial design at the Art Center Europe in Switzerland (1989–91) and the Art Center College of Design, Pasadena, California (1992–95), before working as a designer for Lunar and for frog design, both in Palo Alto, California. In 1999, he went on to establish fuseproject, an integrated creative design agency in San Francisco, and has since forged a reputation as an accomplished designer as well as an innovative design thinker. For Béhar, "Less materials equal less cost and less carbon footprint," and so with any brief he starts with questions rather than answers. How can the amount of material used be reduced? How can the function of a product type be enhanced? How can the environmental impact of the production methods used to manufacture a design be minimized? To this end, he begins the design

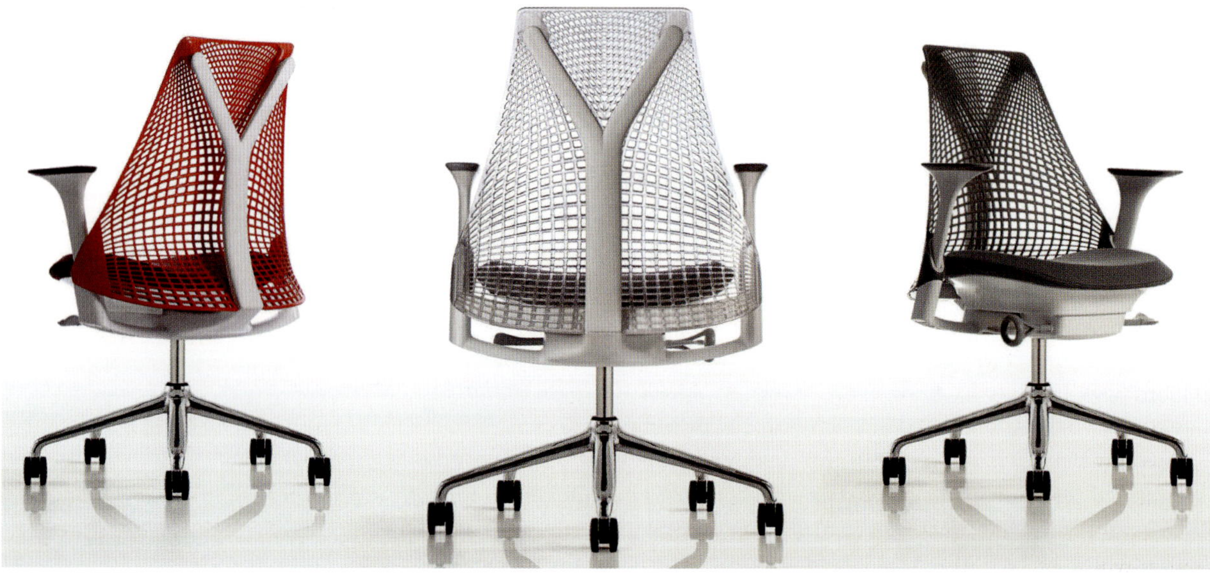

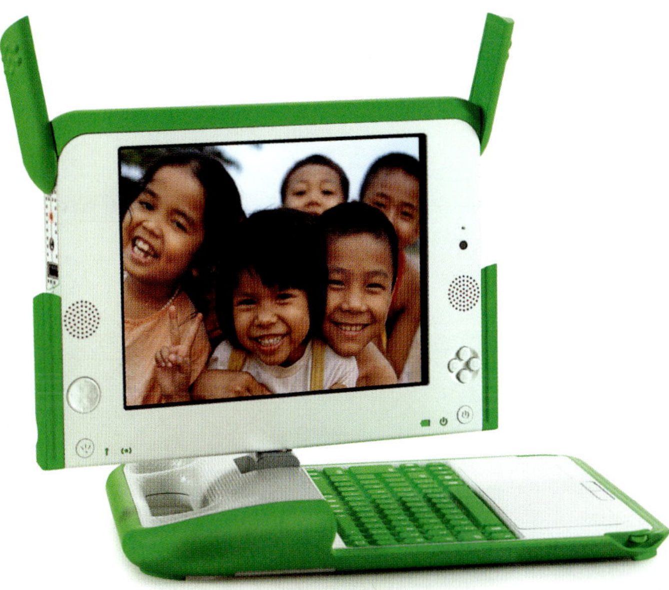

process with numerous drawings, prototypes, material studies and ergonomic studies in order to determine the optimum parameters for the solution. Once these have been determined he and his team at fuseproject work closely with the in-house experts at the company he has been commissioned by to create products that are quantifiably better.

The results speak for themselves. His shoebox for Puma, for example, takes the form of a reusable and recyclable non-woven polyester bag with a die-cut cardboard structure to keep it rigid and therefore stackable. This ingenious "Clever Little Bag" not only uses 65 percent less materials than traditional shoeboxes but is functionally better too, as it is easier for sales assistants to carry in-store and can also be used instead of a plastic shopping bag when sold, and additionally can be employed by the end user as a shoe storage bag. With this design, Béhar has essentially re-imagined traditional shoe packaging and in so doing has managed to deliver more function with a lot less materials.

His Sayl office chair for Herman Miller is another example of innovative design thinking, providing the same functionality as other high-end office chairs yet employing far fewer materials, which makes it 35 percent lighter than its equivalents in the market and also about half the price. In his pursuit of "Design for Good", Béhar also created the Leaf energy-saving LED task light for Herman Miller, an electric charging station for GE and various better-performing Bluetooth headsets for Jawbone.

Understanding that brand and product are inextricably linked, fuseproject has undertaken work for, among others, Y Water, NYC Condom, Birkenstock, Coca-Cola, Danese and Canal+. It was, however, Béhar's XO laptop (2006), designed for the non-profit organization One Laptop Per Child (OLPC), that brought him greatest international recognition. Developed in conjunction with digital guru Nicolas Negroponte and the world-renowned Media Lab at Massachusetts Institute of Techonology (MIT), this compact, highly robust, green-and-white plastic $100 laptop was designed to bring technology and education to millions of children in the developing world. Despite its exacting brief, Béhar was able to provide this design, which features Wi-Fi "Rabbit Ears" antennae, with an engaging toy-like whimsy and a pleasurable tactility. As Béhar notes, "Good design accelerates the adoption of new ideas... accelerates the idea that sustainability is possible at a lower cost and with a better experience," and it is testament to his dogged pursuit of good design that he has received an impressive number of international design awards for his imaginative and innovative work.

OPPOSITE TOP:
Leaf task light
for Herman Miller, 2006

OPPOSITE BOTTOM:
Sayl chair
for Herman Miller, 2010

ABOVE:
OLPC XO-1 laptop
for the One Laptop Per Child (OLPC) non-profit foundation, 2006

Peter Behrens

German, 1868–1940

From the late 1890s until his death in 1940, Peter Behrens was a highly influential architect and design reformer in Germany, whose work mirrored the stylistic and intellectual transition from the Art Nouveau style to Modernism.

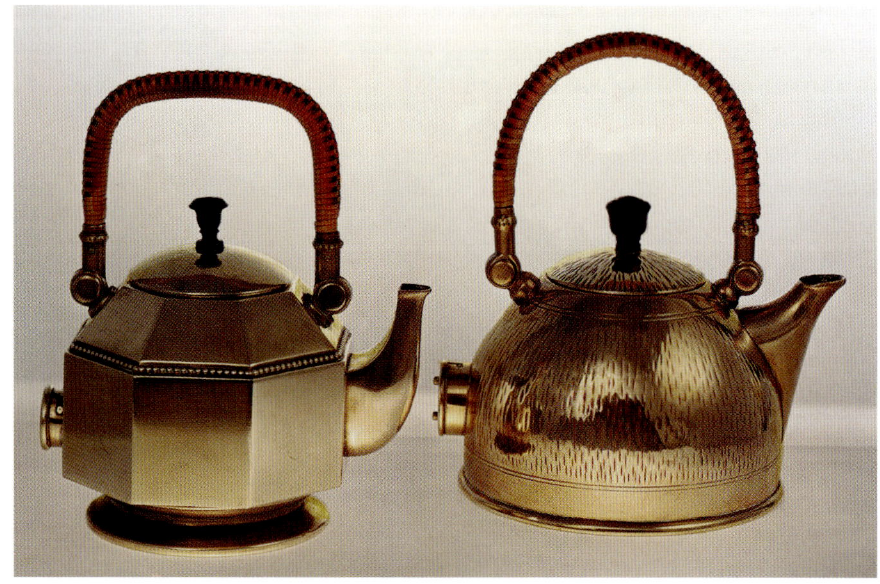

ABOVE:
Brass electric kettles
for AEG, 1908

Starting his career as a painter, Behrens became a member of the Munich Secession in 1892, and the following year took part in the group's first exhibition. Six years later his famous *Der Kuss* (The Kiss) woodcut was published in the Berlin-based journal *Pan*, which was an influential organ of the new Jugendstil (German Art Nouveau) movement. The following year, in 1899, Behrens was invited by Grand Duke Ernst Ludwig of Hesse to become a member of the Darmstadt Artists' Colony, a creative design-reforming venture intended to stimulate co-operation between art and industry. It was here, as part of the colony's complex, that Behrens designed and built his own "artist house", which was conceived as a unified *Gesamtkunstwerk* (total work of art) in which every interior detail from furniture to drinking glasses was designed site-specifically.

In 1902, he designed an influential dining room installation for the Wertheim department store, for which he similarly designed every single item, including the furniture, lighting, carpet, tablecloth, napkins, tableware, glasses and cutlery. These items were far less luxurious than the ones previously designed for Behrens's own residence and were instead based on a strictly geometric grid of rectangles and squares, and were intentionally designed for mass-production so that they could be priced reasonably. The same year, Behrens designed a new typeface, Behrens-Schrift, which fused Roman and Gothic lettering and again reflected his versatility as a designer.

His undeniable talent for architecture, product design and graphics led Behrens to be appointed artistic consultant to the vast and rapidly expanding industrial electric company Allgemeine Elektricitäts-Gesellschaft, better known as AEG, in 1907. One of his earliest forays into industrial design was the redesign of the company's arc lamps, which were intended for industrial usage in factories, railway stations and the like. Behrens's new arc light designs employed simplified forms that were reminiscent of Greek drinking cups and amphora, of which he had a fine personal collection. Indeed, it could be said that with these designs Behrens was pioneering a new Modern Classicism that was not only suited for large-scale industrial production but also gave an object a pleasingly unified appearance.

Certainly, he was acutely aware that the external appearance of an object, even one that was entirely driven by function, was important to its ultimate sales success, once remarking that "a motor ought to look like a birthday present". He went on to design numerous electric appliances for AEG – from kettles and fans to clocks and hair dryers – as well as exhibition pavilions and graphic communications. It was the first time a single designer had been tasked with creating an all-encompassing "total design" corporate identity for a manufacturer.

Behrens's designs for AEG were not only aesthetically refined, but were also fundamentally informed by the technical requirements of industrial mass-production. Through his design of standardized components, some of which were interchangeable between products, he managed to implement a new form of modern design suitable for large-scale industrial production. He also designed buildings for the firm, including workers' housing. However, it is his AEG Turbinenfabrik (Turbine Factory) built in Moabit, Berlin that is generally considered his architectural masterwork.

Behrens's work for AEG utterly embodied the ideals of the Deutscher Werkbund (DWB), which he had co-founded in 1907 in order to promote unity between art, industry and commerce. As a prominent member of the Deutscher Werkbund, Behrens later designed the low-rise Terrassenhaus apartment block as part of the DWB's *Die Wohnung* (The Home) exhibition held in Stuttgart in 1927, which, like other estate buildings on the Weissenhof-Siedlung, reflected the new unadorned International Style of Modernism that emerged during the inter-war period.

Importantly, Behrens had a direct influence on the next generation of architects, with Le Corbusier, Ludwig Mies van de Rohe and Walter Gropius working for him early in their careers. While Behrens's legacy was tarred by the pro-Nazi sympathies that he held during the 1930s, he must still be considered one of the great pioneers of industrial design practice and a founding father of the Modern Movement, with his work reflecting the progressive evolution of Modernism during the early decades of the twentieth century.

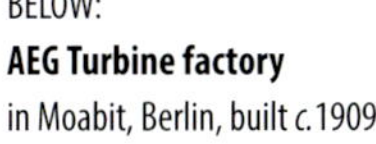
BELOW:
AEG Turbine factory
in Moabit, Berlin, built *c.*1909

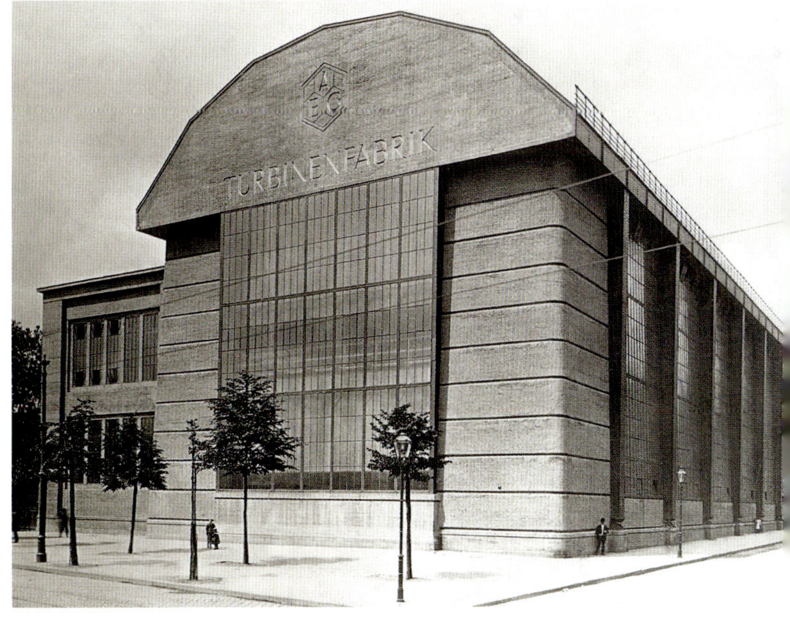

Mario Bellini

Italian, 1935–

Mario Bellini's pioneering design work – from revolutionary electronic products to stylish furniture and lighting – has always been typified by functional innovation and a distinctively Milanese refinement.

Bellini studied architecture at the Politecnico di Milano (Milan Polytechnic University), graduating in 1959, and from 1961 to 1963 worked as a designer at La Rinascente, the influential chain of department stores that was renowned for its promotion of Italian design through its establishment of the famous Compasso d'Oro awards. In 1963 he co-founded a design practice with Marco Romano and the same year became a design consultant to Olivetti. Working for Olivetti in this capacity until 1991, Bellini created numerous landmark products, most notably his Divisumma 18 calculator (1971–73), Divisumma 28 calculator (1972), Lettera 35 typewriter (1974) and Praxis 20 electronic typewriter (1981). With all these designs, he cased their technology with an alluring yet purposeful skin that in turn enhanced their everyday operative functionality.

His remarkable ability to unify aesthetics with utility gave his designs both a strong identity and functional logic. He also created the GA 45 Pop record player for Minerva (1968), which transformed the humble record player into a mobile handbag-like Pop design. His Totem RR 130 FO/ST record and tape player (1970) for Brionvega similarly broke new ground in the realm of consumer electronics by introducing a minimalist aesthetic: when it was closed in on itself, it formed a sculptural solid white cube.

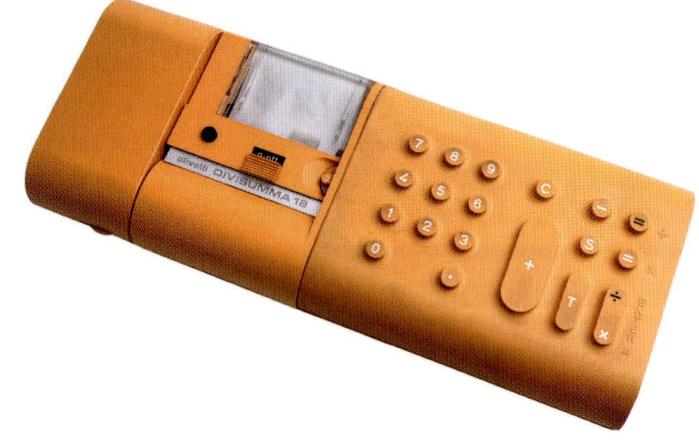

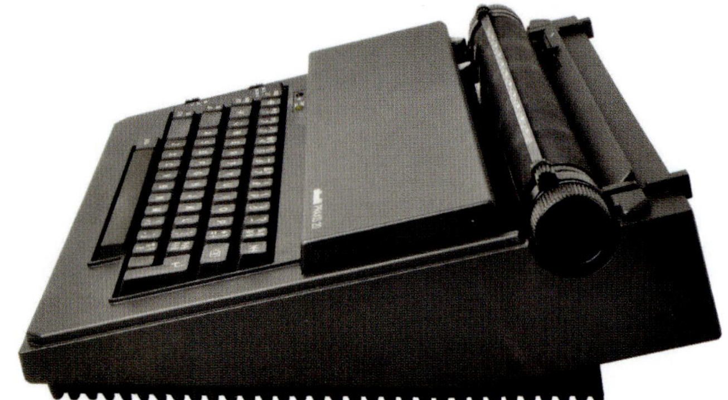

In the field of lighting design, Bellini also revealed his ability to create innovative new forms, such as his Chiara floor light (1960–69) for Flos formed from a sheet of stainless steel and his Area light for Artemide (1974) with its light-diffusing shade of polymerized paper. His furniture designs were also inventive, such as his Le Bambole range for B&B Italia (1970–72) that comprised skinned single blocks of moulded foamed rubber to provide squishy comfort and which Bellini described as like "sitting on a three-dimensional pillow". His

Cab chair (1977) for Cassina, however, is his best-known furniture design, with its skin of saddle leather zipped over a flexible steel frame to provide not only comfort but also a sculptural yet understated elegance.

Bellini has also worked in the automotive industry, designing in 1972 his Kar-a-sutra concept car, which was shown at the *Italy: The New Domestic Landscape – Achievements and Problems of Italian Design* exhibition at the Museum of Modern Art, New York. Between 1978 and 1982, he served as a design consultant to Renault.

Apart from his design work, Bellini was also editor-in-chief of *Domus* magazine from 1986 to 1991 and has taught at the Istituto Superiore di Disegno Industriale (Higher Institute for Industrial Design) in Venice, the Hochschule für Angewandte Kunst (University of Applied Arts) in Vienna, the Domus Academy in Milan and the architecture faculty at the University of Genoa. During his long and prolific career, Bellini has been awarded eight Premio Compasso d'Oro, a fitting testament to his remarkable ability to create pioneering design solutions that possess not only an undeniable functional logic but also an engaging sculptural presence.

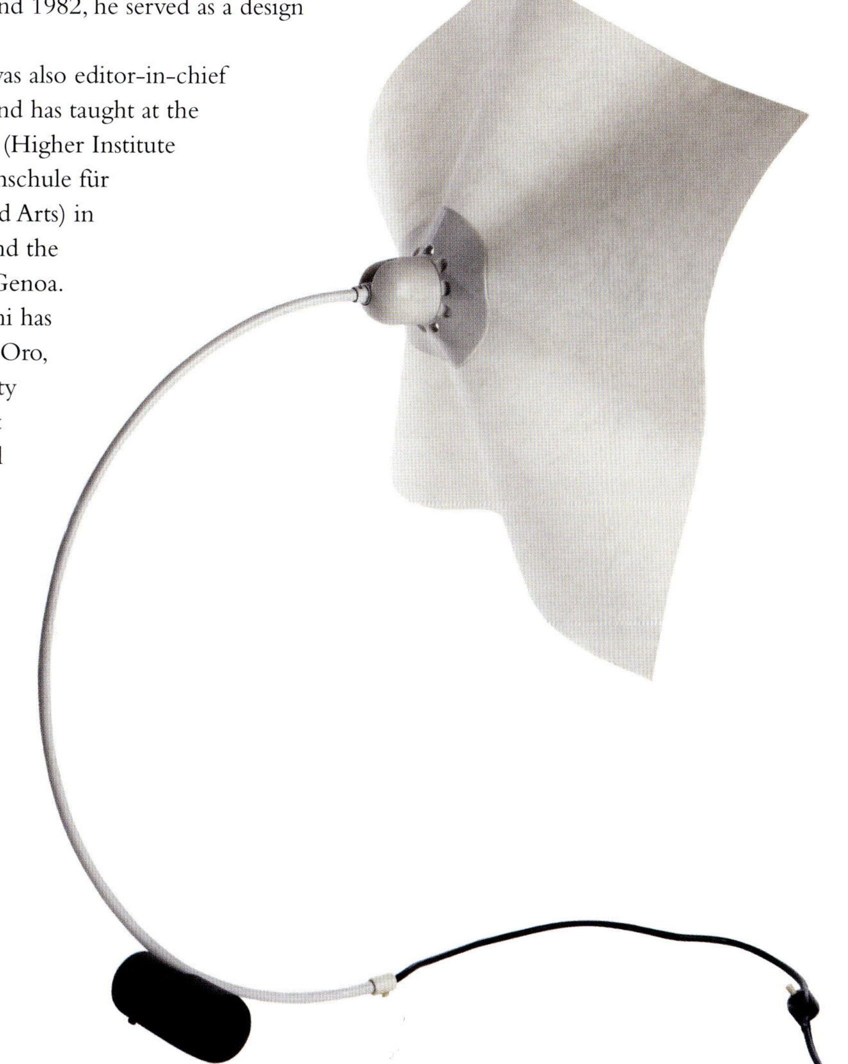

OPPOSITE TOP:
Divisumma 18 printing calculator
for Olivetti, 1971–73

OPPOSITE BOTTOM:
Praxis 20 electronic typewriter
for Olivetti, 1981

RIGHT:
Area light
for Artemide, 1974

William Arthur Smith Benson

British, 1854–1924

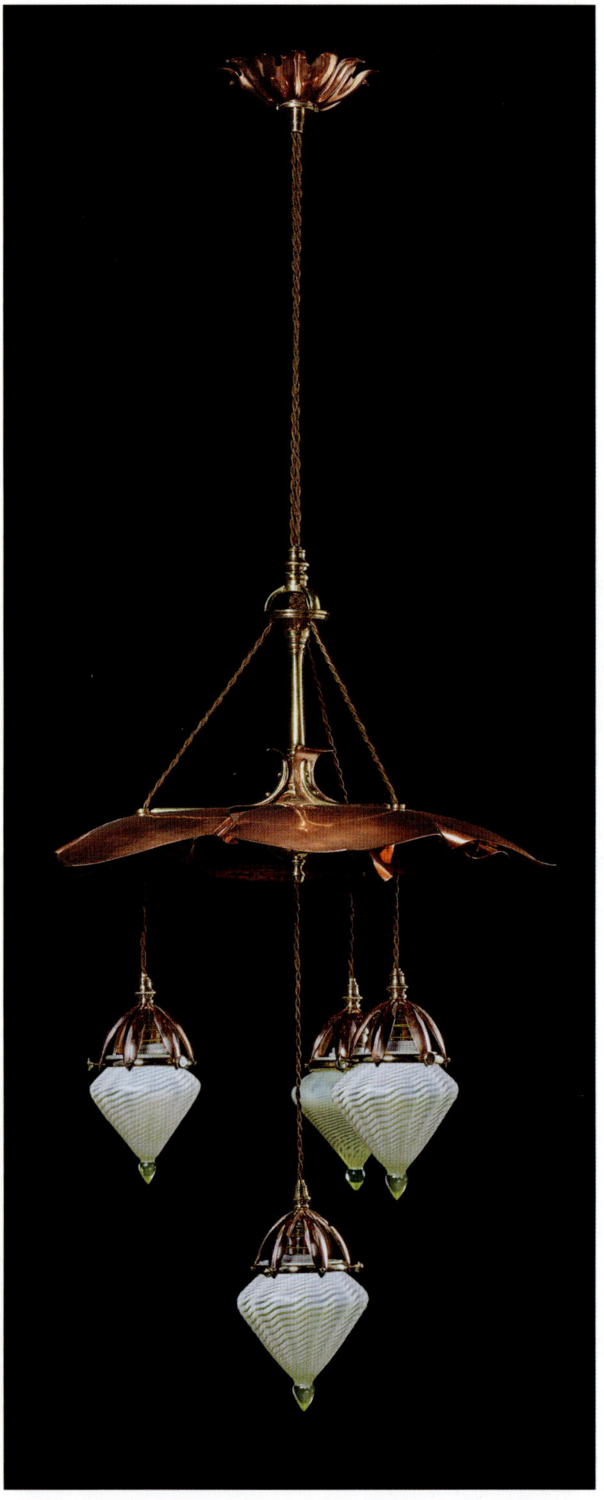

Among the most forward-looking designers associated with the Arts and Crafts Movement, William Arthur Smith Benson, unlike most of his peers, did not shun the machine but instead harnessed its power to create mass-produced designs that were humanized with a craft sensibility. Through this approach he achieved considerable commercial success, unlike those designers who doggedly stuck to handicraft on doctrinal grounds, thereby highlighting a key dilemma of this idealistic design-reforming movement. He was also an important innovator of Rational product development, presaging Peter Behrens's work in this field by some twenty-five years. Benson was, therefore, a very early pioneer of Modern design, even though most of the products he designed and manufactured in his Hammersmith factory were stylistically very much within the Arts and Crafts idiom.

Benson was well connected to the Arts and Crafts Movement through birth and marriage – his sister was married to the designer Heywood Sumner, while his father-in-law was the painter Alfred William Hunt, an associate of the Pre-Raphaelite Brotherhood. Yet, unlike many of those aligned with the movement, Benson appreciated the possibilities of mechanized production from an early age. This can be credited to an uncle of his, who was a keen amateur metalworker with a workshop fully kitted out with machinery. It was from him that Benson gained crucial hands-on knowledge of how to use such equipment and an all-important appreciation of its design potential. Thanks to his family connections Benson also got to know William Morris, who effectively took him under his wing and served as his mentor. In 1880, Benson founded his own decorating firm in London with himself as sole designer. He began designing metalwork conceived for machine production, which was principally made of either brass or copper or an attractive combination of both metals. His machine-made wares were of excellent

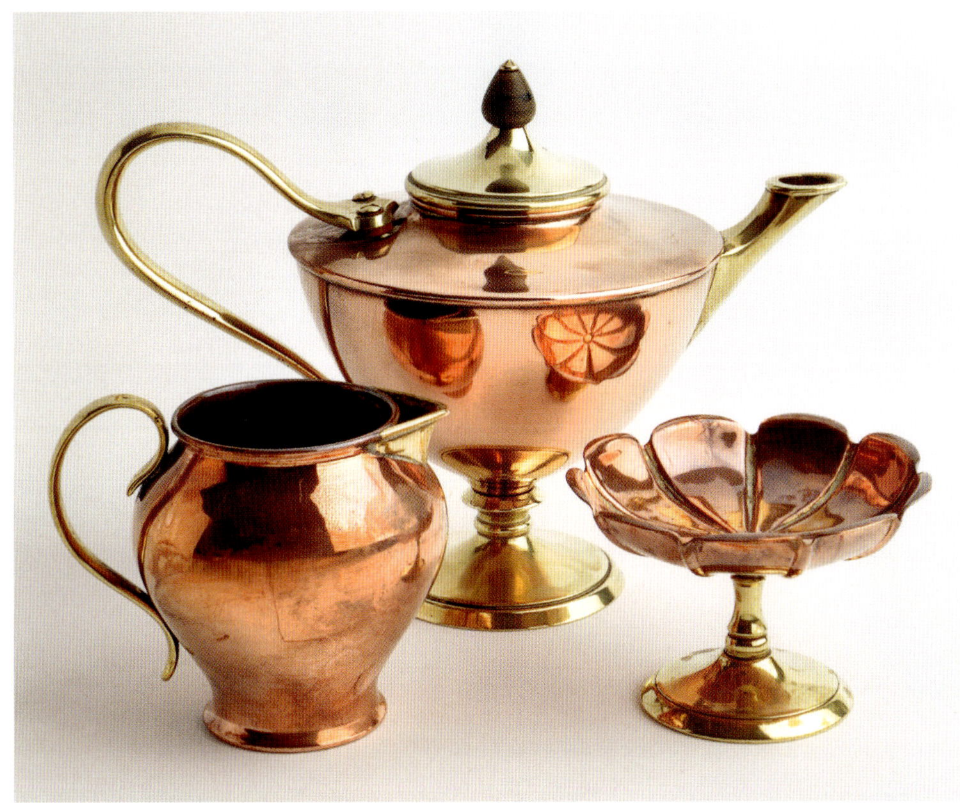

quality and were retailed by Morris & Co. in London and Siegfried Bing's Maison l'Art Nouveau in Paris.

By reconciling "art manufactures" with rational mechanized production methods, Benson drew considerable praise from the German design critic Hermann Muthesius, who suggested that his metalwares should serve as a model for German industrial production. Mr "Brass" Benson, as he became known, was also a pioneer of component interchangeability, whereby standardized parts were joined together in different combinations to create various types of object; for example, an element found on one of his teapots might well also have been used to construct a lamp or an inkwell. This type of mix-and-match assembly enabled Benson to produce hundreds of different patterns at his large purpose-built factory, the Eyot works in Hammersmith, London. Although Benson's brass and copper designs were produced industrially, they did not have an overtly machine aesthetic, and are perhaps best described as having been "crafted" by machine. With their warm metallic glow and sinuous and unfurling forms, Benson's metalwork designs became an essential element of fashionable Art Nouveau interiors during the *fin-de-siècle* years – especially those created by Morris & Co., where he was a director from 1896, following Morris's death. Through his thoughtful and honest use of the machine, Benson was able to produce domestic wares that nonetheless retained craft values, thereby setting an important precedent for the future production of high-quality machine-made goods with an emotionally engaging resonance.

OPPOSITE:
Chandelier for W.A.S. Benson & Co.
*c.*1900

ABOVE:
Tea set for W.A.S. Benson & Co.
*c.*1885

Sigvard Bernadotte

Swedish, 1907–2002

The son of King Gustav VI Adolf of Sweden, Sigvard Bernadotte was born a prince, yet later in life he would prove himself to be a highly accomplished industrial designer. Indeed, Bernadotte was commonly referred to in his home country as the "Design Prince of Sweden" having become one of the most successful practitioners of modern Scandinavian design in the 1950s and 1960s.

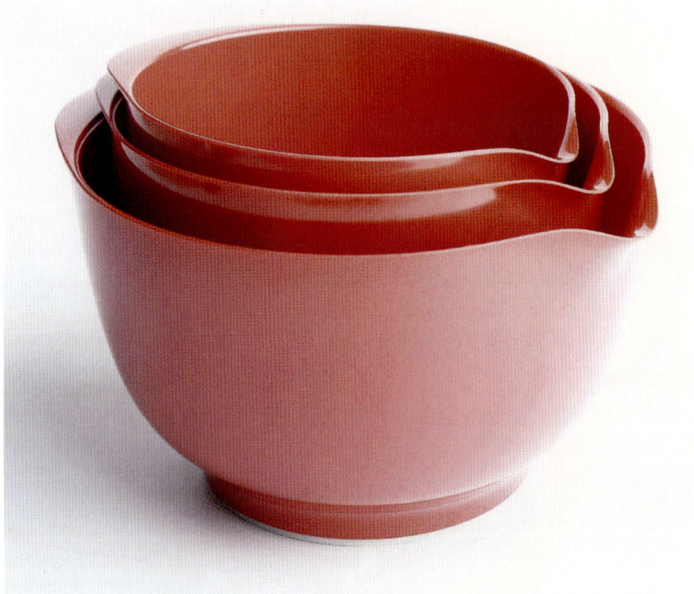

ABOVE:
Margrethe stacking bowls
for Rosti, 1950

Bernadotte studied political science among other subjects at the Faculty of Art at Uppsala University, but subsequently decided to study fine art at the Kungliga Konsthögskolan (Royal Institute of Art) in Stockholm and then design at the Staatschule für Angewandte Kunst (State School of Applied Arts) in Munich. After completion of his studies, he joined the design studio at Georg Jensen and became the first designer there to employ geometric Art Deco forms rather than the more naturalistic Arts and Crafts style that had become synonymous with the workshop's output. His Bernadotte cutlery range of 1939 with its angular handles typified his more Modernistic approach, as did his Bernadotte thermos jug (1938) with its swelling ribbed form.

During the 1930s he travelled extensively in Europe and, crucially for his development as a designer, visited the United States, where he met many leading American industrial design consultants, including Raymond Loewy, Walter Dorwin Teague, Donald Deskey and Henry Dreyfuss. Inspired by the wide-ranging inter-disciplinary nature of their design offices, he left his position as a director of Georg Jensen to establish his own Copenhagen-based industrial design consultancy with the Danish designer Acton Bjørn in 1950.

As one of the first Danish industrial design practices and one of the earliest in Sweden, Bernadotte & Bjørn was hugely influential, receiving international recognition for its innovative work, such as the melamine Margrethe nesting mixing bowls for Rosti (1950) and compact plastic adding machine for Odhner (1952). The consultancy went on to design numerous household products which skilfully exploited the potential of the new plastic materials that were becoming more widely available during the post-war years, such as the wedge-formed Nya Clara can opener (1963) for Nils Johan and the Taffel picnic set for

RIGHT AND BELOW:
Taffel picnic set
for Husqvarna, 1959

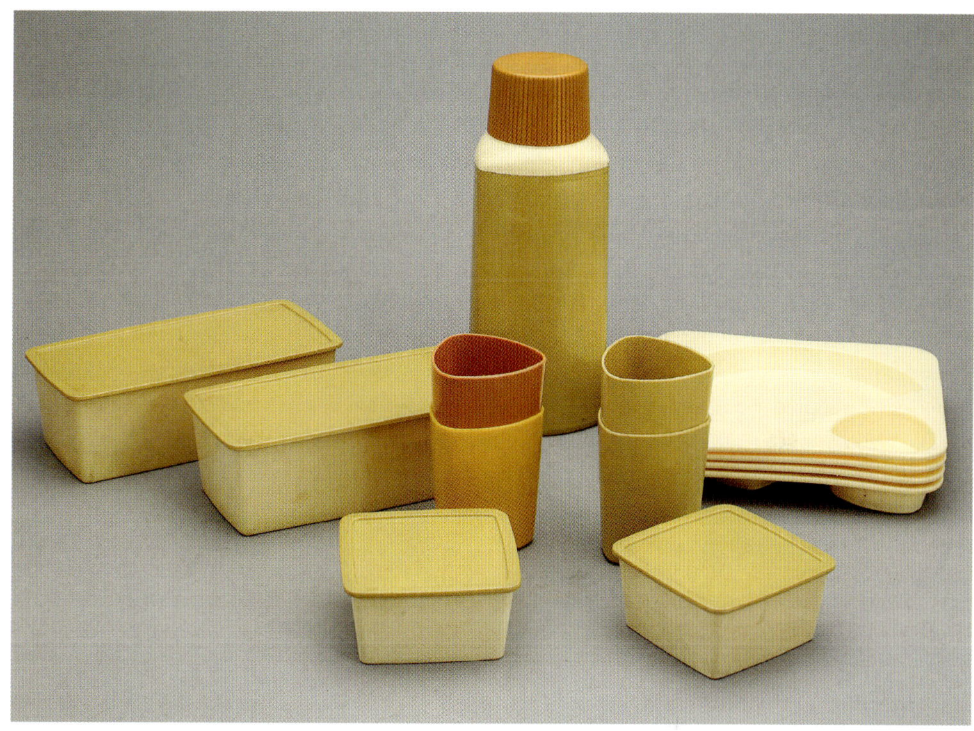

Husqvarna (1959). It also notably created the compact Privat typewriter for Facit (1960), cutlery for SAS and the Beolit 500 portable radio (1965) for Bang & Olufsen, and opened an office in New York. In 1964, Bernadotte independently established the Bernadotte Design Studio, which specialized in the design of heavy industrial equipment such as forklift trucks and outboard motors.

As a leading proponent of modern industrial design practice in Scandinavia, Sigvard Bernadotte co-founded the Swedish Industrial Designers Society (SID) and also became the first European designer to be elected a member of the Industrial Designers Society of America. Between 1961 and 1963 Bernadotte was also president of the International Council of Societies of Industrial Design (ICSID).

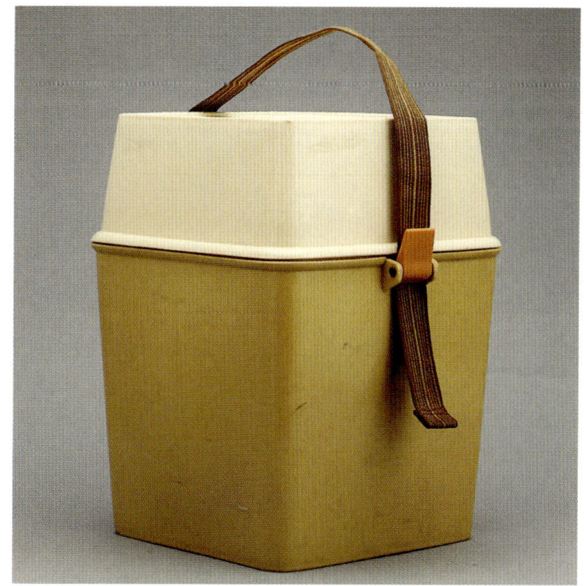

Lucian Bernhard

German/active USA, 1883–1972

Best remembered for his vibrant colour-saturated posters, Lucian Bernhard made an enormous contribution to the evolution of modern graphic design and advertising. Indeed, he was the foremost innovator of what was then known in Germany as *Sachplakat* (object posters) during the early years of the twentieth century. Whether his advertising posters were promoting gloves sold by Ranniger's, cigarettes for Manoli or typewriters for Adler, they had a striking originality with their bold compositions demanding the viewer's immediate attention.

Born Emil Kahn, Bernhard initially attended art school in Munich where he was exposed to the influence of Jugendstil, especially in relation to graphic design. He moved to Berlin in 1901 and entered a poster competition for Priestler, a manufacturer of matches, which he won with a bold composition that showed two red matches with bright yellow heads set against a black background and positioned under the firm's name picked out in an arresting hue of blue. In 1905, he adopted the *nom de plume* "Lucian Bernhard", allegedly because his father disowned him and his family was unsupportive of his creative goals as a commercial artist. The same year he began creating "advertising art" exclusively for the Berlin-based agency Hollerbaum & Schmidt that was striking for its bold directness and reductivist simplicity.

Also in 1905, Bernhard became a founding member of the Verein der Plakatfreunde (Association of Friends of the Poster) in Berlin and was the artistic consultant for this

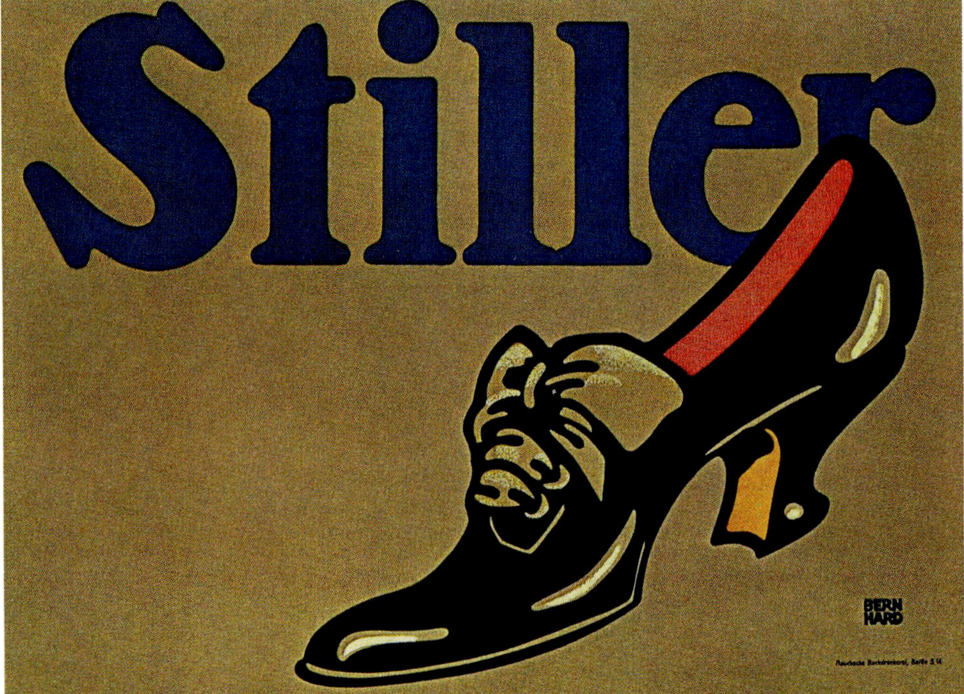

LEFT:
Lithographic poster
for Stiller, 1908

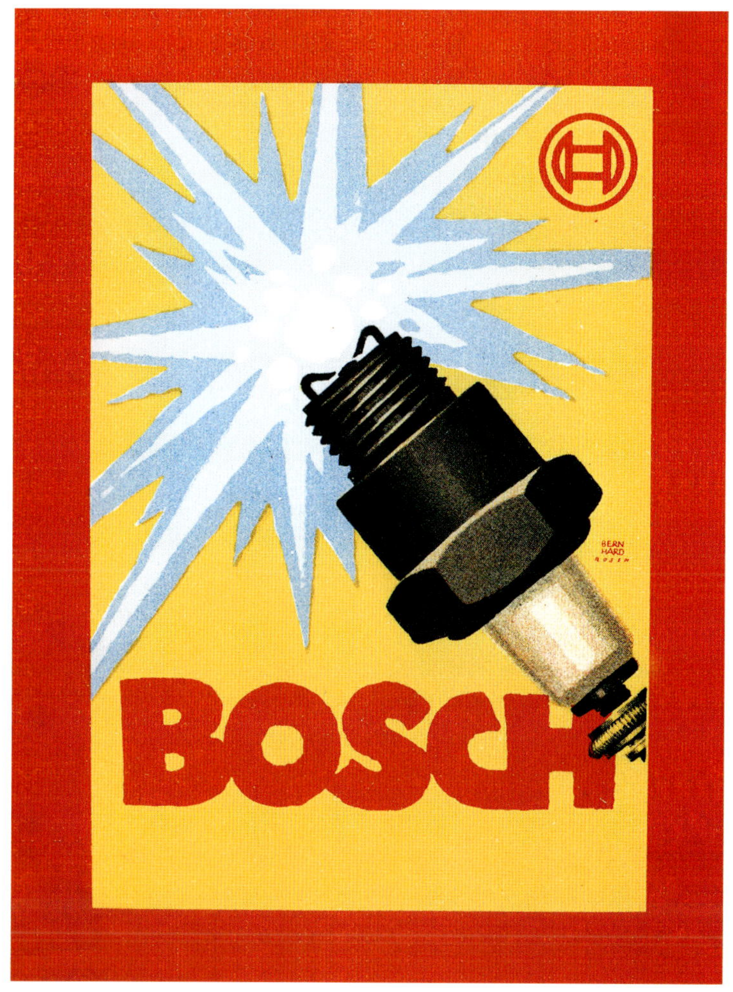

LEFT:
Lithographic poster
for Bosch, *c.*1914

promotional organization. The following year he established his own studio and subsequently became the most celebrated poster designer working in Berlin. In 1907 he co-founded the Deutscher Werkbund (DWB), which was formed to foster a better alliance between art and industry.

Bernhard was appointed artistic director of the Berlin branch of the Deutsche Werkstatten fur Handwerkskunst (Workshops for Craftsmanship) in 1910 and for this design-reforming enterprise he created graphics as well as furniture, lighting, textiles and interiors. In 1920 he became a professor at the Höhere Fachschule für Dekorationskunst (Higher College of Decorative Arts) in Berlin, where he taught poster design along with typography. He emigrated to the United States in 1923 and the following year established a design studio with Elmer Adler in New York, where he created numerous typefaces for the American Type Founders (ATF) as well as for the Bauer Type Foundry in Germany.

With Rockwell Kent, Paul Poiret, Bruno Paul and Erich Mendelsohn, Bernhard founded the Contempora Studio in 1928, and under the aegis of this venture increasingly devoted himself to interior design. The same year he wrote an article for *House and Garden* magazine entitled "Modernism in the Home" in which he described the difference between Modern interior installations designed for the purposes of exhibition and spaces people could actually live in comfortably. From 1930 onwards, Bernhard abandoned his design activities in favour of painting and sculpture, yet it was this area of creativity for which he is best remembered, as he was so instrumental in developing a truly modern graphic language for advertising.

Bertone

Italian, founded 1912

One of the oldest and most renowned automotive design studios, Bertone originally started out as a *carrozzeria* (coachbuilder). The firm's origins go back to 1912 when the young Giovanni Bertone opened a garage for the repair and manufacture of horse-drawn carriages and coaches, with his designs of such vehicles being valued for their high quality and sturdy construction.

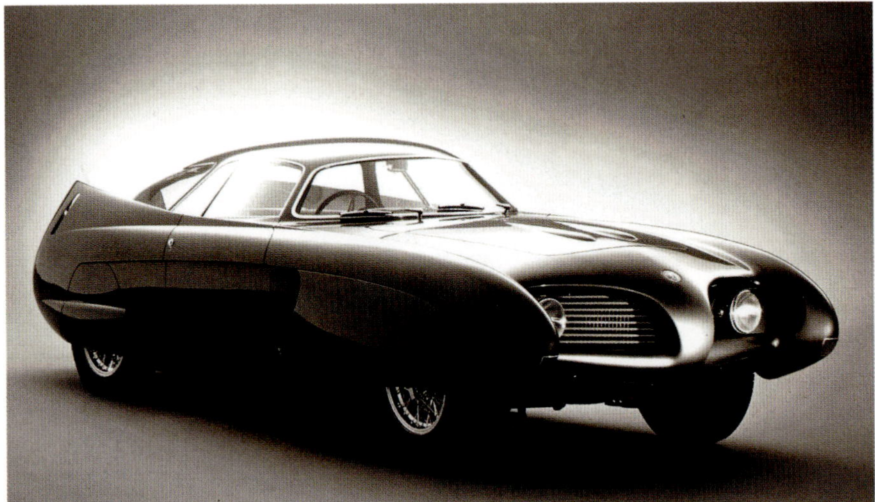

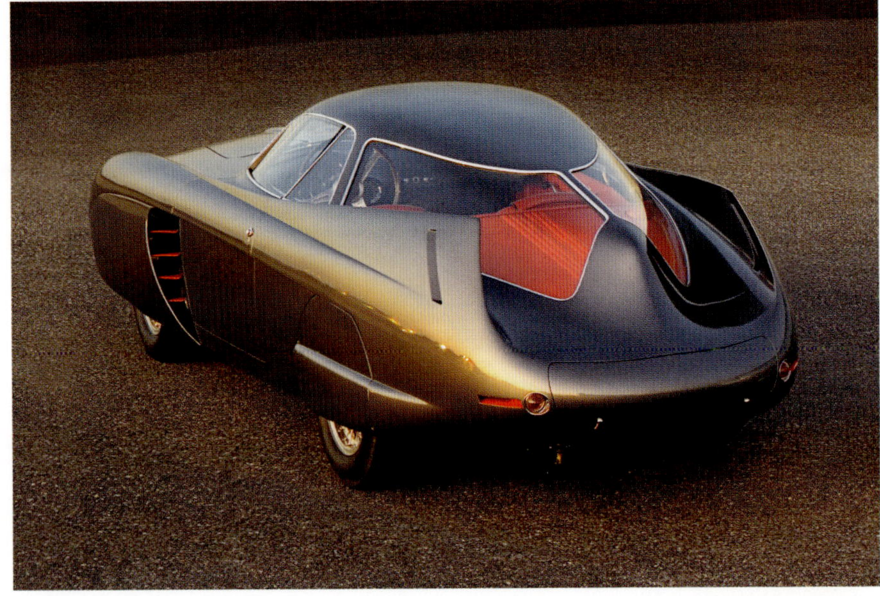

TOP & ABOVE:
BAT 5 concept car
for Alfa Romeo, 1953

In 1914, Giovanni's second son, Giuseppe "Nuccio" Bertone, was born; he would play a leading role in the evolution of the company and become himself a legendary car designer. Although the First World War forced the closure of the Turin-based firm, it re-opened after the cessation of hostilities and expanded into a new and larger plant in 1920 so that it could enter the emerging automotive design sector.

Initially, the company created truck bodies built on a Lancia chassis, but in 1921 it received its first major coachwork contract for the body design of a car, the Torpedo based on the SPA 23 S chassis. This was followed two years later by the Fiat 501 sports car, which had an even more streamlined form for enhanced speed performance.

During the 1930s and 1940s, Carrozzeria Bertone produced a number of other notable models, including the Lancia Aprilia (1937) and the Fiat 2800 cabriolet (1943). It was not until after the Second World War, however, when Nuccio took over the running of the company from his father, that the firm became legendary for its progressive design work, such as the Alfa Romeo BAT 5 concept car of 1953, which used an Alfa Romeo Sprint 1900 chassis and had a progressive streamlined body shape based on aerodynamic studies.

Under Nuccio's leadership Carrozzeria Bertone went on to design other forward-looking cars, most notably the Alfa Romeo Giulietta Sprint Speciale (1960–62), a European-styled Ford Mustang protoype (1965), the sublime Miura for Lamborghini (1966) that is widely credited as the world's first supercar, the futuristic Lancia Stratos HF Zero concept car (1970) and the elegantly styled Maserati Khamsin GranTurismo coupe (1972–75), which together managed to seal Bertone's standing as one of the most innovative car design studios in the world. Unfortunately, Nuccio's death in 1996 led to the company's decline; after unsuccessful attempts at recovery, it was eventually declared bankrupt and closed down in 2014.

BELOW:
Miura sports car
for Lamborghini , 1966

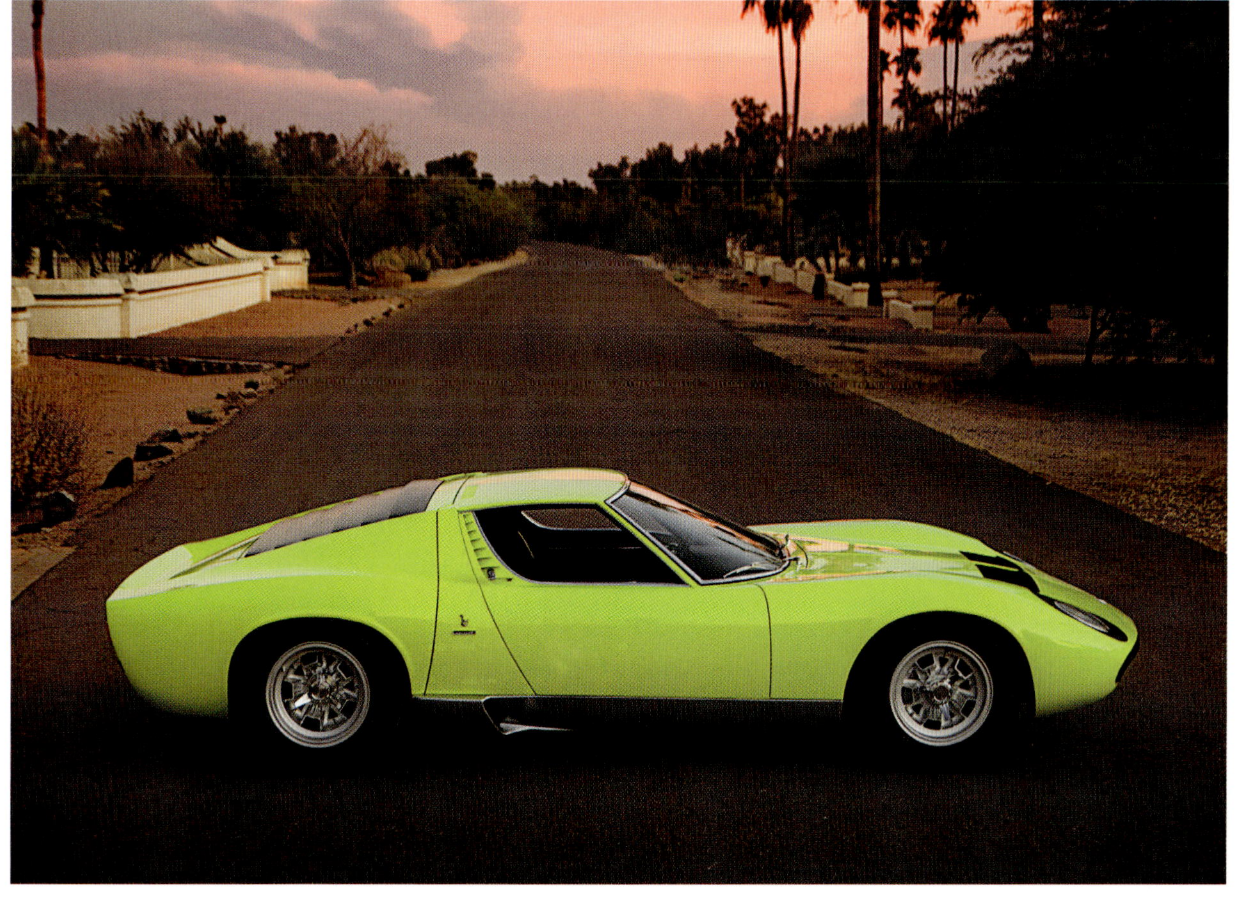

Max Bill

Swiss/active Germany, 1908–1994

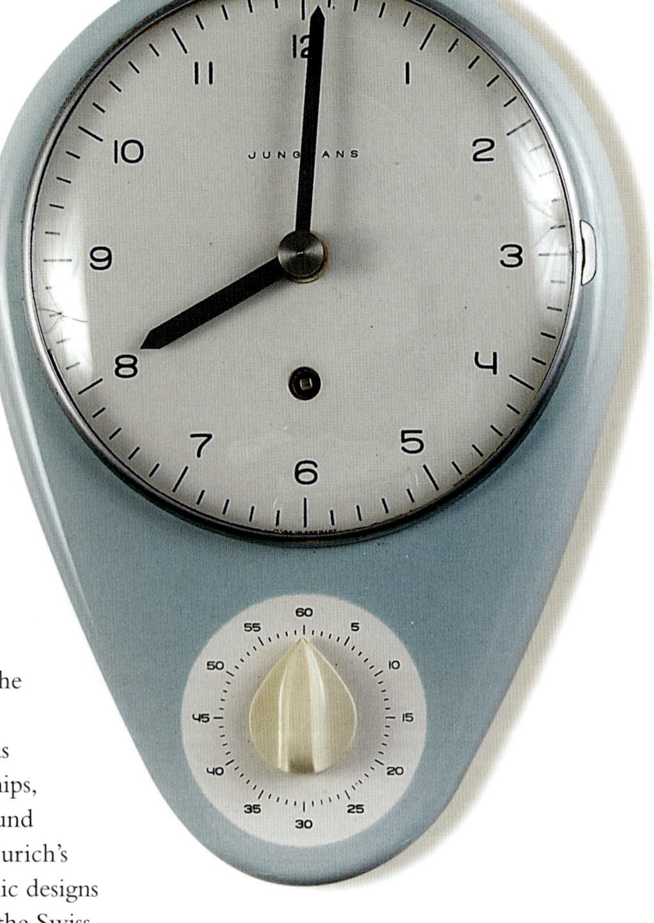

A design visionary and pioneer of Modernist graphic communication, Max Bill took a mathematical approach to art and design that helped him create work with a strong sense of proportional refinement.

Having trained as a silversmith at the Kunstgewerbeschule (School of Applied Arts) in Zurich from 1924 to 1927, he subsequently studied at the Bauhaus in Dessau under Josef Albers, Wassily Kandinsky, Paul Klee and Oskar Schlemmer between 1927 and 1928. In 1929 he returned to Zurich and subsequently worked as an architect, painter, sculptor, graphic designer, product designer and design theorist. Alongside Max Huber, Leo Leuppi and Richard Paul Lohse, Bill became a member of the Allianz group in 1937, which promoted the theories of the Concrete Art movement and its advocacy of abstractionism freed of any symbolic associations – the group later becoming known as the Zürcher Konkrete.

During the 1930s, Bill's graphic design work was typified by the use of bold figure–ground relationships, such as the white O set against the orange background of his poster for the *Negerkunst* exhibition held at Zurich's Kunstgewerbemuseum in 1931. Certainly, his graphic designs from this period epitomized the purist aesthetic of the Swiss School, possessing both a universal clarity and striking boldness of execution.

In 1947, Bill met with the German graphic designer Otl Aicher and his wife Inge Scholl to discuss the founding of a new school of design run along Bauhaus lines. This resulted in the foundation of the Hochschule für Gestaltung or HfG (College of Design) in Ulm in 1953, with Bill being appointed its first rector. Indeed, many of the Ulm school's staff members and guest lecturers had previously taught at the Bauhaus, most notably Johannes Itten, Josef Albers and Walter Peterhans – and therefore it can be seen as the true post-war successor of this remarkably influential design-teaching institution.

ABOVE:
Kitchen clock
for Junghans, 1953

OPPOSITE:
Ulmer Hocker (Ulm stool)
for Ulm HfG, 1954

It was for the school's students that Bill co-designed with Hans Gugelot and Paul Hildinger the famously spartan multi-functional Ulmer Hocker (Ulm stool), which, with its unadorned minimalist form, reflected the strong functionalist agenda that was embodied in the school's teaching doctrine. Bill's wall clocks, kitchen timers and wristwatches designed for Junghans during the 1950s possessed a similar stripped-down quality and revealed his continuing adherence to the Concrete Art movement as well as his talent for mathematically balanced graphic compositions.

Bill also notably designed the Sun health lamp for Novelectric (1951) and a three-legged chair for Horgenglarus, yet perhaps his greatest contribution to design during these post-war years was his instigation of the *Gute Form* (Good Design) campaign, the origins of which can be traced back to a conference speech he made to the Swiss Werkbund (SWB) in 1948 on "beauty as function and based on function". Following this talk, the SWB commissioned him to design an exhibition of Swiss design that would reveal "the principles of pure functional form". The subsequent *Gute Form* touring exhibition of 1949 in turn led the Swiss Werkbund to introduce its annual *Gute Form* prize in 1952, which inspired the establishment of the Rat für Formgebung (German Design Council) in 1953, the founding mandate of which was to promote good design for both economic and cultural purposes.

After disagreeing with Otl Aicher over the structure of the curriculum at the HfG in Ulm, Bill eventually resigned as the school's director in 1956 and the following year set up a studio in Zurich. He subsequently dedicated much of his time to painting and sculpture, but he did continue to teach and also designed a number of exhibition pavilions. Seeing very little difference between his role as an artist and his role as a designer, he declared, "The difference between the design problems which have to be solved every day and works of painting and sculpture is merely one of degree, not one of principle."

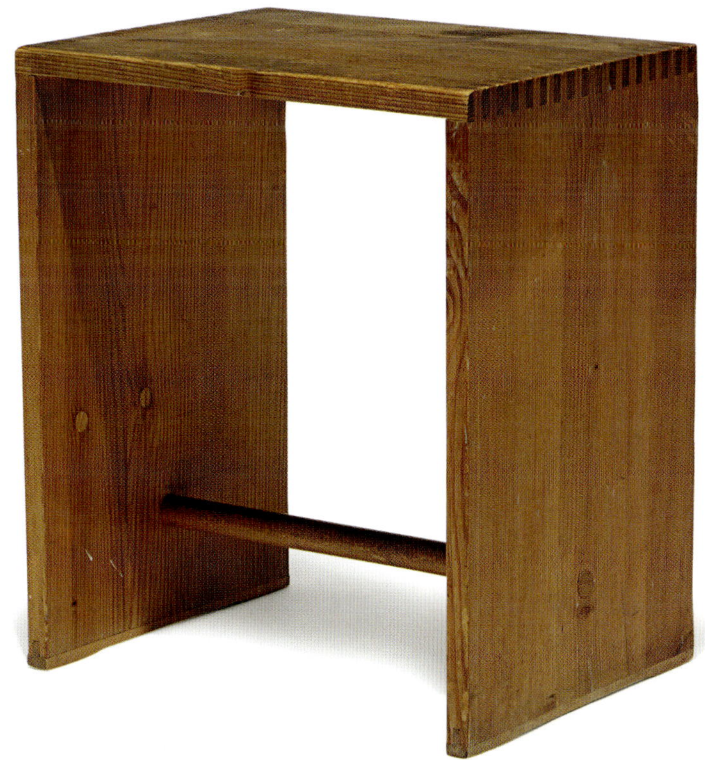

Derek Birdsall

British, 1934–

The British graphic designer and art director Derek Birdsall achieved international renown through his eye-catching cover designs for Penguin Books as well as for his innovative design of various magazines, including *Nova*, and the famous Pirelli calendars.

As a child Birdsall loved stationery shops with their stacks of notebooks, reams of paper, variety of pens and bottles of ink. By his own admission he had a fountain-pen fetish and this ultimately led him to his chosen career, with his first commercial commission being a series of posters for his local cricket club. Although he disliked his grammar school, he did have beautiful handwriting and as a result his art teacher suggested that he go to art school. At Wakefield College of Art he undertook what would be today's equivalent of an art foundation course. After these preliminary studies, he was then faced with the choice of studying either lithography or lettering. He chose the latter and for the next three years at Wakefield he honed his skills in lettering, as well as experimenting with the school's letterpress. He soon acquired his own printing press, and began producing business cards for local companies using type acquired from the college's compositing room.

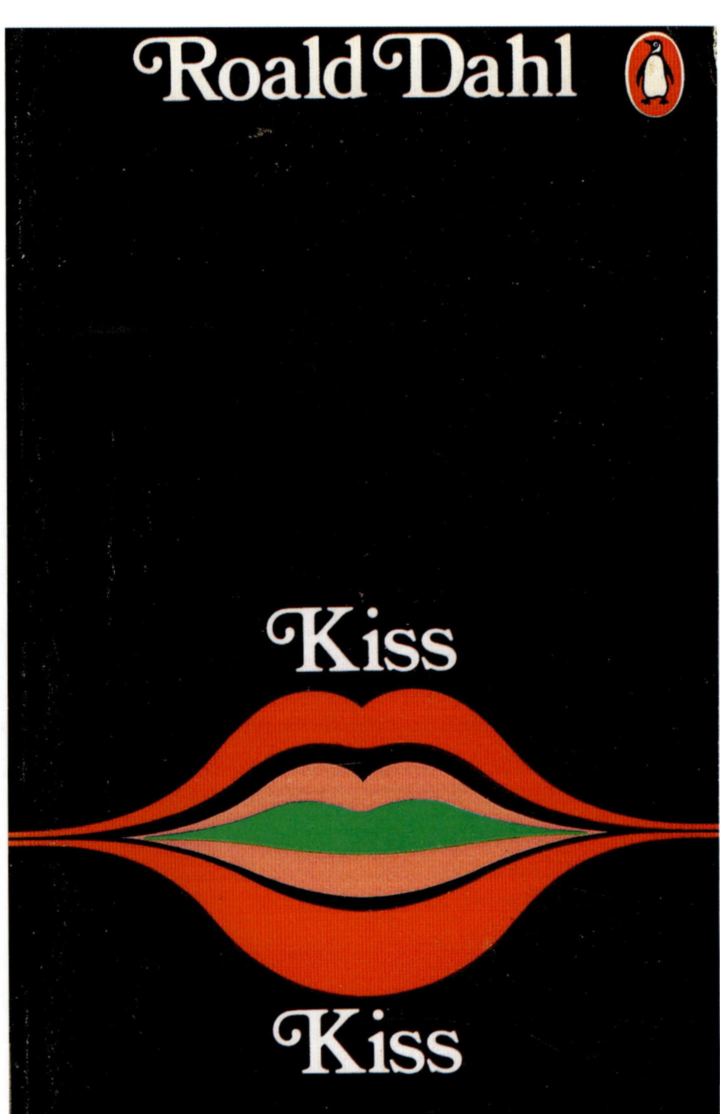

ABOVE:
Book cover for Roald Dahl's *Kiss Kiss*
for Penguin, 1962

In 1952, Birdsall won a scholarship to the Central School of Art and Design, London. There he was influenced by typographer and designer Anthony Froshaug, who, alongside Herbert Spencer and Edward Wright, taught his students to distinguish between beautiful lettering and functional typography, the latter emphasizing clarity, directness and legibility. The legacy of the 1951 *Festival of Britain*, which Birdsall later described as "typographically Victorian", was countered by Froshaug's guidance on the clean modern typography of the Swiss School.

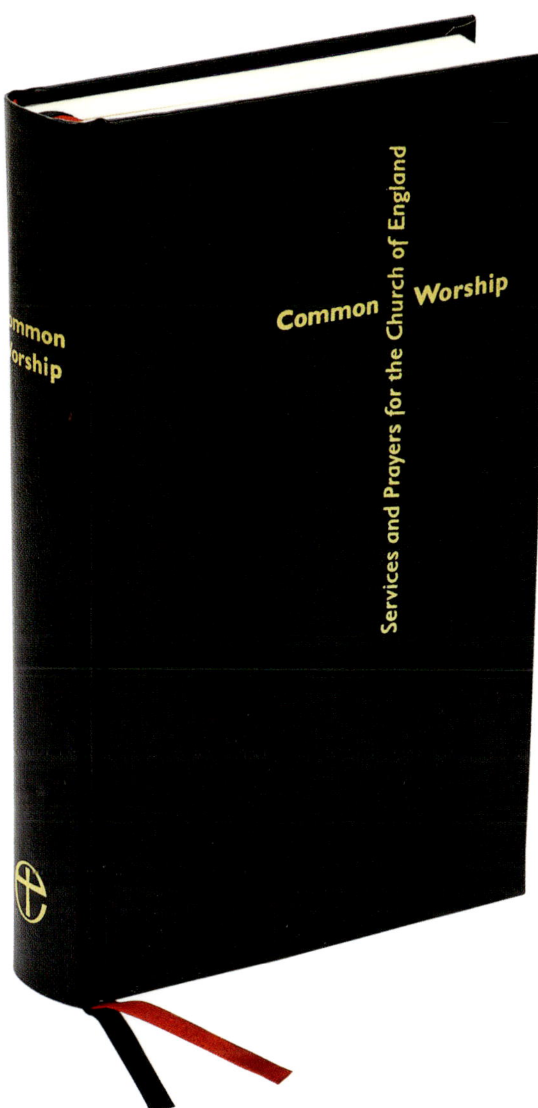

ABOVE:
Book cover for *Common Worship: Services and Prayers for the Church of England*
for Church House Publishing, 2000

Jan Tshichold's work was also an inspiration with its use of asymmetric layouts, Modernist simplicity and decorative restraint. On completion of his studies, Birdsall spent two years of National Service at the Royal Army Ordnance Corps printing unit in Cyprus and in 1957 began his professional design career. His first design job was on a series of leaflets for the printer Banding & Mansell and embodied his typographic style, which he described as having "a sense of poetry; Modernism with a delicate touch". Two years later he formed the BDMW agency with George Daulby, James Mortimer and George Mayhew, and it was here that he acquired a reputation for being the go-to "emergency art director" thanks to his multi-tasking approach, which saw him commissioning and art-directing photography and illustrations as well as creating typography, magazine layouts and book covers, most notably for Penguin.

By skilfully combining typography and imagery, Birdsall designed book covers during the 1960s and 1970s for Penguin that had a powerful visual impact and were hugely influential. During this period he also designed a landmark book for Monty Python for which he was granted temporary membership of this well-known and idiosyncratic comedic group. During the next two decades, Birdsall continued to design numerous beautifully conceived book covers for esteemed cultural organizations around the world, while also working in the realms of editorial design and art direction for both the *Independent* and *The Sunday Telegraph* weekend supplements. In 2000, he was tasked with the redesign of *Common Worship* (an alternative to the *Book of Common Prayer*) for the Church of England, which revealed his extraordinary understanding of typographic organization and his deep respect for the image that words alone can create.

B

Irma Boom

Dutch, 1960–

A gifted graphic designer, Irma Boom has won international acclaim for the iconoclastic beauty of her many book designs. She initially studied at the AKI School of Fine Art, Enscheden and then worked as a designer for the Dutch government publishing and printing office in The Hague, before opening the Irma Boom Office in Amsterdam in 1991.

Skilfully translating the contents of a book into a very personalized graphic interpretation, her designs possess strong visual and tactile qualities, whether it is a book on the history of Dutch postage stamps or a monograph on the work of the American textile artist Sheila Hicks. Tellingly, when the veteran graphic designer Otto Treumann first saw the book devoted to his work that Boom had created, he remarked it was "her" book rather than "his" book, for she had created a design that was about him but in her own unique style. Boom countered saying it was "my book about you" and went on to explain, "It was my own interpretation of the work.... I wasn't trying to be Otto Treumann, I stayed myself."

By being true to her own graphic approach, Boom takes painstaking care when developing the design of a book, each commission beginning with rigorous research into the book's contents and in-depth dialogue with its subjects, editors and authors. Boom's unique approach allows her to create an aesthetic get-up for each and every title that is completely empathetic to the texts and imagery provided. For example, one of her most ambitious projects was a book celebrating the centenary of the Dutch conglomerate SHV, which was published in 1996. This book took Boom five years to design, albeit while also working on other projects, with the first three and a half years devoted to researching the subject matter, scouring the company's archive and attending shareholders' meetings to ensure she was fully immersed in the ethos of the company. The resulting title, which was originally envisioned by Boom as a 4,000-page book, actually ended up having 2,136 pages and weighed in at several pounds. Yet despite its impressive size, the book did not have pagination nor an index, as Boom wanted the title to be "a voyage" for the reader. She explained, "You find things you don't want to find and discoveries happen by coincidence. The only clues are the dates. The book is made in anti-chronological order. It's a book for the reader's mind including doubts, mistakes and changes." And it is this iconoclastic approach, going against established notions of how a book should be laid out, that gives her work such

BELOW:
Book cover for *Irma Boom: Biography in Books*
for University of Amsterdam, 2010 – a minature *catalogue raisoné* of Irma Boom's book designs

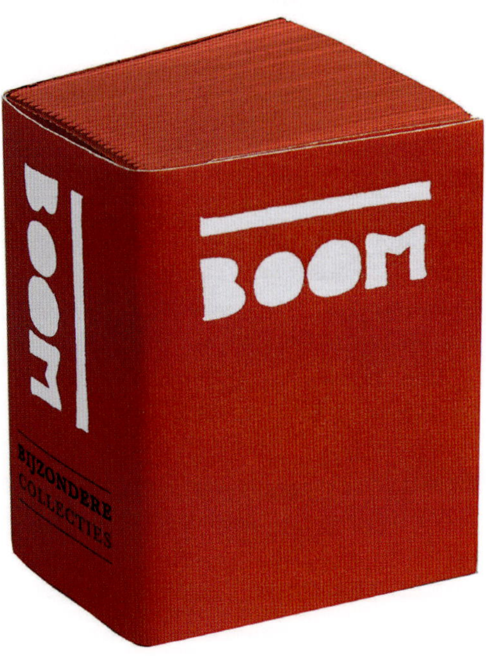

OPPOSITE TOP:
Internal design for *Frits*
for Marthe Foch, 2004

OPPOSITE BOTTOM:
Book cover for *Sheila Hicks: Weaving as Metaphor*
for Yale University Press, 2006

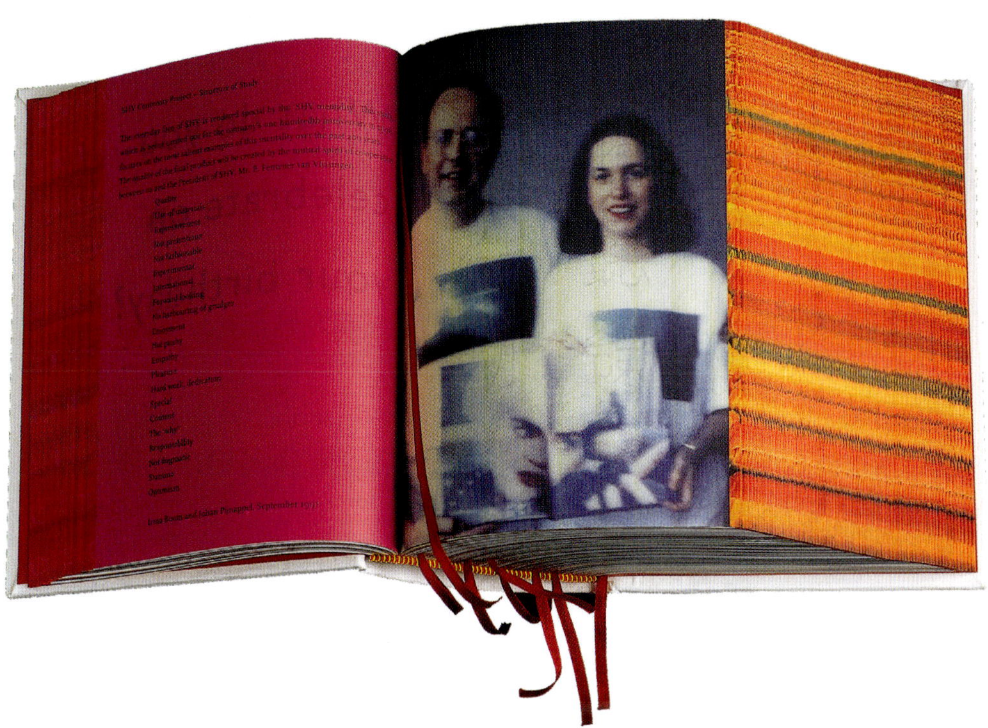

refreshing originality, and firmly establishes her layouts in the realm of book as object rather than reference work.

Since the publication of the SHV title, Boom has become more prolific in her design of books, often working on several titles concurrently, yet even so she requires her clients to give her a free creative rein so that she can produce the best possible outcome, or so she believes. As she freely admits, "I can't even work for someone telling me what size of book to make," yet when she is given full creative licence the results often possess a rare and raw beauty thanks to her bold juxtapositions of type, inclusion of die-cutting surprises, use of flaps and folded pages and curious running of text, which often teeters off the edge of the page. As she notes, "If there is something in common about my books it is the roughness.... They are all unrefined." But perhaps above all else they are infused with her own quirky and passionate spirit, which sets them apart from the formulaic blandness of so much book design today.

Tord Boontje

Dutch, 1968–

The Dutch-born, London-based designer Tord Boontje works on the very cusp of design and craft, using artisanal production methods alongside advanced manufacturing technologies to create objects that have a distinctive poetic quality.

As a child, Boontje grew up in "a very creative environment" and "it seemed natural to pursue design as something I enjoyed". To this end he studied industrial design at the Design Academy in Eindhoven where he was encouraged by his tutors to always experiment and to try to make things that were above all innovative. Around this time, he also worked for a brief period at Studio Alchimia in Milan, which was similarly interested in exploring experimentation for its own sake.

Graduating from the Design Academy in Eindhoven in 1991, he then moved to London the following year and enrolled at the Royal College of Art. There he met the glass sculptor Emma Woffenden, with whom he would later collaborate on one of his earliest projects, the Transglass range (1997). Developed using recycled wine and beer bottles, this series of tableware designs employed simple machines to transform these "found" vessels into various beautiful designs for the home. As Boontje explains, "We have all taken an empty bottle and turned it into something else: we pop a candle into the neck and it is a candelabra, we fill it with flowers and it becomes a vase." With the Transglass series he took this a step further, noting, "A diagonally-cut Soave bottle becomes a jug, two Chardonnay bottles make a carafe. Sicilian table wine transforms into a vase for orchids and the bottoms of beer bottles make a group of drinking glasses."

BELOW:
Transglass vases
1997 – co-designed with Emma Woffenden

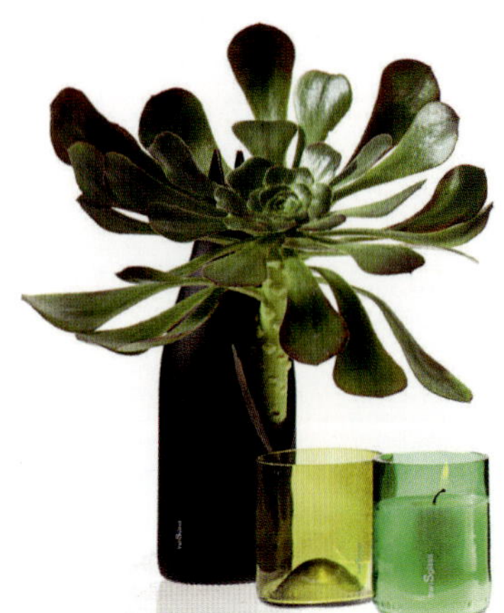

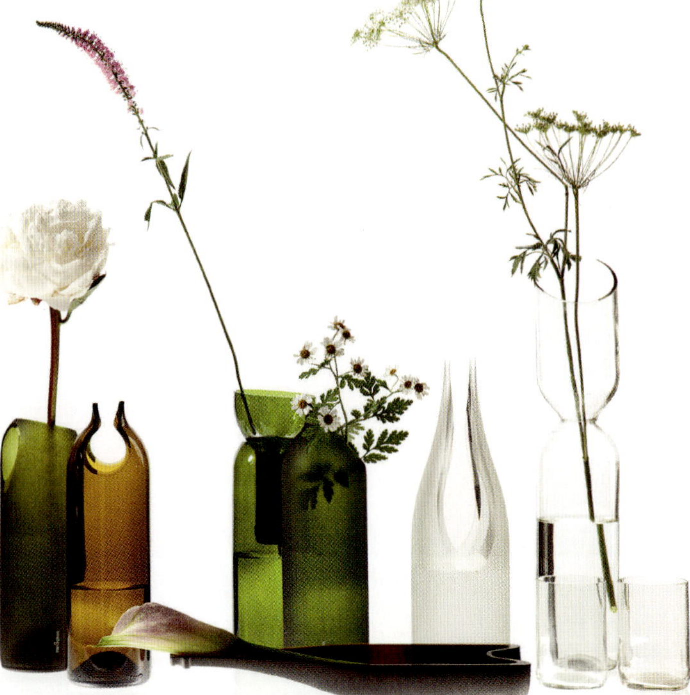

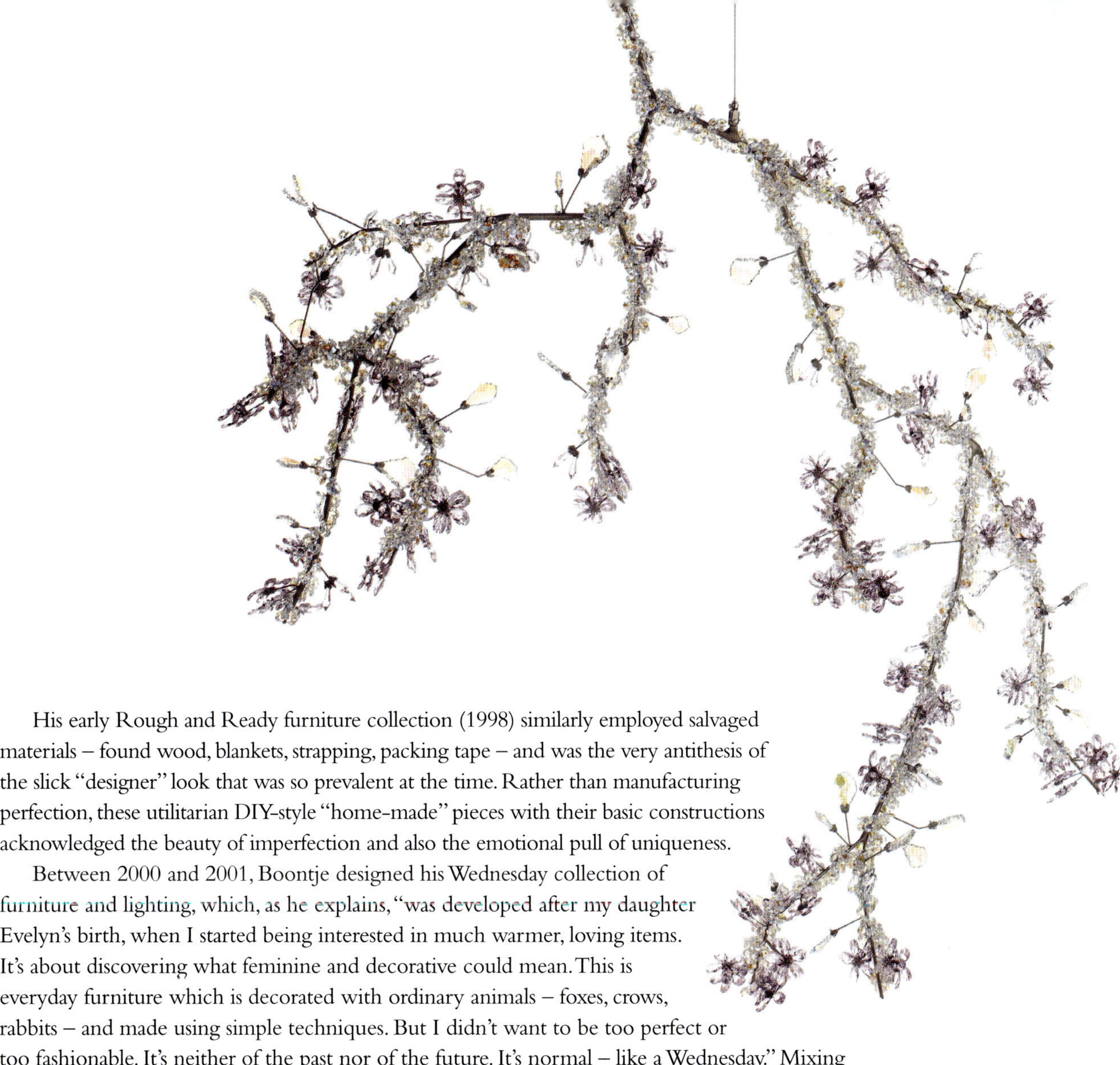

His early Rough and Ready furniture collection (1998) similarly employed salvaged materials – found wood, blankets, strapping, packing tape – and was the very antithesis of the slick "designer" look that was so prevalent at the time. Rather than manufacturing perfection, these utilitarian DIY-style "home-made" pieces with their basic constructions acknowledged the beauty of imperfection and also the emotional pull of uniqueness.

Between 2000 and 2001, Boontje designed his Wednesday collection of furniture and lighting, which, as he explains, "was developed after my daughter Evelyn's birth, when I started being interested in much warmer, loving items. It's about discovering what feminine and decorative could mean. This is everyday furniture which is decorated with ordinary animals – foxes, crows, rabbits – and made using simple techniques. But I didn't want to be too perfect or too fashionable. It's neither of the past nor of the future. It's normal – like a Wednesday." Mixing the hand-made with the machine-made and the digital with the historical, these hybrid pieces, including the lace-like Wednesday light, had an engaging otherworldly fairytale-like quality.

In 2002, his Garland light for Habitat – which, like the Wednesday light, employed photo-etching – brought him widespread recognition, since essentially it was a piece of affordable "design-art". The same year he also designed the exquisite Blossom Chandelier for Swarovski, which took the form of a cherry bough covered in crystal blossoms that were illuminated by tiny programmable LEDs. The chandelier's twinkling effect together with its organic form was utterly romantic and magical, attesting to Boontje's ability to create objects that are infused with a rare poetic sensibility. Between 2009 and 2013, he was a professor at the Royal College of Art in London, and in 2012 set up his own studio/workshop/retail outlet in London's fashionable Shoreditch.

Interested in the creative potential of digital technologies as much as handicrafts, Boontje continues to create playful designs – from lighting and ceramics to tents, door furniture and interior installations – which reveal a very distinctive aesthetic that is both homely and otherworldly, childlike yet sophisticated, textural and sculptural.

ABOVE:
Blossom Chandelier
for Prearo Collection Luce and Swarovski, 2002

Ronan Bouroullec & Erwan Bouroullec

French, 1971– / French, 1976–

The Breton-born brothers Ronan and Erwan Bouroullec are among the most high-profile designers working in today's international design scene and certainly the most prominent French designers since Philippe Starck.

The elder brother, Ronan, studied furniture design at the École Nationale Supérieure des Arts Décoratifs (ENSAD) in Paris, graduating in 1997, while Erwan completed his training at the École Nationale Supérieure d'Arts in Paris-Cergy in 1999. One of Ronan's first designs was the Soliflore vase (1996) made from ABS plastic, first produced by Evans & Wong in France and later by Cappellini. The following year, with a grant from the Fonds d'Incitation à la Création (the Incentive Fund for Creation), the pair created a range of eight white polypropylene vessels, the Vases Combinatoires, which received widespread publicity.

BELOW:
Lit Clos bed
for Cappellini, 2000

OPPOSITE:
Algues screening system
for Vitra, 2004

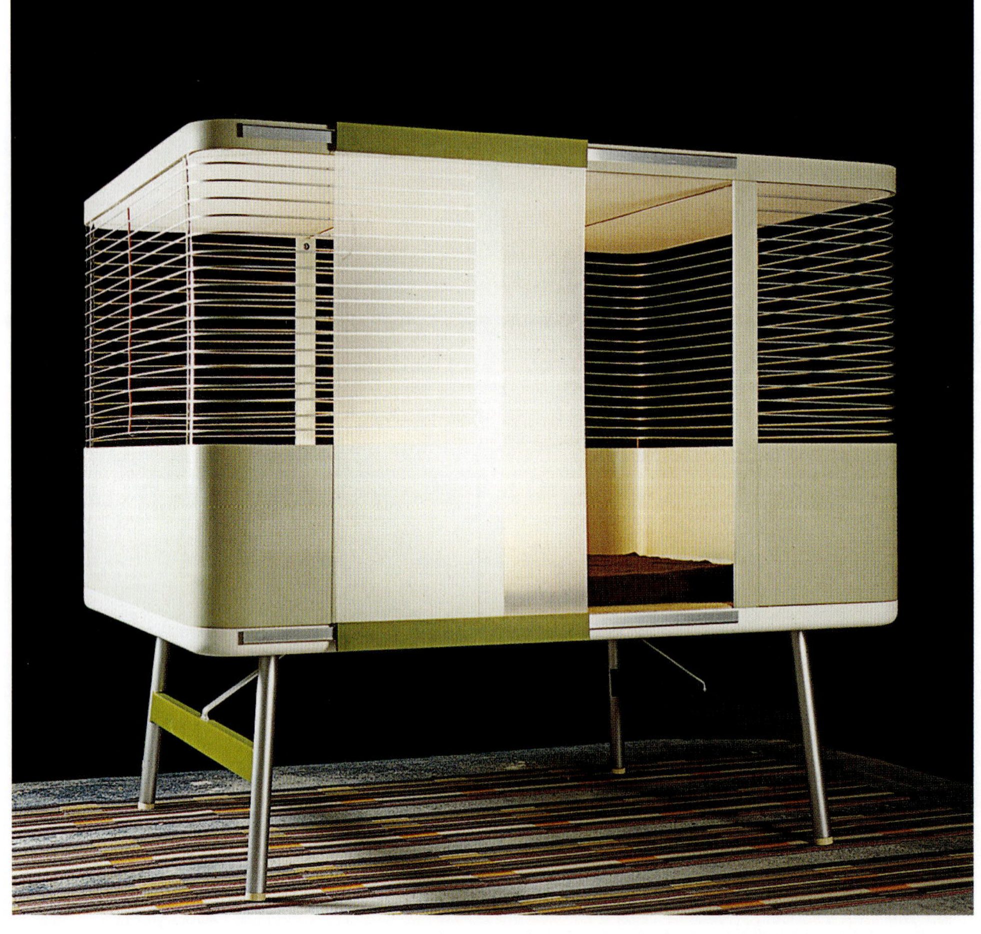

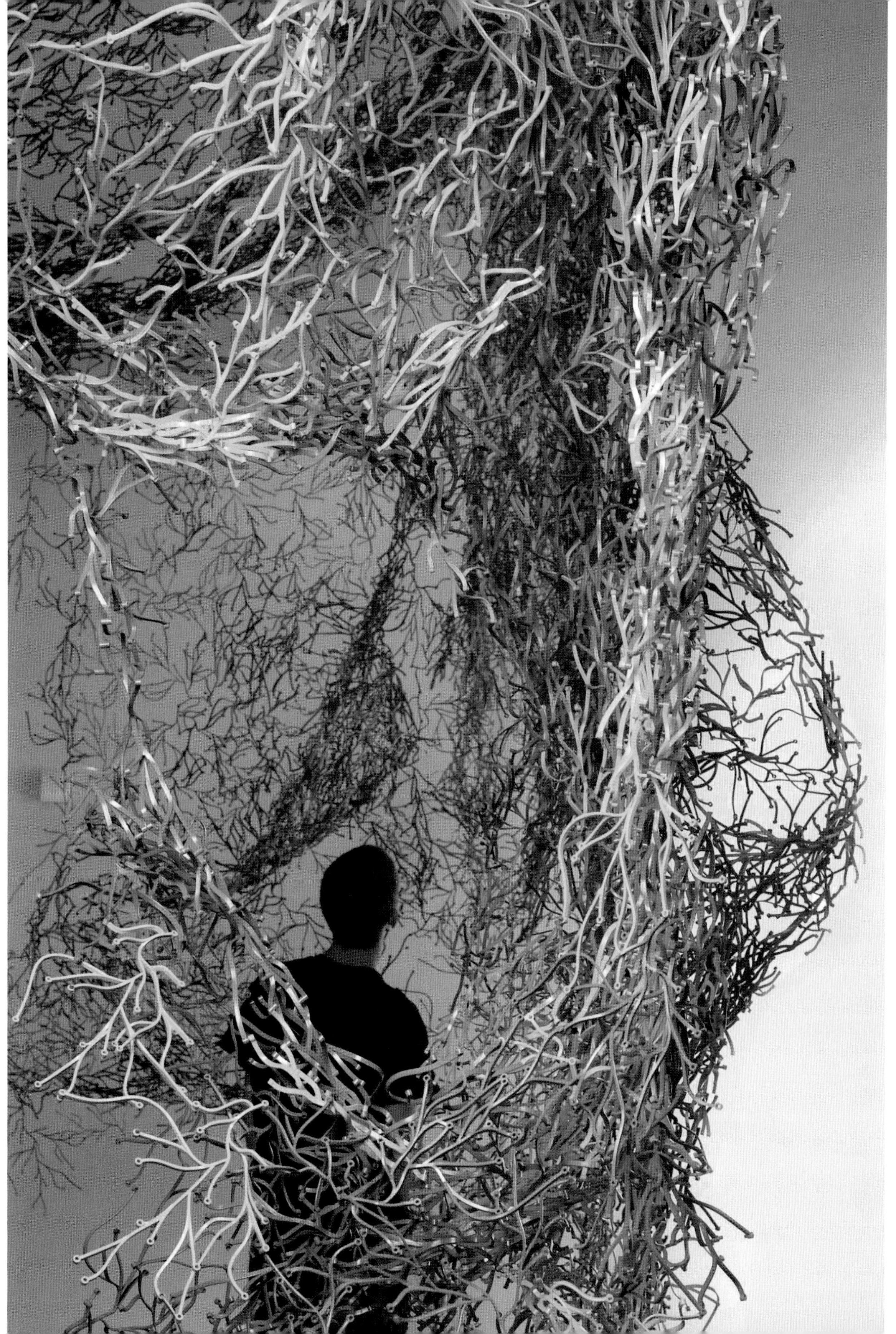

BELOW:
Worknest office chair
for Vitra, 2007

In 1999, following the completion of his studies, Erwan joined his brother's design studio and the pair subsequently designed a range of stainless-steel jewellery, including a curious headband, for SMAK in Iceland, which had been co-founded by the British design maverick Michael Young with the Icelandic illustrator Katrín Pétursdóttir. The same year Ronan created the Hole chair and table for Cappellini and the brothers' Square Vase and their Objets Lumineux pendant lights were also taken up by this Milan-based company. As a body of work, these early designs revealed the siblings' ability to imbue objects with an almost totemic quality through the use of distinctive yet pared-down forms.

It was, however, a white and green cage-like metal structure designed by Erwan and shown on the Cappellini stand at the Milan Furniture Fair in 2000 that was to really announce the brothers' arrival on the world's design stage. This sleeping cabin prototype, known as Lit Clos, was developed with the help of a grant from VIA and was later produced as a limited edition of eight units by the Kreo Gallery in Paris. A curious hybrid bed/bedroom piece, it was intended to provide a private sleeping area within an open-plan interior and as such was a response to new ways of living and working. Certainly it had a strong architectural quality, and its design was meant to promote a feeling of enclosed intimacy while still being sufficiently open to negate any possible feeling of claustrophobia. As Erwan recalls, "Some people said the Lit Clos looked crazy when they first saw it in Milan. For us, it's a practical response to the way that we and our friends like to live."

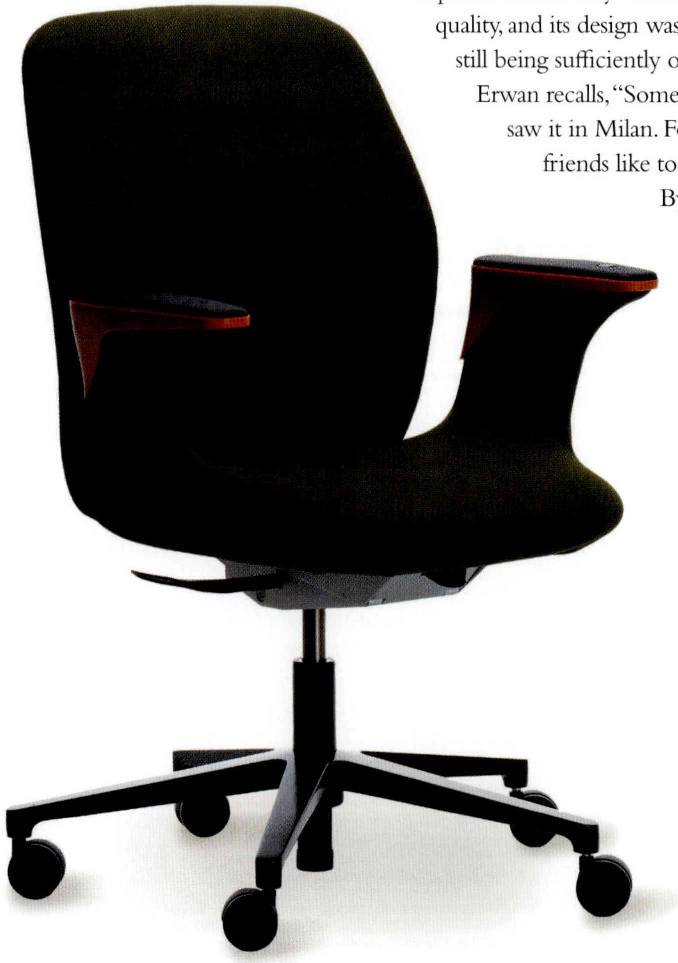

By 2001, the brothers decided to ascribe their designs collectively, for as Ronan notes, "We realized it was pointless to credit one thing to me and another to Erwan, because we both contribute to everything, and it's impossible to identify who does what. You could say that I'm stronger technically and Erwan aesthetically, but that would be an over-simplification. We don't always agree, but we do have a similar sensibility." Indeed, by pooling their creative resources the Bouroullecs are able to create innovative objects that are not only beautiful to look at but also have an undeniable functional logic. As the Design Museum in London has noted, they were also "lucky in beginning their careers at a time when French design was ripe for revival after a fallow period in which the search for home-grown stars to succeed Philippe Starck had proved fruitless. Moreover, a new breed of manufacturers and retailers – both in France and abroad – was eager to snap up talented young designers to emulate the commercial success of the reigning superstars such as Starck, Jasper Morrison and Marc Newson."

Fortuitously the beginning of the Bouroullecs' careers also coincided with a renaissance in French cultural life, from fashion and music to architecture and design. Yet amid this new and emerging post-Starck generation of French designers that included, among others, Christophe Pillet and Matali Crasset, it was the Bouroullecs whose work gained the greatest attention with manufacturers, thanks to its poetic simplicity. During the early 2000s the brothers designed furniture for Habitat, Ligne Roset, Domeaux & Pères and Vitra, packaging for Issey Miyake and filing boxes for Magis, while continuing to produce work for Cappellini and the Kreo Gallery. It was, however, the Algues partitioning screen (2004) for Vitra, made of seaweed-like polyamide modules, that brought them greatest commercial success – with over three million units selling between 2005 and 2007. Although sharing the lyrical qualities of the exclusive "Design Art" movement that was now in full swing, the Bouroullecs' ingenious seaweed screening system was actually a democratic and affordable piece of artful design that also fulfilled a useful function in helping to delineate space within open-plan interiors or filtering light through windows.

Another design for Vitra that demonstrated the Bourollecs' ability to think innovatively was their Worknest office chair (2007), which was born of the desire to create a task chair that, unlike other models, did not employ, as the Bouroullecs put it, a visual language "with obvious references to robots and technology" but was instead more human-centric with its soft accommodating curves and skin-like textile covering. Following on from this, their extraordinary Vegetal chair (2009) for Vitra won the ICFF award in 2009 and their Steelwood chair (2007) for Magis won a prestigious Compasso d'Oro award in 2011. Today the French siblings enjoy working as a team with manufacturers to create designs that have a "subtle yet positive" language "in which formal research retains a primary role".

BELOW:
Copenhague Collection
for Hay, 2012

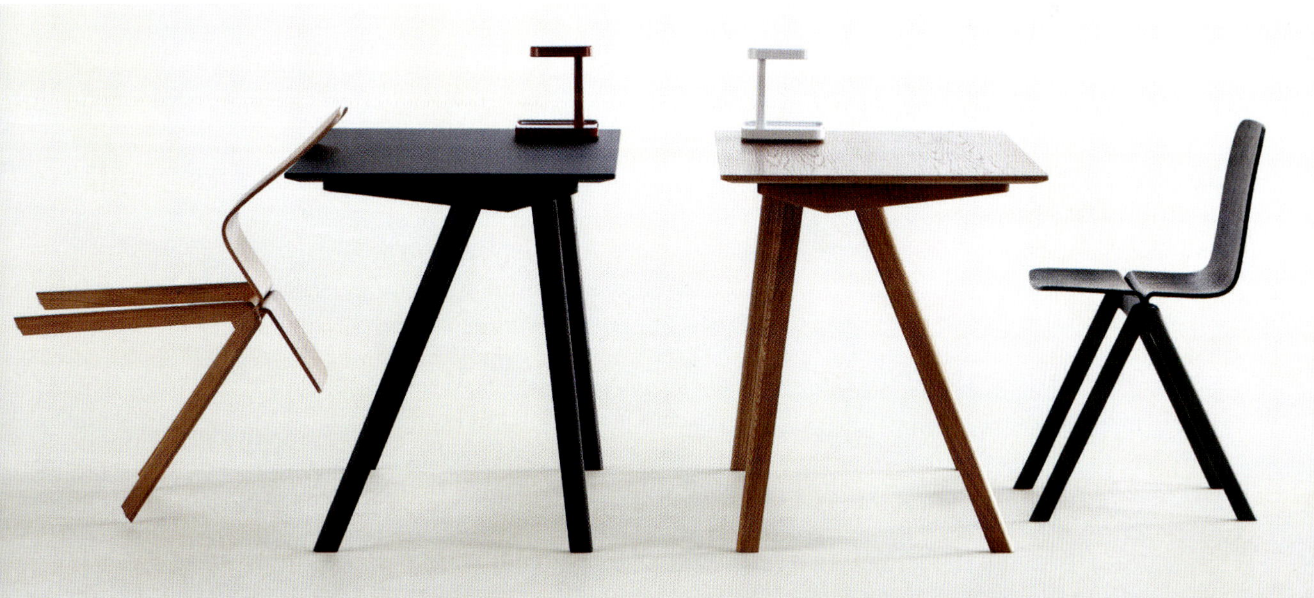

Marianne Brandt

German, 1893–1983

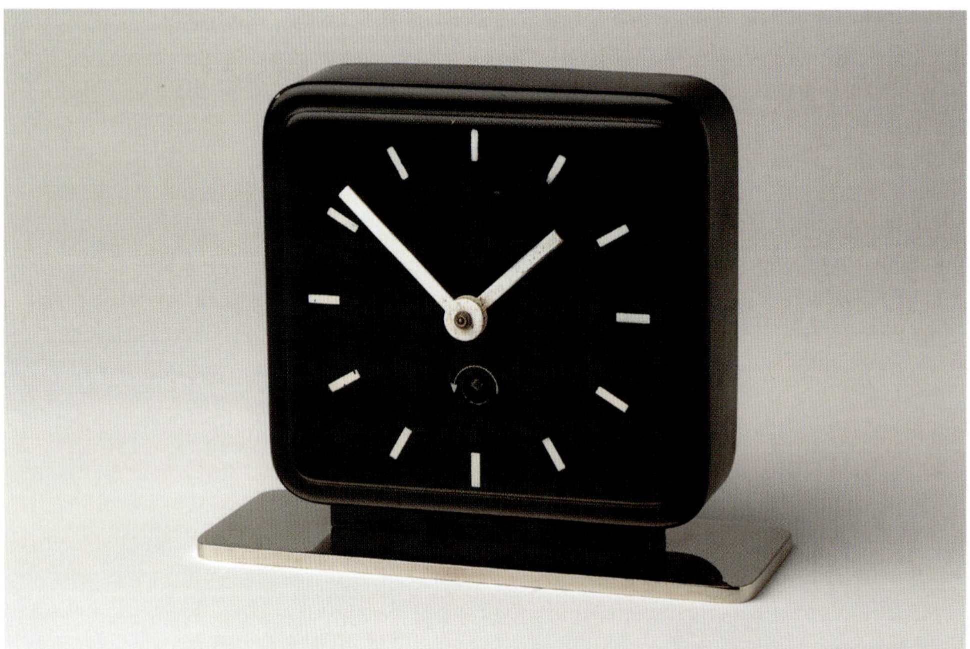

ABOVE:
Table clock
for Ruppelwerk, *c.*1930

Marianne Brandt was one of the very first female industrial designers and helped shape the course of the Modern Movement through her pioneering work at the Bauhaus. Having studied painting and sculpture in Weimar and Paris, and then worked as an independent artist with her own studio, Brandt enrolled at the Weimar Bauhaus in 1923. Here she undertook the school's preliminary course before apprenticing in its metal workshop, under the guidance of László Moholy-Nagy who became a mentor to her. Adopting Moholy-Nagy's Constructivist approach to problem solving, she applied it to the design of objects for everyday use, such as her famous Model No. MT 49 teapot (1924). This harmonious composition of elemental shapes was a masterpiece of geometric simplification that revealed Brandt's interest in logical forms suited to machine production, rather than traditional handcraftsmanship.

After receiving her journeyman's certificate, Brandt was appointed deputy director of the Bauhaus's metal workshop and began working in collaboration with two lighting manufacturers, Körting & Matthiesen AG (Kandem), Leipzig and Schwintzer & Gräff, Berlin. In 1926, Brandt co-designed various utilitarian lighting fixtures for the new Bauhaus building in Dessau with Hans Przyrembel, which again reflected the school's new emphasis on designs intended for industrial production that had been instigated by the institution's director Walter Gropius around 1923. As part of a class project she co-designed with Hin Bredendieck the utilitarian Kandem No. 679 desk lamp (1928) and also designed the diminutive Model 680 bedside lamp for Kandem (*c.*1928), both of which were put into large-scale production

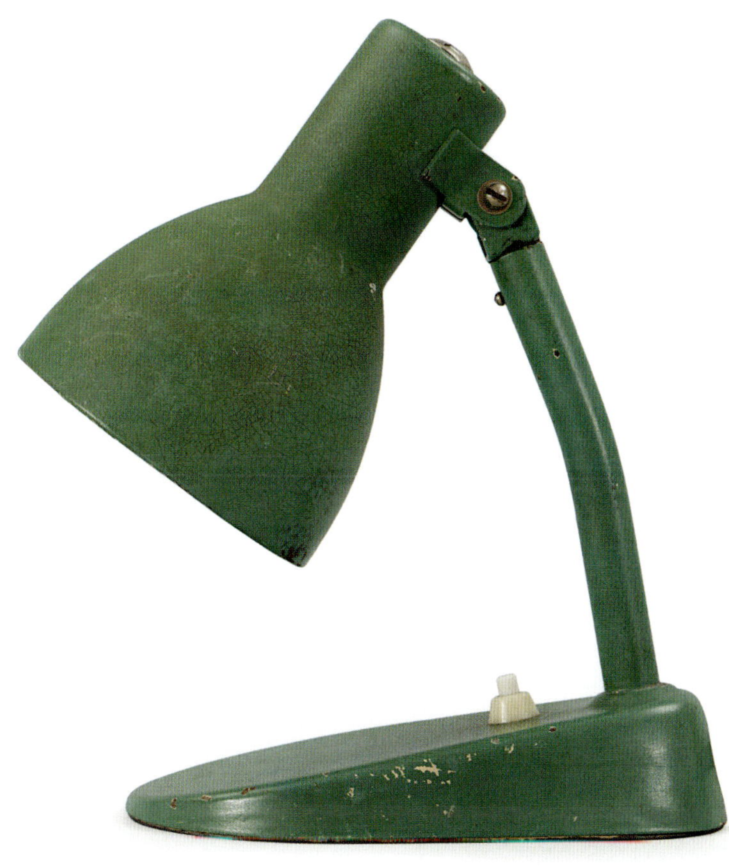

ABOVE:
Kandem bedside lamp
for Körtig & Mattheisen, 1928 – co-designed with Hin Bredendieck

and were commercially successful products. Brandt was director of the metal workshop at the Dessau Bauhaus from 1928 to 1929, although during this period she also briefly worked in Walter Gropius's architecture practice. In addition, as a successful designer who understood the needs of industrial manufacturing, Brandt was also appointed head of the design department at the Ruppelwerk metalware factory in Gotha. During this tenure, which lasted from 1929 to 1932, she created a number of Modernist homewares for the company, including a napkin holder, a tray, a clock, an ashtray and a spherical liquor set holder.

In 1933, with the economic climate worsening in Germany, there was little design work available, so Brandt returned to Chemnitz and devoted herself to painting and also took up weaving and photography. She did, however, during this period manage to license the design of a shallow bowl to the Wohnbedarf department store. She later taught at the Hochschule für Bildende Künste (HfBK, Academy of Fine Arts), Dresden (1949–50) and the Institut für Angewandte Kunst (Institute for Applied Art) in East Berlin (1951–54), and also travelled to China between 1952 and 1953 to curate an exhibition entitled *Deutsche Angewandte Kunst* (German Applied Art) which was held in Beijing and Shanghai. Recalling that the prevailing attitude when she first started at the Bauhaus was that "a woman's place is not the metal workshop", Brandt demonstrated unequivocally that a woman was just as able to design successfully for industrial production as any man, and as such was an inspiration to all female designers who followed in her wake.

Braun

Germany, founded 1921

The Germany manufacturing company Braun became synonymous with design and manufacturing excellence during the post-war period and beyond, thanks to its implementation of a total design policy that was based on rational design principles. The work produced by its design team during this period is still seen as exemplary by many of today's designers, most notably Jasper Morrison and Jonathan Ive, for in many ways it defines the attributes of essentialist design – purity of form and clarity of layout and function.

The origins of Braun go back to 1921 when Max Braun founded an equipment-manufacturing workshop in Frankfurt, which two years later started producing radio components. In 1925, the firm began using early plastic compounds to produce these parts utilizing self-constructed presses. Braun began manufacturing its own radio sets in 1929 and was one of the first companies to produce radios that incorporated the receiver and speaker into a single entity. Three years later, Braun became one of the first European manufacturers to introduce a combination radio/phonograph, which was then followed by the launch of an award-winning battery-operated portable radio in 1935. During the late 1940s and early 1950s, the firm continued to diversify its product line, notably with the introduction of its Manulux dynamo-driven flashlight (1940), the S50 electric razor (1950) and the Multimix kitchen mixer (1950).

After the death of its founder in 1951, Braun was headed up by his two sons, Artur and Erwin, who instigated a comprehensive programme for the implementation of Modern design into its product lines, having identified that there would be a significant demand for electronic products that had a more contemporary aesthetic – designs, in other words, that did not look like pieces of furniture but were instead "honest, unobtrusive and practical devices". This new line of Braun products was developed by designers associated with the Hochschule

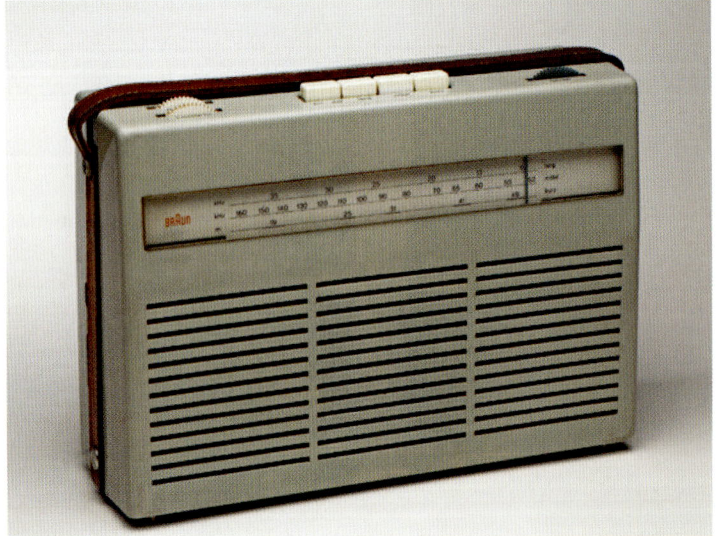

LEFT:
T-22 transistor radio
by Dieter Rams for Braun, 1960

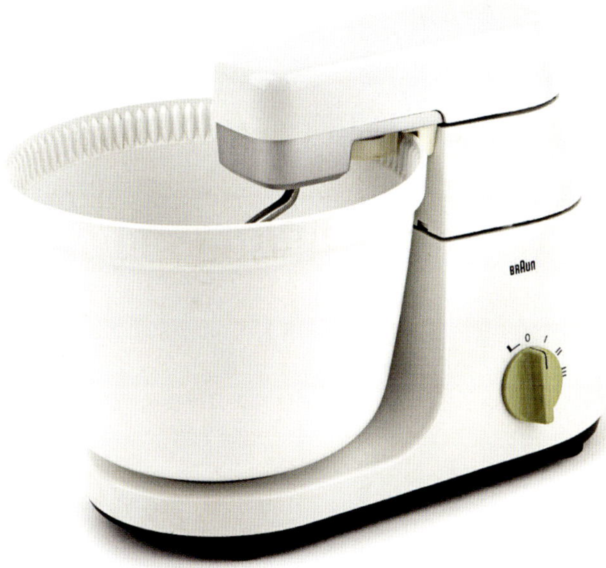

LEFT:
KM 3 food mixer
by Gerd Alfred Müller for Braun, 1957

BELOW:
ET66 calculator
by Dieter Rams and Dietrich Lubs for Braun, 1987

für Gestaltung (School of Design) in Ulm – the ideological successor of the Dessau Bauhaus – including Fritz Eichler, who became head of the firm's new in-house design department in 1956.

Eichler subsequently introduced a new house style that was predicated on geometric simplicity, practical utility and functional clarity. This stridently modern approach was not only applied to products, but also to the company's packaging, marketing materials and graphic projections. During Eichler's tenure, Dieter Rams and Hans Gugelot designed the Phonosuper (1956), a combined radio and record player. Nicknamed "Snow White's Coffin" by competitors, it radically re-imagined products in its category, using a white housing, a clear plastic top and a simple, functional layout. This landmark design, along with other products by Rams, notably the T41 pocket radio (1956) and the P1 portable record player (1959), reflected a new essentialist vocabulary of design that would establish Braun as one of the world's leading consumer electronic brands.

In 1961 Rams was appointed head of Braun's design department, and under his guidance the firm produced a body of work that epitomized good design and reflected Rams's well-known credo, "Less, but Better". In 1967, the Gillette Company acquired a controlling interest in the company and the following year, the international BraunPrize for product design concepts was introduced, which over the succeeding years has helped to promote a better understanding and awareness of good design and the positive benefits it can bring to society.

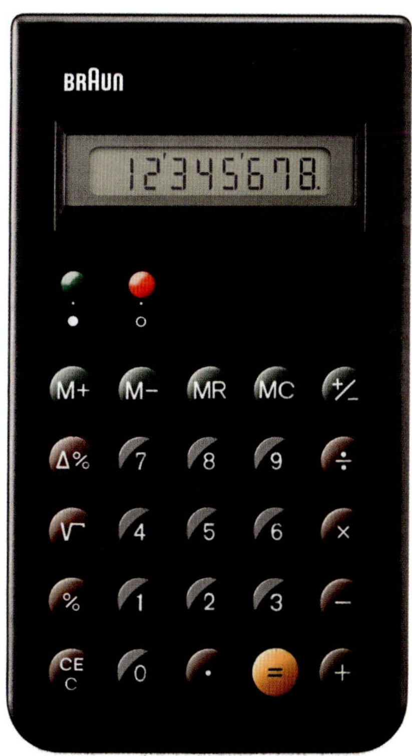

Marcel Breuer

Austro-Hungarian/American, 1902–1981

Hungarian-born and Bauhaus-trained Marcel Breuer was one of the twentieth century's most influential furniture designers, who created numerous landmark chairs during the 1920s and 1930s. His designs innovatively employed new modern industrial materials, such as tubular steel, aluminium and plywood, and thereby introduced a new machine aesthetic into the design and manufacture of furniture. Equally influential were his building projects, which included not only a number of simple and refined Modern residences created for private clients during the post-war years on America's East Coast but also the Y-plan UNESCO Headquarters in Paris (1951), the precast concrete IBM Laboratory in La Gaude, France (1962) and his architectural masterwork: the Breuer Building in New York (1966) – formerly the Whitney Museum of American Art and now The Met Breuer – a monumental edifice with a daring and innovative gravity-defying cantilevered form.

Breuer initially studied at the Akademie der bildenden Künste (Academy of Fine Arts) in Vienna, before training at the Weimar Bauhaus from 1920 to 1924, first undertaking Johannes Itten's preparatory course and then training in the school's cabinet-making workshop. In 1923, Breuer designed his Lattenstuhl (wood-slat armchair), which revealed the strong influence of the De Stijl movement's promotion of geometric abstraction. After obtaining his journeyman's certificate as a cabinet-maker in 1924, Breuer briefly worked for an architect in Paris before joining the teaching staff at the Dessau Bauhaus, where he taught from 1925 to 1928, first as a "junior master" and later heading the cabinet-making workshop. It was during this period that Breuer, inspired by the tubular steel handlebars of his recently purchased Adler bicycle, first had the idea of making furniture out of this modern industrial material. The resulting B3 Wassily armchair of 1926 was a truly revolutionary design and the first of a wide range of furniture designs he produced

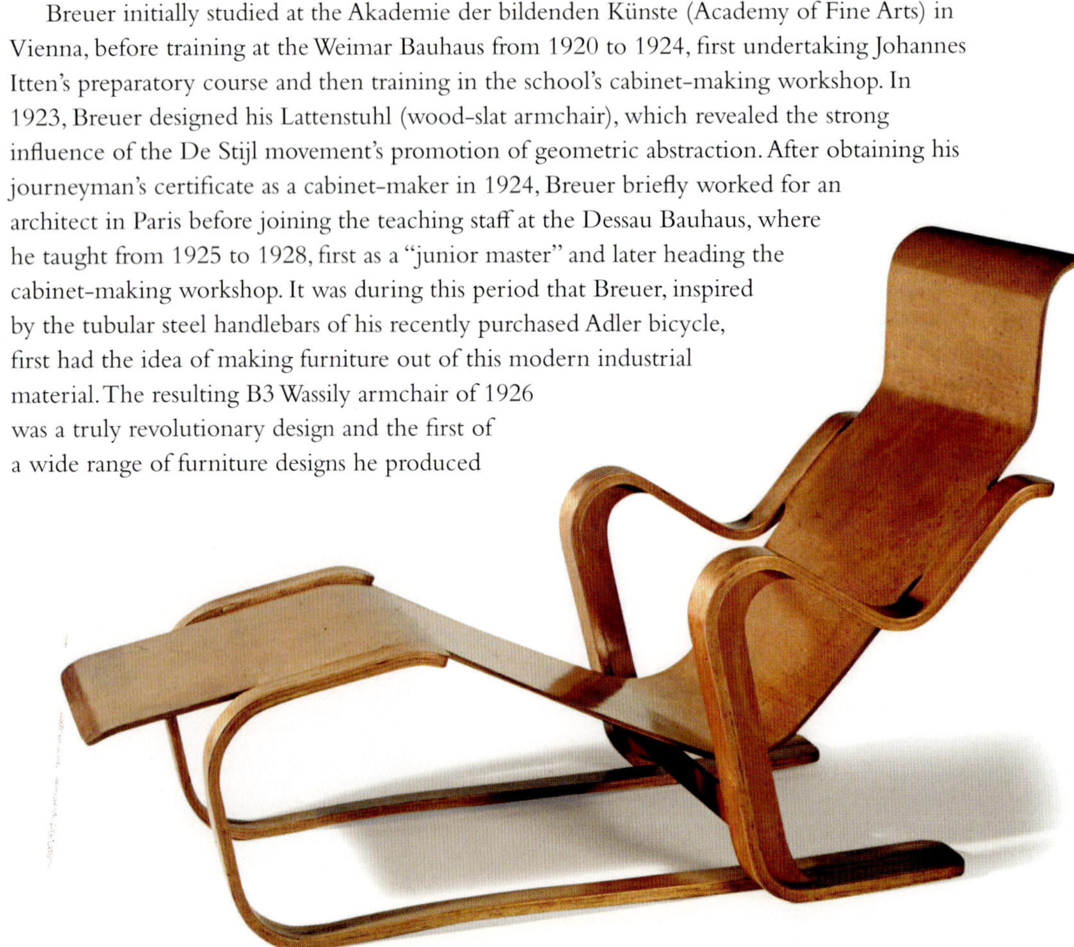

BELOW:
Long chair
for Isokon, 1935–36

that employed this state-of-the-art material. Around 1926 he co-founded Standard-Möbel GmbH in Berlin (with Kalman Lengyel) in order to serially produce and market his designs made from steel tubing. Two years later, Thonet AG took over this venture, with Breuer remaining as a designer.

Because of the worsening political situation in Germany, Breuer decamped to Switzerland in the early 1930s, where he subsequently designed various interesting pieces of furniture – including the Model No. 313 chaise longue (1932) – that utilized a "rustless" aluminium alloy in their constructions and were produced by Embru for the progressive Wohnbedarf store in Zurich. In 1935, Breuer moved again, this time to London, where during a two-year sojourn he designed innovative laminated wood furniture for Isokon, including a nest of tables (*c.*1936) and the famous Isokon long chair (1935–36).

Eventually in 1937, Breuer – like other designers associated with the Bauhaus – emigrated to the United States and the following year became an associate professor at Harvard University School of Design in Cambridge, Massachusetts, and also set up an architectural partnership with Walter Gropius, which was subsequently dissolved in 1941. That same year, Marcel Breuer and Associates was founded, and then moved to New York in 1947. Throughout his career, Breuer was a Modernist in the truest sense of the word, a pioneer of form and function who embraced new materials and technologies to create design solutions that were breathtakingly forward-looking.

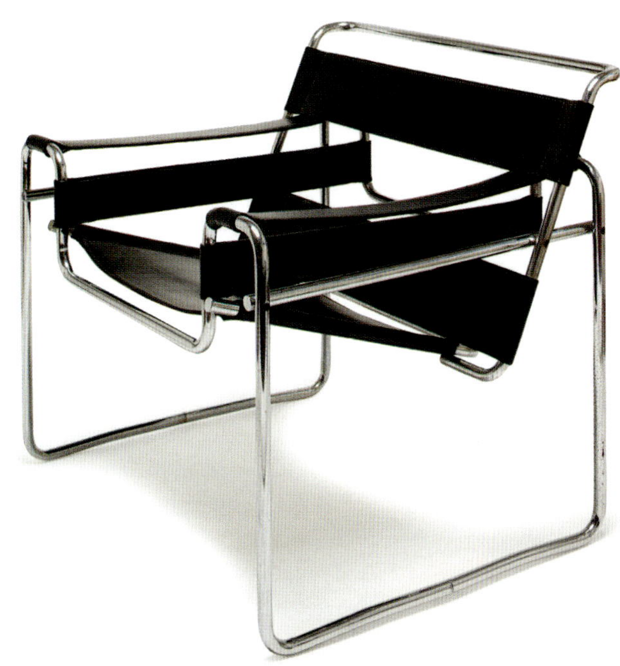

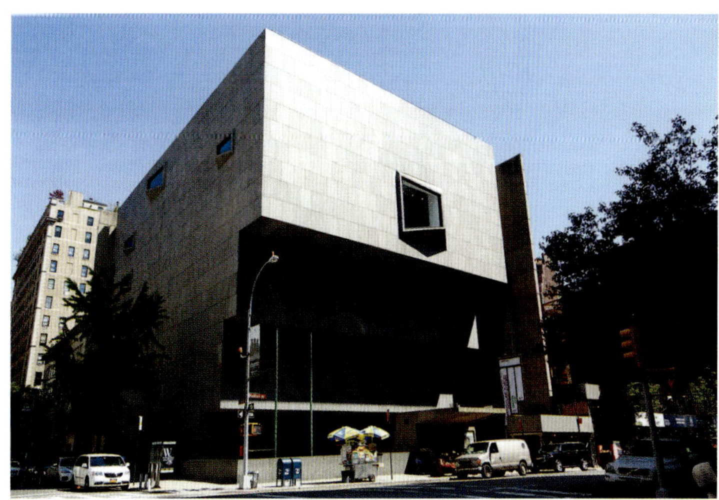

TOP:
Wassily Chair Model B3
for Standard-Möbel (later Thonet), 1926

ABOVE:
The Met Breuer building
in New York, 1966 – formerly the Whitney Museum of American Art

Neville Brody

British, 1957–

London-born Neville Brody is known for having developed a highly expressive language of graphic design, becoming in the 1980s one of the first designers to work in the digital realm. He studied graphic design at the London College of Printing where, influenced by Punk's anarchic "anything is possible" message, he explored, as he puts it, "ideas outside the box" by rebelliously breaking the Modernist rules of graphic design that he was being taught.

Following his studies, Brody worked for a small design studio, Rocking Russian, which specialized in the creation of edgy record sleeves. From 1980, he worked for Stiff Records designing sleeves that captured the youthful zeitgeist of the 1980s New Romantic style.

Recognition for his innovative artwork at Stiff Records led to his appointment as art director of Fetish Records, an independent label for which he designed some of his best-known record-cover art, notably for the bands Cabaret Voltaire and 23 Skidoo. A year later he became art director of the newly formed street style and music magazine *The Face*, and it was here that the 24-year-old Brody was able to fully and freely explore the typographic conundrums of page layouts. His work at the magazine had a forthright avant-garde aesthetic that used experimental fonts as a means of signposting text. He adopted a more toned-down style for the design of sister publication *Arena*, the men's lifestyle magazine where he worked as art director from 1986. Two years later, the Victoria and Albert Museum held a major exhibition of Brody's work and his first monograph *The Graphic Language of Neville Brody* was published.

Brody was perfectly positioned when the Mac revolution of the late 1980s occurred to take full advantage of the new digital opportunities that it heralded. During the late 1980s and early 1990s he designed a number of innovative computer-orientated fonts, including his Industria (1989), Insignia (1989), Arcadia (1990), Blur (1991) and Tyson (1993), which were designed for the digital type library FontShop, of which Brody was a founding partner.

Brody also launched *FUSE* magazine in 1991 as a showcase for experimental typography and visual communications, which went on to spawn a related conference, a quarterly forum and an exhibition. In 1994 the Neville Brody Studio was renamed Research Studios, reflecting its increasing exploration of digital media as a platform for graphic communications. Research Studios created branding, packaging and visual identities for a roster of high-profile companies. In 2011, Brody became the Dean of the School of Communication and Head of the Visual Communication programme at the Royal College of Art, London and three years later Research Studios was rebranded Brody Associates. Through his work, Brody has shown how expressive graphic design and typography can be used to powerfully engage the viewer and the extent to which digital technology provides opportunities for exciting creative experimentation.

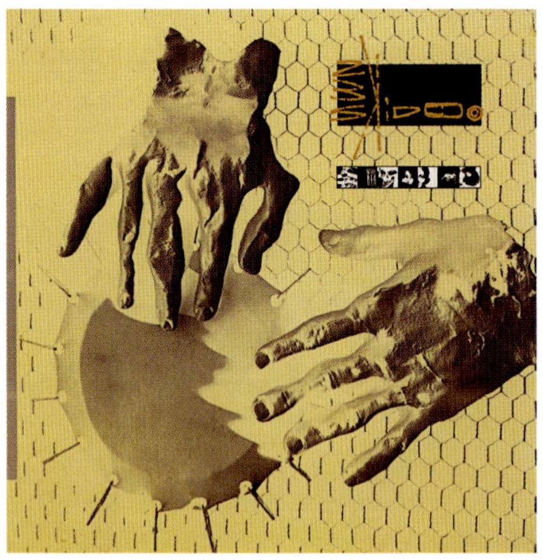

ABOVE:
23 Skidoo's *Seven Songs* album sleeve design
for Fetish Records, 1982

RIGHT:
Fuse Day Manchester poster
1995

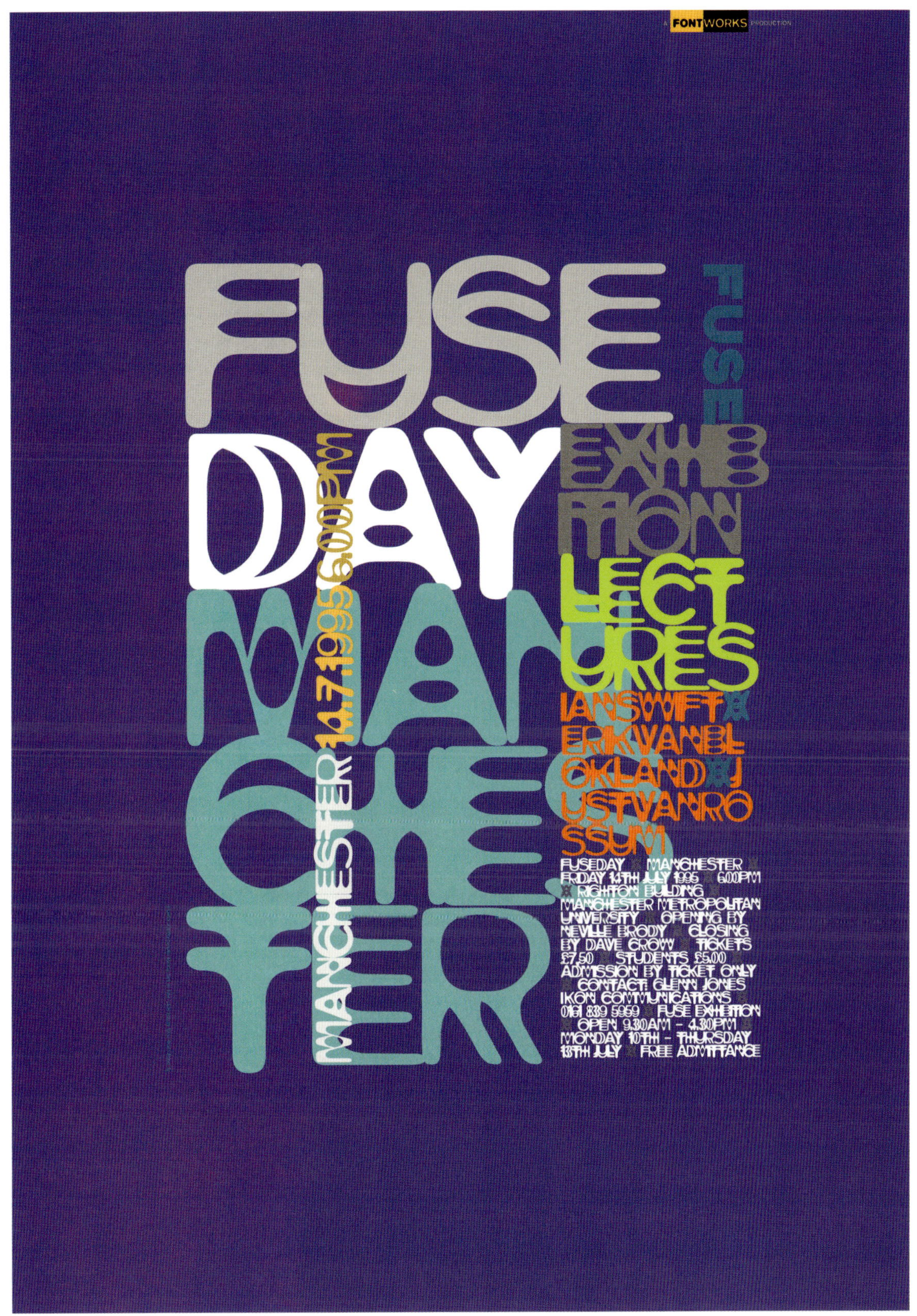
A FONTWORKS PRODUCTION
FUSE
DAY
MAN
CHES
TER
FUSE
EXHIB
ITION
LECT
URES
IANSWIFT
ERIKVANBL
OKLAND J
USTVANRO
SSUM
MANCHESTER 14.7.1995 6.00PM
FUSEDAY MANCHESTER
FRIDAY 14TH JULY 1995 6.00PM
RIGHTON BUILDING
MANCHESTER METROPOLITAN
UNIVERSITY OPENING BY
NEVILLE BRODY CLOSING
BY DAVE CROW TICKETS
£7.50 STUDENTS £5.00
ADMISSION BY TICKET ONLY
CONTACT: GLENN JONES
IKON COMMUNICATIONS
0161 839 5959 FUSE EXHIBITION
OPEN 9.30AM - 4.30PM
MONDAY 10TH - THURSDAY
13TH JULY FREE ADMITTANCE

Daniel Brown

British, 1977–

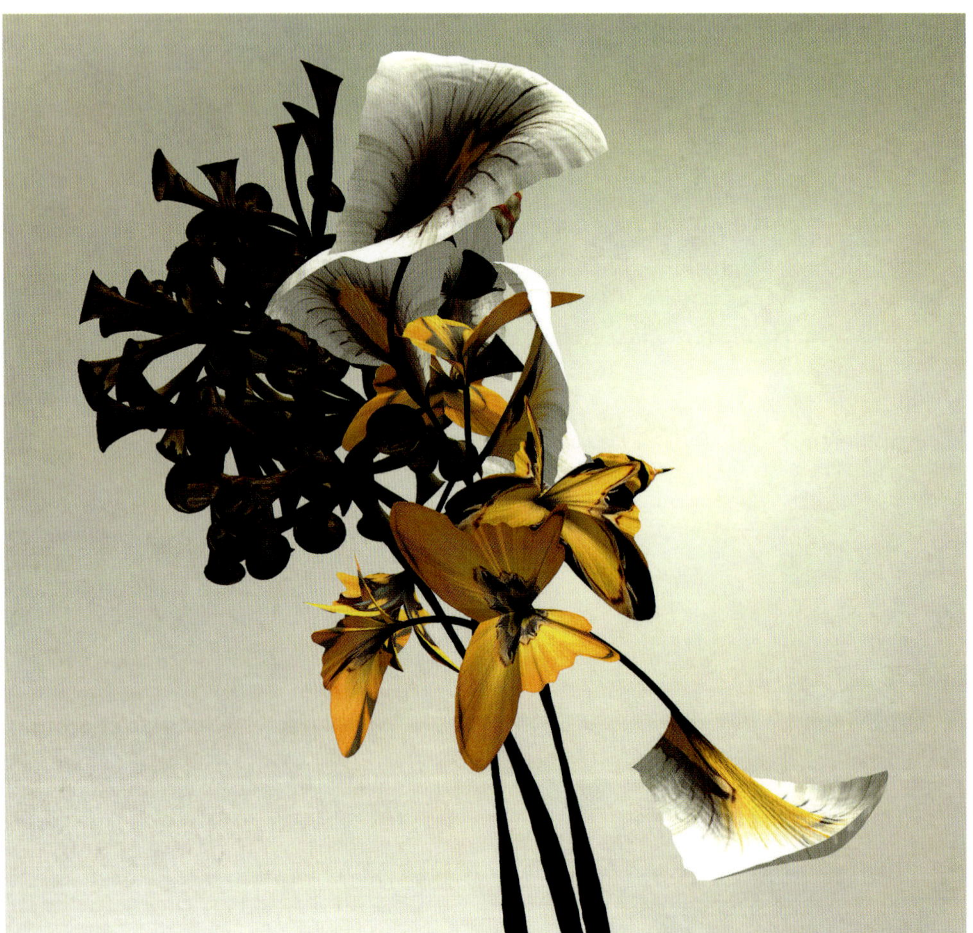

ABOVE:
Generative digital flowers installation
for the D'Arcy Thompson Zoology Museum, 2013 – employing Brown's real-time 3D (OpenGL/DirectX) flowers engine, code-named Darwin

At the vanguard of digital design, Daniel Brown was among the very first designers to successfully explore the extraordinary creative potential of interactive animations. Often inspired by the natural world, his work is distinguished by a poetic refinement that sets it apart from the vast majority of other work found in this emerging but increasingly important field of design activity.

Like many other web-designers of his generation, Brown grew up playing early computer games. His father Paul Brown was also an influential and extremely early pioneer of "systems computer art" or, in other words, computer-generated artwork. Having enjoyed a successful career as a commercial animator in Soho – producing the first computer animation for television in Europe in 1981 – Daniel's father later went on to become Head of Computer Graphics at Middlesex Polytechnic in 1986, then a leading centre for computer graphics education. And it was from him that self-taught Brown received probably the best training available in this new and exciting field of algorithmically based generative digital design. As a young child, he also had access to his own home computer (a Commodore VIC-20) and in 1991, Roy Stringer, an early multimedia pioneer who was a family friend, allowed the teenage Brown to experiment with his state-of-the-art Apple Macintosh. After leaving school, Stringer gave Brown his first job, working for the Learning Methods Unit at Liverpool John Moores University, in 1996, where he researched how new media could be used in various ways to advance learning.

The following year, Brown joined Amaze Limited, which was a spin-off company founded by Roy Stringer and Roger Harnden to commercially exploit their university research. It was here that Brown pioneered new interactive graphical interfaces based on moveable building blocks rather than the traditional menu systems, and during this period he also launched the noodlebox website which, as the Design Museum later noted, "introduced a fluid playfulness to web design, in contrast to the pragmatic, often sterile visual style which then dominated the medium". Later Brown worked as multimedia director for Nick Knight's influential fashion-film-led SHOWstudio website and in 2002 was selected to participate in the Design Museum's *Web Wizards* exhibition. The following year, Brown exhibited in the *Great Brits* show organized by the Design Museum and British Council in Paul Smith's Milan headquarters during the April 2003 Milan Furniture Fair, where he showed a state-of-the-computer-arts self-generating flower installation.

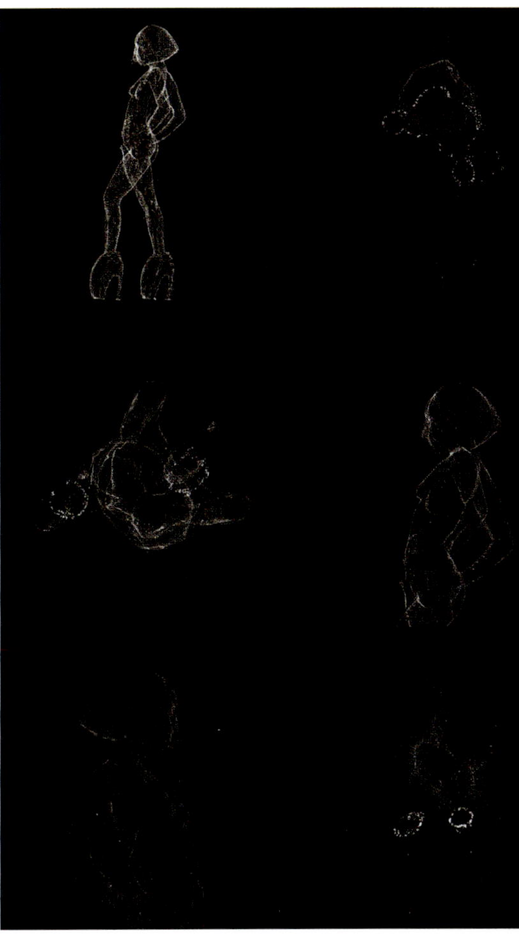

ABOVE:
Lady Gaga Monster Ball
interactive digital installation for Nick Knight/SHOWstudio, 2011

A month later, Brown was in Barcelona for a design conference, and while there he had a diving accident that left him partially paralysed. While he was undergoing rehabilitation back in England at Stoke Mandeville Hospital, he was nominated for the 2004 Designer of the Year award, which he subsequently won for his pioneering work in the field of digital design. Since then, despite his disability, he has created work that continues to be at the very forefront of digital design, including a project commissioned for the D'Arcy Thompson Zoology Museum in Dundee. This extraordinary installation features a series of animated flowers based on the forms and textures of exhibits found in the museum. The realistic-looking three-dimensional digital flowers proceed to "grow" on-screen according to computer algorithms, in much the same way as one would see real plants grow if using time-lapse photography. They are supernatural representations growing in a virtual world that reflect both technical mastery and creative inspiration.

Richard Buckminster Fuller

American, 1895–1983

Richard Buckminster Fuller was an uncategorizable and quixotic visionary, not only a philosopher, architect, designer, engineer and inventor, but also an entrepreneur, mathematician, writer and educator. He was driven by a profound conviction that the Earth's resources needed to be better managed in order to mitigate ecological destruction and to make the world work for all of humanity. He coined the phrase "Spaceship Earth", and proposed what he called an operating manual. He believed this depended on doing "more with less", especially within the fields of building and transportation. Seeing himself as a "comprehensive anticipatory design scientist", Fuller took a holistic view of the world and its problems, and tirelessly attempted to solve them through the implementation of new technologies and design. One of his most extreme visions was to build a protective bubble over the whole of Manhattan. He was able to influence both hippie dropouts in California in the 1960s and technocrats such as the British architect Norman Foster in the 1970s. He was best known for his work with lightweight geodesic dome structures. The structural principle was not his – he had seen a German patent for the system during the Second World War – but Fuller applied it to large-scale architectural projects such as the biosphere, the United States pavilion at the 1967 *International and Universal Exposition* or *Expo 67* in Montreal.

Born in Milton, Massachusetts, to a patrician New England family, Fuller studied at Harvard then joined the US Navy Reserve in 1917. In later life, he claimed it was during his Navy years that he gained all his technical expertise. Without an obvious profession to pursue, he co-founded the Stockade Building Company, manufacturing compressed bricks intended to facilitate the construction of lightweight yet sturdy buildings. The firm failed to make a profit. It was sold to the Celotex Company in 1926 and Fuller lost his job as the company's president. It was the first of a string of business failures. He set up the 4D Company in 1927 to enable the research and development of various innovative prefabricated housing projects, such as his first Dymaxion house (1927–31), none of which were successfully completed in the form that he envisaged.

Fuller became the owner and editor of *Shelter* magazine in 1930. Two years later, he established the Dymaxion Corporation in Bridgeport, Connecticut, and shortly afterwards the first prototype of his Dymaxion car was built (the name

BELOW:
Biosphere museum inside the Buckminster Fuller Dome,
the US pavilion from the 1967 expo on Saint Helen's Island, Montreal, Quebec, Canada

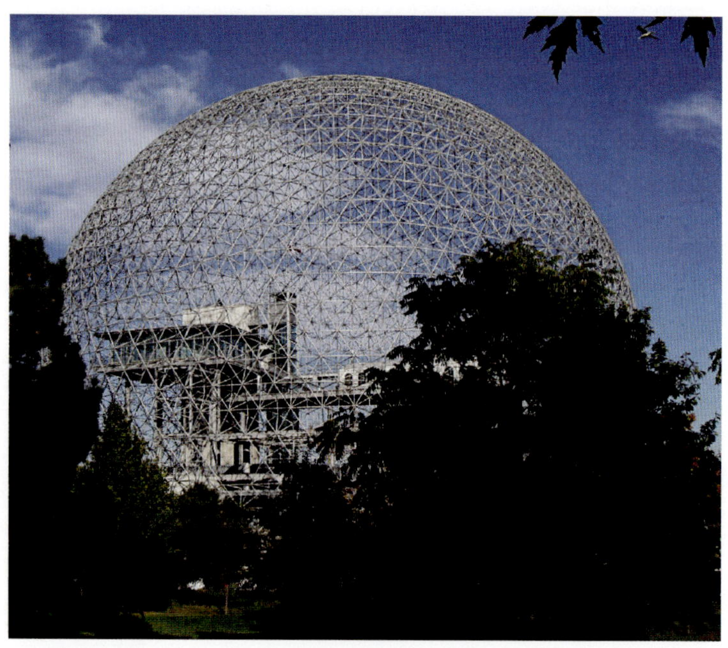

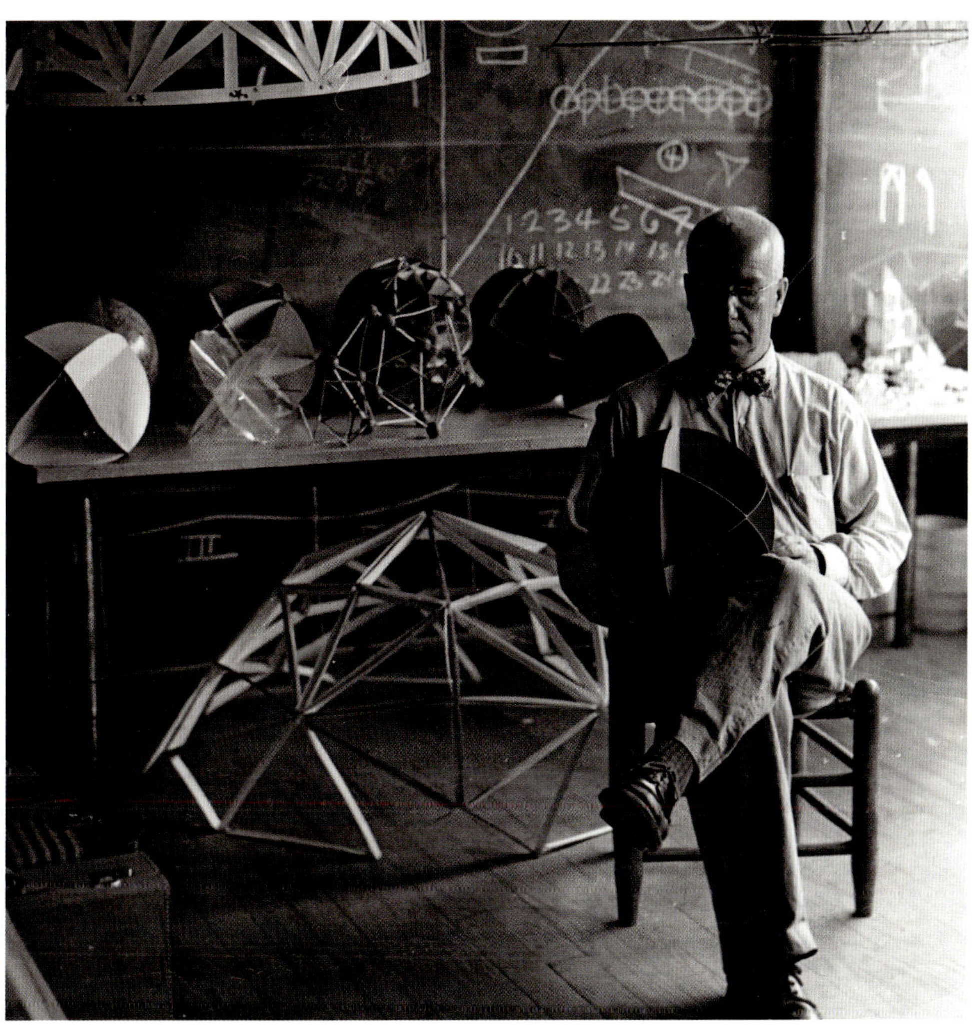

ABOVE:
Richard Buckminster Fuller in his studio at Black Mountain College in Black Mountain, North Carolina

Dymaxion being a contraction of *dy*namic, *max*imium and tens*ion*). A fatal accident, however, resulted in bad press that ultimately doomed the once-promising invention despite it being showcased at the 1939 *New York World's Fair*. During the Second World War, Fuller successfully developed low-cost shelters made from metal grain bins, known as Dymaxion Deployment Units, which were used by the military to house troops and store equipment.

In 1947 Fuller began teaching at Black Mountain College in North Carolina, where he became close to the sculptor Isamu Noguchi, designer Charles Eames and composer John Cage. There he developed the geodesic dome, which later found its first practical application in 1953, when one was installed as a cupola on top of the Ford Rotonda in Dearborn, Michigan. Since then, geodesic domes with their distinctive interlocking grid of icosahedrons have been used throughout the world in various contexts, from military radar domes to Disney World's Epcot Center, and have inspired later generations of architects to develop greener and more ecologically efficient building systems.

Fernando Campana & Humberto Campana

Brazilian, 1953– / Brazilian, 1961–

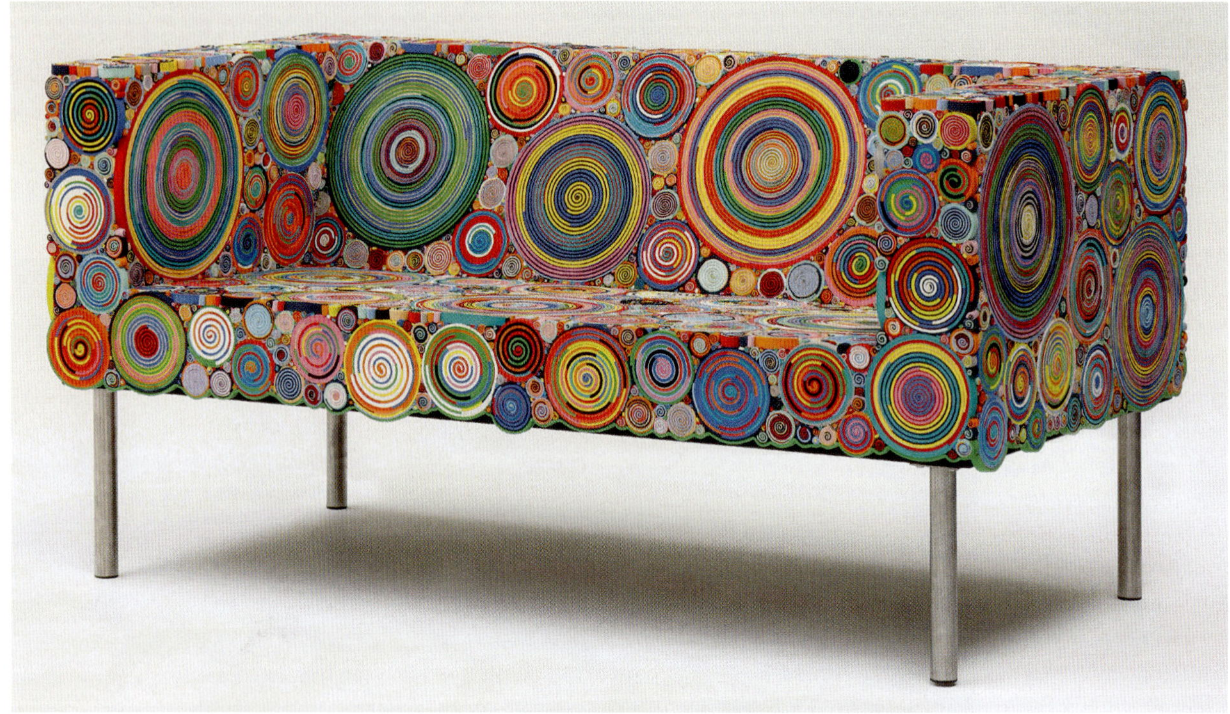

ABOVE:
Sushi sofa
for Campana Objetos, 2003

OPPOSITE TOP:
Blow Up clock
for Alessi, 2003

OPPOSITE BOTTOM:
Favela armchair
for Edra, 1991

Brazilian designers Fernando and Humberto Campana have gained an international reputation for innovative work that spans the worlds of design, craft and art. Often utilizing found objects, they create "design art" assemblages that are inspired by Brazilian street life and carnival culture, and range from the mass-produced to the limited-edition to the unique one-off. The Campana brothers not only produce their own bespoke collections of objects, they have also designed various pieces – referred to as "licensed artworks" – for a number of design-led companies, including Alessi, Baccarat, Edra, Louis Vuitton and Venini. The Campanas are also actively involved in creating urban sculptures and exhibition installations, and work extensively in the interior design sector, notably designing stores for the Spanish shoe brand Camper.

One of the most engaging things about the Campanas' work is how they find poetry in everyday materials and objects, whether it is PVC tubing, thick rope, felt, plastic-covered wire, off-cuts of leather or furry toys. By using an imaginative and experimental approach to the design process that is almost childlike, they manage to transform these "poor" resources or modest *objet trouvés* into precious objects that, as the Design Museum notes, "celebrate the discarded and mundane and are instilled with the spirit of contemporary Brazil" – or as the Campanas put it, reflect a certain "zest for life".

Both born in São Paulo, the brothers began working together in 1983, when they founded Estudio Campana. Elder brother Humberto had obtained a law degree at the University of São Paulo in 1977, and then practised as a lawyer, before deciding to become a sculptor instead. Younger brother Fernando took an architecture degree at the Centro Universitario Belas Artes (University Centre of Fine Arts) in São Paulo, graduating in 1984. Although Brazil had a tradition of Modern design thanks to the work of, among others, Oscar Niemeyer and Lúcio Costa, the Campana brothers felt unfettered by Modernist doctrine because it was not as strongly entrenched in Brazilian culture as in Europe or the United States. Instead, they took their design cues from their surroundings: the creative inventiveness of the people living in São Paulo's slums and the traditional artisanal craft skills still found in Brazil. One such design is their Favela armchair – originally designed in 1991 and later put into production by Edra in 2003 – which is made up of scraps of wood patched together much like the houses found in Brazil's shanty towns.

It was in the early 2000s that the design duo came to prominence on the international design stage, just as the design art phenomenon was gathering pace. Their seating designs from this period, such as the Anemone Chair (2001), the Sushi chair (2002) and the Banquete chair (2002), expressed a new and fresh creative authenticity and originality that made them especially popular among a new and emerging breed of contemporary art collectors – a sort of *arte povera* for the super-rich. Yet not all their designs have been one-offs or limited editions; for instance, they have created numerous moulded PVC shoe and bag designs for Melissa, and also various eye-catching and useful homewares for Alessi made of steel rods, anodized aluminium wire and woven rattan. But even the brothers' designs that are intended for mass-production share the same sense of creative inventiveness and artistry as their more bespoke pieces.

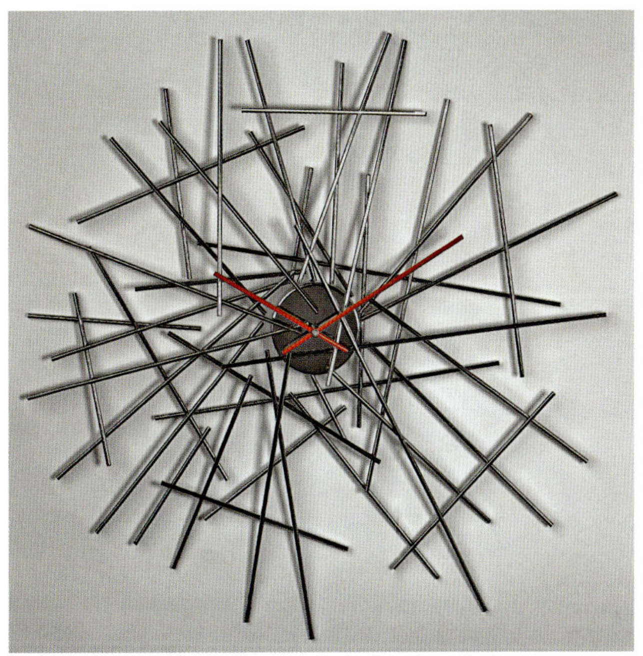

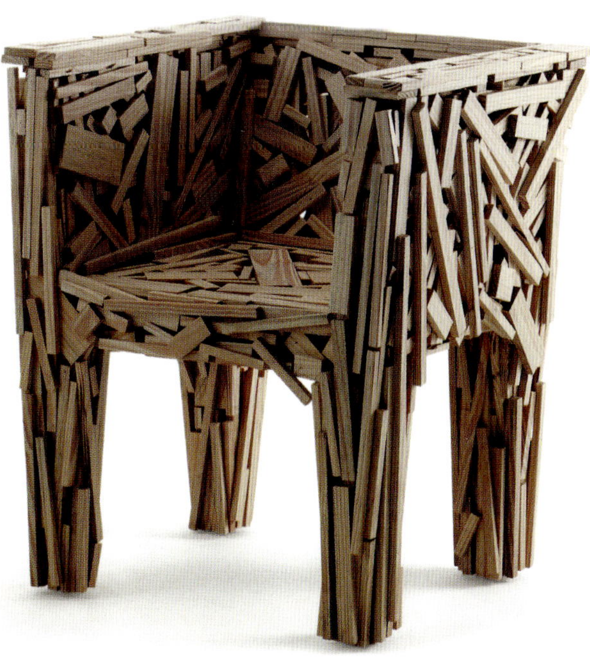

David Carson

American, 1954–

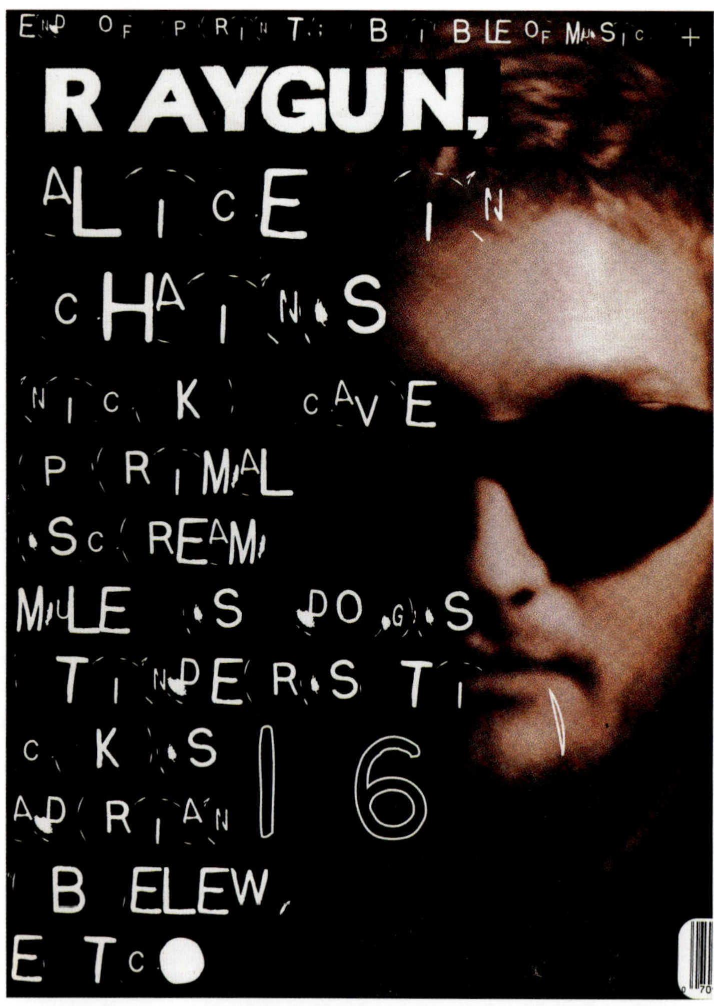

ABOVE:
***Ray Gun* magazine (issue 16)**
1994

The American art director David Carson shook up the world of magazine design during the 1980s and 1990s with his experimental grunge typography and no-rules layouts. As a result, he is regarded as one of the most influential graphic designers of his era, for his distinctive work emphatically showed that typography could be employed as a potent expressive medium. More than anything else, the Texan-born surfer was able to transmit through his deeply personal work a strong sense of creative authenticity, which brilliantly captured the emerging West Coast "dude culture" and ultimately came to define it. Through his work Carson heralded in a new era of graphic design creative freedom that was culturally relevant to the Gen-X generation.

One of the reasons Carson was able to break the rules of Modern graphic design so effectively was because he was not formally trained and therefore the strict rules of the discipline had not been inculcated into him. Instead, he studied sociology at San Diego State University, and during his college days was a professional surfer, at one stage ranking ninth in the world. His first introduction to graphic design came in 1980, when he took a two-week course taught by Jackson Boelts at the University of Arizona. After graduating, he worked for five years as a high school teacher in Torrey Pines, and during this period began to experiment with graphic design, which led him to attend a three-week graphic design workshop in Switzerland in 1983. Crucial for Carson's development as a designer, this course was taught by Hans-Rudolf Lutz who was a leading Swiss pioneer of expressive typography.

In 1984, Carson was appointed art director of the recently established *Transworld Skateboarding* magazine, and during this four-year tenure he imbued the publication with a distinctive rough-and-ready youthful aesthetic that involved the use of so-called "dirty"

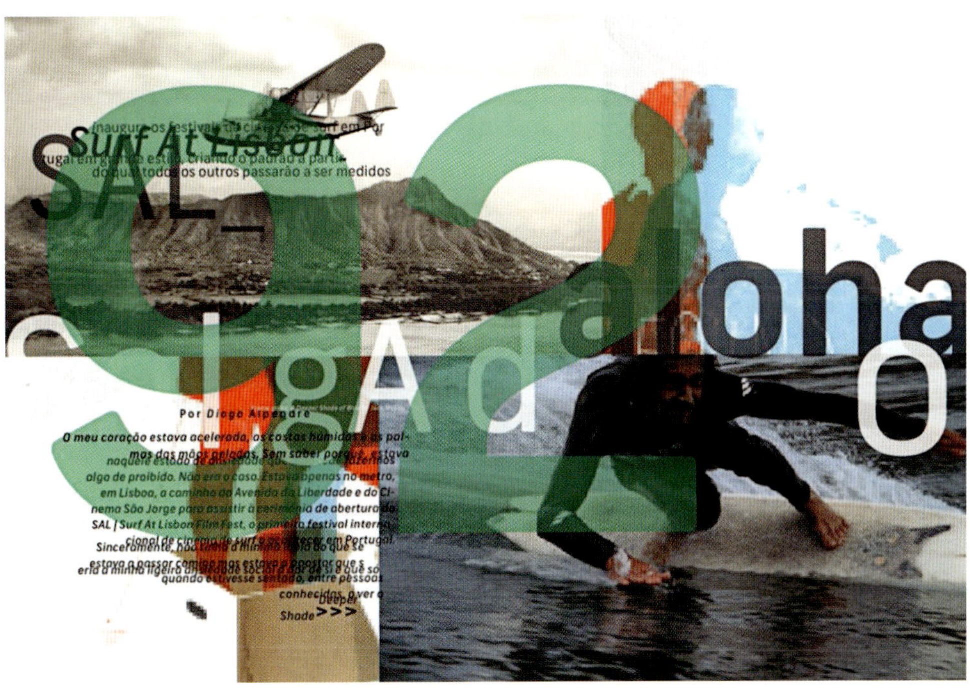

ABOVE:
***SurfPortugal* magazine**
2012

typography, unusual photographic treatments whereby images often looked as if they had been casually slapped down, and, of course, a total disregard for the Modernists' beloved grid. He later did work for its sister magazine, *Transworld Snowboarding*, as well as for the publishers of *Surfer* magazine. He subsequently became art director for the alternative music magazine *Ray Gun* in 1992, where he designed covers and layouts that were utterly radical – sometimes difficult to decode, but always full of vibrant youthful energy, with every issue offering something graphically and typographically fresh. Central to his success was his ability to invoke a sense of the handcrafted – which often came about because that was exactly how his artwork had been created. His design work for *Ray Gun* was also imbued with a feeling of anything-goes coolness, which helped forge an emotional engagement with its readership and set the publication apart from the banal world of glossy magazines.

In 1995, he established his own studio in New York and soon found himself in high demand, with corporate clients wanting him to create "cool" artwork for them that would appeal to his natural audience – the youthfully hip. An engaging speaker, Carson has also lectured all over the world, while his book *The End of Print* (1995) became one of the best-selling books on graphic design of all time. Often imitated, but never equalled, David Carson is quite simply a force of nature who continues to produce work that is full of creative vitality, much like the man himself.

C

George Carwardine

British, 1887–1947

During the 1920s, in response to the expansion of the automotive industry in Britain, the mechanical engineer and inventor George Carwardine established his own company in Bath specializing in the design and manufacture of car suspension systems. While working in this field, Carwardine developed an articulated spring-and-lever balancing mechanism that could be positioned and held in any place, which he described as "equiposing".

In 1932, he patented the design of an articulated task light incorporating this pioneering mechanism, which the Patent Office referred to as "anglepoising". Subsequently christened the Anglepoise, this innovative lighting design was based on pure mathematical engineering principles. It allowed flexible yet precise re-positioning, with the light's construction in many ways mimicking the mechanical function of a human arm. By balancing a weight against a spring through a linking mechanism, Carwardine was able to ensure that the light remained highly stable and could hold any position over three planes.

Carwardine's first light had a simple spun aluminium shade and was initally produced by his own Bath-based company called Cardine – which was not only an abbreviation of his surname but also fittingly the word in Italian for a hinge or pivot. Herbert Terry & Sons, a manufacturer of springs based in Redditch, subsequently produced under licence a short-armed version of this design, known as the Model 1208, which was intended to be used by

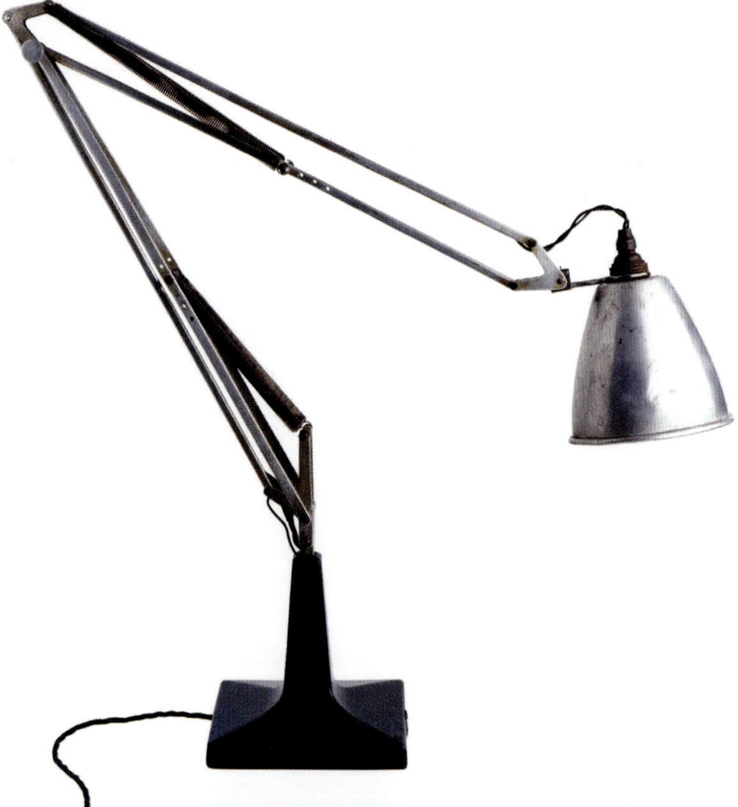

RIGHT:
Early "equiposing" task light for Cardine Accessories Ltd, *c.*1932 (later produced by Herbert Terry & Sons as the Model 1209)

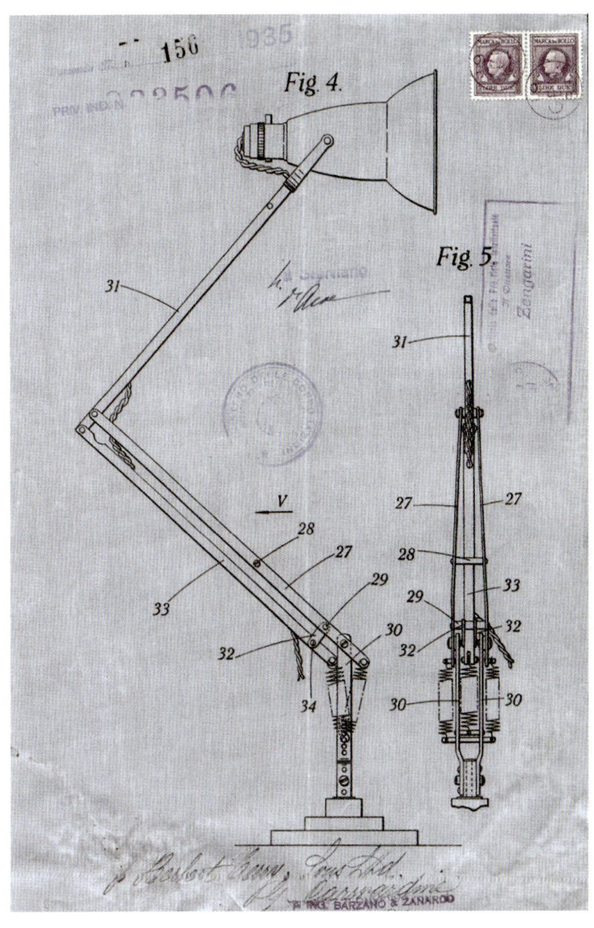

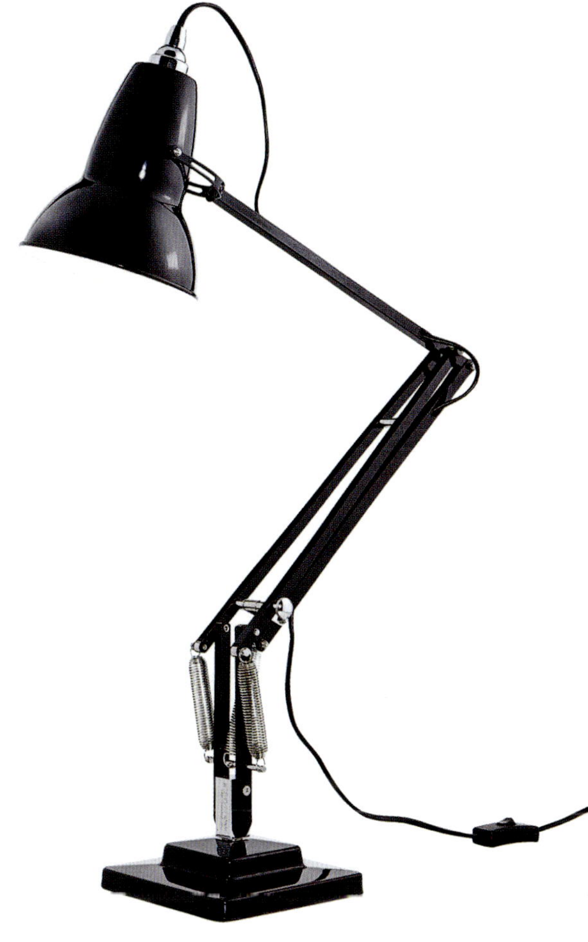

machinists and was in fact the very first "Anglepoise" light. This was followed by the longer-armed Model 1209, which utilized four anglepoising springs, and was similarly intended for industrial and institutional purposes. The Model 1208 became an instant success when it was first introduced in 1933 and it soon became apparent that Carwardine's useful task light could also be marketed for use in homes and offices. To this end, the design was adapted to incorporate three rather than four coiled metal springs, which meant that it was less likely to trap fingers or long hair in its uppermost springs. Launched in 1935, this more refined model, known as the Anglepoise Model 1227, was less utilitarian-looking than its predecessor, but no less functional.

The archetypal Anglepoise, the Model 1227 was widely used in offices, factories and hospitals as well as in domestic environments and was produced in a number of variations, including a ceiling fixture. The base of the Model 1227 evolved from a three-step to a two-step configuration in around 1938 to make it less costly and easier to produce. Hugely influential, the Anglepoise was the blueprint for subsequent generations of task lighting and continues to be produced by its original manufacturer more than seventy years after its original introduction, which is not only testament to its enduring visual appeal but also to its exceptional functionality.

ABOVE LEFT:
Italian patent drawing
for the Model 1227 task light, filed 1935 (showing three-step base produced 1935–38)

ABOVE RIGHT:
Model 1227 task light
for Herbert Terry & Sons (later Anglepoise), originally launched 1934 with a three-step base – this two-step base version introduced *c.*1938

A.M. Cassandre

French, 1901–1968

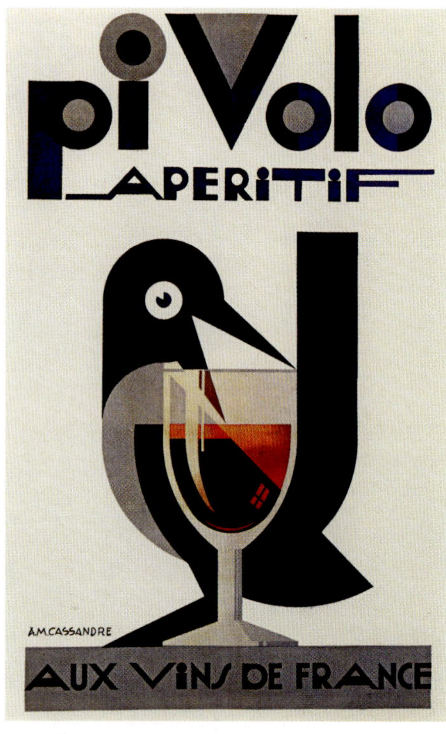

ABOVE:
Poster
for Pivolo aperitif, 1924

Born in the Ukraine to French parents, Adolphe Jean-Marie Mouron would later adopt the pseudonym A.M. Cassandre and go on to become one of the most celebrated avant-garde poster designers of the twentieth century.

Having studied in Paris, he established his own studio in 1922 and the same year began designing posters under the name of "Cassandre". The following year he created a poster for the well-known Parisian furniture store Au Bûcheron. This early and dynamically composed artwork reflected the strong influence of Cubism and Surrealism with its depiction of a bare-chested muscular woodcutter chopping down a tree, and it was later awarded the Grand Prix at the 1925 *Exposition Internationale des Arts Décoratifs et Industriels Modernes* held in Paris. Indeed, this large-format advertising poster with its radiant orange background typified the Art Deco style's bold geometric layout and block-like type, and importantly reflected an early creative bridge between the worlds of fine art and commercial art.

Cassandre's poster advertising the new Pivolo aperitif from 1924 demonstrates his genius for creating a composition that was not only eye-catching but also thought-provoking, playing a visual pun on the product's title. The drink's name derived from an aviation training term meaning "keep your altitude", which also sounded like "*Pie vole haut*" (magpie, fly high) prompting his inclusion of a stylized bird with a mischievous glint in its eye.

During the 1920s and 1930s he also designed posters for, among others, Bugatti, Florent, *L'Intransigeant*, Unic and Pathé, but it was his lithographic travel posters for Nord Express (1927), Chemin du Fer du Nord (1929) and Normandie (1935) that truly revealed his mastery of the poster with their dynamic viewpoints and bold abstraction of form. Cassandre was also a talented typographer whose Bifur (1929) and Peignot (1937) typefaces are some of the most recognizable and well-known Art Deco fonts of all time. His reputation as a design innovator was also recognized in the United States, where he worked on a number of notable commissions including several covers for *Harper's Bazaar* magazine, a series of monthly black and white advertisements for the Container Corporation of America and a striking poster for Ford that featured an all-seeing eye. He also designed the eye-catching YSL monogram for Yves Saint Laurent in 1963 and his own Cassandre typeface in 1968.

Interestingly, Cassandre began a design for a poster by first determining the text and choice of typography and then, once these had been established, they inspired the more pictorial graphic elements of his compositions. It was this unusual approach which undoubtedly allowed him to create dynamic compositions that powerfully conveyed the messages they were intended to deliver, often with an engaging touch of surrealistic humour – and ultimately made him one of the great posters designers of all time.

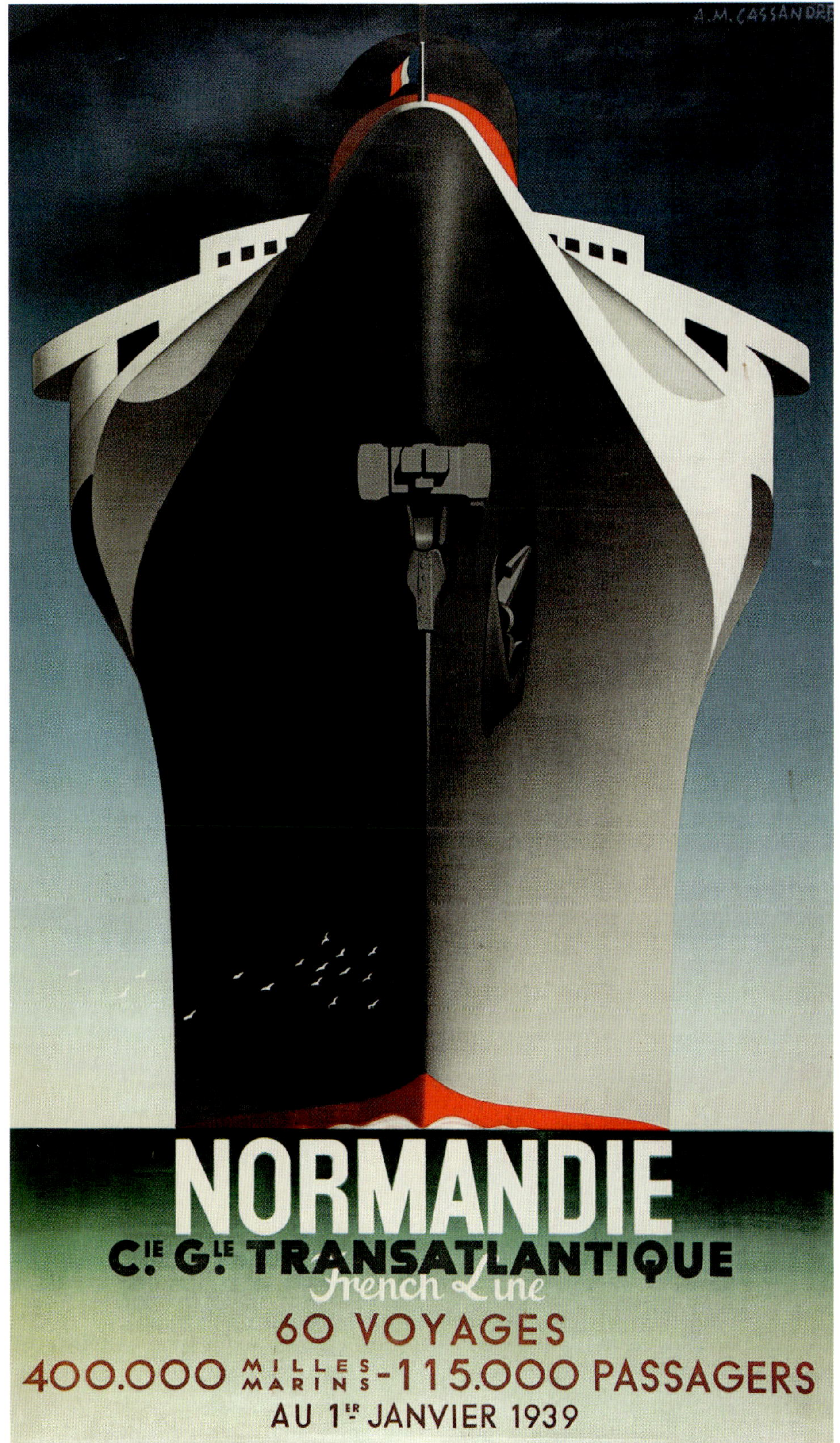

RIGHT:
***Normandie* poster**
for La Cie. Gle.Transatlantique (French Line), 1935 (this version 1939)

Anna Castelli Ferrieri

Italian, 1918–2006

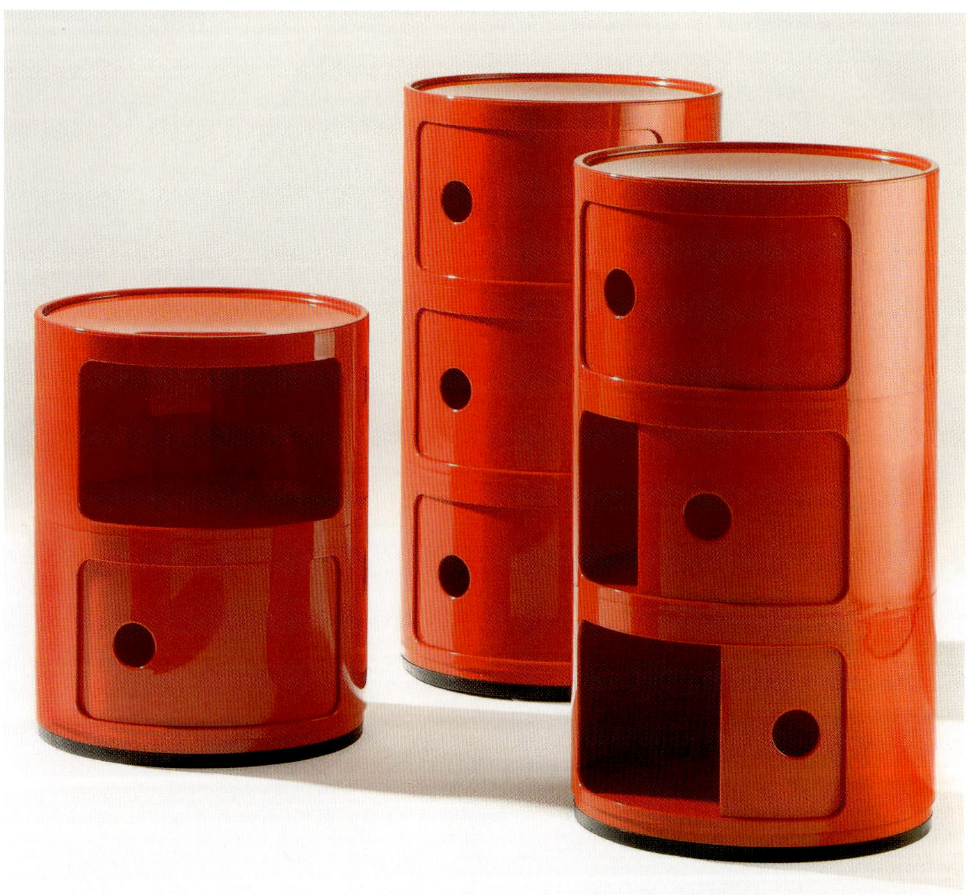

The Milanese architect-designer Anna Castelli Ferrieri was a prominent female pioneer of modern Italian design during the period spanning the 1950s to the 1980s.

The daughter of the noted journalist, film director and screenwriter Enzo Ferrieri who had founded *Il Convegno* journal in 1920 and its related theatre in 1932, she grew up amid the European cultural avant-garde and became one of the first women to graduate from the highly regarded architecture programme at the Politecnico di Milano in 1943. The same year she married the chemical engineer Giulio Castelli, who six years later founded the design-led company Kartell, which was at the leading edge of plastics manufacturing technology. Initially, Castelli Ferrieri was not so involved with her husband's company, as she was a contributor to *Casabella* magazine from 1946 to 1947. From 1949 onwards, however, she was increasingly instrumental in the development of the company's impressive range of high-quality plastic

ABOVE:
Componibili (Model Nos. 4965 and 4966) storage units
for Kartell, 1967–69

OPPOSITE TOP:
Model No. 4870 chair
for Kartell, 1984 – awarded a Compasso d'Oro in 1987

OPPOSITE BOTTOM:
Wheeled dolly with stack of Model No. 4870 chairs

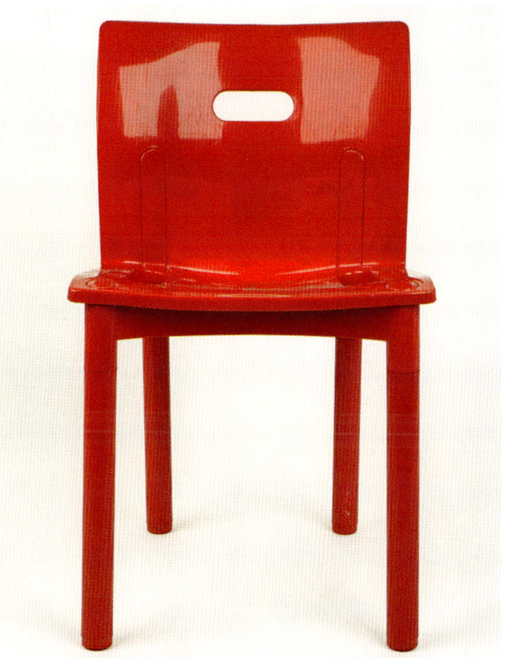

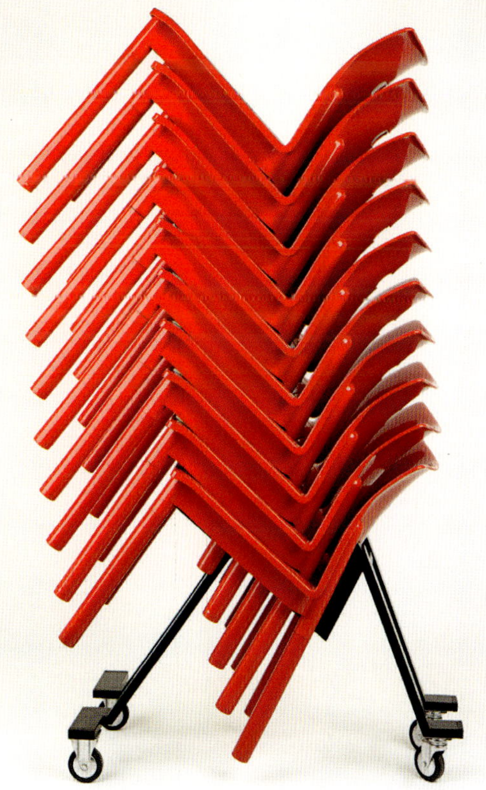

household products and furniture designs. Yet despite being at the forefront of Italian design and architecture at this time, Castelli Ferrieri's remarkable contribution as one of the most significant pioneers of plastics in design has been unsufficiently acknowledged.

While Kartell was still a fledgling company, she collaborated on a number of important architectural and urban planning projects with the architect Ignazio Gardella, including a headquarters building and manufacturing complex for her husband's company in the industrial suburbs of Milan. As the company grew she turned her attention to industrial design, and in 1964 co-designed with Gardella her first product for Kartell, the Model No. 4991 table made of glass-reinforced polyester.

This was followed three years later by her ingenious Model No. 4970 system, which comprised square storage units in two sizes that could be stacked with their openings facing in any of four directions, and were topped with a tray-like element. These components could also be used in conjunction with optional doors and castors. Launched in 1968 and also known as the Multi Box System, this range became the world's first storage system made entirely of injection-moulded ABS plastic. Designed at around the same time but appearing a year later, Castelli Ferrieri's cylindrical Componibili (Model Nos. 4965, 4966, 4967) stacking storage units had a similar construction, and were also injection moulded in a shiny and hard type of ABS. The doors of this range, however, were sliding rather than hinged, which made them even easier to install and use.

As Kartell's art director from 1976 to 1987, Ferrieri Castelli continued to design for the company. Her designs – including various tables and chairs, as well as smaller-scale items such as bowls, mirrors, ashtrays, a chopping board, salad servers and even a laundry basket – attested to her remarkable ability to fuse rational design logic with an elegant stylistic bravado that ultimately came to define the look of Italian design during its acknowledged golden age. As *The New York Times* later noted in her obituary, Castelli Ferrieri was "an emblematic member of a generation of Italian designers that… energetically transformed the world of design with their interest in using new technologies and materials".

Achille Castiglioni

Italian, 1918–2002

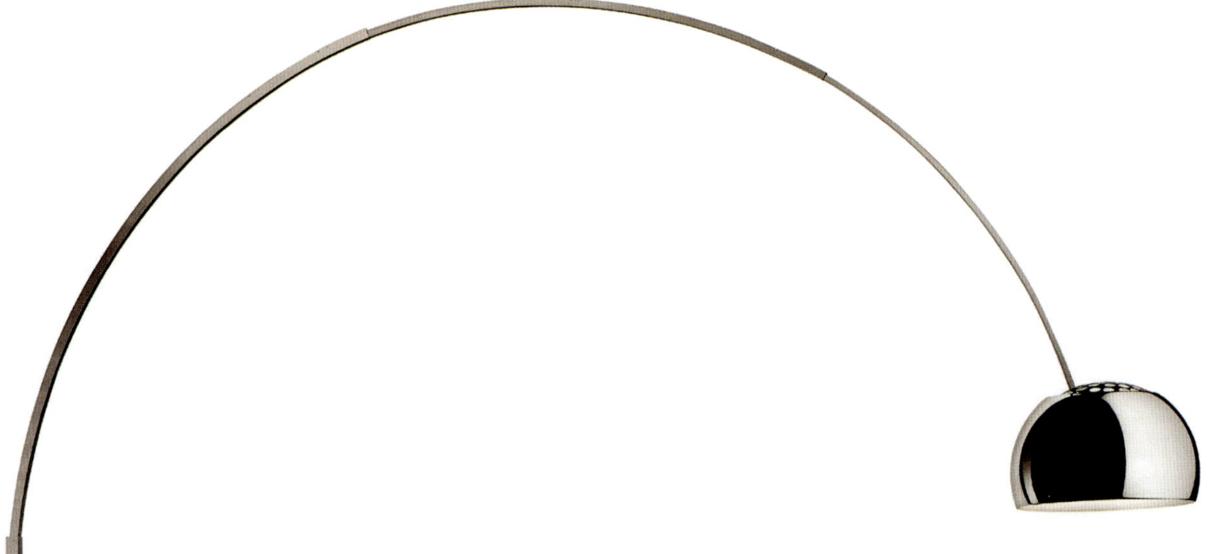

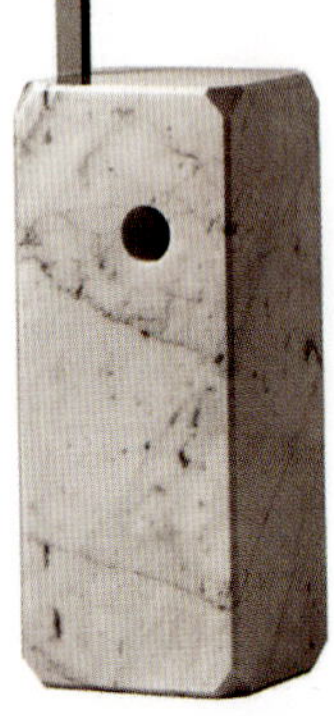

Achille Castiglioni was a hugely talented designer who created dozens of stylishly ingenuous products, many of which are now regarded as exemplars of modern Italian design. Born in Milan, Castiglioni began his industrial design career in his early twenties, following in the footsteps of his two older brothers, Livio and Pier Giacomo, who had already forged a reputation in this field. Like his two siblings, Castiglioni studied architecture at the Politecnico di Milano, and while still a student he began assisting his brothers and their partner Luigi Caccia Dominioni with various designs they were working on, most notably the Caccia cutlery for Ditta Spoggi (1938) and the Model No. 547 radio for Phonola (1938–39).

After graduating in 1944, he joined their design partnership and over the next two decades mainly worked with his brother Pier Giacomo – as Caccia Dominioni and Livio left the studio in 1947 and 1952 respectively. A prominent member of the Milanese design community, Castiglioni joined the organizing committee of the Milan Triennale in 1947 and played an active role in the promotion of modern Italian design both at home and abroad. In 1950, Achille and Pier Giacomo became creative consultants to RAI, Italy's national public broadcasting company, and for the next fourteen years created various eye-catching pavilions and related exhibitions for the broadcaster. The duo also made their mark in the world of furniture design with two early "ready-made" designs from 1957 – the Sella and Mezzadro stools, the former incorporating a bicycle seat and the latter a tractor seat. The Sella was a response to Achille's desire for a more active form of seating that would "move around" while he was making calls from a payphone. The use of found elements in these early seating designs can be seen as a pragmatic repsonse to problem-solving, while also reflecting the conceptual influence of Marcel Duchamp's ready-mades. It was not until the early 1970s that they were put into production by Zanotta – showing just how far ahead of popular taste the Castiglioni brothers really were. Another early design was the Sanluca armchair (1960) for Gavina, the construction of which was informed by extensive research into the ergonomics of sitting and employed state-of-the-art polyurethane foam upholstery, which enabled the creation of a sculptural form the like of which had not previously been seen.

In 1961, the pair began collaborating with the lighting company Flos, their first design being a polished aluminium hanging light which had been specially created for their Splügen Bräu bar in Milan, the interior of which combined modern furnishings with a few nostaglic touches. The following year, Flos launched three other lights by the brothers: the Taccia table lamp and Toio and Arco floor lights – all exceptionally innovative designs that were extremely forward-looking for their day. The sculptural arching Arco lamp for Flos (1962), for example, was inspired by a streetlight and transformed the traditional ceiling light into an autonomous freestanding floor unit that could be moved as required. Apart from furniture and lighting, the brothers also designed products for the pioneering electronics manufacturer Brionvega, including the RR 126 radiogram (1965) which ingeniously consisted of three hinged "boxes" containing the record deck and the two speakers.

After Pier Giacomo's early death in 1968, Achille carried on designing for over thirty years, creating an array of products that were as experimental as they were elegant. These designs possessed a very graphic quality, with their outlines so distinctive you could instantly recognize them just from their silhouettes. Another feature of Castiglioni's designs was humour. He once noted, "There has to be irony both in design and in the objects.... One of my secrets is to joke all the time."

OPPOSITE:
Arco floor light
for Flos, 1962

BELOW LEFT:
Mezzadro (tractor seat)
for Zanotta, 1957 – co-designed with Pier Giacomo Castiglioni

BELOW RIGHT:
RR 126 radiogram
for Brionvega, 1965

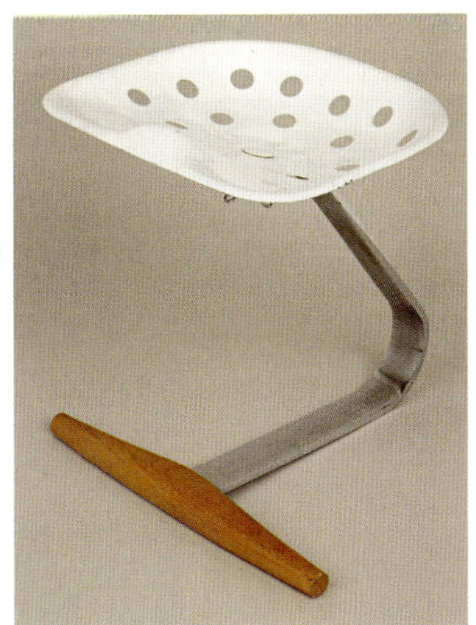

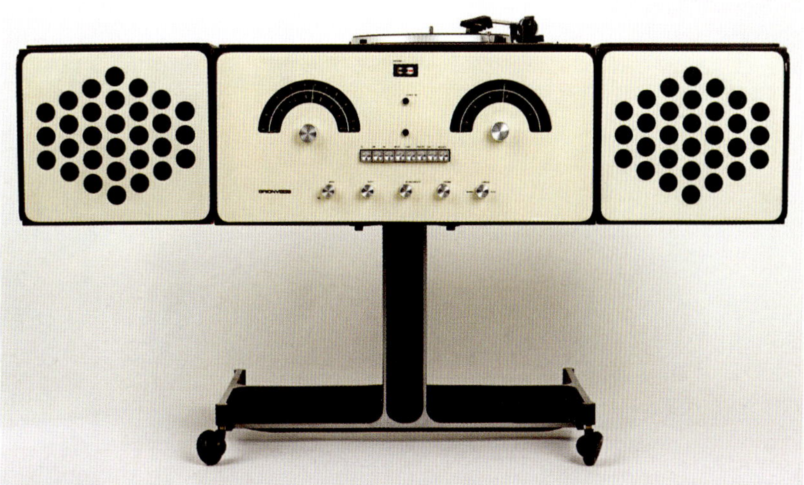

C

Pierre Chareau

French, 1883–1950

During the inter-war period, Pierre Chareau, a leading pioneer of Modernism in France, created buildings and interiors that were astoundingly progressive in terms of both their functionality and the materials they employed.

Born in Bordeaux, he had no formal training and instead began his career as a sixteen-year-old draughtsman in the Paris offices of the British furniture manufacturer and decorating firm Waring & Gillow. While there, he met his British-born future wife, Louise "Dollie" Dyte, whom he married in 1904. During the First World War he was conscripted to the French military, but on his demobilization he returned to Paris and established his own design office in 1919. One of his earliest commissions was from Dr Jean Dalsace and his wife Annie – who would go on to become his most important patrons – and comprised an office/study and a bedroom for their apartment. This project's purpose-designed furniture was subsequently exhibited at the *Salon d'Automne* in 1919.

The following year, he met the Cubist painter Jean Lurçat and again exhibited furniture and interiors at the *Salon d'Automne*, attracting critical acclaim. Two years later, he exhibited at the *Salon de la Société des Artistes-Décorateurs* for the first time and during this period also began collecting works of art by other members of the European avant-garde, notably Amedeo Modigliani, Georges Braque, Paul Klee, Raoul Dufy, Max Ernst and Piet Mondrian.

Chareau subsequently collaborated with Fernand Léger and Robert Mallet-Stevens on the design of film sets for *L'inhumaine* (1924) directed by Marcel L'Herbier. He also opened his own studio-gallery, La Boutique, in 1924 and the following year exhibited furniture and interiors at the landmark *Exposition Internationale des Arts Décoratifs et Industriels Modernes* in Paris. It was there that he met the Dutch architect Bernard Bijvoet, whom he later worked with on a number of commissions, notably the Clubhouse at Beauvallon (1926) and his architectural masterwork: the revolutionary steel and glass Maison de Verre, Paris (1928–32), designed for Jean and Annie Dalsace.

BELOW LEFT:
Façade of Maison de Verre
Paris, 1928–32

BELOW RIGHT:
Detail of the glass bricks
used for the façade of the Maison de Verre

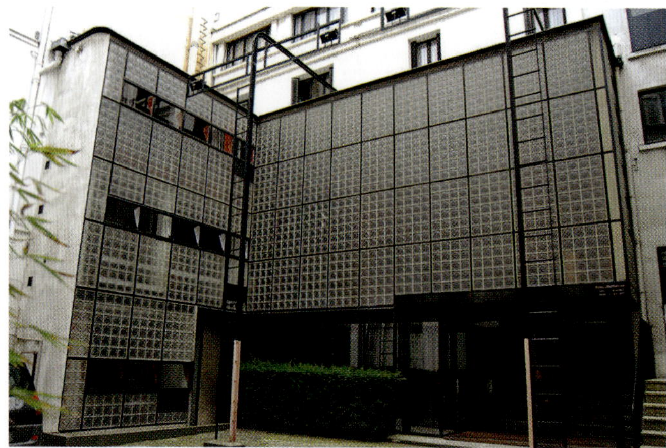

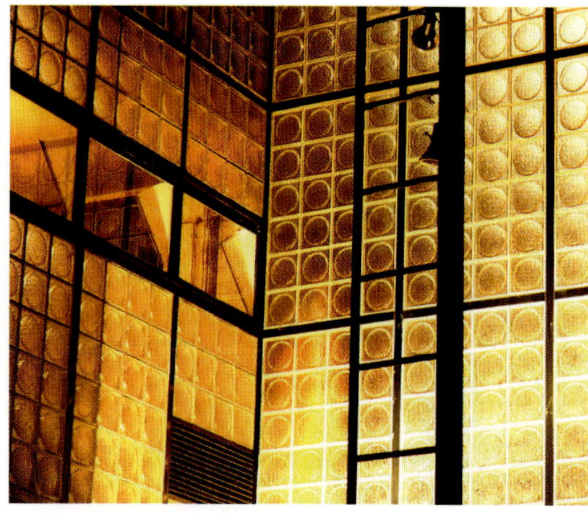

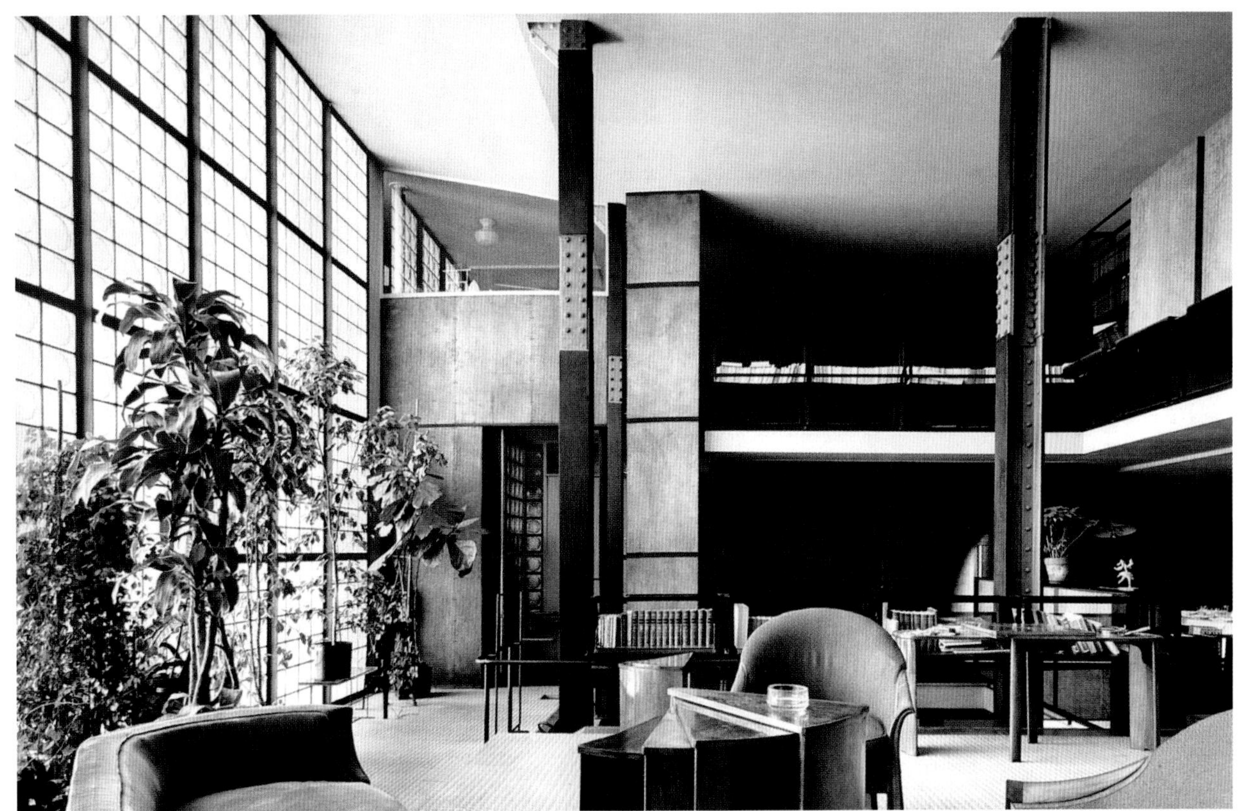

ABOVE:
First floor living room of the Maison de Verre in Paris, 1928–32

This extraordinary "House of Glass" was breathtakingly innovative in its use of industrial materials, including steel beams, translucent glass bricks, perforated sheet metal and rubber flooring tiles. It was an ingenious infill building wedged between two eighteenth-century buildings and squeezed beneath an already-existing top storey. On the ground floor was a very progressive, clinical-looking suite of medical rooms, which was linked by a dramatic open-backed staircase to the modern-style living accommodation above. Throughout the house there were numerous built-in features that not only saved space but also offered a high degree of functional flexibility, such as sliding sheet-metal screens and metal closets that served as walls between the various rooms. Yet despite its unrelentingly industrial aesthetic, this extraordinary dwelling had a surprising visual warmth thanks to Chareau's clever juxtaposition of the industrial materials used in its construction with dove-grey carpeting, gleaming blonde-wood panelling and amply upholstered furniture covered in tapestries and warm-toned velvets.

Like many of the most progressive architect-designers in France, Chareau left the Société des Artistes Décorateurs in 1929 to become a founding member of the UAM (Union des Artistes Modernes). During the 1930s, due to the economic depression, he received few commissions; however, he did design some ingenious collapsible school furniture that was exhibited at the *Salon d'Automne* in 1936 and also designed barracks furniture made from packing crates to be used by soldiers posted overseas in 1939.

In 1940, Chareau emigrated to the United States, where he worked for the French cultural attaché on the design of a number of exhibitions. One of his last commissions was the inventive renovation of a Quonset hut into a working studio in East Hampton, Long Island for his friend the young artist Robert Motherwell in 1947.

Antonio Citterio

Italian, 1950–

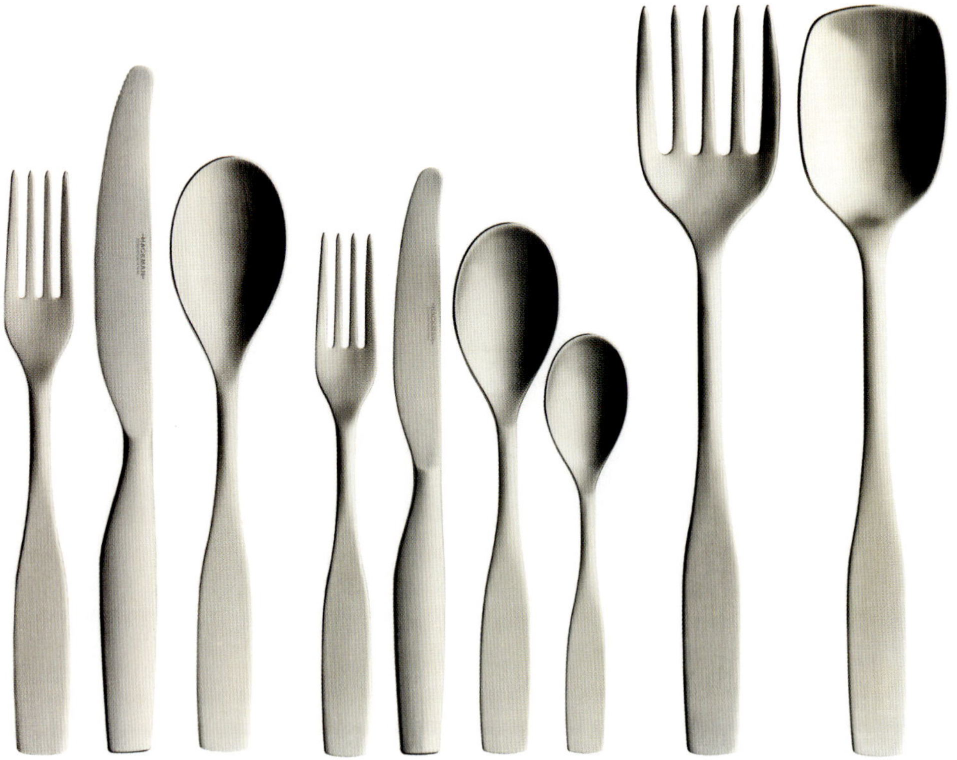

ABOVE:
Citterio cutlery
for Hackman, 1998 (later by Iittala)

Antonio Citterio is one of the most commercially successful Italian designers working today, who consistently creates stylish yet understated furniture and products for a host of leading design-led manufacturers. Above all, his work is defined by an elegant functional refinement, whether it is cutlery, a sofa, an interior or a complete building.

In 1972 Citterio set up his own design studio in Lissone, near Milan, prior to graduating in 1975 in architecture from the Politecnico di Milano. From 1973 he also worked in partnership with Paolo Nava – a creative alliance that lasted until 1981. Having established a design office in Milan the same year, he subsequently worked in collaboration with Gregotti Associati in 1983 on the discreet and subtle renovation of the Raphael Room at the Pinacoteca di Brera (Brera Art Gallery) in Milan.

From 1987 until 1996 he worked with his wife, the American architect Terry Dwan, and together they designed showrooms for, among others, B&B Italia and Vitra as well as shops for Esprit. Citterio has worked extensively in the field of furniture design for Kartell, B&B Italia, Flexform and Moroso – often creating solutions that have dual contract and domestic applications. He has also designed for the office environment – notably his well-known T-Chair (1994) developed with Glen Oliver Löw for Vitra, which provided anatomical support without reducing freedom of movement, and the Ephesos office system for Olivetti Synthesis (1992).

With Löw, he also developed a range of flatware and kitchen tools for the Finnish manufacturer Hackman, which was remarkable for its high manufacturing quality and extremely comfortable egonomics. In partnership with Löw he additionally designed the innovative and influential translucent plastic Mobil storage system (1994) for Kartell, which was awarded a Compasso d'Oro in 1995.

In 1999, Citterio founded with Patricia Viel a new studio known as Antonio Citterio and Partners (later to become Antonio Citterio Patricia Viel and Partners) to specialize in urban planning, as well as the design of residential, commercial and industrial complexes, and interior schemes for offices, showrooms and hotels. The firm is also actively engaged in product design, working for, among others, Ansorg, Arclinea, Axor Hansgrohe, Flexform, Flos, Fusital, Hermès, Iittala, Inda, Kartell, Maxalto, Sanitec Group/Pozzi-Ginori, Technogym, Tre-Più and Vitra. It is, however, Citterio's impressive body of work for B&B Italia that perhaps best exemplifies his approach to design, with these innovative furniture pieces possessing an elegance that is driven not by style but rather by a true understanding of functional simplicity.

BELOW:
Mobil container system
for Kartell, 1994

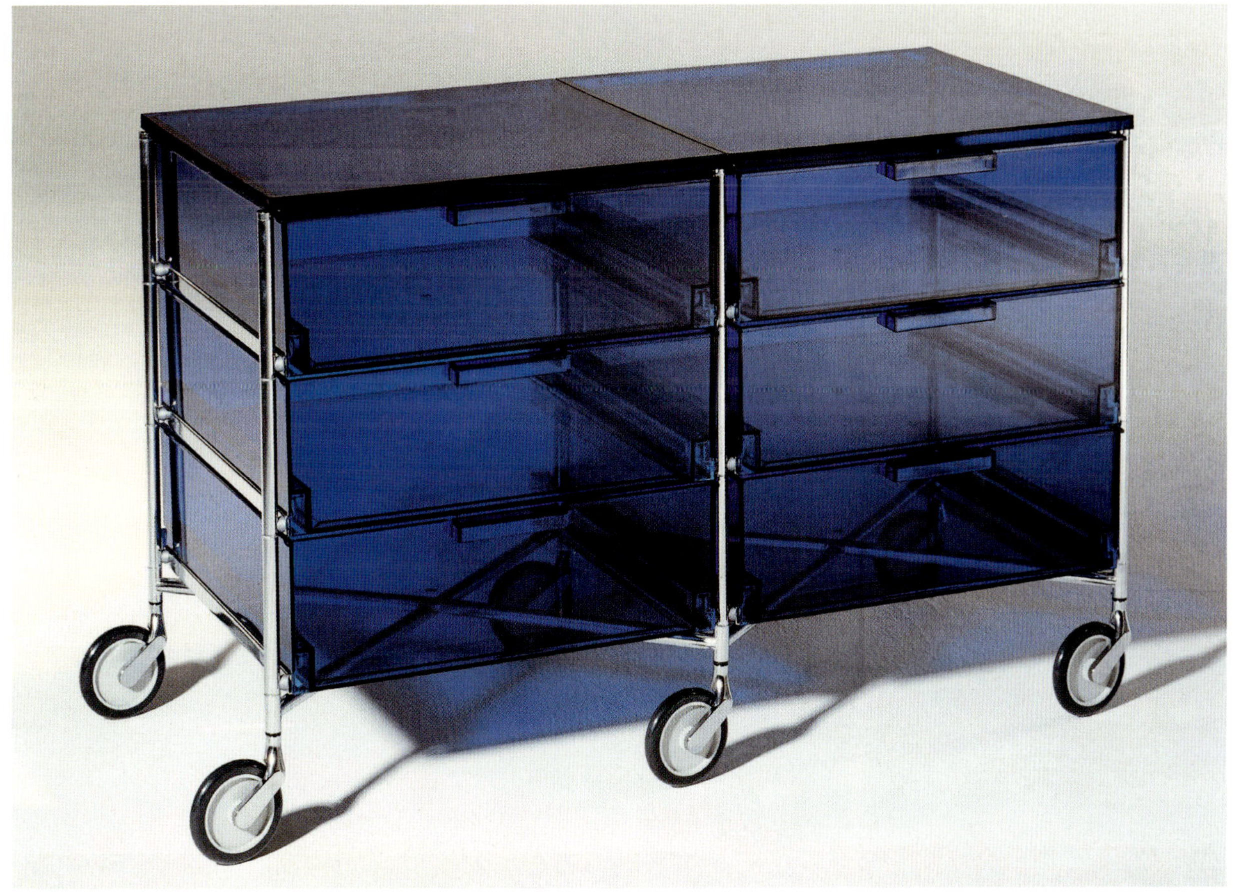

Wells Coates

Canadian/active Britain, 1895–1958

The Canadian designer Wells Coates was a leading protagonist of the Modern Movement in Britain during the 1930s. Rallying against what he termed "ancestor-worship in design", he instead promoted a more scientific approach to design that was based on his engineering background.

Born in Tokyo, the eldest son of Canadian missionaries, Coates travelled widely as a young man, which undoubtedly had a formative influence on his later development as a designer. The fact that his mother had trained as an architect under Louis Sullivan and Frank Lloyd Wright in Chicago before her marriage also unquestionably influenced Coates's later decision to become an architect and designer himself. His engineering studies at the University of British Columbia were interrupted by the outbreak of the First World War and it was only in 1921 that he finally graduated. In 1922, he moved to England to take up a two-year scholarship from the Department of Scientific Research and Industrial Research at London University, receiving his PhD in engineering in 1924.

His first job was as a journalist for the *Daily Express* and it was while working on an eight-month assignment as the newspaper's Paris correspondent that he became interested in the arts. In 1927, he decorated a flat for himself and his new wife, and designed and made some of

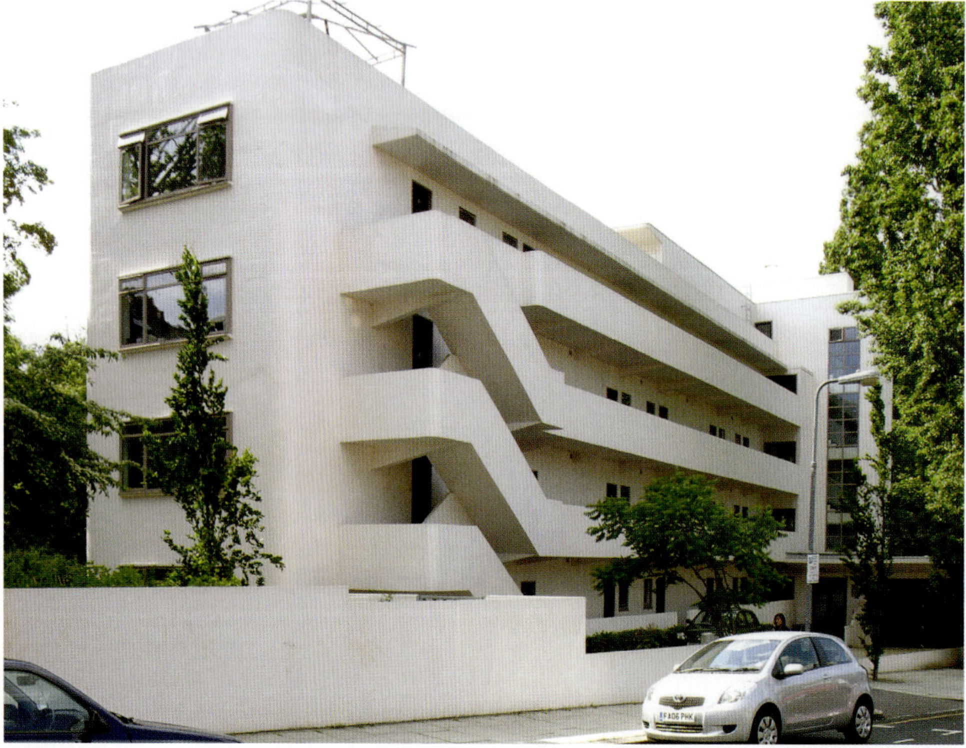

LEFT:
Isokon building
Lawn Road, Hampstead, London, 1933–34 – block of thirty-four flats

its furniture and fittings. This led to a commission to design shop fittings and advertisements for the fashionable textile company Crysede and, a year later, interiors for the firm's factory in Welwyn Garden City. Following this, he received a number of other interior design commissions including studios in London and Newcastle for the BBC.

In 1933, he exhibited his design for the "minimum flat", a progressive vision of contemporary living that was later built as Lawn Road Flats by the owner of Isokon, Jack Pritchard. The same year, Coates created an elegant Modernist tubular steel desk for Practical Equipment Limited (known as PEL) which, with its curved sled-legs, had no sharp edges to damage wooden floors and typified his use of the minimum of means for the maximum design benefit.

Coates also won a radio design competition held by E. K. Cole Ltd in 1932, with an innovative circular model that not only exploited the mass-manufacturing potential of Bakelite – then widely marketed as "the material of a thousand uses" – but also revealed his in-depth understanding of the internal working of radio receivers and the necessary layout of their components. This winning solution was eventually launched in 1934 as the EKCO Model AD-65 and was one of the very first truly Modern mass-produced designs that was made available to British consumers. Coates designed a number of variants of this best-selling radio, which similarly reflected his goal of reducing materials, components and manufacturing costs to make mass-production easier and so undercut the competition. He described his approach to design as "purpose related to purse", and his radios embodied this Modernist mantra. The same year his first of several Sunspan Houses was unveiled at the *Daily Mail Ideal Home Exhibition* in London – an Art Deco light-filled experiment in functional modern living.

In 1933, Coates co-founded MARS (Modern Architecture Research Group), as the British wing of the Congrès Internationaux d'Architecture Moderne (CIAM) and during the war he worked as a designer for the RAF. Later, he taught at Harvard University and in 1956 finally moved back to Canada. Throughout his career, Coates's belief that "the social characteristics of the age determine its art" informed his creation of fashionably avant-garde yet also relatively affordable products that powerfully reflected a new spirit of democratization in British design.

BELOW:
EKCO AD-65 radio
for E.K. Cole Ltd, 1932–34

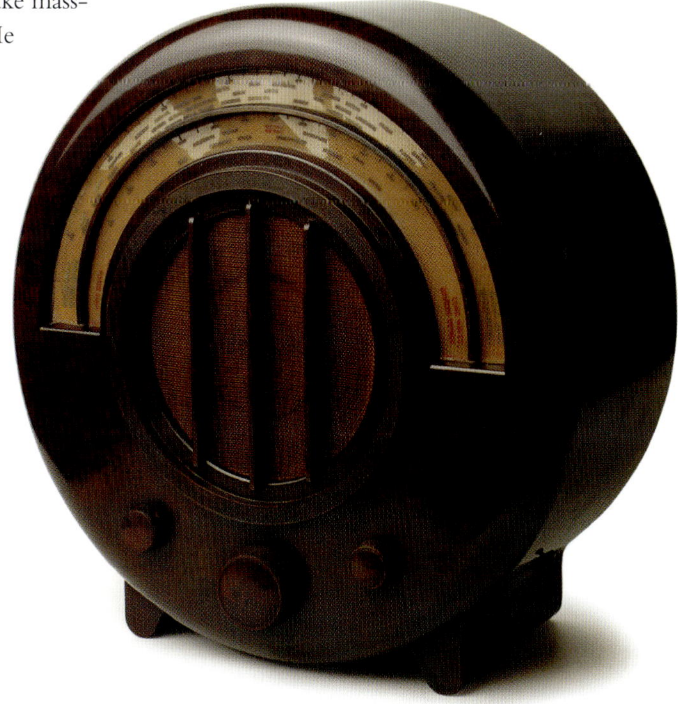

Luigi Colani

German, 1928–

A self-confessed *agent provocateur* of the design world, Luigi Colani is a maverick visionary who likes to think of himself as a 3-D philosopher. Throughout his five-decade-long career he has created sculpturally organic and technically experimental designs that have pulled the future into the present. He was also an early and influential pioneer of bio-design who looked to nature for design inspiration, having once explained, "we should simply bear in mind just how amazingly superior a spider's web is to any load-bearing structure man has made. From this insight, we should look to the superiority of nature for the solutions. If we want to tackle a new task in the studio, then it's best to go outside first and look at what millennia-old answers there may already be to the problem."

German-born, though of Italian and Swiss descent, Colani was christened Lutz but changed his name to the more Italian-sounding Luigi in 1957. He initially studied sculpture at the Akademie der Künste (Academy of Arts) in Berlin and later moved to Paris where he trained as an aerodynamicist at the École Polytechnique. According to Colani, he then read analytical philosophy at the Sorbonne. As he notes, these studies helped him to acquire both a very technical and a highly enquirying mind, which would ultimately determine the kind of designer he would become. As Colani recalls, "I learned to ask myself questions like: Why is something made the way it is? Why does a motorcar look like it does? Is it right or wrong? What is an airplane? Why is it shaped like that?" After the completion of his studies he achieved quite a reputation as a pioneering aerodynamicist, while working for a number

BELOW:
DAF Aero 3000 concept truck, 2001 (left) and **Spitzer-Sllo concept truck**, 2002 (right)

OPPOSITE TOP:
Drop teapot for Rosenthal, 1971

OPPOSITE BOTTOM:
Sitzgerät Colani sitting tool for Top System Burkhard, 1971–72

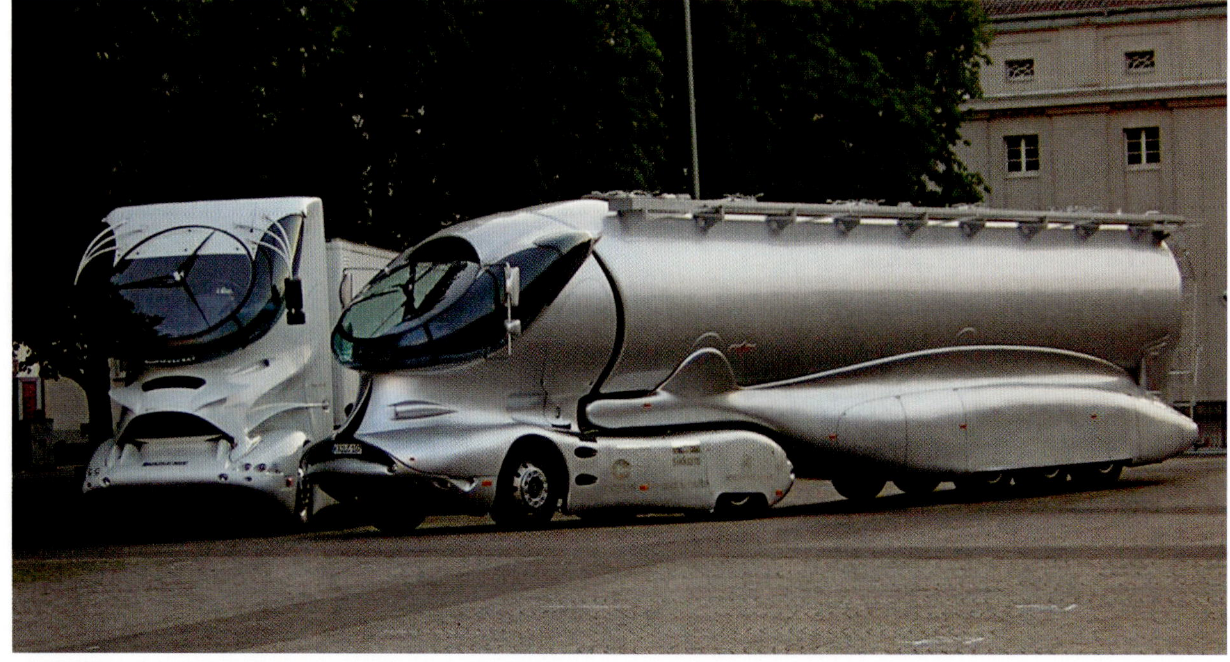

of car-makers and coachbuilders. He eventually established his own design studio in Germany in the early 1970s, which has since specialized in the design of various modes of streamlined transportation, from catamarans and sports coupés to aeroplanes and trucks.

Apart from his work in transportation design, most of which was of a conceptual nature, Colani found success as a furniture designer with his sculptural upholstered chairs for Kusch+Co (1969) and his well-known plastic Zocker seating tools for Top System Burkhard Lübke (1971–72). He is also an accomplished product designer who transformed everyday objects into futuristic sculptural *tours-de-force* – such his ergonomically refined Model No. 042984 baby's bath (1969) for Sulo and his remarkable soft-edge T90 camera for Canon (1984–86). Apart from these sculptural designs, Colani's work has also at times revealed a rather kitsch and chauvinistic quality – for instance, one of the most eye-catching elements of his Horch Mega-Roadster (1996) is its hood ornament featuring a naked woman holding on to a letter H for dear life. In 2007, the Design Museum in London held a major retrospective of Colani's life and work fittingly entitled *Translating Nature*, and in a related interview he noted, "Designers tomorrow must be three-dimensional philosophers. They must ask themselves questions. Are we doing the right thing? Are we employing the materials as intelligently as we should? ... the only choice for designers is to go back to nature."

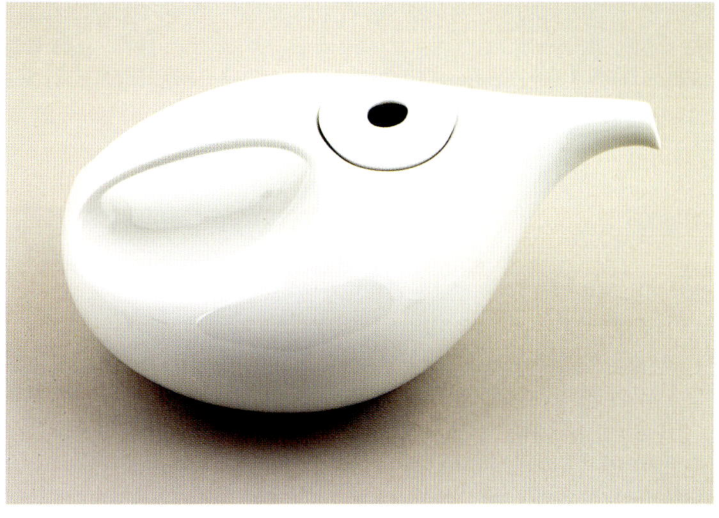

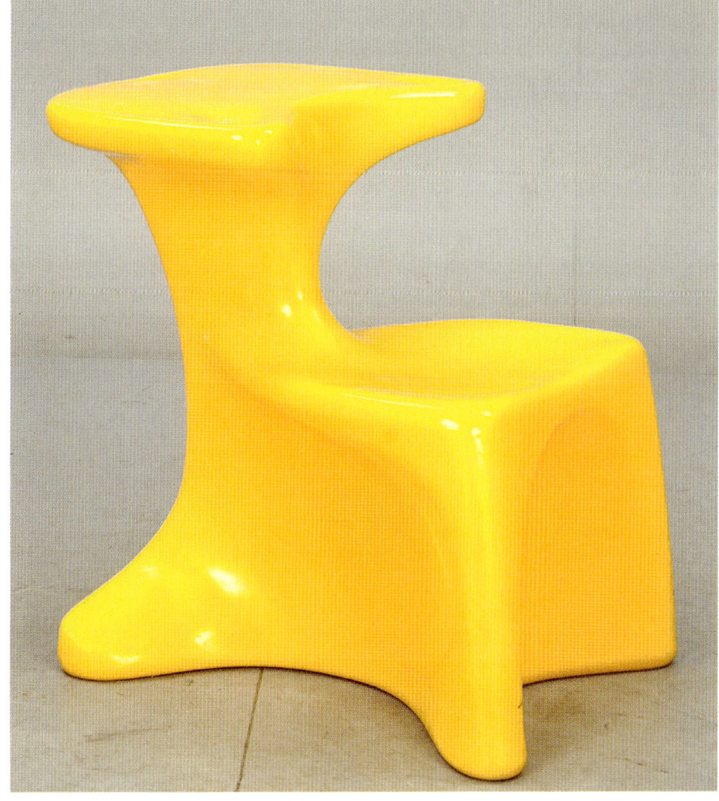

C

Joe Colombo

Italian, 1930–1971

Joe Colombo was one of Italy's greatest design innovators; from his Universale (1965–67), the first adult-sized chair to be moulded entirely in plastic, to his all-in-one Boby trolley (1970), everything Colombo created was intended for what he described as "the environment of the future". Although he actually came to design relatively late in his career, having devoted his twenties to painting and sculpture, in the decade or so he worked as a designer, Colombo was exceptionally prolific, creating some of the most memorable products and habitats of the 1960s.

Cesare "Joe" Colombo had spent his childhood drawing and making Meccano models with his brother Gianni, who would become one of his closest collaborators. He later studied fine art at the Accademia di Belle Arti di Brera (Brera Academy of Fine Arts) in Milan, where he joined the Movimento Nucleare, experimented with abstract painting and sketched a futuristic "nuclear city".

In 1953, he designed a ceiling for a Milan jazz club and the following year created three open-air rest areas featuring "television shrines" at the Milan Triennale. Colombo subsequently studied architecture at the Politecnico di Milano and in 1958 he and Gianni took over the running of their family's electric-conductor factory, using it as a playground for experimenting with the latest production processes and newly developed plastics. In 1962, Colombo opened a studio in Milan, initially working on interiors for ski lodges and hotels but also experimenting in product design.

He saw his role as a futurologist, and whenever he wrote or lectured he emphasized the exciting possibility of harnessing new technologies to produce new design solutions. In his visionary mission to furnish new types of habitat, he explored new production processes and materials, resulting in the Elda armchair (1963), the first really large-scale seating design made of fibreglass, the Small Armchair With Curved Elements (1964) made from three interlocking pieces of plywood, and the landmark Universale chair, which was the result of his desire to make a chair entirely of injection-moulded plastic. Stackable and easy-to-clean, the Universale came with legs in three different heights so it could be used as a barstool, a dining chair and a lounger.

Colombo was also the pioneer of new living-space concepts that were suited to the more nomadic lifestyle of the late 1960s. To this end he rethought the design of storage, from his Combi-Centre (1963) consisting of

BELOW:
Boby storage trolley
for Bieffeplast (later B-Line), 1970

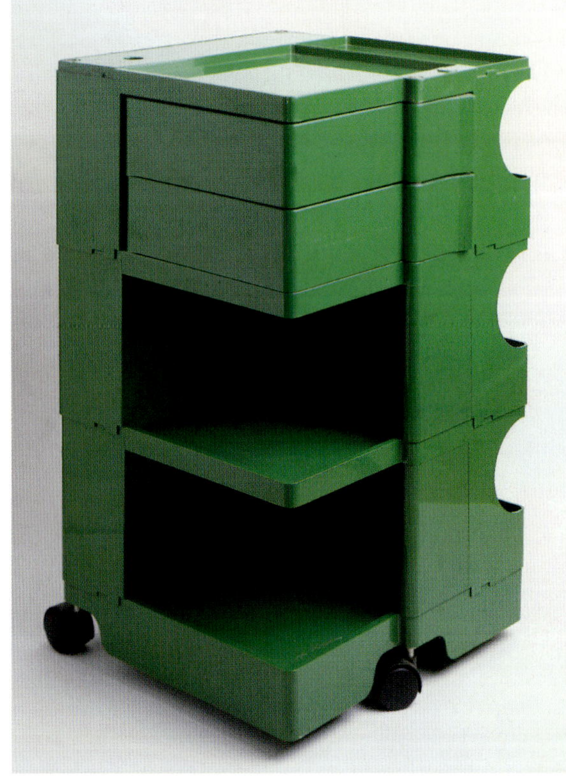

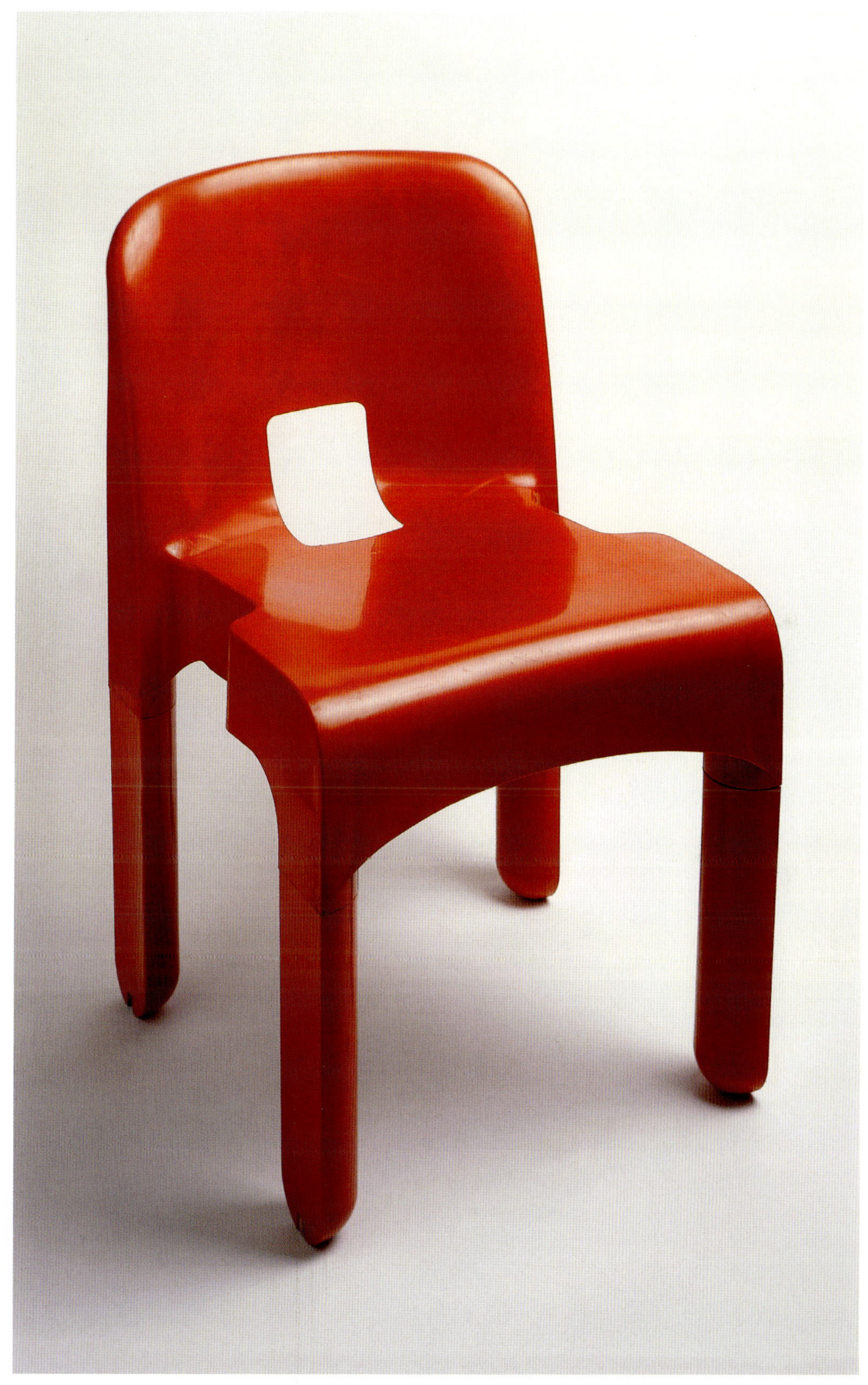

RIGHT:
Model No. 4860
Universale chair
for Kartell, 1965–67

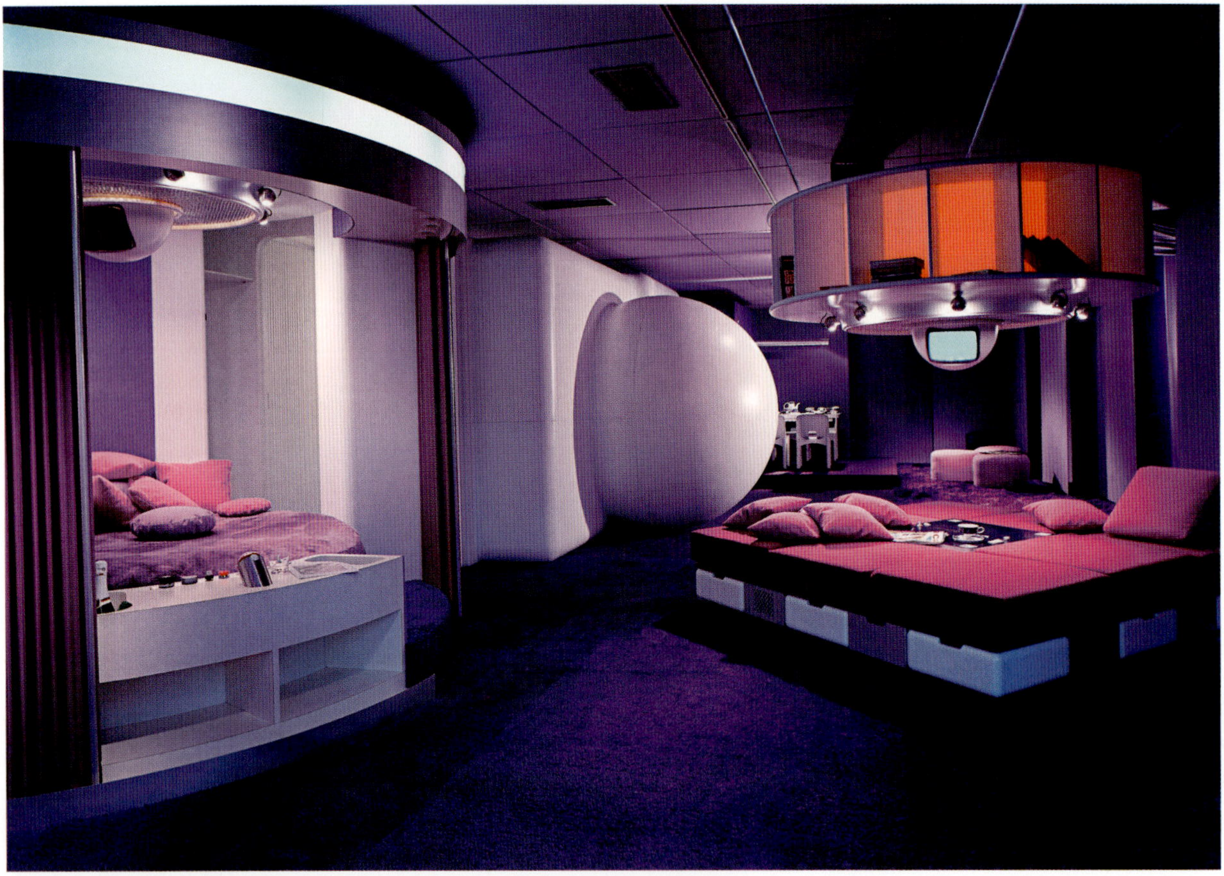

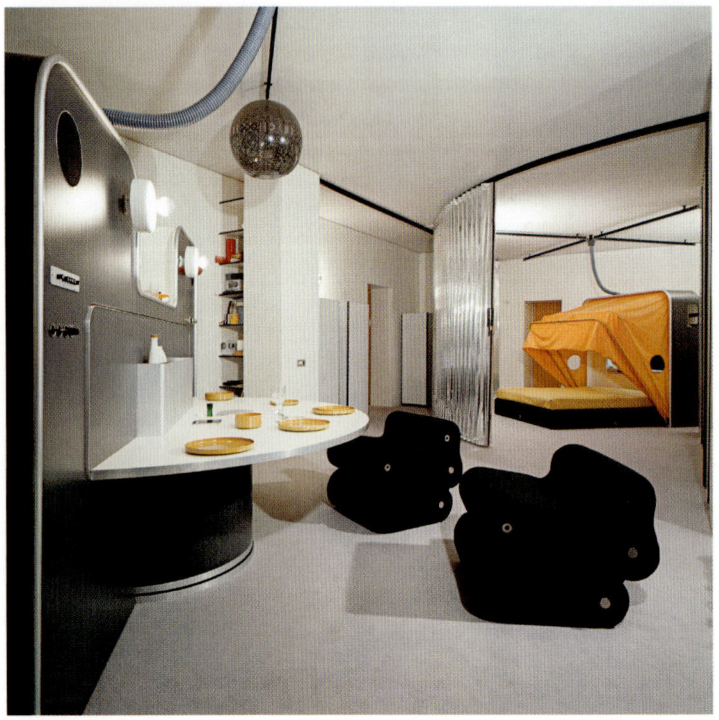

ABOVE:
Visiona 1 installation
at the Cologne Furniture Fair for Bayer AG, 1969

LEFT:
Interior of Joe Colombo's own apartment
on via Argelati in Milan, 1970

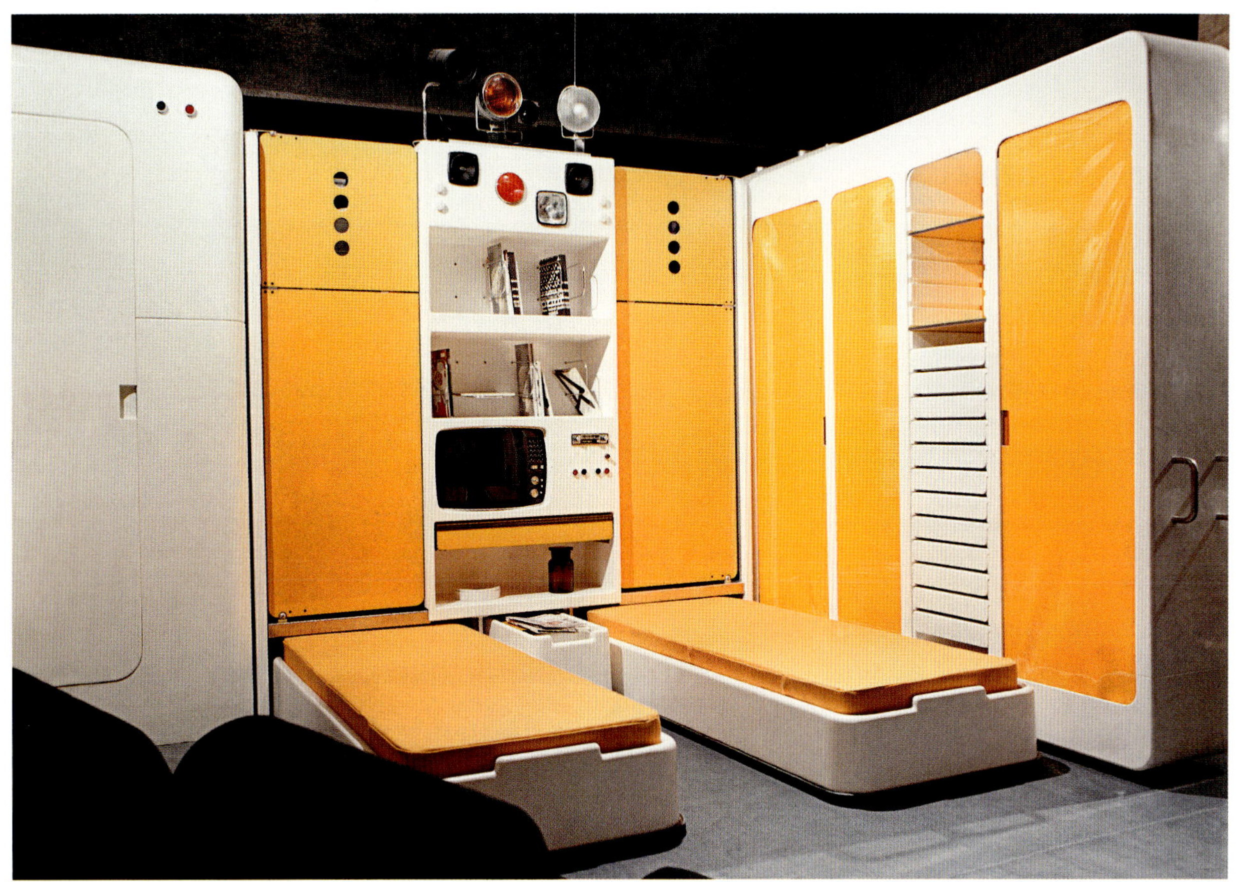

cylindrical units stacked on top of each other on a wheeled base to the innovative mobile Boby trolley of rotating drawers and shelves. His re-imagining of seating solutions led to his Additional Living System (1967) comprising polyurethane cushions that could be configured according to the users' wishes. Two years later he created the Tube chair, composed of four upholstered cylinders that could similarly be configured in multiple ways.

Other innovations included the Ragno outdoor light (1964) that doubled as a seat, the 1966 reversible Two-in-One drinking glasses and the Linea 72 in-flight service tray (1970) for Alitalia. There was a self-indulgence to some of Colombo's designs, notably his Smoke glasses (1964) with their asymmetrical forms enabling the drinker to support a glass with their thumb while leaving the rest of the hand free to hold a cigarette.

It was his living-space installations, however, that were perhaps the best expression of his visionary approach to design. For his Visiona "habitat of the future" (1969) designed for Bayer, he created a series of mobile elements that comprised the contents of an entire house, which required no dividing walls. He then developed the Total Furnishing Unit (1971) in which all essential living spaces – fully equipped kitchen, dining area, bedroom, bathroom and office/study – were contained in a single unit in Colombo's signature colours of white, yellow, red and black. This integrated unit for future living was exhibited at the *Italy: The New Domestic Landscape* exhibition at the Museum of Modern Art, New York in 1972, but sadly Colombo did not live to see it there, having suffered a fatal heart attack on his forty-first birthday the previous year.

ABOVE:
Total Furnishing Unit
1971, designed for the *Italy: The New Domestic Landscape* exhibition held at the Museum of Modern Art, New York, 1972

Terence Conran

British, 1931–

It could be argued that Sir Terence Conran has done more to bring Modern design into people's everyday lives than decades of worthy government-sponsored "good design" promotion ever did. He achieved this initially through his work as a young, up-and-coming designer during the early 1950s, but it was in his later role as an influential design-entrepreneur that he made the greatest impact.

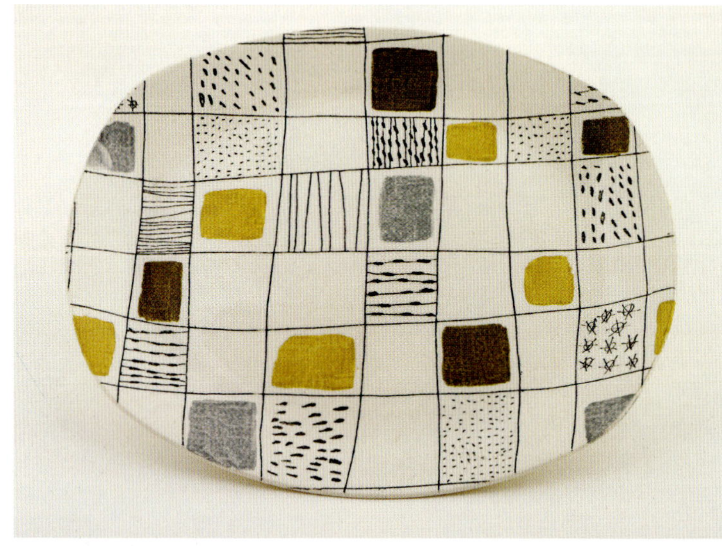

ABOVE:
Chequers serving plate
for W. R. Midwinter, 1957

OPPOSITE:
The young Terence Conran
sitting in his cleverly conceived wicker chair, *c.*1950 – photographed by Ray Williams

Educated at Bryanston School, which had a more progressive approach to education than most boarding schools at the time, Conran later studied textile design at the Central School of Art and Design in London. It was here that he absorbed the Rationalist tenets of the Bauhaus and the Arts and Crafts Movement's guiding principle that, as he put it, "good design should be available to the whole community, not just to a few". While still a student, he established his own furniture-making workshop, sharing space with Eduardo Paolozzi in London's East End, and later, on the advice of his tutor, he left college in order to work as an assistant to the architect Dennis Lennon on various exhibits for the South Bank site of the 1951 *Festival of Britain*. Like other designers of his generation, Conran was greatly inspired by this design-led year-long event – so much so that he went on to establish Conran & Co. in 1952. The same year he also began selling his furniture designs from a basement showroom in Piccadilly Arcade, and the following year he branched out with the opening of the Soup Kitchen in Chandos Place, a stylish yet affordable restaurant that brought simple French cuisine and espresso coffee to London's middle classes and marked the beginning of what would become an empire of design-led restaurants. He established the Conran Design Group in 1956, which famously designed Mary Quant's store in Knightsbridge and the innovative Summa range of flat-pack furniture, and in 1964 opened his first Habitat store on Fulham Road in London to sell, among other things, this furniture range. With its warehouse-like retail space packed and stacked with affordable furniture and a bazaar-like array of constantly changing cookware and accessories, the store was an expression of the Pop zeitgeist of the Sixties, which had heralded a more casual way of living. Indeed, with Habitat, Conran introduced modern design-led retailing to the masses for the first time – and consequently helped to educate the general public in the merits of intelligent design.

The 1970s became the real heyday of Habitat, with the company opening its flagship store on King's Road in 1973 and Conran then publishing his influential *The House Book* in

1974. The success of Habitat enabled the setting up of the Conran Foundation in 1980, with a mission to educate the public and British industry on the values of industrial design. The following year the foundation opened the Boilerhouse exhibition space at the Victoria and Albert Museum, under the enlightened directorship of Stephen Bayley. This groundbreaking initiative ultimately led to the establishment of the Design Museum in Butler's Wharf in 1989 – the world's first museum devoted entirely to the promotion and examination of design. Since then, with Conran's unfailing support, the Design Museum has flourished to become one of the world's leading institutions for the encouragement of design.

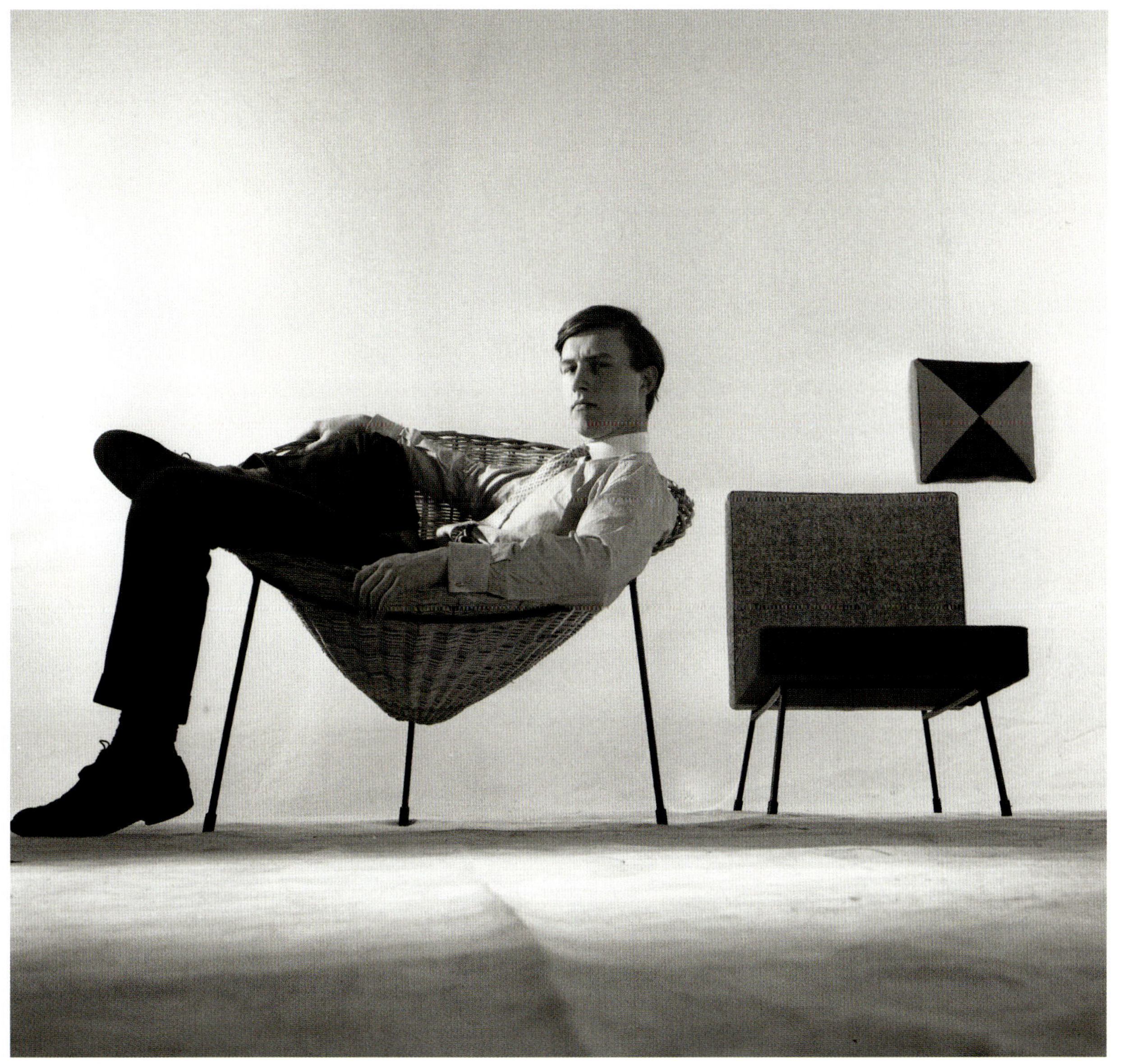

Lucienne Day

British, 1917–2010

It is difficult to comprehend just how drab post-war Britain was; victory had come at a heavy price and government rationing was still a fact of daily life. Yet stirring beneath the surface was a new and optimistic youthful spirit, which would be epitomized by the vibrant modern textiles created by Lucienne Day.

Born Désirée Lucienne Conradi, she was the youngest daughter of a prosperous Belgian re-insurance broker and an English mother who had a keen interest in art, fashion and interior design. Growing up in the leafy and affluent suburbs of London, she shared her mother's enthusiasms and decided initially to study at the Croydon School of Art. From there she went on to study textile design at the Royal College of Art, London in 1937. It was at a dance at the RCA in 1940 that she met her future husband, Robin Day, who had similarly studied at the college, though in furniture design. Despite their different social backgrounds, they found themselves to be kindred spirits who shared a passion for modern design, and two years later they married. As a prodigiously talented and high-profile design couple they went on to transform the landscape of modern British design over the coming years, sharing the belief that good design should be democratic and affordable. Because of continuing rationing during the early 1940s, Lucienne's earliest designs were for dress fabrics, manufactured by, among others, Stevenson & Sons, Marks & Spencer and Horrockses. However, when the manufacturing restrictions were finally lifted in the late 1940s, Lucienne turned her attention to the design of furnishing fabrics as they offered more scope for creative experimentation. Her first foray into this area of design came when she met Alastair Morton, director of

BELOW:
Calyx textile
for Heal & Sons, 1951

OPPOSITE:
Lapis furnishing fabric
for Heal & Sons, 1953

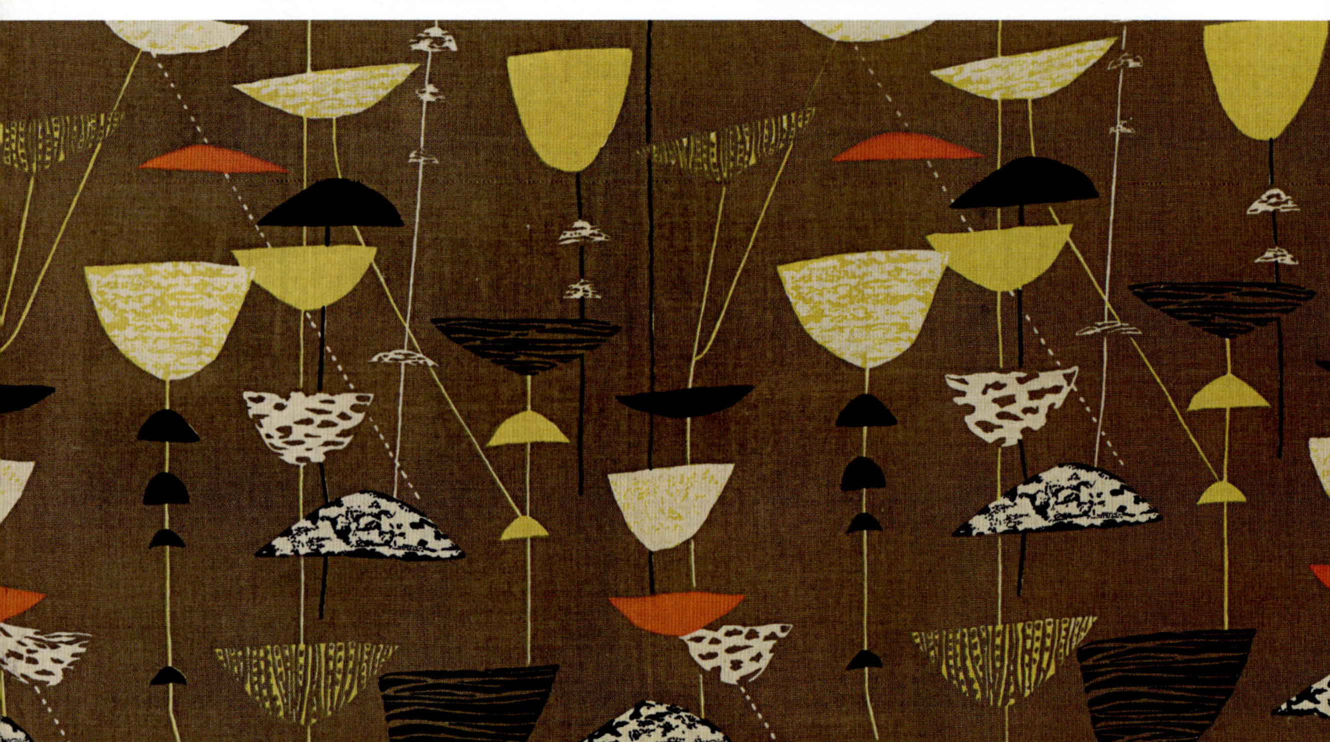

Edinburgh Weavers, one of the most progressive manufacturers of textiles at the time, through the Society of Industrial Artists. Morton subsequently commissioned two screen-printed patterns for furnishing fabrics – Florimel and Elysian (1949) – which in turn caught the attention of Anthony Heal, who invited Day to create similarly modern-style textiles for his family's firm, Heal & Sons.

Influenced by Scandinavian Modernism, Day's early designs were the very antithesis of pre-war textiles, which generally fell into two distinct categories: cottage-style chintzes or neo-Regency pastiches. Instead, she forged a definable contemporary look that was stridently modern. Her major career breakthrough came in 1951 with the launch of Calyx (produced by Heal's) which, with its fresh simplicity, was inspired not only by the work of contemporary artists such as Paul Klee and Alexander Calder but also by forms found in the natural world. As an avid gardener, Day had a keen eye for plant structures and it is unsurprising that the vast majority of her textiles featured patterns based on flowers, herbs and trees. Her palette of earth tones similarly had a subtle naturalness about it, which meant that her work was imbued with homely warmth. During this period, she also created boldly patterned wallpapers, such as Diabolo (1951) for Cole & Son and Provence for John Line & Son (1951) – both of which were shown at the *Festival of Britain* and must have appeared startlingly modern at the time. While during the early 1950s her textile patterns were characterized by a wiry linearity, later in the decade she began using a sketchier style as well as flat blocks or stripes of colours. Her later patterns from the mid 1960s to the early 1970s revealed an assured mastery of composition and colour, as well as a keen eye for contemporary trends.

From 1962 to 1987, Lucienne and her husband worked as joint design consultants for the John Lewis Partnership and were instrumental in forging its distinctive house style, which covered all aspects of the company's corporate identity. During the 1980s, having decided to step back from the design of commercial textiles, she created gorgeous silk mosaic panels made up of thousands of tiny silk squares – which were effectively art-textiles. As both a gifted colourist and formidably talented pattern-maker, Lucienne Day helped define the style of modern Britain and throughout her career created beautiful textiles which, although very much creations of their time, possessed an enduring timeless quality.

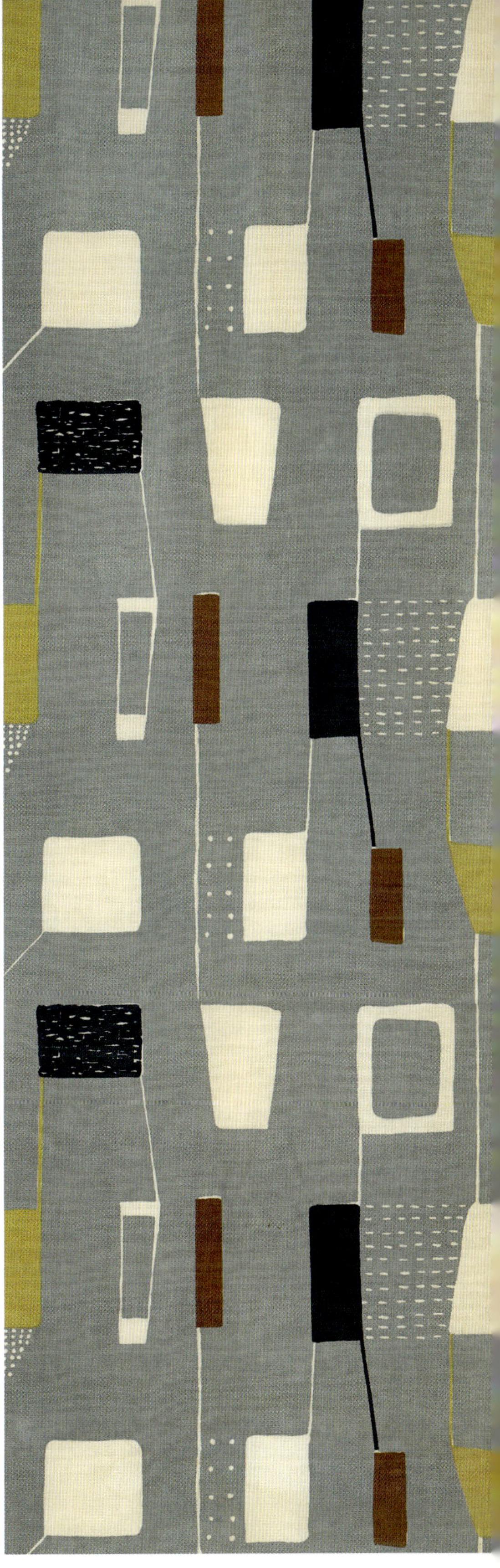

Robin Day

British, 1915–2010

BELOW:
Polypropylene chair
for Hille, 1960–67 – also known as the Polyprop

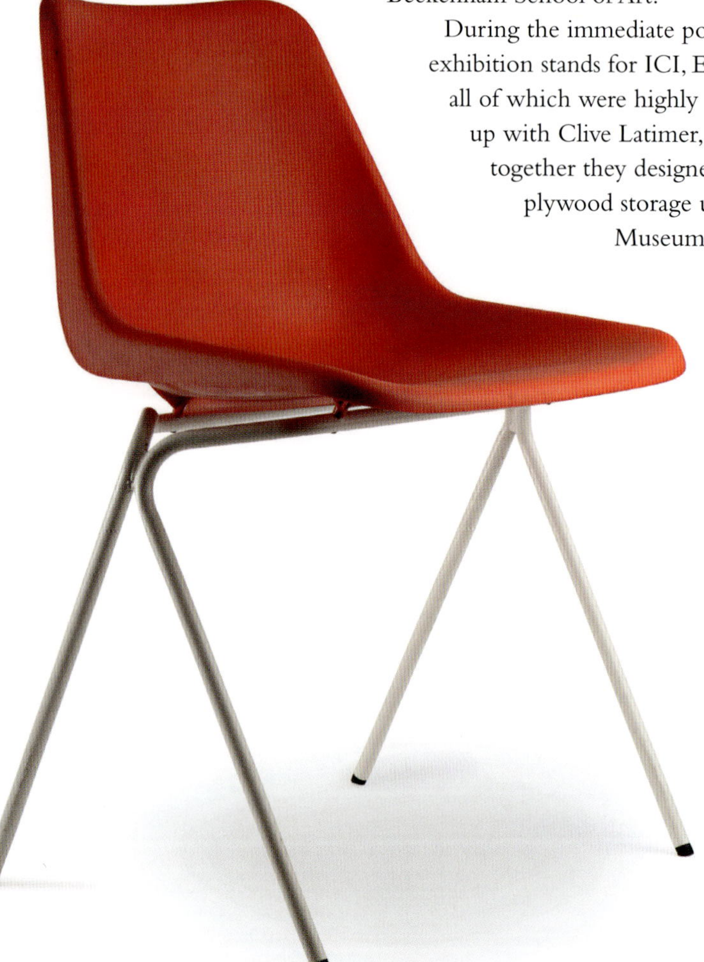

The English furniture designer Robin Day helped define the look of post-war Britain with designs that possessed a functional logic and an aesthetic refinement.

Born in High Wycombe, the epicentre of the British furniture industry, Day grew up in the midst of the town's furniture workshops. He initially studied at High Wycombe Technical Institute and High Wycombe School of Art, before becoming a draughtsman for one of the local furniture factories. He later won a scholarship to the Royal College of Art in London, where he studied furniture and interior design from 1934 to 1938. After leaving the RCA, he remained in touch with the college and in 1940 attended one of its dances where he met his future wife, Lucienne Conradi, who was studying textile design there. The couple were married two years later, and during the Second War World taught at the Beckenham School of Art.

During the immediate post-war period, Day created eye-catching exhibition stands for ICI, EKCO and the Central Office of Information, all of which were highly contemporary in appearance. He later teamed up with Clive Latimer, whom he had met while teaching, and together they designed an innovative system of tubular metal and plywood storage units. This range won first prize in the 1948 Museum of Modern Art's International Competition for the Design of Low-Cost Furniture, and led to a decades-long partnership with the British furniture manufacturer Hille. The same year, Robin and Lucienne Day set up their own design office, although they would always work independently of each other. Three years later, the *Festival of Britain* in 1951 firmly established the Days' professional reputations. For this showcase of British design innovation, Robin designed auditorium seating for the Royal Festival Hall's main concert hall, as well as dining chairs and lounge chairs for its foyers and restaurant. At the Festival, these stylishly modern chairs, innovatively constructed of moulded plywood and steel rod, were also included in Day's dining room/living room installation for the Homes and Garden Pavilion, where Lucienne's Calyx textile design debuted.

Throughout the 1950s and 1960s, Robin went on to develop numerous furniture designs for Hille, including the low-cost Hillestak chair and desk (1951), the institutional Q Stak chair (1953), the Reclining Chair (1952) with its contoured spine-line and tray-like armrests, the minimal 675 chair (1952) and a range of airport seating (1958) for the new Gatwick Airport. It was, however, the Polypropylene chair, or "Polyprop", developed from 1960 to 1967, that would be his greatest achievement. With its universal seat shell made of injection-moulded polypropylene, which could be used in conjunction with a wide variety of interchangeable base options, it met "the need for a multi-purpose side chair at a very low cost". Importantly, this was one of the very first seating designs to fully exploit the high-volume manufacturing potential of thermoplastic, and subsequently sold in tens of millions around the world. Yet despite being a highly utilitarian and extremely durable design, the Polypropylene chair also had an aesthetic purity, with its form shaped not only by functional considerations but also by the nature of its manufacturing process. Over the succeeding decades, Day continued to create innovative and stylish furniture, which similarly reflected his desire to produce beautiful, affordable designs that would enhance the lives of ordinary people.

BELOW:
Royal Festival Hall lounge chair
for Hille, 1951

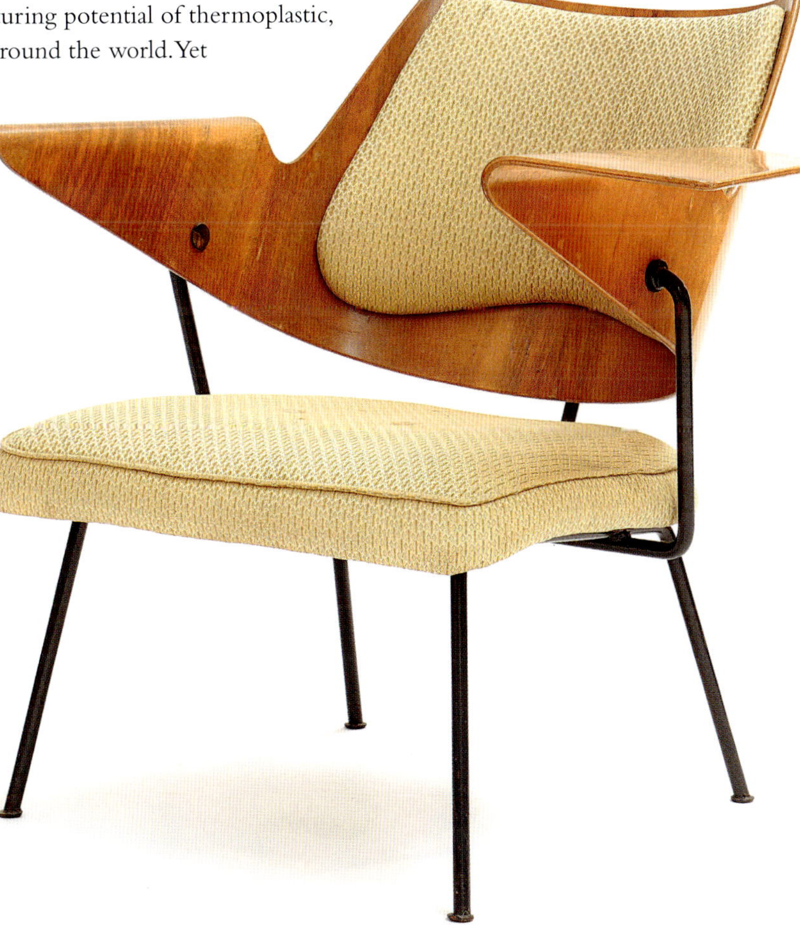

Michele De Lucchi

Italian, 1951–

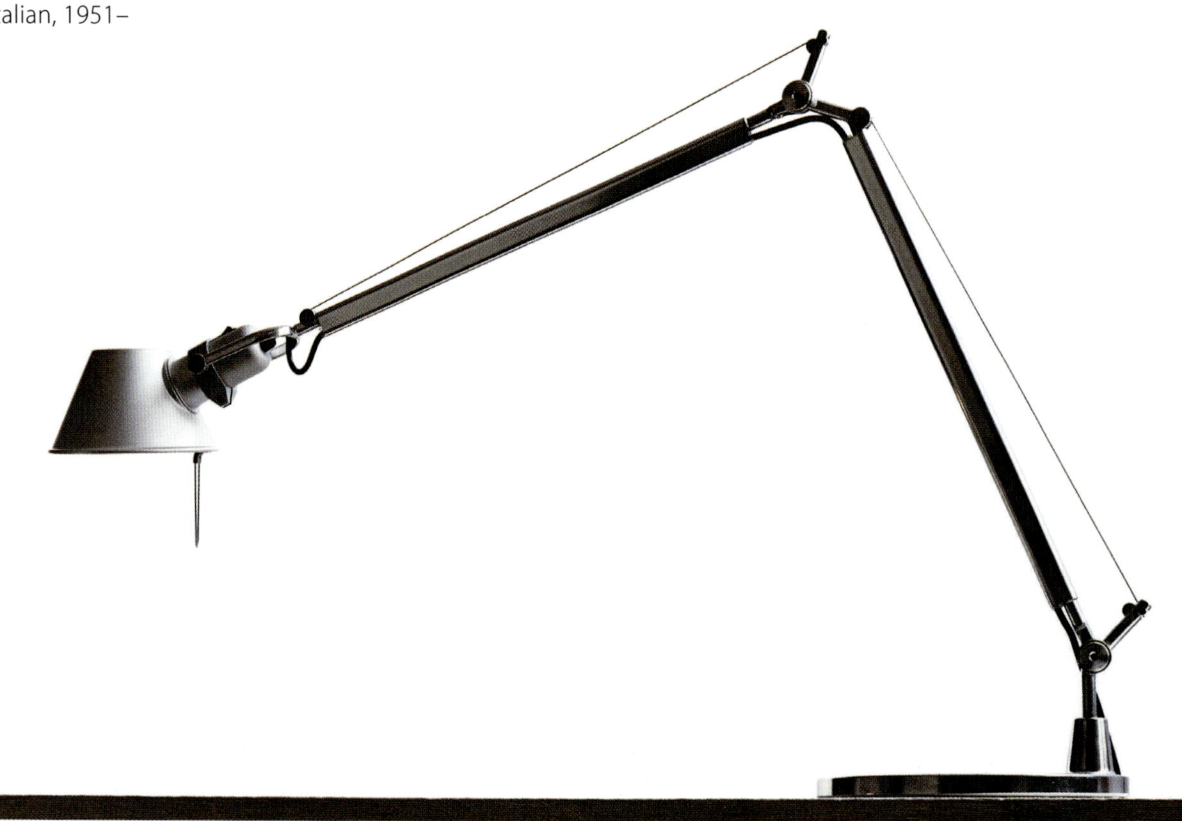

ABOVE:
Tolomeo task light
for Artemide, 1986–87

OPPOSITE:
First chair
for Memphis, 1983

An acclaimed Italian architect-designer, Michele De Lucchi studied in Padua before training to become an architect at the University of Florence; graduating in 1975, he spent a further two years there as an academic assistant. While studying in Florence he co-founded the influential Radical design group Gruppo Cavart in 1973.

Following on from this, in 1976 he collaborated with Andrea Branzi on the organization of a major retrospective exhibition of Italian post-war design of the 1950s, which would eventually be staged in Milan in 1980. He had moved to Milan in 1978 and was now working as a designer for Kartell. Around this time he also began designing various pieces for Studio Alchimia (also known as Studio Alchymia), including his visually striking Sinerpica lamp (1979) and his Sinvola lamp (1979), both of which were included in Alchimia's landmark Bau.Haus 1 collection launched in 1979. In 1980, De Lucchi also created wooden prototypes of various Post-Modern household appliances for Girmi – a table fan, a toaster, an electric iron, a vacuum cleaner, a hairdryer and a heater – which influentially rethought what such objects could potentially look like, using cartoon-like elemental forms and a striking palette of pastel colours. The following year, he became a founding member of Memphis, the New Wave design collective instigated by Ettore Sottsass that went on to become one of the most high-profile proponents of Post-Modernism in the decorative and applied arts. De Lucchi was one of the most creatively prolific members of this influential group, designing around thirty different pieces for Memphis between 1980 and 1987. The best known of these were undoubtedly his Kristall side table (1981) and First chair (1983), both of which incorporated his signature geometric style and pared-down colour palette.

As one of the bright young things of Italian Post-Modernism, De Lucchi had already landed a job as a design consultant with Olivetti Synthesis – Olivetti's office furniture division – in 1979 while still in his twenties, having been spotted by Ettore Sottsass. Then two years later, he joined the design team at Olivetti in Ivrea, where he worked on several projects with Sottsass, who effectively groomed him as his successor. De Lucchi's real breakthrough, however, came in 1987, the year his Tolomeo task light was launched by Artemide. The result of several years of research, the perfectly balanced Tolomeo set a new benchmark in the design of task lighting and perfectly captured the new reductivist aesthetic that would become a defining feature of design in the 1990s. Winning a Compasso d'Oro award in 1989, the Tolomeo became one of the best-selling lighting designs of its time.

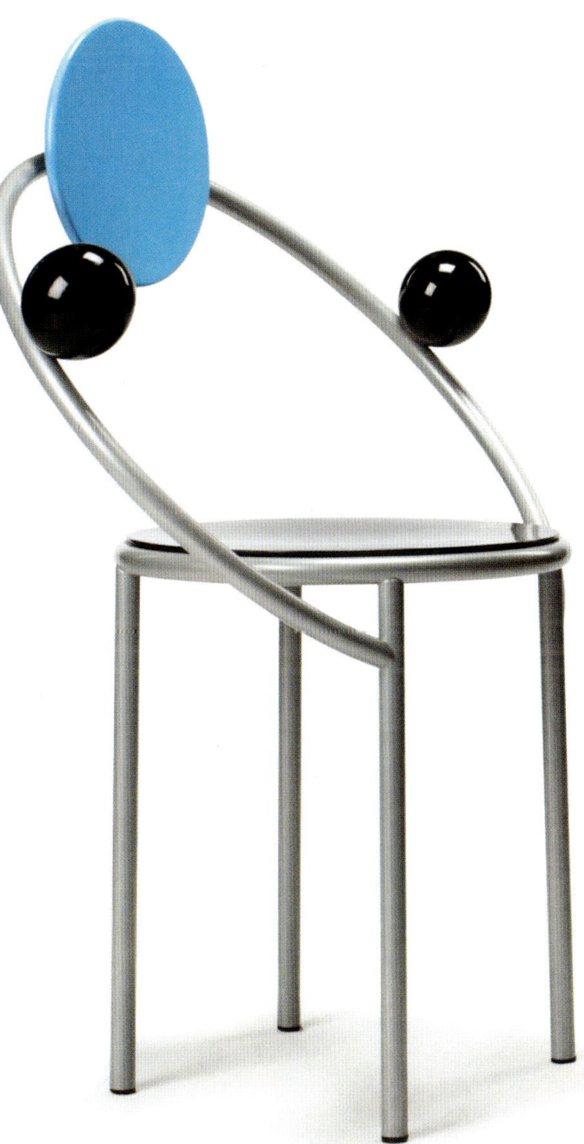

In 1990, bolstered by the success of the Tolomeo, De Lucchi set up his own small-scale manufacturing company, Produzione Privata, to create more experimental designs using craft techniques, while also continuing to design for industry. Between 1988 and 2002, he was Head of Design at Olivetti, and during this tenure received a second Compasso d'Oro for his Artjet 10 printer in 2001. Today, his multidisciplinary office based in Milan undertakes a wide range of work, from exhibition design and residential schemes to retail spaces and large infrastructure projects, with its various buildings notable for their use of eye-catching forms.

De Stijl

Netherlands, founded 1917

In October 1917 in the Dutch city of Leiden, a gathering of like-minded creative individuals founded a new artistic group and aligned journal called *De Stijl* (The Style). This venture was as much a spiritual quest as an art and design reforming movement, in that it sought divine meaning in the mysteries of the universe through the purification of form. Led by the architect Theo van Doesburg, the group initially included Piet Mondrian, Bart van der

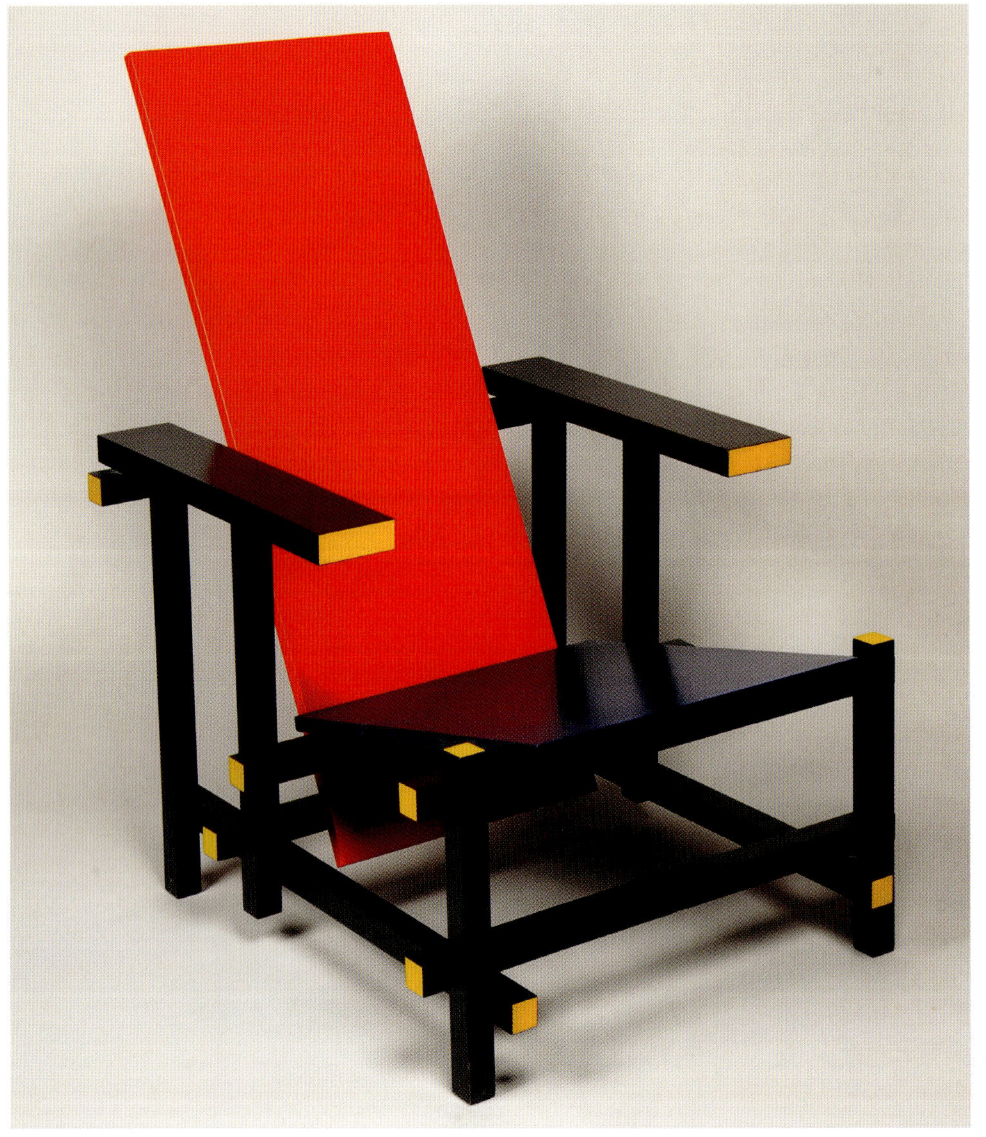

LEFT:
Red/Blue chair
designed by Gerrit Rietveld for Gerard van de Groenekan, 1918 (later painted in 1923)

OPPOSITE:
Axonometric study of Hotel Particulier
by Theo van Doesburg and Cornelis van Eesteren, 1923

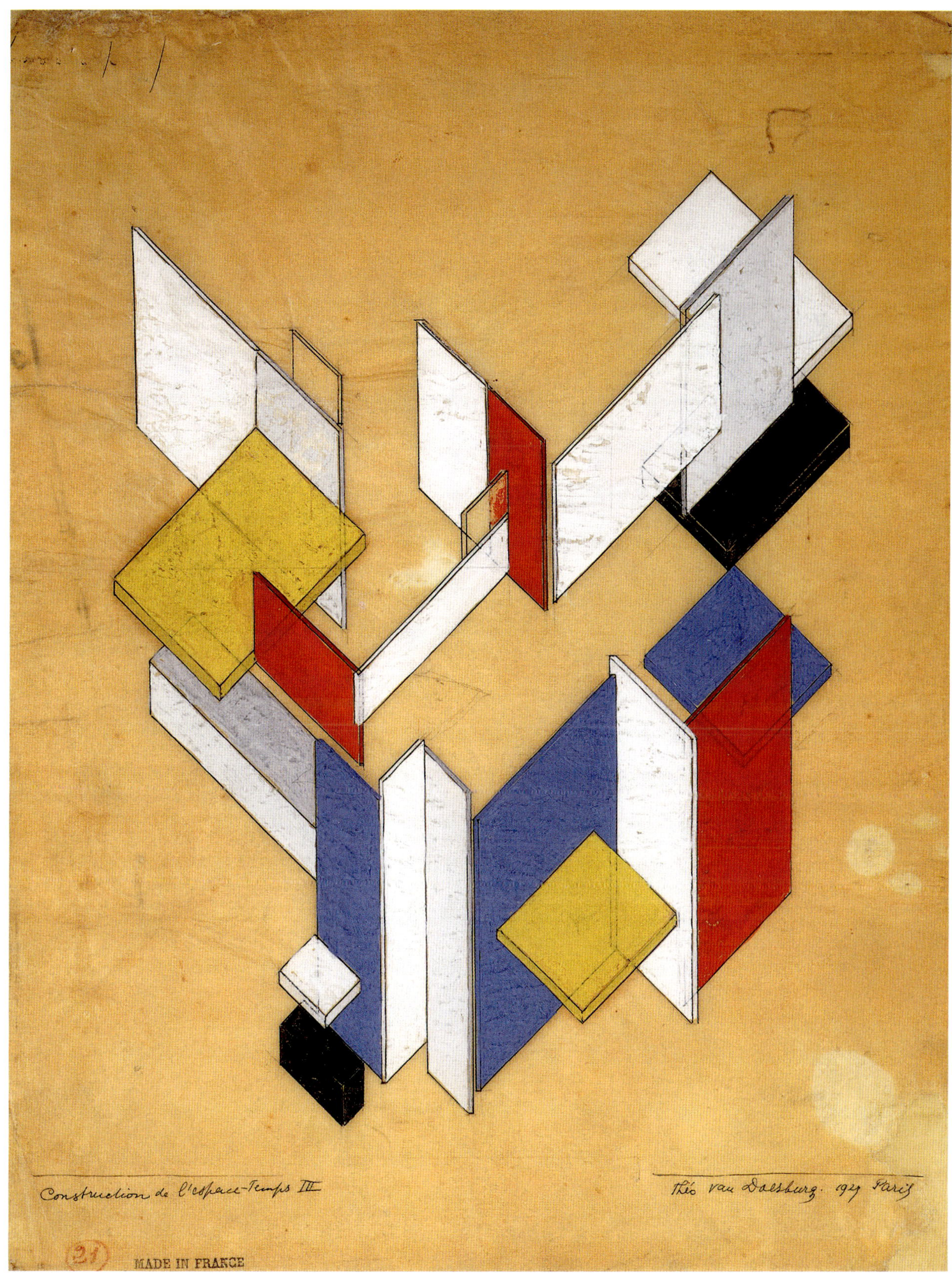
Construction de l'espace-Temps III
Théo van Doesburg. 1929 Paris
21
MADE IN FRANCE

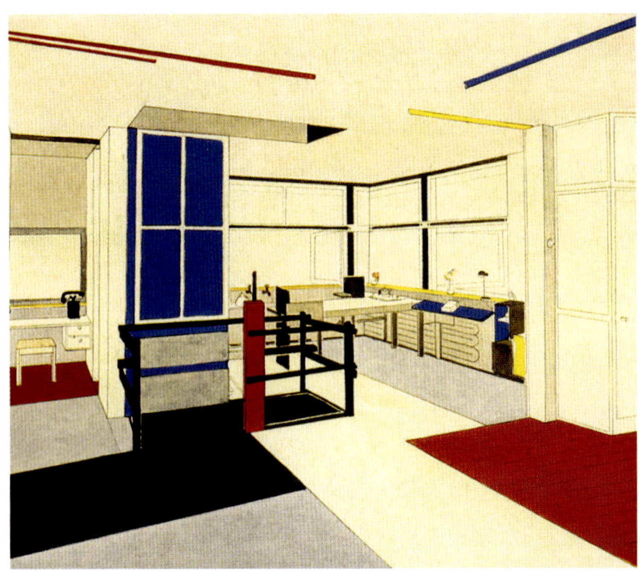

ABOVE:
Drawing of interior of the Schröder House
by Gerrit Rietveld, 1924

Leck, Vilmos Huszár, Jacobus Johannes Pieter Oud, Robert van 't Hoff, Jan Wils and George Vantongerloo. This association of avant-garde individuals drew much inspiration from Cubism, as well as the rectilinearity of Frank Lloyd Wright's architecture. It was, however, the First World War in all its horror that was its great impetus, having prompted a shared desire for a new universal consciousness.

The group's manifesto, published in the first issue of its journal, urged "all who believe in reform of art and culture" to destroy the "tradition, dogmas and the predominance of the individual" that stood in the way of a "new consciousness of the age" to enable "the formation of an international unity in life, art and culture". Socially utopian in essence, this was a call for a cultural purging that would bring in its wake a new spiritual universality. Gerrit Rietveld's slatted chair of 1918 was a visually powerful three-dimensional realization of the De Stijl group's reductivist philosophy. The transparency of its construction suggested the dissolving of matter and gave a sense of spatial infinity, and in this regard the chair could be read as a piece of abstract sculpture. In 1923, at the suggestion of the artist Bart van der Leck, this aesthetically uncompromising design was famously painted in black and primary colours to enhance its rectilinearity and as a result the Red/Blue chair became even more shockingly revolutionary.

Another member of the group, Theo van Doesburg, was also hugely influential in spreading the movement's message, taking evangelizing trips to Belgium, France, Italy and Germany. In 1921 he moved to Weimar and the following year gave a series of lectures on De Stijl at the Bauhaus there. That same year van Doesburg, as an architect who also acted as editor of the group's journal, established important links with the Russian Constructivists, notably El Lissitzky, and the Bauhaus Hungarian László Moholy-Nagy. Thanks to van Doesburg's efforts, Rietveld was subsequently invited by Walter Gropius to exhibit at the Weimar Bauhaus in 1923.

The influence of De Stijl thinking on certain members of the Bauhaus was responsible for the crucial ideological shift that occurred at the school, a move away from arty expressionism towards a new kind of rational objectivity. Certainly, the spatial formalism of Rietveld's Red/Blue chair directly inspired Marcel Breuer's later B3 Wassily Chair (1926). De Stijl architecture and interior designs similarly employed strong geometric planes and primary-coloured elements that helped to delineate space. For instance, in the revolutionary Rietveld Schröder Haus (1924) in Utrecht, sliding screens and folding doors were used to create an exceptionally multifunctional and adaptable living space. It was a home that functioned like a machine, stripped down to the barest of functional essentials, which probably did not make it too easy to live in, but as a statement of De Stijl ideology it was without equal. Like other De Stijl buildings and designs, it not only offered a tantalizing glimpse of a utopian future, but also introduced a new aesthetic purity, and it is for this reason that De Stijl is regarded as the first truly Modernist design movement.

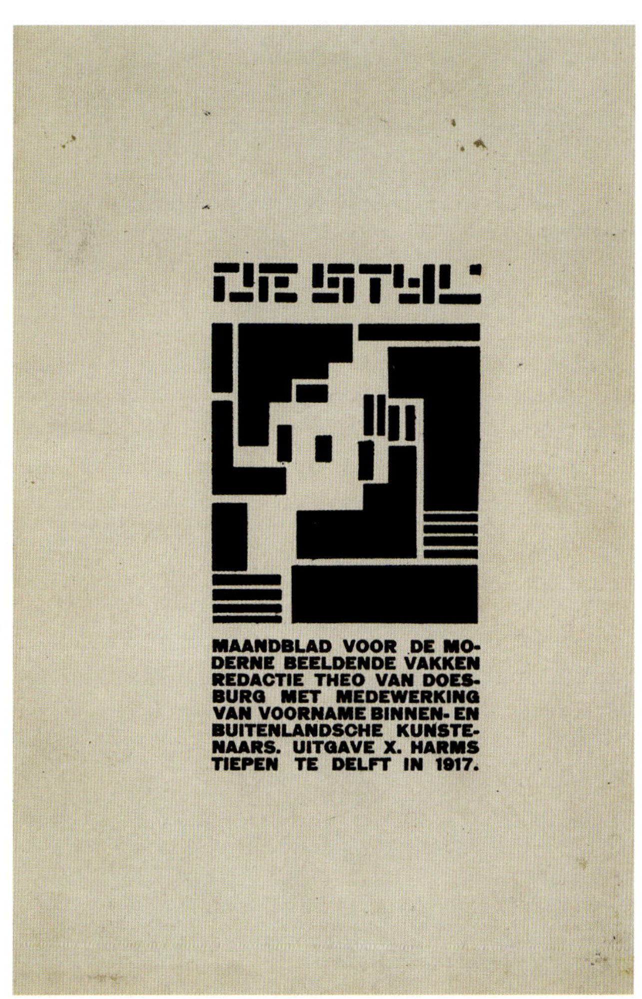

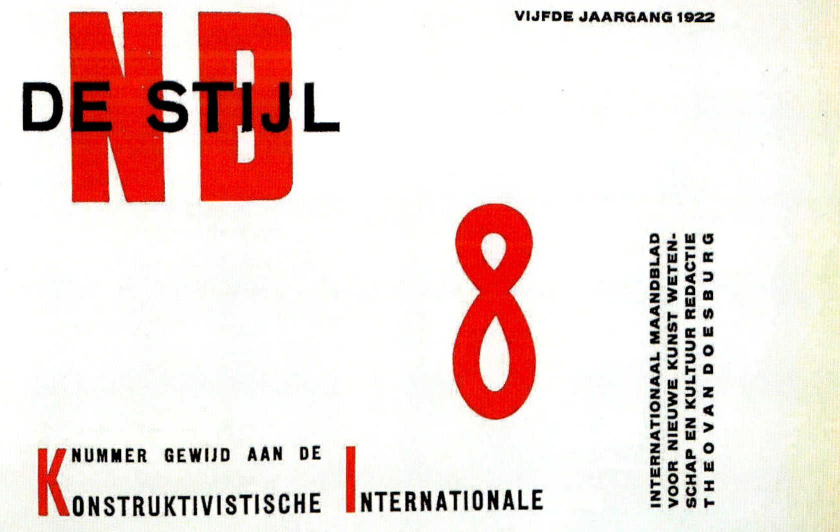

ABOVE:
***De Stijl* magazine**
1917

RIGHT:
***De Stijl* NB 8 magazine**
1922

Christian Dell

German, 1893–1974

Christian Dell was an influential Bauhaus designer who, having trained as a silversmith, successfully made the transition from bespoke craft manufacture to industrial mass-production, most notably in the realm of lighting design.

Between 1907 and 1911, Dell studied at the Königlich Preussische Zeichenakademie (Royal Prussian Drawing Academy) in Hanau, near Frankfurt, while at the same time he apprenticed at J.D. Schleissner & Söhne, the leading silversmithing company in Hanau. From 1911 to 1912 he worked as a silversmith in Dresden, before training under the renowned Belgian architect-designer Henry van de Velde at the Kunstgewerbeschule (School of Applied Arts), Weimar – the precursor of the Weimar Bauhaus – from 1912 to 1913.

Following service in the First World War, Dell worked as a journeyman and later as a master silversmith for Hestermann & Ernst in Munich. In 1920, he joined the silver workshop of Emil Lettré in Berlin, before returning to the city of Hanau and re-enrolling at his alma mater. A year later, he established his own silverware studio there and the following year

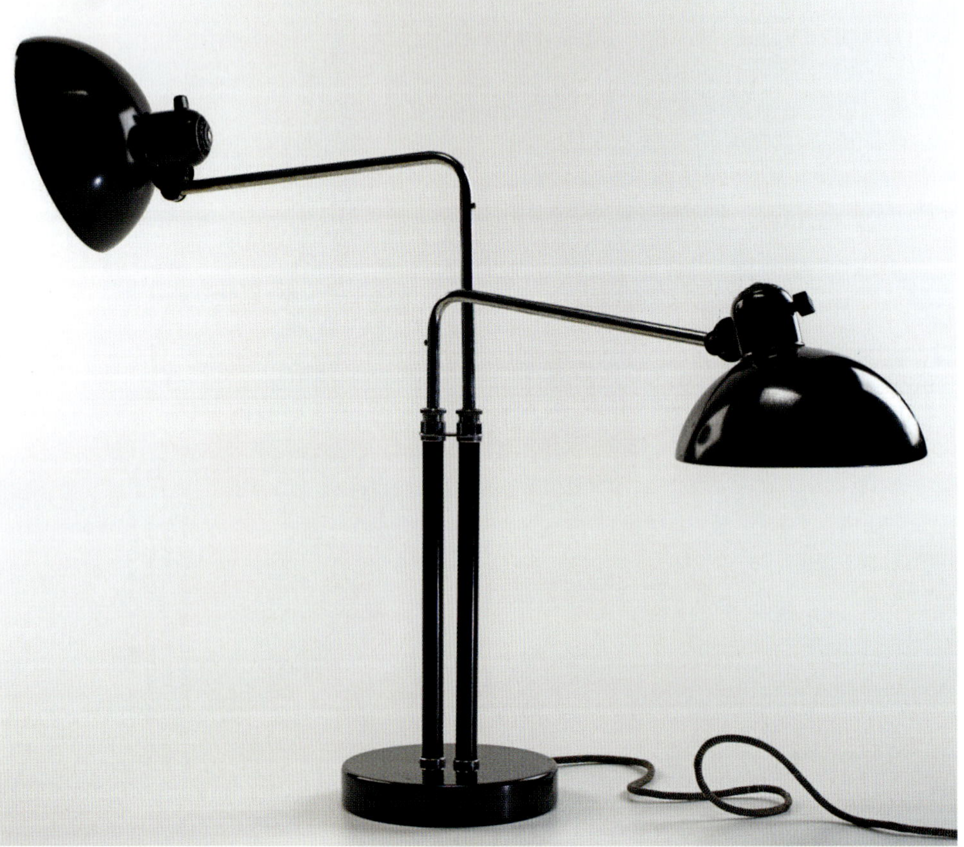

LEFT:
Model No. 6580 double table lamp
for Kaiser & Co., 1932–34

OPPOSITE:
Rondella table lamp
for Rondella, 1927–28

was appointed "craft master" of the metal workshop at the Weimar Bauhaus – working closely with the department's "form master", László Moholy-Nagy. He held this important teaching post for three years until 1925, yet unlike many of his fellow Bauhaus tutors Dell did not subscribe to an outright rejection of historicism but rather favoured an accommodation of it within a modern design idiom.

After leaving the Bauhaus, Dell taught at the Frankfurter Kunstschule (Frankfurt Art School) from 1926 to 1933, heading its metalworking department. Around this period he also began designing products that were eminently suitable for large-scale industrial production. His lighting designs, such as the adjustable Rondella (1927–28) and Rondella-Polo (1928–29) desk lamps and his Idell range, which was later copied by Helo, were subsequently mass-produced by Rondella and Kaiser respectively. These elegant and functional designs, which were based on the Modern ideals of interchangability and standardization, were early realizations of Bauhaus design theory skilfully translated into design practice. In fact, Dell went on to design over 500 lights in total and his Idell range remained in production for over sixty years – a testament to its enduring functional logic and aesthetic durability.

In the 1930s, Dell also began experimenting with newly developed plastics, which he incorporated into some of his lighting designs. After the Second World War, he returned to his craft roots, first working as a silversmith and then in 1948 opening his own jewellery shop in Wiesbaden.

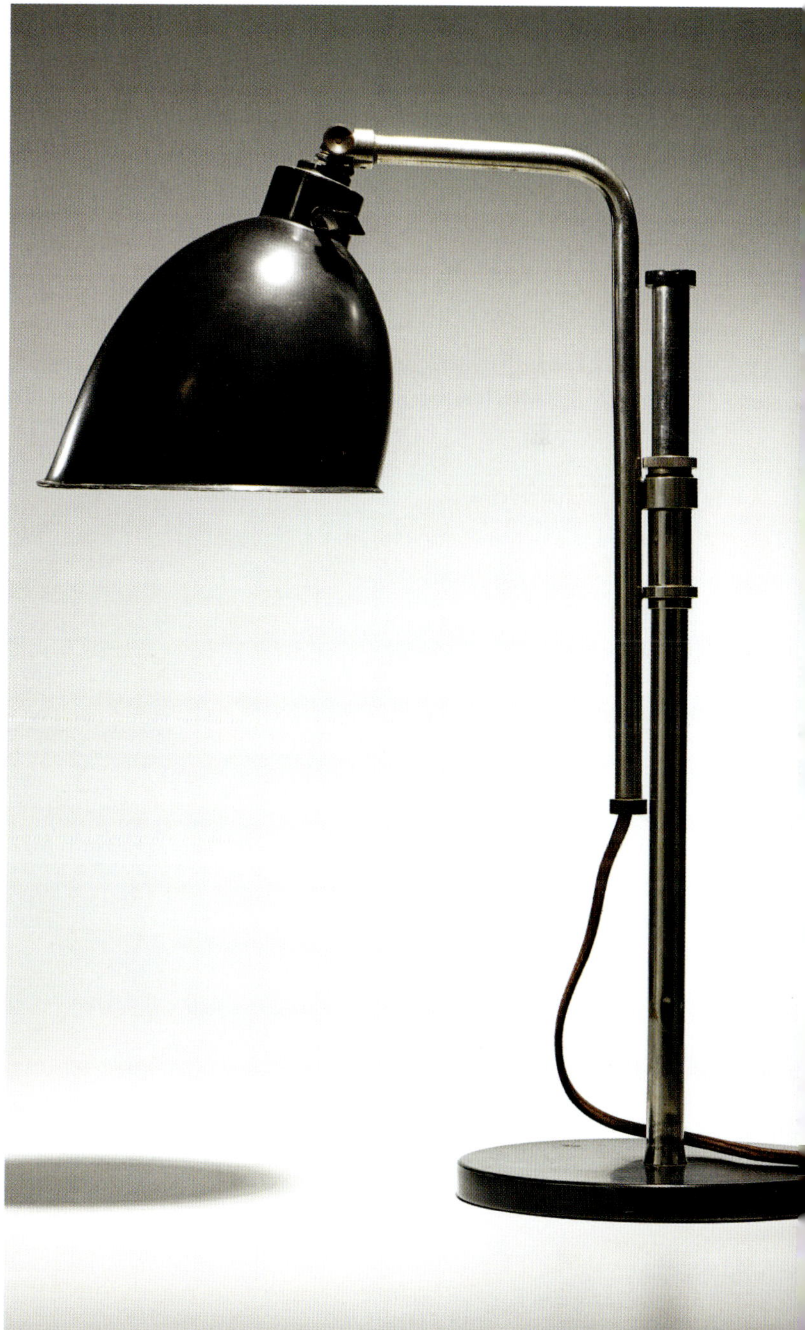

Deutscher Werkbund

Germany, founded 1907

Founded in Munich on 6 October 1907, the Deutscher Werkbund (German Association of Craftsmen) was a design-reforming organization that had an enormous impact on the development of Modern design. Its initial membership comprised twelve leading architect-designers and twelve enlightened manufacturers – including Hermann Muthesius, Richard Riemerschmid, Bruno Paul, Joseph Maria Olbrich and Peter Behrens – as well as the Munich-based Vereinigte Werkstätten für Kunst im Handwerk (United Workshops for Art in Craft) and the Wiener Werkstätte in Vienna.

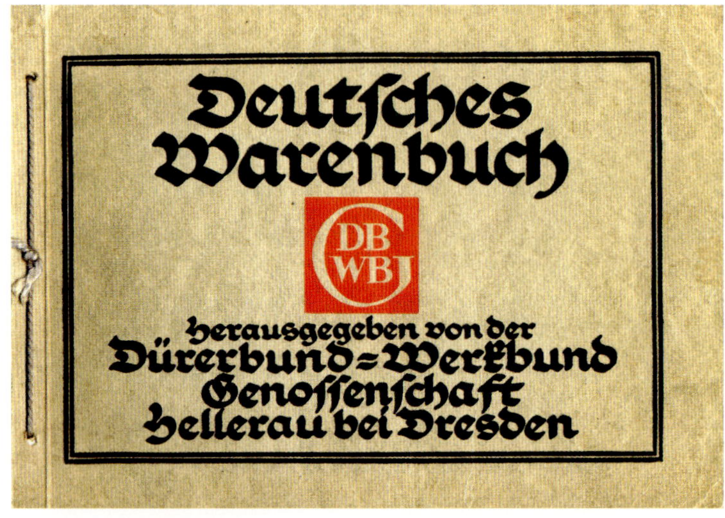

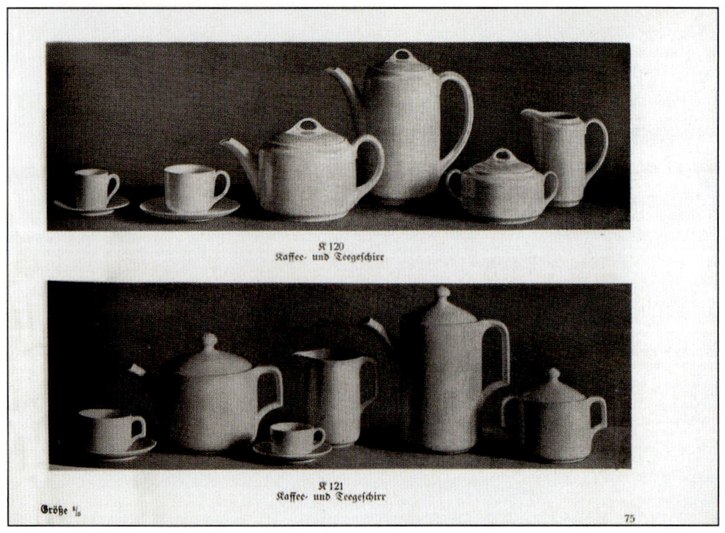

The origins of the Werkbund can be traced to a lecture given by Hermann Muthesius in 1907 in which he warned of the dire economic consequences that would befall German industry if it did not abandon its adherence to historicizing ornament and craft-based education. The lecture caused such a furore within the ranks of the Fachverband für die wirtschaftlichen Interessen des Kunstgewerbes (Association for the Economic Interests of the Arts and Crafts) that a number of its members eventually broke away to form the Deutscher Werkbund. Its primary intentions were to forge much closer alliances between manufacturers and designers and to promote the teaching of the applied arts, especially as they related to industry, in technical schools across the country.

Another of the DWB's central missions was to champion what it saw as "good design" for the benefit of industrialists, retailers and general public alike, and it did this by running a programme of evening lectures and staging exhibitions where exemplars of good design were shown. The association also published *Jahrbücher* (yearbooks) from 1912 until 1920, and *Deutscher Warenbücher* (German Production Directories) from 1916. The former publication illustrated objects made by its members that were thoughtfully designed and well executed,

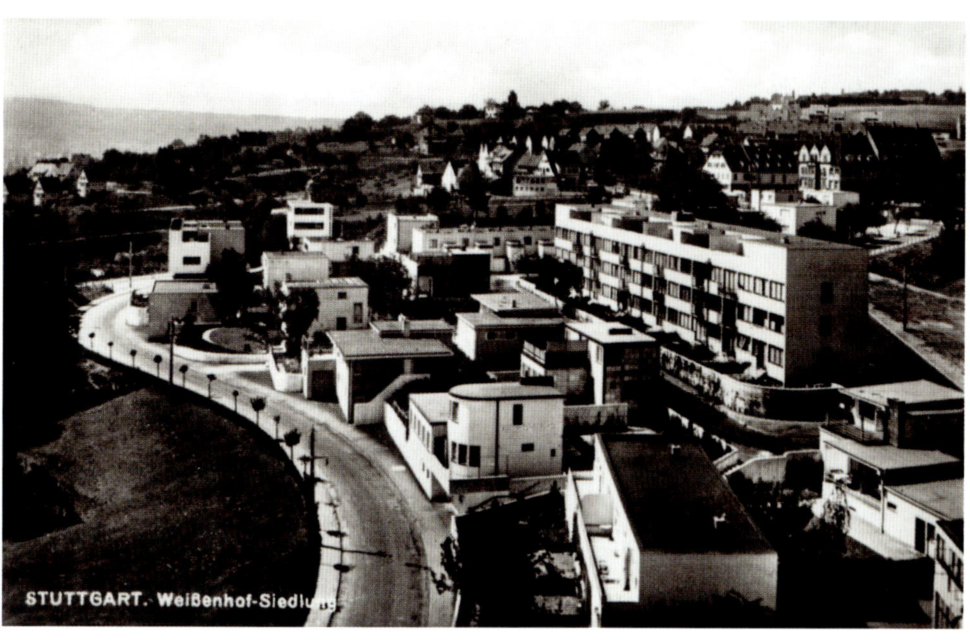

OPPOSITE TOP:
Cover of *Deutsches Warenbuch* (German Production Directory)
1916

OPPOSITE BOTTOM:
Page of *Deutsches Warenbuch* (German Production Directory)
featuring simple utilitarian china, 1916

ABOVE:
Postcard
showing a general view of the Weissenhof housing estate, Stuttgart, 1927

while the latter showcased much more utilitarian wares.

In 1909, the Werkbund established its instructive Deutsche Museum für Kunst in Handel und Gewerbe (German Museum of Art in Trade and Commerce) in Hagen, which not only exhibited examples of good design but also displayed badly designed products so as to create a "battle of objects" that would be instructive to its visitors and help stimulate debate about differences between kitsch and well-designed goods. The DWB was also responsible for staging a number of landmark exhibitions, including the *Deutsche Werkbund Ausstellung* of 1914, held in Cologne, where Walter Gropius and Adolf Meyer's Model Factory was exhibited, and the important *Form ohne Ornament* (Form without Ornament) travelling exhibition of 1924, which showcased functional products that were denuded of all superfluous decoration. It was, however, the Werkbund's *Die Wohnung* (The Dwelling) exhibition held in Stuttgart in 1927 that was the most influential of all. It took the form of a model modern housing estate named the Weissenhof-Siedlung, which comprised twenty-one prototypical buildings containing sixty "dwellings" designed by the leading Modern Movement architects of the day including, among others, Walter Gropius, Ludwig Mies van der Rohe and Le Corbusier.

Disbanded in the 1930s, the Werkbund was re-established after the Second World War, although it never regained its position as the leading voice for design reform in Germany. But by then it had in many ways already achieved its goal of improving German design standards.

Erich Dieckmann

German, 1896–1944

Bauhaus-trained Erich Dieckmann revolutionized Modern furniture design in Germany during the late 1920s and 1930s. Having taken a year's foundation training as an architect and then studied painting, in 1921 he went on to enrol at the Staatliches Bauhaus in Weimar. While there, he not only took Johannes Itten's famous preparatory course but also trained in the school's cabinet-making workshop. During this period, he designed pared-down Modernist furniture including a geometric bed made of padauk and oak for the famous experimental model dwelling known as the Haus am Horn, which was designed by Georg Muche and constructed for the Weimar Bauhaus's landmark exhibition of 1923.

When the Bauhaus school was forced to relocate to Dessau, Dieckmann remained in Weimar and from 1926 to 1930 he headed the cabinet-making workshop and interior design department of the institution that succeeded the Bauhaus, the Staatliche Hochschule für Handwerk und Baukunst (State College for Craft and Architecture) or Bauhochschule – which would later become known as the Bauhaus University. While there, Dieckmann designed an influential range of *Typenmöbel* (standardized furniture) that was manufactured by the school's production unit. Distinguished by the use of simple wooden slatted constructions and often incorporating tubular metal and woven rattan, the chairs he designed were less stridently progressive in their aesthetic than those of his Bauhaus contemporary Marcel Breuer and as such revealed a more pragmatic approach to Modern design. In 1927, Dieckmann participated in the Werkbund *Die Wohnung* (The Dwelling) exhibition in Stuttgart, working on the interior design of the apartment block designed by Ludwig Mies van der Rohe for the Weissenhof estate.

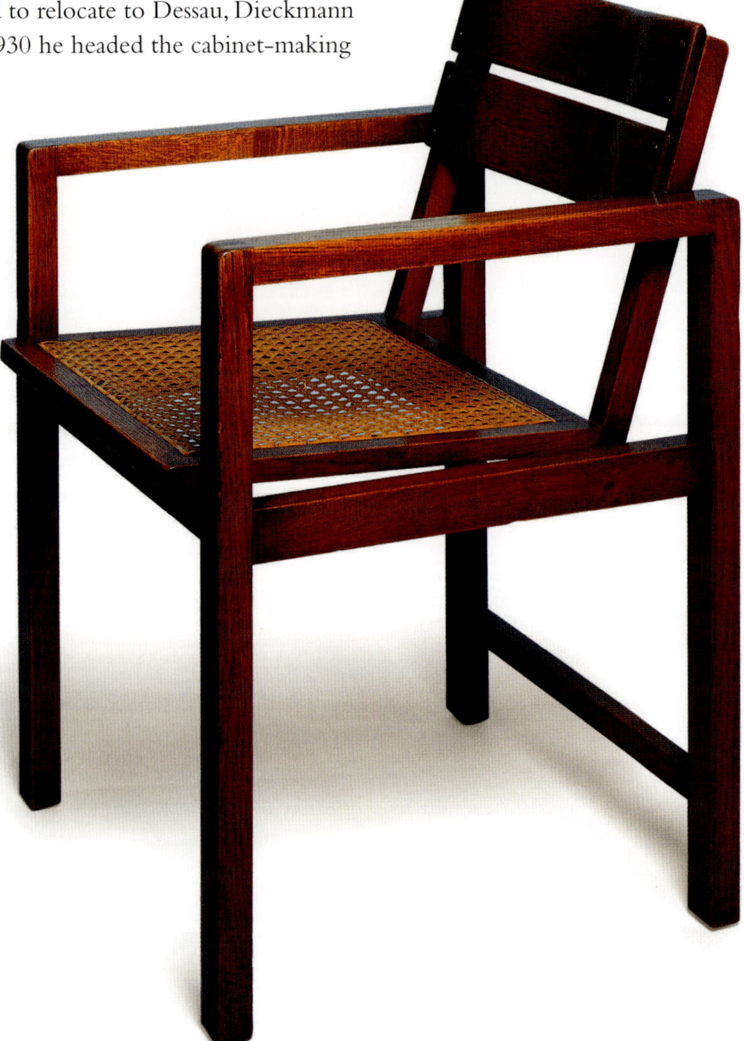

BELOW:
Armchair
made by the furniture workshop of the Bauhochschule in Weimar, c.1926

Between 1930 and 1931, he worked as a freelance furniture designer, creating chairs for a number of German manufacturers, including H. Scheidemantel, Weimar Bau- und Wohnungskunst, Bamberger, Dusco-Werke, F. Kerber, the Korbmacher Verein (Basket-makers' Association) and Cebaso. Many of these designs were subsequently illustrated in his book entitled *Möbelbau in Holz, Rohr und Stahl* (Furniture in Wood, Pipe and Steel), which was published by Julius Hoffmann Verlag in 1931. From 1931 to 1933, Dieckmann also headed the interior design and cabinet-making workshops at the Kunstgewerbeschule (School of Applied Arts) Burg Giebichenstein in Halle. Generally known as "the Halle School", this influential institution, like the Dessau Bauhaus, had already made the philosophical transition from craft manufacture to industrial production, but did not completely depart from the long-established ideals of craft. Eventually, Dieckmann was dismissed from this position by the National Socialists (Nazis) and from 1933 to 1936 struggled to find employment, only managing to find occasional design work with furniture manufacturers based in Oberfranken in Upper Franconia. He did, however, co-design with Fritz Beyer, J. Scherer and Rudolf Henning a number of social housing projects in Berlin, which were commissioned by the Wohnungsfürsorgegesellschaft and GSW Immobilien AG housing associations.

From 1936 until his death in 1944, Dieckmann continued to be a prominent member of the German avant-garde, living in Berlin and working for various government-sponsored design initiatives. It was, however, his beautifully conceived and executed furniture that would be his lasting legacy for it showed that Modern design could integrate craft ideals into products suitable for standardized industrial manufacture.

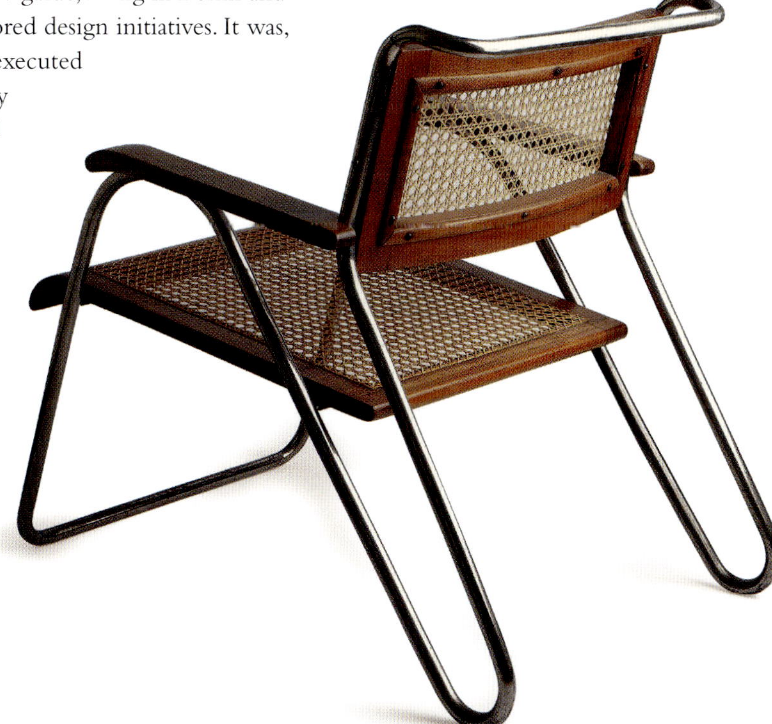

RIGHT:
Model No. 8162 armchair
for Cebaso Stahlrohrmöbel,
*c.*1931

D

Tom Dixon

British, 1959–

An innovative and successful entrepreneurial designer-maker, Tom Dixon imbues his designs for industrial production with a craft sensibility derived from a self-taught knowledge of materials and manufacturing processes.

Born in Sfax, Tunisia, to a British father and a French-Latvian mother, Dixon grew up in London and initially worked as a technician for the interior design course at Chelsea School of Art, and then took a foundation course there in 1979, but dropped out after six months. He subsequently eked out a living as a graphic designer and colourist for animated films, and in 1981 joined the Brit-funk band Funkapolitan as a fresh-faced bassist, and recorded various singles and one album with them. Alongside his musical career, Dixon was also forging a reputation among London's club-goers as a warehouse-party organizer and a "performance welder", along with Mark Brazier-Jones and Nick Jones. These welding happenings were the genesis of the Creative Salvage movement, and in 1983 the trio put on their first show in a shop on Kensington Church Street, where they exhibited various household products made from scrap. For this event they published a Creative Salvage manifesto on a photocopied flyer, which read: "We are convinced the way ahead does not lie in expensive, anonymous, mass-produced high-tech products but in a more decorative, human approach to industrial and interior design."

As a key figure in the Creative Salvage movement, Dixon helped revolutionize design, in much the same way that Punk had irrevocably changed music and fashion just a few years before. Over the next decade, he honed his metalworking skills, and created a number of notable pieces, including his Kitchen chair (1987), S chair (1988–92), Crown chair (1989) and Pylon chair (1989–92). In 1989, Dixon opened his Space studio in an ex-printworks in Vauxhall and began batch-producing his designs in earnest, and three years later established the related Space gallery on All Saint's Road, Notting Hill.

Around this time, the Italian manufacturer Giulio Cappellini began producing the S chair and

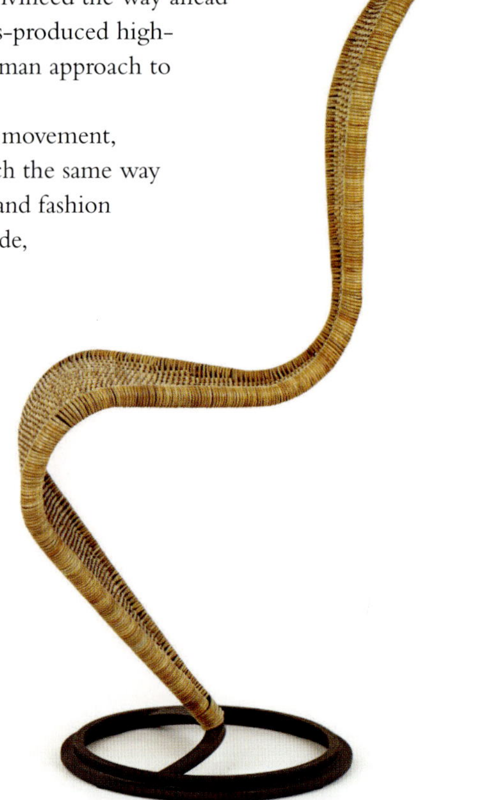

BELOW:
S chair
for Cappellini, 1988 – initially self-manufactured

OPPOSITE TOP:
Jack light
for Eurolounge, 1997

OPPOSITE BOTTOM:
Copper Shade hanging lights
for Tom Dixon, 2005

Bird lounger under licence, which brought Dixon wider international recognition. Soon after this, he became one of a handful of international design superstars in the early 1990s, yet, in contrast to the likes of Ron Arad, Jasper Morrison or Marc Newson, Dixon was always far more hands-on and craft-orientated. In 1994 he co-founded Eurolounge to produce various rotationally moulded designs, including his Jack light (1997), and four years later he was appointed head of design at Habitat, becoming the firm's creative director in 2001. The same year, he independently developed a machine for extruding plastic to make his Fresh Fat Plastic range of products.

During his tenure at Habitat, he must have learnt a lot about selling design as lifestyle, for he set up Tom Dixon Ltd in 2003. Since then, Dixon has created numerous designs that have a distinctive sculptural elegance that reveal his gifted form-giving talents, including his almost ubiquitous Copper Shade lights (2005), his extensive range of sculptural Beat lights (2006), his Wingback chair (2009) and his faceted nickel-plated aluminium Gem low table (2013). He has also worked extensively within the interior and architectural design fields through the auspices of his Design Research Studio, creating extraordinary *Gesamtkunstwerk* (total work of art) spaces.

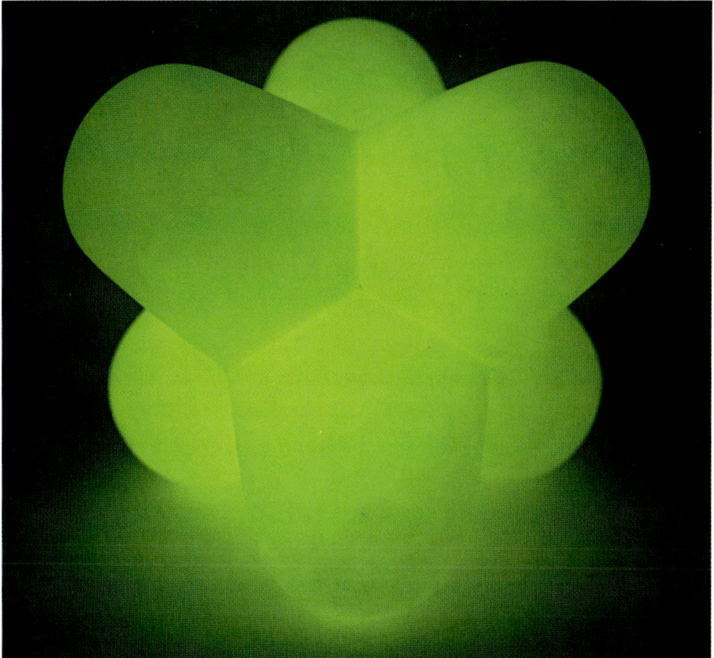

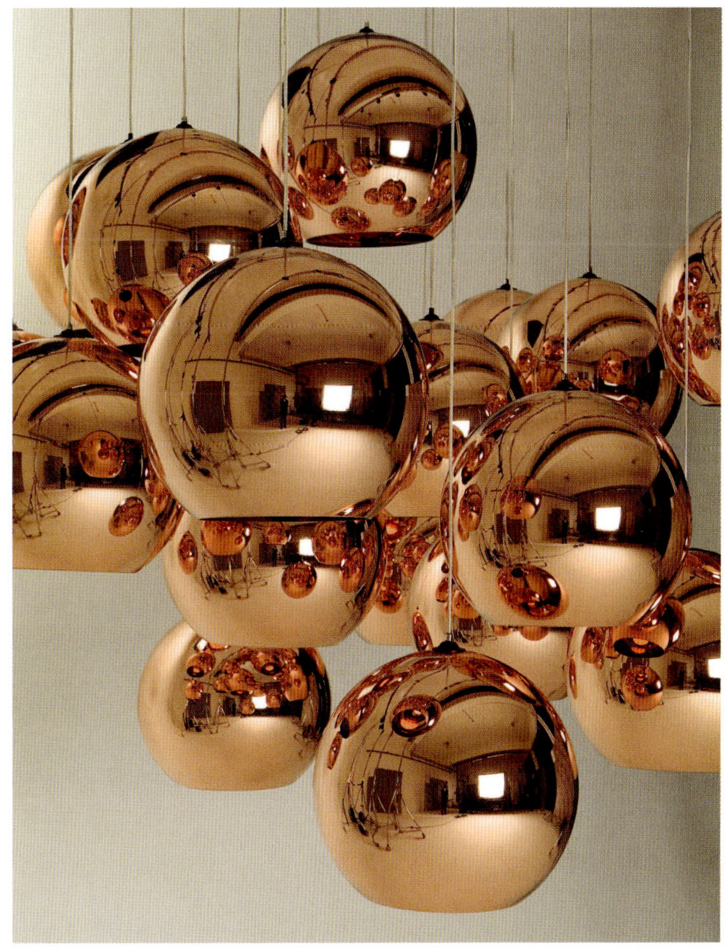

Christopher Dresser

British, 1834–1904

BELOW:
Model No. 2274 teapot
for James Dixon & Sons, 1879

Of all the designers associated with the Aesthetic Movement, Christopher Dresser was by far the most significant in the wider context of design reform. Often cited as the very first person to run a successful design consultancy, he is also generally regarded as "the father of industrial design". An influential design theorist and an accomplished professional designer, Dresser pioneered a pared-down, geometric language of design that we can now see anticipated the formal vocabulary of the Modern Movement, and which was based on his painstaking research into botanical structural forms and his insightful understanding of the art of Japan.

Dresser began his design training at the age of thirteen, when he attended the Government School of Design in London. As part of his studies he specialized in the research of botanical structures, since at the time the natural world was seen as a divine blueprint and there was a belief that if the mysteries of natural forms could be explained it would enable designers to emulate their inherent "rightness" in their own work. As a pioneer of "art botany", he went on to contribute a botanical plate to Owen Jones's influential publication *The Grammar of Ornament* in 1856, and published a number of academic papers on this new subject. So influential were these writings, the University of Jena in Germany awarded him an honorary doctorate in 1859.

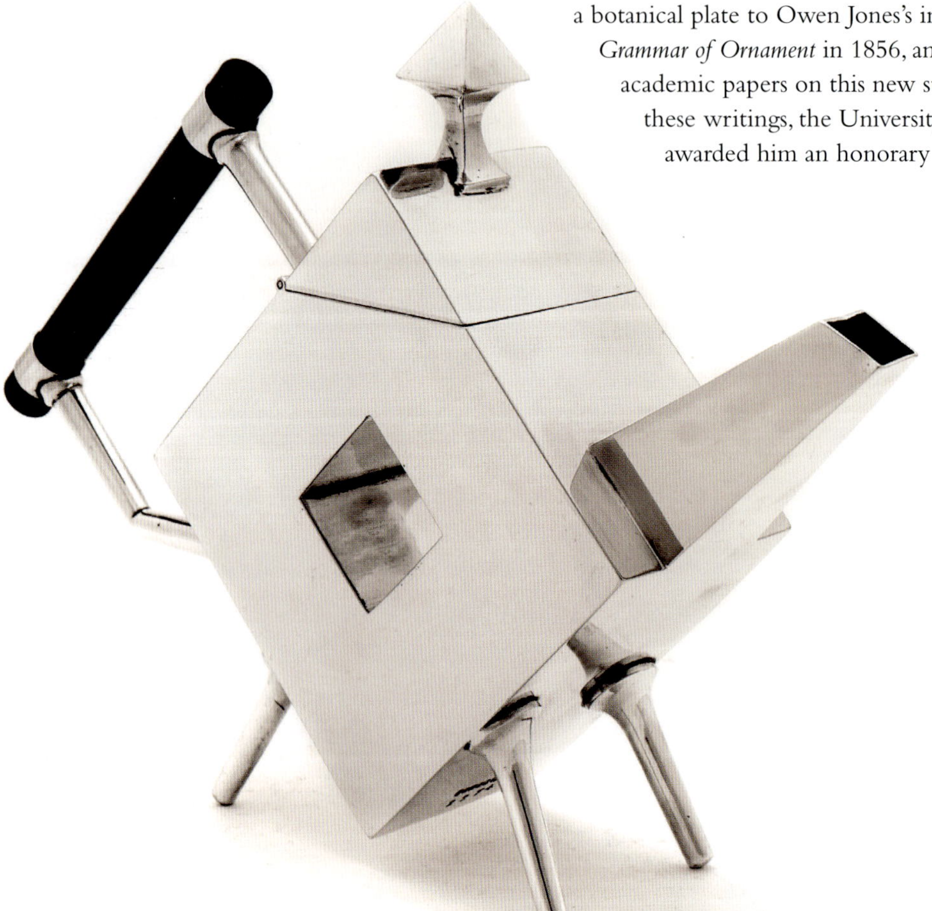

Three years later Dresser visited the *1862 International Exhibition* in London and it was there that he was fully exposed to the rich and varied material culture of Japan. He immediately grasped that there was much intrinsic merit to Japanese design, which so harmoniously balanced form and function, and his designs from the 1860s and 1870s increasingly reflected a Japanese influence in their simplified forms used to express the unique qualities of the chosen materials.

In 1873, Dresser published an influential book entitled *The Principles of Decorative Design*, which explored the relationship between form and function and argued that beauty had commercial value and was therefore an important element of design. Between 1876 and 1877, he extended his knowledge of Japan and its unique design culture considerably by undertaking an extensive four-month research trip as a guest of the Japanese government. As the first Western designer to officially visit Japan in order to study its arts and manufacturing, Dresser gained a unique insight into the country's culture, which he later applied to his design for industry. For instance, his famous Model No. 2274 teapot (1879), although not in any way replicating a Japanese teapot, was utterly inspired by the geometric elementalism found in Japanese design.

As the world's first professional industrial design consultant, Dresser produced designs for at least thirty different manufacturers, including Minton and Coalbrookdale. Some of his ceramic pieces were even emblazoned with his autograph – an early example of an artistic signature being used to sell a designed product. Crucially, through his work Dresser introduced a more rational and forward-looking approach to design that might best be summed up as "art for industry's sake".

BELOW:
Watering can
for Richard Perry & Sons, 1876

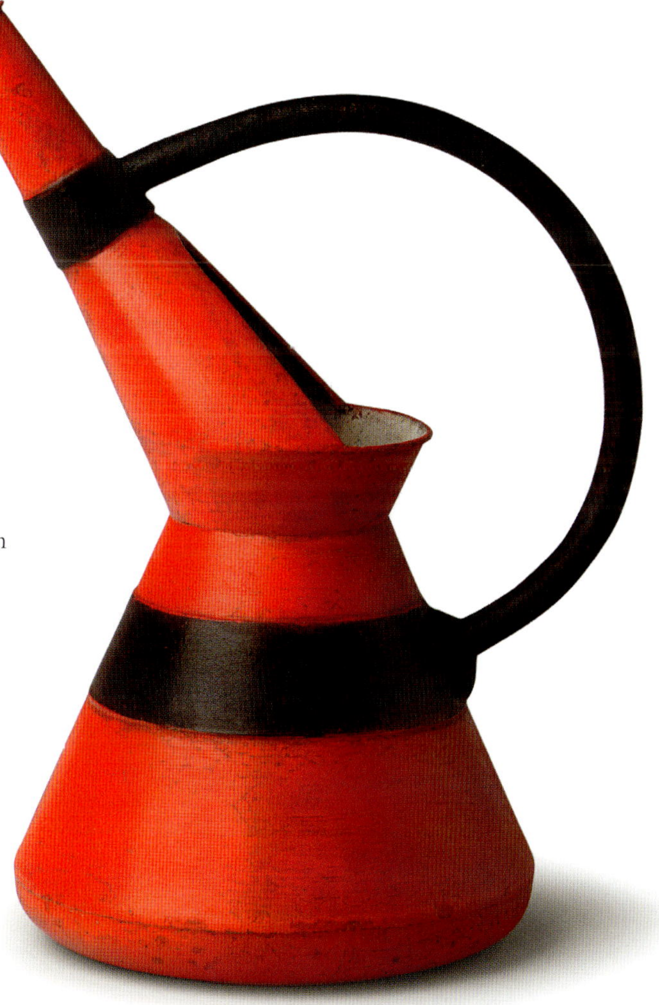

D

Henry Dreyfuss

American, 1904–1972

One of the most celebrated industrial design consultants of the 1930s and 1940s, Henry Dreyfuss was also a pioneering advocate of human factors as applied to design, or in other words ergonomics as well as product design safety. Throughout his prolific and highly successful career, Dreyfuss was guided by his belief that if "people are made safer, more comfortable, more eager to purchase, more efficient, or just happier, the designer has succeeded".

The son of immigrant parents, Brooklyn-born Dreyfuss overcame his humble beginnings to become one of the highest-paid industrial design consultants in the 1930s. Having initially trained at the progressive Ethical Culture School in New York, he went on to apprentice with the industrial designer Norman Bel Geddes. While working in Geddes's office, from 1923 to 1929, he concentrated primarily on theatrical work – designing costumes, sets and lighting for the Strand Theater, New York and for RKO's various vaudeville theatres. Around this time he also worked as a consultant to Macy's store, before establishing his own design office in New York in 1929.

From 1930 onwards, Dreyfuss designed numerous telephones for the Bell Telephone Company, including the Model 302 (1936), the Model 500 (1949), the Princess (1959) and the ubiquitous Trimline telephone (1965). He was also responsible for the design of various vacuum cleaners for Hoover, including the streamlined Model 150 (1936) as well as the classic Big Ben alarm clocks produced by Westclox (1939). Dreyfuss similarly used streamlining in his design of two trains for the New York Central Railroad, the Mercury (1936) and the iconic 20th Century Limited locomotive (1938).

During the 1930s, in addition to product and transportation design, Dreyfuss was tasked with creating his futuristic and utopian 100-foot (30-metre) Democracity diorama for General Electric. This detailed model representing an American city and its surrounding suburbs from the year 2039 was housed in the Perisphere at the 1939 *New York World's Fair*. Equally futuristic was Dreyfuss's later design for the Convaircar (1947) for Vultee – a curious but ultimately doomed car–plane hybrid prototype made of fibreglass that crashed during its test flight. For the most part, beyond the latter rather whimsical design, his work was characterized by a straightforward businesslike approach to the design process, which included working closely with engineers in order to find the most functionally appropriate form. It was this no-nonsense pragmatic "form follows function"

BELOW:
20th Century Limited streamlined locomotive
for New York Central Lines, 1938

OPPOSITE TOP:
Model No. 500 telephone
for Bell Telephone System, 1949

OPPOSITE BOTTOM:
Humanscale 1/2/3
designed by Henry Dreyfuss Associates (Niels Diffrient), 1974 – this manual was released two years after Dreyfuss's death and built on his pioneering research into anthropometrics

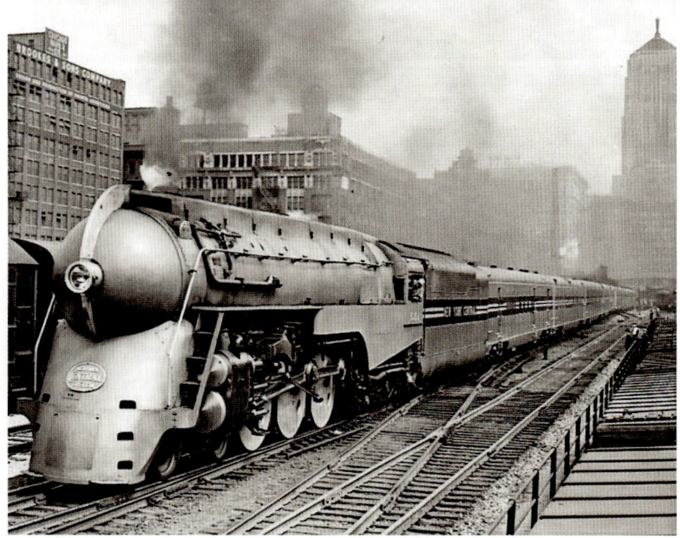

treatment that undoubtedly contributed to the success of his office.

Because he was a prolific patent filer whose designs often had a strong element of technical innovation, Dreyfuss boasted a large corporate clientele including AT&T, American Airlines, Polaroid, Hoover and RCA. While many of his designs exemplified American streamlining, his use of sweeping sculptural forms often had an underlying functional logic, making his products easier and safer to use. Like Raymond Loewy, Norman Bel Geddes and Walter Dorwin Teague, Dreyfuss restyled many products for manufacturers so as to increase consumer demand through stylistic allure; however, his redesigns also frequently enabled easier mass-production or provided enhanced performance. Some of his designs even bore a facsimile of his signature, most notably his bulbous thermal pitcher designed for the American Thermos Bottle Co. in 1935, which suggests an early form of designer-label cachet.

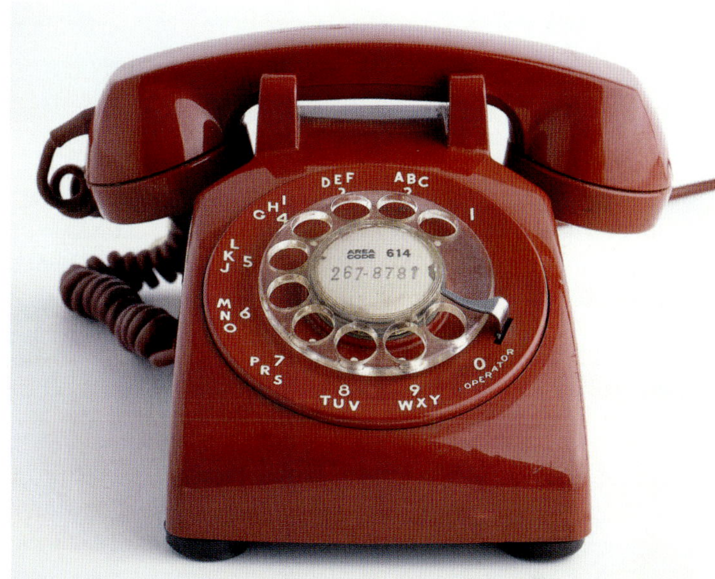

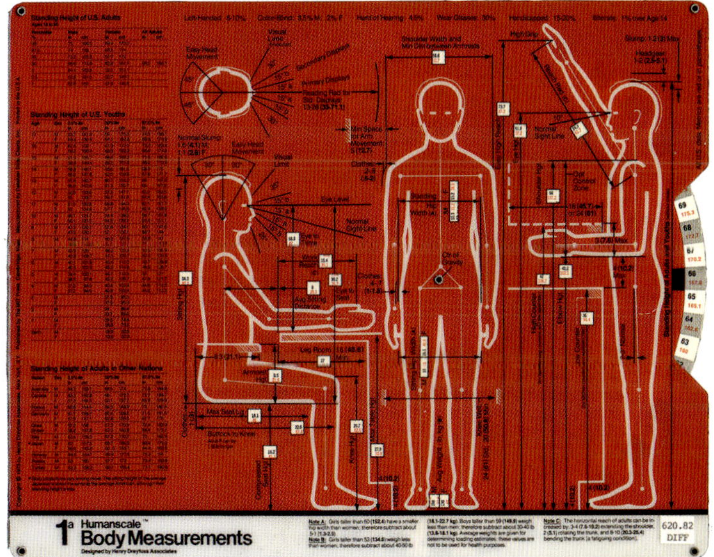

As a founding member of the Society of Industrial Designers in 1944 and the first president of the Industrial Designers Society of America, Dreyfuss was instrumental in helping to professionalize the practice of design. He was also a long-term faculty member of the engineering department at the California Institute of Technology. His greatest contribution to industrial design practice, however, was his research into anthropometrics – the findings of which were published in his influential books *Designing for People* (1955) and *The Measure of Man* (1960). He also published the *Symbol Sourcebook* (1972), a comprehensive guide to international graphic symbols, which acknowledged the increasing communicative importance of universally understood symbols. Later that same year, he committed suicide with his wife who had become terminally ill – a tragic end to one of the greatest design thinkers and practitioners of his era.

James Dyson

British, 1947–

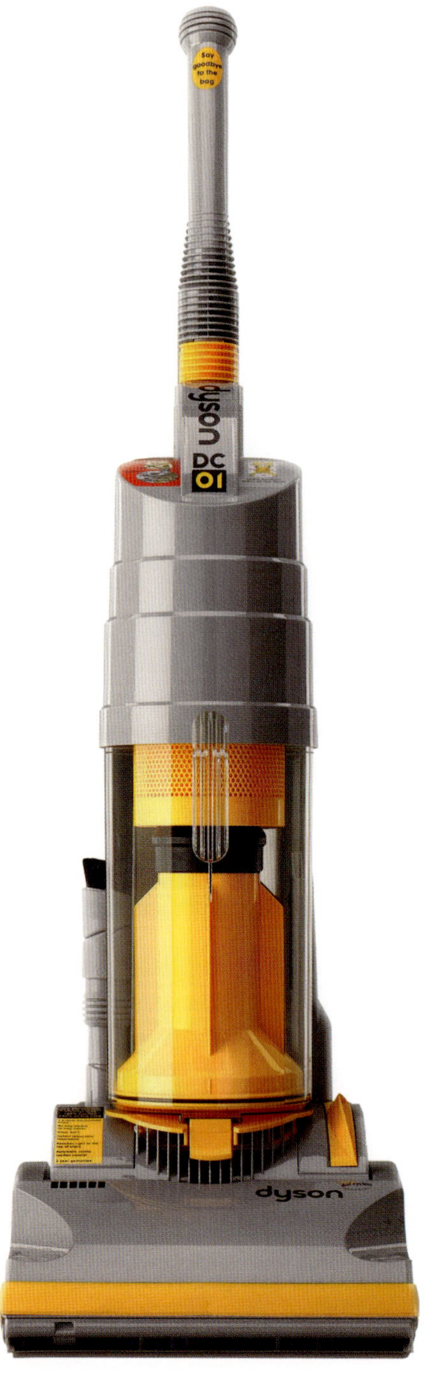

The British inventor and design-led entrepreneur, James Dyson believes in the power of design innovation and is perpetually looking for ways to improve the performance of his products. For him, performance is the key consideration when developing new designs, and the resulting no-nonsense aesthetics of his products are a direct result of this purposeful approach. As Britain's most successful design entrepreneur thanks to his invention of his famous bagless vacuum cleaner in the mid-1980s, Dyson is a hugely influential advocate of good design, actively sponsoring various design education initiatives – not just at college level, but also in the classroom. As he notes, "Throughout history designers and engineers have decided what the future will look like and how it will work. Those that relentlessly invest in research, design and development solve the world's biggest problems."

Dyson initially studied fine art, before training as a furniture and interior designer at the Royal College of Art, London. For his final project there, he designed the flat-hulled, high-speed Sea Truck (1969) for the inventor Jeremy Fry. The rights to this fibreglass vessel were acquired by Rotork, which set up a special marine division, where Dyson worked for four years before leaving to develop his own invention, the Ballbarrow (1974), a variation on the conventional wheelbarrow. Having an innovative plastic ball "wheel" that made it much stabler and easier to steer, the Ballbarrow went on to become a best-seller; however, Dyson did not benefit from its success, having previously sold his interest in it to fund the development of another design concept: a bagless vacuum cleaner.

Taking six years to develop and over five thousand prototypes, the resulting vacuum cleaner used centrifugal force to lift the dust and then separate it from the air, just like cyclone towers used in sawmills to remove particles from the atmosphere. By using a cyclonic method of suction and eliminating the need for a bag, which in conventional vacuum cleaners gets clogged with dust over time thereby reducing suction, the Dyson cleaner had the added benefit of having a constant high level of suction. In 1986, the first

LEFT:
DC01 vacuum cleaner
for Dyson, 1993

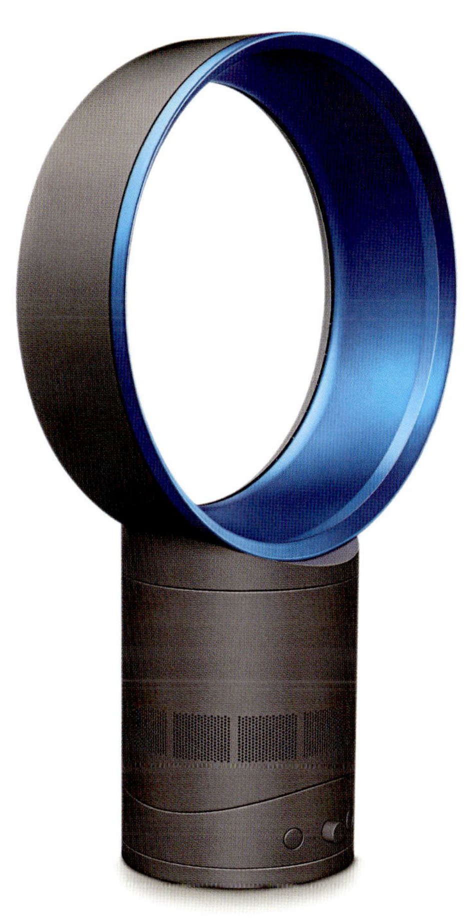

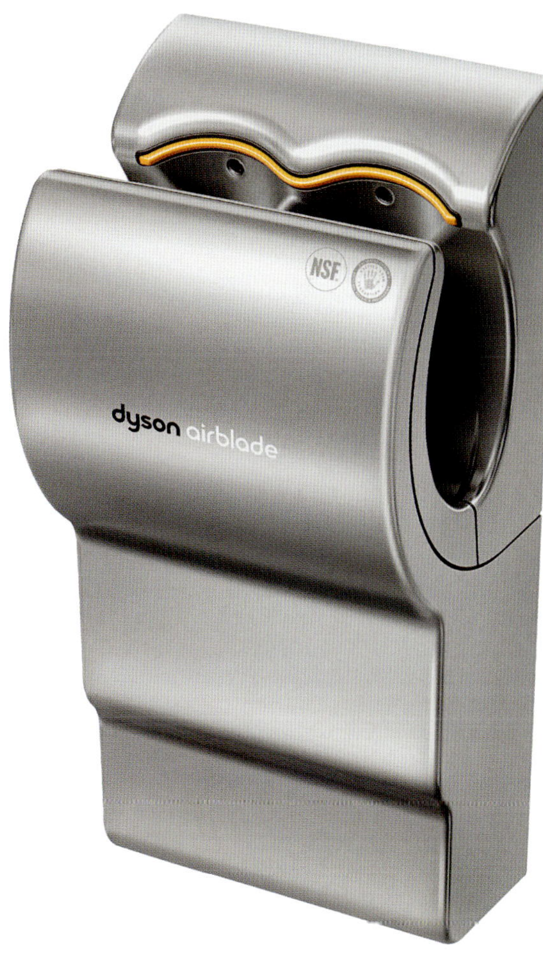

production model of Dyson's cleaner was manufactured under licence in Japan. Known as the G Force, it was produced in pink and lilac ABS plastic to give it a touch of Post-Modern fashionability. However, Dyson found it impossible to find a UK manufacturer for his design; the sale of bags was too lucrative to abandon. Eventually he concluded that the only way to penetrate the UK market was to manufacture the design himself and after several refinements the distinctive silver-grey and yellow DC01 was finally launched in 1993. Within a couple of years, the DC01 had become the UK's best-selling vacuum cleaner. Since then Dyson has refined and developed his bagless vacuum, producing dozens of updated models, while also developing other groundbreaking products incorporating similar proprietary technology, notably hand-dryers and electric fans. As Dyson observes, "Our machines evolve as part of a holistic design process… there is no extraneous window dressing, purpose prevails."

ABOVE LEFT:
Air Multiplier AM01 desk fan
for Dyson, 2009

ABOVE RIGHT:
Airblade hand-dryer
for Dyson, 2004–06

Charles Eames & Ray Eames

American, 1907–1978 / American, 1912–1988

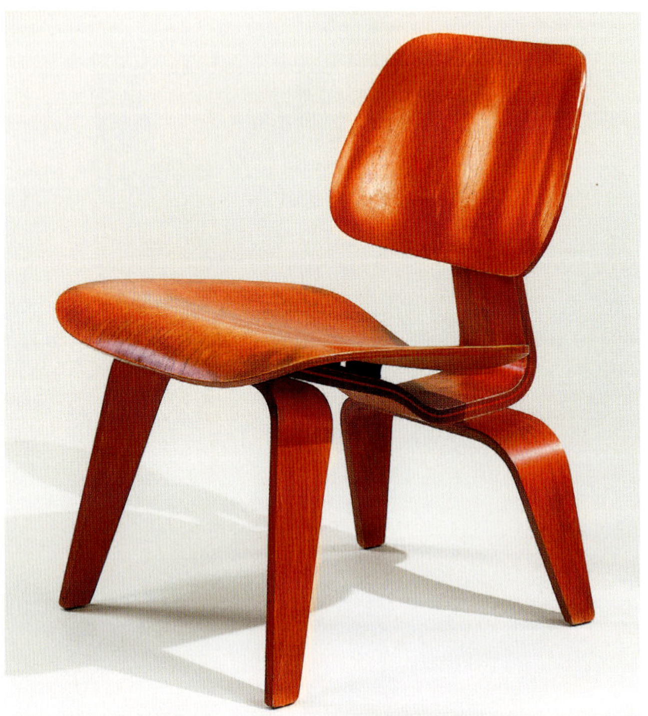

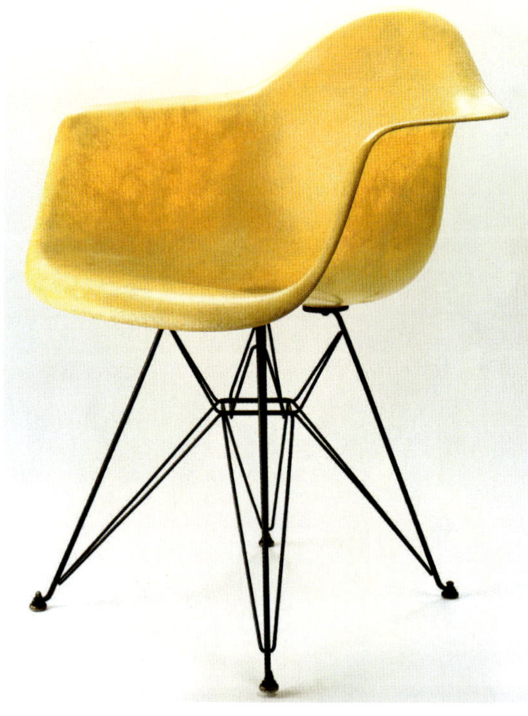

ABOVE LEFT:
LCW (Lounge Chair Wood) chair
for Herman Miller, 1945

ABOVE RIGHT:
DAR (Dining Armchair Rod) chair
for Herman Miller, 1948–50

Best remembered for their numerous iconic furniture designs, Charles and Ray Eames also employed their formidable creative talents to develop ingenious children's toys and puzzles. They designed a number of landmark exhibitions too, and were avid filmmakers who created some of the very first multi-media presentations. Additionally, the Eameses designed two seminal Mid-Century Modern residences – their own house and the Entenza House, both in Pacific Palisades, Los Angeles. Known as Case Study Houses 8 and 9, these prefabricated structures employed new materials and assembly techniques, and stylishly and influentially epitomized the concept of the "modern house".

As the original design power-couple, Charles and Ray possessed in many ways quite different creative talents – she was an artist who had an intuitive eye for colour and form, while he had trained as an architect, and therefore understood the underlying rules of construction and was fascinated by new technologies and materials – and yet they shared a love of poetic whimsy. It was by pooling their inherent skills and interests that they were able to create designs that not only had an extraordinary functional and aesthetic originality, but also had an engaging emotional connection, and it was this sense of connection that set their work apart.

Missouri-born, Charles won a scholarship to study architecture at Washington University in St Louis, while California-born Ray studied painting under Hans Hoffmann at the Art Students League in New York. Their paths crossed in 1940, when Ray enrolled at the Cranbrook Academy of Art in Michigan, where Charles happened to be teaching industrial design. That same year, Charles co-designed with Eero Saarinen a range of highly innovative furniture that won first prize in the prestigious *Organic Design in Home Furnishings* competition organized by the Museum of Modern Art, New York. Having divorced his first wife, Charles married Ray the following year and the newlyweds moved to California, where they began experimenting with the moulding of plywood in the spare room of their Richard Neutra-designed apartment.

In 1942, the Eameses won a contract to supply the US Navy with moulded plywood leg splints and litters, and after the war their landmark Moulded Plywood range of seating (1945), including the famous LCW (Lounge Chair Wood), was put into production by Herman Miller. It was the start of a long and legendary relationship with the Zeeland-based furniture manufacturer, who produced all the Eameses' subsequent furniture designs, including the revolutionary Plastic Shell group (1948–50), which incorporated single-form seat shells made out of moulded glass-reinforced polyester that had been originally developed for radar

BELOW:
Model 670 lounge chair and Model 671 ottoman
for Herman Miller, 1956

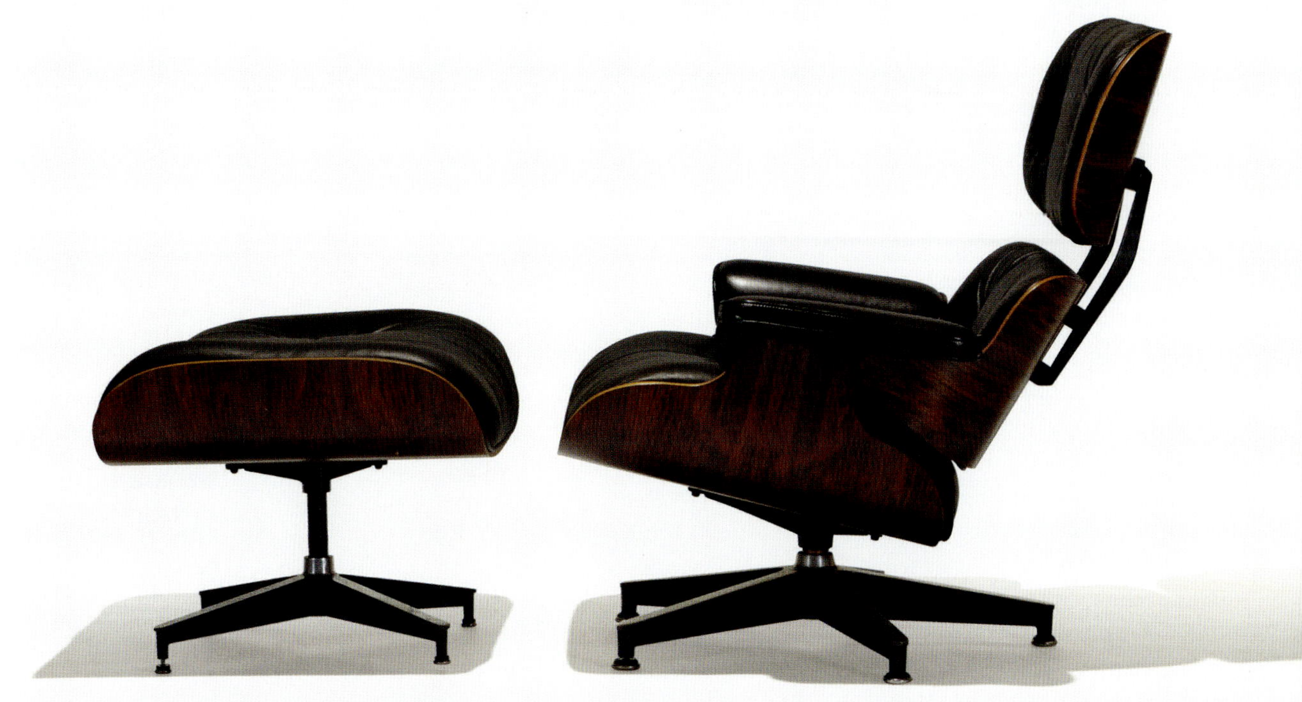

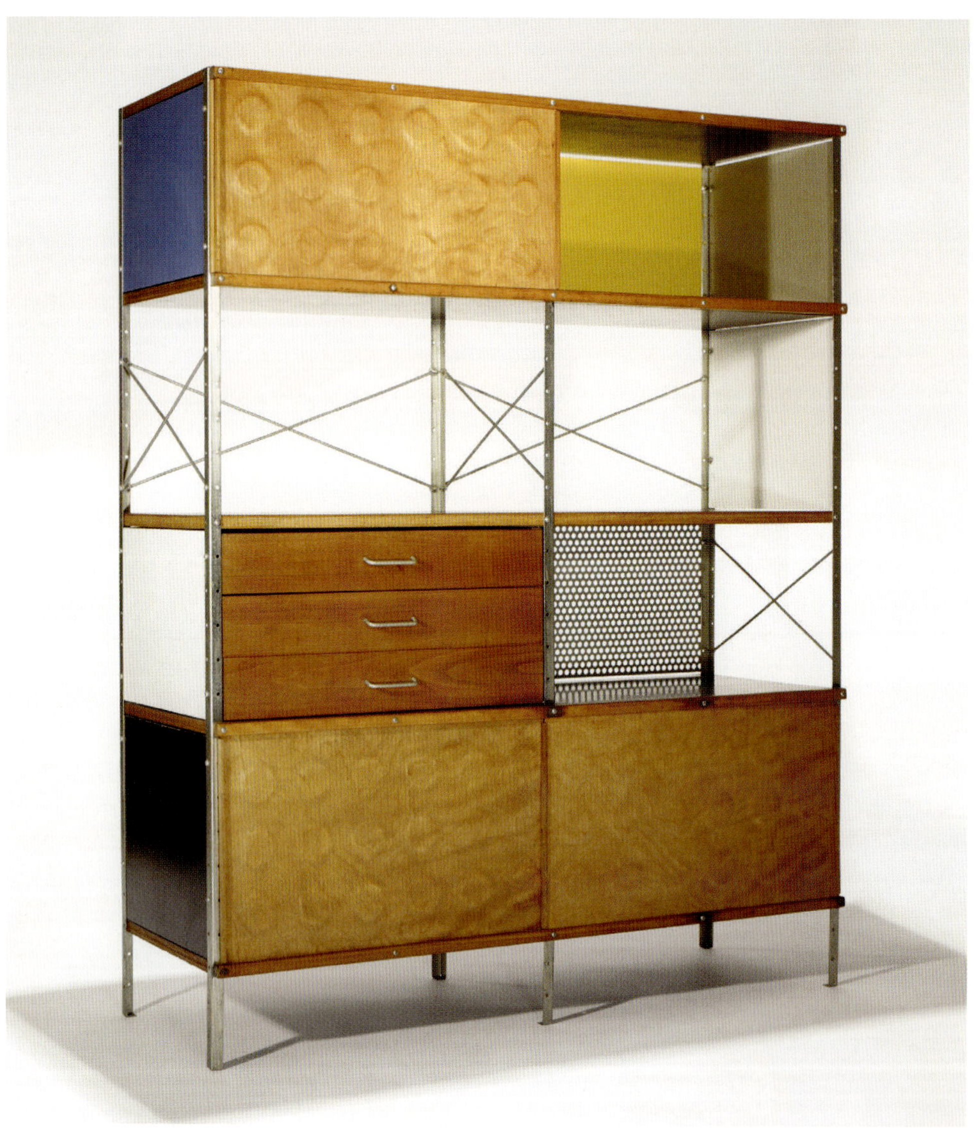

ABOVE:
ESU 420-C storage unit
for Herman Miller, 1952

OPPOSITE TOP:
Case Study House No. 8
(The Eames House), 1949

OPPOSITE BOTTOM:
Crosspatch textile
for Schiffer Prints (designed by Ray Eames), 1947

housings and crash helmets. Developed in collaboration with Herman Miller, Zenith Plastics and the engineering department of the University of California, Los Angeles, the Plastic Shell group seating programme was based on the then-innovative concept of a universal seat shell that could be used with a variety of different types of interchangeable bases. As one of the very first completely integrated seating systems, the Plastic Shell group chairs were also the first to be mass-produced in unlined plastic. Launched in 1950, these landmark chairs were initially available in three colours: "greige", elephant grey or parchment. Later, however, Herman Miller offered more colour options and also a choice of eleven individual bases, including a rocking sled base intended for nursing mothers.

Herman Miller also manufactured the Eameses' Model No. 670 lounge chair (1956), their elegant Aluminum group (1958) and the Soft Pad group (1969) – all of which shared an extraordinary level of detailing. As Charles Eames once noted, "The details are not the details. They make the product. The connections, the connections, the connections. It will in the end be these details … that give the product its life."

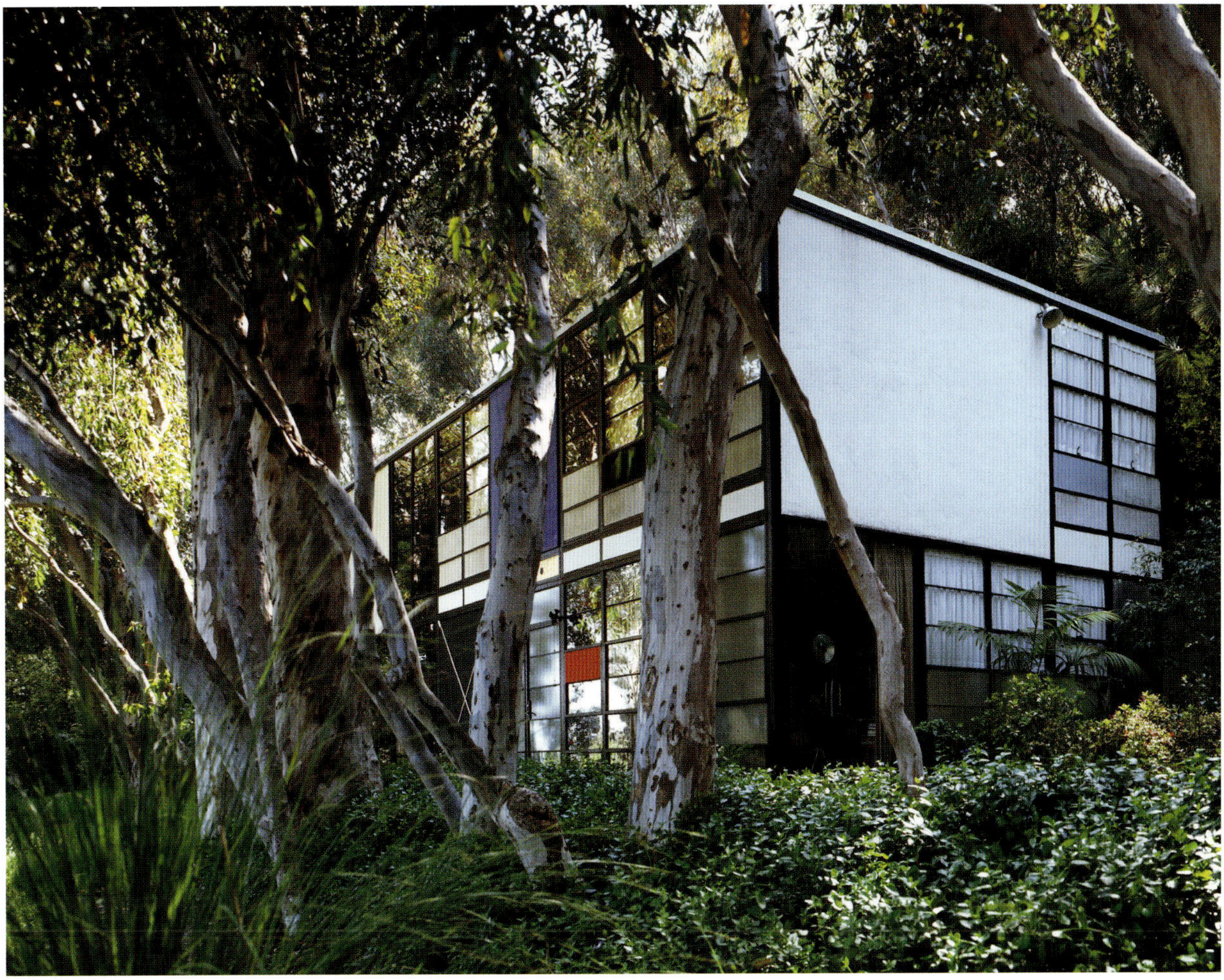

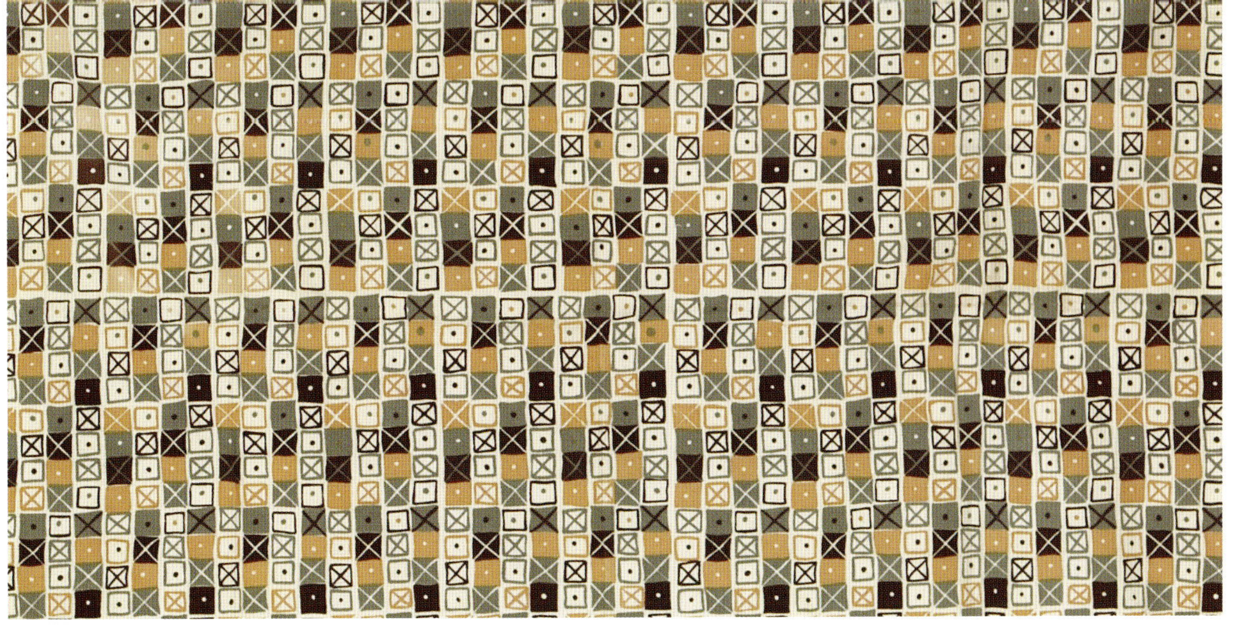

Harley Earl

American, 1893–1969

The acknowledged father of automotive styling, Harley Earl was at an early age exposed to vehicle design and manufacture since his father had founded the Earl Carriage Works in Los Angeles in 1908. This venture was renamed the Earl Automobile Works two years later so as to reflect the transition from horse-drawn to motorized modes of transportation, and began specializing in customizing cars for movie stars and specially built vehicles for use in films.

In 1914, Harley Earl began a degree at Stanford University, but soon abandoned his academic studies in order to train as a designer in his father's auto works. Some of his earliest automotive styling projects were for luxury cars specially created for Hollywood's glitterati, such as the actor Roscoe "Fatty" Arbuckle and the legendary director Cecil B. DeMille. In 1919, the Earl Automobile Works was purchased by Don Lee, Cadillac's West Coast distributor, and subsequently devoted its efforts entirely to car customization. Around this time, Harley Earl pioneered a new way of styling car bodies using clay models, which permitted a freer, more sculptural line and ultimately helped introduce streamline forms into the motoring industry as well as other areas of product design.

While in the early years of the automotive industry, manufacturers had been focused on supplying growing demand, by the early 1920s the market had become much more competitive and they were now thinking of ways to increase their market share. This inevitably led them to the conclusion that they needed to differentiate their cars stylistically from those of their competitors. The chairman of General Motors, Alfred P. Sloan, was one of the first to realize that aesthetics would play an increasingly important role in the car industry and as a result Earl was invited to Detroit by Cadillac's general manage Larry Fisher in 1925.

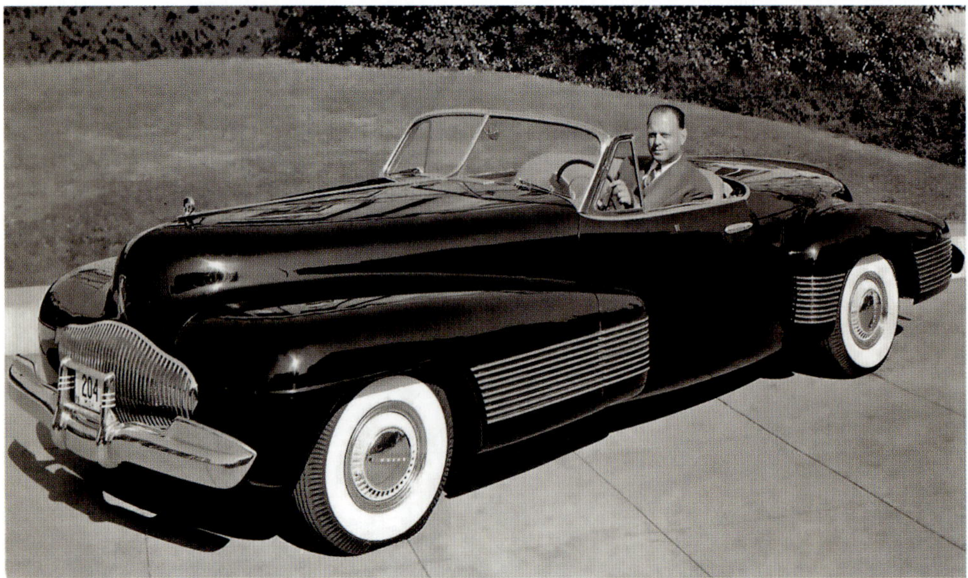

LEFT:
Buick Y-Job concept car for General Motors, 1938 (with Harley Earl in the driving seat)

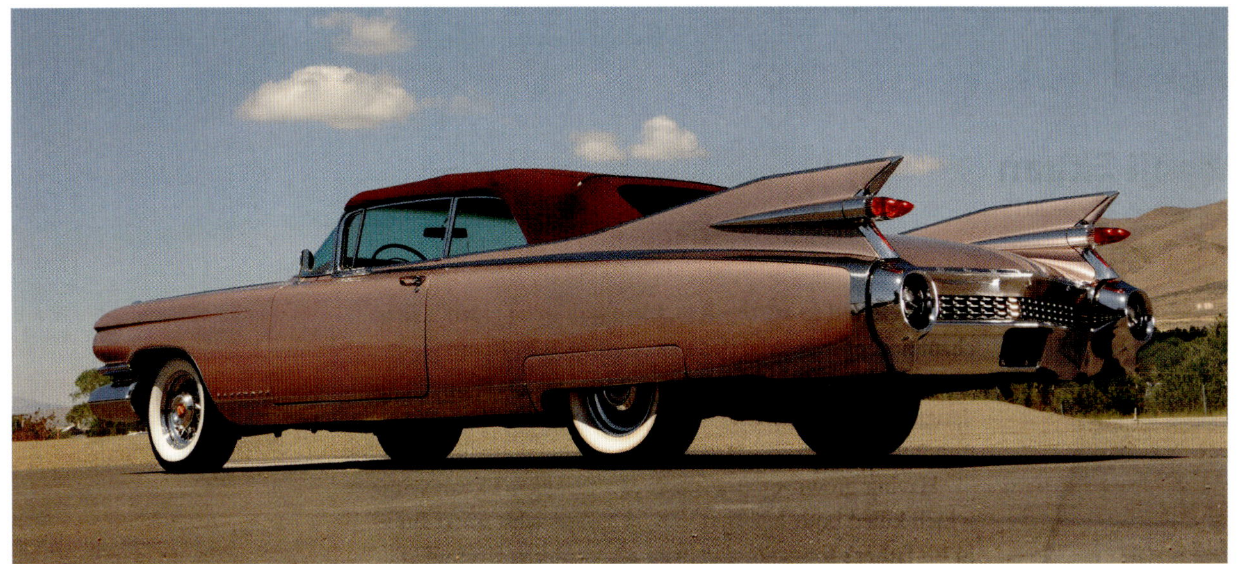

ABOVE:
Cadillac Eldorado
1959

Earl's first brief for General Motors was to bring "something" to the new LaSalle brand, which was pitched between the mid-range Buick and high-end Cadillac models. The resulting 1927 LaSalle was more compact than its Cadillac equivalent and was the first mass-produced car to have a body created by a stylist rather than by an engineer. With this luxury coupé, which boasted a tall and narrow radiator grill and distinctive clamshell fenders, Earl essentially ushered in a new era of automotive styling.

Although Earl's initial assignment was intended to be short-term, Sloan realized that the company would profit if it could produce new cars each year that differed from the previous year's model and so Earl stayed on as GM's body designer. The concept of annual cosmetic changes to promote stylistic obsolescence eventually led to the creation of General Motors' Art and Color Section in 1928, with Earl acting as its supervisor. Renamed the Styling Section in 1937, this very first dedicated style department began to lower and lengthen models in order to make them less boxy in appearance. As Earl was to later note, "my sense of proportion tells me that oblongs are more attractive than squares… just as a greyhound is more graceful than an English bulldog."

Earl employed female stylists in the Styling Section in a bid to reach the increasingly important women's market, and went on to oversee the development of the world's very first concept car – the 1938 Buick Y-Job – with its innovative two-tone paintwork, wrap-around windscreen and "fishtail" rear fender. It was at Earl's instigation that GM also developed a new sports car – the classic 1953 Chevrolet Corvette, which had a body made out of lightweight but strong fibreglass. Around this period, however, his use of styling became increasingly outré, with cars becoming increasingly lower, longer and more chrome-laden, culminating in the 1959 version of the Cadillac Eldorado with its rocket-like tail fins.

While working at General Motors, Earl established his own independent industrial design office in 1945, which was responsible for the design of, among other things, Bissel carpet sweepers and the well-known Greyhound bus. But above all it was his introduction of styling to the automotive industry that was his greatest legacy, and to this day he is still remembered at GM with the words: "Our father who art in styling… Harley be thy name!"

Kenji Ekuan

Japanese, 1929–2015

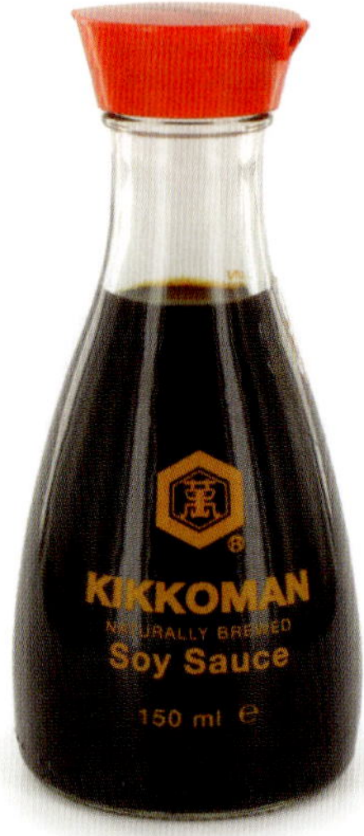

ABOVE:
Soy sauce bottle
for Kikkoman, 1961

OPPOSITE TOP:
Narita Express E259 Series commuter train
2009

OPPOSITE BOTTOM:
E3 Series Shinkansen high-speed train
1997

Often referred to as "the Raymond Loewy of Japan", Kenji Ekuan was an important champion of industrial design consultancy in Japan. Yet his approach to problem-solving was very different to Loewy's: he placed far greater emphasis on the need to democratize design, humanize technology and, as he put it, "to seek the soul in material things". This more mindful approach to industrial design can be attributed to his training as a Buddhist priest.

Having grown up in Hawaii, as a teenager Ekuan witnessed the bombing of Hiroshima, which killed both his sister and his father, who was a Buddhist monk. Initially, Ekuan followed in his father's footsteps and lived as a monk at a temple in Hiroshima, but eventually he decided he wanted to become a "creator of things" in the face of the destruction he had witnessed. To achieve this goal, he studied design at Tokyo University of the Arts. While there he won a scholarship awarded by the Japan External Trade Organization (JETRO) that enabled him to study industrial design the following year in California at the Art Center College of Design, Pasadena – then one of the most progressive design institutions in the United States. After graduating, he returned to Tokyo and in 1957 founded GK Industrial Design Associates – an offshoot of the GK (Group of Koike) Design Group established five years earlier, its name being a tribute to Mr Koike, an associate professor at the university who had helped instigate its founding. With Ekuan as its president, this new industrial design office was instrumental in helping Japan's design-led economic recovery through its creation of beautifully designed products.

In 1961, Ekuan created his best-known design, the iconic Kikkoman soy sauce dispenser with its funnel-shaped body and distinctive red top. The brilliance of this design was that it not only channelled a very purist Japanese aesthetic into a cheap-to-make dispenser but was also so functionally resolved and easy to use. Guided by Ekuan's belief in a fully integrated approach to design, sometimes referred to as "total design", GK Industrial Design Associates, working alongside its sister companies within the GK Design Group, was eventually able to offer an impressively comprehensive range of services to its clients, from market research and product development to communication design and environmental design. Working for, among others, Yamaha, Konica, Kirin Brewery and the East Japan Railway Company, Ekuan and his team created a vast array of different types of products, including public toilets, a parking meter, a sewing machine, saucepans, cosmetic packaging, dental equipment, wristwatches, motorbikes, an all-terrain vehicle and several notable locomotives including the Narita Express 253 (1991), E3 Series Shinkansen bullet train (1997) and Narita Express E259 (2009).

Kenji Ekuan was also a tireless champion of professional design practice, as president of both the Japan Industrial Designers Association and the International Council of Societies of Industrial Design, and through his various publications, including a historical analysis of the role of tools in human society. As Charles Austen Angell, chair of IDSA (Industrial Designers Society of America) Board of Directors, notes, Ekuan "viewed good design as being composed of both the beautiful simplicity of everyday life, and the far reaching goals for a modern society. This was the power of his work."

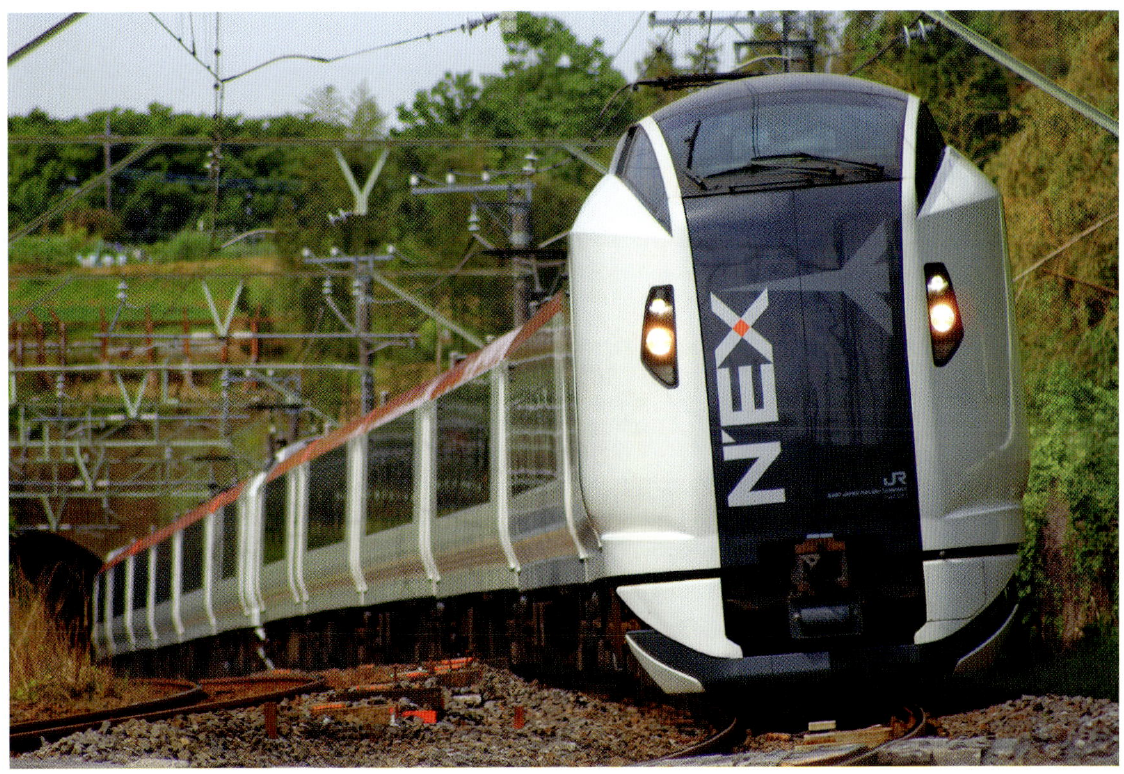
N'EX
JR

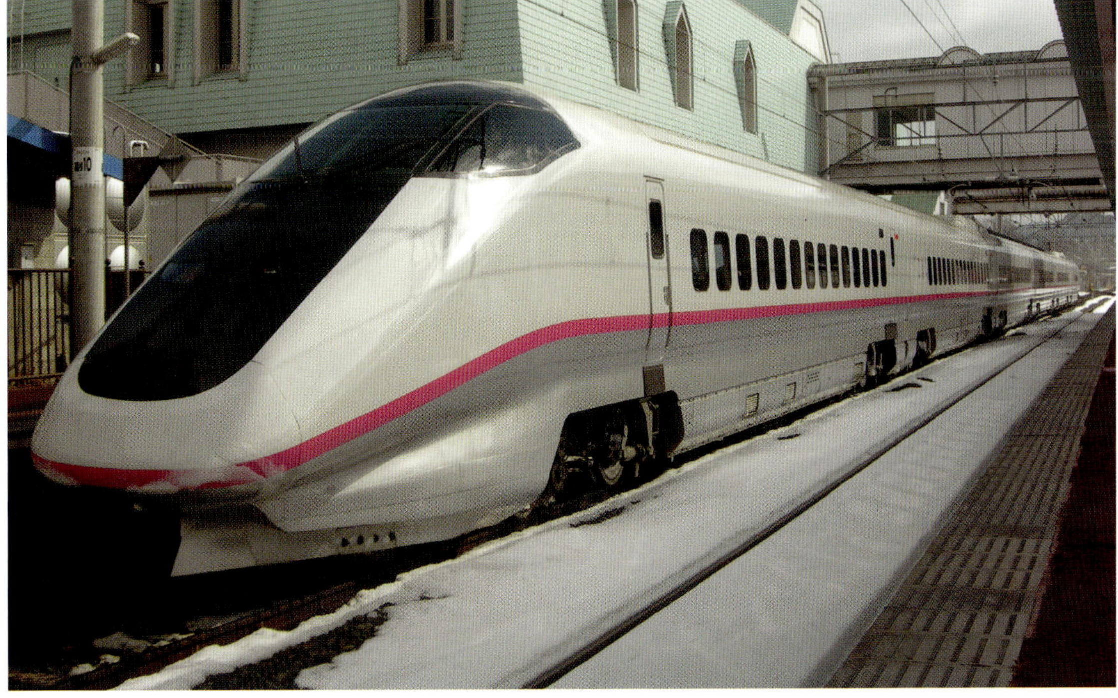

Ergonomi Design Gruppen

Swedish, founded 1979

An early and influential pioneer of user-orientated inclusive design, Ergonomi Design Gruppen (EDG) was at the forefront of design for special needs during the 1970s and 1980s. This specialist design consultancy based in Bromma, Sweden, evolved from two earlier design studios, Designgruppen and Ergonomi Design.

The former was an industrial design consultancy that had been established in 1969 and whose members had previously worked for companies such as AGA, ASEA and IBM, while the latter studio had been founded by Henry Wahlforss and specialized in research-led user-friendly designs for (dis)ability. In 1971, Ergonomi Design moved into the work premises occupied by Designgruppen – a former glue factory – and over the coming years the two design offices became so interconnected that eventually it was decided to merge officially in 1979. As early as 1972, two members of Ergonomi Design – Maria Benktzon and Sven-Eric Juhlin – had begun carrying out in-depth ergonomic studies on the grips of knife and saw handles and then used this data to create a revolutionary new bread knife and cutting board (1973) specifically intended for the elderly and for people with physical disabilities. Manufactured by Gustavsberg, this ingenious design solution featured a sliding cutting guide so that a loaf of bread could be safely and easily sawn rather than cut into slices.

Another landmark design by Ergonomi was the Eat/Drink range (1980) of cutlery, drinking vessels and plates that were again specifically designed for those with physical impairments. RSFU Rehab, a private firm that had initially been established as a grant-aided foundation to give advice on and supply various kinds of medical aids, manufactured this

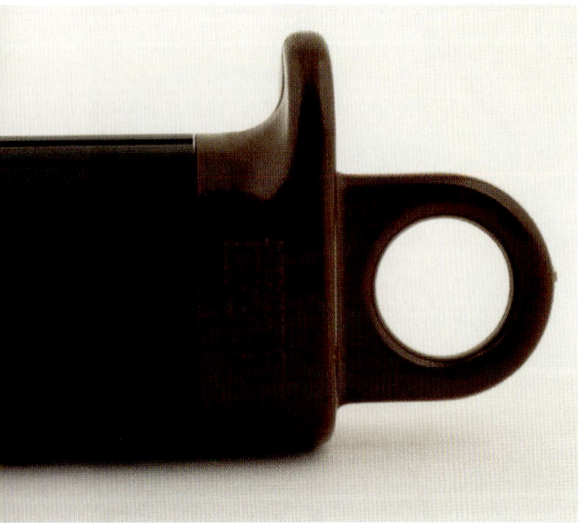

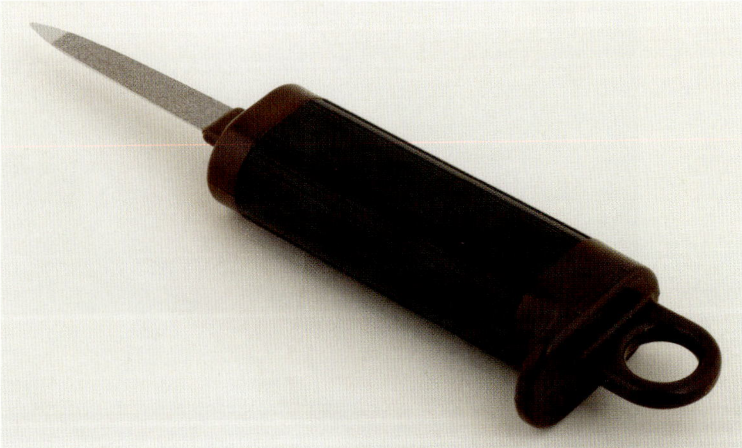

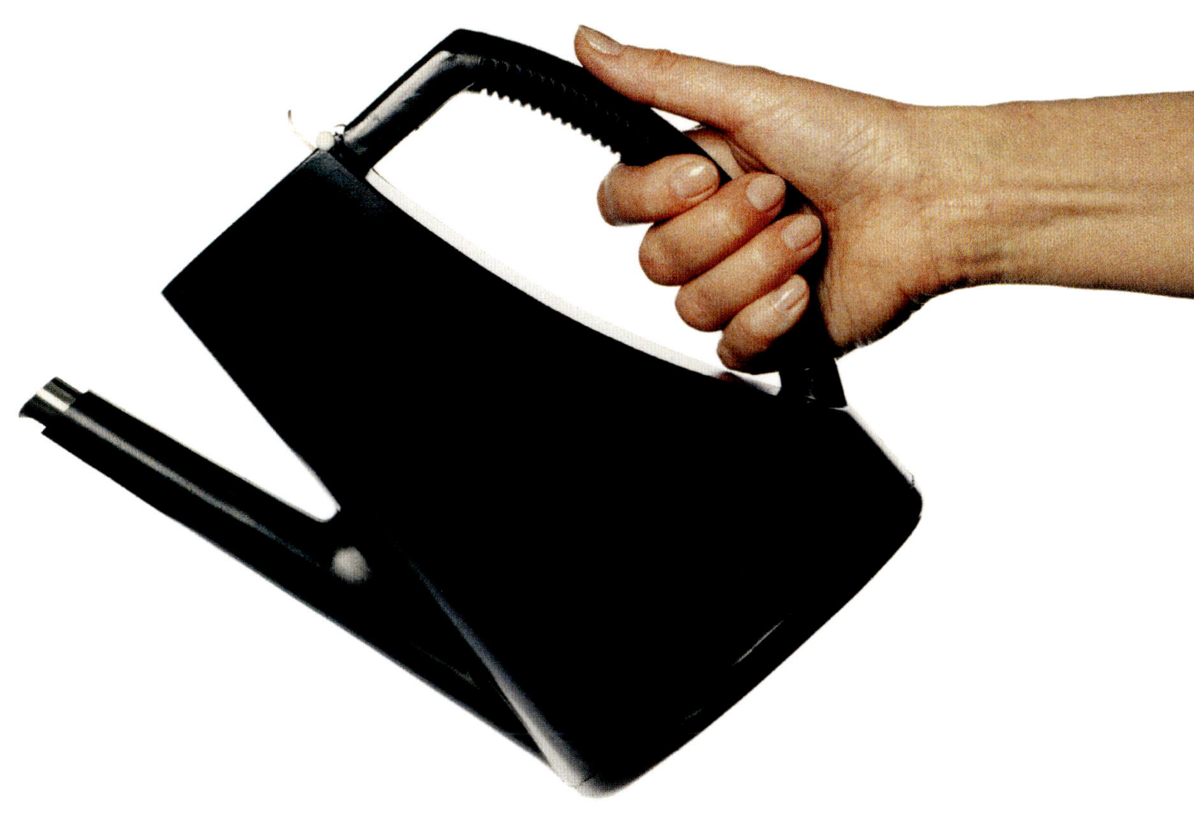

OPPOSITE ABOVE:
Speedglas welding helmet
for 3M, 2009

OPPOSITE BELOW:
Plastic nail file holder
for ETAC, 1970s

ABOVE:
SAS coffee pot
for Scandinavian Airlines (SAS), 1988

painstakingly researched programme of eating utensils. The range was conceived for people with only a single hand, and it was sold inexpensively thanks to having its development and manufacturing costs underwritten by various insurance companies and public bodies. If it had not been for these grants, it is highly unlikely that this landmark real-need design would ever have been produced because it would not have been commercially viable. Ergonomi subsequently designed numerous medical aids that were remarkable for their ergonomic refinement and functional user-friendliness, including a walking cane with a sculpted ergonomic grip (1983) for ETAC, a super-lightweight fibreglass and polycarbonate gripping tong (1984) for F.M. Matsson and feeding spoons with rotating bowls (1986) for RSFU Rehab.

Apart from its award-winning work within this specialized area, Ergonomi (known as Veryday since 2012) has also applied its knowledge of ergonomics to the creation of better-performing and safer products for more general usage – from its in-flight coffee pot (1988) for SAS that has enhanced pouring stability to its Speedglas 9100 welding helmet (2009) for 3M that provides enhanced protection. More than anything else, its work embodies the social ethics of Scandinavian societies, which see good design as the birthright of all, regardless of wealth or physical ability.

Alan Fletcher

British, 1931–2006

The British graphic designer, Alan Fletcher skilfully blended the disparate graphic languages of European Modernism and American Pop culture into his own distinctive visual style. His work was characterized by a creative artistry and was often infused with a subtle sense of playful humour. Such was the influence of his pioneering work, he would eventually become a revered guru to succeeding generations of graphic designers, while Pentagram, the design agency he co-founded, remains to this day at the vanguard of visual communications design.

Born in Kenya, Fletcher attended various art schools including Hammersmith School of Art before opting to study at Central School of Arts and Crafts in London. While there, his tutor Anthony Froshaug thoroughly grounded him in the fundamentals of typography. It was at Central that he also met fellow graphic design student Colin Forbes, with whom he would later collaborate. In 1953 Fletcher enrolled at the Royal College of Art in London, and three years later won an exchange scholarship to Yale University's School of Architecture and Design. The United States was an utter revelation to Fletcher, and he enthusiastically embraced all opportunities this veritable land of plenty offered. At

BELOW LEFT:
***Design* (issue 139) magazine cover**
for Council of Industrial Design, 1960

BELOW RIGHT:
Rorschach Test poster
for Polaroid Corporation, 1989

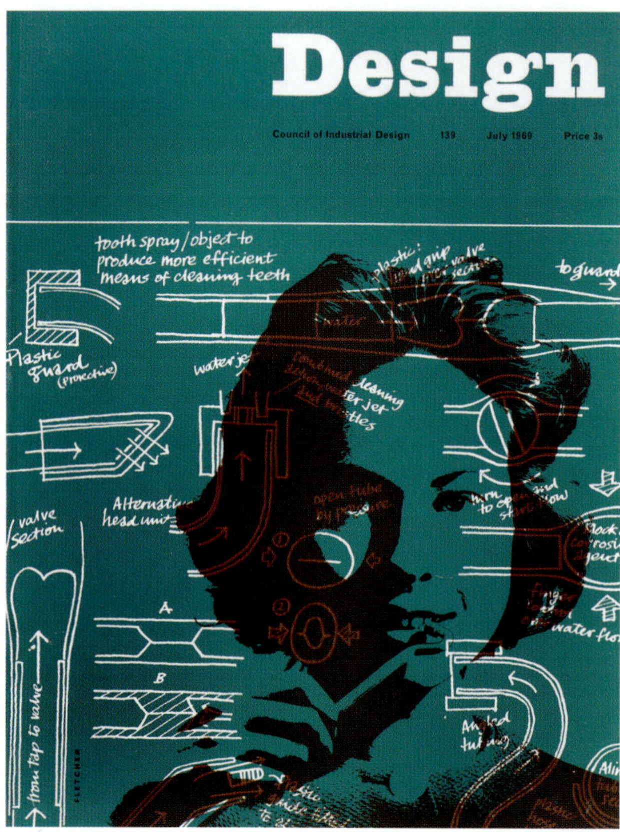

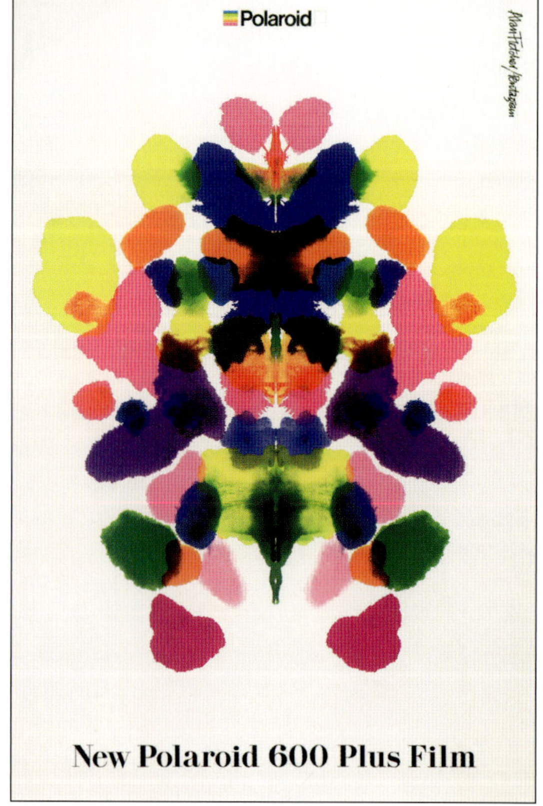

Yale, he was taught by, among others, Paul Rand, Bradbury Thompson, Josef Albers and Alvin Eisenman, and before his return to Britain, Fletcher worked as a freelancer for Leo Lionni at *Fortune* magazine and in Saul Bass's studio in Los Angeles. Working for such talented and professional art directors was a hugely formative experience and, as Mike Dempsey notes, "gave him not only a professional edge but also the confidence to head back to London with the intention of making some waves".

Fletcher eventually returned to London in 1959, journeying via Milan, where he briefly worked in Pirelli's design studio. Meanwhile, his friend Colin Forbes had been appointed head of graphic design at Central and boasted a number of clients, including *Time* and *Life* magazines and Pirelli; on his return to London Fletcher rented a corner of Forbes's studio and two years later the two decided to join forces with the American London-based graphic designer Bob Gill to form their own graphic design consultancy, Fletcher/Forbes/Gill. Based in a mews house just off Baker Street, the trio soon became the most fashionable go-to graphic designers in London thanks to their distinctive graphic style that mixed imagery and text into thought-provoking and visually stimulating compositions with a universally understood clarity. This graphic design studio would eventually evolve in 1972 into the multidisciplinary design consultancy Pentagram.

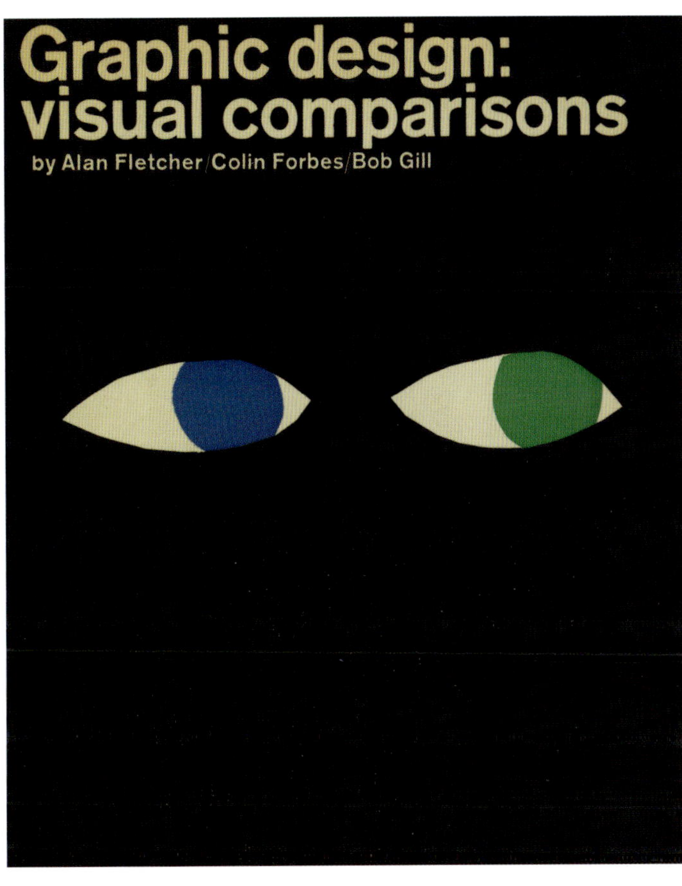

ABOVE:
***Graphic design: visual comparisons* book cover**
for Studio Publications, 1963

The same year, Fletcher turned his hand to product design with the creation of his Clam ashtray for Mebel of Italy that was made from two identical plastic mouldings forming its base and lid, which had wave-like serrations. Over the next two decades he worked under the auspices of Pentagram on numerous high-profile projects, including the celebrated V&A logo for the Victoria and Albert Museum (1989). In 1992 Fletcher left Pentagram and set up his own independent studio in Notting Hill, London, and in 2001 published his best-selling *The Art of Looking Sideways* – an essential primer for graphic designers that encapsulated his visual philosophy.

F

Henry Ford

American, 1863–1946

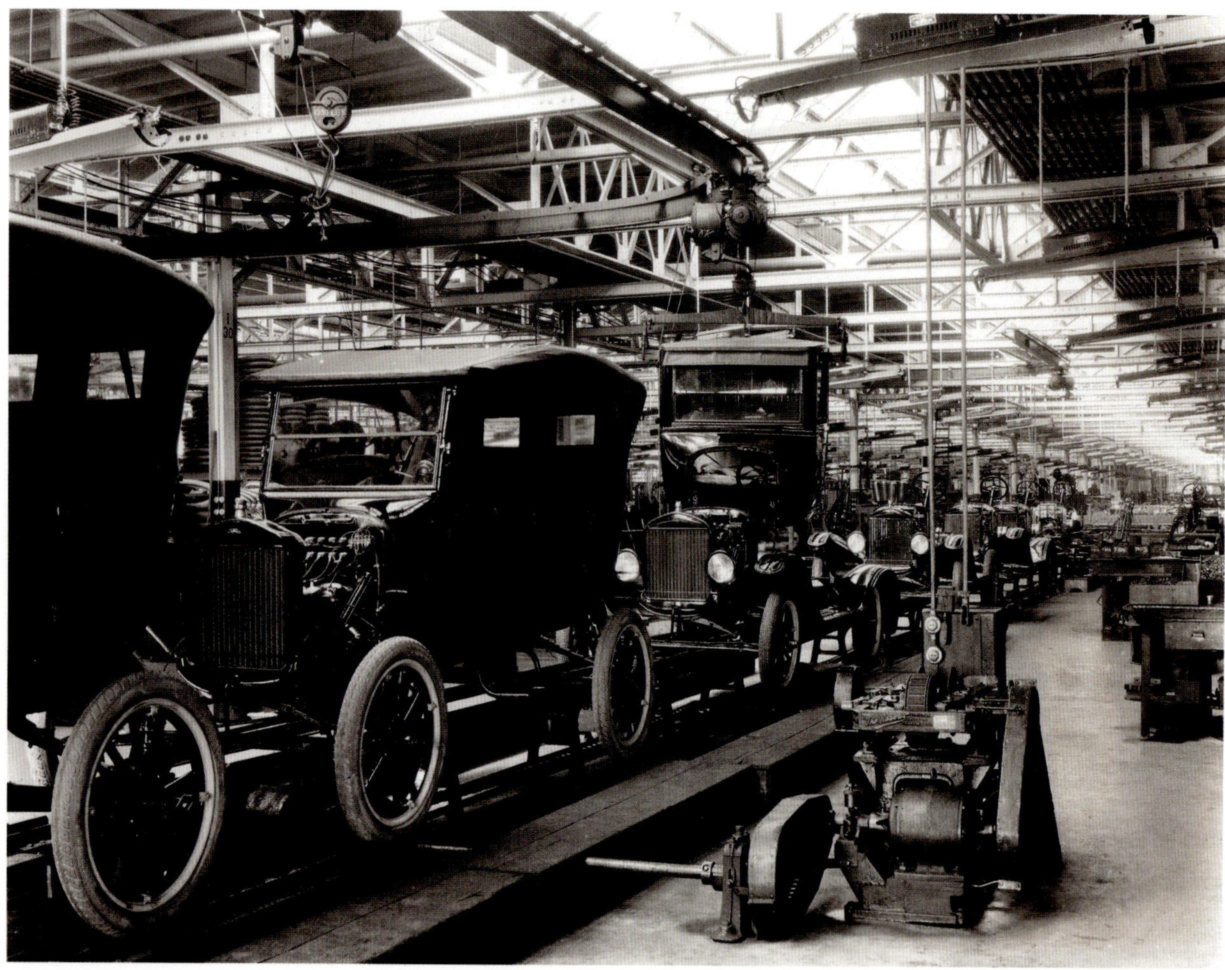

ABOVE:
Ford assembly line
*c.*1913

Henry Ford did not invent the automobile, but it was his vision that made the car accessible to millions of people. After many years of dogged design research and development, he achieved his dream of building "a motor car for the great multitude" with the immortal Model T (1908) – a car specifically designed for high-volume production, which was eventually mass-produced on an unprecedented scale using the world's very first moving assembly line.

Born to a farming family in Wayne County, Michigan, Ford moved to Detroit at the age of sixteen and took an apprenticeship as a machinist. Over the next few years, he learnt how to operate and service steam engines, and also studied bookkeeping. After getting married in 1888, he briefly returned to farm work in order to support his wife and son, but three years later was offered a job as an engineer at the Edison Illuminating Company, where he was promoted to chief engineer in 1893. During this period he developed plans for a horseless carriage, which eventually led him to build the Ford Quadricycle in 1896.

After the development of various other vehicles, Ford, with the backing of twelve investors, established the Ford Motor Company in June 1903 in a disused Detroit wagon factory. The fledgling company's first car was sold only a month later, and was described as "the most perfect machine on the market… so simple that a boy of fifteen can run it". Over the next five years, Ford oversaw a systematic programme of research and development that resulted in a plethora of different models, named alphabetically. Not every model that was developed made it into production, and of those that did, not all were commercially successful, especially those aimed at the top end of the market.

Over time, Ford became increasingly convinced that the company's destiny lay in the manufacture of inexpensive cars – and so was born the Model T, which was introduced in 1908. Described by Henry Ford as the "universal car", this low-cost and reliable model became an instant success; demand for it soared, far outstripping Ford's production capability in its Dearborn assembly plant. Vexed by this problem, Ford looked for ways to accelerate the production flow at his factory and at the same time lower unit cost. Fortuitously for him, the

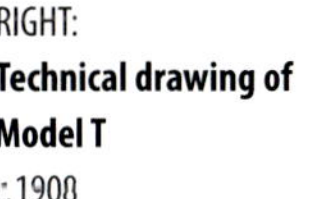

RIGHT:
Technical drawing of Model T
c.1908

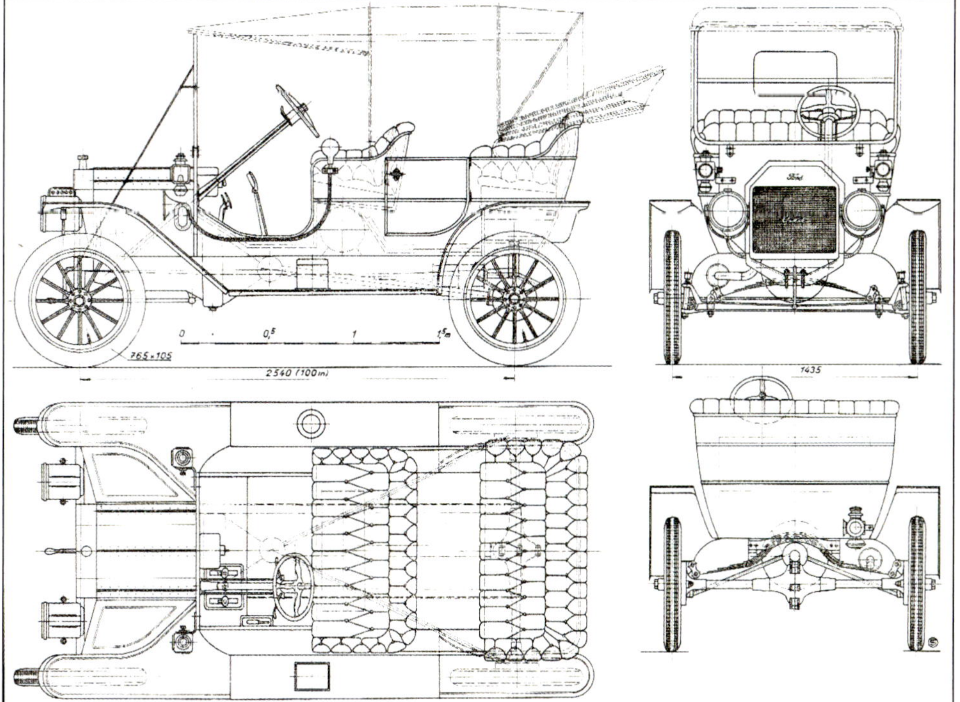

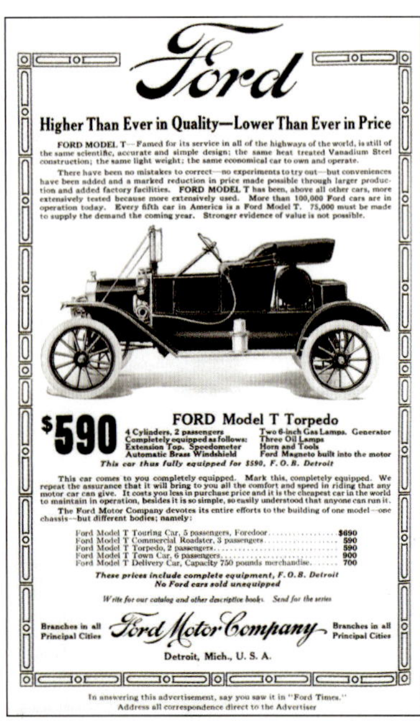

Ford
Higher Than Ever in Quality—Lower Than Ever in Price
FORD MODEL T—Famed for its service in all of the highways of the world, is still of the same scientific, accurate and simple design; the same heat treated Vanadium Steel construction; the same light weight; the same economical car to own and operate.
There have been no mistakes to correct—no experiments to try out—but conveniences have been added and a marked reduction in price made possible through larger production and added factory facilities. FORD MODEL T has been, above all other cars, more extensively tested because more extensively used. More than 100,000 Ford cars are in operation today. Every fifth car in America is a Ford Model T. 75,000 must be made to supply the demand the coming year. Stronger evidence of value is not possible.
$590
FORD Model T Torpedo
4 Cylinders, 2 passengers
Completely equipped as follows:
Extension Top. Speedometer
Automatic Brass Windshield
Two 6-inch Gas Lamps. Generator
Three Oil Lamps
Horn and Tools
Ford Magneto built into the motor
This car thus fully equipped for $590, F. O. B. Detroit
This car comes to you completely equipped. Mark this, completely equipped. We repeat the assurance that it will bring to you all the comfort and speed in riding that any motor car can give. It costs you less in purchase price and it is the cheapest car in the world to maintain in operation, besides it is so simple, so easily understood that anyone can run it.
The Ford Motor Company devotes its entire efforts to the building of one model—one chassis—but different bodies; namely:
Ford Model T Touring Car, 5 passengers, Foredoor $690
Ford Model T Commercial Roadster, 3 passengers 590
Ford Model T Torpedo, 2 passengers 590
Ford Model T Town Car, 6 passengers 900
Ford Model T Delivery Car, Capacity 750 pounds merchandise 700
These prices include complete equipment, F. O. B. Detroit
No Ford cars sold unequipped
Write for our catalog and other descriptive books. Send for the series
Branches in all Principal Cities
Ford Motor Company
Branches in all Principal Cities
Detroit, Mich., U. S. A.
In answering this advertisement, say you saw it in "Ford Times."
Address all correspondence direct to the Advertiser

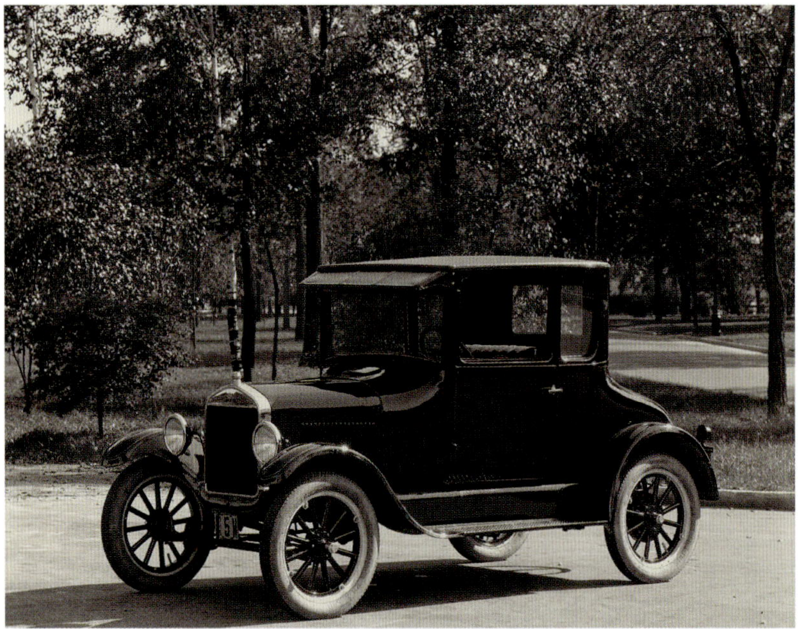

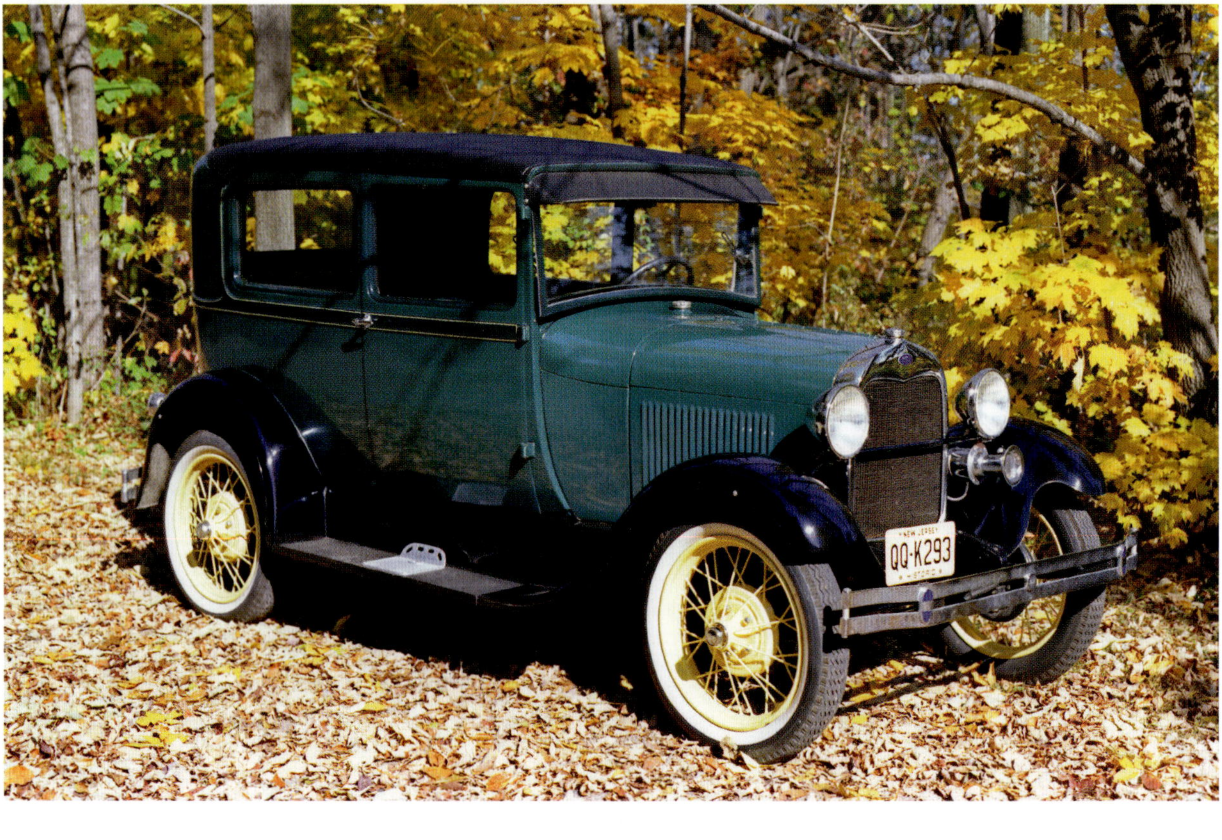

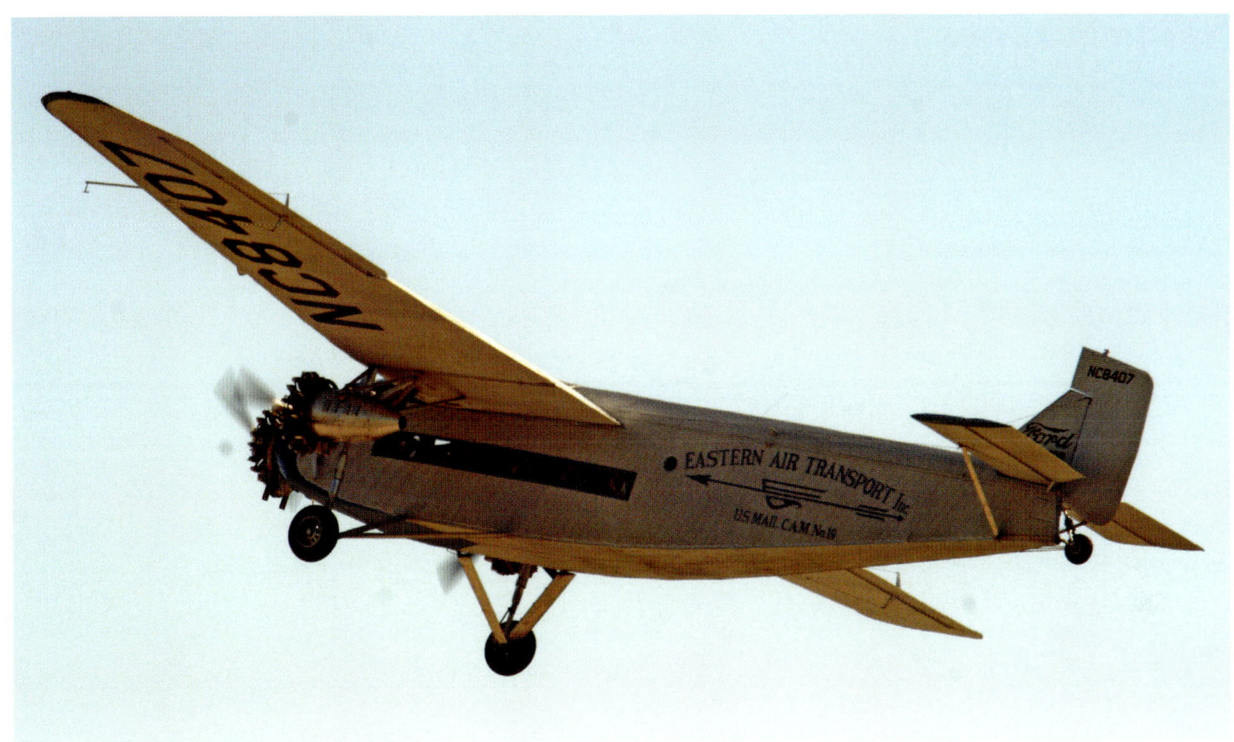

OPPOSITE ABOVE LEFT:
Ford advertisement
for Model T Torpedo, 1910

OPPOSITE ABOVE RIGHT:
Model T
1910

OPPOSITE BELOW:
Model A Tudor Sedan
1929

ABOVE:
Ford 4-AT-E Trimotor aircraft
1926

mechanical engineer Frederick Winslow Taylor had just published *The Principles of Scientific Management* (1911), which proposed applying scientific method to the management of workers based on time-and-motion studies in order to increase manufacturing through-put.

Henry Ford took Taylor's advice fully on board and began to look for ways to achieve better productivity by studying the manufacturing techniques being used at his factory. He quickly realized that the stop-start nature of his production line, which involved dragging components from one work desk to the next, was extremely inefficient. Inspired by a conveyor belt he had seen at a grain mill and also by the pulley systems used in the "disassembly" lines of slaughterhouses, Ford implemented the world's first factory moving assembly line in 1913. This revolutionary production-line system meant that the assembly time of a Model T car's chassis was reduced from twelve and a half hours in October 1913 to two hours and forty minutes by December 1913. As a result more than fifteen million Model Ts were built between 1908 and 1927, altering the lives of countless families across America and abroad. More than this, Henry Ford had revolutionized the production capability of factories and made large-scale mechanized mass-production truly viable for the first time. Within a very short time, manufacturers of every kind were adopting "Fordism", and this had a huge effect on how products were subsequently conceived and designed.

F

Naoto Fukasawa

Japanese, 1956–

The visually refined and functionally honed work of the Japanese designer Naoto Fukasawa has been hugely influential in the world of product design, especially in the look and feel of consumer electronic products. Having almost guru-like status among fellow designers, Fukasawa's designs are guided by his concept of "Without Thought" by which objects are conceived to be as user-friendly as possible, so they can be used literally without thinking. By creating designs that can be understood intuitively and that often have a pleasing tactility, Fukasawa's work is notable for its engaging purity – this is form following subconscious function, which in turn provokes a haptic communication between object and user.

Born in Yamanashi, Japan, Fukasawa studied at Tokyo's Tama Art University, graduating in 1980. He subsequently joined the design team at Seiko Epson, where he worked on the design of products exploiting micro-technology, namely wrist-wearable televisions and miniaturized printers. In 1989 he moved to San Francisco and began working for ID Two (to become IDEO in 1991). Founded by Bill Moggridge, this consultancy was at the very forefront of interaction design, with the majority of its clients being based in nearby Silicon Valley. After several years working for IDEO, Fukasawa returned to Japan and subsequently set up the firm's Tokyo office in 1996, which he directed until 2003. During his stint at IDEO, Fukasawa conducted several "Without Thought" workshops that produced some influential designs notable for their visual simplicity and functional clarity, such as his Epson printer (1998) co-designed with Sam Hecht. It was, however, his "Without Thought" CD player (1999) for Muji that was his real breakthrough product, recalling as it did the earlier essentialist designs of Dieter Rams for Braun, but in a very Japanese way.

In 2003, he established his own design practice, Naoto Fukasawa Design, as well as his own design-led brand, ±0 (Plus Minus Zero), yet continued to retain strong links with IDEO. The same year, he created his Juice Skin or Juicepeel packaging and his doughnut-shaped Humidifier, both of which reflected his genius for re-imaging the design of everyday objects. Two years later, he published *Dezain no Rinkaku* (An Outline of Design) which put forward the notion of design anonymity, arguing that as a designer one should "remove oneself" from the object. With this goal, he based his Déjà-vu chair (2006) for Herman Miller on the archetypal form of the earlier wooden Frankfurter chair from the 1930s. By combining a quintessential seating form with an ultra-modern mirror-polished aluminium frame, Fukasawa's goal was to create a design that would "entwine with people's actions and with the environment, too". Although devoid of the designer's own personality, this chair does have a strong poetic presence. It could be said that by raising the

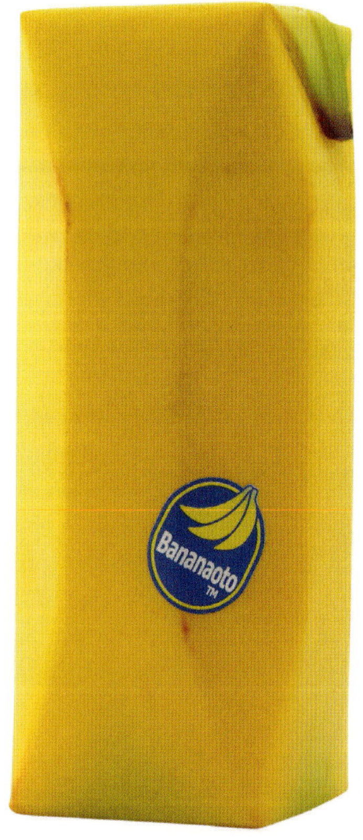

BELOW:
Juicepeel or Juice Skin
fruit-juice carton packaging concept design, 2004

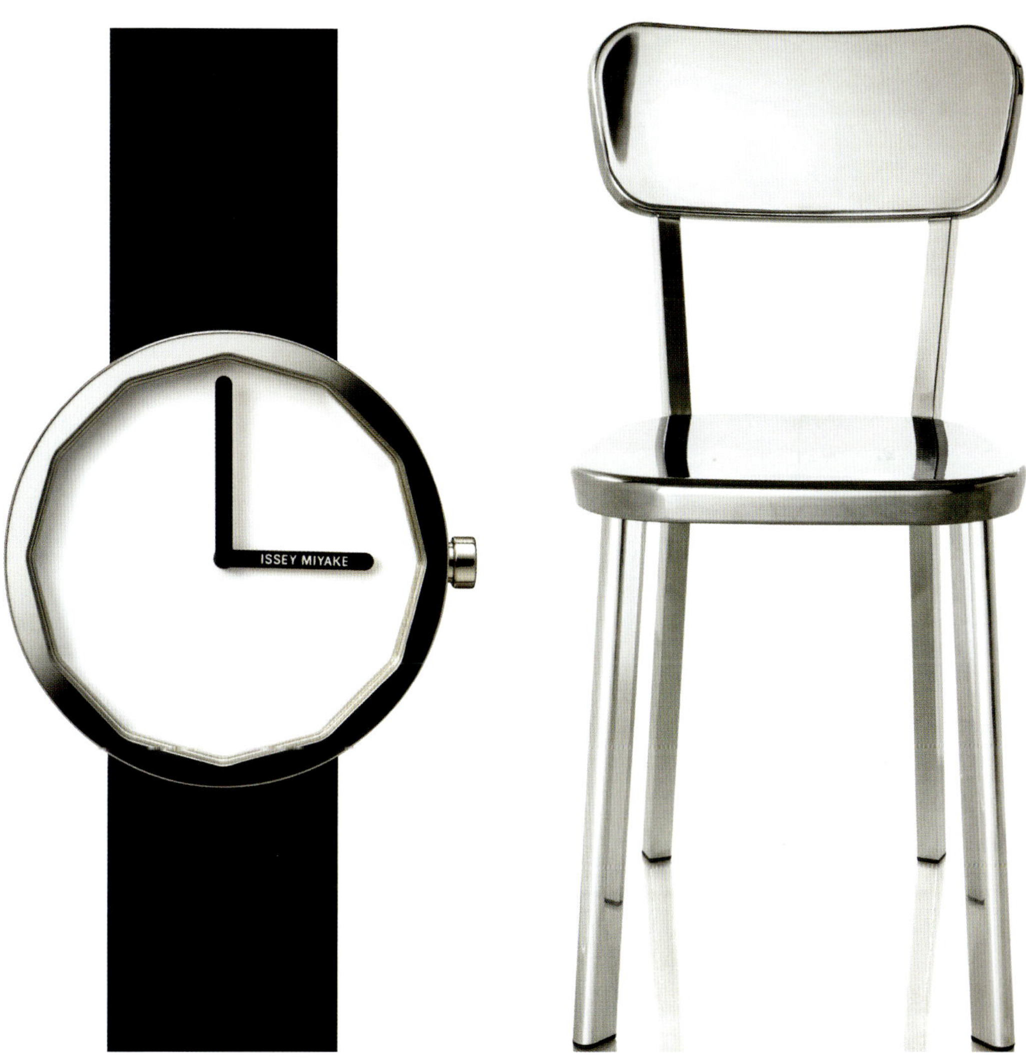

ABOVE LEFT:
Twelve wrist watch
for Issey Miyake, 2006

ABOVE RIGHT:
Déjà-vu chair
for Magis, 2006

aesthetic level and functional capabilities of designs, Fukasawa is a creator of artefacts rather than just plain products. In 2006, Fukasawa together with Jasper Morrison curated a travelling exhibition of some 200 objects, many of them anonymous everyday objects such as the paper clip, the plastic bucket, the wine glass and so forth, entitled *Super Normal: Sensations of the Ordinary*. With this collection of simple objects Fukasawa and Morrison demonstrated that often such items have a quiet modesty that in terms of design transcends normality because they are so perfectly functionally evolved. It is this super normality that Fukasawa tries to infuse into his own designs.

Antoni Gaudí

Spanish, 1852–1926

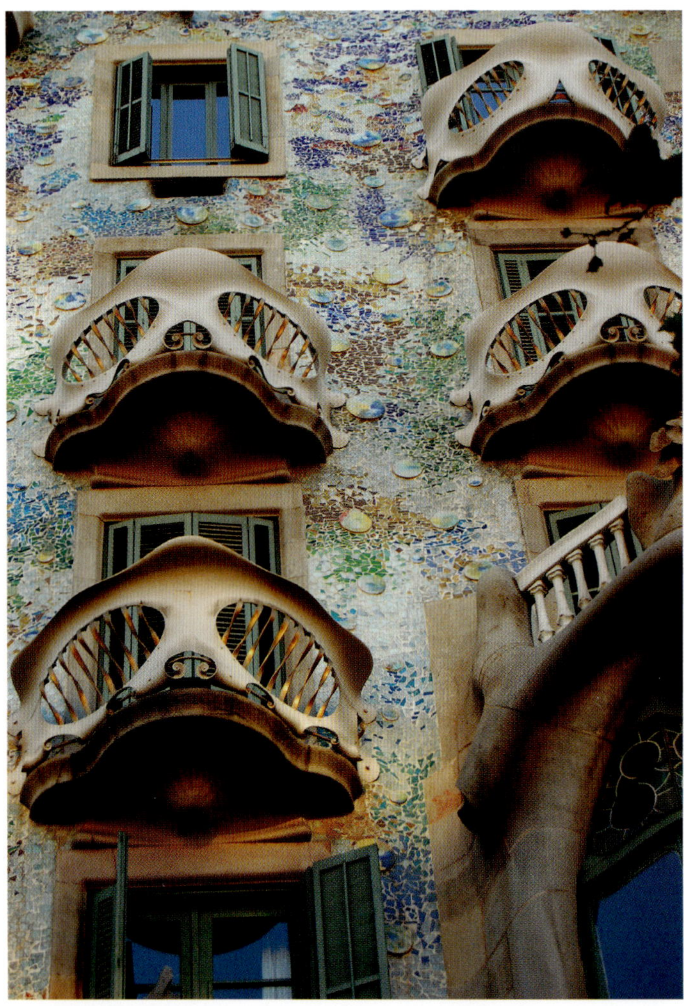

ABOVE:
Detail of the façade of the Casa Batlló
in Barcelona, 1904–06

An architectural genius, Antoni Gaudí forged a distinctive Catalan expression of the Art Nouveau or New Art style that was as sculptural as it was fantastical. A pioneer of the Spanish Modernista movement – or Modernisme as it is referred to in Catalan – Gaudí's idiosyncratic work, although borrowing references from historic styles from Moorish to Baroque, was very much a contemporary expression of its own time. His architectural projects employed progressive building technology to create extraordinary spaces that were notable for their plasticity of form and harmonious balance of materials and colours, while his furniture, often designed site-specifically, had a remarkably forward-looking sculptural quality.

Born in the Catalan city of Reus, Antoni Gaudí i Cornet was the son and grandson of coppersmith boilermakers, and as a child suffered from a rheumatic disease that meant he had to spend long periods at home resting. He used this time, however, as an opportunity to study flora and fauna, and this early understanding of the natural world would crucially inform his later work as an architect and designer. In 1869, Gaudí moved to Barcelona – the city he would come to define creatively – and subsequently studied at the Faculty of Natural Science at the University of Barcelona. Following this, he trained as an architect at the recently established Escuela Provincial de Arquitectura (Provincial School of Architecture), graduating in 1877. The following year he set up his own architecture practice and crucially met the wealthy industrialist Eusebi Güell, who would become his most important and loyal patron.

Also in 1878, Gaudí received his first public commission, to design electrified street lighting for the Passeig de Mar in Barcelona, and created a design for a workers' co-operative settlement in Mataró. From 1882, he collaborated with the architect Joan Martorell, who worked in the Spanish Gothic Revival style, which was strongly associated with Catalan cultural autonomy. Proud of his Catalonian cultural roots, Gaudí also took pilgrimages to

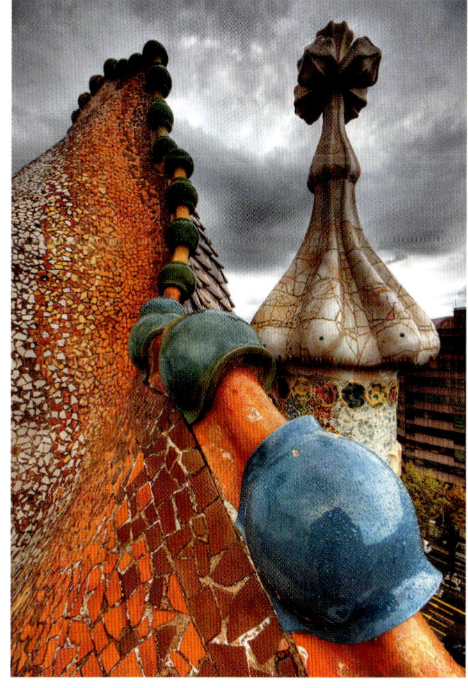

various historical sites in the region, visiting Gothic cathedrals as well as Moorish buildings, which would provide rich decorative and structural inspiration for his own work.

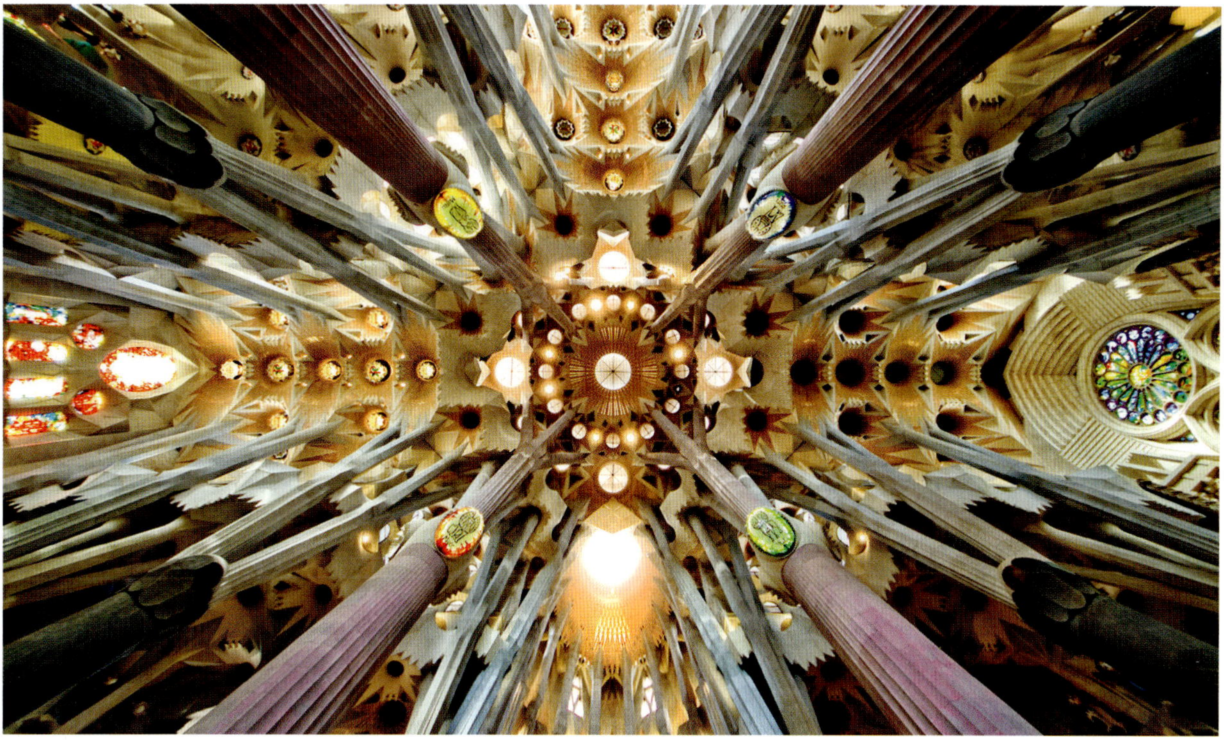

Gaudí's architecture, from the soaring Sagrada Família church to the Park Güell garden complex, borrowed motifs from the Gothic and Moorish styles and then transformed them into wildly exotic melting forms. Defying convention, he used broken tiles as well as old cups and saucers to face the parapet of Park Güell, giving a colourful scale-like mosaic effect that was unlike anything that had ever been produced before. He later used the same curious mix of materials for the four soaring pinnacles of his Sagrada Família, which looks like a fanciful fairytale castle made out of sand. More than any other Spanish designer's work, Gaudí's buildings and designs – such as his armchair with a heart-shaped back designed for the Casa Calvert (1900) – possessed an emotionally charged sense of mystical *duende* and epitomized the sheer theatrical bravado of Spanish Art Nouveau. Today, seven of Gaudí's buildings are on UNESCO's World Heritage List, a fitting tribute to his remarkable contribution to the development of modern architecture and design, not only regionally but also nationally and internationally.

TOP:
Detail of nave ceiling of the Sagrada Família church
in Barcelona, designed by Antoni Gaudí between 1883 and 1926

ABOVE:
Detail of the roof of the Casa Batlló
in Barcelona, 1904–06

Milton Glaser

American, 1929–

As both a graphic designer and an illustrator, Milton Glaser consistently created visually engaging work infused with bold colour and quirky humour. As he once noted, "To design is to communicate clearly by whatever means you can control or master," and certainly his famous I ♥ NY logo (1976–77) used to promote tourism in New York City is a masterful lesson in the communicative power of universal graphic symbols.

Having initially trained at the High School of Music & Art in Manhattan, Glaser went on to study at the well-regarded Cooper Union art school in New York, graduating in 1951. He was subsequently awarded a Fulbright Scholarship, which enabled him to study at the Accademia di Belle Arti e Liceo Artistico (Academy of Fine Arts and Art School) in Bologna, Italy, under the still-life painter Giorgio Morandi. On his return to New York in 1954, Glaser founded Push Pin Studios with Seymour Chwast and Edward Sorel, soon to be joined by Reynold Ruffins.

In 1957 the studio published its first *Push Pin Graphic* magazine that helped to disseminate its freer approach to graphic design, which countered the then-predominant Modernist Swiss School style of graphics. Push Pin's approach was more pictorial and often incorporated quirky perspectives, flattened planes, bright colours, as well as the sampling of previous typographic styles and referencing of art historical subjects.

During the 1960s, inspired by psychedelic art, Glaser created numerous poster designs, notably Dylan (1967), Rainbow Palette (1966) and From Poppy with Love (1969), which brought him widespread recognition – to such an extent that he was asked to create a cover depicting the economist Milton Friedman for *Time* magazine in 1969. Around this time, he founded *New York* magazine with Clay Felker, which went on to become a blueprint for later city magazines. The playful quality of his graphics led Glaser to be commissioned to illustrate several children's books and to design the Childcraft toyshop in New York in 1970 and the Sesame Place Play Park in 1981–83. Such was the international fame of his work and that of his Push Pin colleagues that a major exhibition entitled *The Push Pin Style* was staged at the Louvre's Musée des Arts Decoratifs in Paris in 1970 with an accompanying catalogue published by *Communication Arts* magazine.

In 1974, he founded Milton Glaser Inc and two years later devised the I ♥ New York logo. During the 1970s, apart from redesigning a number of magazines including *Paris Match*, *Village Voice* and *Esquire*, he also created numerous corporate identities. Throughout the 1980s and 1990s, Glaser continued to work on a variety of projects, and several exhibitions of his work were held that helped cement his reputation as one of the great masters of twentieth-century graphic design who, believing strongly in a hands-on creative approach, once remarked "computers are to design as microwaves are to cooking".

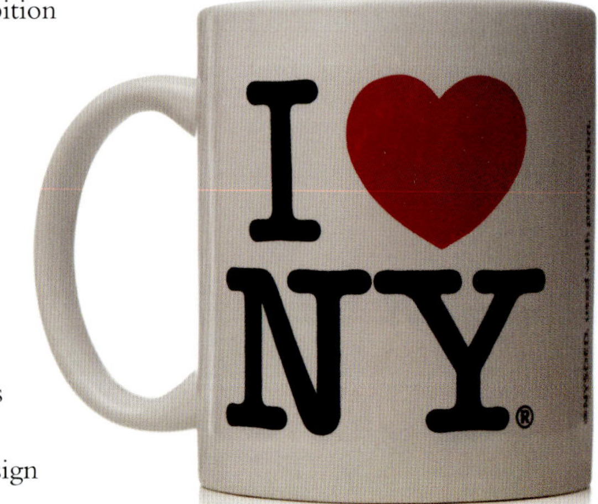

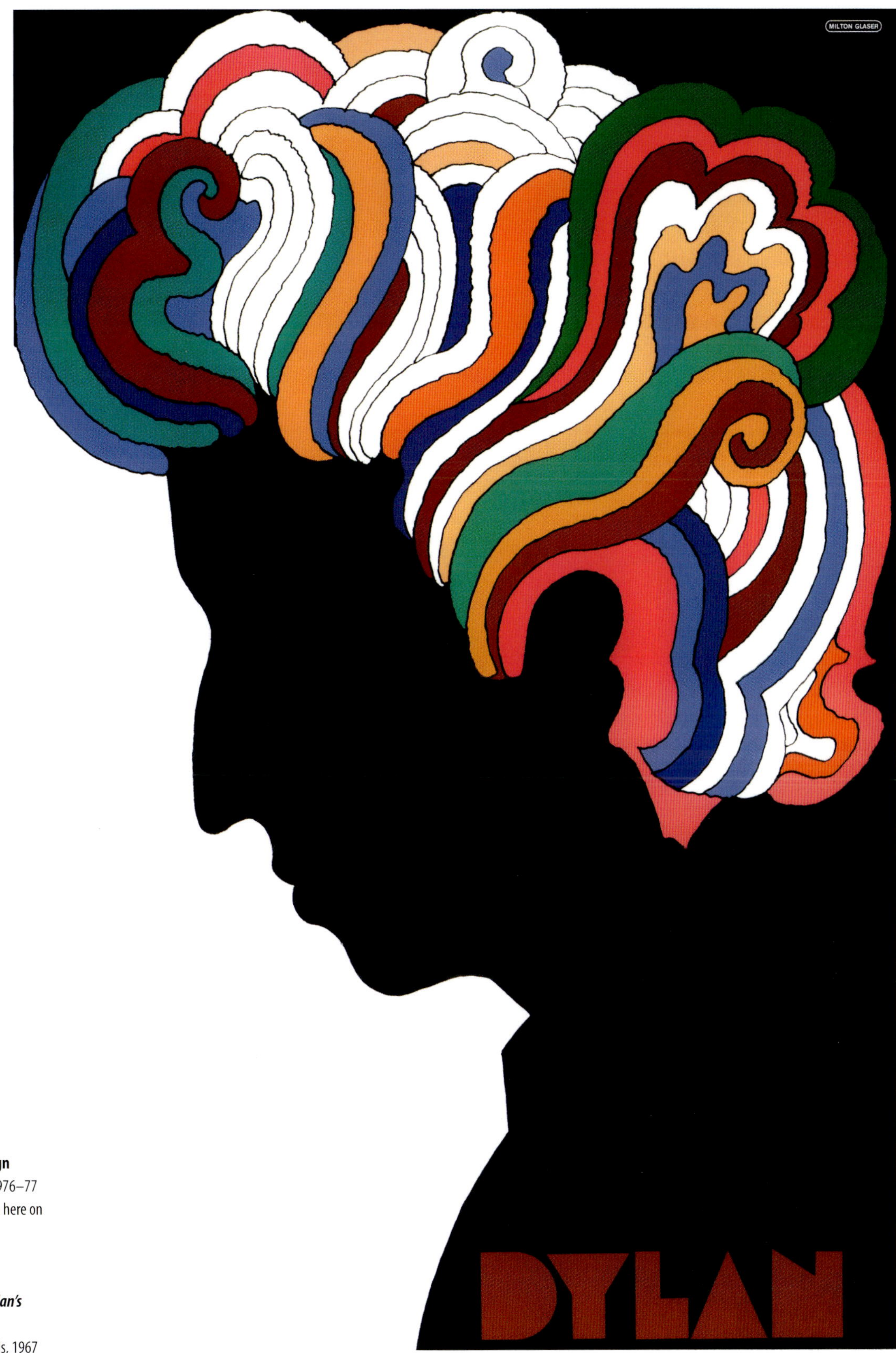

OPPOSITE:
I Love NY campaign
for New York City, 1976–77
– iconic logo shown here on a mug

RIGHT:
Poster for *Bob Dylan's Greatest Hits*
for Columbia Records, 1967

Kenneth Grange

British, 1929–

The leading British industrial designer Sir Kenneth Grange has noted that, for him, "the starting point of a design is the belief that I can design something better" – a sentiment shared by most designers. Grange, however, has an impressive track record of updating different product typologies, so that his new designs are often clearly marked improvements on what has gone before. From Kodak cameras and Kenwood food mixers to Anglepoise lights and London taxis, Grange has created visually understated yet exceptionally innovative designs that have helped shape modern Britain.

Born in the East End of London, Grange inherited an appreciation of design and manufacturing from his mother, who worked in a spring factory and was "completely in love with manufacturing". He later won a scholarship to study drawing and lettering at Willesden School of Arts and Crafts, and after the completion of his studies worked in various architects' offices, including those of Arcon, Bronek Katz and Reginald Vaughan, Gordon and Ursula Bowyer, and eventually Jack Howe in 1952. At these different architectural practices, all of which actively participated in the 1951 *Festival of Britain*, Grange absorbed the new post-war spirit of optimism that went hand-in-hand with the belief that Modern design could build a better society.

While working for Jack Howe, he designed light fittings and interior balustrades, and was encouraged to take on freelance work, which included creating exhibition stands for Bakelite Ltd and the Atomic Energy Authority. The latter was so impressed with Grange's work that

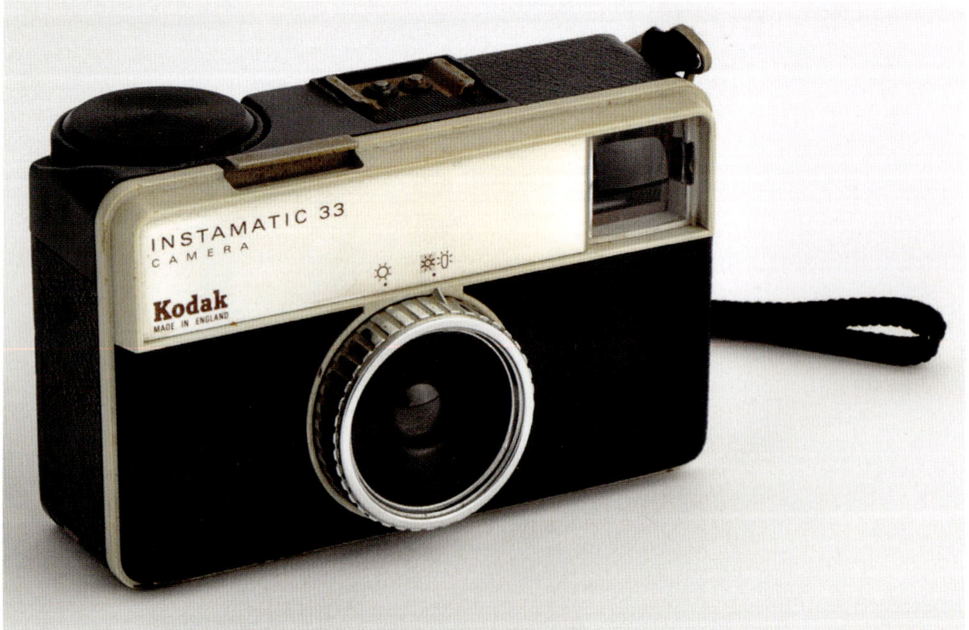

LEFT:
Instamatic 33 camera
for Kodak, 1968

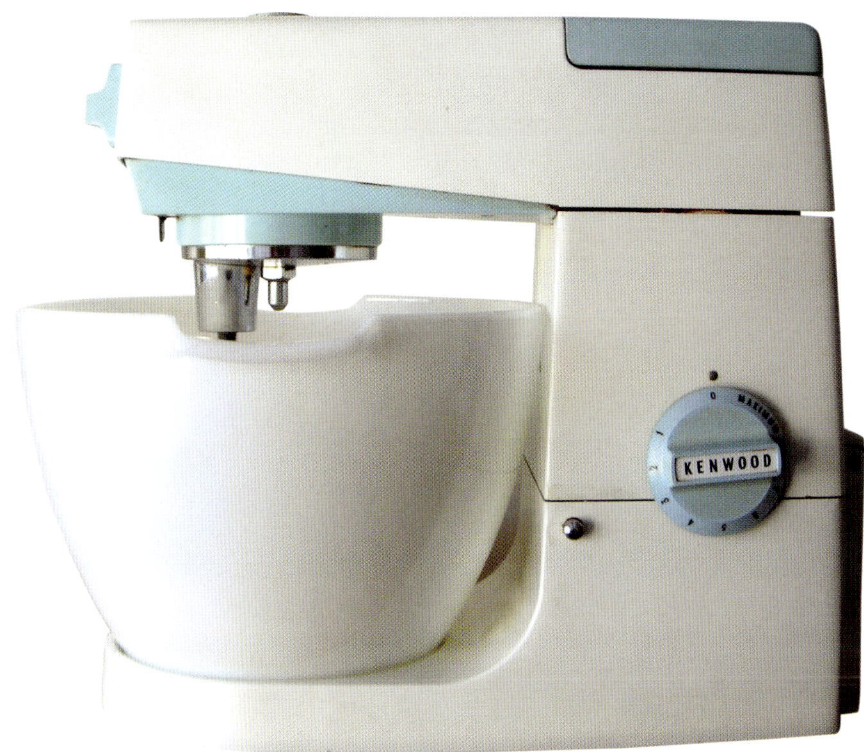

LEFT:
A701A Chef food mixer
for Kenwood, 1960

it asked him to create a much larger display for an exhibition in Geneva. This project turned into "a big, big job" and Grange had to hire three full time assistants which was how his design consultancy accidentally came into being.

Officially established in 1956, his design office received one of its first commissions from Jack Howe, who asked Grange to design the interior of the Kodak pavilion at *Expo 58*, the 1958 Brussels World's Fair. As Grange recalls, "I was arranging the products on the stand and someone overheard me say, 'It's a shame these are so ugly; I could make this [display] really good if they weren't.' The next day, the phone rang. It was the head of development at Kodak, and he said, 'I understand you're going to design a camera for us.'" The resulting Brownie 44A by Grange had both a well-conceived layout and a clean Modern aesthetic, which helped it win a Design Centre Award in 1960. That same year, Grange designed the A701A Chef food mixer (1960) for Kenwood. For this design, Grange essentially took the company's existing food mixer and devised a sleeker plastic and enamelled metal housing for it, replacing the curves of the earlier model with more angular lines. Crucially, the dynamic styling of Grange's A701A mixer with its gleaming surfaces distinguished it from other domestic appliances on the market, making it a must-have product for households across Britain.

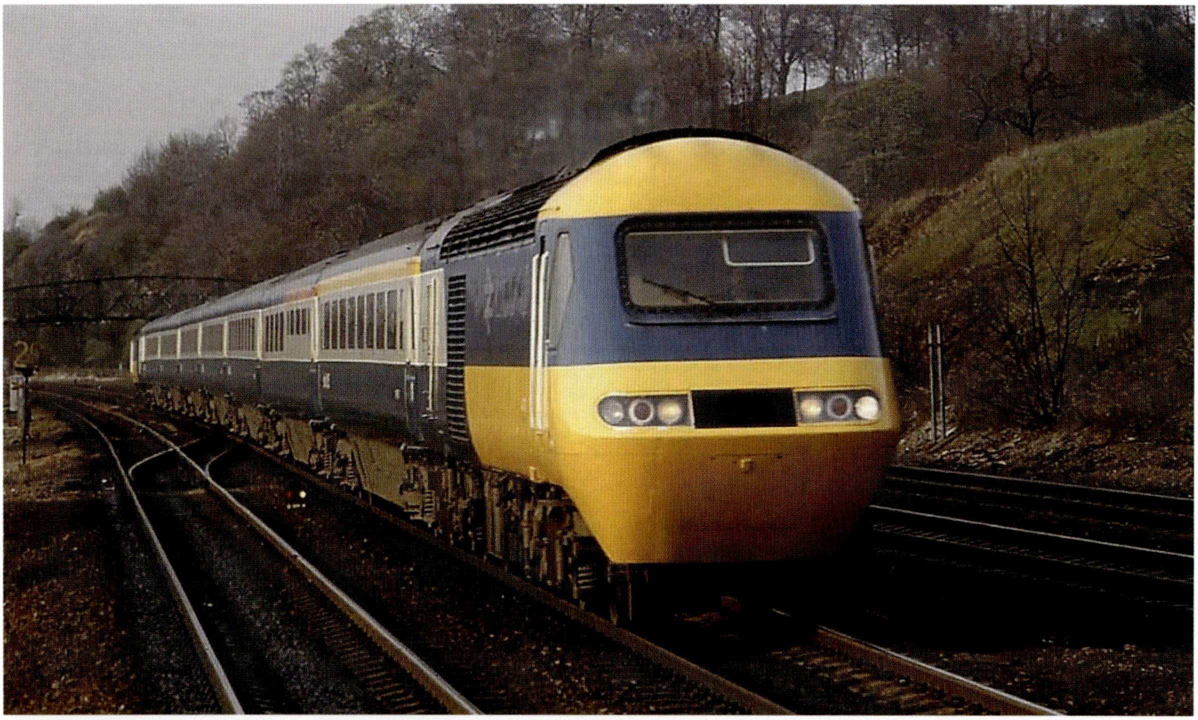

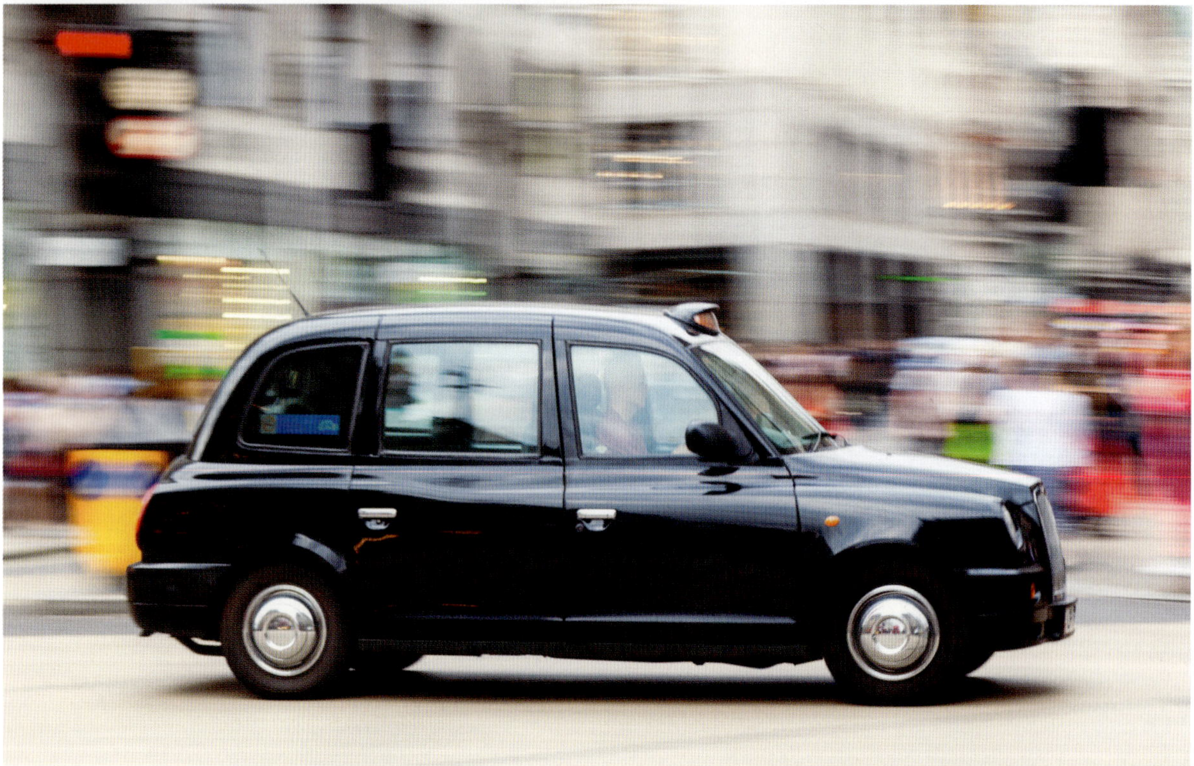

Grange went on to design numerous other products for Kenwood over the coming decades. In 1972, he famously co-founded a multidisciplinary design consultancy with Theo Crosby, Alan Fletcher, Mervyn Kurlansky and Colin Forbes, known as Pentagram, with Grange concentrating on the firm's many industrial and product design commissions, most notably: the external body of British Rail's 125 InterCity high-speed train (1971–76), the Kodak Pocket Instamatic camera (1975), the Parker 25 range of pens (1979), the Protector wet razor for Wilkinson Sword (1992) and the TX1 re-styled classic London black cab for LTI (1997). Later Grange created various lighting designs for Anglepoise Ltd, including the Type 75 (2004), which perfectly encapsulates the central attributes of classic British design – precision engineering twinned with an understated beauty, born of purposeful form following practical function.

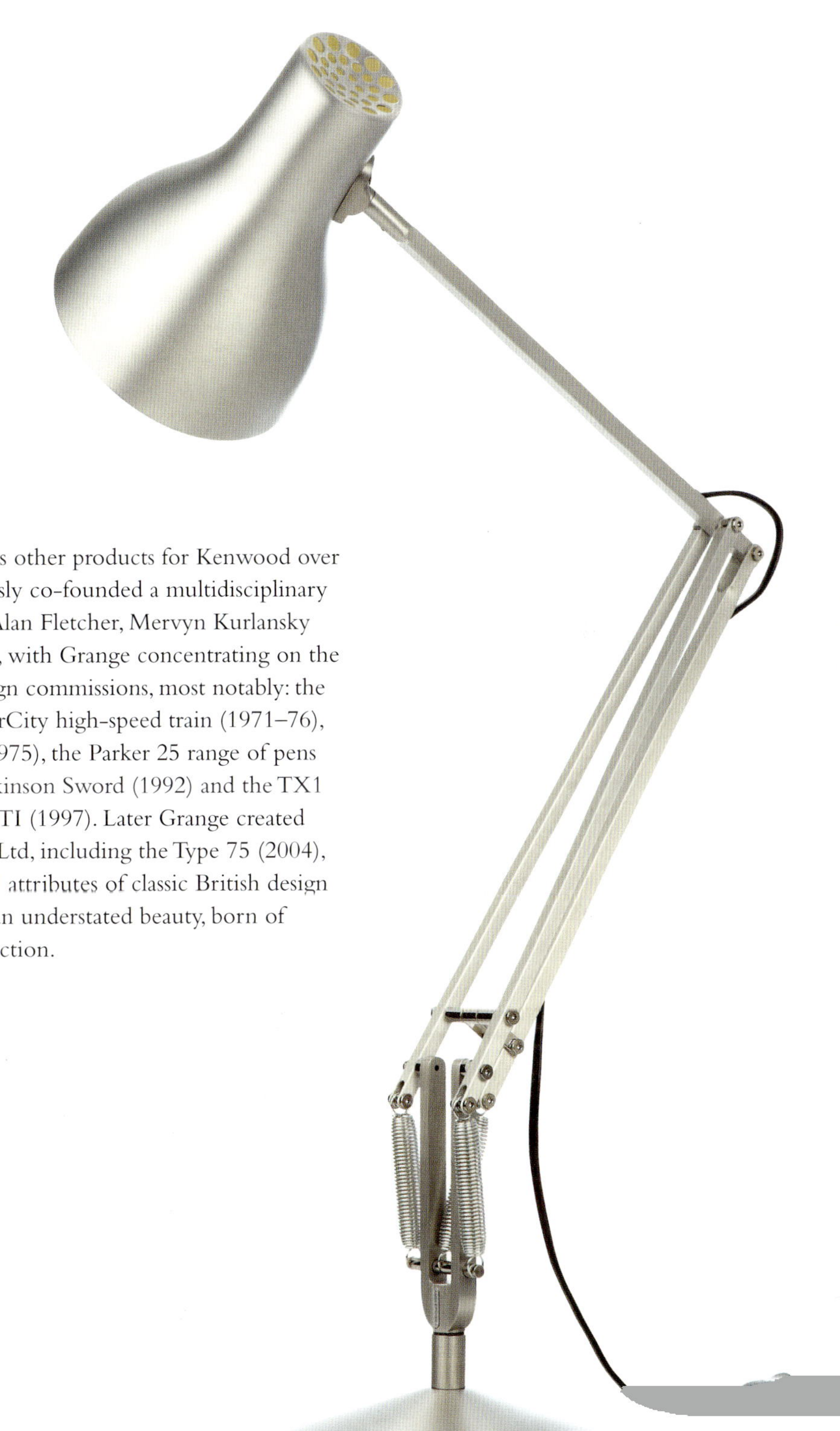

OPPOSITE TOP:
InterCity 125 train
for British Rail, 1971–76

OPPOSITE BOTTOM:
TX1 London taxi
for LTI, 1997

RIGHT:
Type 75 Anglepoise light
for Anglepoise, 2004

Michael Graves

American, 1934–2015

Michael Graves did not invent Post-Modern architecture on his own, but he was certainly the most visible and perhaps the most accomplished exponent of this movement as it swept the world in the 1980s. His distinctive and monumental Portland Government Building (1982) and the Humana skyscraper in Louisville (1985) were the exemplars of the style. Graves also received widespread recognition as the creator of Post-Modern "designer" homewares, with his kettle adorned with a bird-shaped whistle (1985) becoming Alessi's best-selling product for more than a decade. But more than this, he was also an influential educator, who viewed design and architecture as a conduit for creative invention, much like art or poetry, rather than as a means through which to instigate social change. He understood the power of symbolism when used in a building or an object, and the related human need for emotional connection.

Born in Indianapolis, Indiana, Graves initially studied architecture at the University of Cincinnati and then at Harvard University Graduate School of Design, graduating in 1959. The following year he won the Rome Prize, which enabled him to study for two years at the American Academy in Rome. This Italian period had a strong formative influence and undoubtedly gave rise to his adoption of Classical motifs within his design of buildings. Returning to the United States in 1962, he began teaching architecture at Princeton University – in fact he would teach there for the next thirty-nine years, eventually becoming the college's Robert Schirmer Professor of Architecture. Graves also established his own practice in Princeton, opening a second office in New York City. During this early part of his career, he was a member of the so-called "New York Five" along with Peter Eisenman, Charles Gwathmey, John Hejduk and Richard Meier – a group of young architects who espoused a purist form of Modernism that harked back to the work of Le Corbusier.

BELOW:
9093 kettle
for Alessi, 1985

Throughout the 1970s Graves designed a series of houses that were unequivocally Modernist in spirit, but in the early 1980s his buildings became emphatically Post-Modern. They were inspired by the reaction against the abstraction of commercial Modernism and a search for architecture that offered memories of past traditions, meaning and ornament. Graves reacted against his Harvard teachers, Gropius and Breuer. It was initially a very successful strategy, and he subsequently received many commissions for his distinctive totemic buildings.

Graves was a brilliant draughtsman, with an intuitive colour sense that seemed to coarsen with a growing

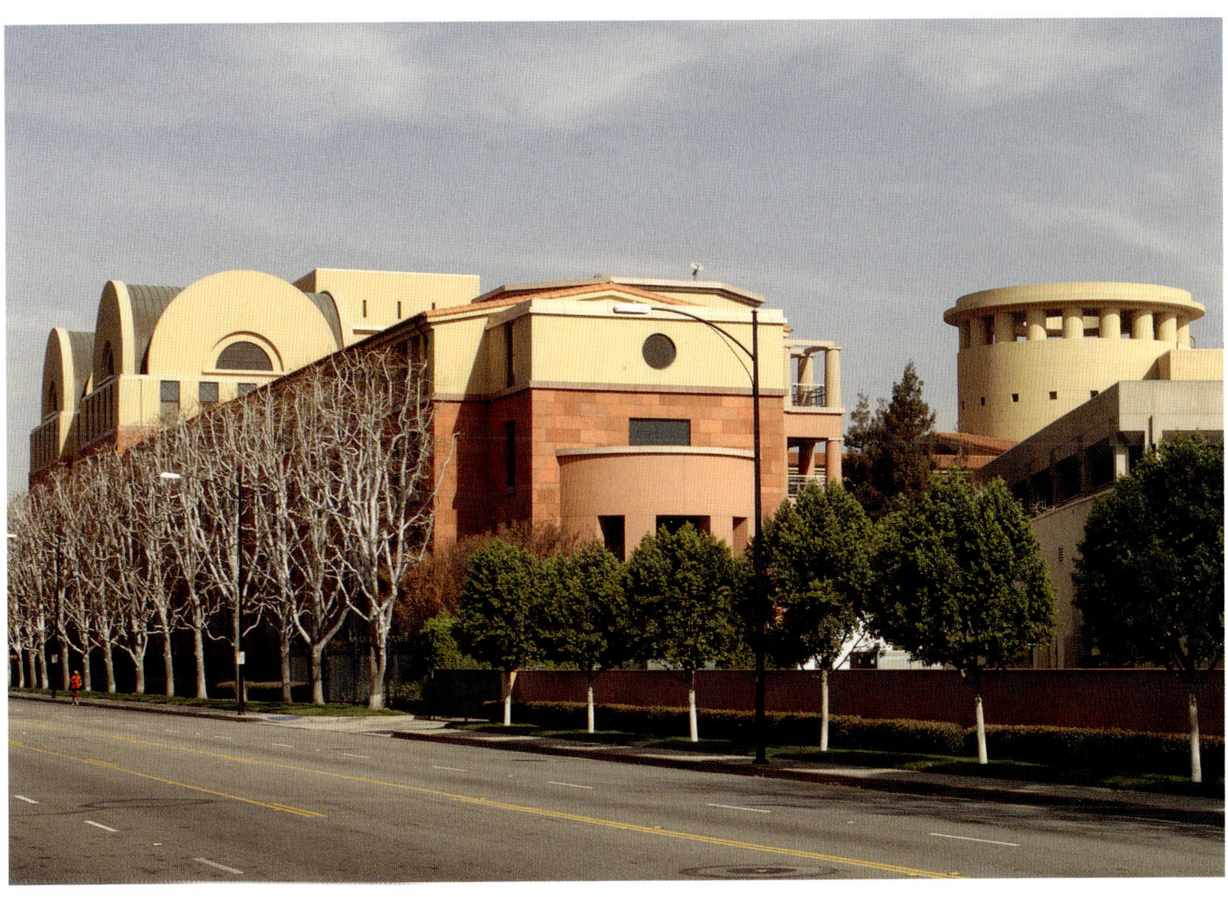

ABOVE:
Team Disney – Michael D. Eisner Building
Burbank, California, 1986–91

workload. From deftly deploying the Classical language of architecture, his commissions for the Disney Corporation turned into crude cartoons. One façade was based on the facetious pun of a giant order of dwarves. Graves designed Disney's corporate headquarters in Burbank, California, a hotel in Disneyland, Paris, and Walt Disney World's Swan and Dolphin Hotels in Florida. As Michael Eisner, the former president of the Disney Corporation, once noted, "Michael Graves is an architect for whom design has no boundaries. There is no such thing as an insignificant object," and certainly Graves lavished symbolic detailing on all his buildings, making each one unique in character and thereby giving them a strong sense of place.

He also worked in the fields of furniture and product design, famously creating his Art Deco-style Plaza dressing table and stool for Memphis (1981), as well as numerous homewares for Alessi and Target, and an assortment of pens, ties and accessories for ACME. After becoming wheelchair-bound in 2003 due to an acute viral infection that caused waist-down paralysis, Graves spent the remaining twelve years of his life working as a passionate advocate for the disabled. To this day his office is guided by his strong belief in the transformative effect of human-centric design.

Eileen Gray

Irish/active France, 1878–1976

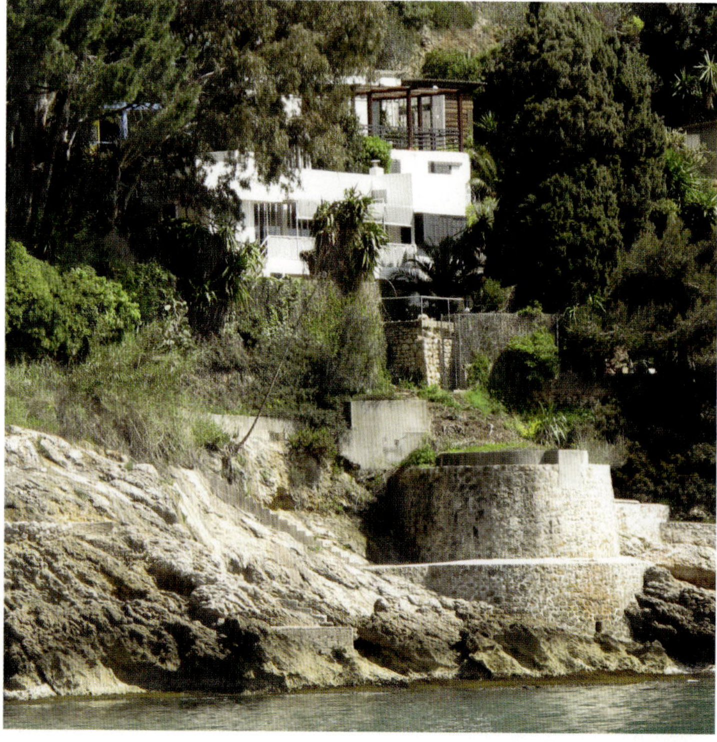

ABOVE:
E-1027 villa
Roquebrune-Cap-Martin, 1926–29

An innovative furniture designer and progressive architect, Eileen Gray worked initially with Japanese lacquer, later moving on from Art Deco to build at least one Modernist masterpiece. Born Kathleen Eileen Moray Smith, she was the daughter of Scottish painter James McLaren Smith and Eveleen Pounden who became the nineteenth Baroness Gray and whose name her family adopted when she inherited the title. Eileen Gray enrolled in the painting course at the Slade School of Art in London in 1897 and two years later travelled with her mother to Paris in order to visit the 1900 *Exposition Universelle*. She fell in love with the city and eventually moved there in 1902. She continued her painting studies, taking classes at the Académie Colarossi and the Académie Julian. In 1905, she returned to London to care for her ailing mother and began learning lacquering techniques from an art restorer based in Soho.

The following year she returned to Paris and met the Japanese lacquer master craftsman Seizo Sugawara. Gray subsequently perfected her technical skills with Sugawara, becoming one of the first Western practitioners of Japanese lacquering, which involved the use of toxic materials and laborious techniques. In 1907 she moved into an apartment on rue Bonaparte, which she furnished with her own designs. In 1910, she and Sugawara established a studio in rue Guénégaud and over the next twenty years they collaborated on the creation of numerous well-known designs, such as the famous Serpent or Dragon armchair (1917–19), later owned by Yves St Laurent. She exhibited her lacquer designs for the first time in 1913 at the *Salon des Artistes Décorateurs* and received her first important commission from the couturier Jacques Doucet. Gray was also commissioned to redecorate and furnish an apartment in rue de Lota by Mme Mathieu Lévy, also known as Suzanne Talbot (1919–22). This was her first real commission for an interior, and she pulled it off with characteristic panache. It was for this apartment that she designed the Lota sofa and developed her ingenious "block" screens, epitomizing the East-meets-West sensibility of her version of the Art Deco style.

In 1922 Gray opened a showroom, the Galerie Jean Desert, a name chosen to suggest a non-existent male proprietor, on the rue du Faubourg Saint-Honoré. The same year, she took part in a group exhibition in Amsterdam, which brought her work to the attention of the Dutch architect Jan Wils, a founder member of the De Stijl group. The following year Gray exhibited her Bedroom-Boudoir for Monte Carlo at the *Salon des Artistes Décorateurs*, reflecting the influence of the Dutch avant-garde with her use of bold geometry. That year she also exhibited her "block" screens at the *Salone d'Automne*, alongside Le Corbusier and Robert Mallet-Stevens, whose pioneering Modern designs inspired her own forward-looking ideas. Between 1926 and 1929, Gray oversaw the construction of her remarkable E-1027 house at Roquebrune-Cap-Martin in the south of France, a highly original architectural masterpiece designed with some input from the Romanian architect and critic Jean Badovici.

As well as the Lota sofa, Gray designed a sequence of furniture pieces, such as the Bibendum club armchair (1926) in tubular steel and leather upholstery, mostly made in very small quantities. Gray's later furniture was distinguished by a fascination with mechanisms, notably the E1027 adjustable table and satellite wall mirror (1927). In 1937, at the invitation of Le Corbusier, she exhibited an ambitious unbuilt scheme for a holiday complex complete with a restaurant and theatre within his Pavillon des Temps Nouveaux at the *Exposition Internationale des Arts et Techniques dans la Vie Moderne* in Paris. Badovici later took over the E-1027 house and allowed Le Corbusier, who built himself a hut on an adjacent site, to paint a series of intrusive murals over Gray's chaste white walls. Gray designed the Tempe à Pailla, a second house for her own use, close by on the outskirts of Menton. She subsequently retreated into retirement and relative obscurity until collectors of Art Deco rediscovered her in the 1970s. Her reputation has grown ever since.

BELOW:
Interior of the E-1027 villa
in Roquebrune, 1926–29

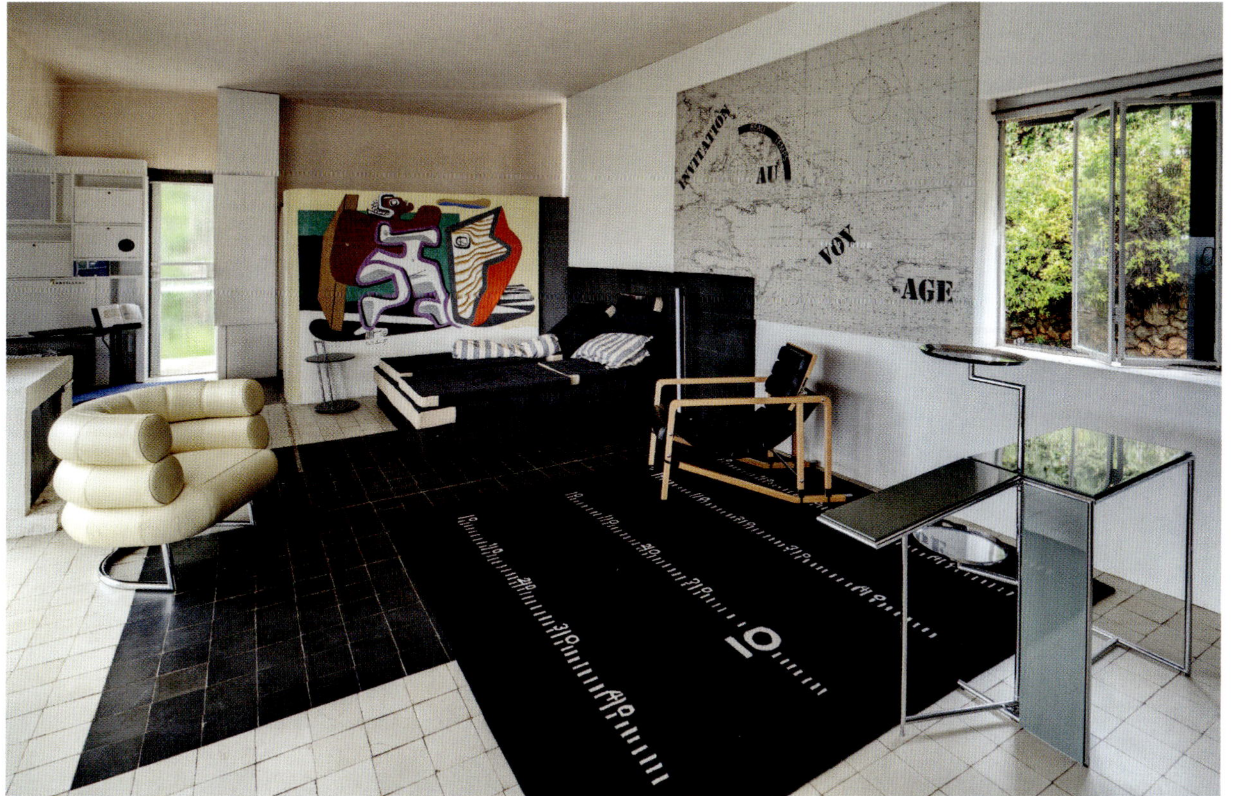

Konstantin Grcic

German, 1965–

The German designer Konstanin Grcic describes his approach to design as "defining function in human terms" and consequently he has developed a very distinctive design vocabulary based on a rigorous analytic method but gently humanized with a subtle sense of humour. His success as a designer ultimately lies in his understanding of materials and manufacturing processes, which can be attributed to his craft background.

Grcic initially trained as a cabinet-maker in Germany, before training at John Makepeace's Parnham College – a school for wood craftsmanship based in Dorset, England. He then studied furniture design at the Royal College of Art, London – and for his final project there, created a slab-like wooden chair (1990) that was beautifully executed and exquisitely proportioned. After graduating, he worked in Jasper Morrison's design office in London for a year before returning to Munich and setting up his own practice in 1991. The following year he took part in Cappellini's Progetto Ogetto project curated by Jasper Morrison and James Irvine, which was testament to the high regard in which his design peers held him.

His major break, however, came in 1994 when he began designing for the German homewares manufacturer Authentics and included the 2 Hands laundry basket (1996) and H20 bucket (1997). At the time plastics were enjoying a huge revival of popularity, and Grcic's designs, which were contemporary re-interpretations of archetypal forms, were highly successful, both commercially and critically. These were followed by the Mayday portable light (1999) for Flos, winner of a Compasso d'Oro award in 2001, which incorporated a carrying handle and a large hook so it could be easily hung wherever illumination was needed. Similarly iconoclastic was his extensive Chair_One range (2004) for Magis, employing a universal seating section constructed of cast aluminium that was shaped from flat geometric planes, rather like a football.

BELOW:
ALLSTAR office chairs
for Vitra, 2014

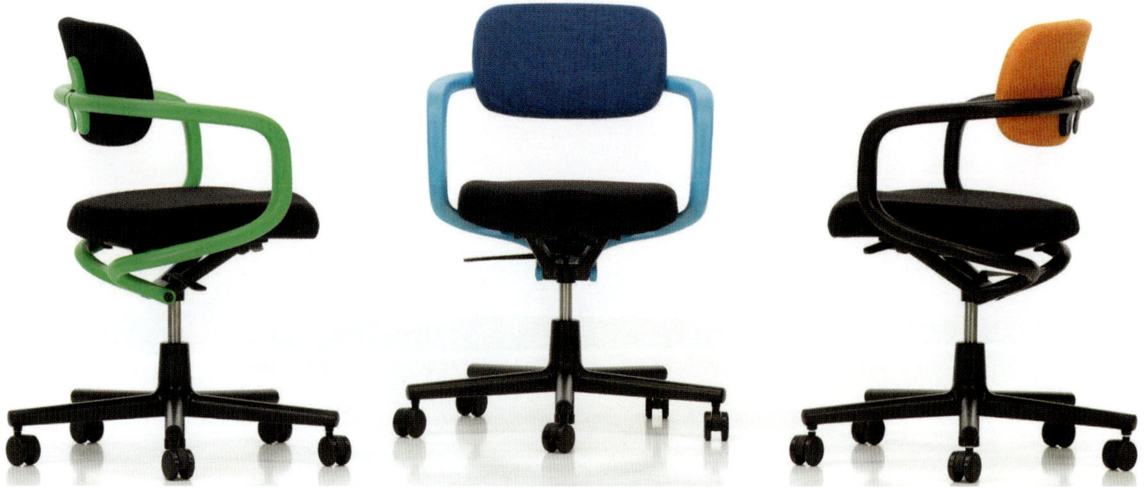

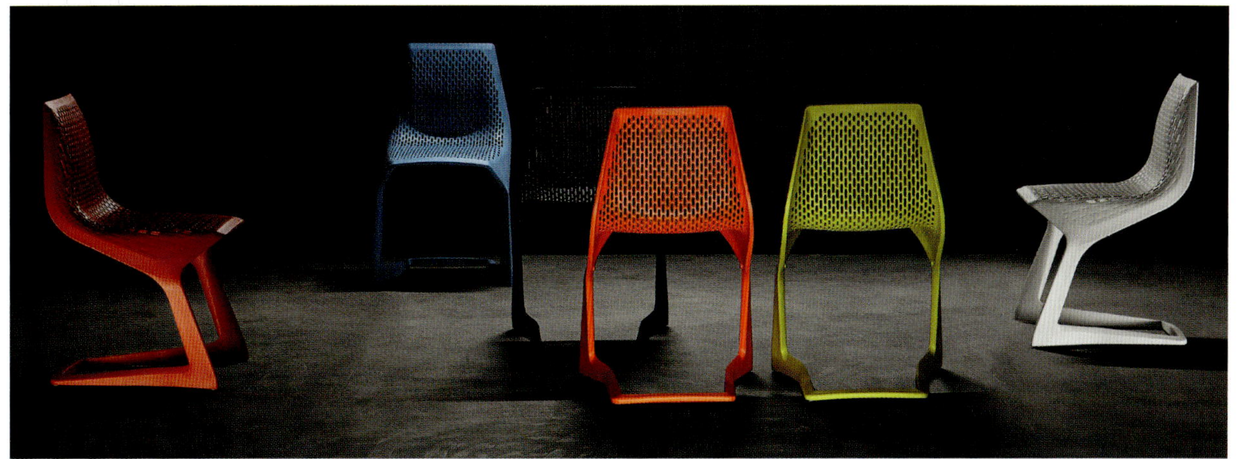

This edgy design came with various base options, and despite its hard-edged "stealth-bomber aesthetic" was actually quite comfortable. His monobloc Miura barstool (2005) for Plank had a similarly faceted design, but as Grcic explains, "its shape was conceived by working in a much more sculptural manner" with all its complex surfaces designed entirely by computer.

In late 2006, BASF commissioned Grcic to come up with a new application or product using one of its newly developed plastic resins, Ultradur® High Speed, a form of polybutylene terephthalate (PBT) with a high flow rate and an impressive strength-to-weight ratio. Working closely with engineers and technicians at BASF and Plank (the manufacturer of his Miura bar stool), Grcic spent several months refining a design for a new stacking chair – research and development time that proved wholly justified, with the resulting product constituting a significant benchmark in both plastics-moulding technology and furniture design. When the fully recyclable MYTO cantilevered monobloc chair was eventually presented for the first time in 2007 at the plastics industry's largest trade exhibition, the *K 2007* fair in Düsseldorf, it caused a complete sensation. The main concept behind the chair was a supporting frame that seamlessly dissolved into a mesh-like perforated seat section, and it earned the design a Compasso d'Oro in 2011, the design world's highest accolade.

Today, Grcic continues to create research-led furniture, lighting, architectural fittings, consumer products and installations that have a strong underlying functional logic as well as a pared-down aesthetic refinement, which ultimately reflects Grcic's desire for simplicity and exceptional functional utility.

ABOVE:
MYTO stacking chair
for Plank Collection, 2006–08

BELOW:
Chair_One concrete-based chairs
for Magis, 2004

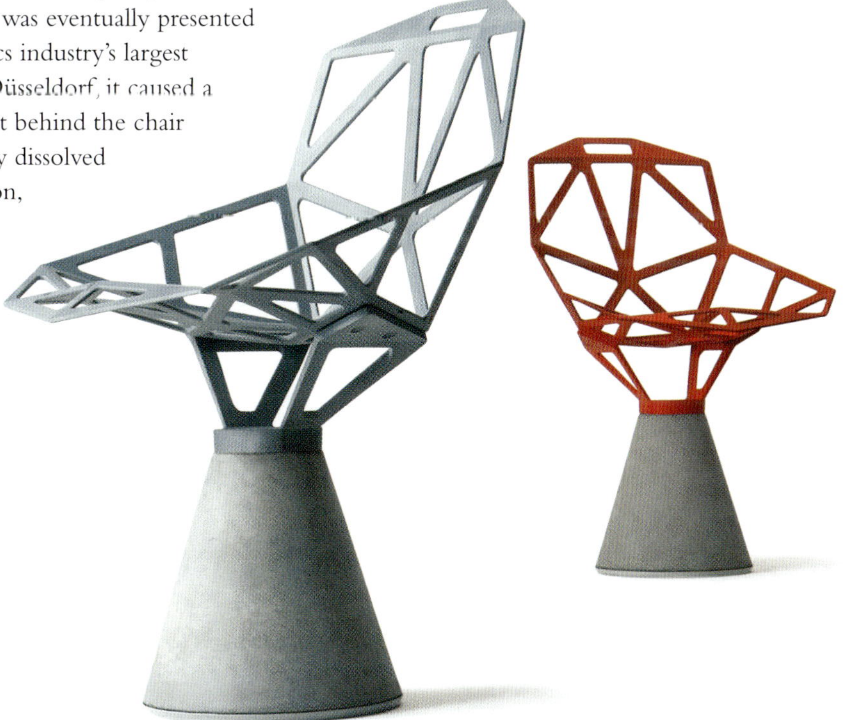

April Greiman

American, 1948–

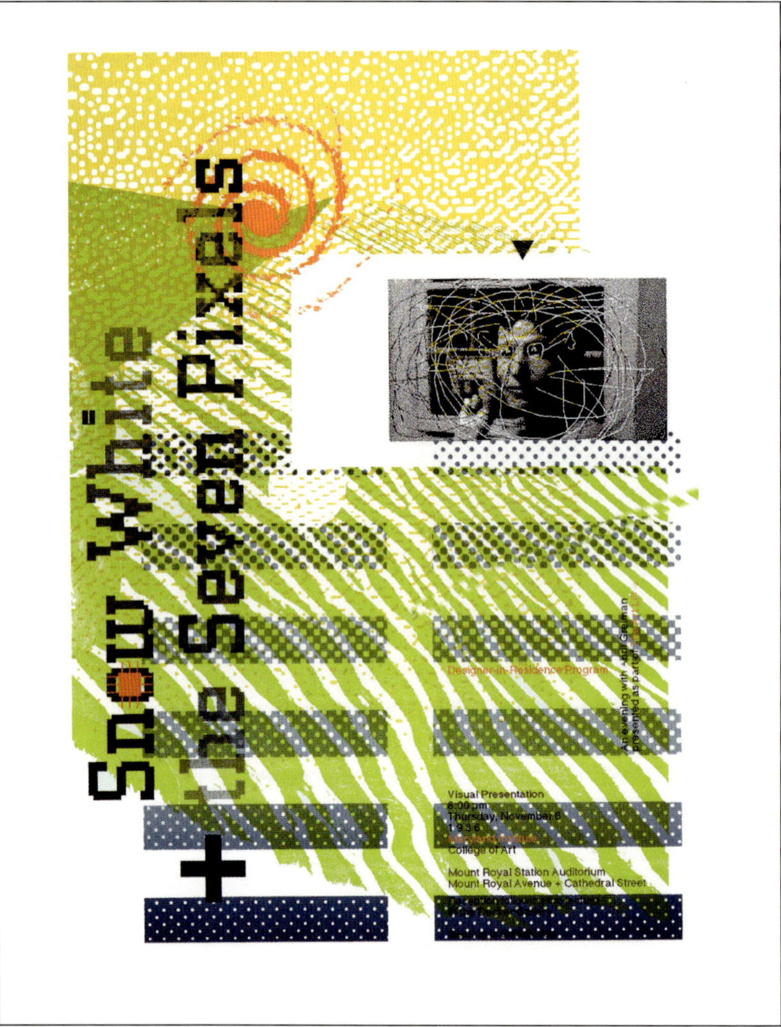

ABOVE:
Snow White + the Seven Pixels poster
for the Maryland Institute College of Art, 1986

April Greiman was among the first graphic designers to fully explore and experiment with the creative potential offered by emerging digital technologies in the early 1980s. Through her visually intriguing work she went on to help define what eventually became known as the California New Wave – a brand of Post-Modern graphics that was highly avant-garde for its day. Since then, she has over the last thirty years continued to work on various projects using a hybrid-based approach that attempts to fuse the visual arts with digital technology in order to produce thought-provoking and sensorially stimulating work.

Greiman initially studied graphic design and ceramics at the Kansas City Art Institute from 1966 to 1970. Following this, she trained at the Allgemeine Kunstgewerbeschule (General School of Arts and Crafts) in Basel, Switzerland, which was internationally renowned for its postgraduate graphic design programme that offered an intensive study of design principles as well as a broad overview of different techniques and processes. While there, Greiman studied under two of the greatest proponents of "new" Swiss graphic design and typography – Armin Hoffmann, who introduced a more expressive quality to Swiss School graphic design, and Wolfgang Weingart, who was a similarly influential founding father of Swiss New Wave graphic design and typography who dared to break the grid.

During her studies, Greiman became increasingly convinced that, as she put it, "all designers come to a task with a unique way of ordering that is particular to their past experiences, and perhaps even their genetic structure," and as a result began to rely increasingly on creative intuition, which she believes is "our highest form of intelligence".

By now thoroughly grounded in European avant-gardism, Greiman returned to the United States in 1971, and for the next five years taught at the Philadelphia College of Art, while also working as a graphic designer in New York.

In 1976, she moved to California and began developing her own distinctive style of graphics that combined the emerging New Wave vibe of West Coast Post-Modernism with her rigorous Swiss School training. The resulting work, including her cover for *WET* magazine (1979) co-designed with Jayme Odgers which is now hailed as a paradigm of Post-Modern graphic design, was typified by a strong sense of visual depth, whereby certain elements seemingly float in space and messages appear as though they are being filtered through different layers of a complex three-dimensional grid.

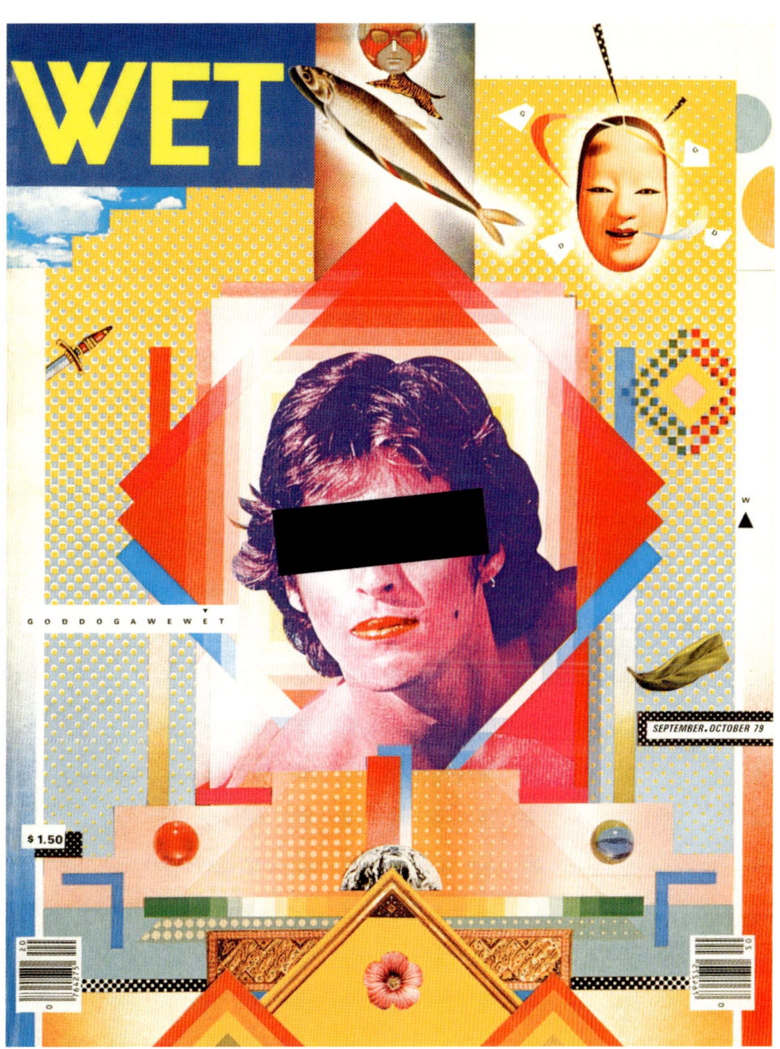

ABOVE:
***WET* magazine cover**
September/October 1979 – co-designed with Jayme Odgers

During the early 1980s Greiman began using then state-of-the-art Apple Macintosh software to create eye-catching graphic design work that continued playfully to subvert the holy grid of Modernism and incorporate eclectic references that acted as poetic visual hooks, such as in her Does it Make Sense? offset print (1987) for *Design Quarterly* and her most famous poster, Snow White + the Seven Pixels (1986), created for a presentation she was giving at the Maryland Institute College of Art.

From 1982 to 1984, Greiman was director of design at the California Institute of the Arts, and in 1990 published her first book, entitled *Hybrid Imagery: The Fusion of Technology and Graphic Design*. In 2002 she established a Los-Angeles-based consultancy called Made in Space that specializes in what she describes as "transmedia" design, working mainly in the areas of corporate identity and branding.

Walter Gropius

German/American, 1883–1969

Walter Gropius's early architectural projects, such as the Fagus factory in Alfeld, Germany (1911) with its Cubist form and curtain walls, made him one of the key pioneers of the Modern Movement. But his greatest contribution was as an educator in Germany and subsequently, in exile from the Nazis, in the United States. He was the founding director of the Bauhaus, the most influential art and design school of the twentieth century, and appointed his successors, Hannes Meyer and Ludwig Mies van der Rohe.

Gropius's great-uncle was the architect Martin Gropius, who had studied under Karl Friedrich Schinkel – Germany's great nineteenth-century Neo-Classicist. Given this, it is unsurprising that Gropius took the decision to pursue a career as an architect, initially studying in Munich and Berlin. He only completed four semesters before his studies were interrupted by military service. Subsequently, he travelled to Spain (1907–08), where he met Karl Ernst Osthaus, a well-connected patron of the European avant-garde. Osthaus arranged for Gropius to become an assistant to Peter Behrens in Berlin (1908–10), who at various times also employed Ludwig Mies van der Rohe, Le Corbusier and Adolf Meyer. Behrens's proto-Modernist turbine factory and utilitarian product designs for AEG had a strong formative influence on Gropius's subsequent development as an architect and designer.

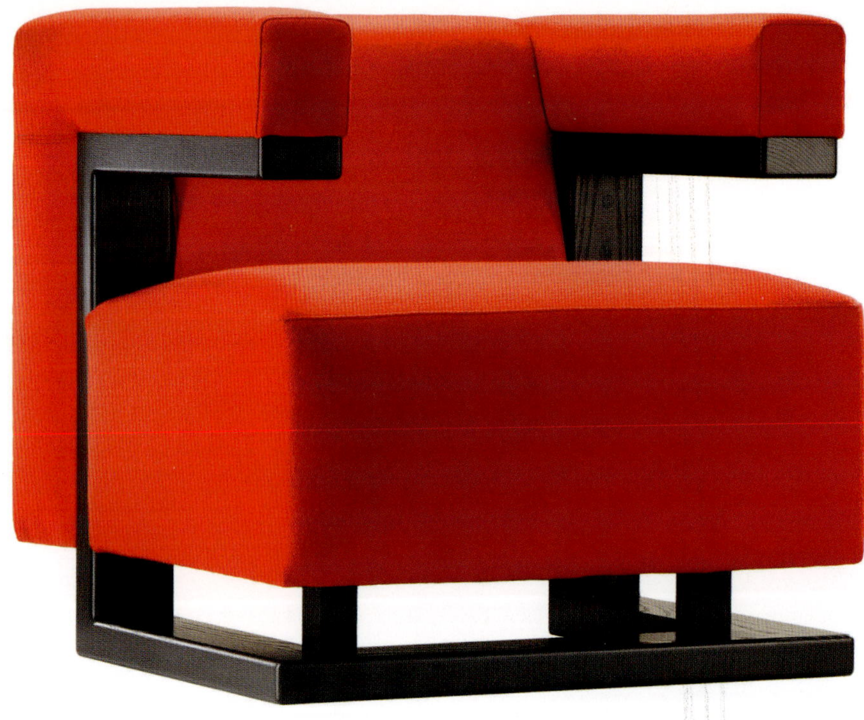

LEFT:
F51 armchair
designed for the director's room at the Bauhaus school in Weimar, 1920 (re-issued by Tecta)

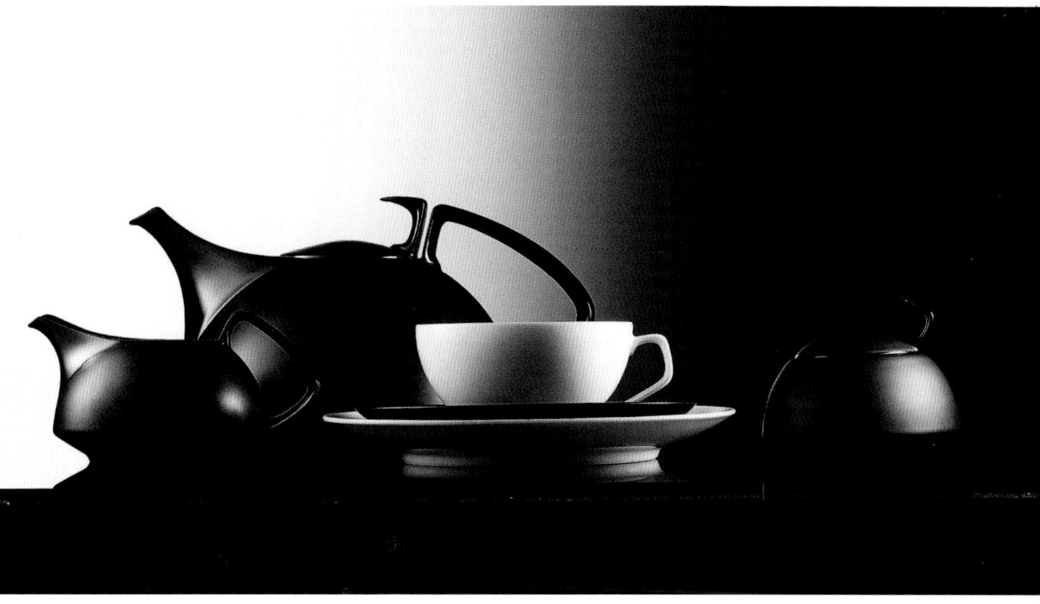

RIGHT:
TAC tea set
for Rosenthal, 1969

In 1910, Gropius and Meyer established their own practice in Berlin and the following year designed the Fagus factory, which incorporated one of the first completely glazed façades – a wall of glass supported by narrow brick pillars and iron frames that bathed the interior in natural light. Gropius and Meyer went on to create an equally innovative model factory for the 1914 Deutscher Werkbund exhibition held in Cologne. Gropius's career was interrupted again by military service in the First World War. He was decorated for gallantry yet, like so many of his generation, the conflict made him feel that the world had, in his words, "come to an end" and that a better one needed to be built from its ashes.

The founding of the Staatliches Bauhaus in Weimar in 1919 was a concrete expression of this sentiment – a new design school for the dawning Machine Age created from a traditional art school. The radical character of the school, and the politics of some of its students, alienated the city. After various offers, Gropius relocated the school to Dessau in 1925, where the mayor financed him to design the Bauhaus's emphatically Modern main building and a number of studio houses to accommodate its senior teachers. Gropius also designed the Törten housing estate in Dessau (1926–28) to provide affordable housing for workers, which comprised terraces of cube-like residential units.

After stepping down as the Bauhaus's director in 1928, Gropius eventually moved to England in 1934, where he established a partnership with the British Modernist architect Maxwell Fry. Three years later he moved to the United States, where he was appointed professor of architecture at the Harvard Graduate School of Architecture and Design. He brought Marcel Breuer, a Bauhaus graduate and former teacher, with him.

Gropius's later career as an architect was prolific and international, ranging from American high-rises to a university in Iraq, but failed to match the impact of his early work. In 1946, he founded The Architects Collaborative (TAC) with seven younger American partners, which subsequently designed a succession of buildings that took on an increasingly corporate character, culminating in the urbanistically problematic Pan Am tower (1960–63) in New York. In his later years, Gropius continued to work as a designer, producing the well-known Rosenthal tea set (1969); for him, design was "simply an integral part of the stuff of life, necessary for everyone in a civilized society".

The Guild of Handicraft

British, active 1888–1907

The Guild of Handicraft was a hugely influential experiment in design as social mission. It was first and foremost the brainchild of Charles Robert Ashbee, a visionary British design thinker who was also a highly accomplished architect-designer and a leading member of the Arts and Crafts Movement.

Though born into a respectable Jewish middle-class family, Ashbee had a rather unconventional upbringing – his mother was a German-born suffragist, while his father, Henry Spencer Ashbee, was a noted collector of erotica who scandalously published a three-volume bibliography of erotic literature written under the pseudonym Pisanus Fraxi. It was while Ashbee was at King's College, Cambridge, studying history that he became caught up in the spirit of philosophical idealism and became influenced by the writings of John Ruskin and by the socialist philosopher Edward Carpenter – both of whom highlighted the disastrous social consequences of the industrial system.

William Morris's romantic socialism, which advocated a simple life and called for design reform through a revitalization of craft, was also a huge inspiration to Ashbee, and after Cambridge he decided to become an architect, training under the Gothic Revivalist George Bodley. During this period, Ashbee lived at Toynbee Hall, a social-reforming educational mission established by Samuel and Henrietta Barnett in London's East End. It was here that Ashbee subsequently founded the Guild of Handicraft in 1888 as a sort of proactive social-design experiment.

RIGHT:
Silver-mounted decanter designed by Charles Robert Ashbee for the Guild of Handicraft, 1904–05

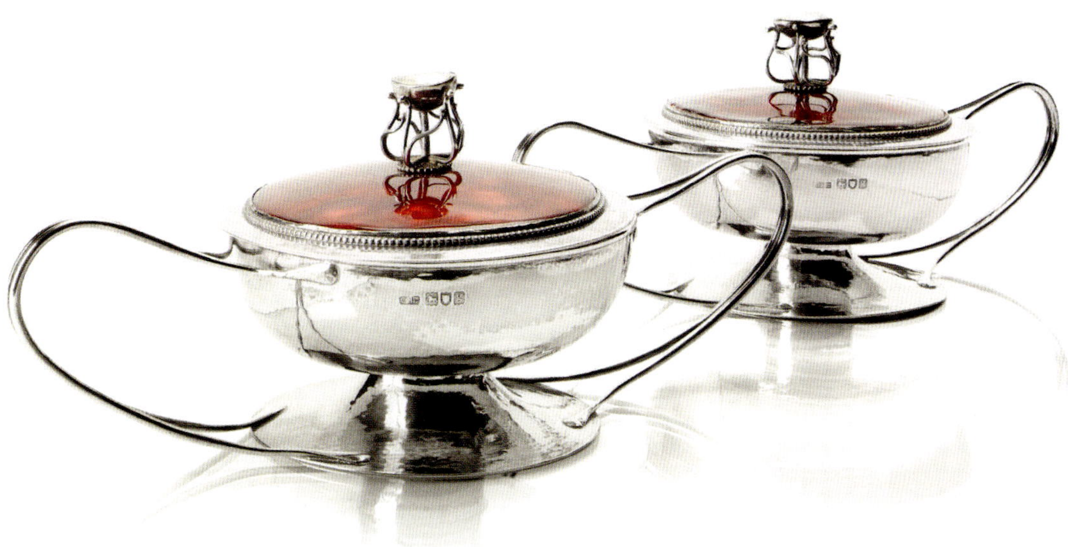

ABOVE:
Pair of twin-handled bowls with covers designed by Charles Robert Ashbee for the Guild of Handicraft, 1900

The guiding aim of Ashbee's enterprise was to provide practical training in handicraft to the very poorest people living in the surrounding slums, thereby giving them a means by which to earn an honest livelihood. The beautifully executed wares that the guildsmen subsequently produced were displayed in shows put on by the Arts and Crafts Exhibition Society, and sold through the later guild-run shop in Brook Street, in London's West End. In 1891 the Guild moved to larger premises at Essex House in Mile End Road, and there the community made furniture, fixtures and fittings, often related to Ashbee's architectural commissions. Bolstered by the success of the Guild, Ashbee became caught up with the idea of realizing the Arts and Crafts Movement's vision of a self-sustaining rural community of artistic craftspeople – a veritable Arcadia where workers could produce meaningful creative work in pleasant and healthful surroundings.

Eventually, Ashbee and his guildsmen made the decision to relocate the Guild to the countryside. In 1902, he and some fifty guildsmen together with their families moved to Chipping Campden, a historic market town in the Gloucestershire Cotswolds. For five years, the Guild more or less attained the Arts and Crafts dream of living and working in rural utopia, with the skilled craftsman spending part of each day creatively engaged in making beautiful work and the rest of it tilling the land to provide food for their families. During this period, Chipping Campden became a magnet for like-minded creatives, and was visited by numerous architect-designers of international repute, including Josef Hoffmann, Koloman Moser, Elbert Hubbard and Frank Lloyd Wright, who came to see this social design experiment in action and were so inspired by it they established their own design-reforming enterprises. Although relatively short-lived, the Guild's legacy was immense, since its utopian ideals ultimately helped inspire some of the philosophical foundations of the later Modern Movement.

G

Hans Gugelot

Dutch/active Germany, 1920–1965

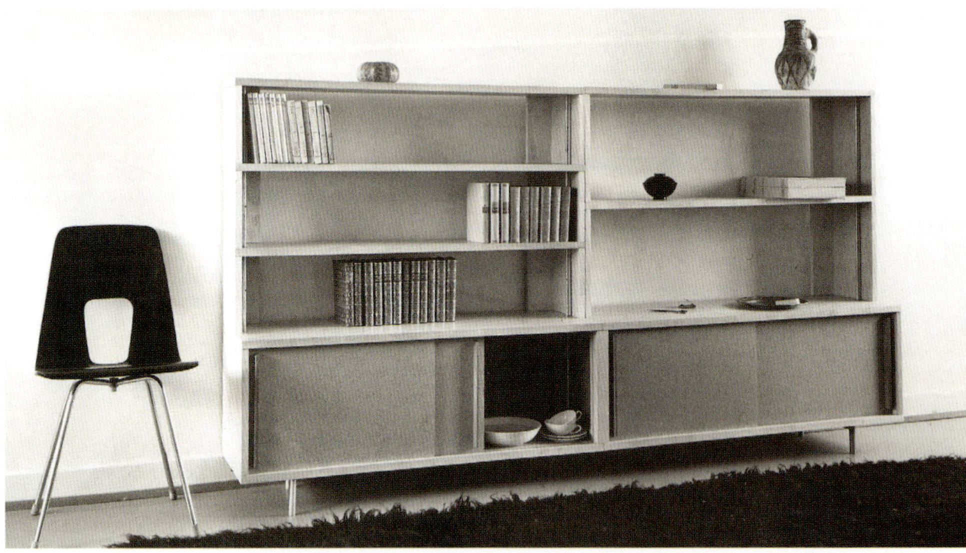

ABOVE:
M125 modular furniture system
for Wohnbedarf, 1950–53 and 1956 (later Bofinger)

Indonesian-born, but of Swiss and Dutch descent, Hans Gugelot initially studied engineering in Lausanne and later trained as an architect at ETH or the Eidgenössische Technische Hochschule (Federal Institute of Technology) in Zurich, graduating in 1946. He subsequently worked for various architectural firms before joining Max Bill's design office in 1948, where he stayed for two years. During this period, he designed his first pieces of furniture, including his adjustable 1363 armchair for Wohnbedarf (1948–49) and a simple side chair with moulded plywood seat and back sections for Horenglarus (1949).

In 1950, Gugelot established his own design practice and began developing a new programme of modular furniture, known as the M125 range (1950–53). Ingeniously constructed of various prefabricated panels, doors, shelves and standardized fittings, the M125 was a landmark furniture system, which could be assembled and disassembled with ease and the elements combined to make a wide range of furniture pieces, from wardrobes and cupboards to shelving units and desks. This rationally conceived programme of furniture had the added benefits of being easy to transport and possible to reconfigured according to changing needs. Another advantage was that it could be extended over time through the purchase of additional elements. In 1954 Max Bill appointed Gugelot as a staff member to the Hochschule für Gestaltung (School of Design), known as HfG, in Ulm, a new design school that would function essentially as a post-war continuation of the Dessau Bauhaus in that it was intended to promote a Rationalist approach to design. The same year, Gugelot together with Max Bill and Paul Hidinger created the HfG stool for the school's students – later known as the Ulmer Hocker. This multifunctional piece of minimalist furniture is now widely regarded as one of the great icons of post-war German design.

Also in 1954, Gugelot met Erwin Braun for the first time and the following year developed various new products for Braun that were launched to critical acclaim at the *Deutsche Rundfunk- Phono- und Fernseh-Ausstellung* (German Broadcasting, Phonograph and Television Exhibition) in Düsseldorf. In 1956 the Phonosuper SK4, which Gugelot co-designed with Dieter Rams, was also launched. Setting a new aesthetic standard for electronic products, this record-player-cum-radio as well as other later designs created by Gugelot for Braun, such as his Sixtant 1 electric shaver (1961), exemplified the new pared-down Rationalist look of post-war German design and became highly influential on the development of electronic products for decades to come.

In 1956, Gugelot's M125 furniture system was improved and extended further and began to be made by the German furniture manufacturer Wilhelm Bofinger. As one of the leading industrial designers in Germany during the 1960s, Gugelot worked for numerous German manufacturing companies, notably creating an ingenious trade fair stand system for Max Weishaupt (1963). He also designed a new slide projector for Kodak of Stuttgart, culminating in the Carousel S-AV 1000 (1964). This sleek design, like his earlier work for Braun, was celebrated for being beautifully engineered and logically laid out so as to make its operation as simple as possible.

One of his last projects was the development of a concept sports car that was intended to have the first-ever self-supporting chassis made from a plastic compound. Sadly, Gugelot died from a heart attack before he could complete the project. Yet despite his all-too-short career, he had an enormous impact on design, for he practised what he preached through his development of design systems based entirely on a logical, process-driven approach to problem solving.

BELOW:
Carousel S slide projector
for Kodak, 1963

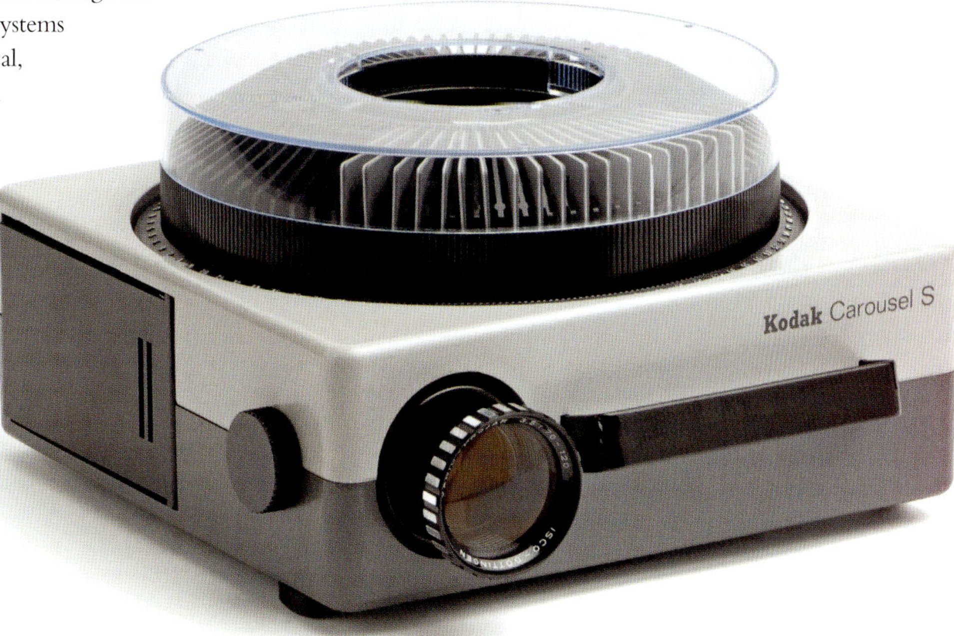

Zaha Hadid

Iraqi/British, 1950–2016

The first woman to win the Pritzker Architecture Prize, Zaha Hadid was a force of creative genius, who not only designed extraordinary buildings that pushed the furthest technical boundaries of what was physically possible but was also an accomplished designer of furniture, lighting, homewares, fashion items, installations and interiors. Like her radical architecture, her progressive design work was characterized by the use of dynamic flowing lines that seamlessly melded one geometric plane into another.

Born in Baghdad, Hadid grew up in a country vastly different to today's Iraq. At the time it was an outward-looking, liberal and secular society with a burgeoning economy – but all that changed when the Ba'ath party seized power in 1963. Hadid's politician father was leader of the Iraqi Progressive Democratic Party, and she had been brought up to be independent-minded. After gaining a mathematics degree from the American University in Beirut, she moved to London in 1972 in order to train at the Architectural Association, which at the time was the most exciting and progressive architecture school in the world.

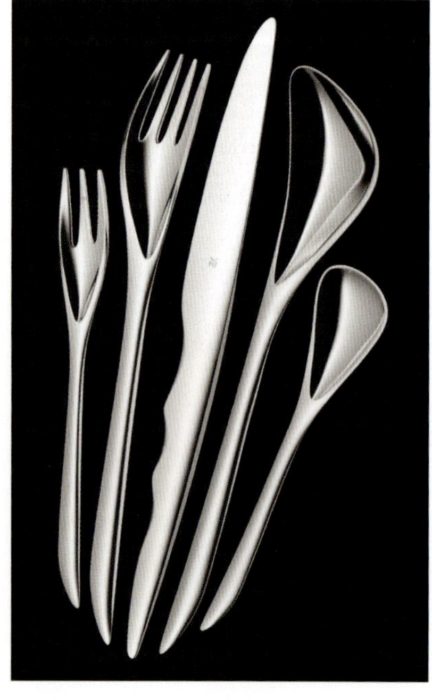

ABOVE:
Zaha cutlery
for WMF, 2007

OPPOSITE:
Vortexx chandelier
for Zumtobel, 2005

Upon graduating from the AA in 1977, she briefly joined the Office for Metropolitan Architecture (OMA), which had been founded two years earlier by fellow AA graduate Rem Koolhaas along with Madelon Vriesendorp and Elia and Zoe Zenghelis. Hadid subsequently taught at her alma mater, eventually leading her own studio there. While continuing to teach at the AA, she opened her own architecture practice in 1980. Three years later she won a prestigious competition for the design of a cliff-top resort, The Peak in Hong Kong, with plans that reflected the influence of Russian Suprematism with its dynamic deconstruction of spatial planes. Although this progressive building was never built, Hadid created furniture at this time for an apartment in London which reflected her architectural ideas, albeit on a smaller scale.

In 1994, she had her first real break, with a commission to design the Vitra fire station in Weil am Rhein, Germany, and by the early 2000s her architectural career had begun to take off. Among her best-known work is the London Aquatics Centre (2011) for the 2012 Olympics. As a product designer, she created the sculptural Z-Play modular seating units for Sawaya & Moroni in 2002, and three years later the dynamic Vortexx chandelier for Zumtobel. From then she designed exhibitions, interiors, products, fashion and furniture for design-led companies including Alessi, Artemide, Melissa, Serralunga, Swarovski and Triflow, to name but a few. Hadid also found considerable success within the rarefied design-art market, most notably with her sculptural pieces designed for Established & Sons, such as her Aqua table (2005) and clustering Nekton stools (2007). Like her remarkable gravity-defying buildings, Hadid's designs have a distinctive sculptural organic presence that was derived from a sophisticated understanding of spatial form and its manipulation. Similarly, she relied heavily on CAD-systems to transform her forward-looking visions into modern-day realities.

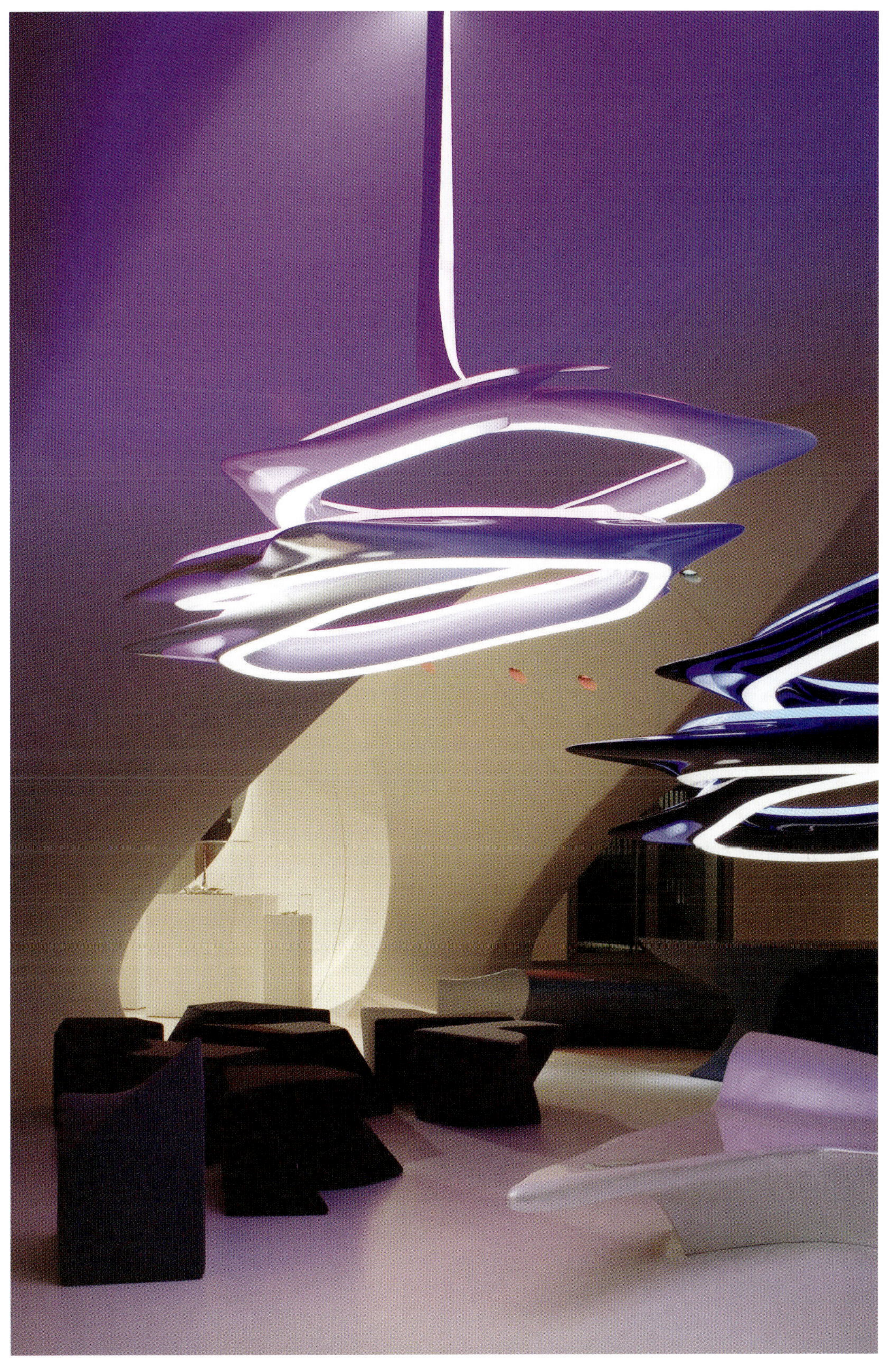

Thomas Heatherwick

British, 1970–

The British designer Thomas Heatherwick works across an impressively broad creative spectrum that encompasses buildings, urban infrastructure, product design and sculpture, as well as strategic design thinking.

At the heart of Heatherwick's approach lies, as his studio notes, "a profound commitment to finding innovative design solutions, with a dedication to artistic thinking and the latent potential of materials and craftsmanship … achieved through a working methodology of collaborative rational inquiry, undertaken in a spirit of curiosity and experimentation". The results are often breathtakingly imaginative and extraordinarily beautiful – from his etheral Seed Cathedral that was the UK Pavilion for *Expo 2010 Shanghai, China* to the Olympic Cauldron for the London 2012 Olympic Games which, with its copper petal-like stems, formed a poetic kinetic sculpture that epitomized "the extraordinary, albeit transitory, togetherness that the Olympic Games symbolize". When Heatherwick creates something, he designs not just for physical function but for emotional connection as well – and that is what makes his work so special: it engages both the head and the heart.

Born in London, Heatherwick was introduced to architecture and design at an early age by his father, who took him to see, among other things, the latest carbon-fibre cars at Earl's Court and a house of the future at Milton Keynes. His mother, who collected and dealt in beads, was also highly influential in his aesthetic development as a child, as was his attendance at the Rudolf Steiner School in Hertfordshire, which, like other Steiner educational establishments, fosters a culture of independent creative thinking.

BELOW:
Spun chairs
for Magis, 2010

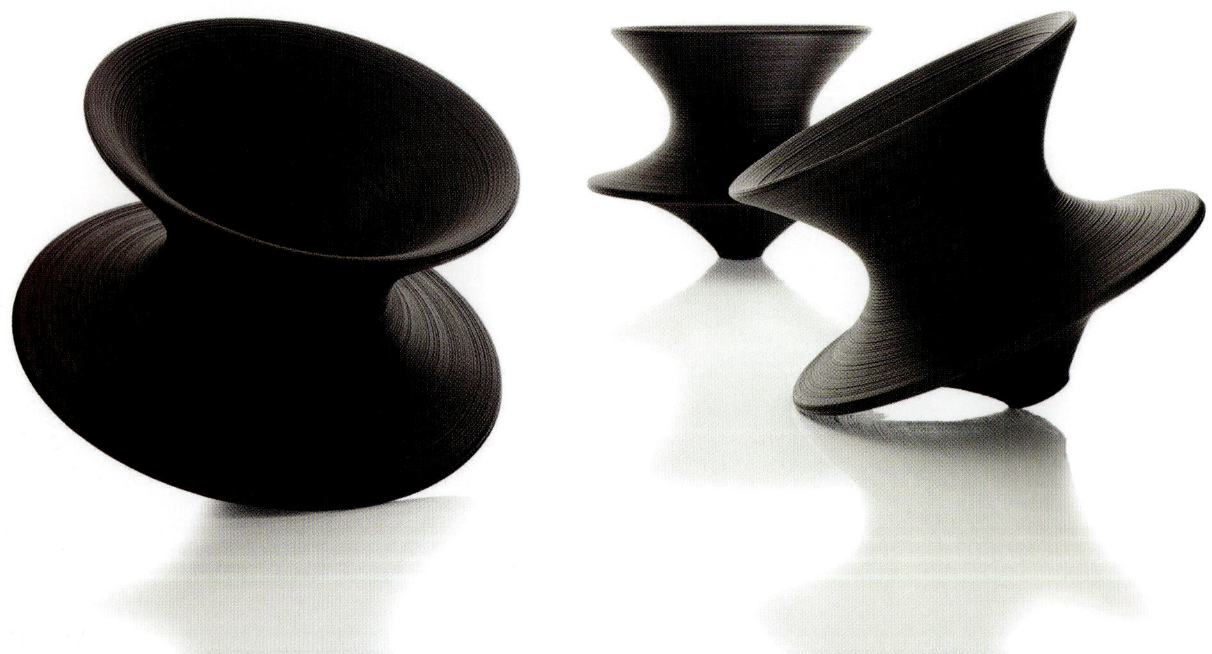

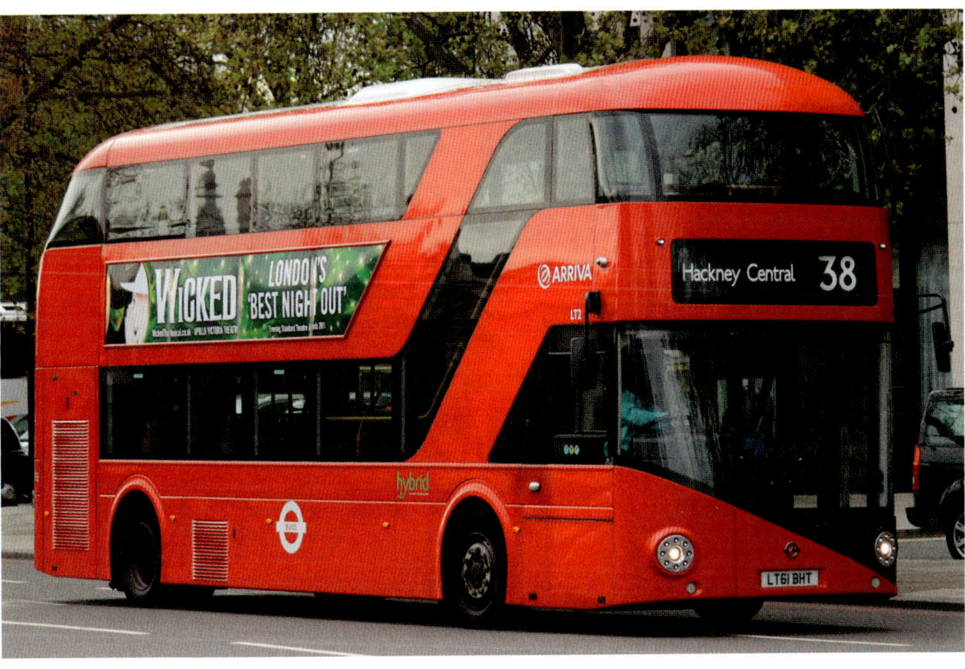

ABOVE:
LT2 New Routemaster London bus
for Transport for London, 2010 – manufacturer Wrightbus

Between 1989 and 1991, Heatherwick studied three-dimensional design at Manchester Polytechnic, and for his final project he created a pavilion that was later purchased for the park of the Cass Sculpture Foundation in Chichester. He continued his studies at the Royal College of Art, and shortly after graduating founded his own London-based studio in 1994, which was initially a one-man operation based in a former button factory in north London. Since then Heatherwick Studio has grown exponentially in both scale and creative breadth – having undertaken hundreds of projects all around the world, the practice now comprises a team of 160 dedicated and talented individuals, including architects, designers and makers working from a combined studio-workshop facility in London's Kings Cross. As Heatherwick explains, "At the root of what we do is rationality. Finding a design solution is like solving a crime. We're a bit like an investigative team. We analyse. We explore lines of inquiry. Then we eliminate things until we're left with the solution."

Among Heatherwick's most interesting projects are his range of Zip Bags for Longchamp (2004), his ingenious Rolling Bridge (2004), the Spun chair for Magis (2010) made of rotationally moulded polyethylene, his New Routemaster London bus (2010), and the controversial Garden Bridge project (2013), which will provide London with a new green park across the River Thames. A highly talented and original thinker, Heatherwick is an architect-designer-sculptor who manages to bring a rare sense of imagination to the creative process, time and time again.

Josef Hoffmann

Moravian (Czech)/Austrian, 1870–1956

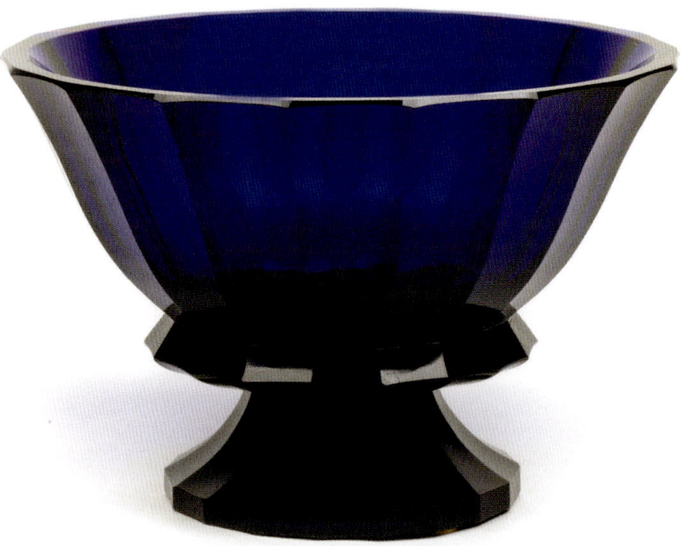

ABOVE:
Glass tazza
for Meyr's Neffe, *c.*1917–19

The legendary Austrian architect and designer Josef Hoffmann had a long and illustrious career spanning almost five decades. As a leading member of the Vienna Secession he pioneered a new geometric language of design, while as one of the founders of the Deutscher Werkbund he was instrumental in forging crucial links between art and industry.

Hoffmann studied architecture at the Akademie der bildenden Künste (Academy of Fine Arts) in Vienna, under Otto Wagner, who was the most famous architect working in Vienna during the *fin-de-siècle* period and an influential and outspoken pioneer of Modernism. Hoffmann later worked in his mentor's architecture practice and Wagner's insistence that form should follow function had a crucial bearing on Hoffmann's own avant-garde approach to design.

In 1897, Hoffmann became a founding member of the Vereinigung Bildender Künstler Österreichs (Union of Austrian Artists), a coterie of like-minded artists and architects that sought to reform design and counter the prevailing conservatism of the Association of Austrian Artists. This new group became known as the Vienna Secession in acknowledgement of its members' act of seceding from the prevailing historicism of the academic tradition.

Hoffmann travelled to Britain in 1900, and while there met various leading members of the British Arts and Crafts Movement, including Charles Robert Ashbee and Charles Rennie Mackintosh. The former's Guild of Handicraft inspired Hoffmann to establish the Wiener Werkstätte (together with Kolman Moser) three years later, while the latter's work influenced his own adoption of rectilinear forms. The Wiener Werkstätte was established with the financial backing of the wealthy banker Fritz Wärndorfer, who had been the main patron of the Vienna Secession. Hoffmann was appointed the director of this design-reforming venture, a co-operative workshop run along guild lines whereby skilled artisans

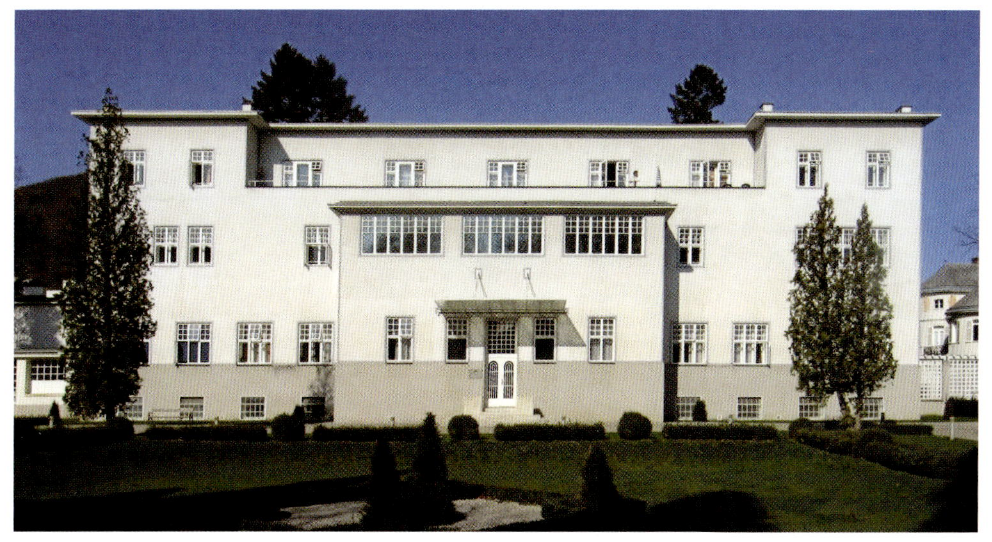

LEFT:
Purkersdorf Sanatorium
in Purkersdorf
Wien-Umgebung, Austria,
1904–05

BELOW:
Sitzmaschine armchair
for J. & J. Kohn, *c.*1905

worked in collaboration with professional designers to create objects of aesthetic beauty and exacting manufacture.

Many of Hoffmann's more luxurious metalware designs for the Wiener Werkstätte had an almost architectonic quality, while some of his less expensive products incorporated a distinctive pierced grid that became known as the "Hoffmann-Quadratl". This type of grid-like motif was also used on many of his seating designs, notably the Sitzmaschine chair (*c.*1905) manufactured by Jacob & Josef Kohn. It also appeared in his cut and etched glassware designs for J.&L. Lobmeyr and Loetz Witwe.

Apart from his work in the field of applied art, Hoffmann also ran a highly successful architecture practice, which often undertook complete *Gesamtkunstwerk* (total work of art) schemes, whereby not only the building was designed by Hoffmann but also its interiors, fixtures and fittings. Among such unified projects were the Purkersdorf Sanatorium (1904–05), the Palais Stoclet, Brussels (1905–11), his undoubted masterpiece, and the Cabaret Fledermaus (1907).

In 1905, Hoffmann resigned from the Vienna Secession and two years later became a founding member of the Deutscher Werkbund, the aim of which was to forge closer links between designers and manufacturers in order to improve the quality of manufactured products. As one of the pioneering architects of the early Modern Movement, Hoffmann participated in the landmark *Deutsche Werkbund Ausstellung* exhibition held in Cologne in 1914. He also subsequently participated in the *Exposition Internationale des Arts Décoratifs et Industriels Modernes* held in Paris in 1925 and the *Stockholmsutställningen* (Stockholm Exhibition) of 1930. A role model for succeeding generations of architects, Hoffmann's importance lay in his outright rejection of historicism and his pared-down vocabulary of rectilinear form that can be seen to have presaged the geometric simplicity espoused by later proponents of Modernism.

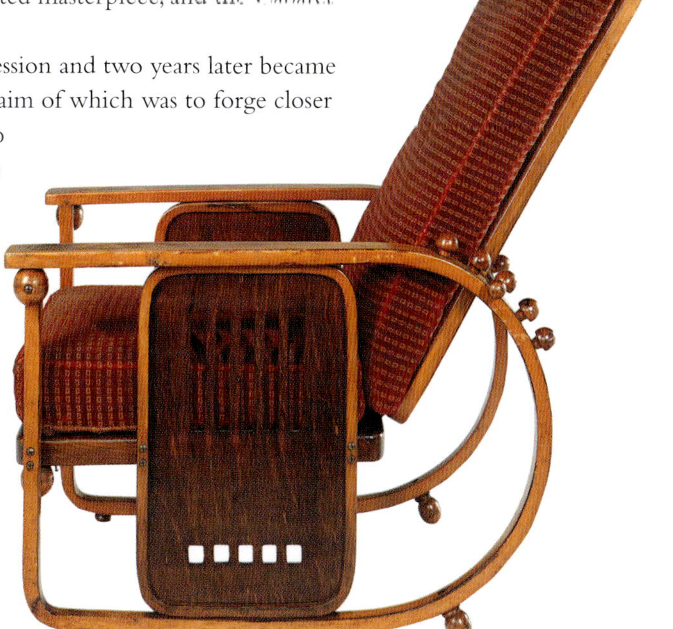

Victor Horta

Belgian, 1861–1947

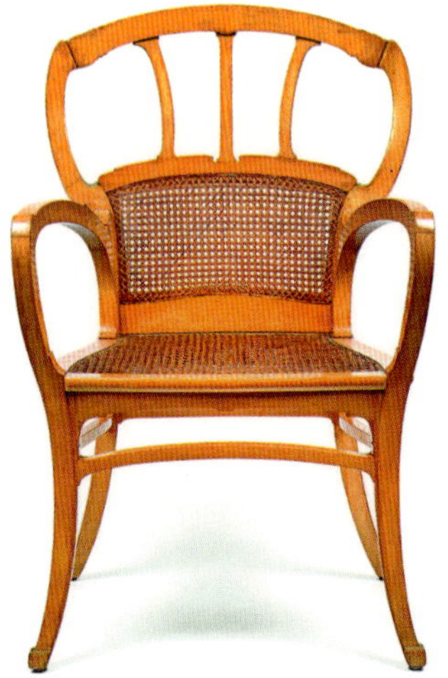

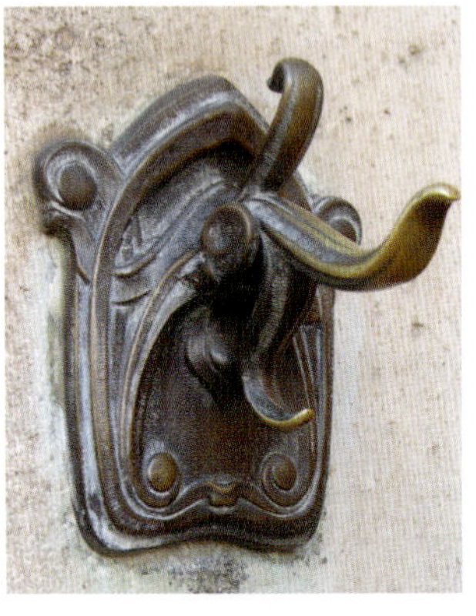

TOP:
Armchair for Villa Aubecq
1899

ABOVE:
Doorbell/knocker of the Maison et Atelier Horta
in Brussels (now the Horta Museum), 1898–1901

The Belgian architect and designer Victor Horta was an important pioneer of the Art Nouveau style and created some of the most extraordinary *Gesamtkunstwerk* (total work of art) architectural schemes of the *fin-de-siècle* period, which were sublime expressions of this new stylistic revolution.

Horta had initially studied at the Académie des Beaux-Arts and the Royal Atheneum in Ghent, before spending two years in France (1878–80), where he worked in the studio of the Parisian interior designer Jules Debuysson. He then moved to Brussels in 1881 in order to complete his studies at the Académie Royale des Beaux-Arts, while concurrently working for the Neo-Classical architect Alphonse Balat. It was during this period that Horta became influenced by the ideas of the French Gothic Revivalist architectural theorist Eugène-Emmanuel Viollet-le-Duc, who advocated a more holistic approach to the design of buildings whereby their interiors were seamlessly integrated into the overall design. Viollet-le-Duc also championed the use of pioneering engineering techniques and modern materials, most notably cast iron. Inspired by Viollet-le-Duc's writings, Horta would later create *Gesamtkunstwerk* buildings that utilized cast iron for their structural components, such as the Hôtel Tassel in Brussels, designed between 1893 and 1894. This town house, created for the Belgian scientist and professor Emile Tassel, is generally considered to be the founding work of the Art Nouveau style. It was also the earliest private residence to feature ironwork used both structurally and decoratively, with its swelling stalk-like supporting columns and the tendril-like balustrading of its sweeping staircase. The house incorporated an innovative steel-structured two-storey bow window that filled it with light, while the general sense of dynamic organicism was further enhanced by swirling motifs painted on the walls and patterned in the mosaic flooring. In fact, Horta became so identified with the Art Nouveau style that the term "Horta line" was often used to describe the highly stylized natural motifs so characteristic of this new international style.

During the 1890s Horta created a number of similar *Gesamkunstwerk* buildings in Brussels, notably the Maison Autrique (1893), the Maison Winssinger (1894–97), and the Hôtel Solvay (1894–1900). But perhaps the best known, thanks to its intact survival, is the Maison et Atelier Horta that he created for himself between 1898 and 1901, which is now the Horta Museum. This magnificent jewel-like building is bathed in light throughout thanks to a vast glass canopy ceiling over the main staircase, and is adorned with site-specifically-designed furnishings. From furniture to light fixtures and door handles, these exquisite features reflect Horta's extraordinary ability to create a seamless flowing unity between architecture and decoration. Apart from working on his architectural schemes, he also taught at the Free University in Brussels and the Académie Royale des Beaux-Arts, Brussels, where he was director in 1913–16 and again from 1925 to 1931.

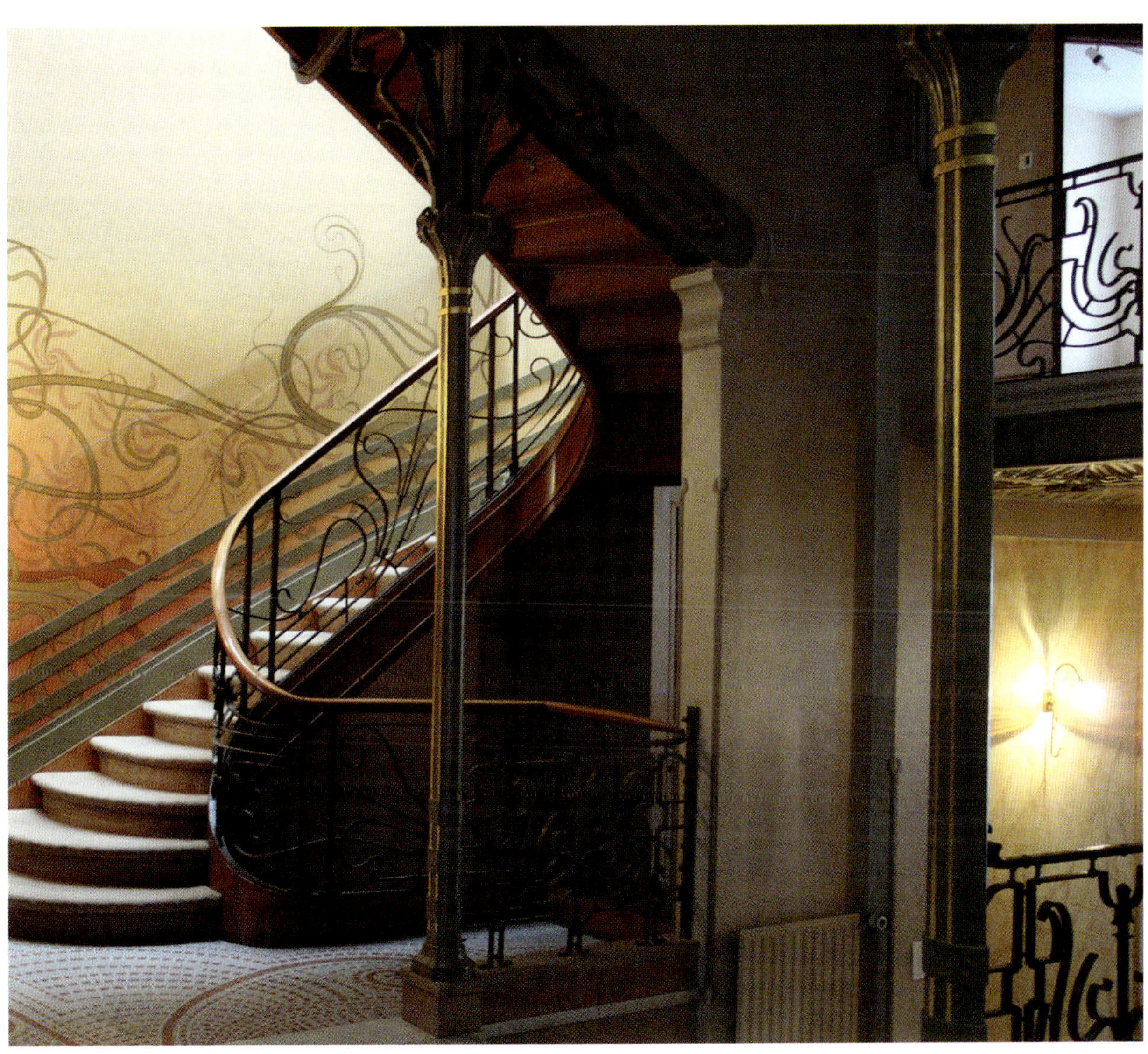

ABOVE:
Staircase of the Hôtel Tassel
in Brussels, 1893–94

In latter years, he continued to experiment with modern materials, such as reinforced concrete, but adopted a more geometric style in tune with the then fashionable Art Deco style, as demonstrated by his Palais des Beaux-Arts, Brussels (1919–28). As one of the great innovators of Art Nouveau, Horta not only pioneered the use of open-plan layouts but also helped advance a new concept of decoration, holistically linking it to the built fabric of a building so that the whole became greater than the sum of its parts, much like an organism found in nature.

IDEO

American, founded 1991

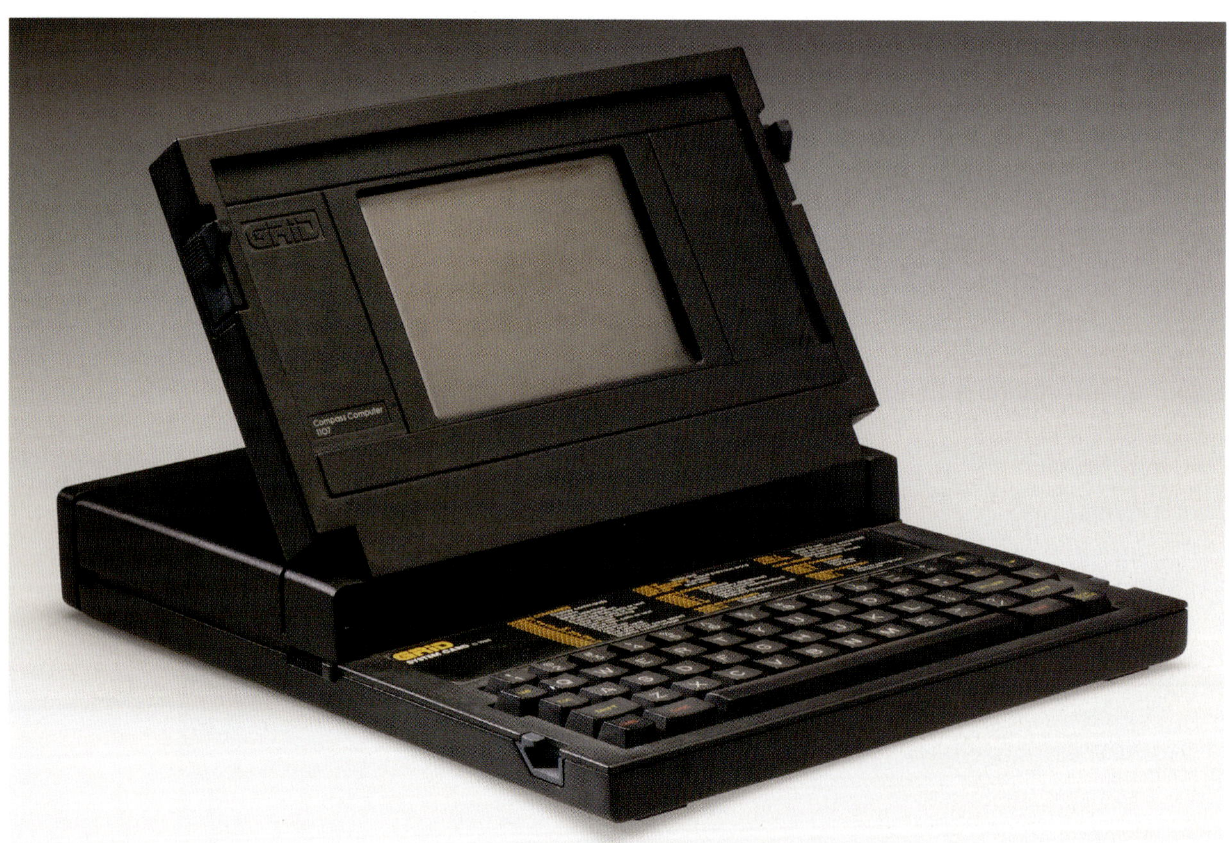

One of the largest and most influential design practices in the world, IDEO describes itself as "a design and innovation consulting firm" and applies strategic design thinking to the development of innovative products, services, environments and digital experiences. Like other contemporary design consultancies, IDEO's problem-solving talents are also being increasingly applied to the structural makeup of companies – so that they are designed to work better and more efficiently in terms of management and organization.

Founded in 1991 in Palo Alto, California, IDEO was the result of a merger of four design offices: Bill Moggridge's studios based in London and San Francisco, David Kelley's DKD design-engineering firm that had started as a spin-off from research he did at the engineering department of Stanford University, and Mike Nutall's Matrix Product Design in Palo Alto. Moggridge was already well known for his design of the GRiD Compass laptop computer (1979), while David Kelley had helped design the first mouse for Apple and Nuttall had worked on the design of another computer for Convergent Technologies.

ABOVE:
Compass portable computer
for GRiD Systems Corp., built 1982 – designed 1979 by Bill Moggridge, Stephen Hobson and Glenn Edens

RIGHT:
Heart monitor
for AliveCor, 2014

From its inception, IDEO was guided by a belief in the power of empathetic thinking to create better-performing user-centric design solutions. Over time, as David Kelley explains, "We moved from thinking of ourselves as designers to thinking of ourselves as design thinkers," and this gave the consultancy a "methodology that enables us to come up with a solution that nobody has before". Similarly, the design team at IDEO focuses a great deal on the idea of product or service experience – how a design works, looks, feels and sounds, or in other words the critical interaction between a design solution and its user. This played a decisive part in the transformation of design focused on the object to a form of design based on systems and the digital world.

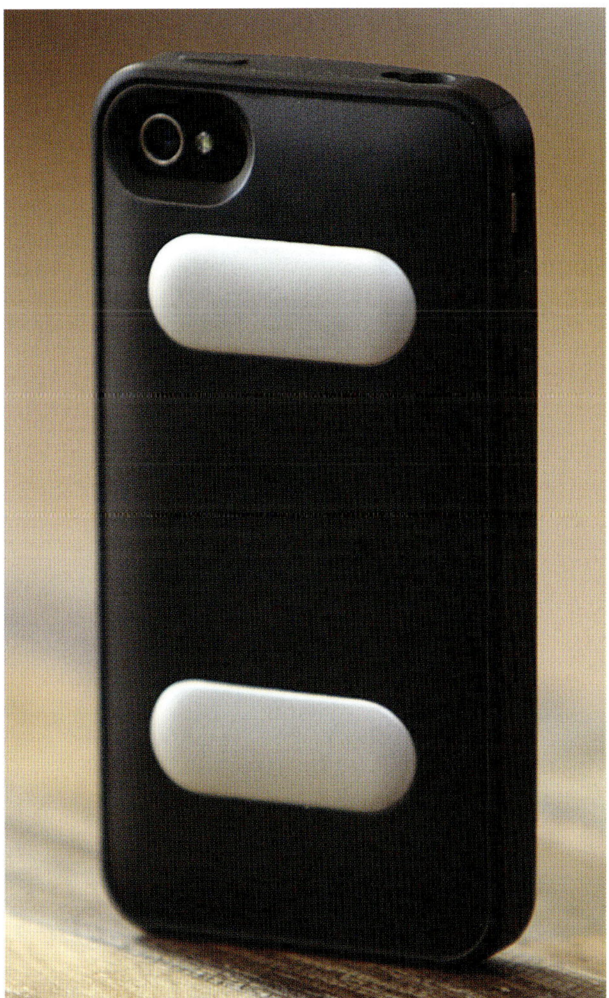

Over the last three decades, IDEO has worked on projects as diverse as creating the perfectly shaped Pringle potato chip for Procter & Gamble, developing a "smart" slim-lined heart monitor for AliveCor and designing a palliative-care facility in San Francisco. A professor at Stanford University, a close collaborator of Steve Jobs and IDEO's chairman, Kelley committed himself to promoting "creative confidence building" as widely as possible after a life-changing diagnosis of seemingly terminal throat cancer in 2007, which he happily survived. His TED talk of 2012 on "How to build your creative confidence" debunked the myth that there is a strict division between "creatives" and "non-creatives" and offered empowering design-thinking ways to help non-designers build self-belief in their own creative abilities.

Today, design thinking is still central to IDEO's approach, which aims to balance "the needs of people, the possibilities of technology, and the requirements of business success", or, in other words, find the optimum innovative overlap between desirability, feasibility and viability. It is a winning formula, for today IDEO has offices around the world, from London and Munich to Tokyo and Shanghai, and over 600 people working across an impressively broad range of design disciplines. The company's motto states, "We create impact through design," and ultimately that is just what their roster of clients is looking for.

Maija Isola

Finnish, 1927–2001

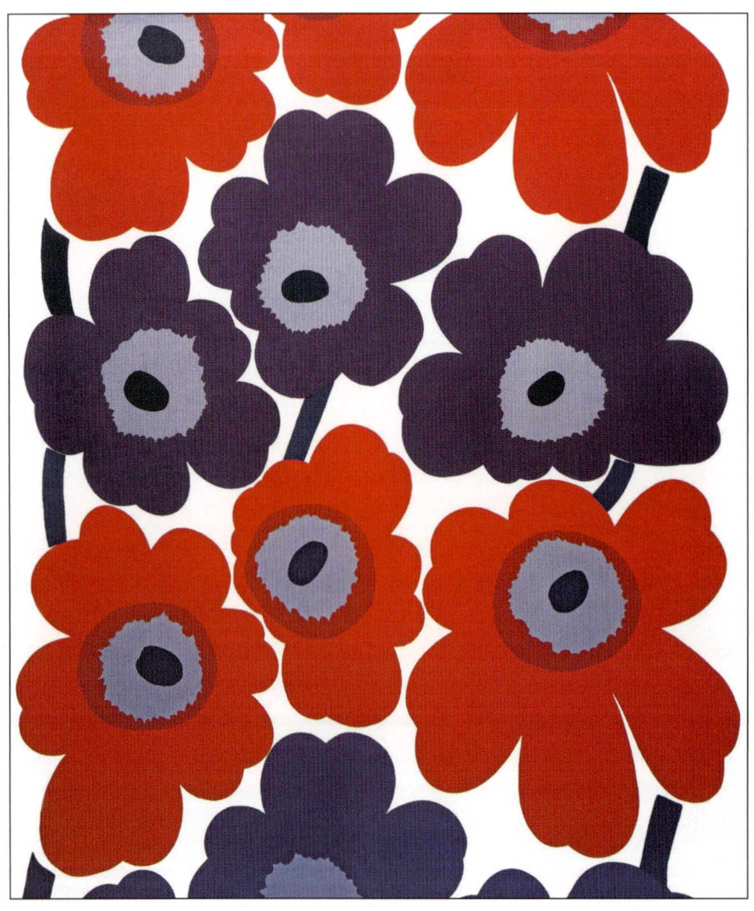

From the early 1950s up to the mid-1970s, Finland experienced a golden age of design, as a new generation of youthful designers, emboldened by the earlier international success of Alvar and Aino Aalto in the 1930s, pioneered a distinctively Finnish identity in design. Among this new crop of Finnish creative talent was Maija Isola, who produced some of the most renowned textile patterns of the twentieth century, including her famous poppy print, Unikko (1964), which has become synonymous with the Marimekko label.

Having studied painting at the Taideteollinen Korkeakoulu (University of Art and Design) in Helsinki, Isola was appointed principal designer at Printex in 1949. This textile company, founded by Vilho Ratia, was then under the art direction of his creatively talented wife, Armi. During her stint at Printex, Isola designed numerous furnishing textiles for the firm, many of which were inspired by the African art she had first encountered on a trip to Norway in 1949. From 1951, she also began designing bold and colourful fashion/interior prints for Printex's newly established sister company, Marimekko. The first fashion show presenting Marimekko's bold new designs – touted as the Marimekko-projekti – took place at the Kalastajatorppa restaurant on the outskirts of Helsinki in 1951. The patterns on show must have seemed like a breath of fresh air after the prolonged shortage of clothes and materials that been experienced in Finland both during the war and its aftermath. Rather than wartime grey cloth or cheap artificial silk, Isola had opted for inexpensive cotton sheeting, which she had transformed into boldly abstracted patterns using silk-screen printing and often incorporating simple hand-drawn patterns or stripes. Her textile designs for Marimekko and Printex were subsequently included in the landmark *Design in Scandinavia* exhibition that toured America and Canada (1954–57), and were also shown in the *Formes Scandinaves* exhibition held in the Musée des Arts Décoratifs, Paris in 1958, and at *Expo 58* in Brussels.

ABOVE:
Unikko (Poppy) textile
for Marimekko, 1964

OPPOSITE:
Kaivo textile
for Marimekko, 1964

By the mid-1950s, Isola had begun incorporating floral motifs into her textiles, often using a photographic process whereby she would project plant forms onto the printed screen to create the pattern required. Over time, as she matured as a designer and became increasingly confident, so her patterns became ever bolder. It was the large-scale patterns Isola created for Marimekko during the mid-1960s that would eventually become her most famous, notably Unikko (1964), Kaivo (1964) and Melooni (1963) – with the latter two reflecting the influence of American Colour Field painting through their incorporation of strong geometric patterns printed in flat, contrasting colours.

During her career, Isola also spent time in Yugoslavia, Italy and Algeria, and the exposure to these very different cultures inspired her work and helped broaden her design outlook. Taken as a body of work, her designs had an impressively wide stylistic breadth. During the early 2000s there was a resurgence of interest in Isola's work, and in 2005 two major retrospectives were held in Helsinki and Glasgow, which revealed that her iconic designs still had a remarkable freshness about them and remain completely timeless.

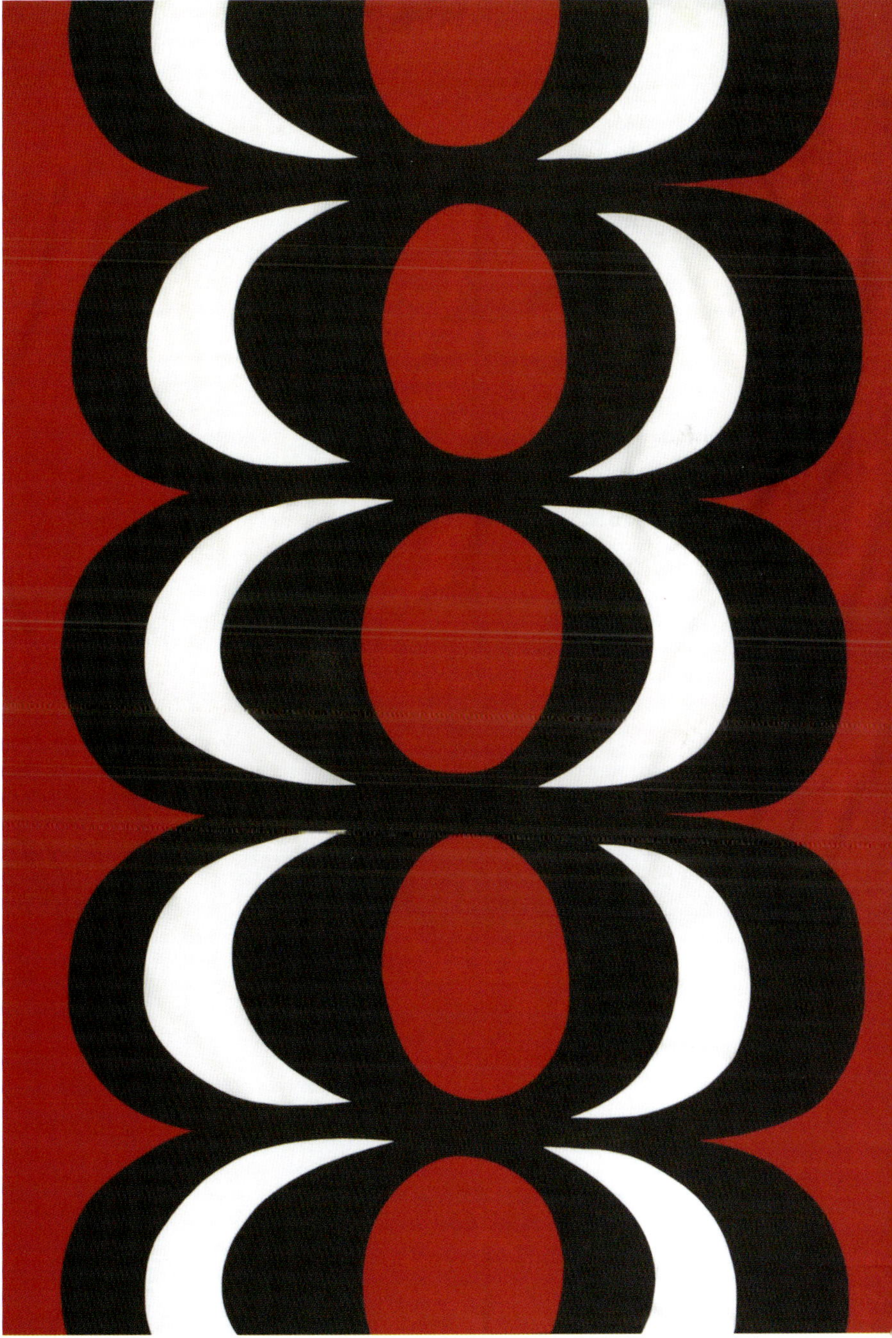

Alec Issigonis

British, 1906–1988

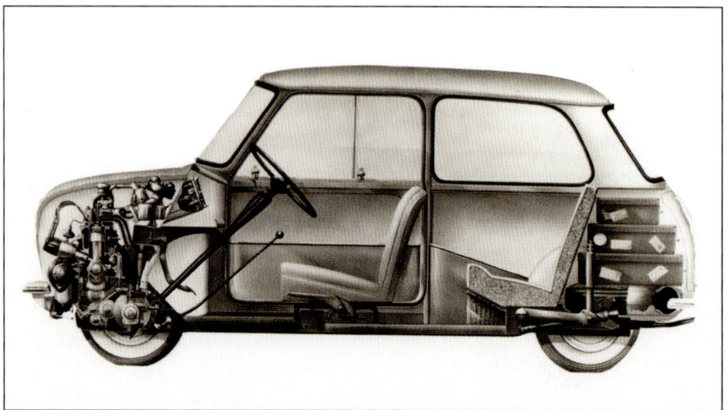

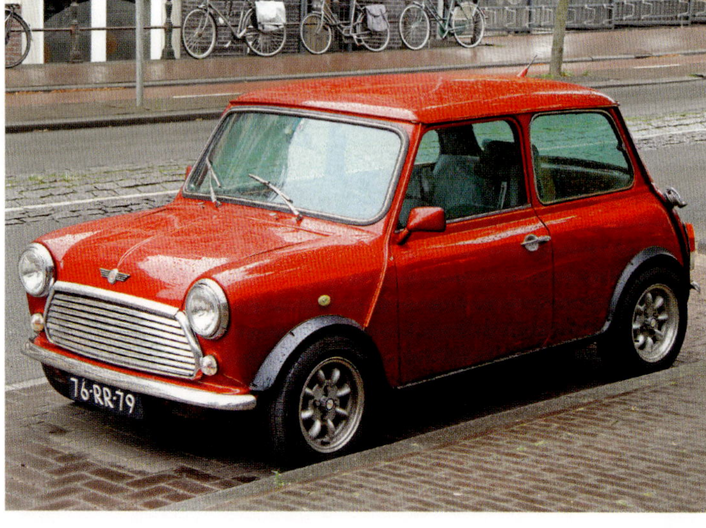

TOP:
Sectional view of original Mini car
*c.*1957

ABOVE:
Morris Mini-Minor (Mark 1)
for British Motor Corporation, 1959

Among the most famous automotive designers of all time, Alec Issigonis is best remembered as the creator of the Mini, a car that captured the optimistic and youthful spirit of the Sixties. He did, however, also design two other models that rank among some of the best-selling cars in British motoring history – the diminutive Morris Minor (1948) and the compact yet fun-to-drive Austin 1100 (1963).

Issigonis's success as an innovator lay in his understanding that the design of a car was utterly linked to its engineering, and therefore had to be conceived holistically. He was also stridently independent and took pride in not compromising his design vision to the vagaries of market research, which he dismissively referred to as "bunk". He had a low opinion of "pure mathematics" as applied to automotive design, deriding it as "the enemy of every truly creative man". For him it was freshness of vision that was of utmost importance; as he once observed, "When you're designing a new car for production never, never copy the opposition."

Issigonis was born in the port town of Smyrna in Turkey, which then had a sizeable Greek population. His British father was of Greek descent and owned a marine engineering business, while his mother came from a wealthy German brewing family. After the First World War, having spent much of it under house arrest, Issigonis and his parents were evacuated from Turkey, but while en route to Britain his father died. After arriving in Britain in 1922, Issigonis studied engineering for three years at Battersea Polytechnic. He subsequently worked as a draughtsman for Humber and later as a designer for Rootes Motors in Coventry, before becoming a suspension engineer for Morris Motors in Oxford in 1936. It was here that Issigonis designed a small two-seater in 1943, which was launched five years later as the Morris Minor. This much-loved automobile with its distinctive curvaceous lines had a unitary body that made it suitable for large-scale mass-production. Generally considered the first modern British car, the popular Morris Minor was the first all-British car to exceed one million sales.

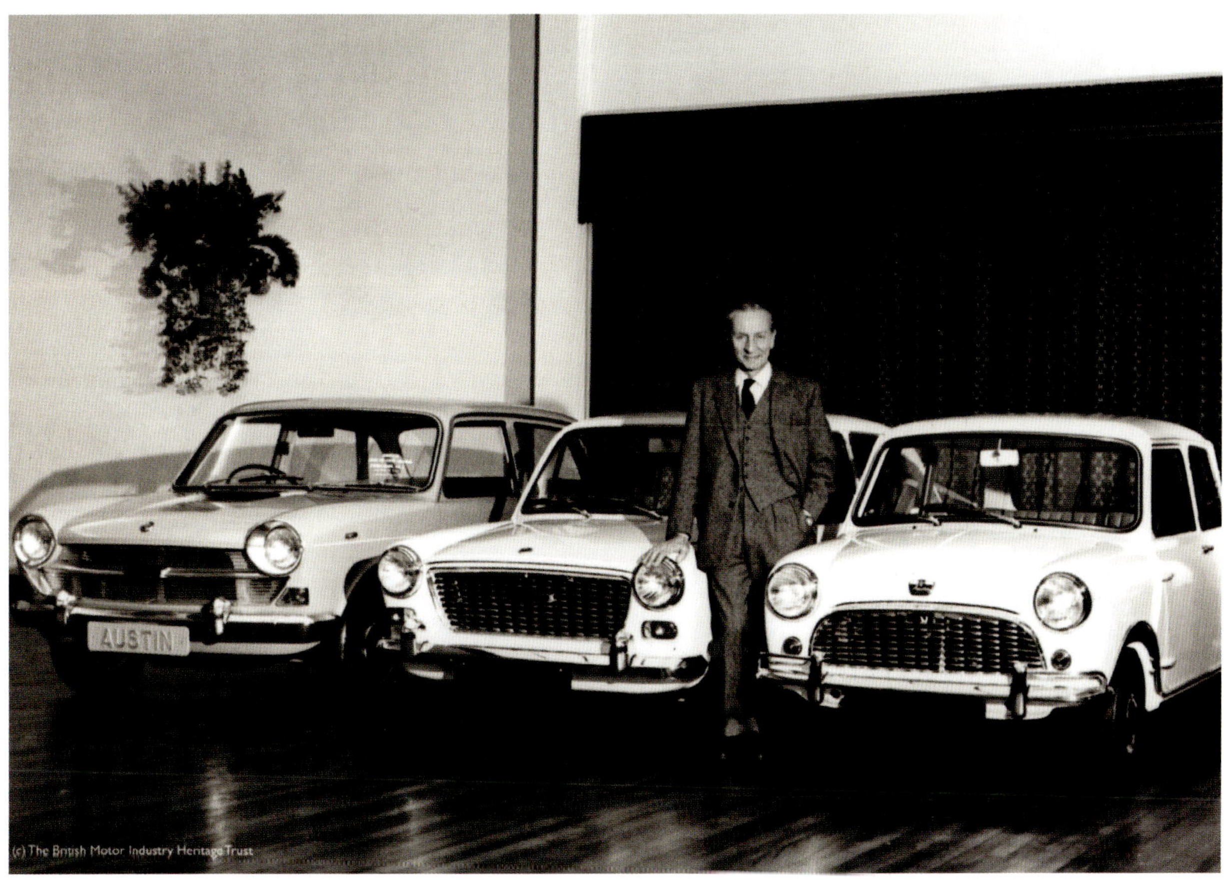

ABOVE:
Alec Issigonis
with three of his best-known car designs. Left to right: the Austin 1800 (1964), the Austin 1100 (1963) and the Mini (1959)

Issigonis stayed with Morris until 1952, the year it was merged with the Austin Motor Company to form the British Motor Corporation (BMC). After a three-year stint at Alvis on a luxury car project that was eventually shelved, he re-joined BMC in 1955 and two years later was tasked with the development of another small car in response to petrol shortages resulting from the Suez Crisis, and also to the increasing popularity of the German-imported Volkswagen Beetle in Britain. The compact, fuel-efficient, inexpensive and boxy Morris Mini-Minor was subsequently launched in 1959. Three metres (ten feet) long, this front-wheel-drive vehicle had a radical layout that incorporated a space-saving transverse engine. This freed up 80 percent of the car's space to accommodate the driver and three passengers.

The Mini was initially sold under both the Morris and Austin prefixes, and it was not until 1969 that Mini became a marque in its own right. Between 1959 and 1986, more than five million Minis were sold, reflecting not only its remarkably democratic design but also the emotional pull of this surprisingly seductive vehicle. The most significant car design of the 1960s, the Mini embodied a new carefree Britain and became a beloved symbol of both the nation and the era – and this can be attributed almost entirely to Issigonis's perfect unification of engineering, design and styling.

Toyo Ito

Japanese, 1941–

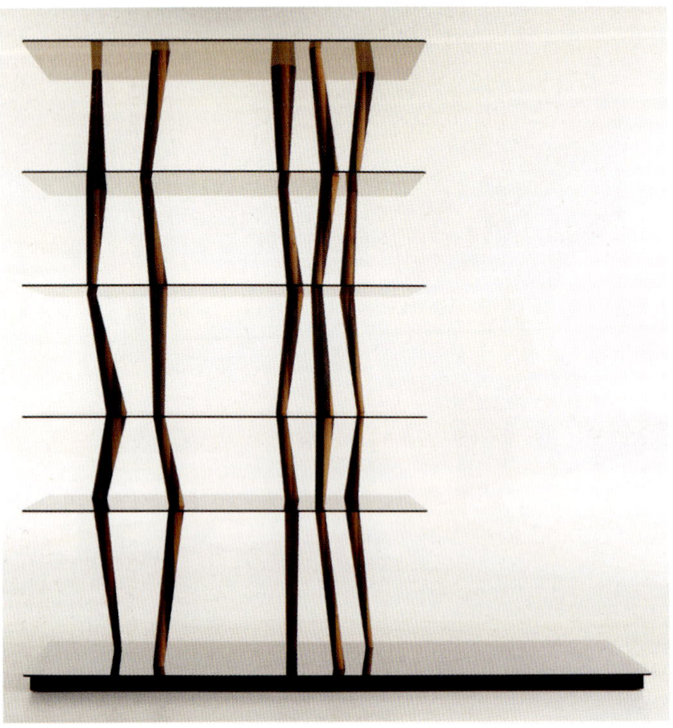

ABOVE:
Sendai crystal bookshelf
2014 – a glass version of Toyo Ito's earlier Sendai bookcase-sculpture (2005)

Winner of the Pritzker Architecture Prize in 2013, the Japanese architect Toyo Ito is well known for his extraordinary buildings, which are celebrated for their light-filled ethereality that conveys a sense of uniqueness and, paradoxically, universality. As a gifted form-giver, Ito has also been able to bring these qualities into the realms of product and furniture design.

Born in Seoul, Korea, to Japanese parents, Ito studied architecture at the University of Tokyo, graduating in 1965. He subsequently worked in the office of Kiyonori Kikutake Architects and Associates from 1965 to 1969. Following this, he established his own Tokyo-based architecture practice, Urban Robot (URBOT), in 1971 – renaming the office Toyo Ito & Associates, Architects some eight years later. Working on a mix of structurally and formally innovative private and public architectural commissions during the late 1970s and early 1980s, Ito's reputation continued to grow.

It was, however, the remarkable Tower of Winds in Yokohama (1986–88) that firmly established his credentials as one of the foremost architects of the era. This was followed by his design of the seven-storey Sendai Mediatheque (1995–2000) – a state-of-the-art library-cum-gallery that was widely published in the international design press thanks to its innovative latticed tubular-column construction. For this project's interior spaces, Ito incorporated foyer seating by Karim Rashid, and tasked Ross Lovegrove with designing a 180-seat cinema and furniture for its audio-visual library. This project helped forge strong links to the international design community and set Ito expanding his work to include object design.

He was subsequently invited by Alessi to participate in its Tea and Coffee Towers project of 2003, which, as the manufacturer explained, would create "a new landscape of objects designed by contemporary architects … that combines the expression of architecture with the language of design", thus echoing the remit of its earlier Tea and Coffee Piazza project (1979–83). Ito's contribution was a white porcelain set embellished with tiny green frogs, which in comparison to the other nineteen "Towers" created by, among others, Future Systems, Greg Lynn and David Chipperfield, had a distinctive Zen-like subtlety.

The same year, Ito also designed the Ripples bench (2003) for Horm – ingeniously made from laminated planks comprising a multilayer of five different woods, which were then

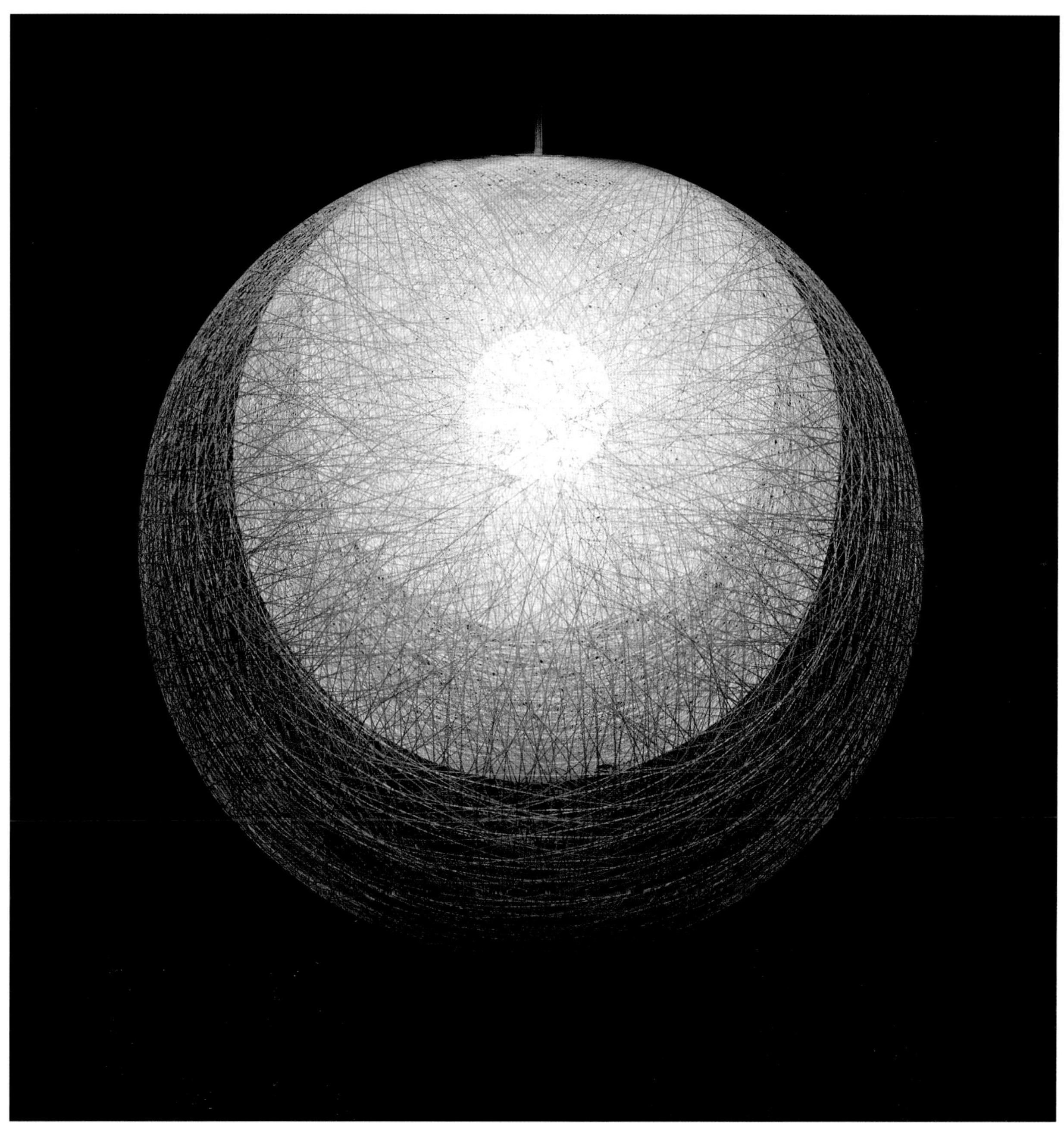

ABOVE:
Mayuhana pendant light
for Yamagiwa, 2007

scooped out to provide contoured seating dips, producing a remarkable polychromatic effect. This design received a Compasso d'Oro award in 2004, firmly placing Ito as a new creative force in the design world.

Since then he has created the Sendai shelving unit/exhibition sculpture (2005) and Kaze shelving unit for Horm (2005); reinforced concrete Naguisa street furniture for Escofet (2004); the Bo cup and saucer for the Oribe Design Center (2007); the Fin doorhandle for Olivari (2008); and the white porcelain KU tableware service (2006) and fourteen-piece MU cutlery set (2013) for Alessi. All of which reflect Ito's desire to counter, as he puts it, "the fixity" of buildings and products with "an ineffable immaterial quality".

I

Jonathan Ive

British/active USA, 1967–

The most influential designer of our times, Jonathan Ive has through his designs for Apple changed the way we work, communicate and ultimately live. The way he has been able to do this is by using a human-centric approach to problem solving, which has enabled him to create better and more intuitive interfaces for users to access technology. As Apple founder Steve Jobs once noted, "You've got to start with the customer experience and work backwards to the technology," and this is exactly what Ive has done time and time again, resulting in spectacular product outcomes.

The son of a silversmith who also worked as a design teacher, Ive grew up surrounded by a culture of design, and from an early age learnt from his father that a can-do attitude married with craft skills could enable one to make things for oneself. This early understanding of hands-on design manufacture gave Ive an outlier's advantage, as well as the belief that one could, with hard work and skill, transform dreams into physical realities.

He subsequently studied art and design at Newcastle Polytechnic (now Northumbria University) before becoming in 1989 a partner at Tangerine, a London-based design consultancy. One of Tangerine's earliest clients was Apple and, while there, Ive worked on the design of the Macintosh Sketchpad in 1990 and the Powerbook laptop in 1991. On the back of these, he was offered a full-time position by Apple in 1992 as part of its in-house design team based in Cupertino, California.

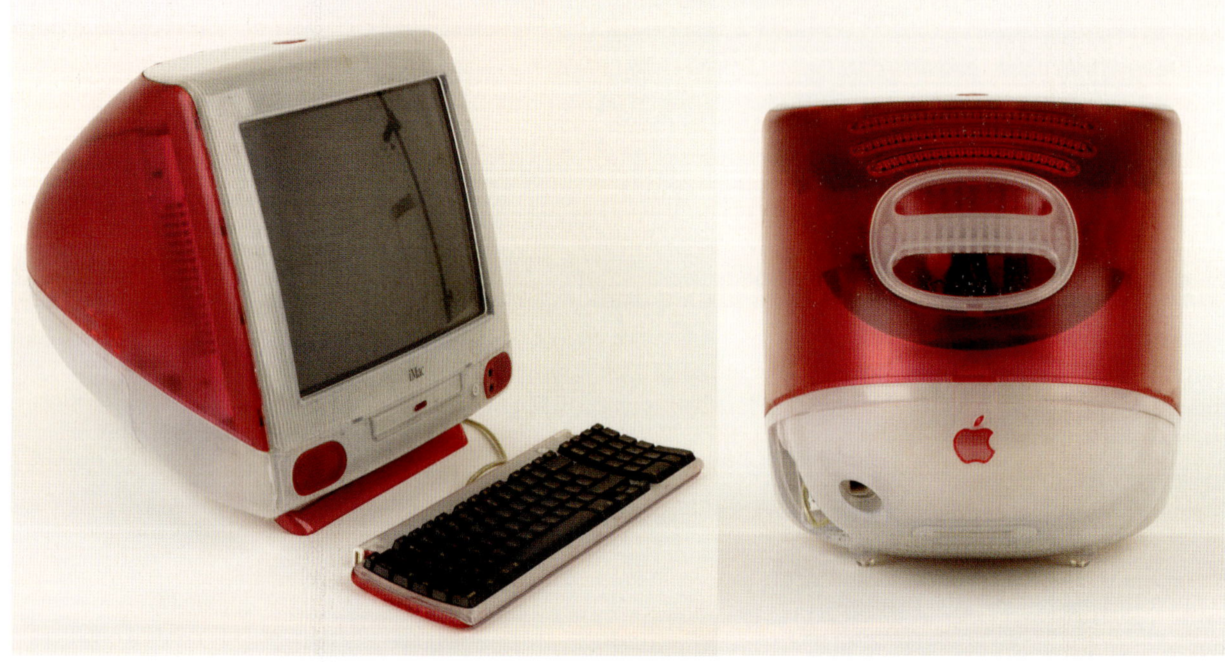

BELOW:
iMac computer
for Apple, 1998

During the 1990s, however, Apple was a deeply troubled company unable to compete properly in the marketplace, so much so that its legendary founder Steve Jobs, having been controversially ousted twelve years earlier, was re-appointed its CEO in 1997. On meeting, Ive and Jobs instantly hit it off, and shortly thereafter Ive was appointed Apple's senior vice-president of industrial design. The following year saw the launch of Ive's iMac – a completely revolutionary new computer design that would not only become a game-changer for the fortunes of the then struggling company but also for the desktop-computer industry as a whole, which up till then had relied on cream or grey boring box-like housings.

At the launch of the first iMac in 1998, Jobs waxed lyrically that it looked as if it was "from another planet, a good planet, a planet with better designers". Marking an important paradigm shift in computer styling, with its seductive, unified gumdrop form made from a two-tone colour combination of gleaming opaque and translucent polycarbonate, the iMac had a visual freshness that massively distinguished it from all computers that had gone before. It was, as the advertisement for it stated, "Chic, not Geek". That same year, over two million iMacs were sold, returning Apple to profitability for the first time in three years. Ive subsequently designed the first iPod in 2001, which likewise revolutionized the MP3 player (MP3 is a digital audio file format) market with its easy-to-use technology. He followed this up with the first iPhone in 2007 and the iPad in 2010 – both of which have similarly come to dominate the smart-phone and computer-tablet markets respectively, thanks to their superior design which means they offer far better functional performance than their competitors.

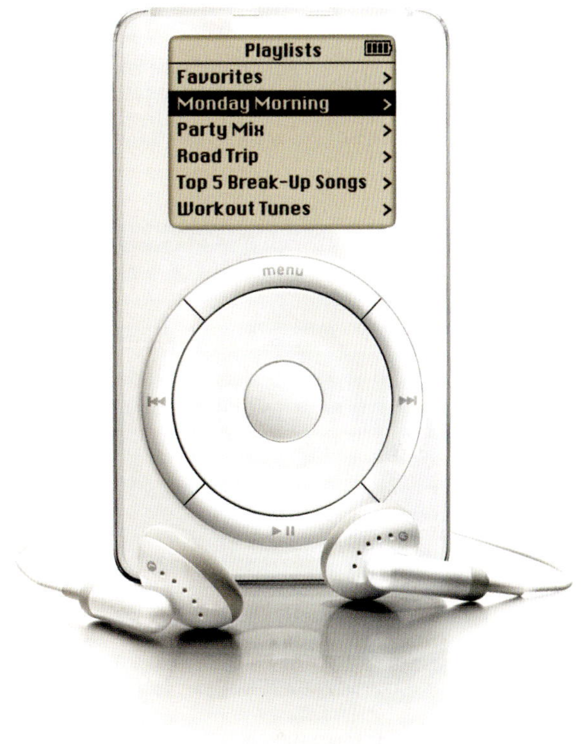

ABOVE:
iPod MP3 player
for Apple, 2001

The real genius of Ive, however, lies in his innate understanding of simplicity, for as he observes, "there is a profound and enduring beauty in simplicity; in clarity, in efficiency. True simplicity is derived from so much more than just the absence of clutter and ornamentation. It's about bringing order to complexity." And in our information-saturated digital age, that is what we most want from any product, which is why his beautifully conceived designs have become such potent objects of desire: ultimately they help make our lives easier to navigate.

Arne Jacobsen

Danish, 1902–1971

BELOW:
Series 7 (Model 3107) chair
for Fritz Hansen, 1955

OPPOSITE:
Egg chair and ottoman
for Fritz Hansen, 1956–58

Arne Jacobsen's work was the very embodiment of Danish Modernism – combining the functionalist ideals of the Modern Movement with a very Nordic reverence for the natural world. It is a tribute to his genius as a designer that many of his designs have remained in production for decades and are now probably more popular than ever.

Born in Copenhagen, Jacobsen trained as a mason at the Skolen for Brugskunst (School of Applied Arts), Copenhagen, before studying architecture at the Kongelige Danske Kunstakademi (Royal Danish Academy of Arts), also in Copenhagen. While still a student, he won a silver medal at the 1925 *Exposition Internationale des Arts Décoratifs et Industriels Modernes* held in Paris for a strikingly innovative armchair made of woven cane. After the completion of his studies in 1927, he travelled in Europe and became inspired by the work of the early pioneers of the Modern Movement. On his return to Denmark, he worked as an associate for two years in the City Architect's Office in Copenhagen where he designed a music pavilion, shelters and entrance gates for Enghave Park in Copenhagen – all of which reflected the influence of European Modernism.

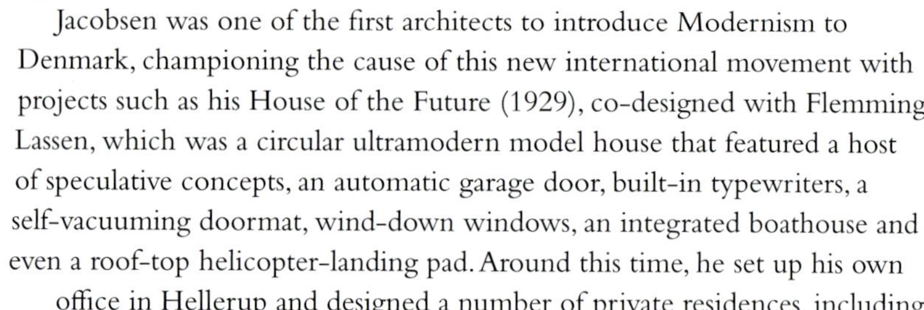

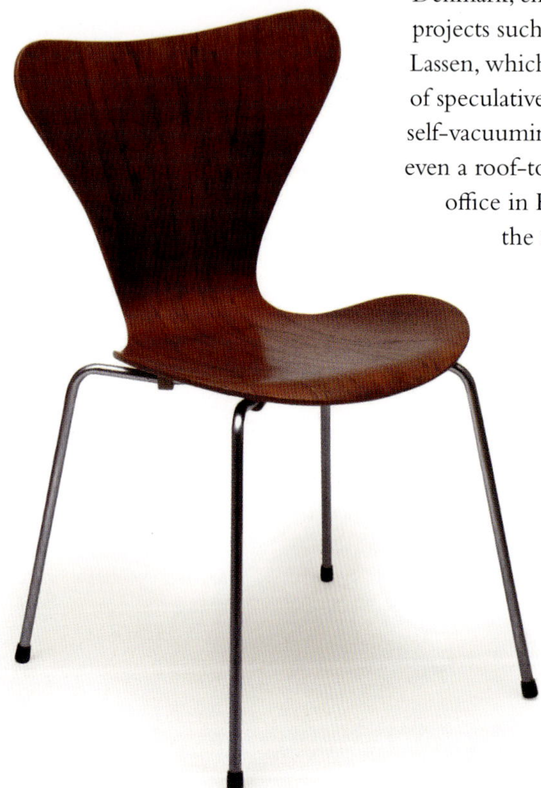

Jacobsen was one of the first architects to introduce Modernism to Denmark, championing the cause of this new international movement with projects such as his House of the Future (1929), co-designed with Flemming Lassen, which was a circular ultramodern model house that featured a host of speculative concepts, an automatic garage door, built-in typewriters, a self-vacuuming doormat, wind-down windows, an integrated boathouse and even a roof-top helicopter-landing pad. Around this time, he set up his own office in Hellerup and designed a number of private residences, including the functionalist Rothenborg House (1930) in Klampenborg, which was conceived as a *Gesamtkunstwerk* (total work of art). It was, however, the Bellevue complex (1930–34) sited next to the beach in Klampenborg that was his first major public project. Comprising three apartment blocks with stepped and jutting balconies, which had an appropriately nautical air, an airy and light-filled restaurant furnished with specially designed chairs that were made by Fritz Hansen, and an adjoining theatre with a round-edged façade and an interior filled with wave-like rows of steam-bent plywood auditorium seats, the Bellevue project revealed Jacobsen's humanist approach to Modernism. This was reiterated in his competition-winning design for Århus Town Hall (1937–42), co-designed with Erik Møller, which was notable for its use of soft flowing lines that predicted the bold organic forms of Jacobsen's later designs.

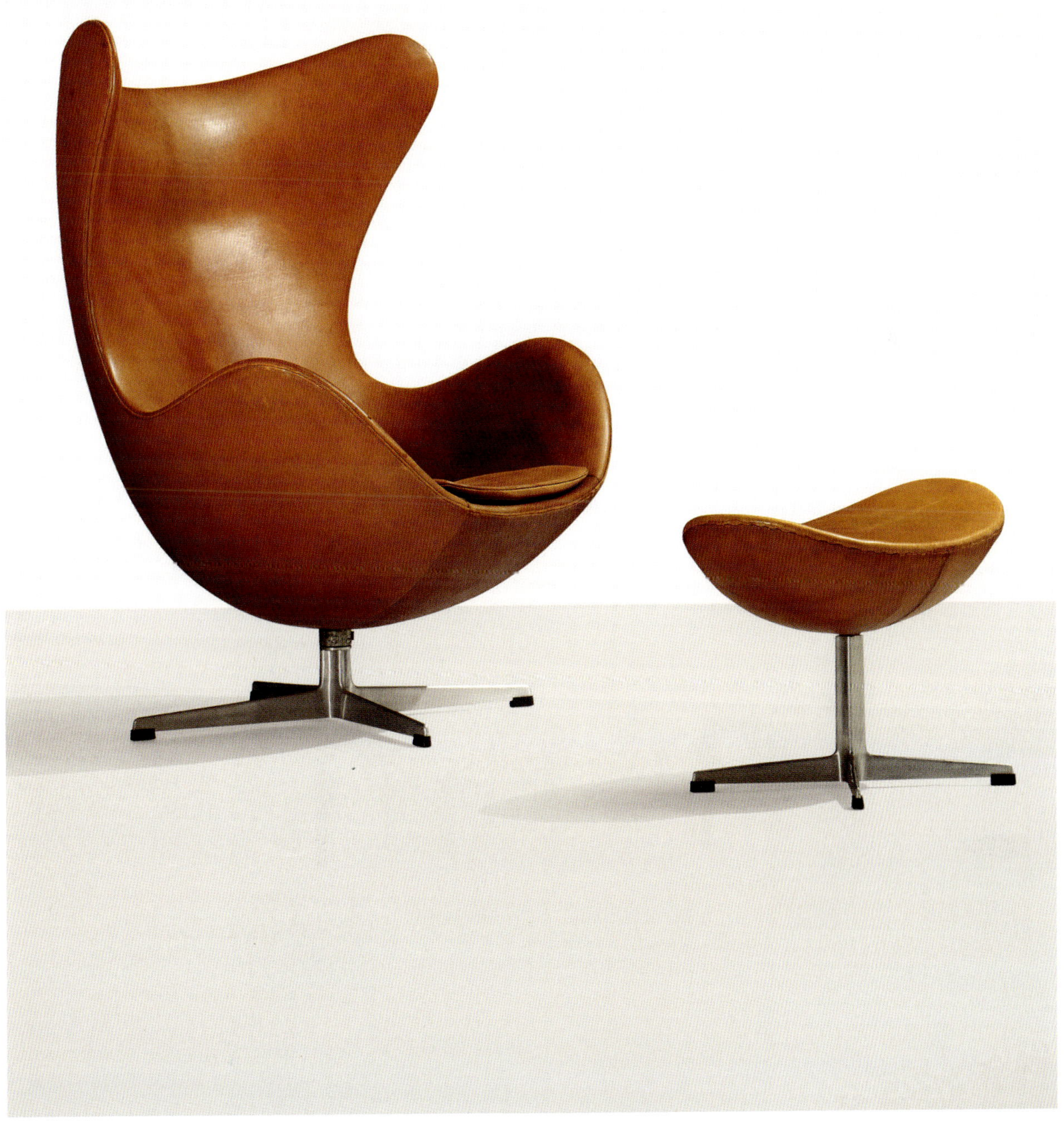

During the Second World War, Jacobsen lived in neutral Sweden; after the cessation of hostilities he returned to Denmark and began designing furniture specifically for high-volume production. His first notable success in this area was the three-legged Model 3100 Ant chair (1951–52), originally designed for the canteen at Novo Nordisk but then put into production by Fritz Hansen. This chair with its biomorphic-shaped seat shell made of moulded plywood heralded a new organic sculptural confidence in Danish design. It also acted as the blueprint for his Series 7 chairs, which innovatively used a universal seat shell in conjunction with various different bases. The basic version of this chair, the Model 3107, would go on to become one of the best-selling seating designs of all time.

Frequently, Jacobsen's designs for furniture and lighting were created for a specific architectural project and only later put into production. One such project was the SAS Air Terminal and Royal Hotel, Copenhagen (1956–60) – a Modernist *Gesamtkunstwerk* for which Jacobsen designed every detail, from textiles and light fittings to cutlery and furniture. The integrated interiors of the hotel had a strong futuristic quality and included two of Jacobsen's best-known designs, the Egg and Swan chairs (1956–58). Apart from his numerous furniture designs produced by Fritz Hansen, Jacobsen also created the AJ lighting range for Louis Poulsen (1955–60), the Cylinda-Line tableware collection for Stelton (1967), a range of sleekly profiled cutlery for Georg Jensen, the stylish Vola bathroom taps for I.P. Lunds, and various woven and printed textiles for August Millech, Graucob Textilen and C. Olesen. Many of these designs were included in his architectural masterwork, St Catherine's College, Oxford (built 1960–64), which was another wholly unified scheme for which he designed various site-specific furniture, fixtures and fittings. This extraordinary project reflected better than any other architectural project Jacobsen's overriding belief in the importance of harmonious proportions and was remarkable for the way it integrated the various buildings on the campus with the surrounding landscaped garden – indeed, for Jacobsen, the outside spaces were completely integral to the college's overall design.

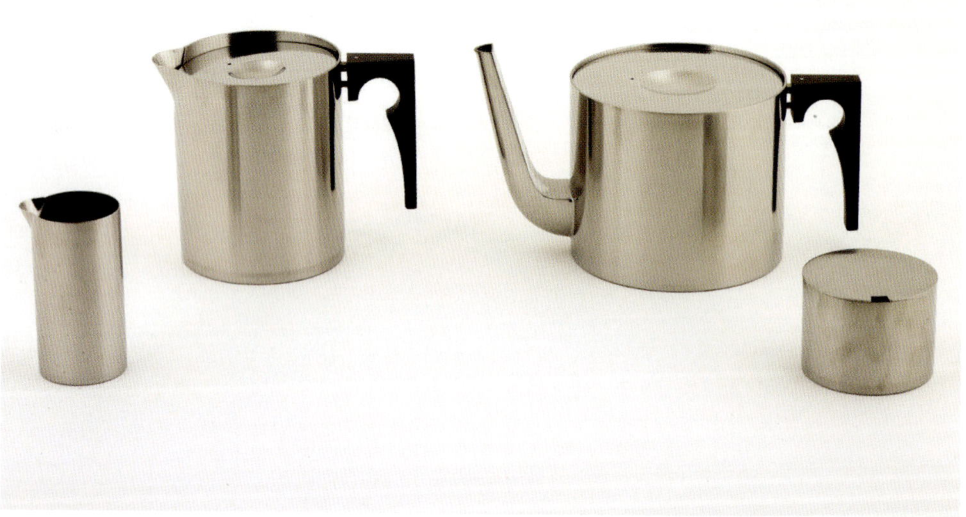

LEFT:
Cylinda-Line tea set
for Stelton, 1967

RIGHT:
AJ cutlery for Georg Jensen
1957

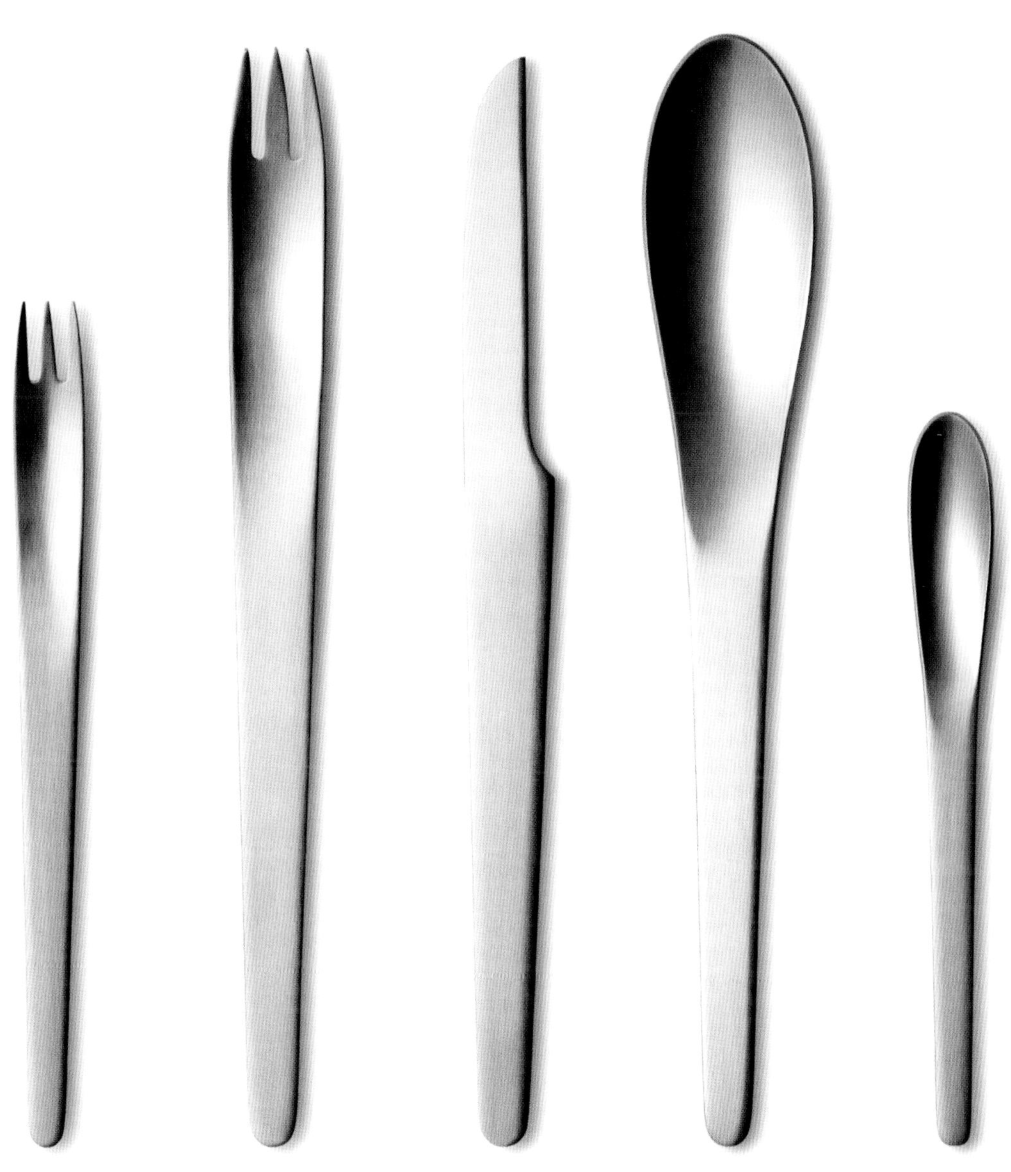

Hella Jongerius

Dutch, 1963–

During the late 1980s and early 1990s there was a resurgence of avant-garde design in the Netherlands thanks to the country having a number of world-class teaching institutions that were intent on pushing the boundaries of design education. Among these was the renowned Design Academy Eindhoven (DAE), with many of its alumni going on to become the pioneers of New Dutch Design, a Post-Modern/conceptual design movement. A notable member of this group was Hella Jongerius, who studied industrial design at the academy from 1988 to 1993. For her final project Jongerius created her innovative Bath Mat (1993) made from half-droplets of polyurethane – an off-the-shelf cushioning material that had previously been used in the bronze-working industry.

After graduating she set up her own design studio, Jongeriuslab, in Rotterdam in 1993 and the same year exhibited with the design collective Droog at the Milan Furniture Fair. Like other designers associated with New Dutch Design, Jongerius enjoys exploring the creative potential of traditional craftsmanship in her pursuit of conceptual designs that have a rather quirky craft-meets-industry aesthetic. For instance, her Soft Urn and Soft Vase series (1994) for Droog Design, featuring archetypal vessel forms cast in either soft un-dyed polyurethane rubber or coloured silicone rubber, explored how synthetic materials age over time. Examples from both series were included in the landmark *Mutant Materials in Contemporary Design* exhibition held at the Museum of Modern Art, New York in 1995.

By fusing craft with industry, the low tech with the high tech, the traditional with the new, Jongerius creates work that is far removed from the sterile perfection of so much of

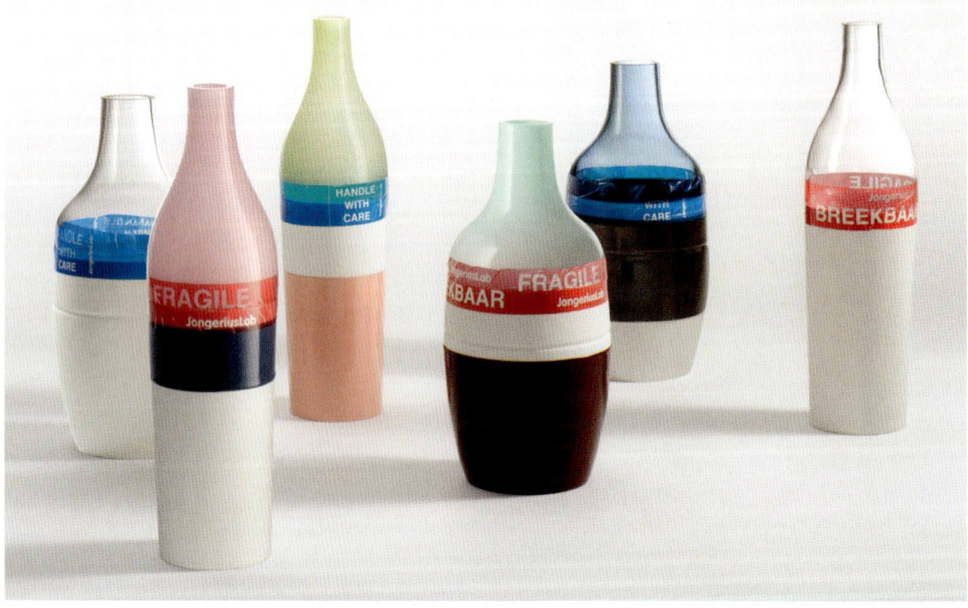

BELOW:
Long Neck and Groove Bottles
for Jongeriuslab, 2000

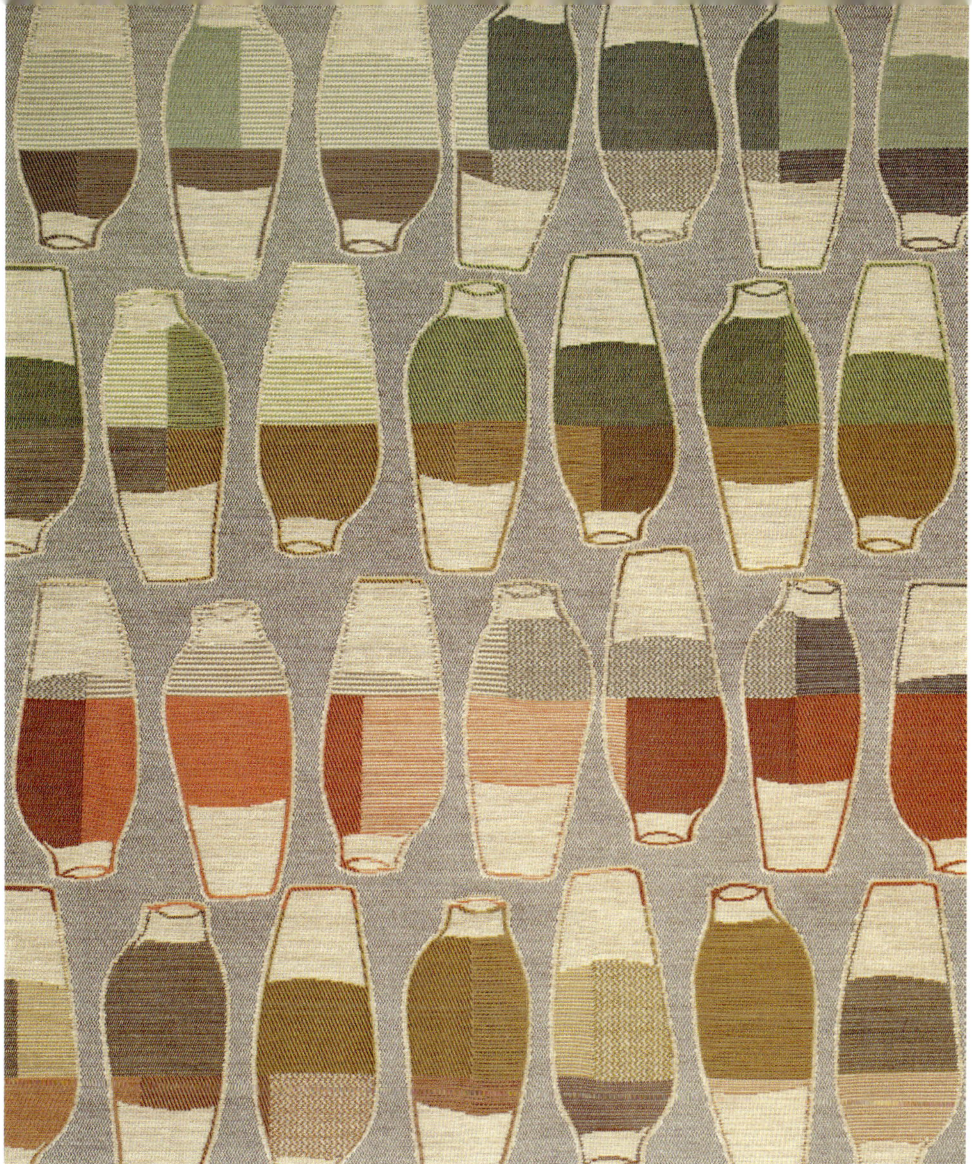

ABOVE:
Vases textile
for Maharam, 2012–13

today's mass-produced design. Instead, her pieces have a curious hybrid quality. In 1998, she began teaching at the Design Academy Eindhoven, and between 2000 and 2004 she headed up the college's Living Department. During this period, she also created some pieces that were notable for their unconventional approach to design and making, for instance the B-Set range (1997) of intentionally imperfect industrially produced glazed-porcelain tableware for Royal Tichelaar Makkum and her porcelain Prince and Princess vases (2000) based on traditional Ming forms and "embroidered" with coloured silicone rubber. It was, however, her range of Long Neck and Groove Bottles (2000), which constructionally fused two disparate materials – glass and ceramic – using simple packing tape, that would bring her greatest international recognition.

The following year, Jongerius participated in the *Workspheres* exhibition at the Museum of Modern Art, New York, and in 2002 began designing eye-catching textiles for Maharam and created the Crystal Frock chandelier for Swarovski. From 2005, she has worked closely with the Swiss manufacturer Vitra, both as a designer in her own right and as art director for colours and materials used for the firm's contemporary and classic collections.

Susan Kare

American, 1954–

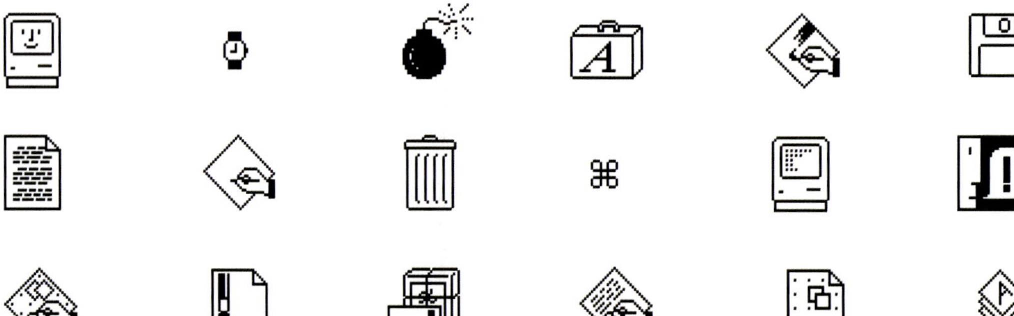

ABOVE:
GUI (graphical user interface) icons for Apple
*c.*1983–84

A great unsung hero of early digital font design, Susan Kare was also responsible for creating the first computer icons for Apple's Macintosh computer – thereby changing the face of computing forever and defining the visual language of computers for decades to come. Yet until recently Kare's important design contribution to our digital revolution has been largely overlooked.

Having studied at Mount Holyoke College and then New York University, Kare initially worked as a curator at the Fine Arts Museums of San Francisco. In the early 1980s, however, a high-school friend, Andy Hertzfeld, recruited her to help design the screen graphics for the original Apple Macintosh computer, which was one of the first commercial computers to boast a GUI, or graphical user interface. This meant that it allowed users to interact with it using images rather than text commands, which made it much easier to operate than previous models. A talented computer scientist, Hertzfeld was one of the main authors of the Macintosh system software, specifically developing its core operating system and its innovative user-interface tools. As part of Apple's small but dedicated design team, Kare, with her background in the arts, began to create a family of easy-to-understand yet slightly whimsical computer icons that were originally inspired by familiar objects – notably the trash can, the bomb, the paint can, the ticking watch, the floppy disk, the font suitcase and so forth. These ingeniously clever yet graphically simple icons made the Apple Mac the first-ever user-friendly desktop machine, so much so it was marketed as the "computer for the rest of us". Kare's smiling computer icon – the Happy Mac – symbolized in just a few simple lines what the Apple Macintosh was all about, and helped to give computers a more human face, quite literally.

With these icons that were stylized representations of real-world objects, Kare was able to make computer commands familiar and easy to understand – a huge breakthrough given that earlier computers had used deeply off-putting command lines, which relied on users having to type in text instructions. She was also one of the pioneers of digital fonts, notably

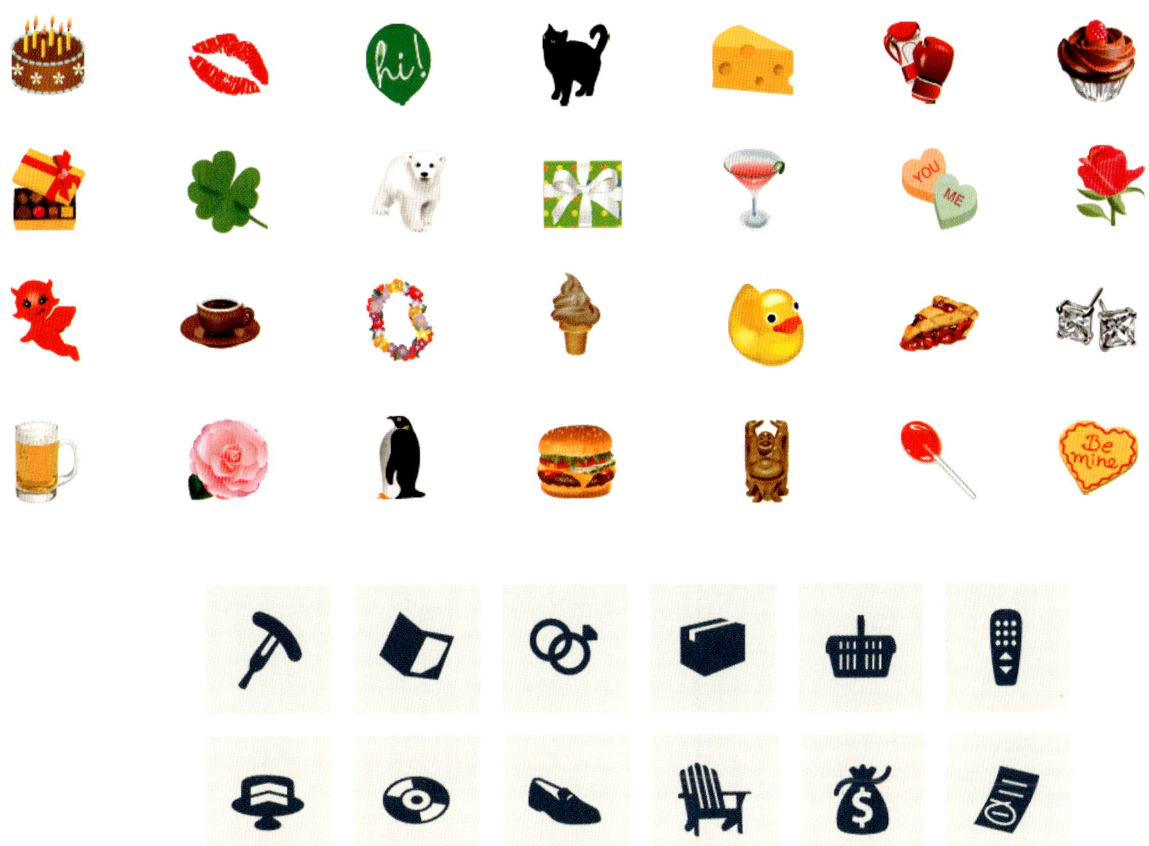

TOP:
Gift icons for Facebook
from 2007

ABOVE:
Transaction icons for PayPal
2009

creating some of the original Macintosh "city" fonts such as Chicago, New York, Monaco, San Francisco, Geneva and Cairo. In 1985, when Steve Jobs was famously ousted from Apple, Kare left shortly thereafter, and subsequently joined NeXT, the new computer company Jobs founded, as its creative director. As one of the leading interface designers working in Silicon Valley, she was also responsible for designing icons used for Microsoft's Windows 3.0 operating system, and worked as a designer for IBM.

In 2007, she began creating hundreds of virtual gifts for the social-networking website Facebook – including a birthday cake, a box of chocolates, a cupcake, an ice-cream, a four-leaf clover, a cocktail, a rubber duck, a pair of diamond earrings – which, like her earlier icons, had a direct clarity that could be universally understood. As Kare noted in an interview with *Wired* magazine in 2013, "The basic problem that you're trying to solve by designing an icon for a screen has not changed: you aim to create an image that's visual shorthand for a concept. If you do your job well, that image becomes meaningful as a symbol – something easy to recognize and remember." For over thirty years, Kare has created functional graphic imagery, often with a humorous metaphorical twist, which has made the world of computers easier to navigate and understand, and because of this she must be considered one of the world's most influential designers.

Jock Kinneir & Margaret Calvert

British, 1917–1974 / British, 1936–

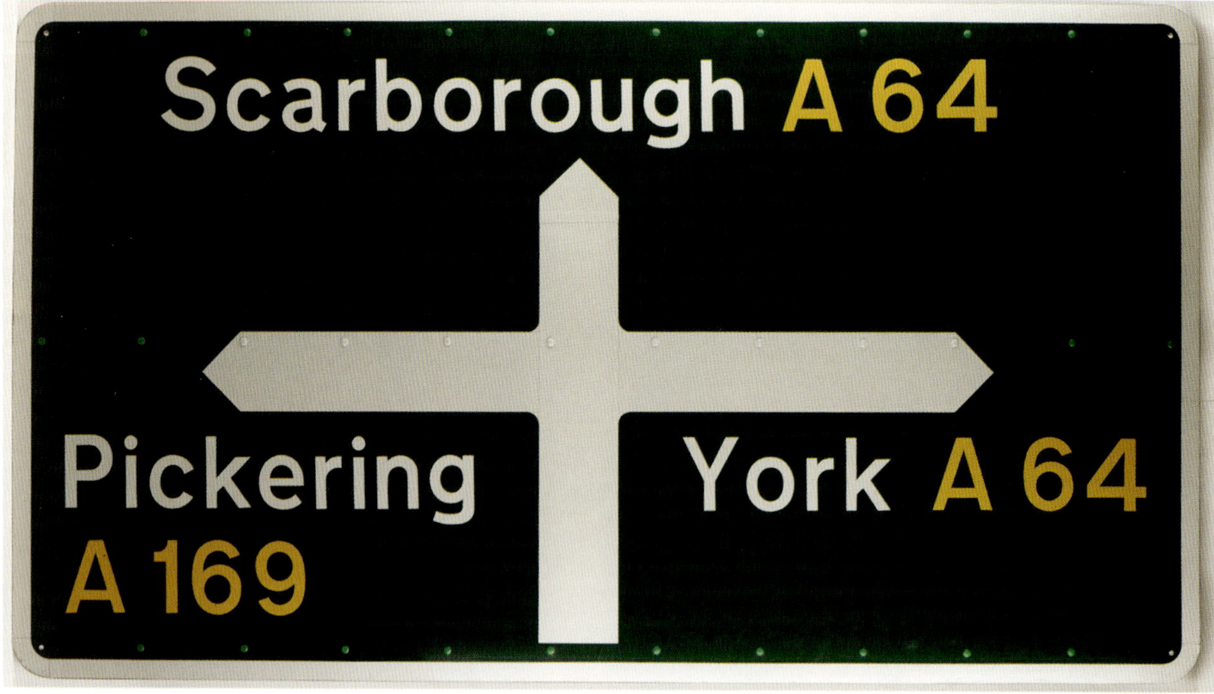

ABOVE:
Road signage system
for the Ministry of Transport, UK, 1957–67

Britain's distinctive motorway and road signage, designed by Jock Kinneir and Margaret Calvert during the late 1950s and 1960s, is probably the most effective and influential system of its kind anywhere. By utterly embodying the British design sensibility of graceful yet purposeful function, it has an unassailable visual logic that has made it an exemplar of Modern communication design.

Richard "Jock" Kinneir initially studied at Chelsea School of Art before working as an exhibition designer for the Central Office of Information. In 1949 he joined the Design Research Unit (DRU), a progressive multi-discipline design consultancy that had been founded six years earlier by Milner Grey and Misha Black. Kinneir remained at the DRU until he set up his own office in 1956. His first significant commission was the design of signage for the new Gatwick Airport and for this project he was assisted by one of his students at Chelsea, Margaret Calvert. Together they created a modern airport signage system that had a remarkable sense of clarity and formal consistency. Importantly, this way-finding design came to the attention of Sir Colin Anderson, who had recently been appointed chairman of a new Advisory Committee on Traffic Signs for Motorways by the Ministry of Transport in 1957. This working group was charged with overseeing the design of signage for the country's new motorway system and Kinneir, being the most obvious candidate, was commissioned to undertake it. Using an in-depth research-led approach, Kinneir, assisted by Calvert, developed a new motorway signage system that was cleverly based on the concept of letter tiles laid out on a grid. By using this method, the overall size of specific signs could be determined by the amount of information they needed to contain, while the width of the signs' borders and other key elements were set in proportional relationship to the cross stroke of the capital letter "I".

To maximize clarity and legibility, the duo also created a bespoke rounded sans serif typeface, known as Transport, which could be easily read from a car travelling at high speed. Similarly, they used a combination of upper- and lower-case lettering to enhance readability, rather than purely capitals as had previously been used on British road signage. By codifying the size and placement of the easy-to-read lettering, Kinneir and Calvert had effectively developed a highly adaptable and functional signage system, which was first trialled on the Preston bypass in 1958 before being introduced the following year on the M1 motorway.

After the new motorway signage had been installed, the government set up the Worboys Committee to review the design of signage on all of the nation's other roads. This led to a new commission for Kinneir and Calvert, to design – over a period of several years – an exhaustive range of all-new traffic signs. They included the iconic Children Crossing sign, which was based on a childhood photograph of Calvert. In 1965, Kinneir and Calvert's thoughtfully conceived and gently refined signage system was introduced, and subsequently became a blueprint for other road signage systems all over the world. The same year, the duo started work on a new visual identity programme for British Rail that included their easy-to-read Rail Alphabet typeface, which is still used to this day. They also developed a distinctive signage for the Tyne & Weir Metro in 1980, and between 1987 and 1991, Calvert was head of graphic design at the Royal College of Art.

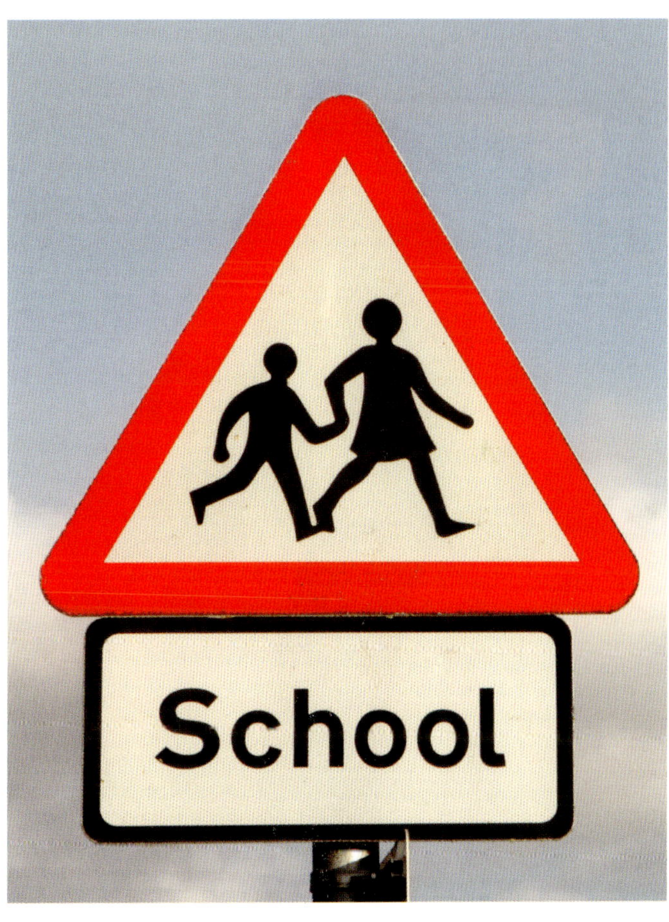

ABOVE:
Children Crossing sign (part of the road signage system for the Ministry of Transport, England, 1957–67) based on a childhood photograph of Margaret Calvert

Shiro Kuramata

Japanese, 1934–1991

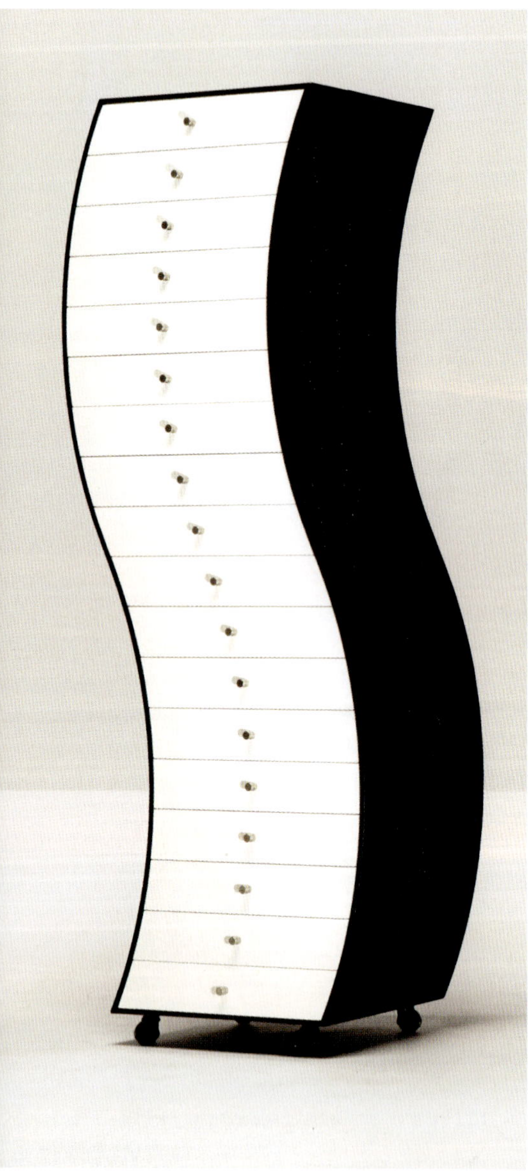

ABOVE:
Furniture in Irregular Forms Side 1
for Cappellini, 1970

OPPOSITE:
Sing Sing Sing chair
for Terada Tekkojo, 1985

With his intuitive feeling for materials, his understanding of spatial relationships and his imaginative and experimental approach to design, Shiro Kuramata created poetic furniture, lighting, homewares and interior installations that transcended everyday function and eroded the traditional boundaries between art and design. His masterful handling of materials stemmed from his studies in woodcraft at Tokyo Higher School of Industrial Design, while his ability to create compelling spatial tensions between an object and its surroundings can be traced to his training as an interior designer at the Kuwasawa Design Institute. Kuramata's earliest design work involved the creation of retail showcases, window displays and forward-looking interior spaces for department stores, restaurants, boutiques and offices.

He established his own design office in 1965 and two years later encountered conceptual art for the first time at the *Design for Living* exhibition held at Matsuya department store in Ginza, Tokyo. This show made a huge impression on him and he began designing what might be best described as concept furniture, with his Pyramid furniture chest-of-drawers (1968) and Spring table (1970) already revealing his ability to devise playful yet still quasi-functional solutions that had a strong visual presence. As Deyan Sudjic has noted, "Along with fashion designer and friend Issey Miyake, architects Arata Isozaki and Tadao Ando, and film-maker Akira Kurosawa, Kuramata belonged to the remarkable generation of talented young Japanese who transformed the way that Japan was viewed by the world.... After the war, their generation was the first to come to maturity with a chance to express itself. Kuramata's work was clearly Modern in the way that it used materials, and specifically Japanese in its simplicity and elegance. Yet Kuramata was always prepared to experiment."

Kuramata delighted in transforming commonly used "poor" materials such as acrylic, chipboard and strength-reinforcing steel expanded mesh into precious objects of rare poetic beauty. As one of the leading figures of the Japanese avant-garde he went on to collaborate with the Memphis design group in the early 1980s, notably creating the Kyoto table out of glass-chipped terrazzo (1983). Although often described as a minimalist, Kuramata was actually more of a dematerialist who produced refined elemental designs that were highly sculptural and were typified by an inherent tension between the object and the defining space surrounding it.

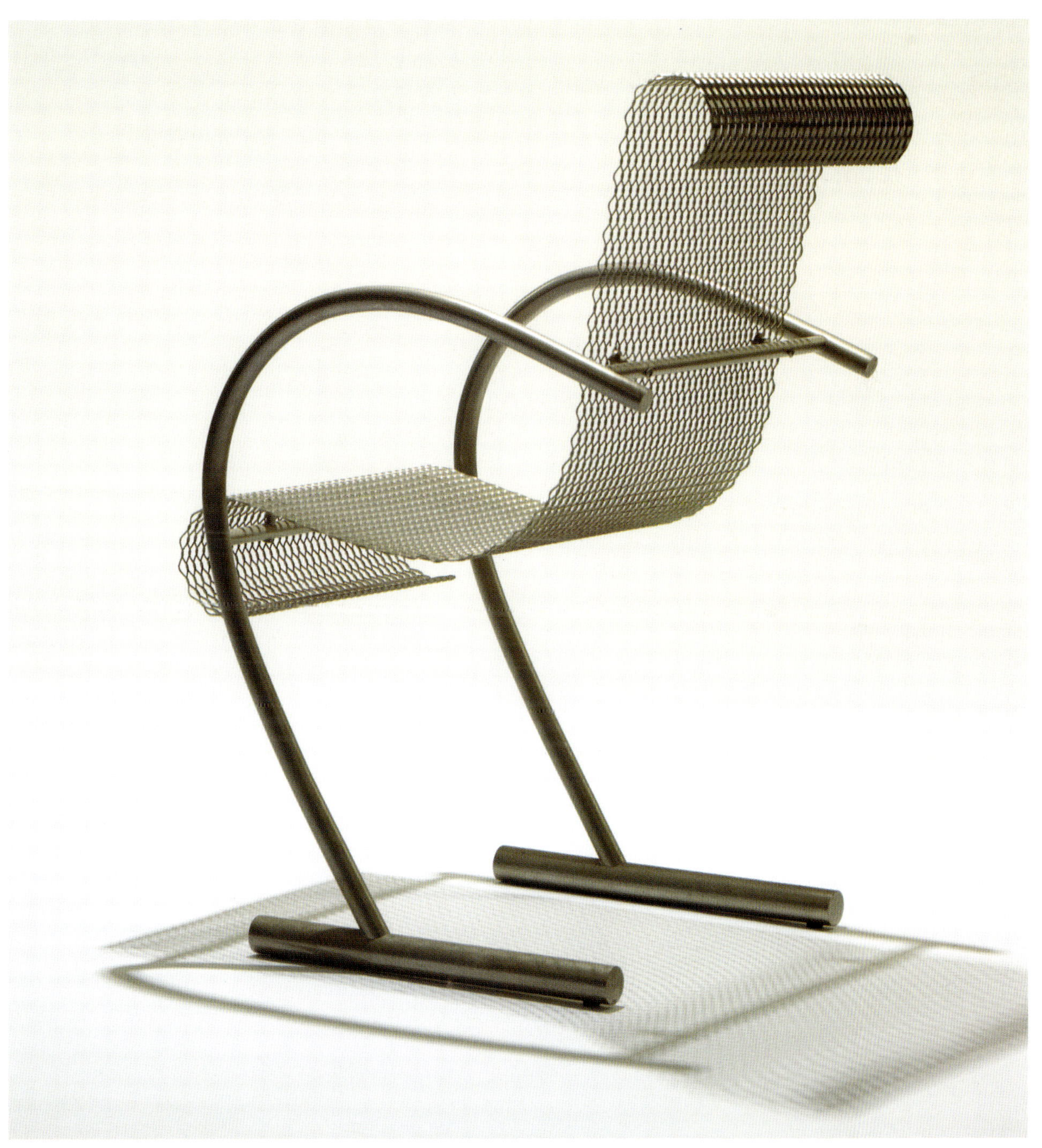

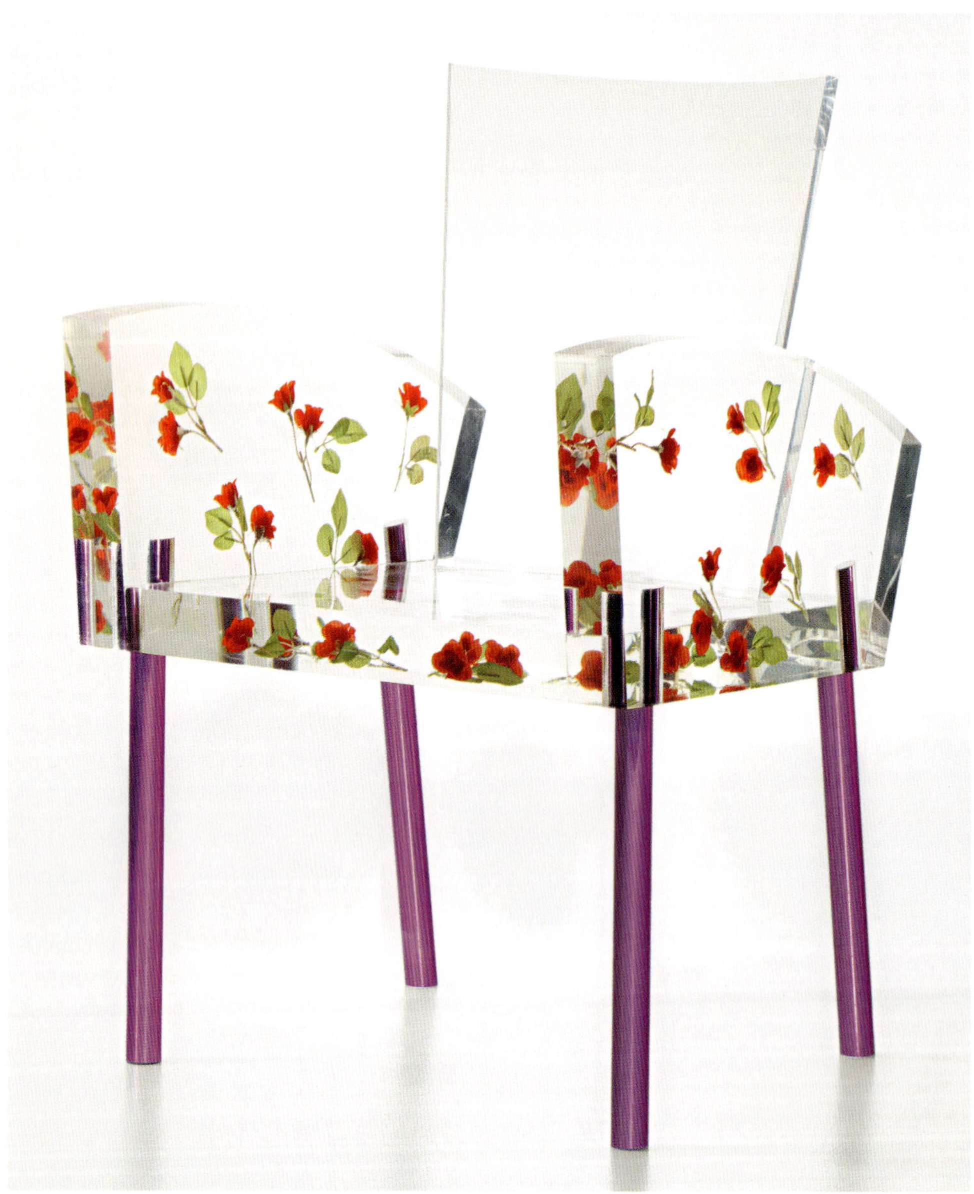

ABOVE:
Miss Blanche chair
for Ishimaru Corporation, 1988

OPPOSITE:
Model No. 2 and Model No. 1 vases
for Ishimaru Corporation, 1989

One of the most characteristic themes found in Kuramata's later designs is that of transparency. This was most eloquently expressed in his extraordinary Miss Blanche chair of 1988, which, with its artificial roses suspended in cast acrylic, exemplified his alchemical way of using synthetic polymers to create magical and otherworldly designs that bridged the age-old cultural traditions of the East and the Modernist design credo of the West. As Aaron Betsky, the former architecture curator of the San Francisco Museum of Modern Art, explained, "Kuramata showed us that a chair is not just an object to sit on but a way to dream and defy gravity." During the three remaining years of his all-too-short life, Kuramata continued to explore the jewel-like qualities of cast acrylic to dramatic effect – from his series of well-known vases to his Feather stool (1990). Kuramata's idiosyncratic work synthesized the cultures of the East and the West and in so doing expressed an exciting new internationalism in design.

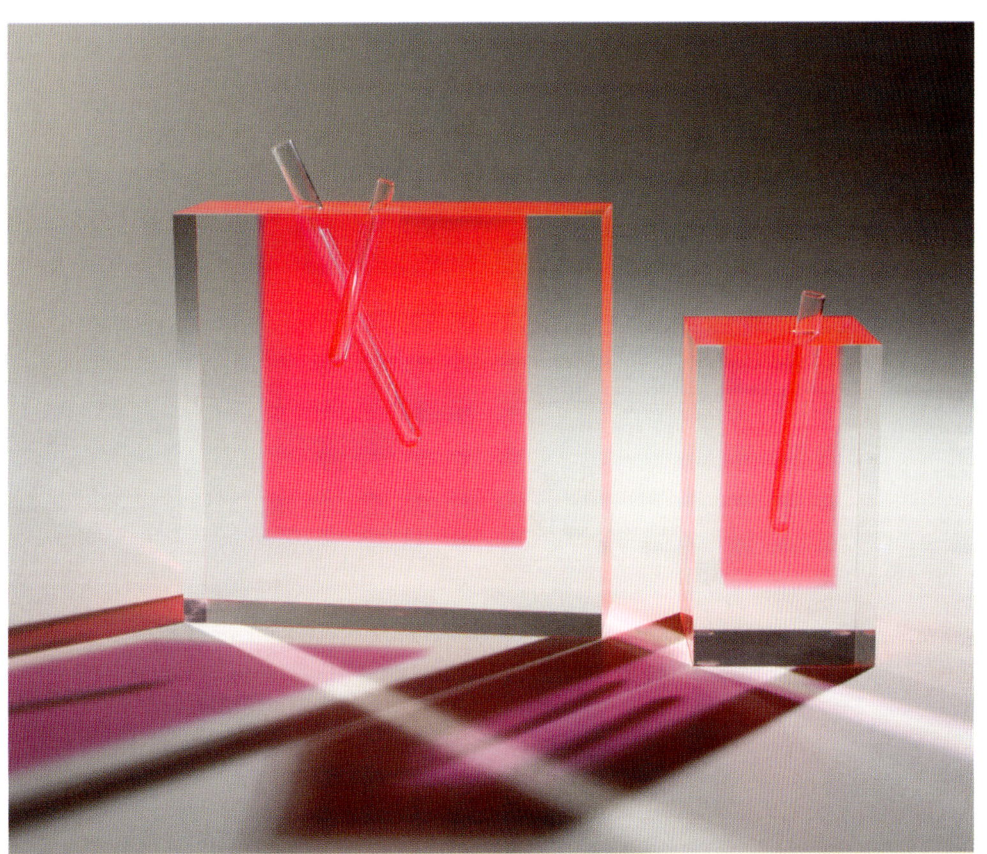

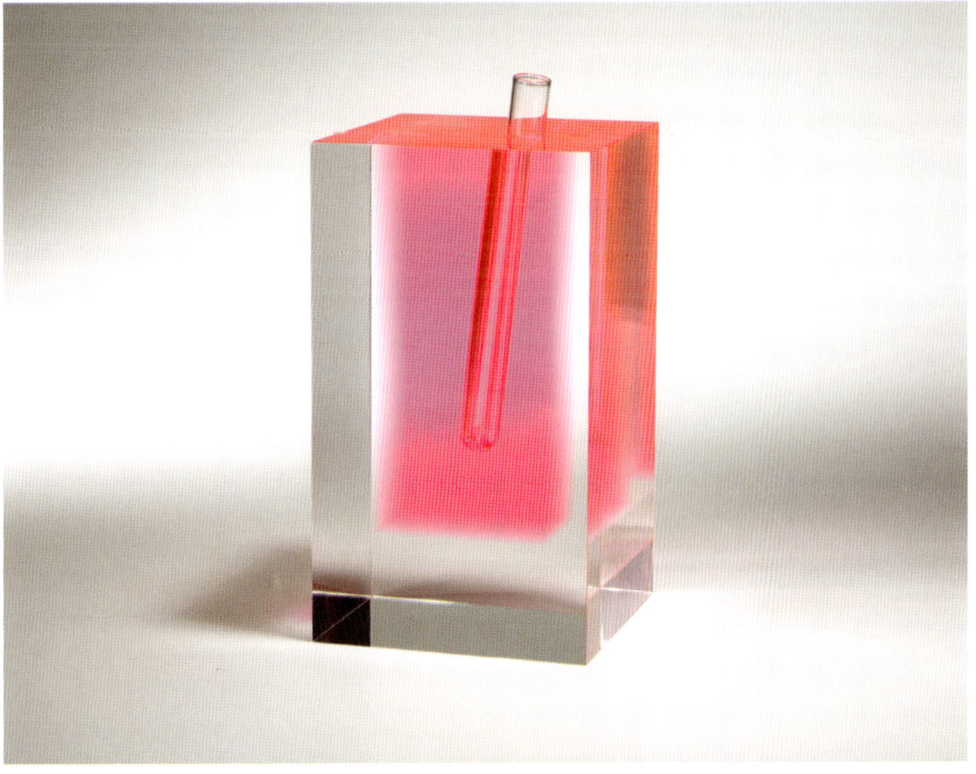

Le Corbusier

Swiss/French, 1887–1965

OPPOSITE:
L'équipement d'une Habitation (equipment for the home) model apartment installation for the 1929 *Salon d'Automne* - co-designed with Charlotte Perriand and Pierre Jeanneret

A seminal figure in the evolution of Modern architecture and design, Le Corbusier's uncompromising Modernist "visions" fundamentally changed how our homes were designed and our cities planned. During his prolific career he regarded himself as a sort of design crusader for a new Modern industrial age based on scientific empiricism. And in his single-minded quest for the rational, Le Corbusier often overlooked the human condition. As a result, his design theories tended to be rather hard-line, yet despite this his work and thoughts were of immense appeal to those attempting to build a brave new Modern world, during both the inter-war period and the post-war years, when there was a general consensus that well-designed social housing and better-planned cities were urgently needed.

Born in Switzerland as Charles-Édouard Jeanneret-Gris, he initially studied at the École d'Arts Appliqués (School of Applied Arts) in La Chaux-de-Fonds, and while there was urged by one of his tutors, Charles L'Eplattenier, to take up architecture. With this in mind, at the tender age of seventeen he assisted the architect René Chapallaz on the design and construction of the Villa Fallet (1905), a Jugendstil Alpine chalet built for one of the school's teaching staff, which is generally regarded as Le Corbusier's first building as he was responsible for drafting its plans and overseeing its construction.

In 1908 he moved to Paris and worked in the architectural practice of Auguste Perret, who was a leading specialist in reinforced concrete structures. While there, he met the influential German design critic Hermann Muthesius and the German architect and industrial designer Peter Behrens, for whom he later worked in Berlin from 1910 to 1911. He returned to Switzerland in 1912 and taught at his alma mater, and also worked on a concept for a prefabricated dwelling, known as the Dom-ino House (1914–15). Returning to the French capital in 1917, he subsequently adopted the pseudonym "Le Corbusier" – in reference to his maternal grandfather's surname Lecorbésier. Between 1918 and 1920, he edited the journal *L'Esprit Nouveau* (The New Spirit) and in 1923 published his influential book *Vers une Architecture* (Towards an Architecture).

In 1925, Le Corbusier caused quite a stir among the international design community with his Pavilion de l'Espirit Nouveau at the *Exposition Internationale des Arts Décoratifs et Industriels Modernes* in Paris. Countering the French interior design tradition, Le Corbusier's pavilion was a provocative statement of Modernist intent, which – with its airy spatial quality and sparse, functional furniture – reflected the Modern Movement's obsession with health and hygiene as well as the unrelenting progression of the modern industrial age. His concept of the house as "a machine for living in" would later include the creation of furniture that functioned as "equipment" and to this end he designed – in partnership with his cousin, Pierre Jeanneret, and Charlotte Perriand – a revolutionary range of tubular steel furniture, which included the famous Model No. B306 chaise longue (1928) and the LC2 Grand Confort club chair (1928).

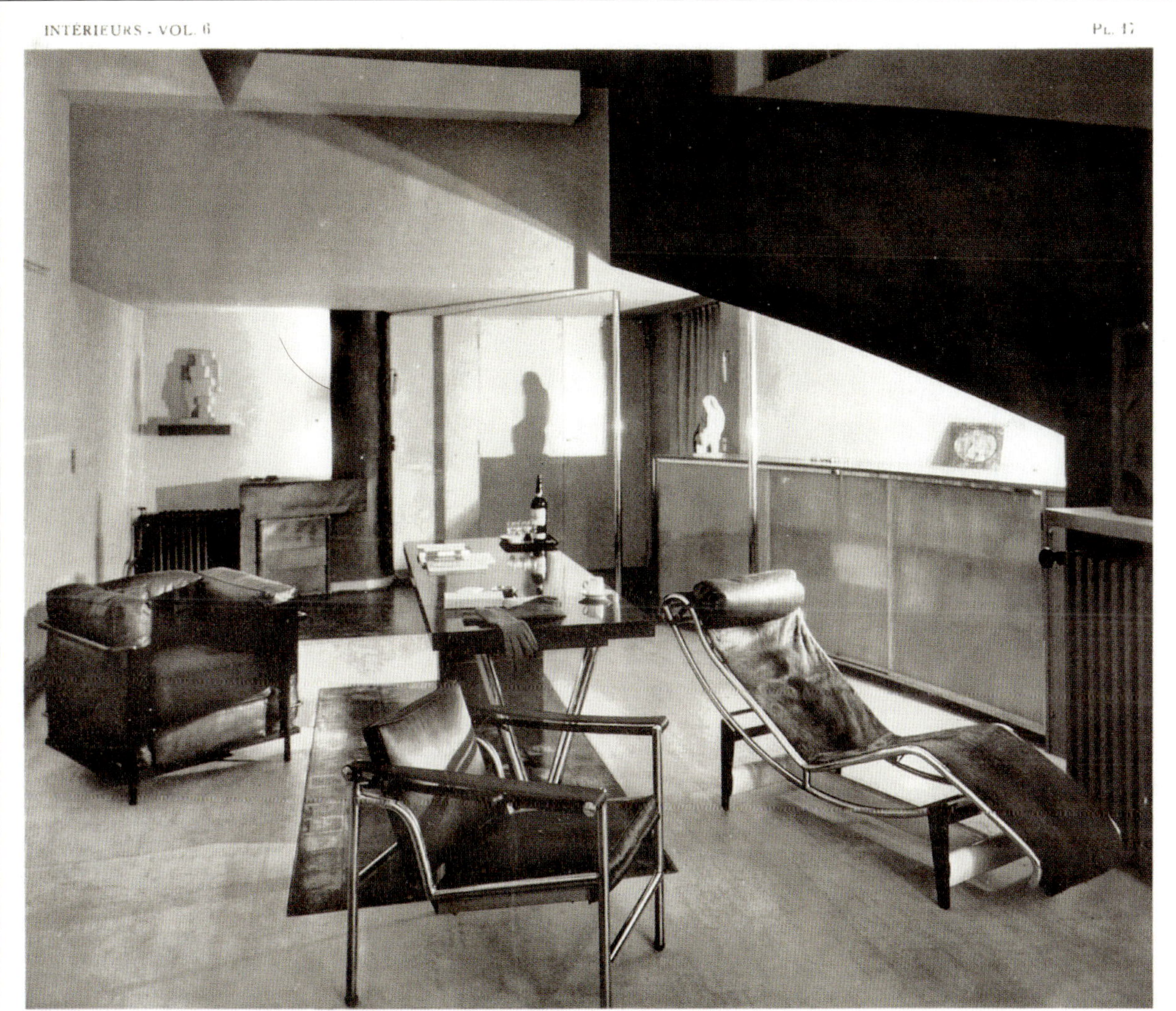
INTÉRIEURS - VOL. 6 PL. 17

Ensemble. — Le Corbusier, P. Jeanneret et Mme Ch. Perriand, décorateurs à Paris

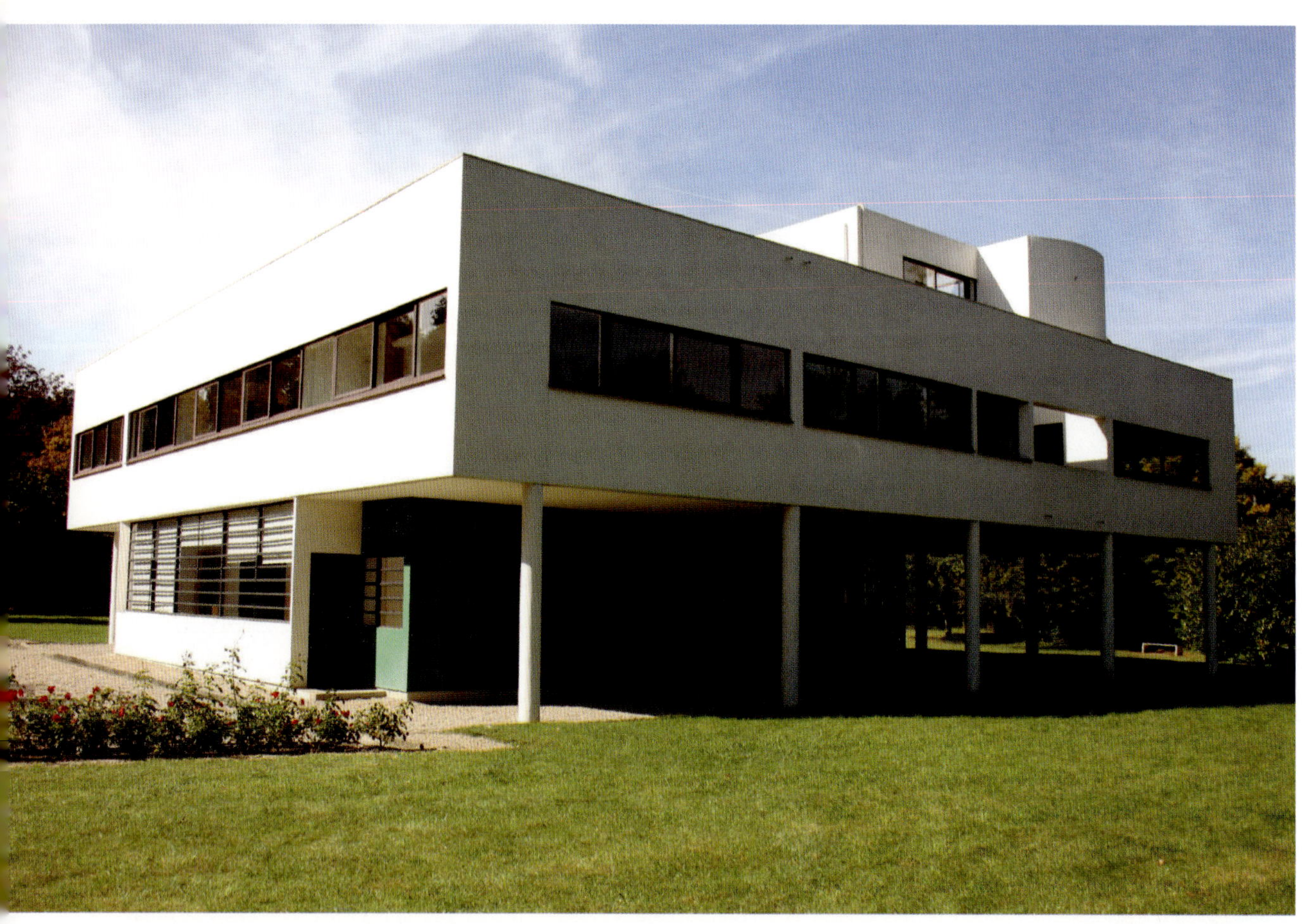

ABOVE:
Front and side elevations of the Villa Savoye
Poissy, 1928–31 – co-designed with Pierre Jeanneret

OPPOSITE:
Detail of the exterior of Corbusierhaus apartment building constructed as a *Unité d'Habitation* (housing unit)
Berlin, Germany, 1957

Between 1928 and 1931, Le Corbusier and Jeanneret designed the Villa Savoye in Poissy, on the outskirts of Paris. This Modernist *Gesamtkunstwerk* (total work of art) built of reinforced concrete was a revolutionary house that epitomized the aesthetic and functional purity of the International Style. Le Corbusier also designed far larger-scale projects that were infinitely more utilitarian in their intent – notably his unrealized La Ville Radieuse city plan (1924), the Cité de Refuge block built in Paris for the Salvation Army (1929–33) and the Unité d'Habitation residential-housing project in Marseille (1947-52).

Towards the end of his career, however, a new sculptural quality evolved in his buildings, notably the Notre-Dame-du-Haut church in Ronchamp in eastern France (1950–54) with its roofline suggesting the peaked habit of a nun. Recent research has revealed that Le Corbusier had Fascist sympathies and supported the idea of eugenics, which could well explain the lack of human empathy revealed in his supposedly utopian urban plans. Despite this, it cannot be denied that he was a design visionary at the absolute vanguard of the Modern Movement who was completely convinced that the implementation of Modernism would make the world a better place.

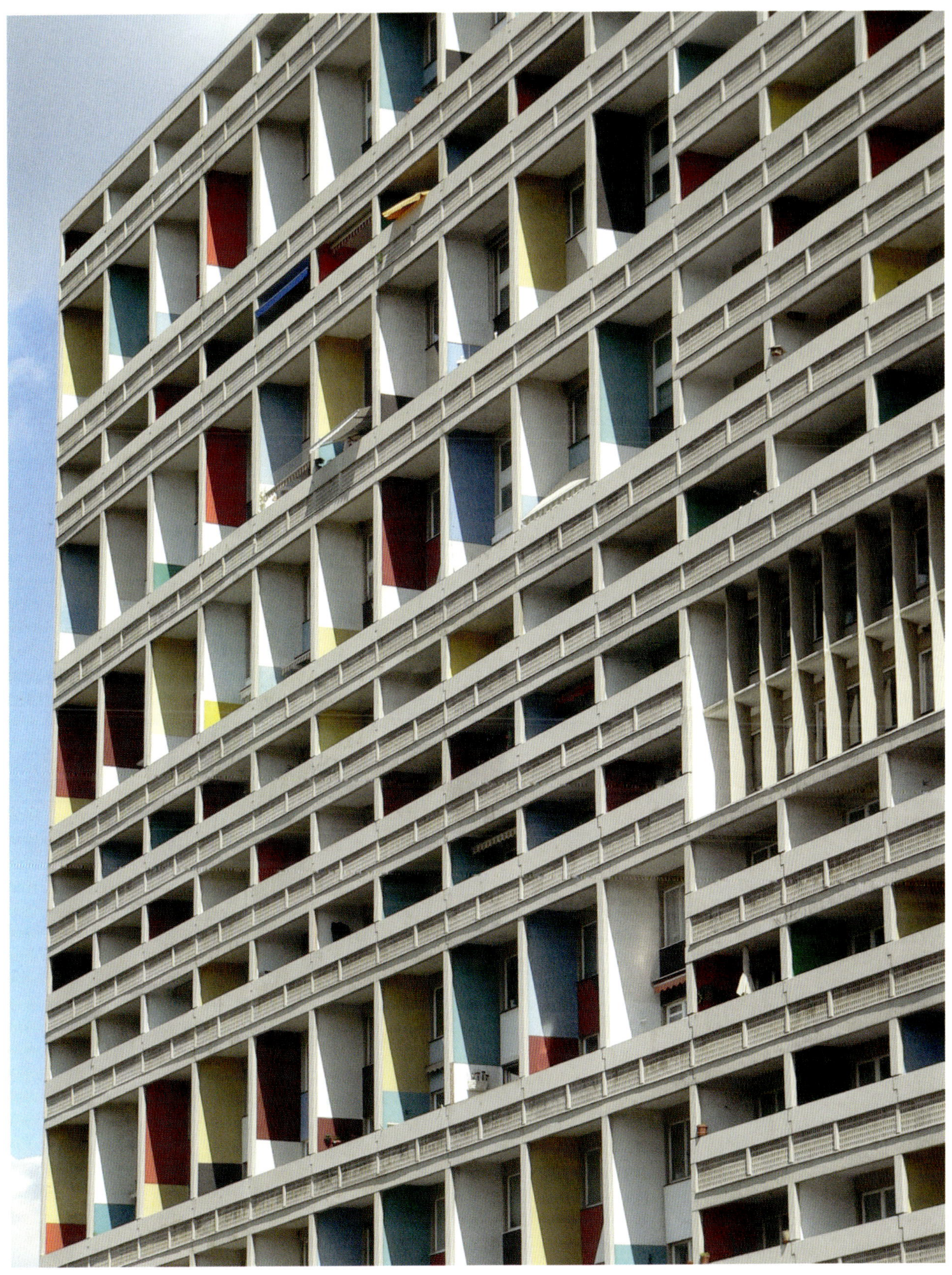

Raymond Loewy

French/American, 1893–1986

One of the most preeminent pioneers of industrial design consulting in American, Raymond Loewy summed up his approach to design with the maxim "Never leave well enough alone". Certainly, he took a commercially pragmatic approach to the design of objects that ensured their success in the marketplace, which made him the darling of many manufacturers who realized the impact his designs could have on their bottom lines. Indeed, it could be said that Loewy was instrumental in designing America's consumer culture.

Born in France, Loewy showed an early propensity for design problem solving, building and then flying at the age of fifteen a model airplane that won the James Gordon Bennett Cup. He also demonstrated early business acumen by designing and then patenting another model plane, the Monoplan Ayrel, powered by rubber bands, which he licensed to a manufacturer and which was subsequently sold throughout France. This early foray into design taught Loewy that "design could be fun and profitable". With the money he earned from his invention he was able to fund his studies at the Sorbonne in Paris and later at the École de Lanneau, graduating as an engineer in 1918. Having served in the French army during the First World War, after demobilization Loewy decided to emigrate to the United States in 1919.

On his arrival in New York, he was astounded by, as he put it, "the chasm between the excellent quality of American production and its gross appearance, clumsiness, bulk and noise". With his undoubted flair for design, he initially found work as a window dresser working for Macy's, Saks Fifth Avenue and Bonvit Teller, and later enjoyed a brief stint as a fashion illustrator for, among others, *Vogue*, *Harper's Bazaar* and *Vanity Fair*. He also designed a logo for the department store Neiman-Marcus in 1923 and advertisements for the White Star Line in 1928. In 1929, he established his own industrial design office in New York and as a venerated showman had cards printed with the credo: "Between two products equal in price, function and quality, the better looking will outsell the other."

BELOW:
Redesigned copier machine
for Gestetner, 1929

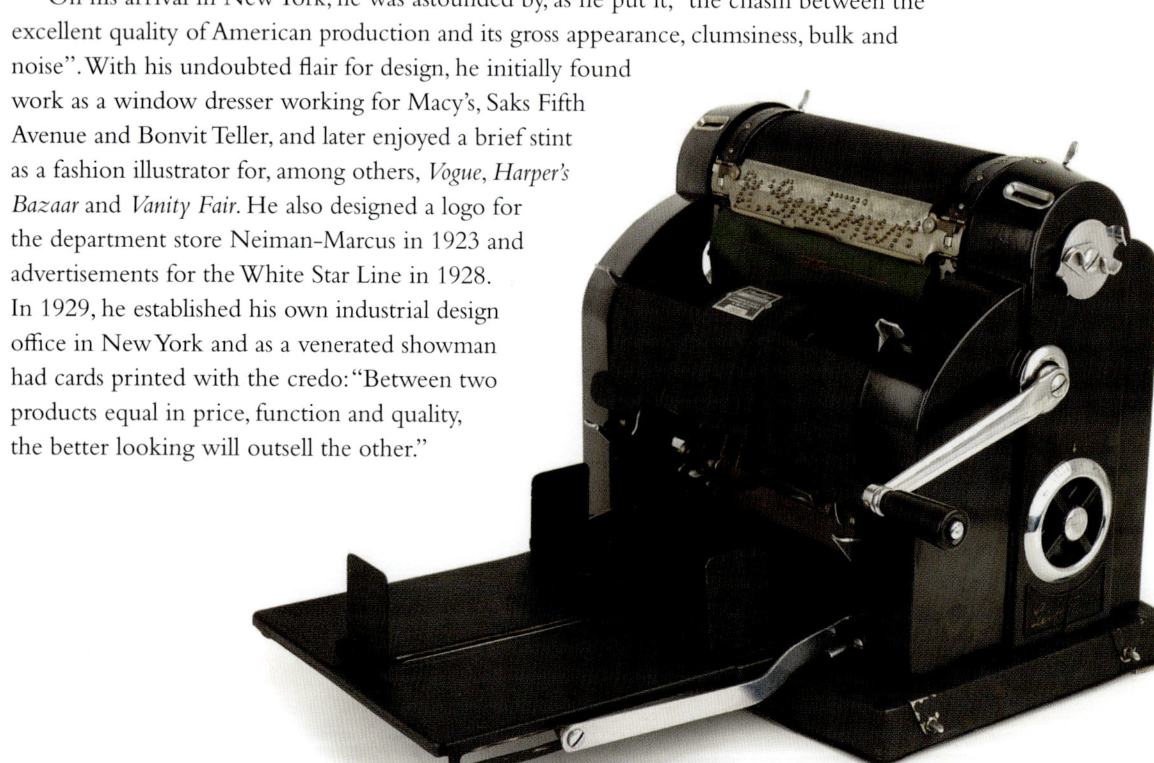

RIGHT:
Coldspot Super-Six refrigerator
for Sears Roebuck, 1934

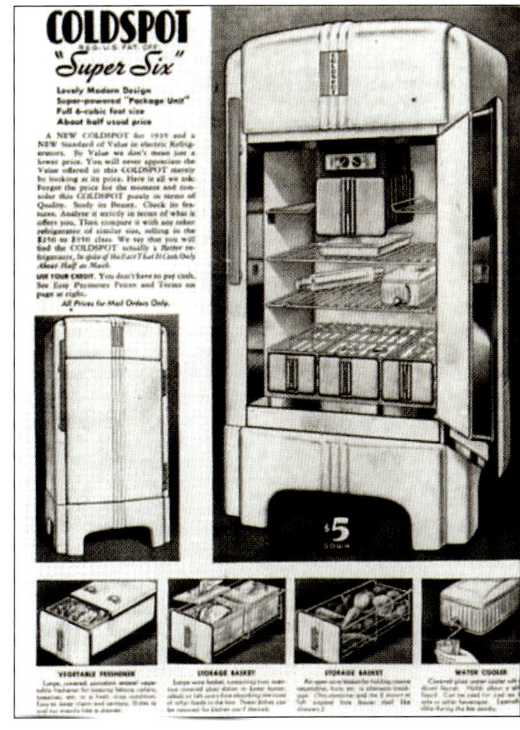

His first design brief soon followed, with the British manufacturer of business machines Sigmund Gestetner commissioning him to redesign the casing of a mimeograph machine. Loewy transformed the look of the machine by giving it a streamlined form, later describing the rationale of this approach as a means of providing "beauty through function and simplification". For the Gestetner project, he used modelling clay to create the casing's sleek shape – a technique he employed to great effect in his later automotive designs. Importantly, the resulting machine not only looked better, but also with its simplified form was far easier to manufacture, clean and service than earlier models.

In 1932, Loewy also gave the streamlined treatment to his first car, known as the Hupmobile, which was far less boxy in appearance than other cars at the time. Two years later he designed an improved version of this car that featured integrated headlights and an even more streamlined body. Around the same time, Loewy designed the Coldspot Super-Six refrigerator (1934) for Sears Roebuck, which similarly boasted a streamlined form. As the first domestic appliance to be marketed on its aesthetic appeal rather than on its practical function, advertisements for it invited consumers to "Study its Beauty". But Loewy's new design went further than just good looks – its streamlined form meant it was easier and therefore cheaper to produce, and this was reflected in its competitive retail price. To manufacturers who were struggling during the Great Depression to make their products more alluring to price-sensitive consumers, Loewy came to be seen as a veritable design saviour. His services, however, did not come cheap: he charged annual retainer fees of $10,000–$60,000 per company, which equates to around $135,000–$815,000 today. By now Loewy was enjoying the status of a celebrity design consultant and in 1934 the Metropolitan Museum of Art in New York displayed a mock-up of his glamorous design office with its Moderne-style furnishings. During this period, apart from re-planning various well-known department stores, Loewy also designed three iconic locomotives with aerodynamic sweeping forms that not only looked more appealing

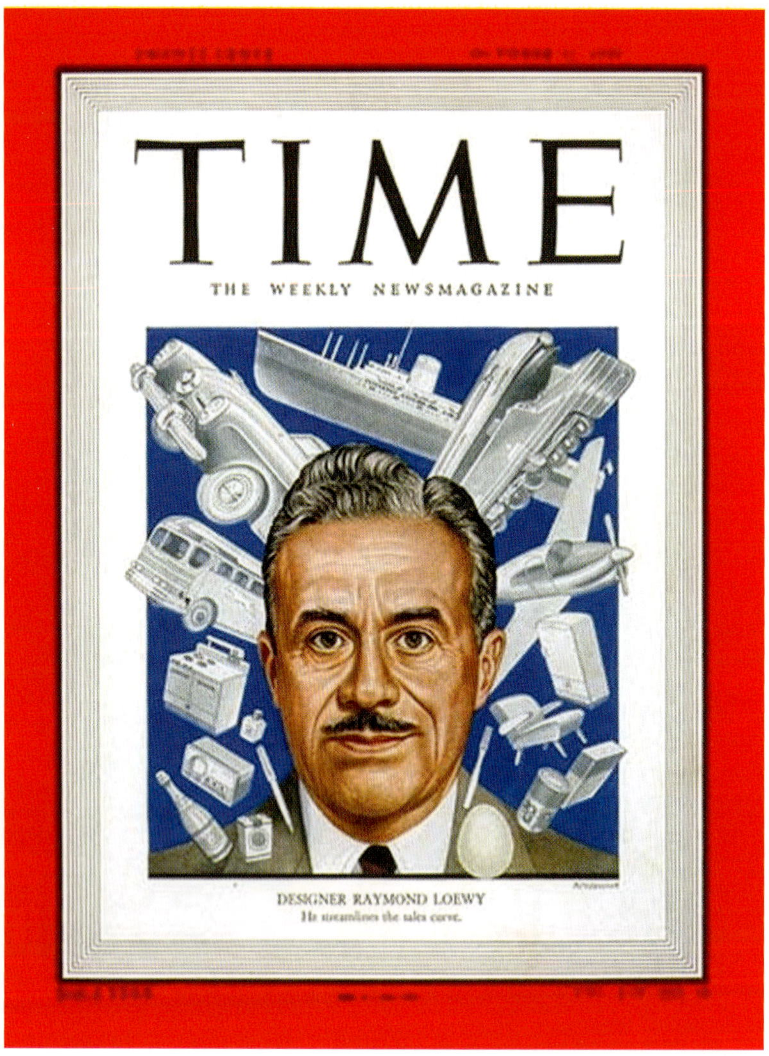

LEFT:
Cover of *Time* magazine featuring a portrait of Raymond Loewy
31 October 1949 – with the memorable byline "He streamlines the sales curve."

than existing models but performed better too. He went on to famously remodel coaches for Greyhound in 1946 and became increasingly celebrated for his corporate identity work, notably his repackaging of Lucky Strike cigarettes (1942).

Loewy became the first designer to feature on the cover of *Time* magazine, in 1949, with his portrait accompanied by the memorable caption, "He streamlines the sales curve." Certainly, when conceptualizing a design Loewy always had the end-user at the forefront of his mind, employing a pragmatic approach to design, which he termed MAYA (Most Advanced, Yet Acceptable). As "The Man Who Shaped America", he powerfully demonstrated that the commercial success of a product is determined as much by its aesthetics as by its function. While few design consultants have been as influential or prolific as Loewy, his work is often misunderstood as that of just an accomplished stylist. He was, however, far more than that, being a prodigiously talented industrial designer who significantly improved the function and manufacturability of the products he redesigned and an important pioneer of many design innovations. By glamorizing design practice, Loewy was also hugely instrumental in raising the status of industrial design, not only among manufacturers but also among the public at large.

RIGHT:
Studebaker Champion sedan
for Studebaker, 1950

BELOW:
Greyhound Scenicruiser motorcoach
for General Motors, 1946–55

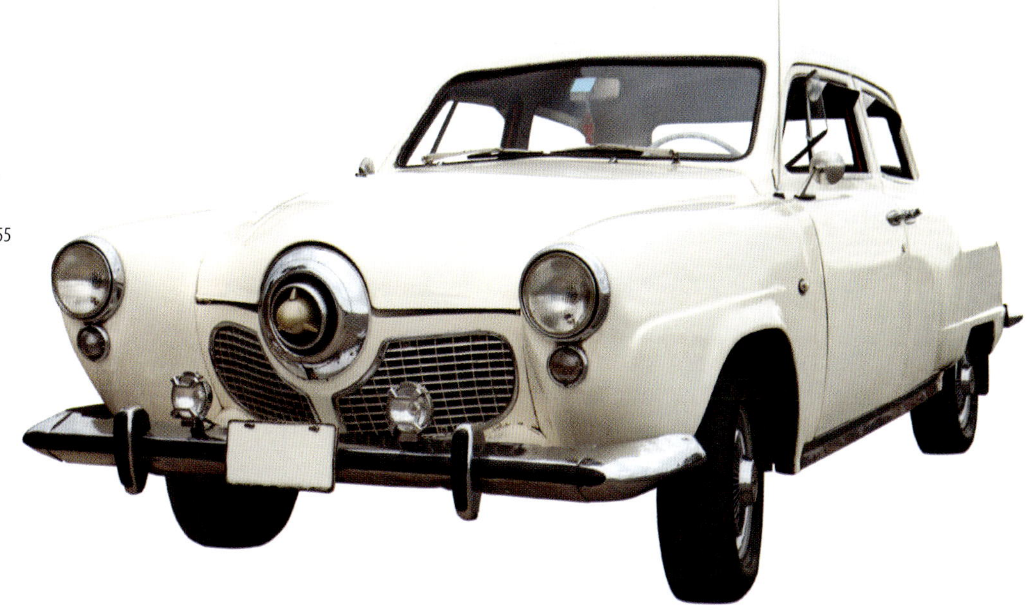

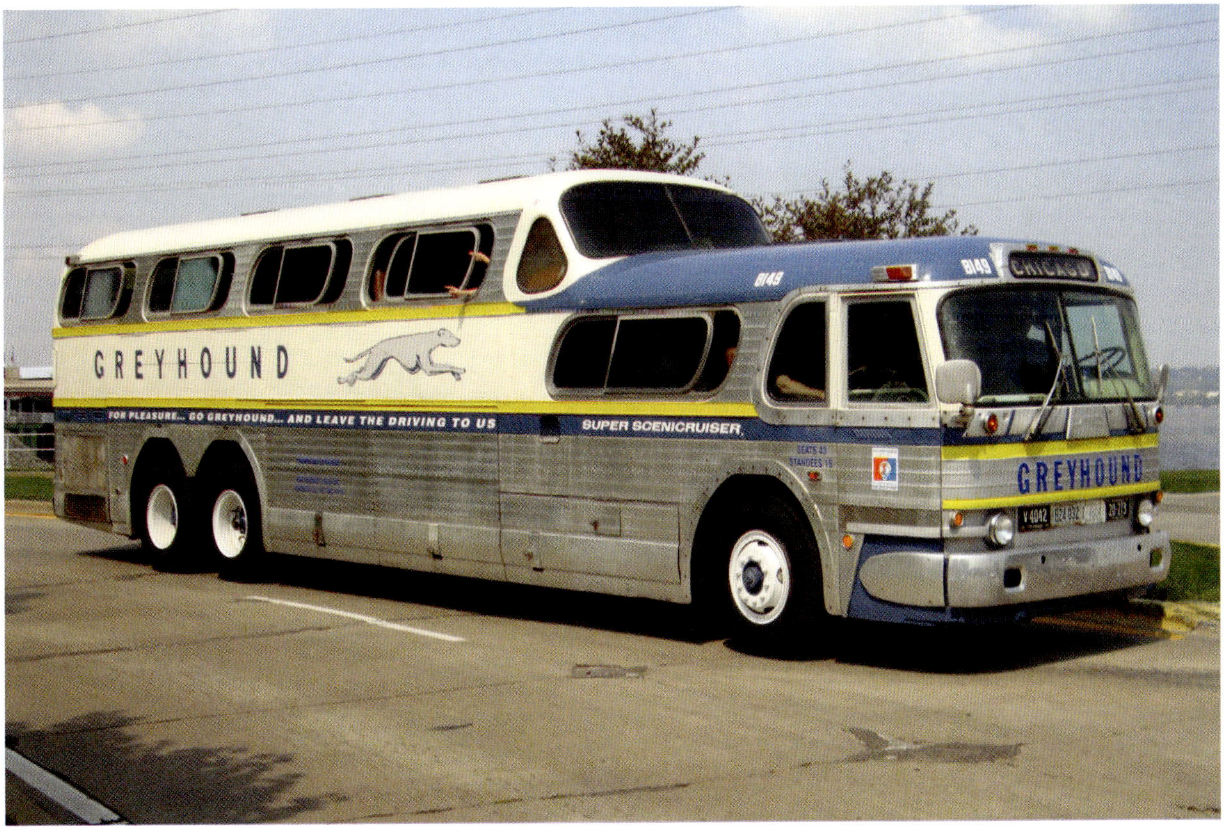

London Transport

Britain, founded 1902

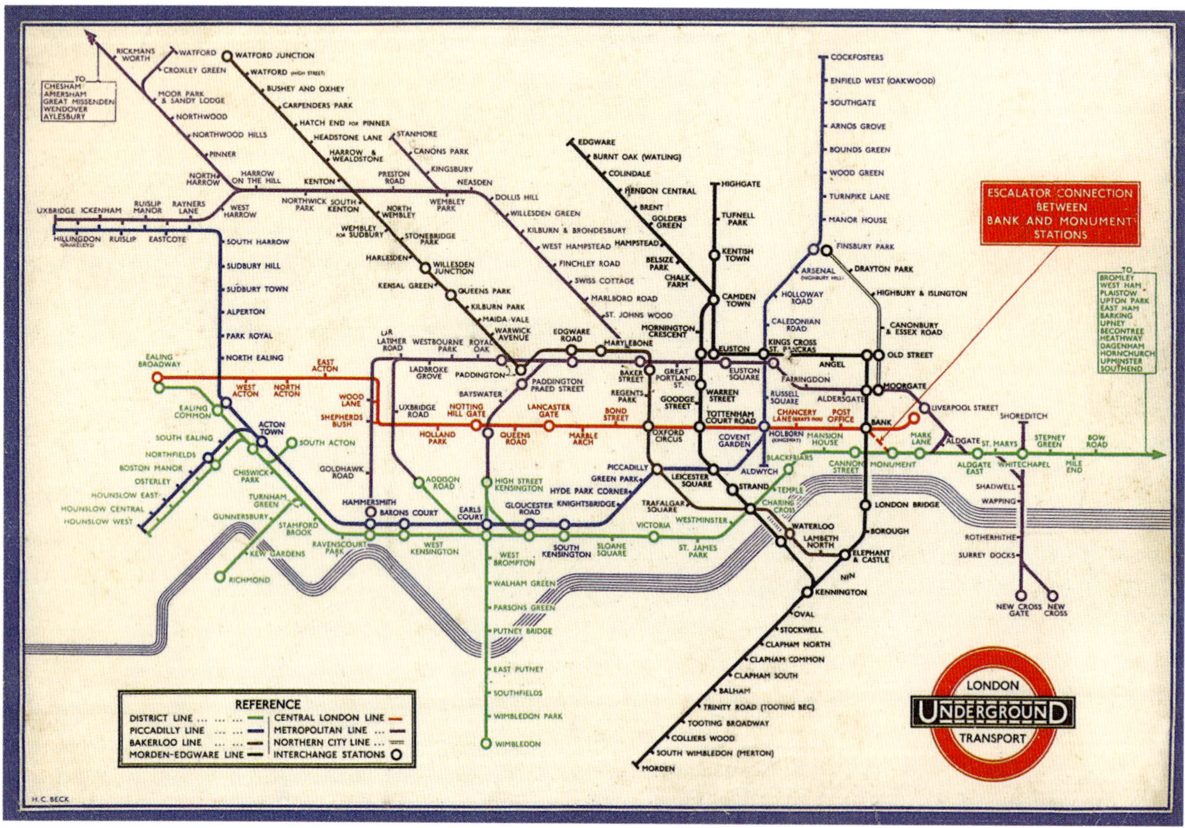

ABOVE:
London Underground map redesigned by Henry Beck, 1933

London Transport's distinctive corporate identity is recognized throughout the world thanks mainly to the design vision of one man: Frank Pick. In 1906 he joined the Underground Group, which had been founded four years earlier, initially as an assistant to the corporation's newly appointed deputy director, Sir George Gibb. However, in 1908 he was promoted to the Group's publicity manager, and that same year he commissioned the talented typographer and acknowledged father of Modern calligraphy Edward Johnston to create a new and far more legible typeface to be used throughout the Underground system – the result was Johnston Sans.

In 1918, again at Pick's instigation, Johnston redesigned the Underground's pre-existing roundel symbol, which had been introduced in 1908 and comprised a solid red circle with a horizontal blue bar running across it. Although this device was perfectly serviceable – it could be easily read from surrounding advertising billboards and gave prominence to the name of the station – it was not a particularly elegant solution. In contrast, Johnston's visually striking "bullseye" design, with its bold red circle targeting the eye into the horizontal blue

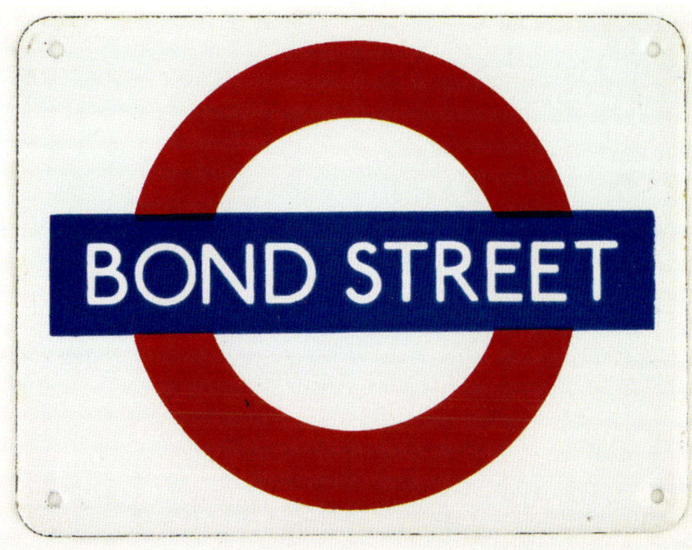

ABOVE:
Bond Street Underground sign
The famous London Underground roundel sign was first designed by Edward Johnson in *c.*1918, and then updated in 1925

text-holding stripe, was a work of genius. The new standardized roundel symbol was first used on publicity material in 1919 and then introduced to station exteriors and platforms in the early 1920s.

As part of his vision of an integrated design programme for London Transport, Pick also commissioned numerous eye-catching posters from well-known artists, such as Edward McKnight Kauffer, Edward Bawden, Frank Newbould, Dorothy Dix and Fred Taylor to name but a few, all of which helped to promote travel on the London Underground, while also solidifying the company's identity. As part of his pioneering total design policy, Beck also engaged the architect Charles Holden to modernize existing stations and design various new ones. In total, Holden designed more than fifty London Underground stations, which were influenced by Modern Movement architecture in Scandinavia and the Netherlands and represented a high-point in English Rational design. But perhaps the most iconic of all the Modernist London Underground stations was the one built at Park Royal (1935–36), which was designed by Herbert Arthur Welch and Felix Lander.

Another crucial part of London Transport's identity was the London Underground map, which over the years had – as more and more stations had been added to the system – become increasingly complex and difficult to follow, as it attempted to show the exact geographic location of each line and station. Commissioned by Pick, the engineering draughtsman Henry Beck redesigned the map in 1933 using a diagrammatic approach that showed the spatial relationship of the stations to one another, rather than the relative distances between them. This ingenious approach to map-making also made use of colours as symbols: each line was given its own easy-to-distinguish colour, for example green for the District Line and dark blue for the Piccadilly Line.

The map was given even more visual clarity by being worked up from an octagonal grid, so that the lines and stations were "locked" at 180, 90 or 45 degrees to each other. Henry Beck's London Underground map not only allowed passengers to navigate their way across the capital more easily, but also helped give London Underground a very clear and recognizably modern brand identity. London Transport's pioneering design policy included the commissioning of hardwearing yet distinctively patterned textiles from Enid Marx and, of course, the iconic red Routemaster bus designed by Douglas Scott in 1954. Over the succeeding decades, London Transport has continued to use a holistic "total design" approach based on Pick's belief in the crucial interrelationship between form and function.

Adolf Loos

Austrian, 1870–1933

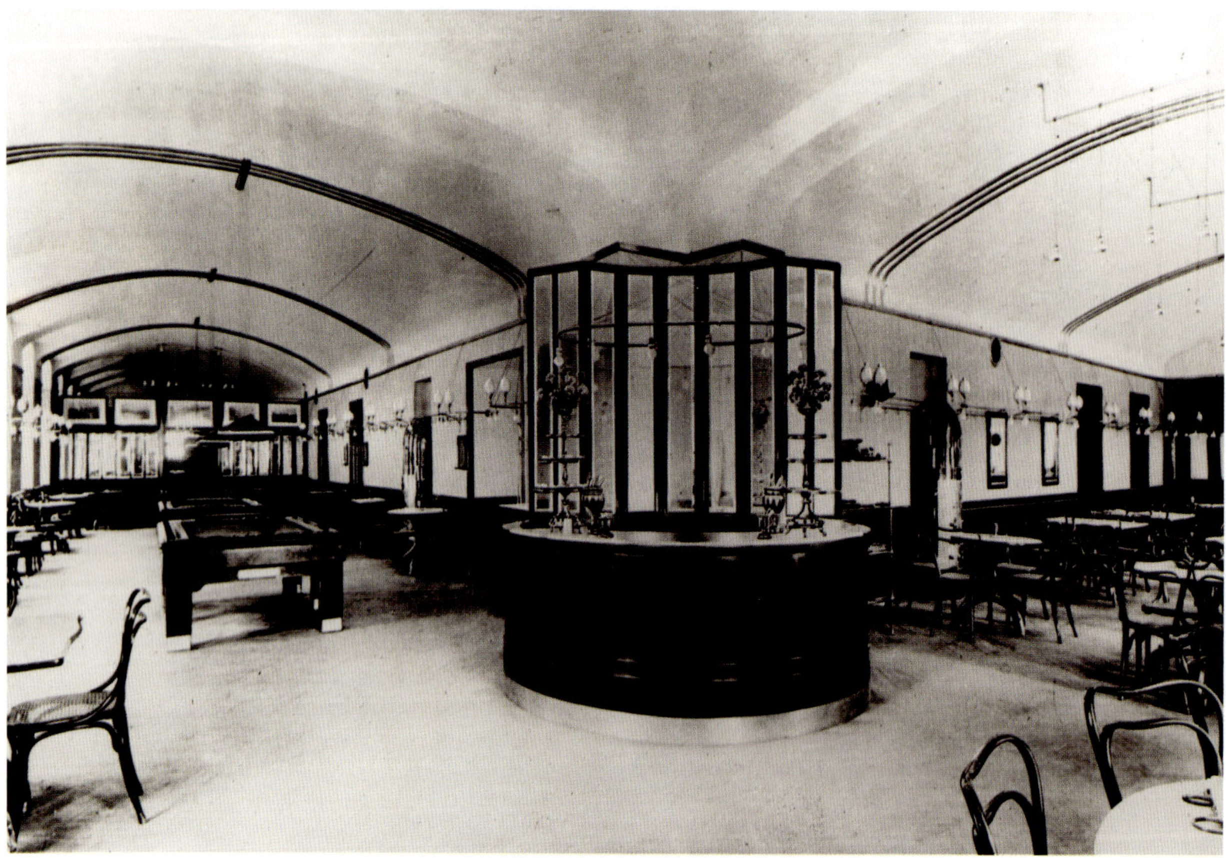

ABOVE:
Interior of the Café Museum
in Vienna, 1899

OPPOSITE TOP:
Ornament and Crime lecture poster
1913

OPPOSITE BOTTOM:
Armchair
for F.O. Schmidt, *c.*1899

The Viennese architect Adolf Loos helped forge the theoretical foundations of the Modern Movement, being one of the first design practitioners to understand that the only way to mass-produce well-designed objects was to accept the machine as a fact of modern life and to design specifically for it. Unlike many of his contemporaries, Loos realized that design for industry needed a completely different and more rational approach that was based on standardization rather than on individuality. In other words, a new approach that was more scientific than artistic, and which identified the most logical forms, materials and manufacturing processes that would be suitable for mechanized production. For Loos, a designed object should not be an expression of personal creativity but of the spirit of the machine that made it.

Having studied architecture in Germany, at the technical school in Dresden, Loos devised an interior scheme for the Café Museum located close to the gilt-domed Secession Building in Vienna in 1899. This project introduced the new functionalist spirit of design advocated by Loos: his simple red-painted bentwood chairs, manufactured by J. & J. Kohn, contrasted with the space's light-green walls, which were lit by minimalist light fixtures that were notable for their display of bare bulbs hanging from simple brass rails. Nicknamed the Café Nihilismus, this comparatively stark space marked a departure from the sinuous exuberance of the Jugendstil style, introducing instead a reductivist aesthetic. To a large extent the Café Museum acted as a cultural seedling from which a new form of design and architecture would grow, whereby the inevitability of industrialization was accepted for the benefit of the many rather than for the few.

Loos's most influential work was, however, his essay *Ornament und Verbrechen* (Ornament and Crime) of 1908 in which he laid out the case for a more rational approach to design and manufacturing. This text marked an intellectual turning point that led to the rejection of nineteenth-century historicism and the hedonism of the *fin-de-siècle* Art Nouveau style in favour of a more purposeful design mindset, which presaged the unadorned functionalism of the Modern Movement. Loos argued from a quasi-scientific standpoint that ornamentation in design and architecture was retrogressive and ultimately responsible for cultural backwardness and degeneracy – he memorably linked tattoos to a proclivity for criminality. Like William Morris before him, Loos understood the human and economic costs of superfluous decoration, yet he was a pragmatist who realized that simplicity needed to be tied to mechanization rather than to handicraft. He also had a more extreme definition of simplicity, which meant stripping designed objects entirely of all decorative superfluity.

The same year he published his famous tract, Loos designed the American Bar in Vienna, which incorporated a proto-Modernist, pared-down geometric theme. His acknowledged architectural masterwork, however, was the Goldman & Salatsch Building (1910–12) – now known as the Looshaus – located in Vienna's Michaelerplatz, the façade of which caused much controversy as it expressed a new form of stripped-down functionalism and marked an utter rejection of historicism with its lack of traditional decorative details. Loos's rallying cry for unadorned functional forms had a major influence on the next generation of designers, who went on to shape the Modern Movement. As Loos once ironically quipped, "Whatever is good in Le Corbusier's work, he learned from Loos."

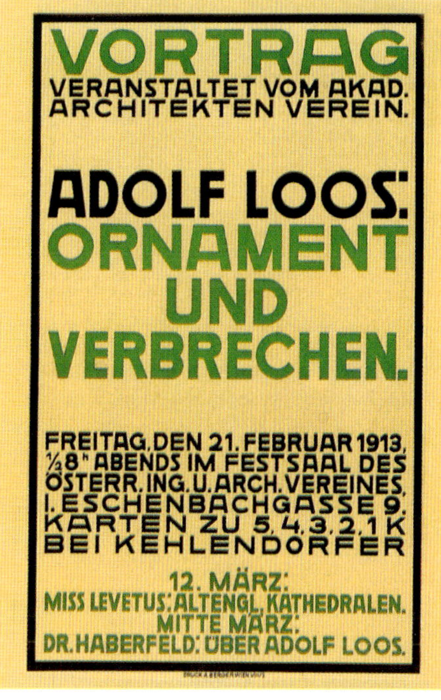

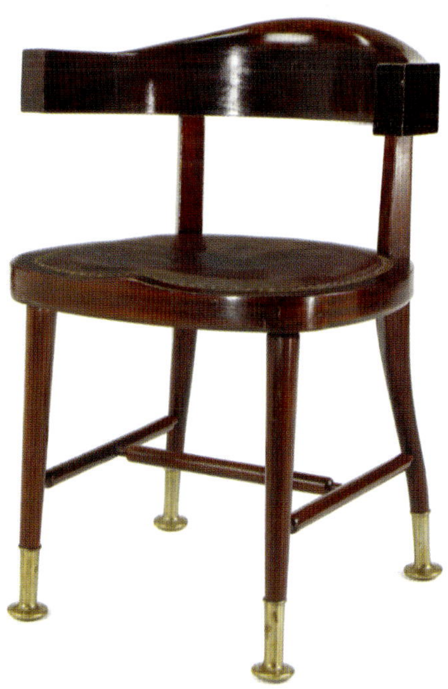

Ross Lovegrove

British, 1958–

A visionary designer and a gifted form-giver, Ross Lovegrove is inspired as much by the creative potential of futuristic technologies as he is by the wonders of the natural world. With his deeply humanistic approach to problem solving, he is able to imbue his work with a poetic spirit, which reflects his optimistic belief in the future. By skilfully combining what he describes as "really weird" newly developed materials with sculptural organic forms, Lovegrove produces work with an almost alchemic quality that he terms "supernatural".

Born in Wales, Lovegrove initially studied industrial design at Manchester Polytechnic, before taking a master's degree at the Royal College of Art, London, graduating in 1983. Immediately following this, he spent a year in Germany working for the design consultancy frog design on the development of Walkmans for Sony and computers for Apple. Between 1984 and 1986, he worked in Paris as an in-house designer for Knoll International, where he contributed substantially to the development of the Alessandri Office System. During this period he was also a member of the Atelier de Nîmes, alongside Philippe Starck and Jean Nouvel, and in this capacity worked as a design consultant to Louis Vuitton, Cacharel, Dupont and Hermès.

Returning to Britain in 1986, Lovegrove formed a partnership with fellow RCA designer Julian Brown. This resulted in the Basic thermos flask for Alfi (1988–90), which employed a polycarbonate bubble-like housing that was highly influential and heralded a new transparency trend in product design. Lovegrove subsequently established his own design office, Studio X, in London in 1990. Working for a diversity of clients, including Alias, Apple, Artemide, BioMega, Ceccotti, Cappellini, Driade, Hackman, Herman Miller, Idée, Issey Miyake, Japan Airlines, Luceplan, LVMH, Moroso, Tag Heuer, Toyo Ito Architects and Yamagiwa, Lovegrove's reputation grew throughout the 1990s and 2000s, as he was uniquely able to create products that pulled the future into the present, while capturing the abstract essence of nature.

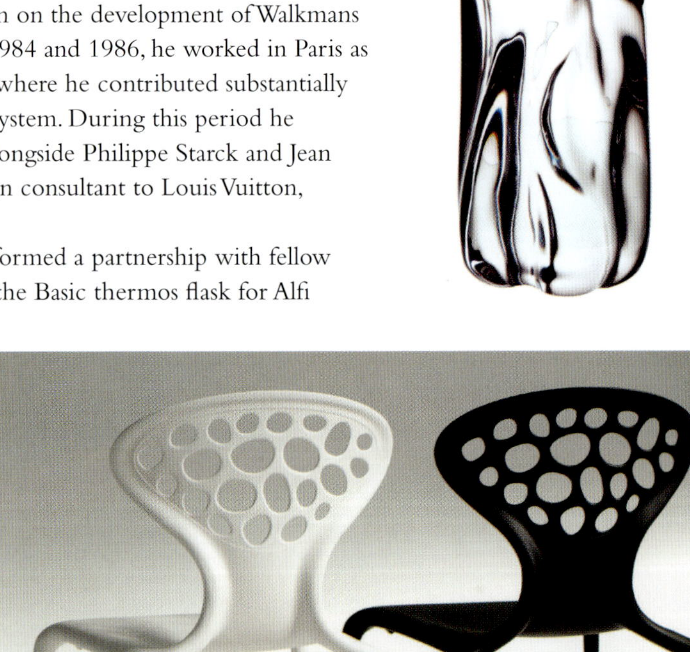

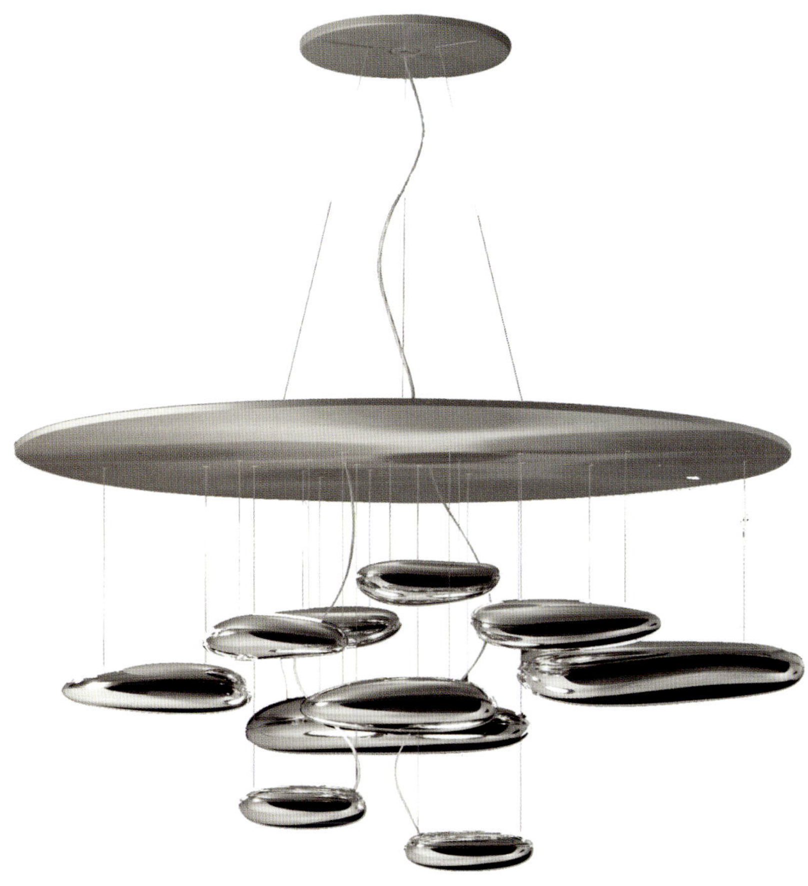

OPPOSITE TOP:
Ty Nant water bottle
for Ty Nant, 2000-02

OPPOSITE BOTTOM:
Supernatural chair
for Moroso, 2005-08

ABOVE:
Mercury ceiling light
for Artemide, 2007

Whether it is his Supernatural chair (2005–08) or the Mercury ceiling lights (2007), the Ty Nant water bottle (2000–02) or the HU wristwatch (2005–08), the Muon audio-speakers (2005–07) or his extraordinary DNA staircase (2003), Lovegrove's designs all share a functional logic that is based on a highly considered understanding of how humans interact with things on both a physical and psychological level, as well as an in-depth knowledge of high-tech materials and manufacturing processes. His futuristic designs have an almost biological quality, with their sculptural organic forms wrapping purposeful function, much like a natural organism.

Beyond his commissioned work, Lovegrove has also always explored more experimental and creative projects, which often speculate on future design concepts or new materials and processes in an approach that balances the scientific with the artistic. These explorations often inform his more commercial industrial design; however, as a well-known futurist, he has always been commissioned to develop highly progressive conceptual designs too, most notably his all-electric carbon-fibre Twin'Z concept car (2013) for Renault. As Lovegrove notes, "If you have an ability to communicate through drawings or whatever, you can envisage things that have never existed before. So you can dream in an incredible way."

M/M (Paris)

French, founded 1992

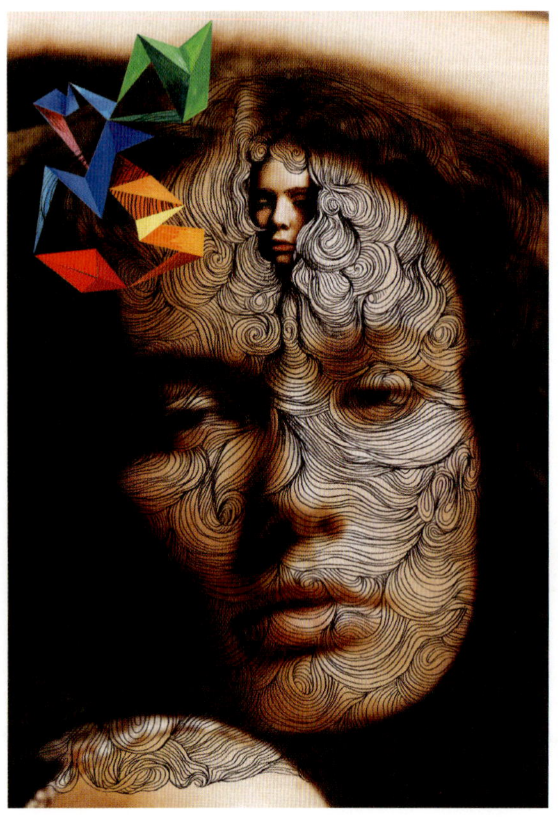

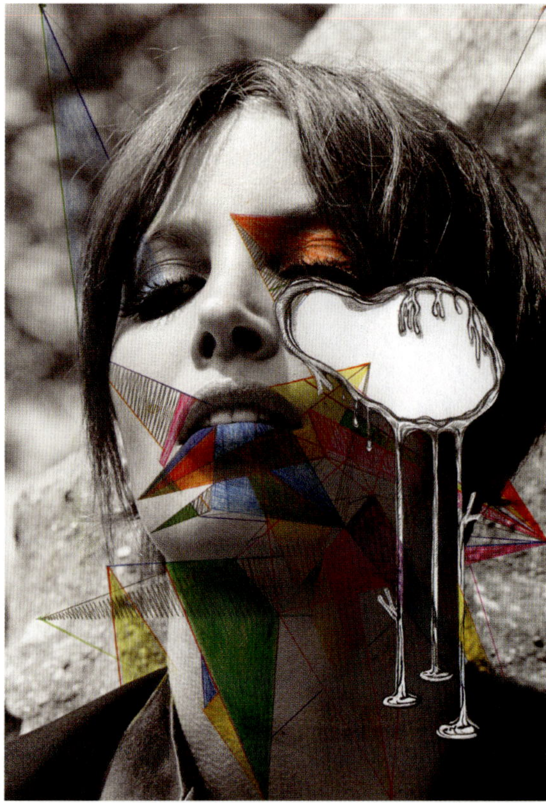

ABOVE LEFT:
Balenciaga (Melia) silkscreen poster
2001

ABOVE RIGHT:
Balenciaga (Christy) silkscreen poster
2001

A highly acclaimed creative direction studio, M/M (Paris) is a powerful force not only in French culture but also in the globalized worlds of fashion and music. This innovative visual communications studio was co-founded by Michael Amzalag and Mathias Augustyniak in 1992.

The pair had previously met while studying at the École Nationale Supérieure des Arts Décoratifs (ENSAD), but the former left after two years of study in order to art direct a music magazine, while the latter went on to take a master's degree in graphic design and art direction at the Royal College of Art, London. After Augustyniak graduated in 1991, they began working together, mainly for clients in the music industry, designing sleeves for various obscure French artists and bands. As Augustyniak recalls, "At that time in France, a lot of money was being spent marketing music, which was French to the max.... Back then – in the early 1990s – more established French design companies, such as Grapus, were doing all the work in the cultural field, work generated by the left-wing government of that era. We just took what was left." For these two, graphic design was not just a means to earn a living, but rather a way to disseminate ideas.

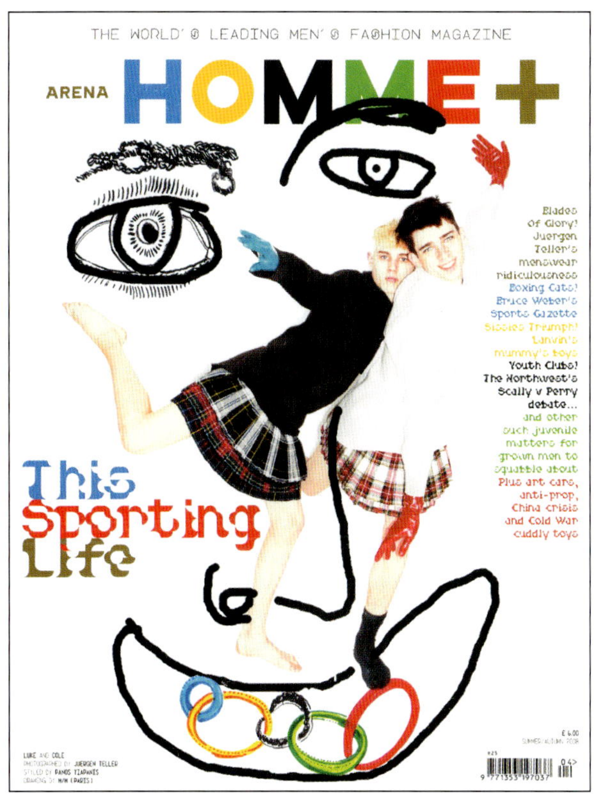

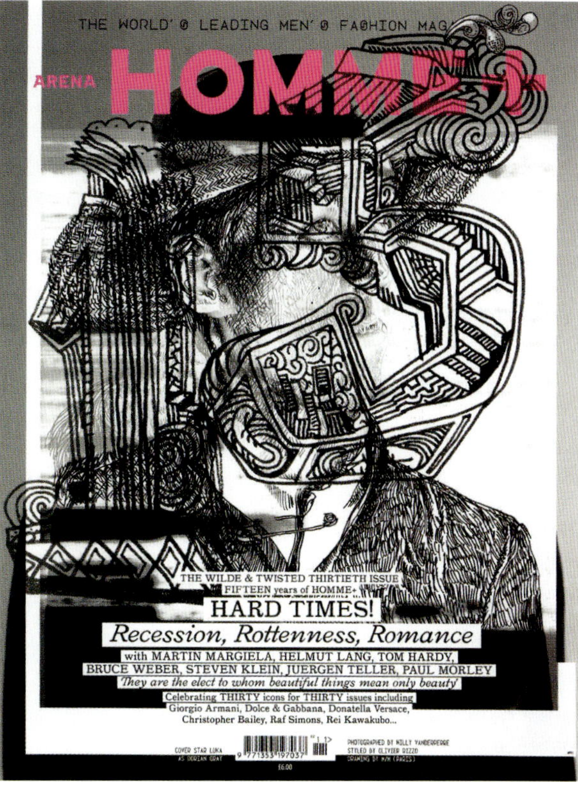

ABOVE LEFT:
Cover for *Arena Homme+*
Issue 29, Summer 2008/Autumn, 2008

ABOVE RIGHT:
Cover for *Arena Homme+*
Issue 30, Winter 2008/Spring 2009

Through a friend of a friend, they acquired their first "fashion job" in 1993 for the European launch of Yohji Yamamoto's Y's range. A few months later, they began designing for the French fashion designer Martine Sitbon and then several months after that they met the people behind the art magazine *Documents*, which ultimately led them to begin working in the fine-art realm. Importantly, the fashion industry with its never-ending cycle of seasonal collections meant that their clients in this world needed something visually fresh on an almost constant basis, so they learnt to keep on their creative toes. As they explain, "When we are working for fashion companies, we still try and mix in other projects in different fields. This is very important to our fashion work, which we see as looking at culture through fashion eyes. We always try and link one project to another. We want our work to be considered on a larger scale."

One of their most successful fashion campaigns was for Balenciaga; it featured fashion-show invitation cards and posters with photographs of models artistically defaced with colourful doodles and image manipulation. Countering the airbrushed perfection of most fashion imagery, M/M's work in this field has, in contrast, a sense of creative authenticity thanks to its handcrafted raw quality, which makes it immediately appealing. Between 2001 and 2003, they were the art directors and creative consultants to French *Vogue*, and since 2006 have also worked as consultants to *Purple Fashion* magazine. In the realm of men's fashion, from 2007 to 2009 they also worked as creative directors for *Arena Homme+*, a bi-annual publication that evolved from *Arena* magazine. Today, M/M (Paris) enjoy an impressive roster of clients who value their unique creative vision that is not only visually compelling but also emotionally engaging.

Charles Rennie Mackintosh

British, 1868–1928

The Glaswegian architect-designer Charles Rennie Mackintosh was a leading proponent of the Art Nouveau style during the *fin-de-siècle* period and an important pioneer of proto-modern architecture and design. In many ways he can be seen as the crucial link between British nineteenth-century design reformers and the nascent Modern Movement emerging in Continental Europe.

Born in Glasgow, Mackintosh from any early age had a deep appreciation of the natural world, thanks to his father who was a keen gardener. While growing up he was also encouraged to take rambles in the countryside surrounding Glasgow to strengthen his clubfoot, and on these excursions he sketched the buildings, flora and fauna he came across, becoming an accomplished young draughtsman. At the age of sixteen Mackintosh began an apprenticeship in the architecture practice of John Hutchison and that same year, 1884, he began taking evening classes in drawing and painting at Glasgow School of Art. In 1889, he joined the highly regarded architecture practice of Honeyman & Keppie in Glasgow and the following year won a scholarship that allowed him to travel to Italy, via Paris, Brussels, Antwerp and London. This trip was effectively a cultural pilgrimage and left him with the belief that all great "architecture has been the direct expression of the needs and beliefs of man at the time of its creation... we must clothe Modern ideas with Modern dress".

In 1895, Mackintosh began exhibiting with fellow students Herbert McNair and the MacDonald sisters, Frances and Margaret (he married the latter in 1900). The work of "The

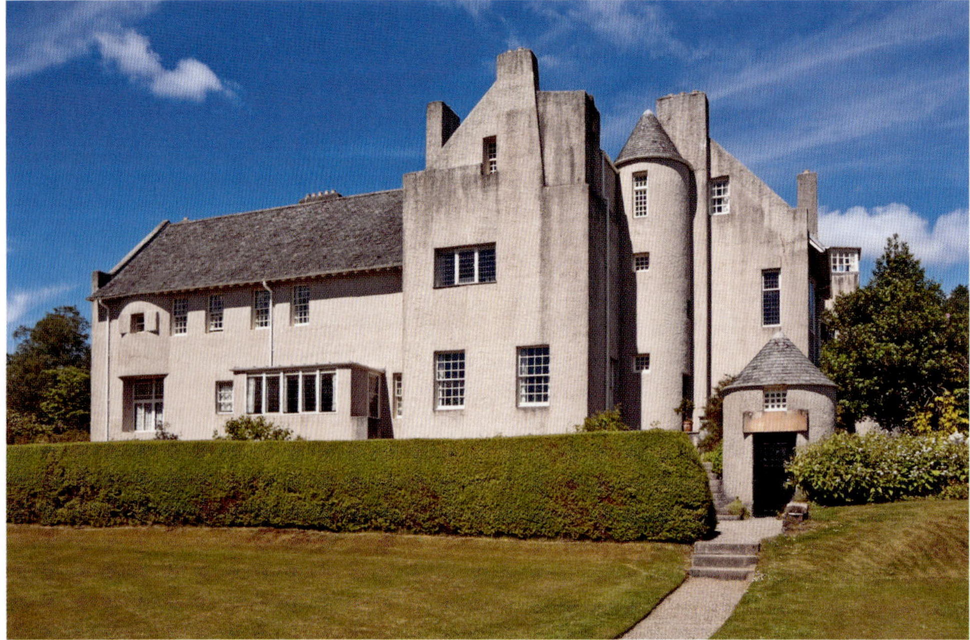

LEFT:
The Hill House, garden elevation
1902–04

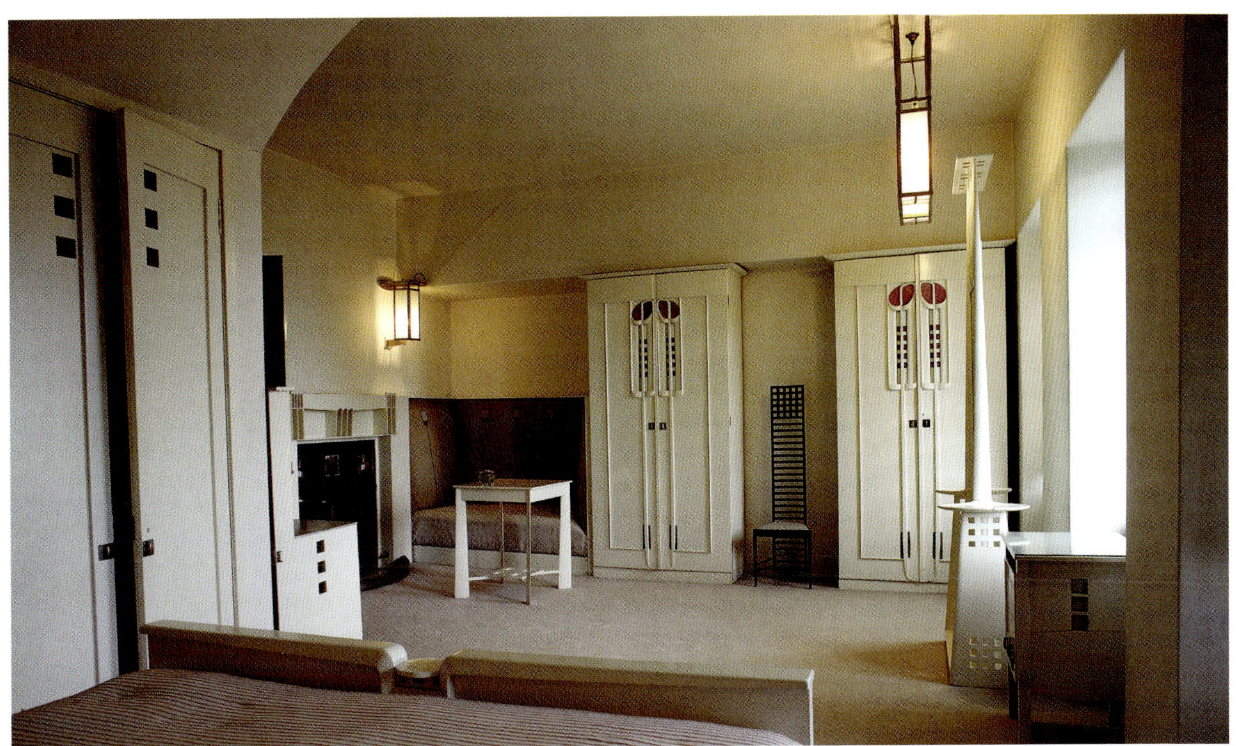

ABOVE:
Bedroom at The Hill House
1902–04

Glasgow Four" possessed such a distinctive ethereal style that they were nicknamed "The Spook School" by their detractors in the press. In 1900, The Four's Scottish Room was shown at the eighth Secessionist exhibition in Vienna, leading Herman Muthesius to note that "they had a seminal influence on the emerging new vocabulary of forms, especially and continuously in Vienna, where an unbreakable bond was forged between them and the Vienna movement".

In Scotland, Mackintosh was also making his architectural mark, working on the Glasgow School of Art (1897–99 and 1907–09) and The Hill House in Helensburgh (1902–04), a sublimely beautiful *Gesamtkunstwerk* project. He also designed four tearooms in Glasgow for their proprietress, Katherine Cranston, who gave him a creative and financial carte blanche. The resulting interiors included some of Mackintosh's most seminal designs, such as the famous high-back chair designed for the Argyll Street tearoom with its elliptical back rail intended to halo the sitter's head. He also designed installations for the *Prima Esposizione Internazionale d'Arte Decorativa Moderna* (First International Exhibition of Modern Decorative Art) in Turin (1902) and the Dresden Werkstätten exhibition of 1903–04. But, although his reputation as a leading design visionary was growing in Europe, he became increasingly frustrated by the lack of recognition in his own country, where he struggled to find patronage, thanks as much to the progressive nature of his work as to his increasingly erratic temper and growing alcohol dependency.

Mackintosh did, however, complete one notable project in the 1910s: the interiors and remodelling of a house in Northampton owned by the industrialist Wynne J. Bassett-Lowke. This residence at 78 Derngate was a remarkable composition of geometric elements and can be considered the first proper example of Modern Movement architecture in Britain. Mackintosh was a complex but visionary designer, whose work synthesized the national and the international, fused vernacularism with modernity, and looked to the future but paid homage to the past.

Vico Magistretti

Italian, 1920–2006

The Italian architect-designer Vico Magistretti created furniture and lighting designs that combined elegant beauty with functional ingenuity. So much so that his work came to exemplify the stylish Milanese sophistication associated with the term "Made in Italy".

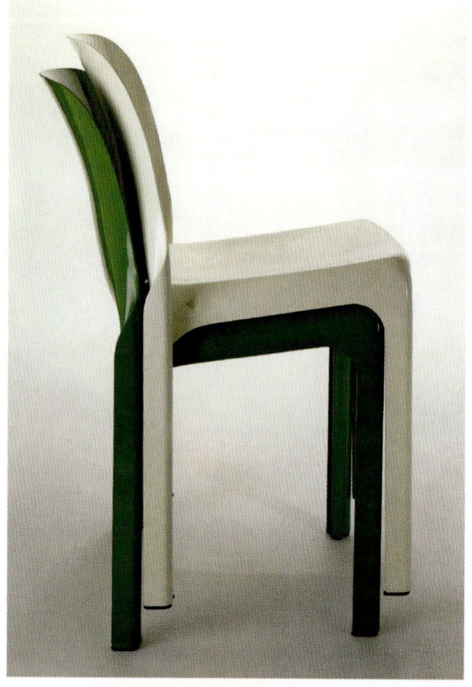

Magistretti was fortunate that during the Second World War he managed to escape deportation to Germany by moving to Switzerland, where he studied at the Italian Champ Universitaire in Lausanne. There he took a course on architecture and urban planning given by one of Italy's most influential architects, Ernesto Rogers. He later trained as an architect at the Politecnico di Milano, graduating in 1945. It could be said that Magistretti was at the right place at the right time, for during the immediate post-war period Italian industry deployed cutting-edge design as a means of invigorating the national economy through an export-led recovery – and who better placed than recently graduated architects to help manufacturers get the war-torn country back on its feet? Certainly, Rogers's belief that design practice should encompass everything "from the city to the spoon" was highly influential to this younger generation of Milanese architect-designers, and it unquestionably had a hugely formative effect on Magistretti's subsequent career.

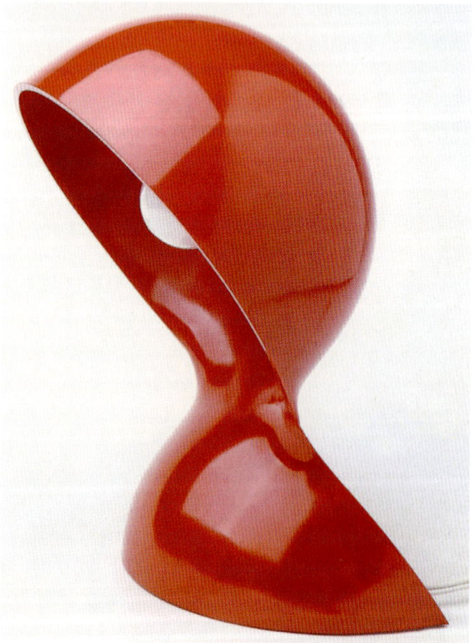

After completing his studies, Magistretti designed a tubular metal bookcase and a simple deckchair for a low-cost furnishings exhibition organized by RIMA (Italian Assembly for Furniture Exhibitions). He subsequently participated in exhibitions arranged by the textile manufacturer Fede Cheti in 1949, displaying a ladder-like bookcase and a simple nest of tables that revealed an underlying rationalism. During the 1950s Magistretti designed a number of buildings in Milan, notably the Torre al Parco in via Revere (1953–56) in collaboration with Franco Longoni, and an office block in corso Europa (1955–57) – both of which firmly established his credentials as one of the leading Italian architects of his generation. His Neo-Liberty-style Villa Arosio in Arenzano (1956–59) certainly stimulated much discussion within architectural circles, for with this project Magistretti showed that Modernism could be successfully reconciled with vernacularism. For his clubhouse for the Carimate Golf Club of 1959–62, Magistretti similarly incorporated vernacular-inspired yet still modern elements, including a rush-seated armchair that countered the International Style's obsession with the industrial aesthetic.

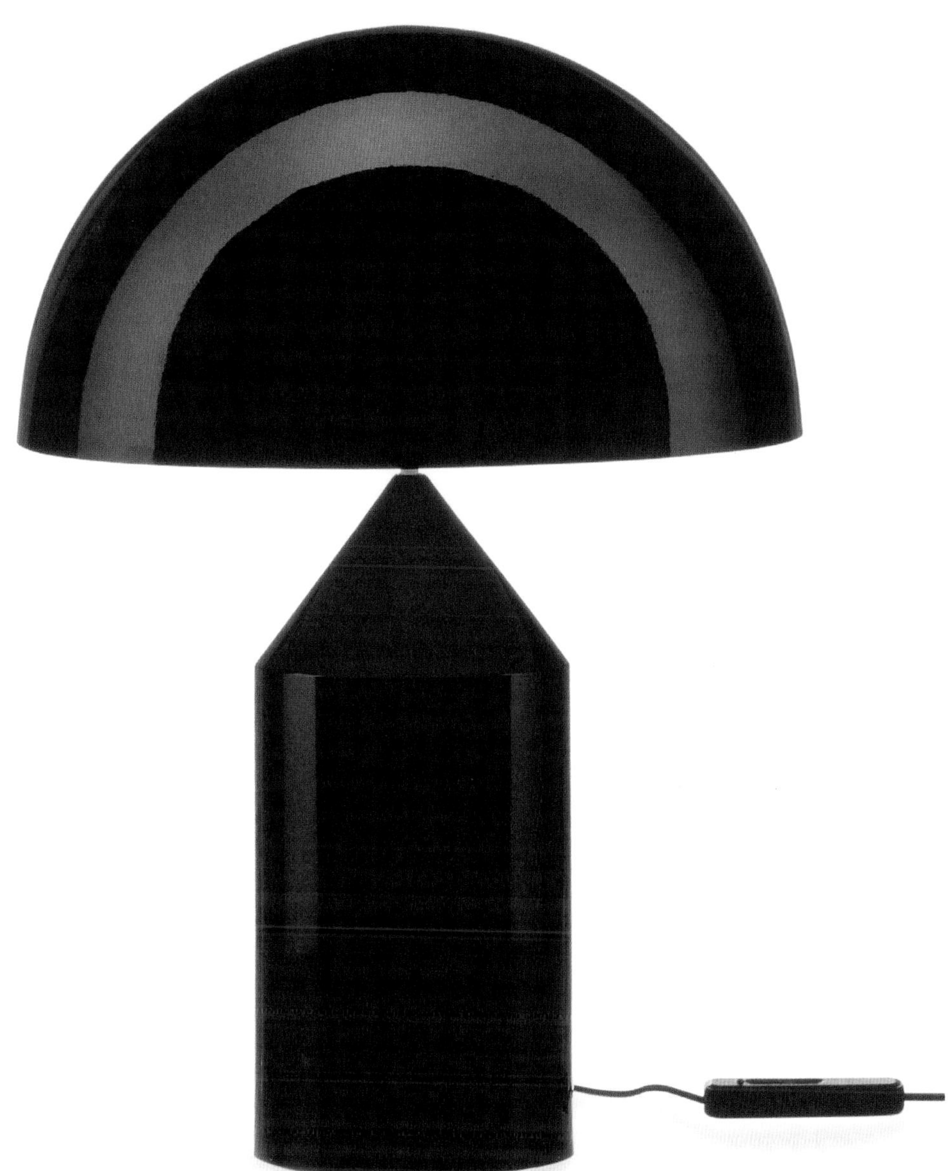

OPPOSITE TOP:
Selene chairs
for Artemide, 1969

OPPOSITE BOTTOM:
Dalù light
for Artemide, 1969

ABOVE:
Atollo table light
for Oluce, 1977

In 1960 Magistretti met the furniture manufacturer Cesare Cassina, who subsequently put the Carimate chair into production. Over the coming years, Magistretti created a number of other landmark designs for Cassina, including the Maralunga sofa (1973) with its moveable headrest, the leather-clad Cab chair (1977) and the collapsible Nuvola Rossa bookcase (1977). He also designed extensively for Kartell, with his innovative Selene chair (1969), Vicario armchair (1971) and Demetrio tables (1966) setting a new aesthetic standard for plastic furniture. Many of his numerous lighting designs for Artemide have acquired iconic status, among them the Eclisse (1966), the Chimera (1969) and the Atollo (1977). Over his long career, Magistretti received several Compasso d'Oro awards for his design work, which was notable not only for its functionality, elegance and innovative use of materials and processes, but also for its use of strong graphic outlines that gave it an enduring Modern classical quality.

Angelo Mangiarotti

Italian, 1921–2012

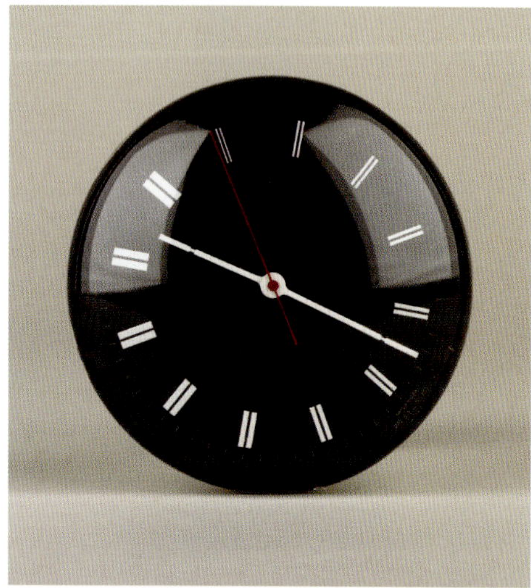

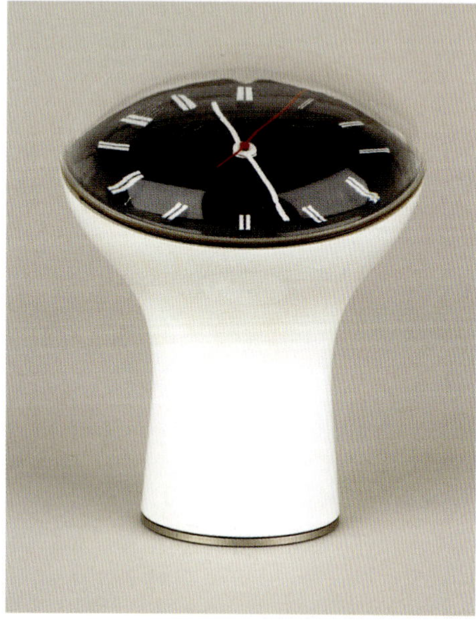

ABOVE:
Secticon Model C1 table clock
for Secticon Portescap (Le Porte-Échappment Universel), c.1960–62

The Italian architect and designer Angelo Mangiarotti was a master form-giver, who pioneered a very unique, muscular yet precise language of design. As he was once to note, "Happiness comes from correctness," and certainly his designs were three-dimensional realizations of this sentiment.

Like so many designers of his generation in Italy, Mangiarotti studied architecture at the Politecnico di Milano, graduating in 1948. He subsequently moved to the United States, where he participated in the competition for the design of Chicago's Loop business district and from 1953 to 1954 was a visiting professor at the Institute of Design at the Illinois Institute of Technology in Chicago. It was here that he met Ludwig Mies van der Rohe and Frank Lloyd Wright – both were to have a hugely formative influence on the young Mangiarotti. On his return to Italy in 1955, he set up a design studio with Bruno Morassutti in Milan and subsequently designed, among other things, a range of plywood furniture (1953), a chewing gum dispenser (1955), his well-known range of Secticon clocks (1955–62), his stackable Cavalletto furniture collection (1955) and the modular Multiuse furniture range (1955) – the last three designed in collaboration with Morassutti. He also became a founding member of the ADI (Associazione per il Disegno Industriale/Industrial Design Association) in 1956 and four years later established his own independent design office, working as an architect, industrial designer and urban planner. Although he designed residential and office buildings, it was his large-scale industrial architecture that impressed the most, being bold, uncompromisingly modular and prefabricated. These designs had an interesting quasi-Brutalist quality, and although firmly rooted within the canon of the International Style, they also predicted the unrelenting industrial aesthetic that would become synonymous with the High-Tech style of the 1970s.

Like his architecture, Mangiarotti's product and furniture designs possessed a striking sculptural monumentality, most notably his Eros series of tables (1971) for Skipper that were made of marble and incorporated in their constructions innovative gravity joints. His glass vases and marble bowls for Knoll likewise revealed his instinctive understanding of materials' properties. Apart from his architecture and design work, Mangiarotti was also an accomplished sculptor and teacher, who taught at numerous institutions including the Istituto Superiore di Disegno Industriale

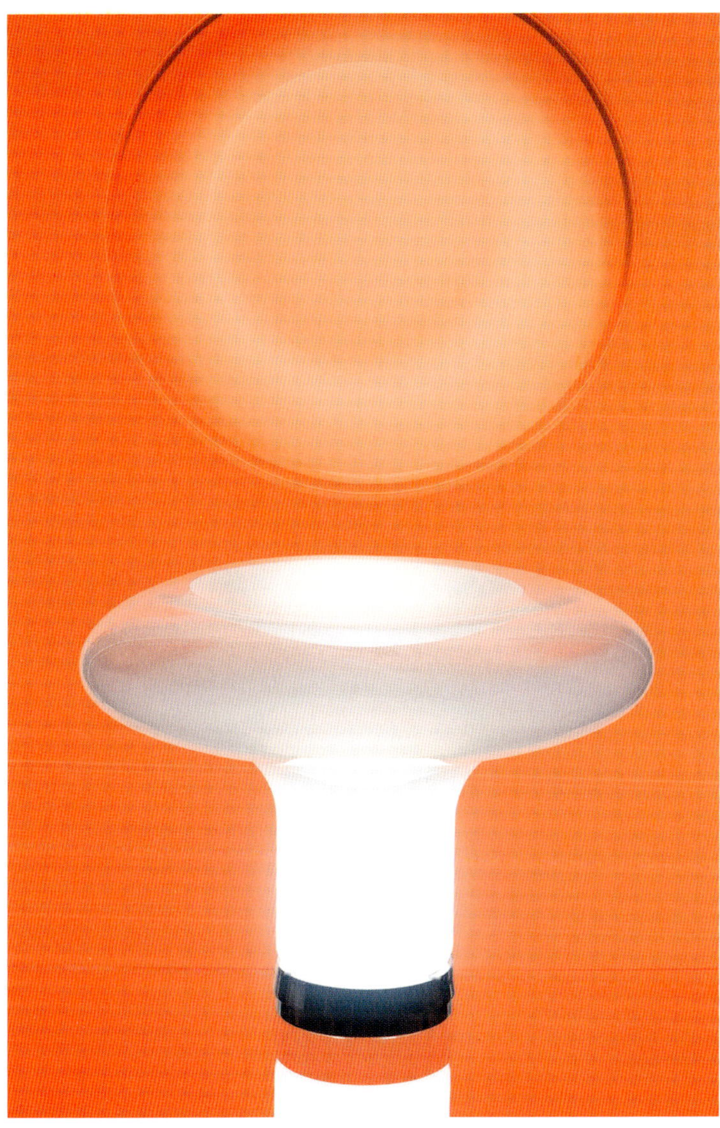

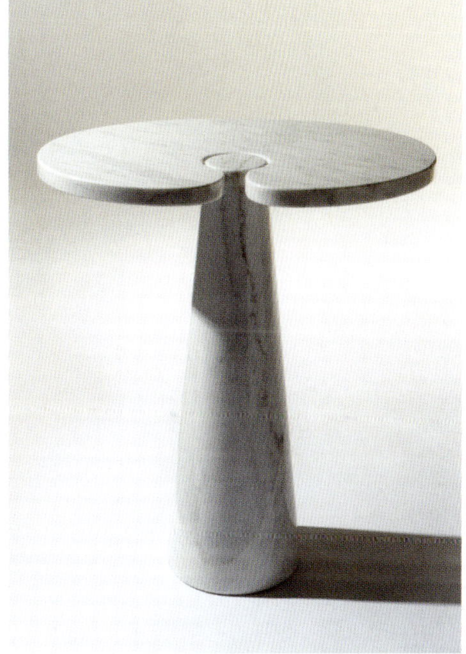

ABOVE LEFT:
Lesbo table light
for Artemide, 1966–67

ABOVE RIGHT:
Eros table for Skipper
1971

(Higher Institute of Industrial Design) in Venice, the University of Hawaii, the University of Palermo and the University of Florence, as well as his alma mater. In 2002 a major retrospective exhibition of his work was held at the Triennale di Milano museum, which led to a rediscovery and re-evaluation of his significant contribution to Italian design and architecture.

Herbert Matter

Swiss/active USA, 1907–1984

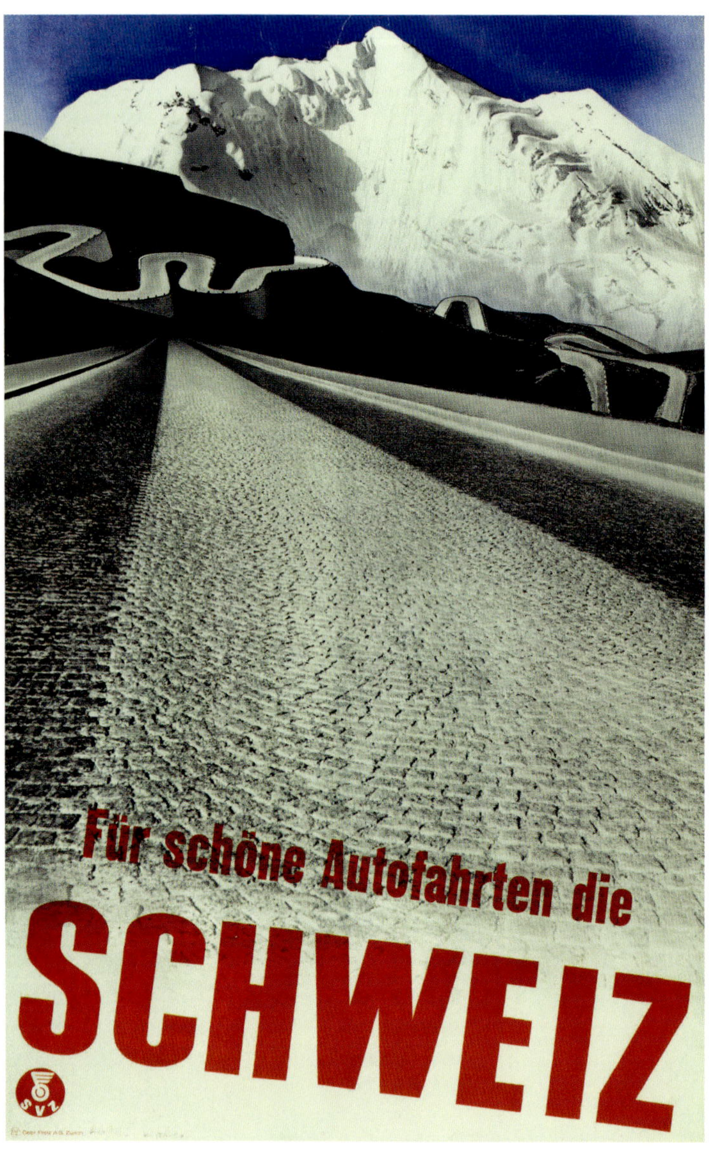

ABOVE:
German version of the All Roads Lead to Switzerland travel poster for the Swiss National Tourist Office (SNTO), 1935

An influential pioneer of modern graphic design, Herbert Matter introduced new photomontage techniques to create boldly dynamic work that brought a fine-art sensibility to the commercial arts. His artistic studies started at the École des Beaux-Arts in Geneva, but in 1927 he decided to move to Paris and train at the Académie Moderne, which had been established by Fernand Léger and Amédée Ozenfant. The latter had previously co-founded the Purist art movement with Le Corbusier and as a result from 1929 to 1932 Matter worked for the architect on exhibit displays and building projects, while also working for the Deberny et Peignot type foundry and collaborating with A.M. Cassandre on various poster designs.

Matter had an in-depth understanding of photographic and printing techniques that enabled him to perfect over-printing, which gave his posters a striking visual depth as well as a strong dynamic contrast between image and type. This was exemplified by a series of posters designed for the Swiss Tourist Board (1932–35), which included his renowned All Roads Lead to Switzerland poster with its dramatic landscape of a straight road angling into a vanishing point set against a dramatic backdrop of a snow-clad mountain and looping mountain road. The bold red typography set at the angle of the road further enhanced the dynamic quality of the composition. This series of posters projected a confident modern identity for Switzerland during the 1930s and earned Matter widespread international acclaim.

In 1935 Matter travelled to the United States with Trudi Schoop's dance troupe, acting as its photographer, and while there decided to settle in New York City. He initially worked as a freelance photographer for *Harper's Bazaar,* then under the art direction of Alexey

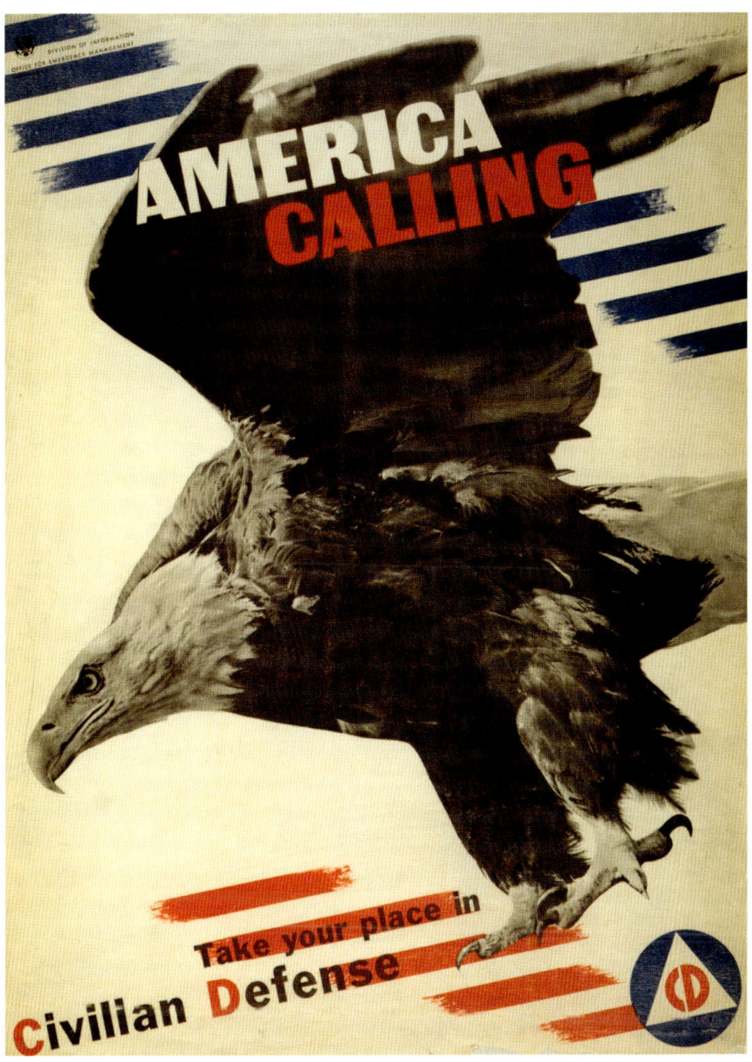

RIGHT:
America Calling, Take Your Place in Civilian Defence lithographic poster
for the US Office of Emergency Management, 1941

Brodovitch. In 1939 Matter undertook exhibit design for the Swiss National Pavilion at the *New York World's Fair* and two years later began creating an innovative series of posters and advertisements for the Container Corporation of America (CCA). During the Second World War, he was commissioned by the US Government to design propaganda posters including his famous America Calling poster (1941) featuring an American eagle. In 1943 he moved to Venice, California, to work with Charles and Ray Eames for the next three years helping to forge a strong graphic identity for the Eames office, and during this period he also designed covers and layouts for John Entenza's *Arts & Architecture* journal.

Returning to New York in 1946, Matter became a consultant to Knoll Associates, and subsequently designed numerous eye-catching advertisements and posters as well as the company's distinctive K trademark. One of his best-known advertisements (1956) featured an Eero Saarinen Tulip chair in two sequential images – one showing the chair and the sitter wrapped in brown paper and the other showing them unwrapped – with the transmitted message having such clarity there was no need for copy. By marrying the visual clarity of the Swiss School with American popular culture, Matter's work came to define the look of avant-garde graphic design in the United States during the post-war period.

David Mellor

British, 1930–2009

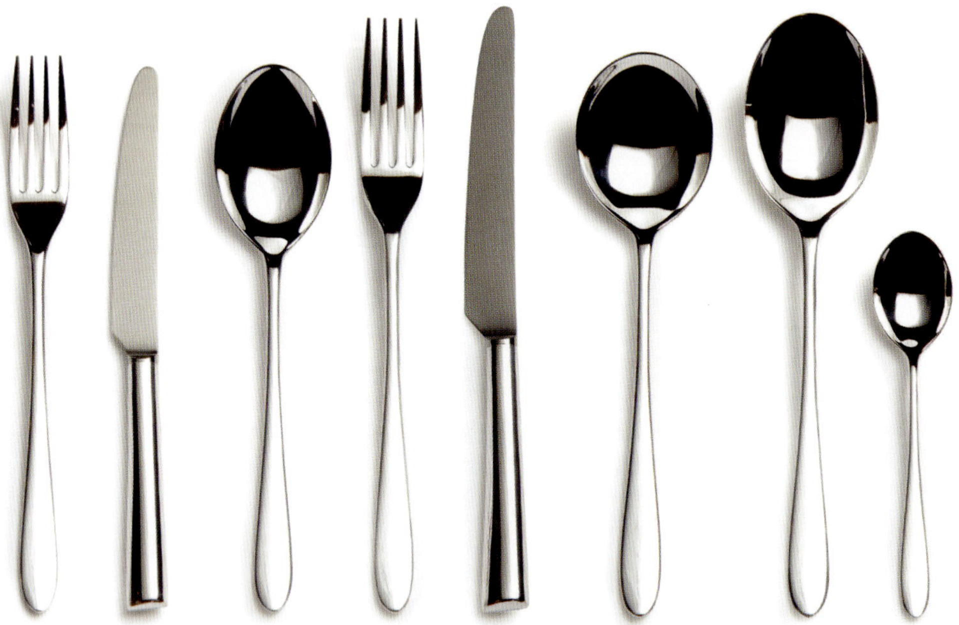

ABOVE:
Pride cutlery
for Walker & Hall (later by David Mellor), 1953–54

Once described by Sir Terence Conran as "Britain's greatest post-war product designer", David Mellor was a skilled metalware specialist whose quest was always for perfection. He had not only a highly developed eye for detail but also a genius for combining form with function, born from an understanding of both craft and industry. Renowned for his cutlery and tableware, Mellor was also one of the very few successful designer-makers of his generation, whose workshop produced designs for his elegant jewel-like shop on London's Sloane Square, which was a prominent showcase for his pioneering design talent.

Born in Sheffield, the epicentre of Britain's cutlery industry, Mellor came from a working-class background, his father being a toolmaker. From an early age, this Yorkshire lad showed a strong affinity for metalwork, so much so that he went on to study silversmithing at Sheffield College of Art, and then later at the Royal College of Art in London. As the design commentor Stephen Bayley notes, "Somewhere along the way he learned Eric Gill's philosophy of art, with its religiose commitment to the morality of making things, which was to remain a lifelong influence."

Scandinavian Modernism also had a huge formative influence on Mellor's development as a designer, for while studying at the RCA he was awarded a scholarship that enabled him to travel to Sweden and Denmark in 1952, which gave him first-hand experience of the Nordic belief in good design for all. After completing his studies at the British School in Rome, Mellor returned to Sheffield in 1954 and established his own workshop. Thanks to a resurgence of interest in contemporary silversmithing, he received various special one-off commissions, and that same year he was hired by local firm Walker & Hall as a consultant designer.

Having been initially conceived at the RCA, Pride (1953–54) was his first flatware pattern to be put into mass-production, by Walker & Hall. This design's contemporary aesthetic not only captured the optimistic post-war spirit but also reflected a generational shift towards more casual modes of entertaining. Mellor went on to design many other praiseworthy flatware patterns, such as Canteen (1965), devised specifically for institutional usage, and a range of white plastic disposable cutlery (1969) for Cross Paperware that was produced in its millions.

Apart from becoming the "king of cutlery", Mellor worked as a successful industrial consultant, notably designing a bus shelter (1959) used throughout Britain and the national traffic light system (1966) for the Department of the Environment. In 1969, he opened his eponymous London store, which enabled him to sell his cutlery and cookware designs directly to the public, and also helped raise his public profile.

In 1973 he began self-producing his cutlery at Broom Hall in Sheffield, and eventually in 1990 he moved his design and manufacturing facility to The Round Building in Hathersage, Derbyshire. This former gasworks had been skilfully adapted by the architect Michael Hopkins into a stylish factory/studio/showroom, and subsequently won a BBC Design Award. In 2006, the Hopkins-designed David Mellor Design Museum at Hathersage was opened, and to this day the company that bears his name continues to thrive, with his talented son, Corin, having followed in his father's professional footsteps.

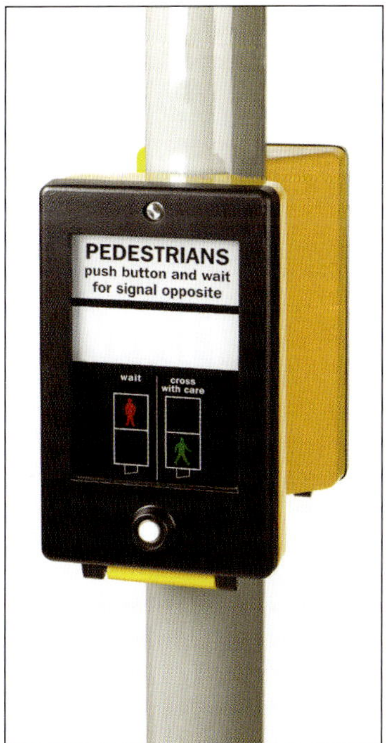

LEFT:
Pedestrian signal box
for the Department of the Environment, 1965–69

RIGHT:
National traffic light system
for the Department of the Environment, 1965–69

Memphis

Italy, founded 1980

Following in the Italian Radical Design footsteps of Global Tools and Studio Alchimia, Memphis was a far more populist venture than its predecessors and helped to transform what was then known as New Wave design into a new and highly influential international design style, Post-Modernism. It is difficult to comprehend the startling impact Memphis must have had when it first splashed on to the design world's stage with its provocative debut at the Milan Furniture Fair in 1981.

Memphis was essentially a riotous design circus, with the enigmatic architect/designer Ettore Sottsass taking the role of ringmaster for its band of youthful design renegades, which included not only Italian designers such as Michele De Lucchi and Marco Zanini but also foreign practitioners, notably George Sowden, Nathalie Du Pasquier, Martine Bedin and Masanori Umeda (later to be joined by Hans Hollein, Shiro Kuramata, Peter Shire and Michael Graves). Courting publicity, Memphis did what no Anti-Design group had really managed to do before: popularize Post-Modernist theory by repackaging it into, as the design critic Alice Rawsthorn puts it, "a fun, seductive form that millions understood".

Although Sottsass had been associated with Studio Alchimia, he had found its focus on "banal design" and "redesign" too creatively restrictive, and his founding of Memphis was an attempt to find a new creative approach to design that was less intellectualized and rhetorically laden. Essentially a design collaborative, its name had been inspired by the lyrics of a Bob Dylan song, "Stuck Inside of Mobile with the Memphis Blues Again", which had been playing at the group's first gathering in 1980, getting stuck on the last three words repeatedly. The name also had a suitably ironic double meaning, being both the home of the ancient Egyptian capital of culture and the Tennessee birthplace of Elvis Presley. Indeed, double-coded messages were as much a feature of Memphis design as was the use of eye-catching colour combinations, bold totemic forms and plastic laminates with New Wave style geometric and biomorphic patterning.

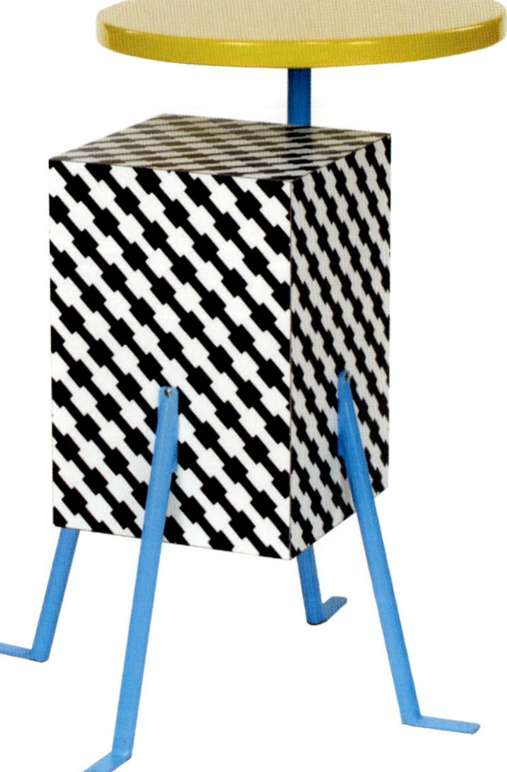

LEFT:
Kristall side table
by Michele De Lucchi for Memphis, 1981

OPPOSITE:
Tahiti lamp
by Ettore Sottsass for Memphis, 1981

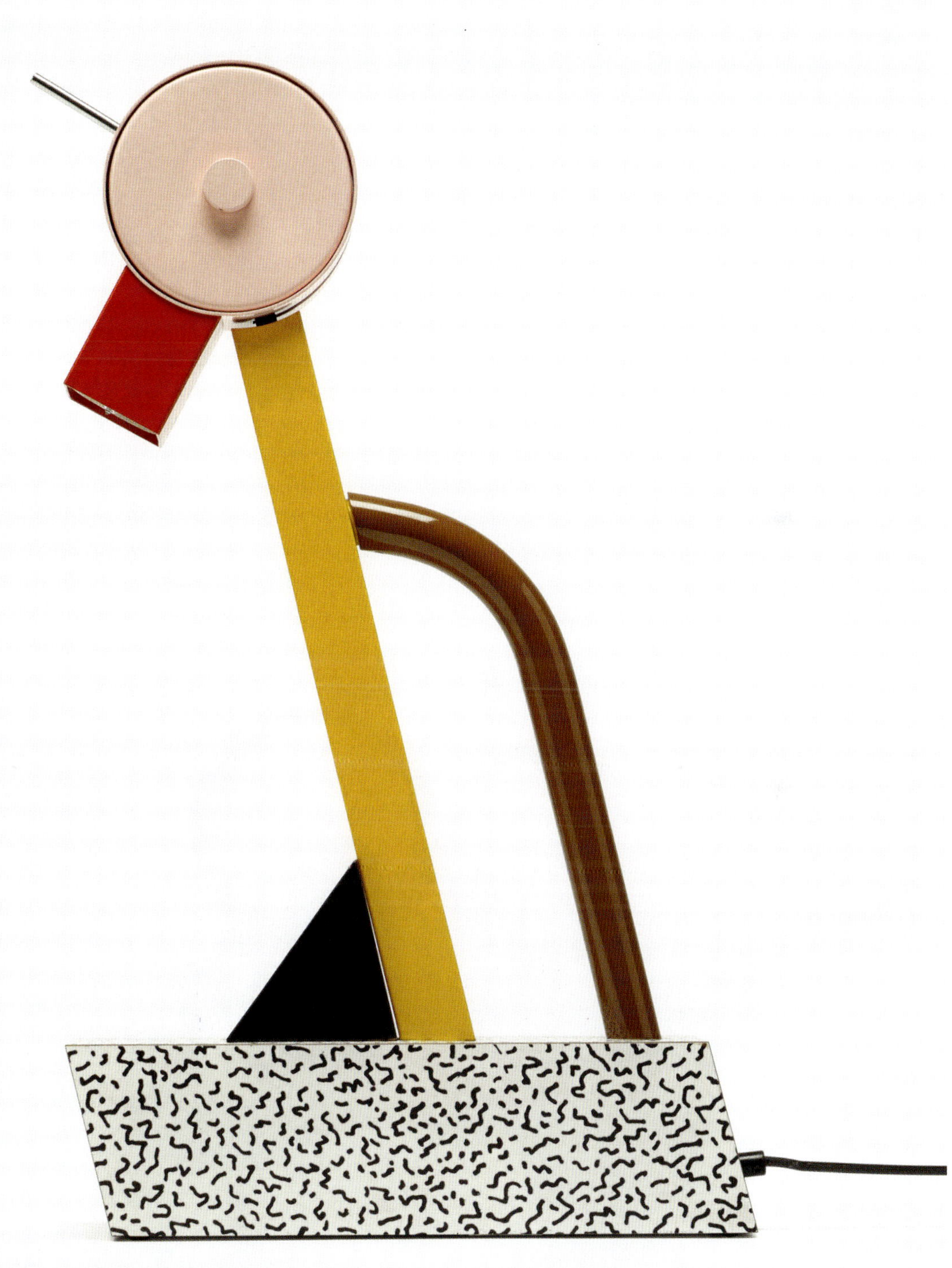

There was nothing visually subtle about Memphis designs, and they heralded a new language of Post-Modern Italian design that was exuberantly playful and captured the emerging optimism of the early 1980s as the world's economy began to heave itself out of recession. Memphis caught the attention of the design press around the world and in so doing helped disseminate Post-Modernism globally, with the famous photograph of Ettore Sottsass along with seven other members of the group sprawled in Masanori Umeda's Tawaraya boxing-ring-cum-conversation-pit (1981) becoming an especially iconic image, for it powerfully reflected a new sense of freedom and youthful humour in design. Through the diverse nationalities of its members, Memphis also heralded a new age of internationalism in design. As the Design Museum has noted, "Memphis was seen as equally sensational outside the closed confines of the design community. The packed opening party, cool graphics and hip young designers – male and female, from different countries – proved irresistible to the mass media. Perfectly in tune with an era when pop culture was dominated by the post-Punk flamboyance of early 1980s New Romanticism, Memphis was also a colourful, clearly defined manifestation of the often obscure Post-Modernist theories then so influential in art and architecture." Although relatively short-lived, with its star waning when Sottsass left in 1985, Memphis was an important spawning ground of youthful talent, with many of its youthful associates going on to have important independent design careers.

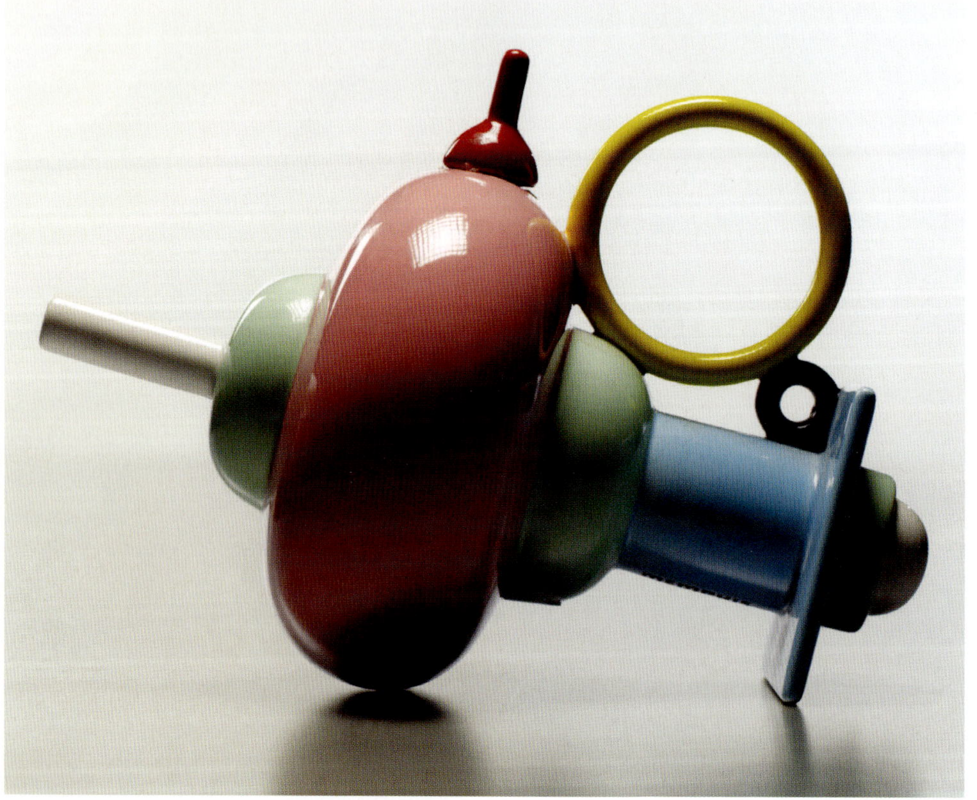

LEFT:
Colorado teapot
by Marco Zanini for Memphis, 1983

OPPOSITE:
Murmansk fruit dish
by Ettore Sottsass for Memphis, 1982

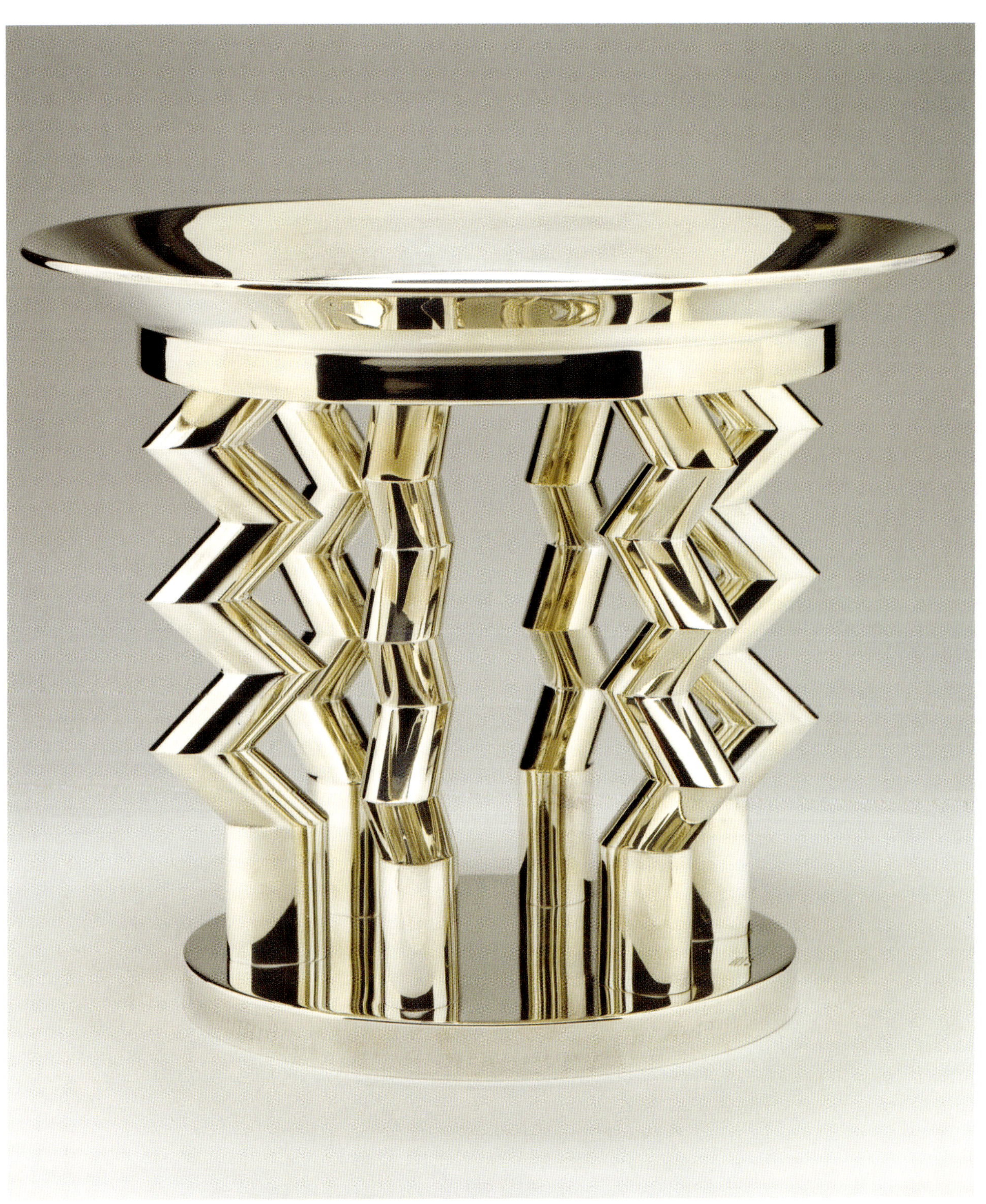

Alessandro Mendini

Italian, 1931–

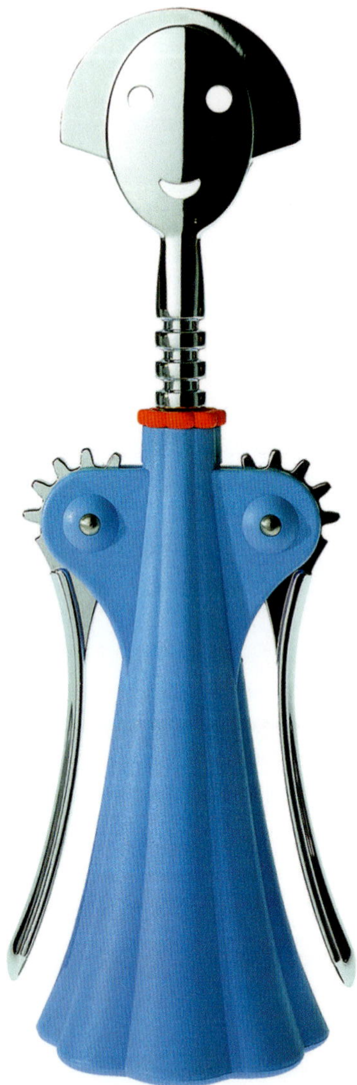

ABOVE:
Anna G corkscrew
for Alessi, 1994

The Milanese architect-designer Alessandro Mendini was fundamental to the intellectualization of Italian Radical Design throughout the 1970s and also, subsequently, to Post-Modernism. More than any other designer, he understood that "an object is something that tells a tale", and therefore used design as a powerful form of rhetoric.

Having graduated as an architect from the Politecnico di Milano in 1959, he joined Nizzoli Associati the following year and became a partner in this leading Italian design practice. Later, as the editor of *Casabella* from 1970 to 1976, he helped to disseminate the Radical Design agenda. He also set up Global Tools, a new movement of counter-architecture and -design, which was founded at the magazine's offices in 1973. The following year Mendini dramatically set fire to two identical "ideal" chairs outside *Casabella's* offices – both bore the name Lassù (Up There) and their symbolic burning was intended to blur the boundaries between art and design.

Mendini went on to create equally intellectually challenging work for Studio Alchimia (sometimes called Studio Alchymia), which was established by the architect Alessandro Guerriero in 1976. For Studio Alchimia's ironically named Bau.Haus 1 collection shown in 1979, Mendini contributed his Proust armchair and the Kandissi sofa, both designed the previous year. The former was conceived as part of the Redesign series, whereby Mendini transformed anonymous supermarket goods, antique reproduction furniture and acknowledged Modern design "classics" with the application of "banal" decoration into Post-Modern design statements. This redesign strategy had an almost nihilistic quality, with Mendini believing it was no longer possible to create "original" designs but only redesign. However, with this type of work he gave rise to a new kind of design, one that was free from the constraints of large-scale mass-production and was essentially an amalgam of references – in other words, an edited object infused with polemic. In 1980, Mendini curated the *L'Oggetto Banale* (The Banal Object) exhibition for the Venice Biennale and the following year created with other designers the Mobili Infinito collection for Studio Alchimia. He also held the editorship of *Domus* from 1979 until 1985, and under his guidance the magazine helped to widely publicize the emerging Neo-Modern style, as it was then called.

In addition, Mendini designed boldly patterned furniture pieces for Zabro Editions, an Anti-Design offshoot of Zanotta, that were in a similar vein to those produced by Memphis. It was, however, his role as art director of Alessi's Tea and Coffee Piazza project (1979–83) that

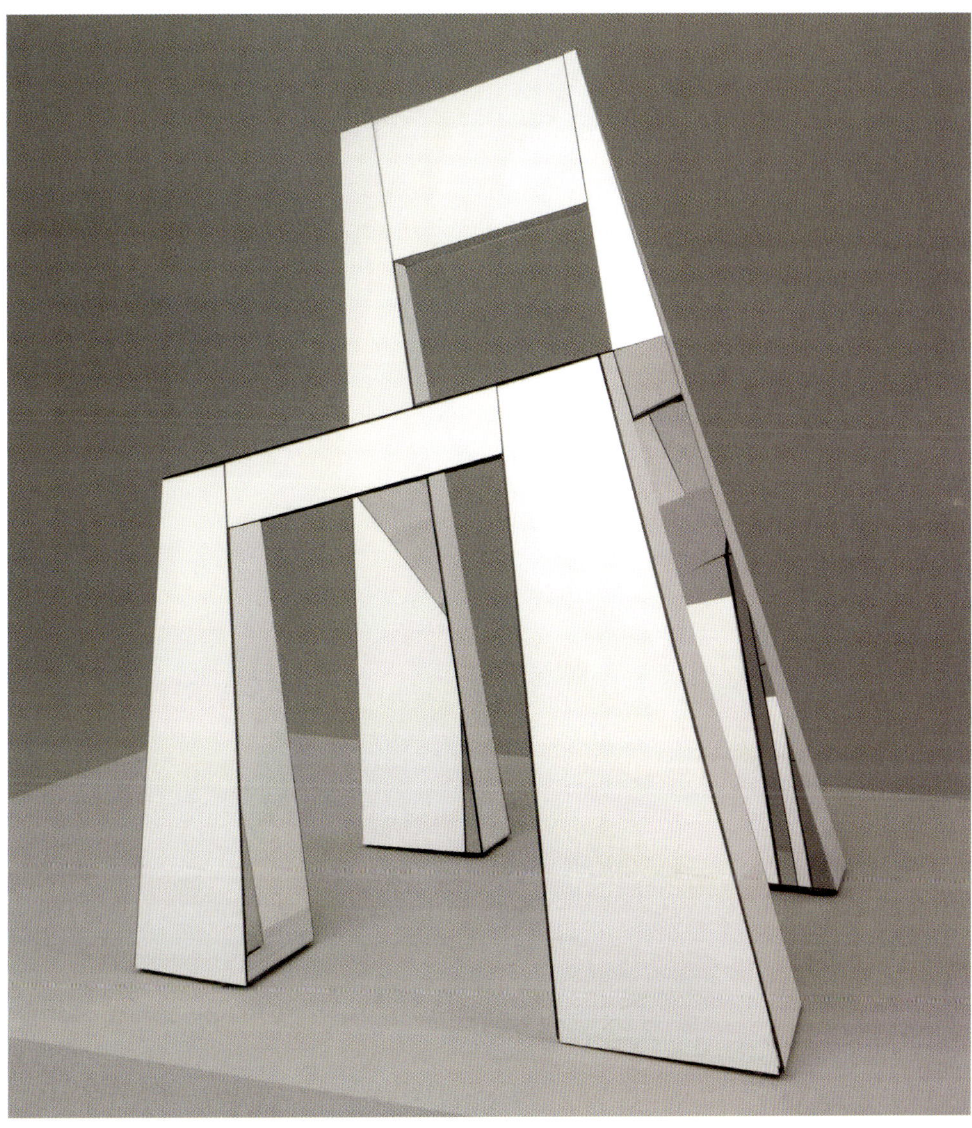

ABOVE:
Scivolando chair from the Collezione Oggetti Senza Tempo (Timeless Object Collection)
for Studio Alchimia (manufactured by Gavina), 1983

significantly contributed to the internationalization of Post-Modernism, thanks to the participation of various avant-garde designers from all around the world. During the early 1980s Mendini continued designing for Alchimia and during the 1990s and 2000s produced a number of notable designs for Alessi, including the Anna G corkscrew (1994). In 1989, he co-founded Atelier Mendini with his architect brother Francesco, and the same year they designed, with Yumiko Kobayashi, the Paradise Tower in Hiroshima, Japan. Since then the studio has designed numerous buildings and exhibitions infused with a sense of poetic symbolism. Above all, Mendini has shown that designing is an act of intellectual discourse and that experimental collaboration can lead to thought-provoking designs which are about far more than just fulfilling function.

Max Miedinger

Swiss, 1910–1980

The Swiss typeface designer Max Miedinger was the creator of Helvetica, a typeface that represents the apotheosis of typographic modernity. It is the world's most ubiquitous typeface, which graphic designers either love or loathe. For some, it represents Swiss School perfection, while for others it stands for all the stultifying Modernist rules they rally against.

Designed in 1957, this non-expressive typeface was the brainchild of Eduard Hoffmann, the president of the Haas type foundry in Münchenstein, Switzerland, who wanted to develop a modernized version of the well-known Akzidenz-Grotesk typeface. This earlier typeface had been created at the end of the nineteenth century by the H. Berthold type foundry in Berlin. To achieve his goal Hoffmann approached Max Miedinger to develop a new typeface that would capture a new sense of Modern idealism.

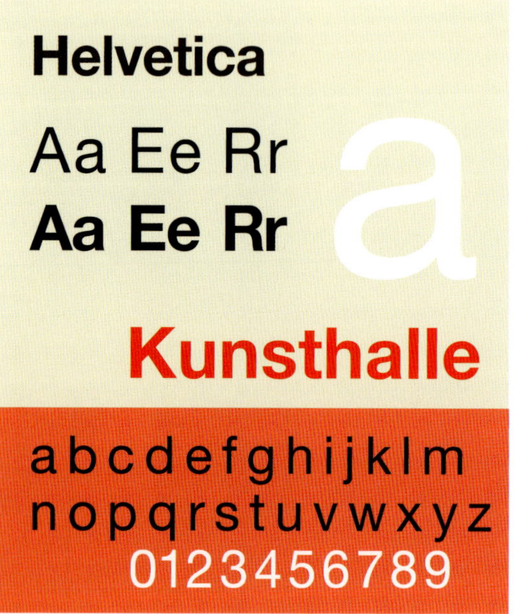

ABOVE:
Helvetica typeface
for Haas type foundry (later Linotype), 1957

At the time, Miedinger was working as a sales representative for the Haas type foundry, although he had previously trained as a typesetter in Zürich and taken evening classes at the Kunstgewerbeschule (School of Applied Arts) in Zürich. Miedinger painstakingly created the new typeface with much input from Hoffmann, who helped him hone it to utter polished perfection by suggesting subtle improvements to various letters. Although there had been a long tradition of sans serif lettering, especially in Germany, no typeface had previously been created that had such a harmoniously balanced figure–ground relationship – where each letter sat perfectly in its surrounding space. The typeface also incorporated very distinctive horizontal terminals among some of its lower-case letters, which gave it a sense of refined precision and modern crispness. Exuding a very Swiss sense of order and clarity, it exemplified the universal legibility associated with the International Typographic Style of the post-war period, which is sometimes referred to as the Swiss School.

Originally entitled Neue Haas Grotesk, the font's name was changed to Helvetica at the suggestion of the marketing director at the Stempel foundry in Frankfurt, which, like Haas, was owned by Linotype. It was the perfect name for the perfect Swiss typeface – derived from Helvetia, the Latin name for Switzerland. After its release in 1957, Helvetica became the go-to typeface for most graphic designers, as it powerfully conveyed a sense of contemporary modernity in a neutral, efficient and straightforward manner. As Massimo Vignelli, who used it time and time again in his corporate identity work, noted, it was "good for everything, pretty much".

In comparison to the plethora of hand-drawn lettering that was so prevalent in advertising during the late 1950s and early 1960s, Helvetica cut through the graphic mess of 1950s Americana and provided a straight-talking message that had a distinctly official tone. Because of this, it became associated with corporate America, and consequently capitalism, with numerous well-known companies using it for their logos. It also became the typeface of choice for many governments, who liked its official-looking directness, tempered by a seemingly humane smoothness.

With the advent of the Apple Mac, and later the Windows PC operating system, during the early 1980s Helvetica became even more ubiquitous than previously, as both operating systems originally used it as their default typeface setting. Today, Helvetica continues to be the most used typeface on the planet, yet because of its neutrality we often do not even notice it being used. It is beautiful and timeless, but due to its overuse Helvetica can be seen to have become something of a typographic cliché.

BELOW:
Eduard Hoffmann's notebook
documenting the early development of the Neue Haas Grotesk typeface (later called Helvetica)

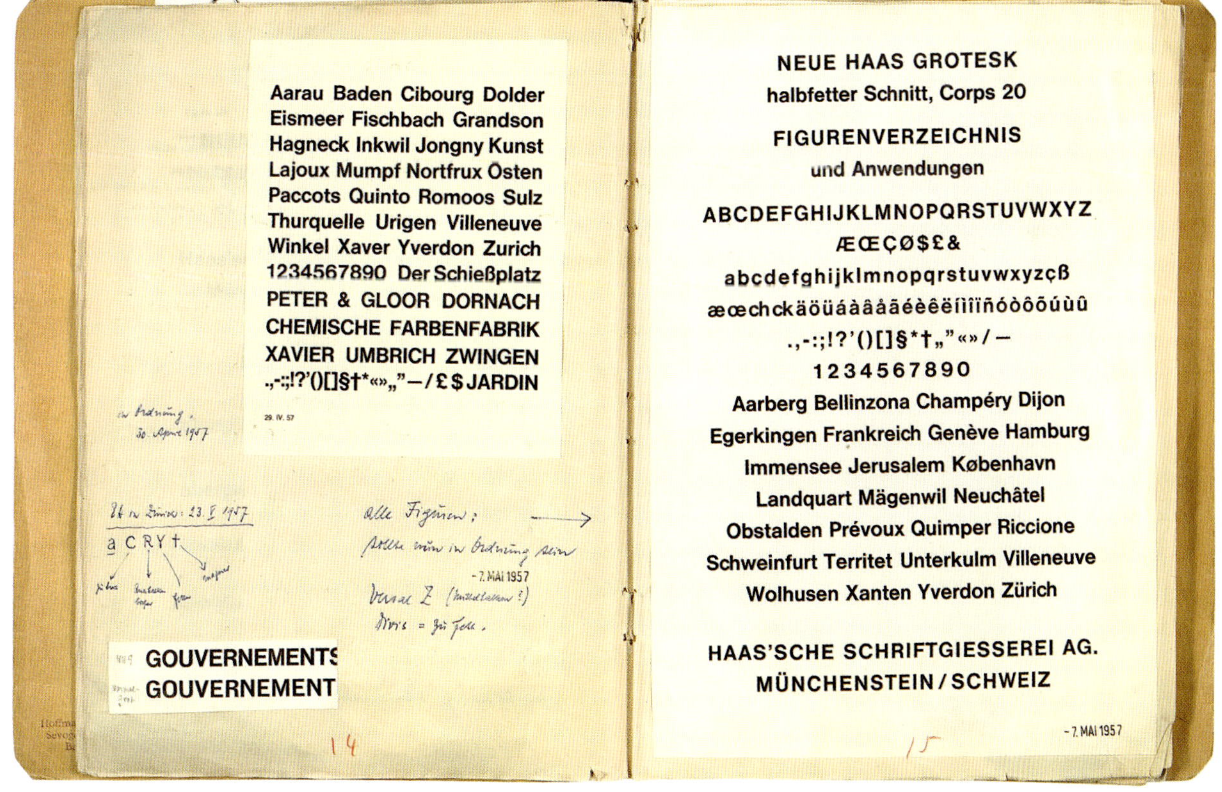

Aarau Baden Cibourg Dolder
Eismeer Fischbach Grandson
Hagneck Inkwil Jongny Kunst
Lajoux Mumpf Nortfrux Osten
Paccots Quinto Romoos Sulz
Thurquelle Urigen Villeneuve
Winkel Xaver Yverdon Zurich
1234567890 Der Schießplatz
PETER & GLOOR DORNACH
CHEMISCHE FARBENFABRIK
XAVIER UMBRICH ZWINGEN
.,-:;!?'()[]§†*«»„"—/£$JARDIN

GOUVERNEMENTS
GOUVERNEMENT

NEUE HAAS GROTESK
halbfetter Schnitt, Corps 20
FIGURENVERZEICHNIS
und Anwendungen
ABCDEFGHIJKLMNOPQRSTUVWXYZ
ÆŒÇØ$£&
abcdefghijklmnopqrstuvwxyzçß
æœchckäöüáàâåãéèêëíìîïñóòôõúùû
.,-:;!?'()[]§*†„"«»/—
1234567890
Aarberg Bellinzona Champéry Dijon
Egerkingen Frankreich Genève Hamburg
Immensee Jerusalem København
Landquart Mägenwil Neuchâtel
Obstalden Prévoux Quimper Riccione
Schweinfurt Territet Unterkulm Villeneuve
Wolhusen Xanten Yverdon Zürich
HAAS'SCHE SCHRIFTGIESSEREI AG.
MÜNCHENSTEIN / SCHWEIZ
- 7. MAI 1957

M

Ludwig Mies van der Rohe

German/American, 1886–1969

OPPOSITE:
German Barcelona Pavilion for the *Barcelona International Exposition*, 1929 (reconstruction)

BELOW:
MR10 chair for Thonet, 1927

One of the greatest and most influential architects of the twentieth century, Ludwig Mies van der Rohe helped transform European Modernism into the International Style. He defined what Modern architecture was, through his innovative buildings that incorporated open-plan layouts and industrial materials such as steel and glass. Having worked as a draughtsman, Mies van der Rohe moved to Berlin in 1905, where he studied at the Kunstgewerbeschule (School of Applied Arts) while also working in the architecture practice of Bruno Paul. While there, he designed his first building, the Riehl House in Potsdam-Neubabelsberg in 1907, which reflected the influence of Jugendstil. The following year, Mies joined Peter Behrens's design office and became inspired by the Neo-Classicism of Frederick Schinkel's architecture. In 1912, he opened his own office in Berlin and subsequently designed houses in a stripped-down Neo-Classical style. During the First World War he undertook military service, then after the war joined the revolutionary November Group of Expressionist artists and architects. Mies organized the group's exhibitions from 1921 to 1925 and it was during this period that he propagated his Modernist approach to architecture through his idealized plans for "skin and bones" offices, houses and apartment blocks.

In 1925, he joined the Deutscher Werkbund, becoming its vice-president the following year. Mies subsequently organized the Werkbund's landmark *Die Wohnung* (The Dwelling) exhibition of 1927, showcasing the Weissenhof-Siedlung – a model housing estate in Stuttgart with buildings designed by the most progressive architects of the day. It was at a meeting to discuss this exhibition that the Dutch architect Mart Stam showed Mies a drawing of a cantilevered chair he had constructed from welded gas pipes. Somewhat controversially, Mies went on to design his own cantilevered chair the following year. Made of resilient yet springy tubular steel, Mies's MR10 chair and MR20 armchair were first shown at the Weissenhof-Siedlung exhibition and were his first notable seating designs.

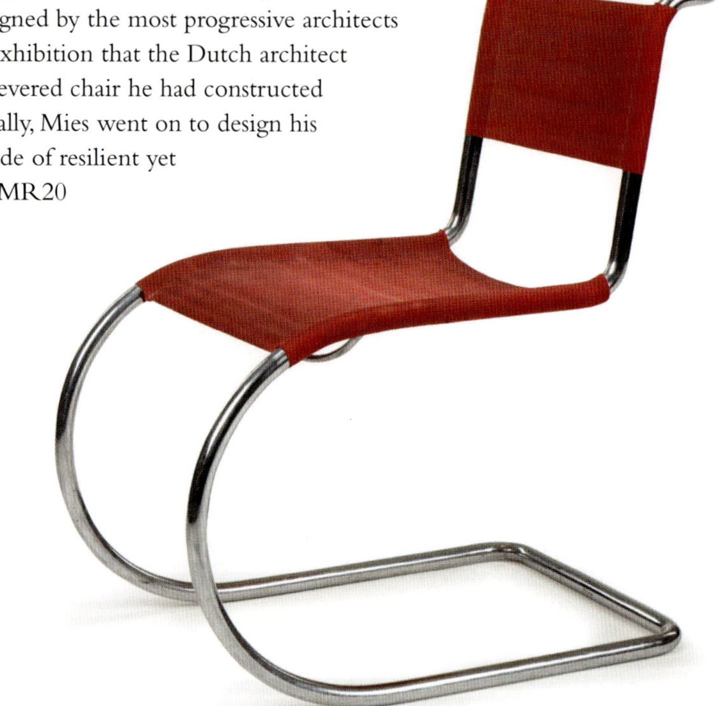

Such was his reputation that Mies was selected to design the German Pavilion for the 1929 *Barcelona International Exposition*. The resulting structure was one of the great landmark buildings of twentieth-century architecture, harmoniously blending Modern elemental forms and industrial materials such as steel and glass with materials more traditionally associated with luxury, namely marble, red onyx and travertine. A classical temple built in the Modern idiom, this open-plan building

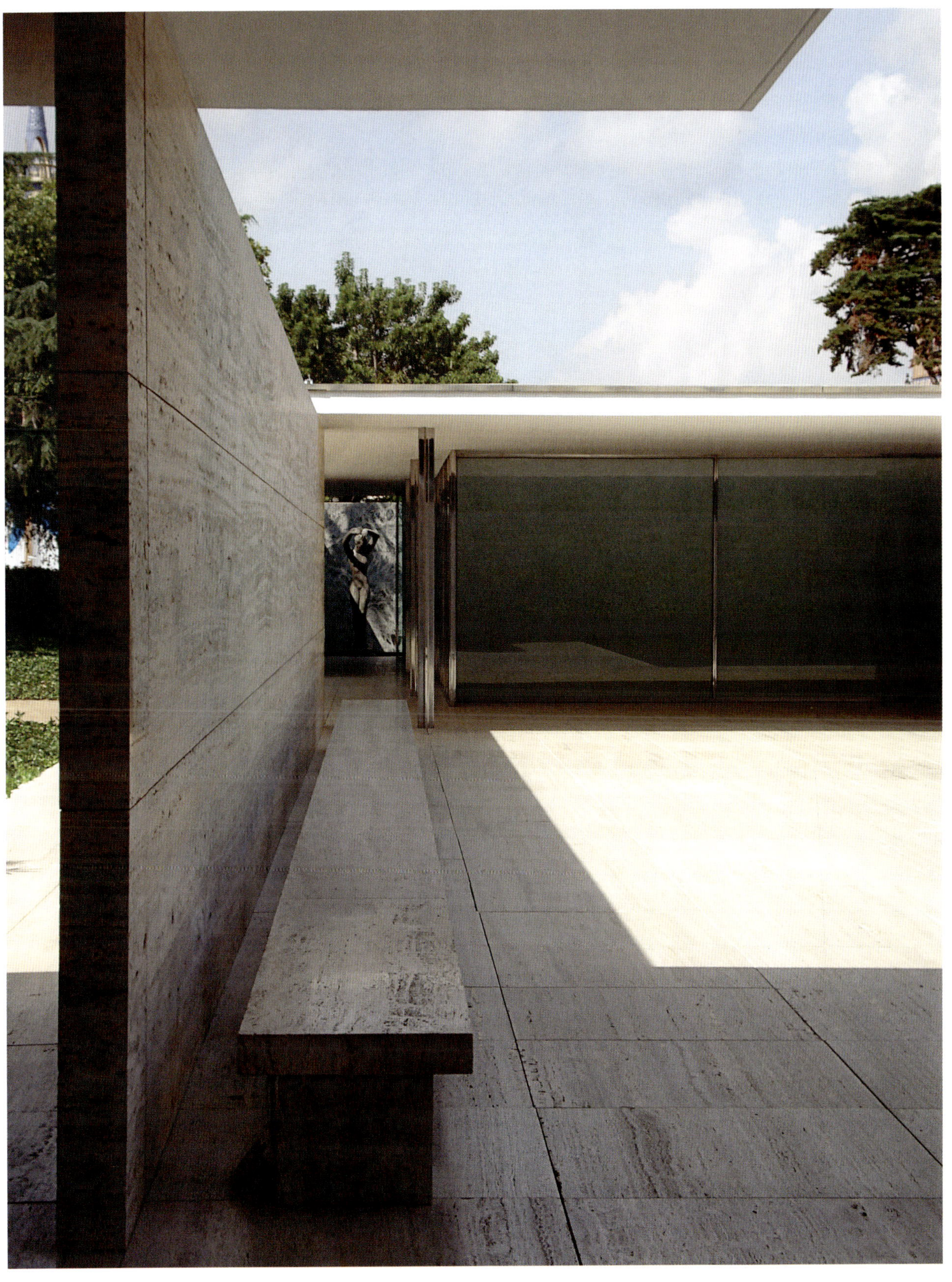

conveyed a forward-looking and positive message about contemporary Germany. It was furnished with site-specifically designed chromed-steel and buttoned leather seats – Mies's famous Barcelona chair – that were in effect modern-day thrones for the Spanish king and queen to sit on. Free of the constraints of everyday practicalities, the sparsely furnished pavilion was a dramatic spatial composition that eloquently confirmed Mies's famous dictum "less is more".

In 1930, he became the last director of the Dessau Bauhaus, and during his short tenure there the study of architecture was given increasing prominence, a tendency already instigated by Hannes Meyer. Because of its association with left-leaning politics, however, the Bauhaus was shut down by the National Socialists in September 1932, although Mies briefly re-established it as a private school in Berlin (closed in 1933). Eventually, Mies emigrated to America in 1937, where he established his own design office in Chicago and became director of the architecture department at the Armour Institute (later Illinois Institute of Technology) in Chicago. This move marked a second phase in his career and allowed him to put architectural theory into practice on a significant scale – among his most notable buildings from this period are the Farnsworth House, Plano, Illinois (1946–51), his masterwork Seagram Building, New York (1954–58) and the Neue National Gallerie in Berlin (1962–68).

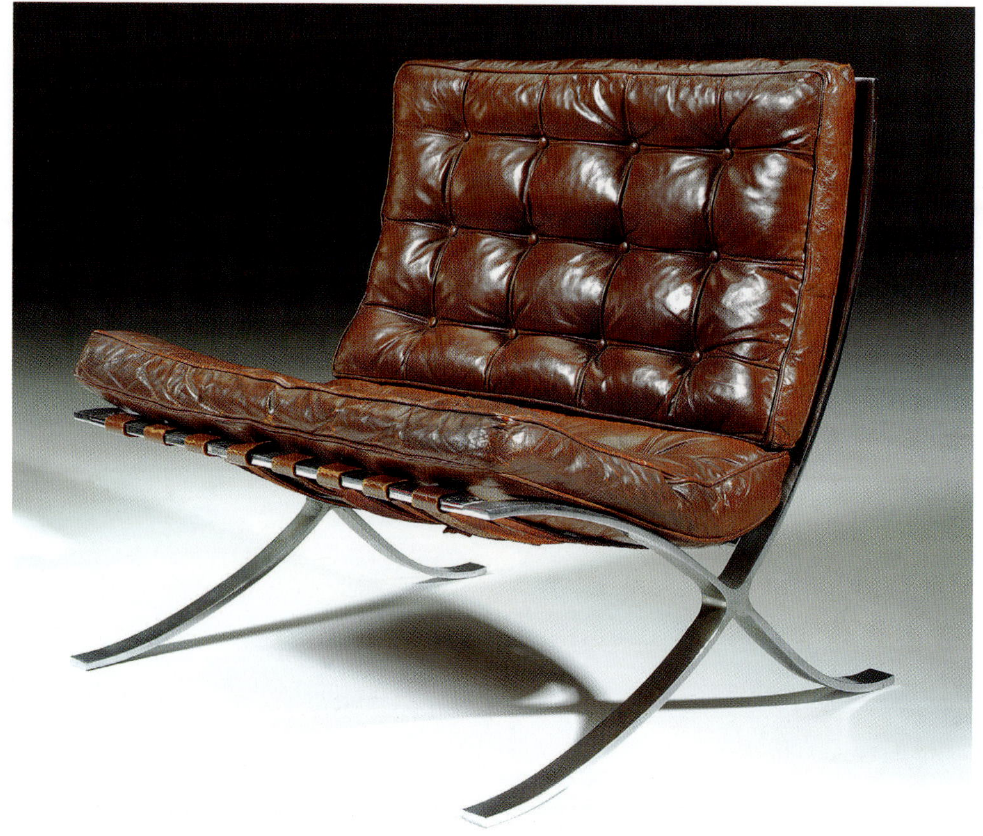

LEFT:
Barcelona chair
for Berliner Metallgewerbe
Josef Müller, 1929

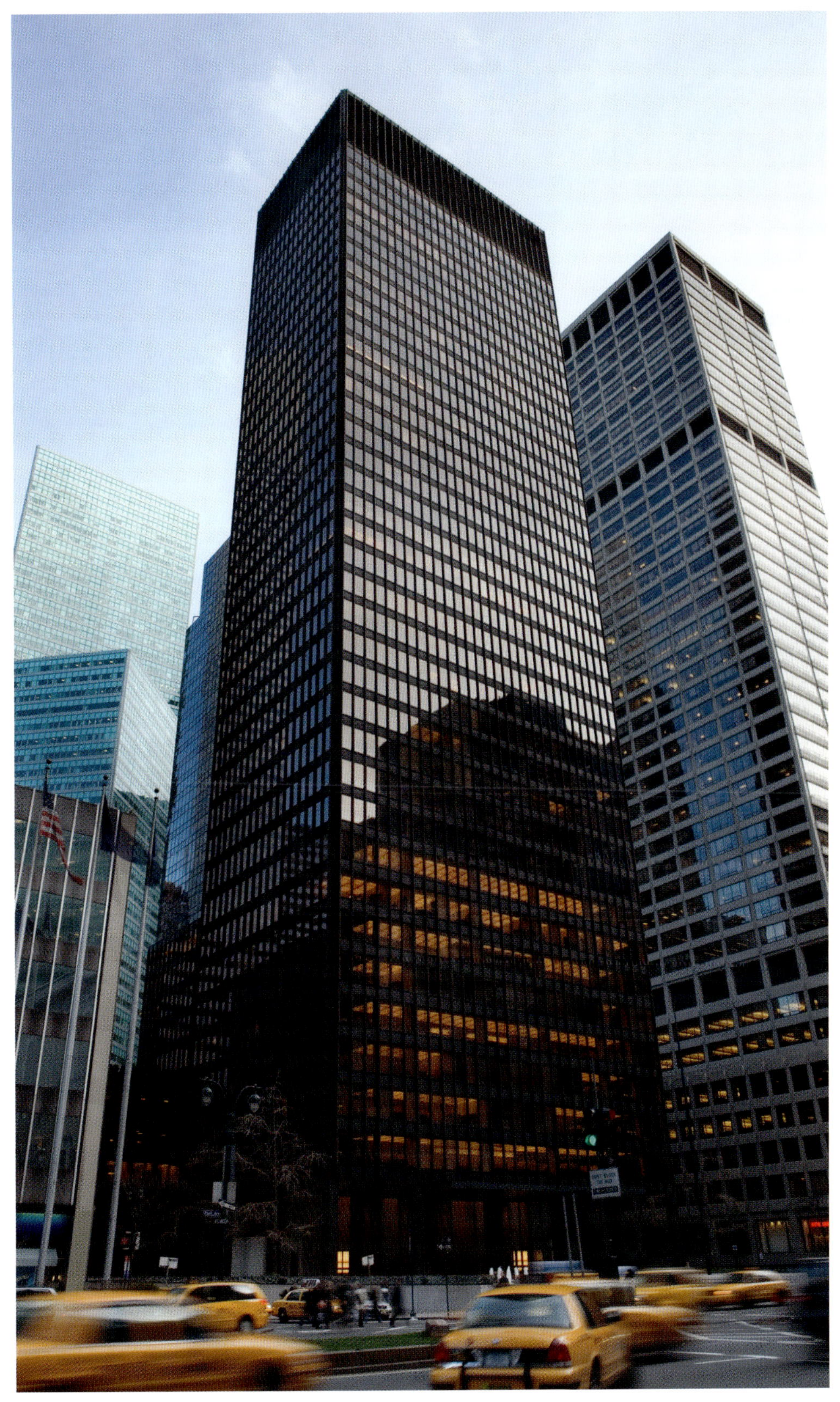

RIGHT:
Seagram Building
in New York City, 1954–58

László Moholy-Nagy

Hungarian/American, 1895–1946

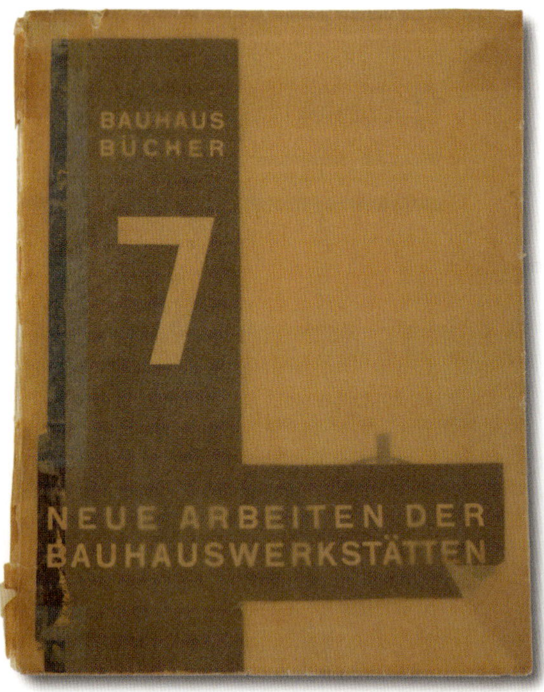

LEFT:
Cover of *Bauhaus Bücher 7* published by Albert Langen Verlag, 1925

The Hungarian-born graphic designer and typographer László Moholy-Nagy was highly instrumental in defining the stripped-down yet dynamic look of Modernist posters and publications. Although he had initially studied law, he decided to pursue an artistic career after being wounded in the First World War. He began going to life drawing classes in 1918 and soon became influenced by the work of the German Expressionists and Russian Constructivists. Having become associated with various prominent members of the Hungarian avant-garde, Moholy-Nagy moved to Berlin in 1920 and exhibited in various progressive art shows.

In 1922 he created his first "photograms" and that same year, while exhibiting at the Der Sturm gallery, he met Walter Gropius, the director of the Bauhaus in Weimar. The following year, Gropius invited him to join the school's teaching staff and he took over the teaching of the school's famous foundation course that had been established by Johannes Itten. He was also appointed the new *Formmeister* (form master) of the Bauhaus's metal workshop, a position previously held by Paul Klee. Moholy-Nagy brought a more rational Constructivist spirit to the Bauhaus and as a result the school's curriculum became increasingly focused on teaching art as applied to industry, which led to a much greater emphasis on functional utilitarianism in its output. While at the Bauhaus, Moholy-Nagy not only created exhibition posters, notable for their visual directness and dynamic compositions, but also eleven *Bauhausbücher* (Bauhaus books) published by Bauhausverlag. Comprising simple three-colour printing, bold typefaces in different sizes and weights, and much use of white space, these books exemplified what became known as "New Typography". After leaving the Bauhaus in 1928, Moholy-Nagy set up his own studio in Berlin and the following year curated and designed the Deutscher Werkbund's *Film und Foto* exhibition in Stuttgart. Around this time he also published an influential book entitled *Neues Sehen: Von Material zu Architektur* (The New Vision: From Material to Architecture), which was based on his Bauhaus lecture notes.

To escape Nazi persecution, Moholy-Nagy moved to Amsterdam in 1934 and then to London, where he lived from 1935 to 1937, working as a commercial artist and architectural

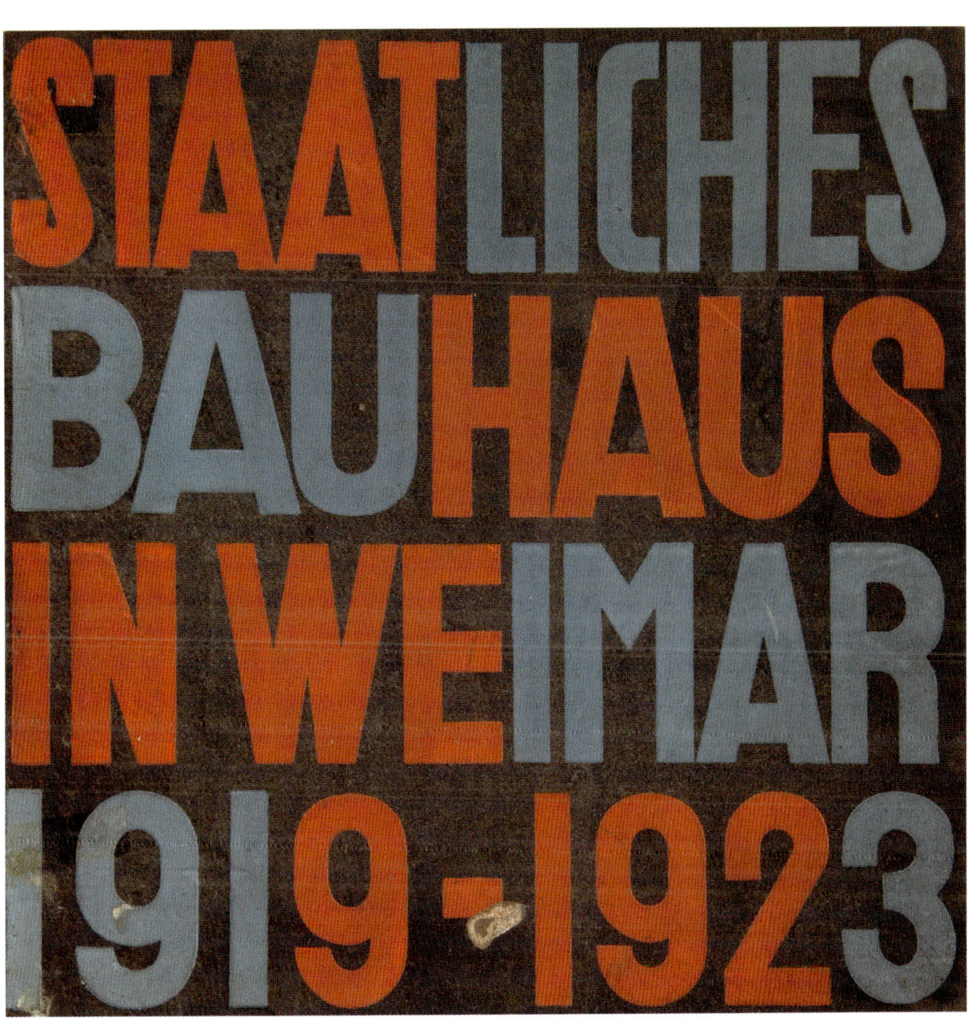

ABOVE:
Cover of the *Staatliches Bauhaus im Weimar 1919–1923* catalogue
for Bauhaus Verlag, 1923 – co-designed with Herbert Bayer

photographer. In 1937, at the invitation of Chicago's Association of Art and Industry, he moved to the United States to establish a new school of design in Chicago – known as the New Bauhaus School of Design. It ran into financial difficulties the following year, however, and had to close temporarily. Luckily Walter Paepcke, the influential chairman of the Container Corporation of America who was a prominent champion of Modern design in the US, came to the rescue by offering personal financial support and the college re-opened as the Chicago School of Design in 1939. From 1939 until his death in 1946, Moholy-Nagy was its director and helped advance the tenets of European Modernism in American design, thereby contributing to the development of what became known as the International Style.

Carlo Mollino

Italian, 1905–1973

Carlo Mollino was an extraordinarily gifted architect and furniture designer whose work during the late 1940s came to epitomize the stylistic bravado of Italian post-war design. Unlike many of his contemporaries in Italy, however, Mollino did not subscribe to any Rationalist canon of design, instead preferring a more personalized approach typified by the use of sweeping expressive forms, which in 1948 the American designer and critic George Nelson dubbed "Turinese Baroque".

As the son of Eugenio Mollino, a prominent engineer based in Turin, Carlo Mollino studied engineering and art history before enrolling at the Turin Polytechnic School of Architecture, from which he graduated in 1931. He initially worked in his father's architecture practice and in 1933 won his first major architectural competition, for the design of a modern-looking headquarters building for the Federazione Provinciale Fascista degli Agricoltori (Farmers' Fascist Provincial Union) in Cuneo. That same year, he designed the interiors of his own residence, the Casa Miller, which had a strong Surrealistic quality. He also memorably used this home as a photographic studio for his numerous erotic female studies. Certainly Mollino had a passion for life – skiing, fast cars and beautiful women – and this was reflected in his flamboyant approach to design and his dictum "Everything is permissible as long as it is fantastic". With this guiding motto, Mollino sought to create work that had an authentic creative expression and was not formulated by Modernist dogma.

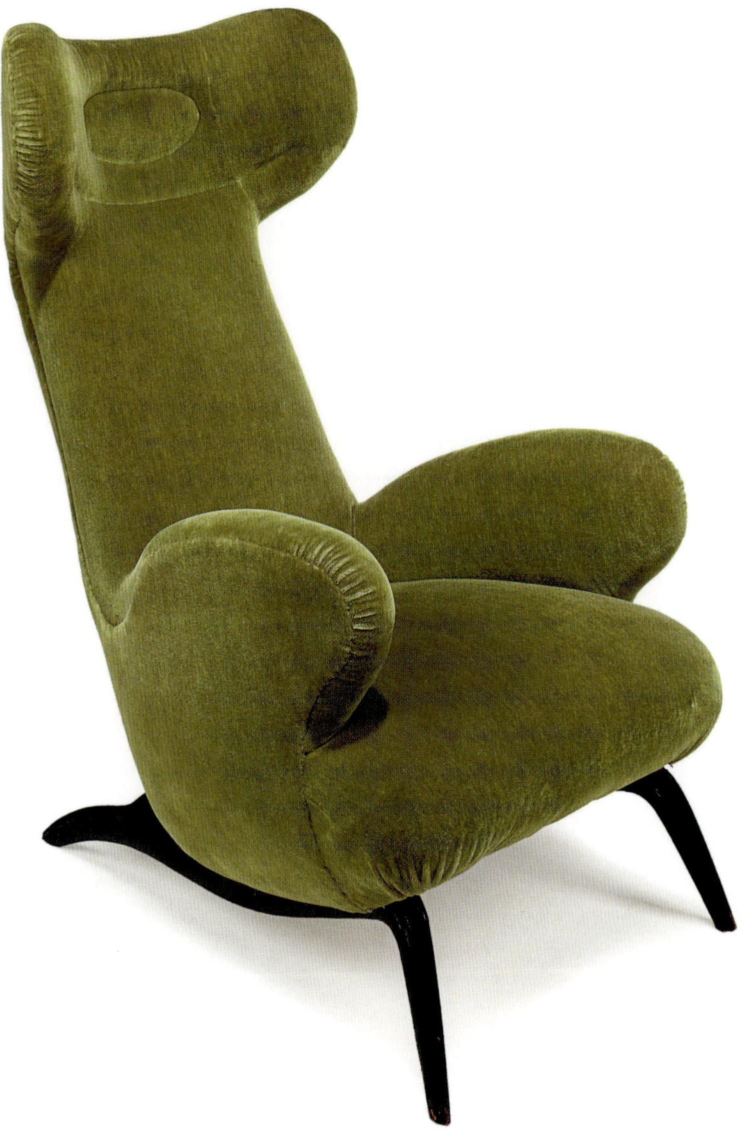

Being well grounded in the historical styles of the past, he confidently explored his own, highly original vocabulary of form. In 1937, he designed the Società Ippica (Equestrian Association)

headquarters in Turin – a riding-school building that accommodated up to 115 horses and boasted an indoor arena and clubhouse – which is generally considered his architectural masterwork, although it is no longer extant. From the mid-1940s to the mid-1950s, Mollino worked on an impressive number of architecture and interiors commissions that ranged from private residences and hotels to Alpine resorts and commercial complexes, many of which were featured on the pages of *Domus* magazine. For a number of these commissions, he also designed site-specific furniture that was very often biomorphic in form and was for the most part executed by the Turin joinery shop of Apelli & Varesio. Some of these pieces, such as his serpentine Arabesque table series (from 1949), each made from a wave-like piece of moulded plywood, were later batch-produced.

From 1952 until 1968, Mollino taught a course on the history of architecture at his alma mater, and certainly his exuberant biomorphic styling inspired the next generation of post-war Italian designers to create products that had a stylistic bravado and typified what became known as the "Italian Line". Apart from his buildings, interiors, furniture and lighting designs, Mollino was also an accomplished automotive designer, with his Osca 1100 racing car winning its class at the Le Mans 24-hour race in 1954. His remarkable talent for sculpting form into function and for infusing a sense of thrilling theatricality into his designs has ensured that today his work is highly prized by design collectors. As the renowned Mollino collector Fulvio Ferrari has noted of this uniquely gifted design maestro, "He continued the tradition of those eclectic Italian Renaissance artists whose work expressed the harmonious coming-together of science and art, logic and poetry, beauty and practicality"

OPPOSITE:
Lounge chair for Casa M-1
1946 – executed by Giovanno Cellerino

RIGHT:
Arabesque table
*c.*1949 – executed by Apelli & Varesio

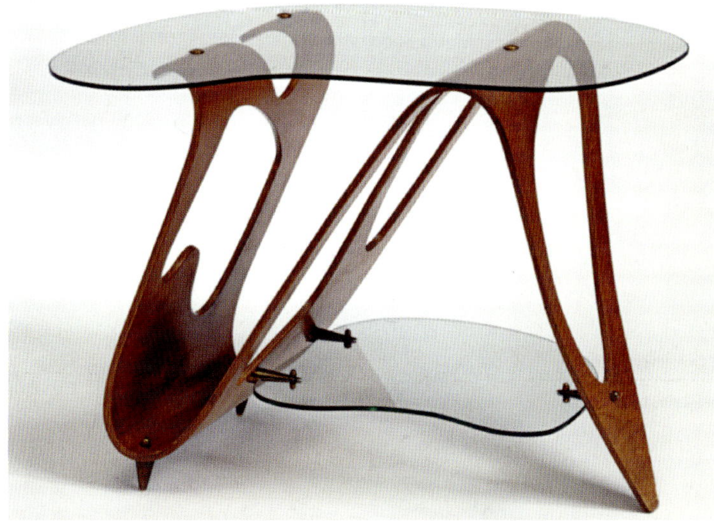

William Morris

British, 1834–1896

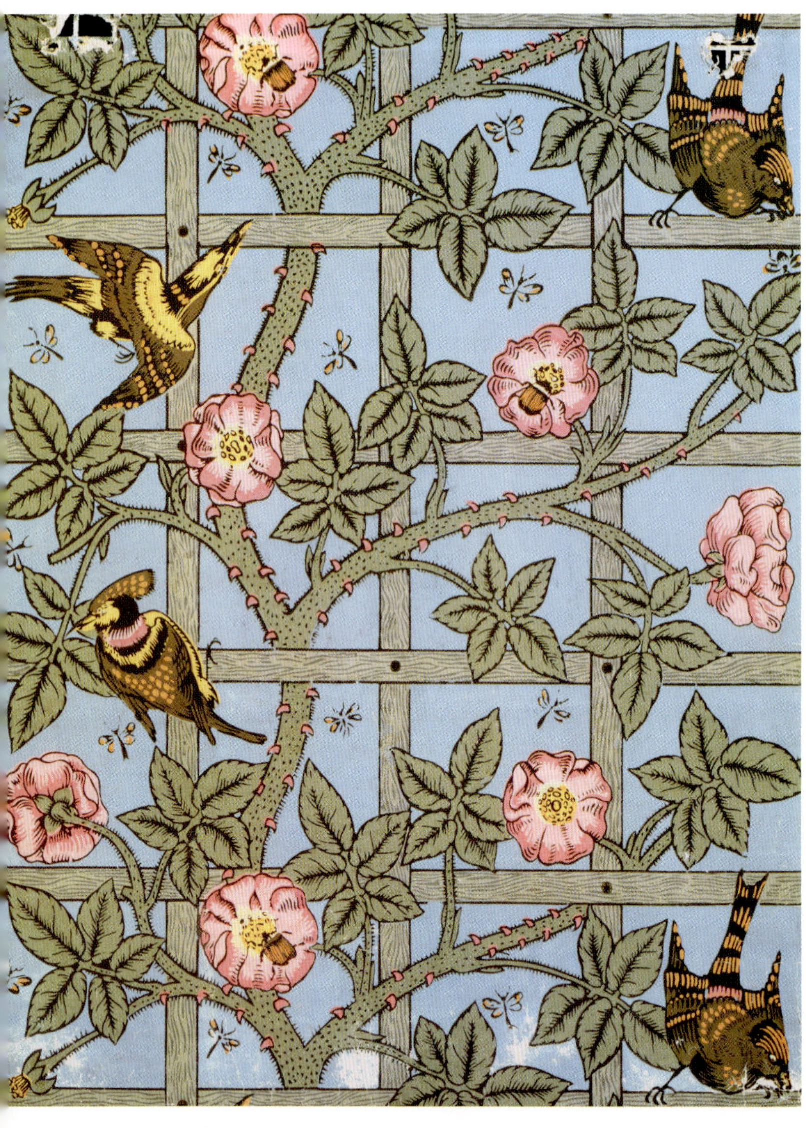

ABOVE:
Trellis wallpaper
1862 (first produced 1864)

Arguably the most important design visionary of the nineteenth century, William Morris was the founding father of the Arts and Crafts Movement, while his socially reforming words and deeds laid much of the philosophical bedrock upon which the Modern Movement would be built. Yet, despite being a prominent design reformer, a gifted designer, a successful entrepreneur, an acclaimed novelist, a popular poet, a leading political activist and a far-sighted conservationist, his life was beset with paradoxes.

Morris was fundamentally a revolutionary thinker, whose life and work were shaped by the dream of a medieval Arcadia as well as the vision of a fraternal utopia. Looking to the past in order to make sense of the future, he was driven by his avowed "hatred of modern civilization" whereby the industrialization of Victorian society had reduced men to, as he put it, "wage slaves". As a social reformer, he crucially put design theory into hands-on practice in order to demonstrate that it was possible to find a more ethical way of making things. Yet he was frustrated by the fact that his ideological adherence to handcraft meant that the simple designs he produced under the auspices of Morris & Co. were by necessity relatively expensive to manufacture and therefore not as affordable and democratic as he would have liked.

Born into a prosperous family, Morris initially studied theology at Oxford University, where he first met his life-long colleague Edward Burne-Jones. While at Oxford, Morris became intellectually inspired by the writings of John Ruskin, as well as those of Charles Kingsley and Thomas Carlyle. Both he and Burne-Jones were also influenced by the Pre-Raphaelite Brotherhood, indeed to such an extent that they both decided to abandon their theological studies to pursue "a life of art". While Burne-Jones pursued painting, Morris initially articled as an architect in George Edmund Street's practice, but he was persuaded to hone his painting skills after meeting his hero, Dante Gabriel Rossetti. Morris struggled with the medium, but happily found that he had an aptitude for design when he began decorating his new marital home, Red House in Bexleyheath to the southeast of London.

Designed by Philip Webb in close collaboration with Morris, Red House was intended to be a veritable "palace of art" and was an embodiment of Morris's dreams of a medieval Arcadia. Furnished with Pre-Raphaelite embroidered wall hangings, murals, stained glass, metalwork and heavy painted furniture designed by Morris and his circle of friends, the home was an artistic triumph that reflected Morris's understanding of materials, texture, colour and pattern.

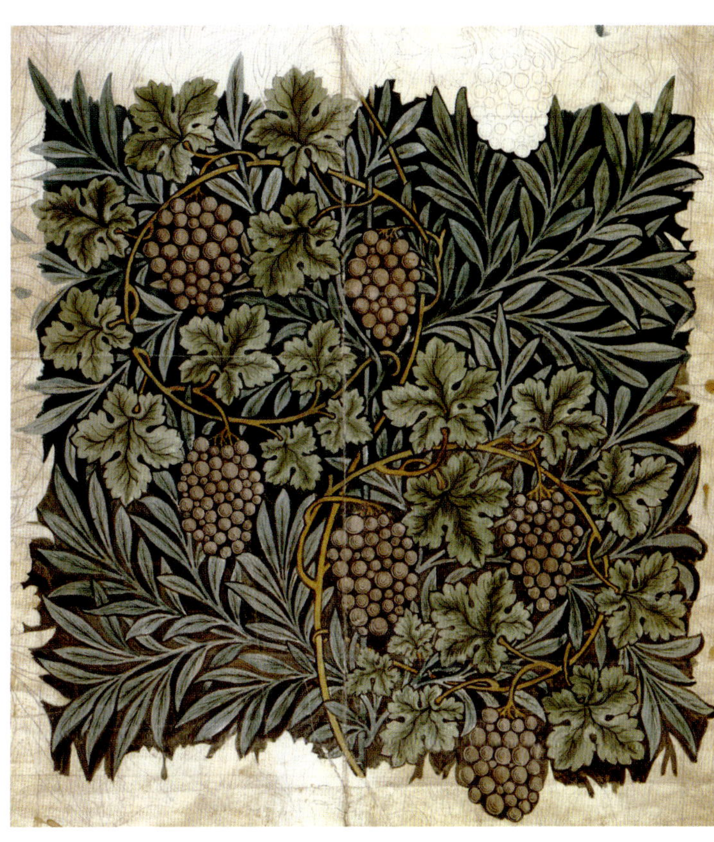

ABOVE:
Ink and watercolour design
for Vine wallpaper, 1874

Bolstered by the success of Red House, Morris went on to found Morris, Marshall, Faulkner & Co. (later Morris & Co.) in 1861, not only to infuse design with art but also to revitalize the age-old craft traditions. With its underlying social mission of bringing "joy through labour" to its employees, "the Firm" under Morris's guidance tended to shun the machine in favour of handcraft wherever possible, but this meant that although his goal was to produce affordable "Good Citizens' Furniture", such as Philip Webb's Sussex chair (*c.*1860), most of his time was taken up instead with, as he put it, "ministering to the swinish luxury of the rich". As a deeply committed socialist, Morris was reluctant to embrace any form of mechanization that would have seen his skilled craftsmen become mere machine minders, yet if he had done so he could have fulfilled his vision of producing affordable, well-designed objects for the many rather than for the few. Such was the paradox of Morris's design-reforming mission, which aimed towards a then unachievable goal: affordable yet high-quality goods and creatively engaged workers. Nevertheless, at the heart of whatever Morris did was his humanist belief in fellowship that in turn provided a deeper understanding of the inter-relationship between design, manufacturing, wellbeing and environment, which is as relevant today as it ever was.

Jasper Morrison

British, 1959–

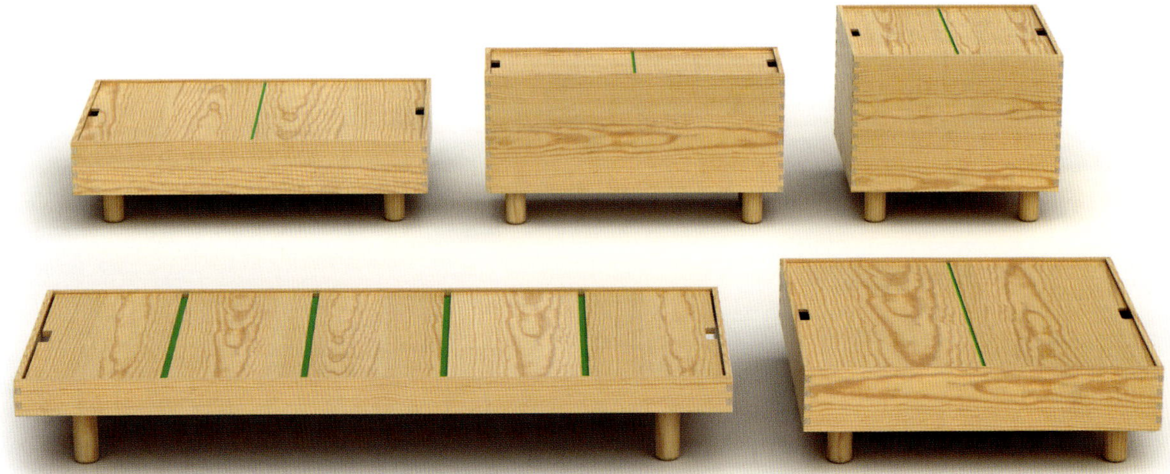

Jasper Morrison is highly respected for his ascetic designs that often possess an understated elegance and a gentle humour. He has not only worked on a diverse range of products – from furniture and lighting to cookware and kitchen appliances, and even a tram for the German city of Hanover (1997) and a pair of bus shelters for Vitra's headquarter site (2006) – but has also created influential installations, curated thought-provoking exhibitions and published various books, including *A World Without Words*, which reflect his inquisitive eye that finds the remarkable within the ordinary.

Morrison grew up in London and also in New York, when his advertising-executive father was posted there. He initially studied design at Kingston Polytechnic, before taking an MA in furniture design at the Royal College of Art, London. While he was a student he became interested in the work of the Modernist pioneers such as Gerald Summers, Le Corbusier, Jean Prouvé, Eileen Gray and Richard Buckminster Fuller – all of whom had taken a form-follows-function approach to design that had eliminated virtually any hint of superfluous decoration.

The young Morrison also witnessed the launch of the Memphis design group at the Milan Furniture Fair in 1981, which had a formative influence on his design thinking. As he recalls, it was "just fantastic. Here was proof that none of the old design rules mattered any more." While still a student, Morrison self-made some of his own designs, but he also decided to contract out the manufacture of some of his pieces with a view to larger-scale production. With this aim, he scoured London on his Honda moped looking for small workshops that could make up his designs using "found" industrially produced components. An example being his Flower Pot table (1984) – ingenuously simple, it was a circle of glass supported on a stack of terracotta pots.

ABOVE:
The Crate Series storage units
for Established & Sons, 2007

OPPOSITE:
Air-Chairs
for Magis
1999

Graduating from the RCA in 1985, the following year Morrison opened his own London-based studio, Office for Design, its straightforward name being an indication of his no-nonsense approach to design. Some of his earliest designs were successfully put into production by SCP in London and Cappellini in Italy, such as the minimalistic Side Table (1986) and the Thinking Man's Chair (1986). From the early 1990s onwards, Morrison had become firmly established within the rarefied ranks of international superstar designers, and found himself being commissioned by an impressive array of clients, including Alessi, Flos, FSB, Magis, Rosenthal, Rowenta and Vitra.

In 1992, Morrison, with his friend James Irvine, curated the influential Progetto Oggetto homewares project for Cappellini, and in 1999 he designed the super-elegant Low Pad chair for them, inspired by the earlier PK22 chair by Poul Kjaerholm. The same year, he designed the inexpensive gas-assisted injection-moulded Air-Chair for Magis, which became an instant critical and commercial success. Virtually indestructible, this stacking design with its archetypal chair form was not only structurally and materially unified but also totally recycable, and reflected Morrison's rare talent for essentialist design. Through his career, Morrison has been fascinated by archetypal products, with many of his designs being contemporary evolutions of historic paradigms.

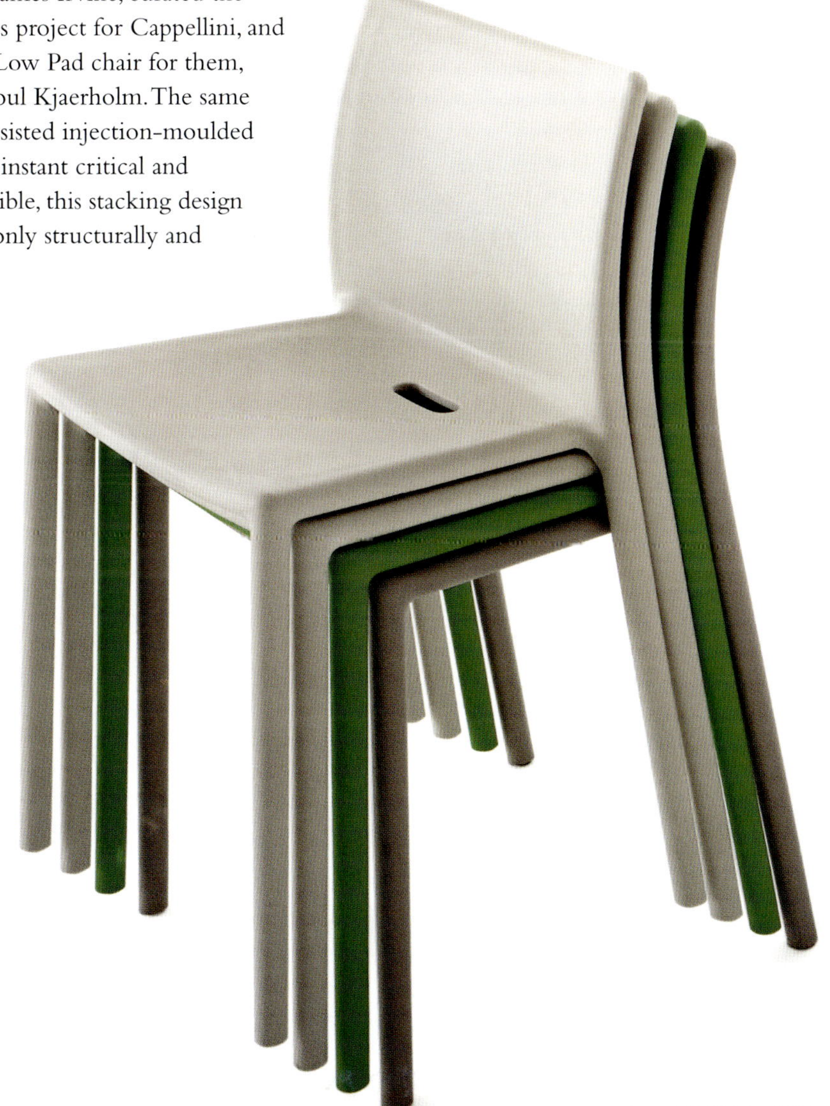

This interest in "ideal" functional objects led Morris, together with Naoto Fukasawa, to curate the *Super Normal: Sensations of the Ordinary* travelling exhibition in 2006, which included many anonymous everyday objects. The show opened the design world's eyes to the extraordinary nature of "ordinary" things, and as such was highly influential.

George Nelson

American, 1908–1986

An accomplished design innovator and influential theorist and communicator, the American architect George Nelson was a true polymath. Having studied architecture at Yale University and the Catholic University in Washington DC, Nelson won a Rome Prize that enabled him to study at the American Academy in Rome. After returning to the United States, he became an associate editor at *Architectural Forum* and *Fortune* in 1935, and also contributed a dozen profiles of pioneering Modern architects, including Frank Lloyd Wright, Walter Gropius and Hans and Vassili Luckhardt to the *Pencil Points* journal, from 1935 to 1936.

He subsequently joined the faculty of architecture at Yale University in 1941, and here he developed numerous innovative architectural concepts and planning ideas, including that of the pedestrianized shopping mall, which was part of his Grass on Main Street proposal of 1942. Another innovation was the concept of built-in storage, which came to him as a sort of eureka moment while writing a chapter on storage for his book *Tomorrow's House*, co-written with Henry Wright in 1944. Putting theory into practice, Nelson subsequently designed with Wright the hugely influential Storagewall, which was featured in *Life* magazine in January 1945, with a dedicated article explaining that it was "a device planned for keeping household articles neatly and conveniently in the otherwise wasted hollow space within a wall".

The following year, Nelson succeeded Gilbert Rohde as the director of design at Herman Miller, and during his tenure there, which lasted until 1972, he brought in a number of highly talented designers – Charles Eames, Isamu Noguchi, Alexander Girard – to create truly Modern rather than modernistic furniture items. He himself also designed various key pieces of furniture for Herman Miller, including a system of modular storage units that rested on slatted platform benches (1946); a home-office desk (1946); a molded plywood tray table (1949); the Marshmallow sofa (1956); the Swagged-Leg Group of chairs, tables and desks (1958); Comprehensive Storage System shelving system (1959); the Catenary chair and table (1963); the Sling sofa (1964); and, perhaps most importantly, the Action Office I system (1964–65). Attempting to address the needs of the ever-evolving office environment, the Action Office I system (co-designed with Robert Propst) provided greater freedom of movement for office workers as well as better layout flexibility. Although it

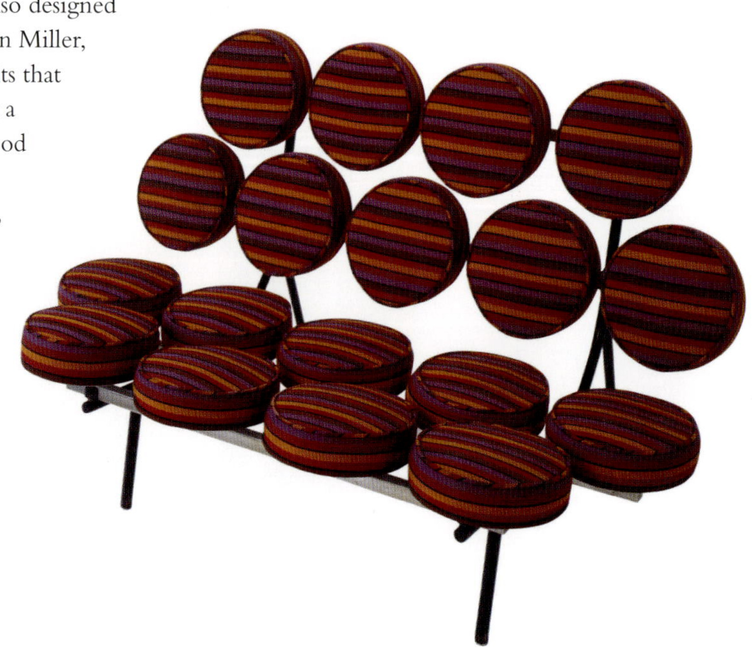

BELOW:
Marshmallow sofa
for Herman Miller, 1956 – upholstered in Jacobs Coat textile by Alexander Girard (designed 1959)

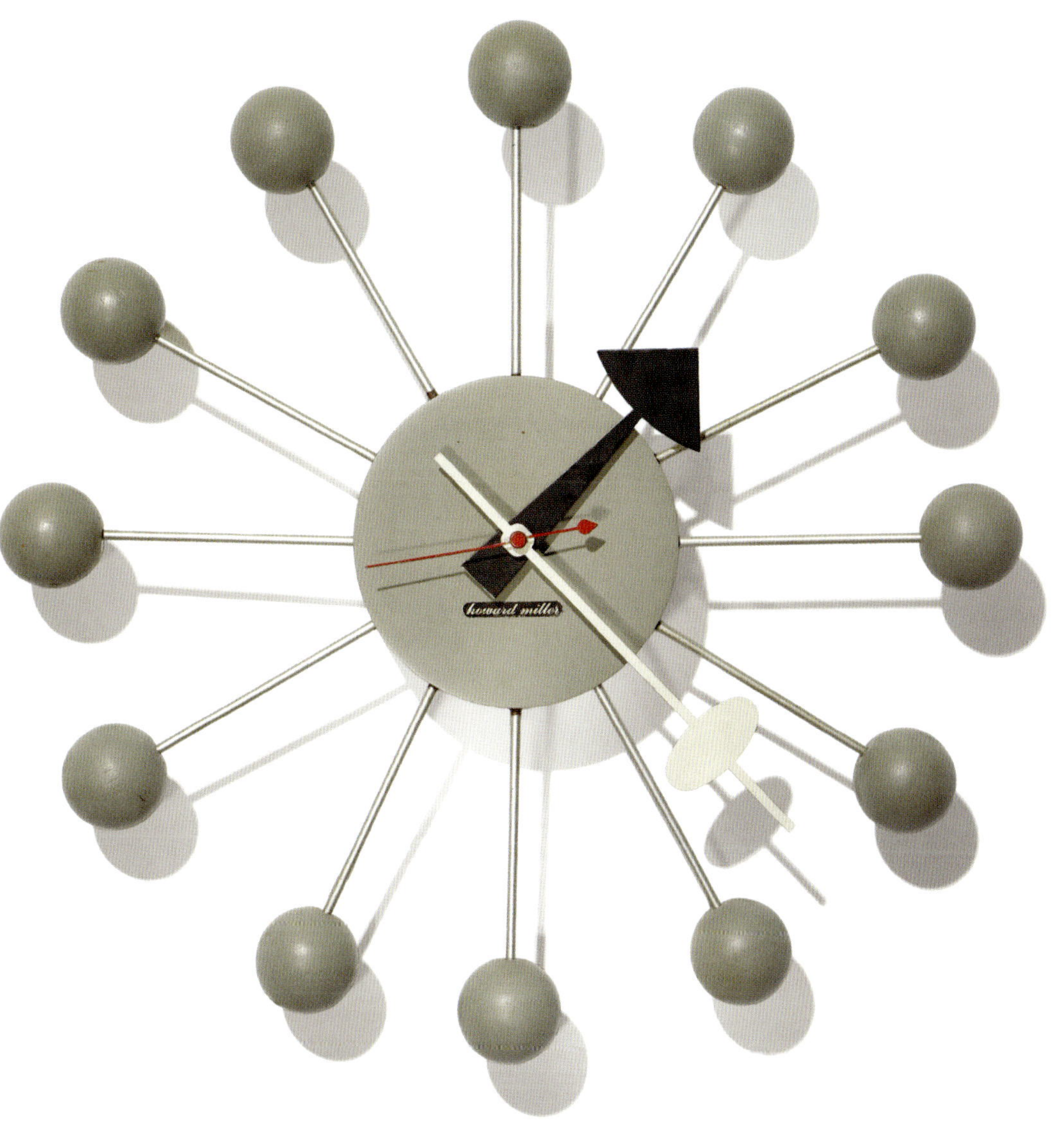

ABOVE:
Model 4755 Ball wall clock
for Howard Miller Clock Co., 1949

was most suited to smaller offices, the system can be seen as an important benchmark in the development of "contract furniture", in that it helped to humanize the office environment. Nelson also developed an ingenious modular prefabricated house, the Experimental House (1952–57), a model of which was published widely in the late 1950s.

During the 1960s and 1970s, he continued to publish books on design theory, devise exhibitions and interior spaces, and teach at both Harvard and the Pratt Institute School of Architecture. His influence on American design practice in particular was huge. As both an architect and a designer, Nelson always understood the crucial interconnections between people, places and things, and he tirelessly promoted the life-enhancing role that good design can play, noting on one occasion, "Total design is nothing more or less than relating everything to everything."

Marc Newson

Australian, 1963–

From iconoclastic furniture, sculptural lighting and unconventional housewares to futuristic aircraft interiors, a Ford concept car and a sublimely beautiful speedboat, Marc Newson has worked across a startling range of disciplines. Although he trained as a jewellery designer, he regards himself as being ostensibly self-taught, having learnt far more about contemporary design through reading magazines such as *Domus* and *Ottagano*. This has meant that Newson has never felt constrained by design rules.

His career breakthrough came in 1986 when his painstakingly riveted aluminium Lockheed lounger was exhibited at a gallery in Sydney. Making reference to 1930s streamlined airplane fuselages, this design was also inspired by an eighteenth-century chaise longue, and consequently had an undeniable Post-Modern elegance. The following year he designed his similarly constructed Pod of Drawers. However, soon after this Newson adopted a more Rational industrial approach that was sleekly futuristic. Early designs that reflected his new aesthetic direction included the Embryo chair (1988) and the Orgone lounger (1989). Having struggled to make a living from design, Newson moved to Japan in 1989 and began working for the Tokyo design entrepreneur Teruo Kurosaki, which enabled him to put some of his existing designs into production and to develop new ones, notably the Wicker chair (1990), exhibited by Kurosaki's company Idée at the Milan Furniture Fair. Having had his work shown in Europe, Newson soon found himself with design commissions from Cappellini and Flos, for furniture and lighting respectively.

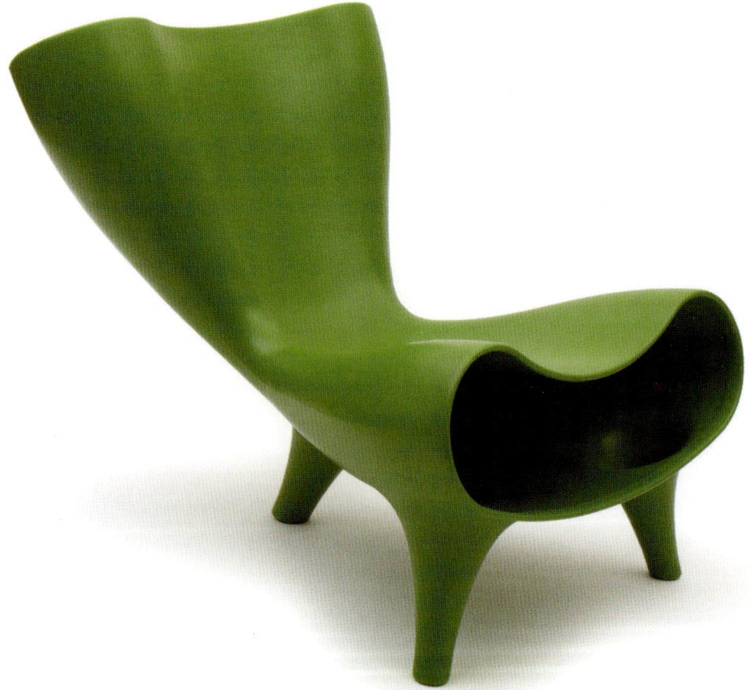

LEFT:
Plastic Orgone chair
for Marc Newson Ltd, 1998

OPPOSITE TOP:
MN Bicycle
for Biomega, 1999

OPPOSITE BOTTOM:
Hemipode watch
for Ikepod, 2006

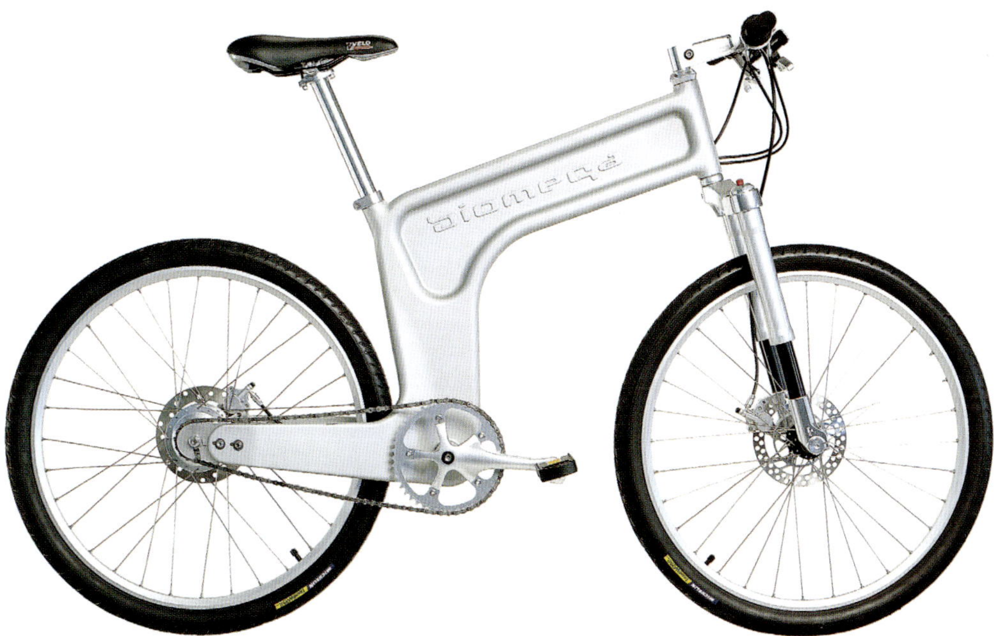

Moving to Paris in 1992, Newson established his own design studio and was soon being commissioned by manufacturers around the world. Five years later, he moved his studio to London and soon afterwards landed two dreams jobs that took his career to a new and professionalized level – the cabin interior and livery of a Dassault Falcon 900B long-range executive jet (1998) and the retro-inspired toy-like 021C concept car for Ford (1999), which incorporated innovations such as swivelling pedestal seats, side doors that opened from the centre and a boot that pulled out like a drawer. While product-design commissions were received from existing clients as well as the likes of Nike and Gap, Newson found himself in demand as an interior designer. Yet despite this he also found time to produce limited-edition and unique pieces that were free from the constraints of mass-production or clients' briefs. This venture into the world of "design-art" not only proved lucrative but also enabled Newson to explore unfettered creativity, resulting in some extraordinary designs such as his Voronoi Shelf (2007) made of white Carrara marble.

One of the most influential designers practising today, Newson is currently working as a consultant to Apple, having already assisted in the design of the Apple Watch (2015). Over the years he has received numerous awards, yet at the heart of his approach to design remains a committed belief in good design which, as he notes, "has always been about creating objects … that have a sense of quality".

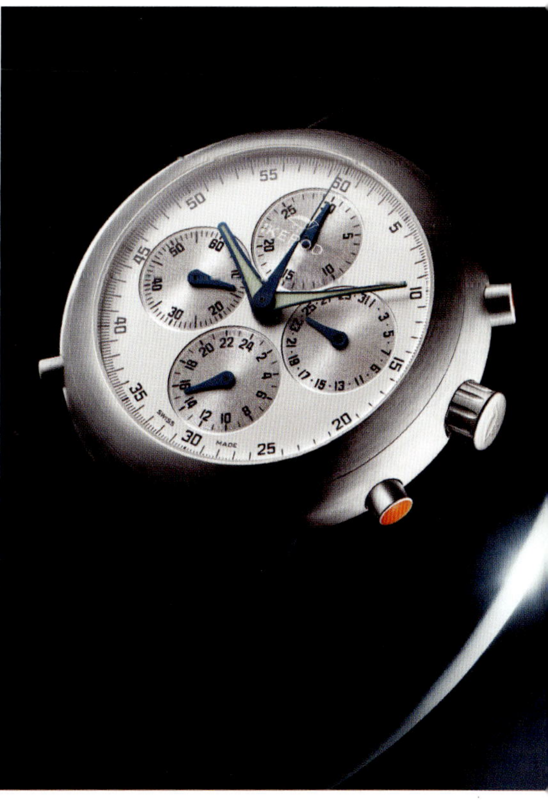

Marcello Nizzoli

Italian, 1887–1969

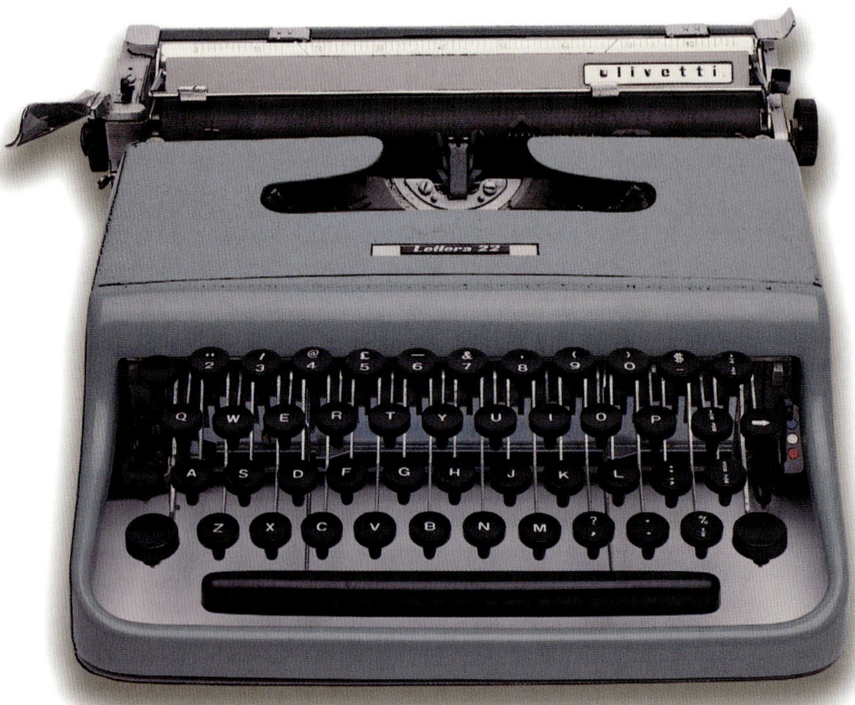

ABOVE:
Lettera 22 typewriter
for Olivetti, 1950

A prolific and multi-talented designer, Marcello Nizzoli played a key role in the development of Modern industrial design in Italy. Having studied at the Accademia di Belle Arti in Parma, he participated in the first *Nuove Tendenze* (New Trends) exhibition held in Milan in 1914, showing two paintings and four embroideries alongside the work of other artists aligned to Futurism. He subsequently produced a series of tapestries and established his own design studio in Milan in 1918.

During the 1920s, Nizzoli was associated with the Rationalists and exhibited at the *Biennale Esposizione delle Arti Decorative* held in Monza in 1923. Following this event he received a variety of commissions, including posters advertising Campari liqueur and Fiat lubricants. From 1934 to 1936 he collaborated with the architect Edoardo Persico, with whom he co-designed a shop in Milan for the Parker Pen Company (1934) and a number of exhibition spaces including the critically acclaimed Sala delle Medaglie d'Oro (Hall of Gold Medals) at the *Italian Aeronautical Exhibition* held in Milan in 1934.

From 1931, he also worked as a freelance graphic designer for Olivetti, and seven years later was hired by the company to work in its in-house advertising department, where he managed to forge a distinctive corporate identity for the firm. He also began designing products for Olivetti in 1940, eventually becoming the firm's chief product designer. In this capacity, he created a number of innovative typewriters, including the Lexikon 80 (1948), with its distinctive sloping form that introduced a new sculptural sensibility into the design of office equipment, and the immensely popular portable Lettera 22 (1950), which was awarded a Compasso d'Oro in 1954. In addition, Nizzoli designed a number of adding machines for the company – notably the Elettrosumma 14 (1946) and the Divisumma 14 (1947). Frequently he was responsible for the design of the advertisements that promoted these and other Olivetti designs too, and as part of Olivetti's "total design" strategy was even tasked with designing workers' housing for the company, and eventually its headquarters building in Ivrea (1960–64) in collaboration with G.A. Bernasconi and A. Fiocchi.

Apart from his extensive work for Olivetti, Nizzoli created designs for the sewing machine manufacturer Necchi, including the Mirella of 1957, which had a unified housing made of white and black enamelled aluminium. Aesthetically light years ahead of any other sewing machine then being made, it won a Compasso d'Oro award and had an unequivocally contemporary look that reflected Nizzoli's genius for artful yet functional compositions as well as his refined eye for graphic detailing. Nizzoli's other commissions included the design of cigarette lighters for Ronson (1959) as well as a petrol pump and an illuminated petrol-station sign for Agip (1960). Nizzoli's promotion of rational yet visually pleasing sculptural forms that had a strong graphic identity came to define the Stile Industriale (Industrial Style) of Italian post-war design.

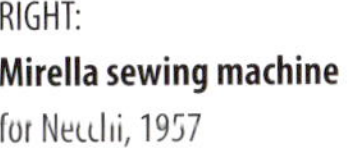

RIGHT:
Mirella sewing machine
for Necchi, 1957

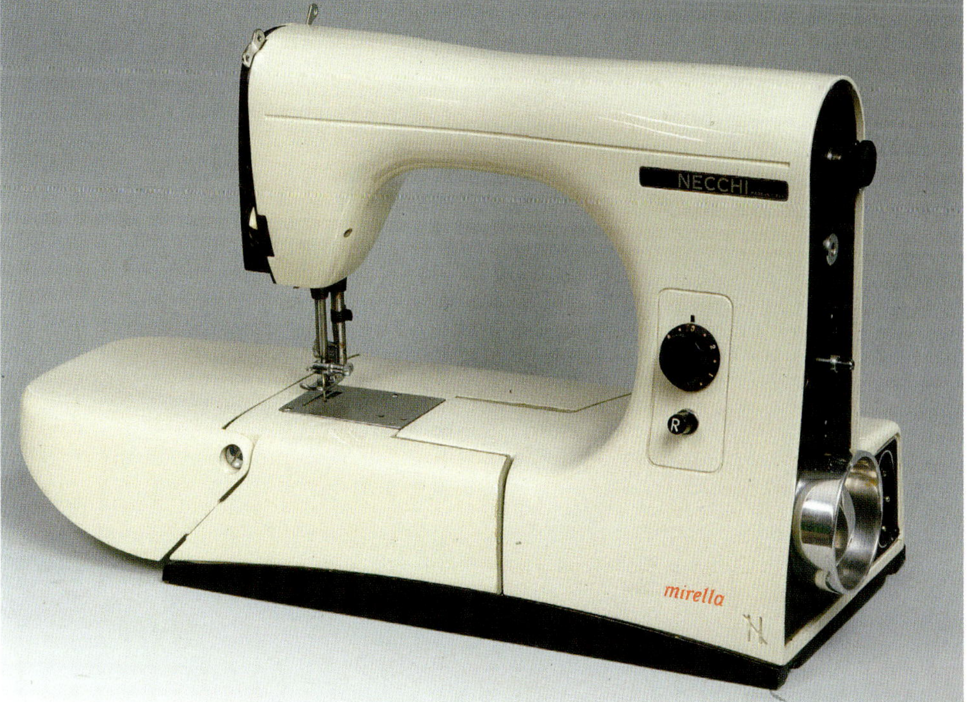

Isamu Noguchi

American, 1904–1988

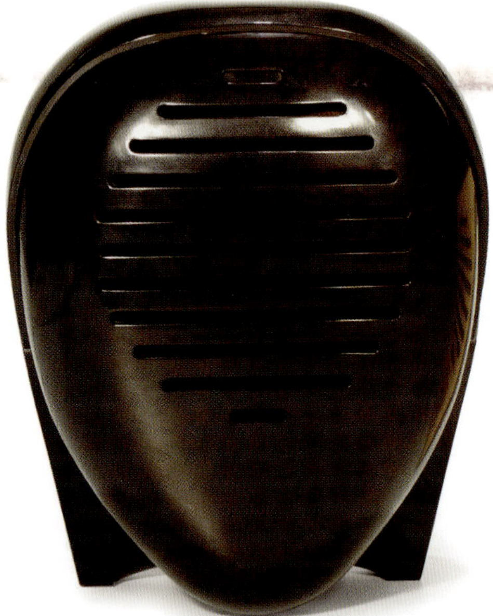

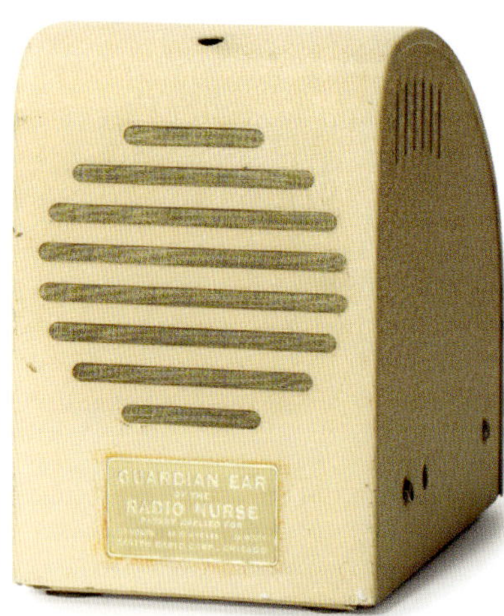

ABOVE:
Guardian Ear and Radio Nurse baby monitor
for Zenith Radio Corporation, 1937

Isamu Noguchi was an ingenious and gifted sculptor who was also critically acclaimed for his groundbreaking design work. By introducing a Japanese aestheticism to the contemporary domestic landscape, he created a gentler and more sculptural version of Modernism.

Noguchi was born in Los Angeles, but spent his early childhood in Japan. Returning to the United States at the age of fourteen to attend high school in Indiana, he then studied medicine at Columbia University, but abandoned this training in 1924 in order to pursue his love of sculpture. He went on to study sculpture in New York and subsequently won a Guggenheim Fellowship in 1927. This enabled him to travel to Paris, where he worked as an assistant in Constantin Brancusi's studio from 1927 to 1929.

There followed a brief period back in Japan, during which Noguchi developed an interest in forms and philosophy of Zen gardens. Back in New York once more in 1932, he began work mainly as a sculptor, although he also designed twenty-one highly progressive stage sets for the legendary modern dancer and choreographer Martha Graham, as well as a number of innovative playgrounds that incorporated sculptural equipment.

Equally influenced by a sense of sculpture was his work in the industrial design field, with his Guardian Ear and Radio Nurse baby monitor (1937) for Zenith displaying a remarkably refined synthesis of form and function. Noguchi's biomorphic design for the monitor/transmitter took the shape of an abstracted head which, with its bar-like incisions, was reminiscent of the protective helmets used in the traditional Japanese martial art of kendo. The highly stylized form of the receiver, moulded in Bakelite, was also closely related to Noguchi's rather Surrealistic sculptures from this period.

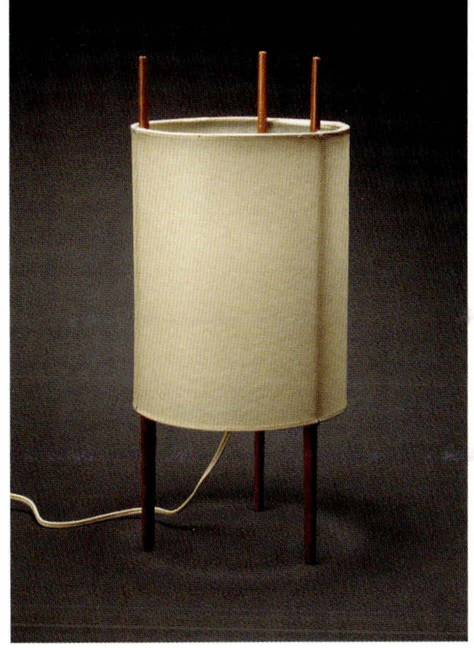

In 1939, the president of the Museum of Modern Art in New York, Anson Conger Goodyear, commissioned Noguchi to design a table for his weekend house. Recalling his interlocking sculptures, the resulting biomorphic design was a sculptural *tour-de-force* in laminated rosewood and glass that was remarkable for its asymmetrical organic form. This bold free-form design would become the blueprint for Noguchi's later walnut and glass IN-50 coffee table designed in 1944–45 for Herman Miller. Three years later the company launched another table designed by Noguchi, the IN-61 Chess Table, the form of which strongly reflected the influence of Alexander Calder's sculptures. These tables, like others designed by Noguchi, suggested sculptural landscapes; as he once noted, "You must be aware that every garden is a landscape, and every garden can be considered a table… especially Zen gardens."

LEFT:
Cylinder model no. 9 table lamp
for Knoll, 1947–48

BELOW:
IN-50 coffee table
for Herman Miller, 1944–45

During the 1940s Noguchi created a series of light sculptures known as Lunars and in 1950 moved to Japan, where he was asked by the city of Gifu to help revive its stricken paper-lantern industry as part of the country's post-war reconstruction. He designed his first Akari light in 1951, which, like the other models he was to design, had a mulberry-paper and bamboo shade supported on a thin metal-rod frame. With the range eventually comprising over one hundred variants, the sculptural Akari lights became an almost omnipresent feature in Mid-Century Modern interiors. As a masterful form-giver, Noguchi brought a unique artistic expression to design through his vision of art as an "overall concept".

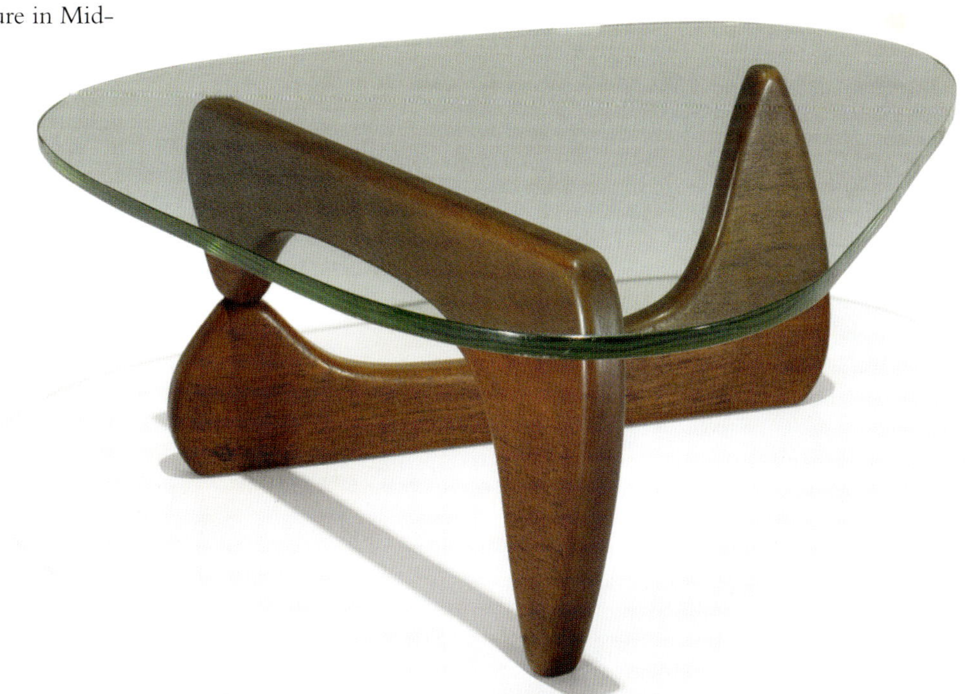

Eliot Noyes

American, 1910–1977

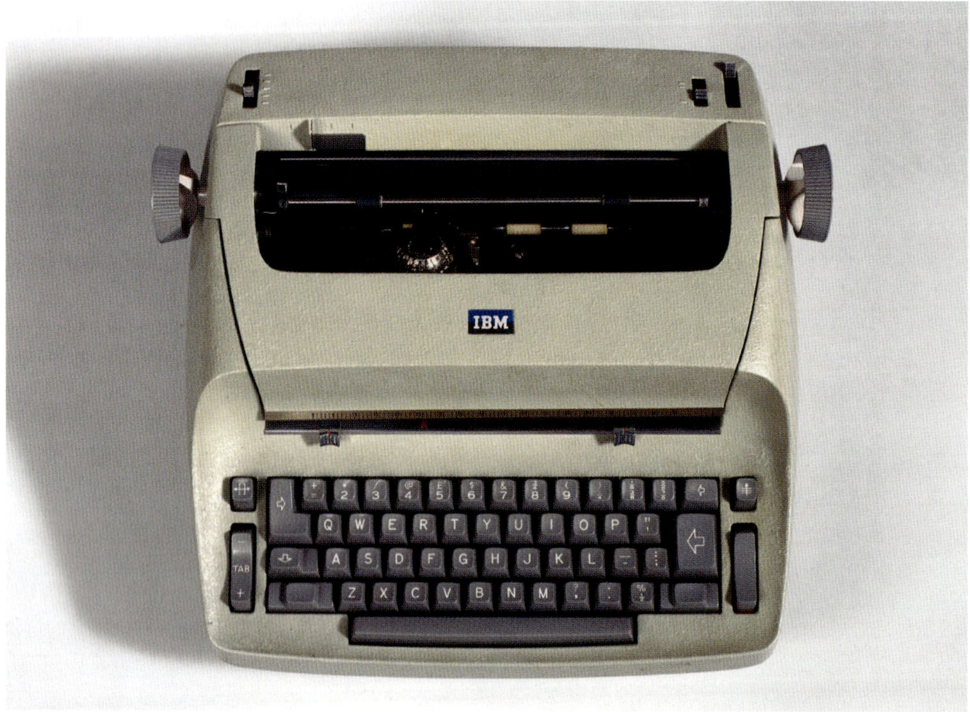

ABOVE:
Selectric I typewriter
for IBM, 1961

The American architect and industrial designer Eliot Fette Noyes was a tireless champion of Modern design, who was employed as a consultant by a host of blue-chip American corporations and worked as a curator at the Museum of Modern Art, where he helped disseminate the ideals of good design to a global audience. Noyes studied classics at Harvard before moving to the architecture school, where he was a student of Walter Gropius. On graduating, he joined the successful Boston-based architectural firm of Coolidge, Shepley, Bulfinch & Abbot in 1938, and the following year began working at Gropius and Marcel Breuer's architecture practice in Cambridge, Massachusetts. Gropius subsequently recommended Noyes for the newly created position of director of industrial design at the Museum of Modern Art, New York – a position he held from 1940 to 1942, and then from 1945 to 1946. During this tenure, he curated the landmark *Organic Design in Home Furnishings* competition and related exhibition held in 1940, the goal of which was to inspire designers to create avant-garde Modern furniture that could be afforded by the middle classes.

After leaving MoMA, Noyes was design director of Norman Bel Geddes's industrial design practice for a year, before opening his own design office in New Canaan, Connecticut, in 1947. While working at Bel Geddes's consultancy, one of Noyes's clients had been IBM, and as a result in 1956 he was appointed the company's design director. In this capacity Noyes pioneered a "total design" programme, which included not only the products the company manufactured but also its buildings, logos and marketing materials. With this all-encompassing remit Noyes's goal was, as IBM notes, "much more than consistency of look and feel. It marked perhaps the first time in which a business organization itself – its management, operations and culture, as well as its products and marketing – was conceived of as an intentionally created product of the imagination, as a work of art." Describing his own role as a "curator of corporate character", Noyes was also responsible for the design of several revolutionary products, most notably the Selectric I typewriter (1961). With its innovative rotating "golfball" typing head and static carriage, the Selectric I went on to become one of the best-selling office electric typewriters of all time. Vigorously opposed to the idea of annual marketing-driven styling changes, which had been pioneered by Harley Earl at General Motors and had now become a widespread practice within corporate America, Noyes instead doggedly established a strong and strategic corporate identity for IBM through the design integrity of the products it manufactured as well as through its commissioning of innovative graphics from Paul Rand and building designs from leading architects, most notably Marcel Breuer.

Apart from his work for IBM, Noyes also served as a consultant to many other companies, including Pan Am, Westinghouse, Xerox and Mobil, for whom he designed an innovative petrol pump in 1968. With his commitment to "total design", Noyes not only reshaped entire corporations through the power of design, but also established new standards for design practice in America.

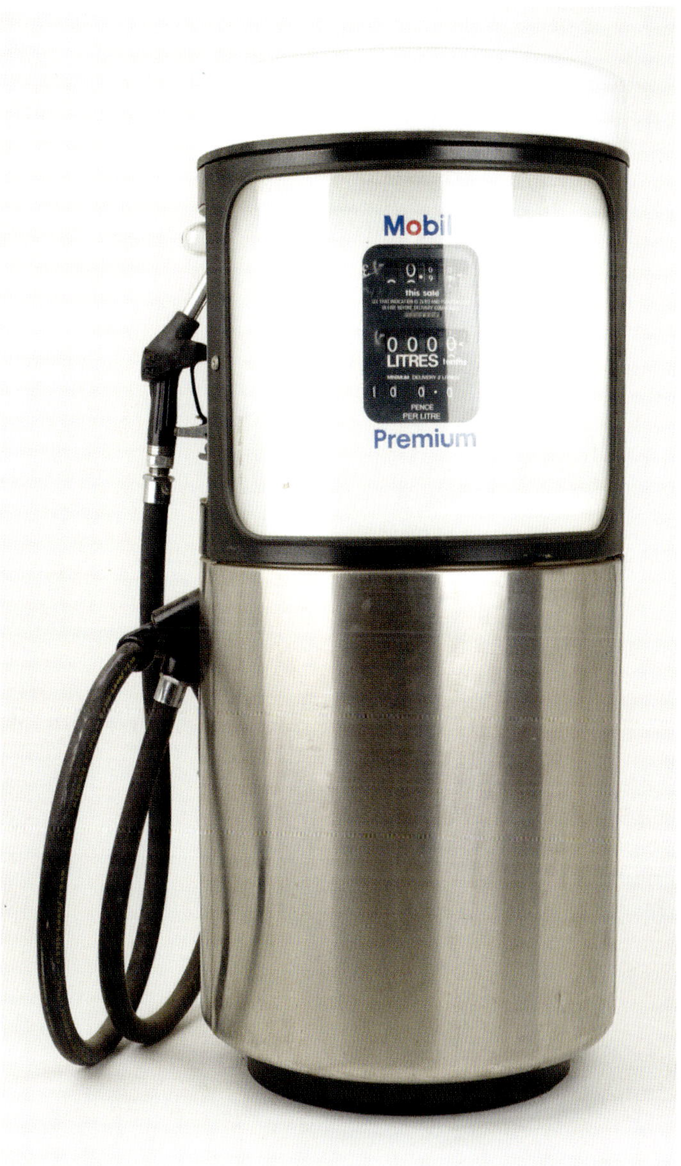

ABOVE:
Petrol pump
for Mobil, 1968

Verner Panton

Danish/active Switzerland, 1926–1998

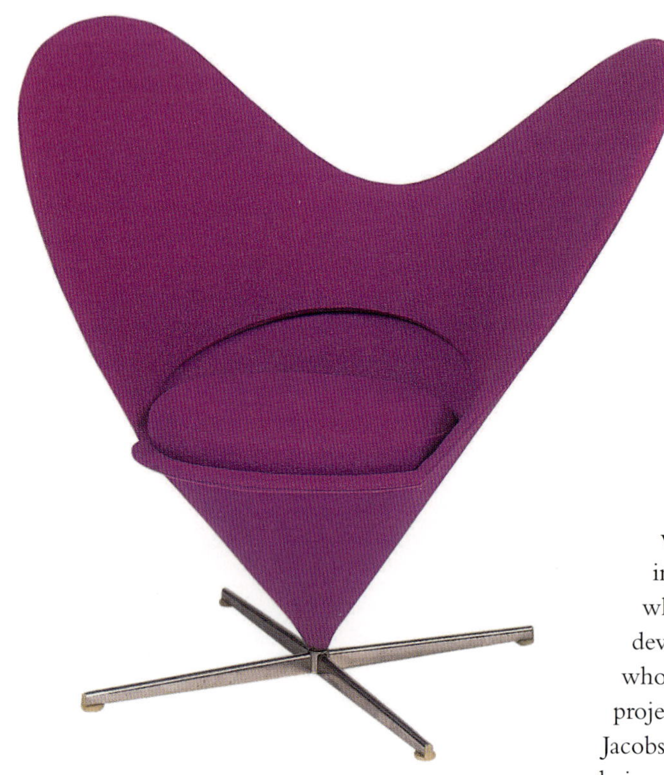

ABOVE:
Heart chair for Plus-Linje
1959

Verner Panton was a visionary designer who popularized a space-age Pop aesthetic during the 1960s and early 1970s. His iconoclastic furniture, lighting, ceramics and fully integrated interior installations had a very distinctive signature style – functionally innovative and futuristic designs with bold sculptural forms in eye-catching colours that often broke existing conventions through their use of new materials and cutting-edge manufacturing processes.

While training as an architect at the Kongelige Danske Kunstakademi (Royal Danish Academy of Arts) in Copenhagen, Panton studied under the lighting designer Poul Henningsen, whose use of mathematical proportions in design influenced him hugely. Another architect-designer who had a strong formative influence on Panton's development as a designer was Arne Jacobsen, for whom he worked between 1950 and 1952 on various projects including the famous Ant chair. After leaving Jacobsen's office, Panton began working as a freelance designer and bought a Volkswagen camper van which he turned into a mobile design studio. With this customized vehicle he travelled around Europe every few months in order to visit fellow designers and make speculative calls on manufacturers and distributors whom he hoped would license his designs or commission him to design new ones.

His first break as a designer came in 1955 when Fritz Hansen put his Bachelor chair and Tivoli chair into production. It was, however, his Cone chair, originally designed for his parents' Komigen inn on the island of Funen, that really got him noticed. It was so admired by Percy von Halling-Koch, the founder of Plus-Linje, at the hotel's opening that he put it into production. The design was subsequently featured in *Mobilia* magazine with naked shop mannequins and models draped over the chairs, which caused quite a stir. In New York, the police ordered a similar display to be removed from a store window because it attracted such a large crowd of people – which only added to Panton's notoriety.

As a visionary designer who revelled in experimentation, Panton went on to develop his first inflatable furniture pieces made of PVC in 1960. The same year, he created a "total environment" for the Astoria Hotel in Trondheim, Norway, which included the lobby, cloakroom and three restaurants, all of which had floors, walls and ceilings covered in a specially

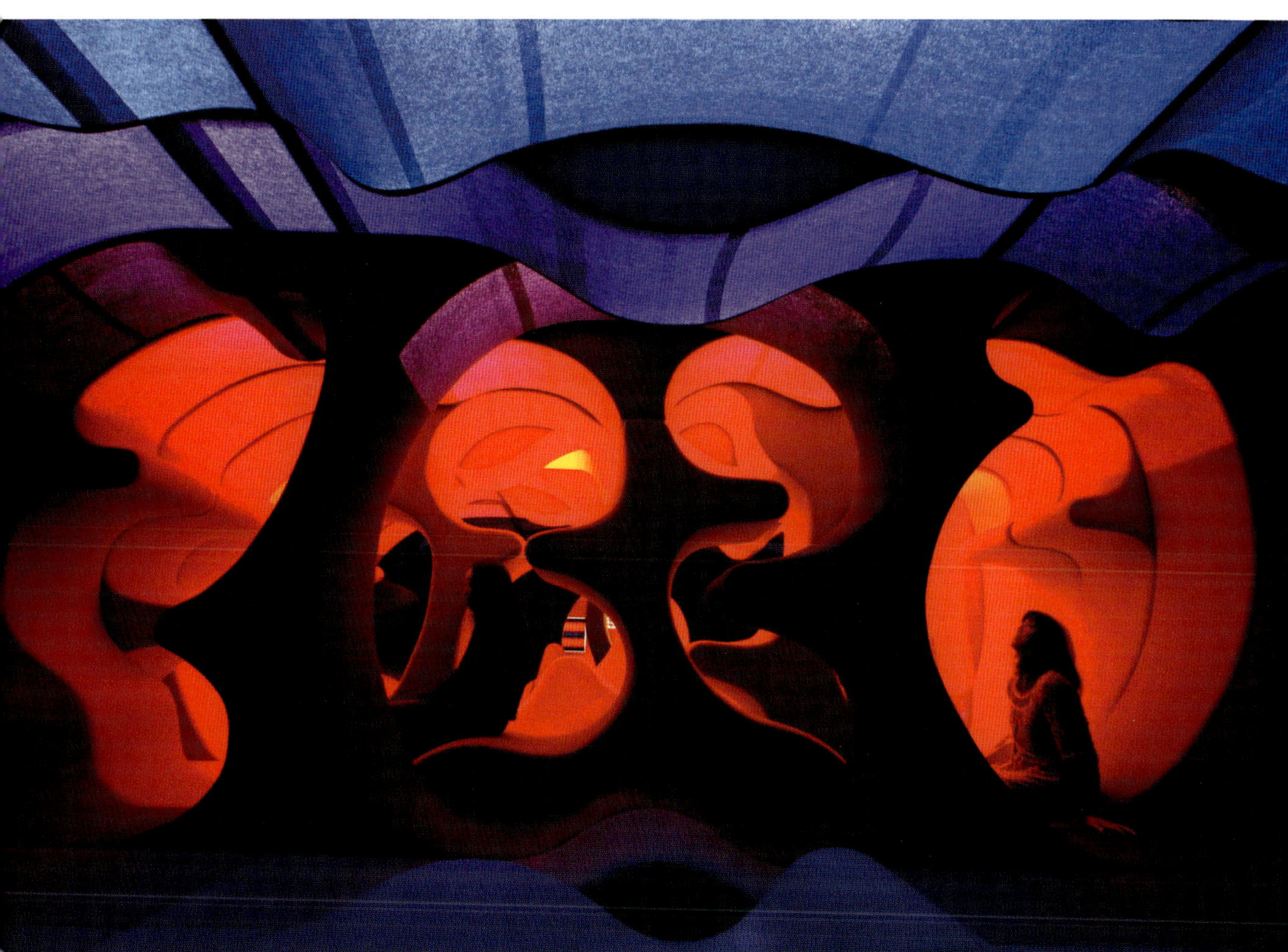

ABOVE:
Visiona II installation
at Cologne Furniture Fair, 1970

designed Op-Art-inspired range of textiles – Geometry I to IV – which gave a sense of visual unity. These colour-saturated interiors were also furnished with various versions of his Cone chair, including the Heart chair and Wire Cone chair, as well as his distinctive Topan lights.

A decade later, he created the landmark Visiona II installation for the German chemical company Bayer on board a Rhine pleasure cruiser for the 1970 Cologne Furniture Fair. This "Phantasy Landscape" was a hallucinogenic riot of bold colours and unconventional forms; its series of cave-like rooms furnished with inviting latex-foam upholstered furniture and sculptural lighting re-imagined ways of living. Above all else, Panton wanted the installation to provide an unforgettable sensory stimulus, and to this end each room had its own sound, smell and colour.

The fluid forms found in this remarkable space-age installation were also echoed in Panton's design for a revolutionary plastic cantilevered chair. Originally launched in 1967, the landmark Panton chair was the first single-material, single-piece injection-moulded plastic chair and took years of development and commitment from the Swiss furniture manufacturer Vitra in order to overcome the plastic-moulding technological challenges it presented. Initially it was produced in rigid cold-pressed GPR (fibreglass-reinforced polyester), but it was later slightly modified to incorporate strengthening ribs that enabled it to be injection-moulded in ABS plastic. This change of polymer and moulding process heralded the advent

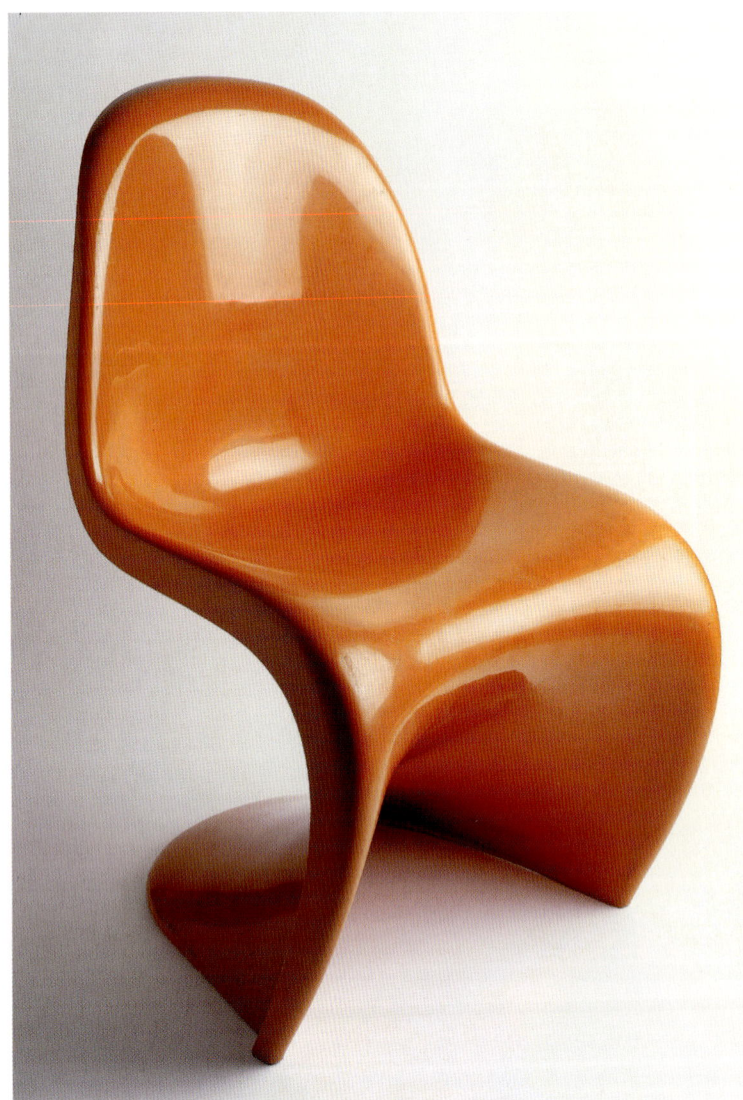

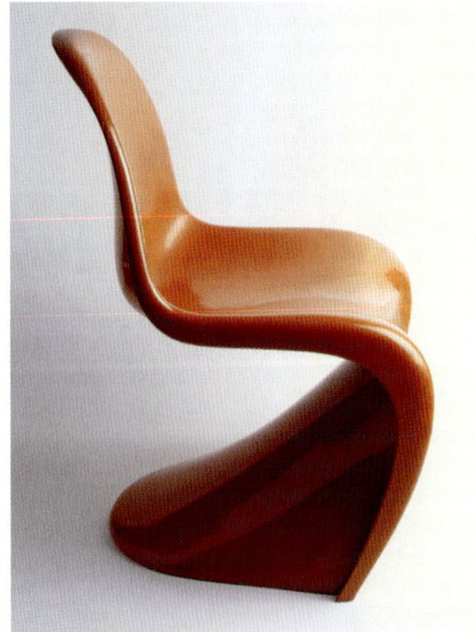

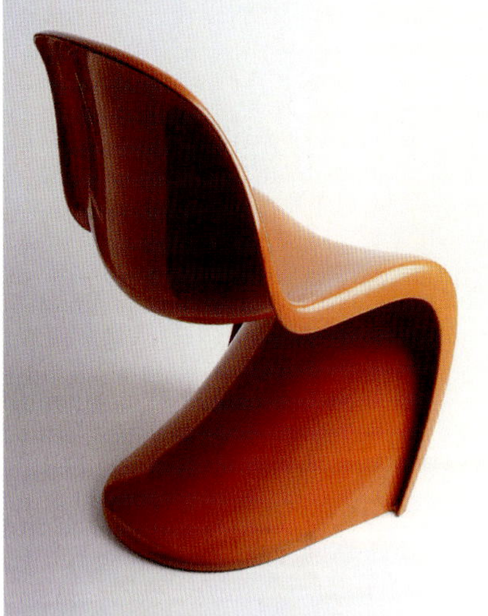

of the so-called monobloc plastic chair. During the 1970s Panton continued designing for various manufacturers as well as undertaking interior design commissions, and in 1980 was tasked with renovating the interior spaces of the circus building in Copenhagen, the results of which reflected the increasing influence of Post-Modernism with its foyer's cartoonized Ionic columns. During the rest of the 1980s Panton continued to create designs within the Post-Modern idiom, such as the Vilbert chair for IKEA (1993–94), yet they did not have the visual bravado of his earlier designs. In the mid-1990s, however, with the reappraisal of mid-twentieth-century design, Panton's earlier work was essentially rediscovered by a new generation and in 1998 a major exhibition, *Verner Panton: Light and Colour*, was designed by Panton and held at the Trapholt Museum in Kolding, Denmark.

ABOVE:
Panton chair
for Vitra, 1965–68

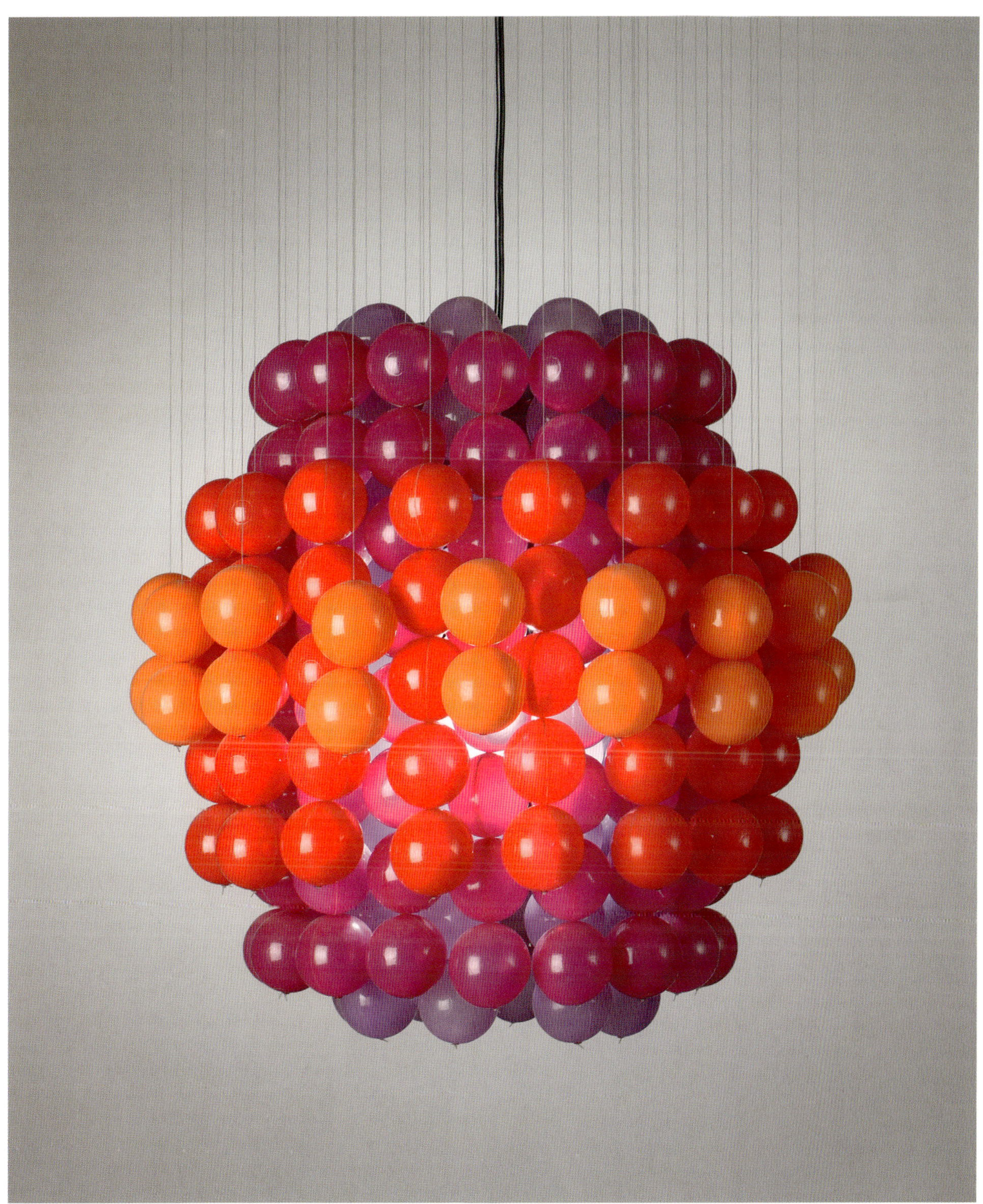

ABOVE:
Wonderlamp hanging light
for J. Lüber, 1964–70

Victor Papanek

Austrian/American, 1923–1998

The Austrian-born designer, educator and writer Victor Papanek published the enormously influential book *Design for the Real World: Making to Measure* in 1971. While it included the much-quoted, somewhat overheated claim, "There are professions more harmful than industrial design, but only a few of them," Papanek's belief in "the role of designers as crucial mediators of humanitarian ideals" encouraged a worldwide movement to adopt his idea of socially responsible design.

Following the annexation of Austria by Germany in 1938, Papenek moved to Britain, where he briefly attended public school, subsequently emigrating to the United States. There he worked temporarily for Frank Lloyd Wright, took an undergraduate degree at the Cooper Union in New York City, graduating in 1950, and then went on to study design at MIT (Massachusetts Institute of Technology), receiving an MA in 1955. During this period he came under the influence of Richard Buckminster Fuller, who would later write the preface for *Design for the Real World*, a book that was based on the premise that designers ought not to be designing for marketing departments in order to seduce consumers to buy products that they did not really need, but rather respond to the design needs of the masses, and most especially those of the poor, sick or elderly.

Teaching at various design schools and colleges, Papanek encouraged his students to create "real solutions" for "real needs", such as a cheap tin-can wireless radio for use in developing countries (costing 4 pence), a prototype of an affordable educational television set (costing £3.50) and a modular cooling unit to enable the better preservation of food. He went on to publish a number of other books, including *Nomadic Furniture* (1974 – co-authored with James Hennessey), *Design for Human Scale* (1983) and *The Green Imperative* (1995).

Papanek saw himself as a design crusader and applied the principles of social responsibility to a variety of projects, many undertaken in collaboration with UNESCO and the World Health Organization. Unlike most designers, he looked beyond the needs of the developed world and instead tried to use design as a tool that could improve the quality of life in developing countries and for overlooked sectors of society in the United States and Europe. Papanek was also acutely aware of the environmental impact of design and manufacturing, noting, "Design, if it is to be ecologically responsible, must be revolutionary and radical (going back to the roots) in the truest sense. It must dedicate itself to nature's 'principle of least effort', or in other words … doing the most with the least. That means consuming less, using things longer, recycling materials.… In many areas designers must learn how to de-design."

BELOW:
Victor Papanek, head of the Department of Product Design at North Carolina State College's School of Design, photo *c.*1960–69

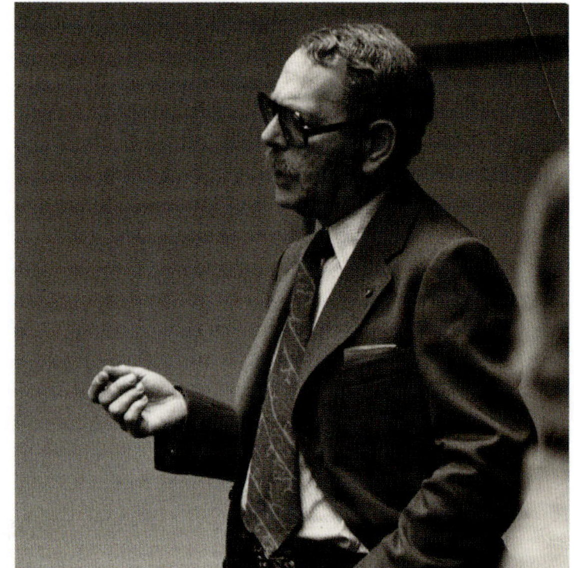

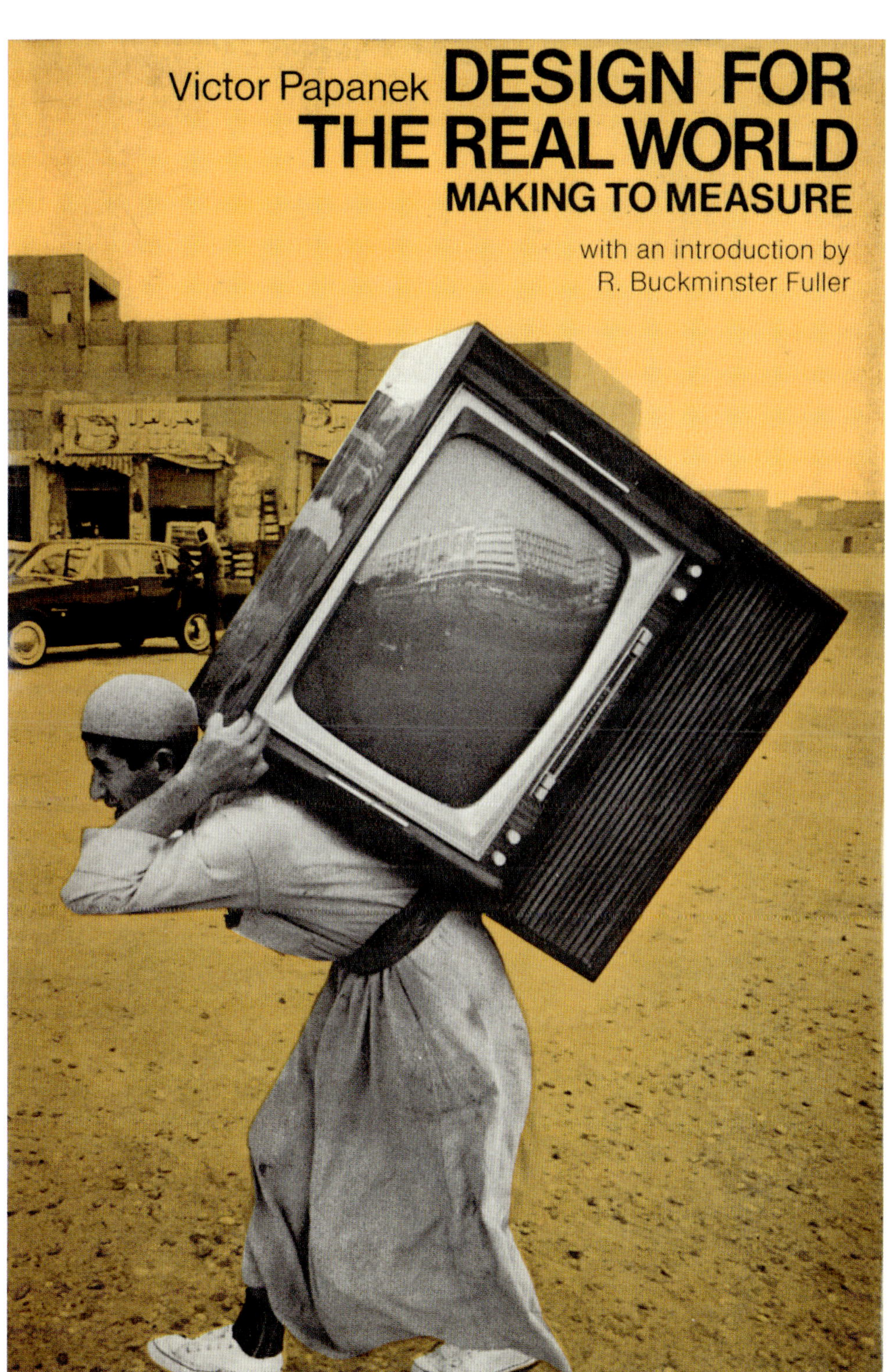

LEFT:
Cover of Victor Papanek's *Design for the Real World: Making to Measure*, first published 1971 (Swedish edition), 1972 (English edition)

Pentagram

British, founded 1972

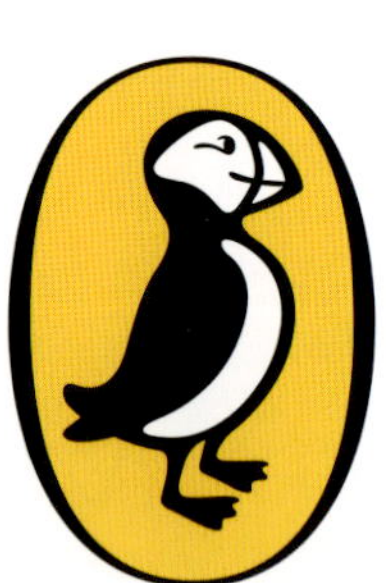

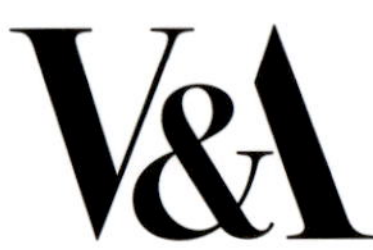

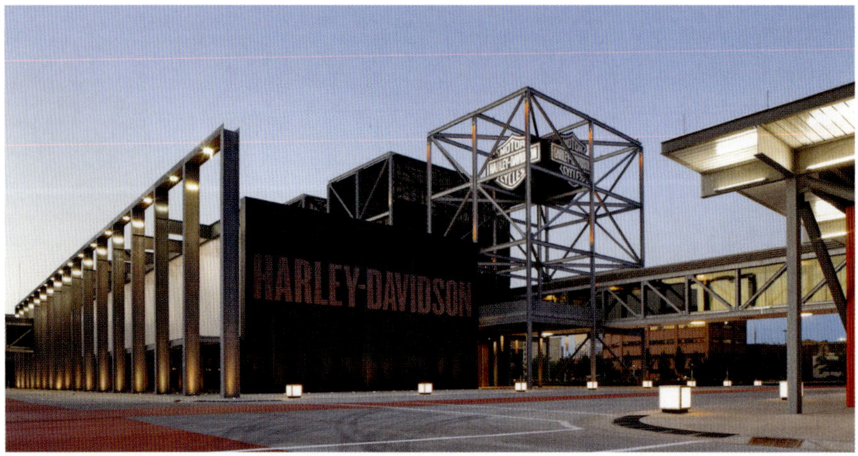

ABOVE:
Graphic identities for:
Penguin Group (Penguin Books and Puffin Books), 2003; V&A (Victoria & Albert Museum), 1989–90

Today, Pentagram is one of the most respected multidisciplinary design agencies in the world, with offices in London, New York, Berlin, Austin and San Francisco. One of the reasons for its success is that it is, and has always been, a designer-led consultancy with each partner running their own specialist in-house teams within their own given area of expertise. As current Pentagram partner Angus Hyland explains, "This makes us like an atelier of small businesses, working more or less independent from each other in terms of projects, but sharing profit, portfolio and space. We regularly join up teams especially across disciplines when a project requires a collaborative focus." Indeed, it could be said that this is the agency's greatest strength: its whole is more than the sum of its parts.

The origins of Pentagram go back to a design studio founded in 1962 by Alan Fletcher and Colin Forbes, who had met while studying graphic design at Central School of Arts and Crafts in London, and the American graphic designer, Bob Gill. Known as Fletcher/Forbes/Gill, this agency boasted Penguin Books and Shell as clients, and in 1964 published an influential book entitled *Graphic Design: Visual Comparisons*, which expounded their belief that, rather than having a preconceived graphic style, a designer should let the content creatively guide their work.

In 1965 the consultancy became Crosby/Fletcher/Forbes, following the departure of Bob Gill and the joining of architect Theo Crosby. With the addition of Crosby, it broadened its scope, being able to offer clients a more multidisciplinary design service. The South African graphic designer Mervyn Kurlansky joined the studio in 1969, having previously worked as graphic director of Knoll's planning unit, and then in 1972 the renowned British industrial designer Kenneth Grange became the fifth member of the team. The same year the agency was renamed Pentagram – reflecting the fact that it now had five partners.

With Grange on board, the office could offer its clients a total design package; for instance, a corporate identity programme devised for Reuters included not only the creation of its corporate logo but also the design of its computer monitors. Under the auspices of Pentagram, Grange created various landmark consumer products, including his Parker 25 range of pens for Parker (1979) and his gleaming bright-red plastic Protector razor for Wilkinson Sword (1992), and on a larger scale he was also responsible for the body styling of British Rail's 125 Intercity high-speed train (1971–76).

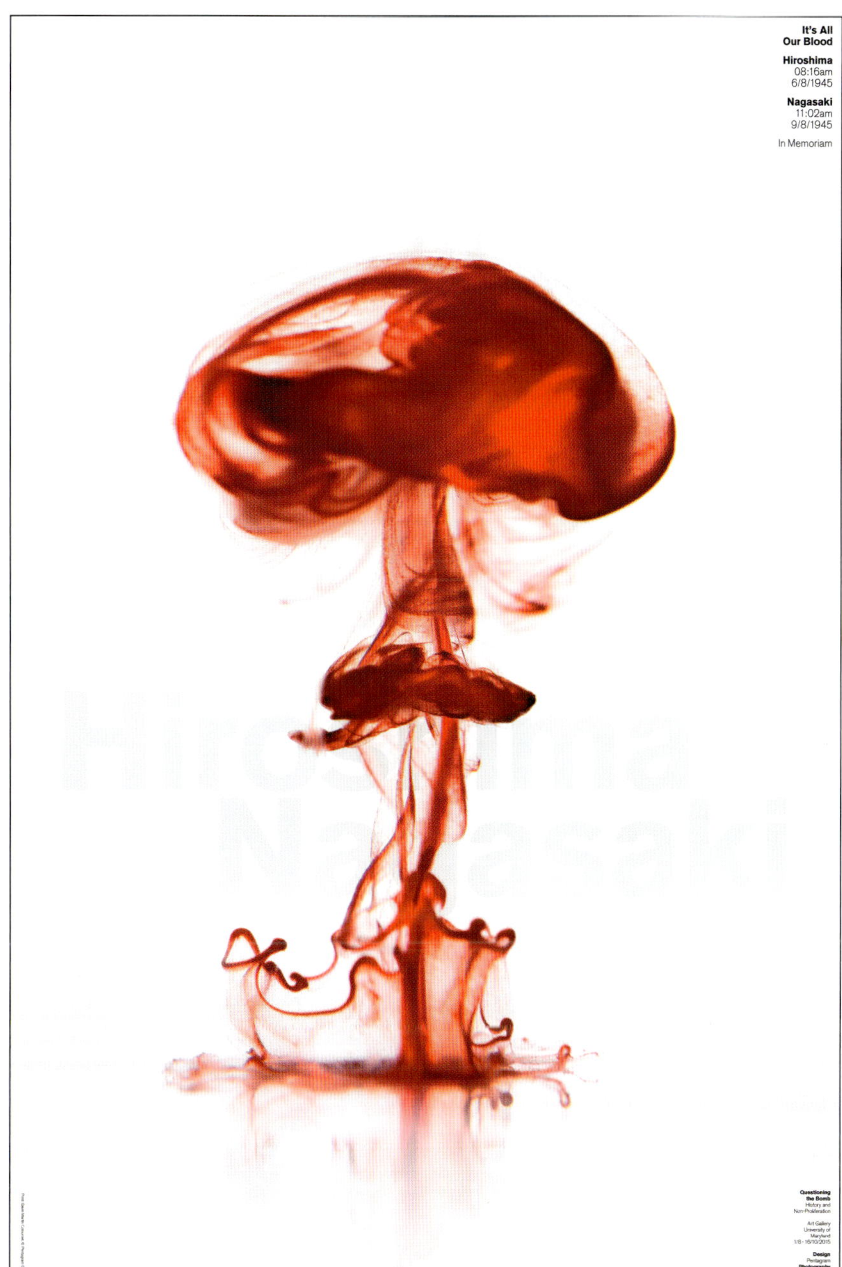

OPPOSITE:
Harley-Davidson Museum in Milwaukee, Wisconsin, completed 2008 – designed by James Biber and team, in association with Michael Zweck-Bonner, both Pentagram partners

RIGHT:
It's All Our Blood poster for *Question of Bombing* exhibition for University of Maryland Art Gallery, 2015 – designed by Harry Pearce

Today, the "federally" structured agency continues to work creatively across an impressively broad range of disciplines that spans advertising, architecture and interior design, book and magazine design, branding and identity work, data visualization, logo creation, packaging, video presentations, and website and interactive design, while also helping clients implement overall design strategies. Pentagram's impressive portfolio spanning five decades of passionate commitment to good design is without equal, not only in terms of its sheer breadth of work, but also in terms of its professional consistency – all of which is a reflection of its partners' creative intelligence and their personal dedication to design innovation and excellence.

Charlotte Perriand

French, 1903–1999

Renowned for her avant-garde furniture designs that were often startlingly progressive for their day, Charlotte Perriand introduced a Modern "machine age" aesthetic while working in Le Corbusier's architecture studio during the late 1920s and 1930s. She initially trained as a furniture designer at the school of the Union Centrale des Arts Décoratifs (UCAD) in Paris, but she rejected the school's craft-based approach and instead sought inspiration in the new machine aesthetic evinced in the motorcars and bicycles she saw in the streets of Paris.

In 1926, following the completion of her studies, Perriand undertook her first interior design project, the transformation of her and her husband's rented attic apartment into a stridently Modernist statement. Around this time, she strode into Le Corbusier's studio to see if he would hire her as a furniture designer, but was rebuffed with his famous putdown, "We don't embroider cushions here," and was promptly shown the door. A few months later, however, Le Corbusier saw Perriand's Bar sous le Toît – a rooftop bar in glass, steel and aluminium – at the *Salon d'Automne* exhibition in Paris, realized his error and, after apologizing, invited her to join his studio. Prior to this, Le Corbusier had furnished his exhibition installations and buildings with pre-existing furniture, such as Thonet's Model No. 9 armchair and a club chair. He had, however, already outlined in his 1925 book *L'Art Décoratif d'Aujourdhui* (The Decorative Art of Today) his perceived requirements of furniture and identified three distinct types: *besoins-types* (needs-type), *meubles-types* (furniture-type) and *objets-membres humains* (human-limb objects).

Distilling those ideas, over the next few years Perriand in collaboration with Le Corbusier and Pierre Jeanneret developed various landmark seating designs that utilized tubular steel in their constructions – most notably, the B301 sling-chair (1928) designed "for conversation", the B302 swivelling chair (1928–29), the B306 chaise longue (1928) intended to function as

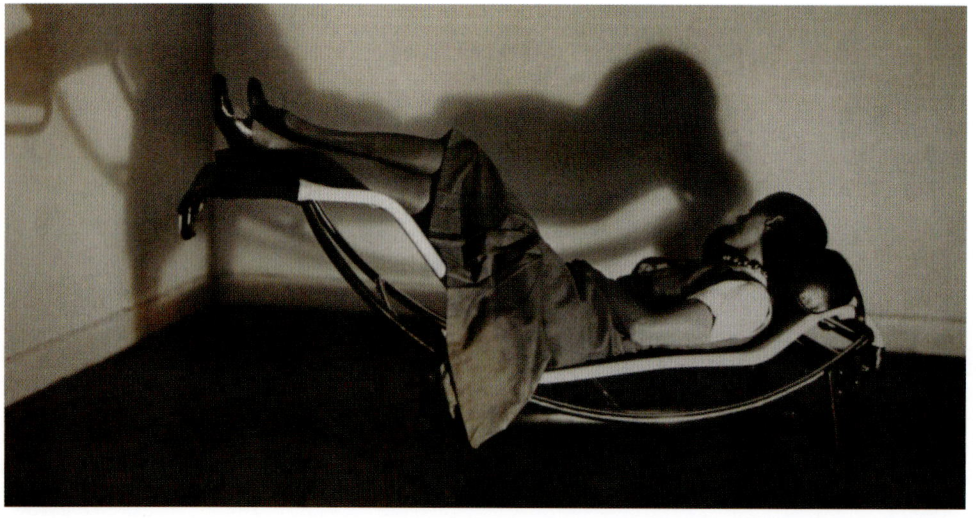

LEFT:
Photograph of Charlotte Perriand
posing on the B306 chaise longue, wearing a necklace made of ball bearings, 1928

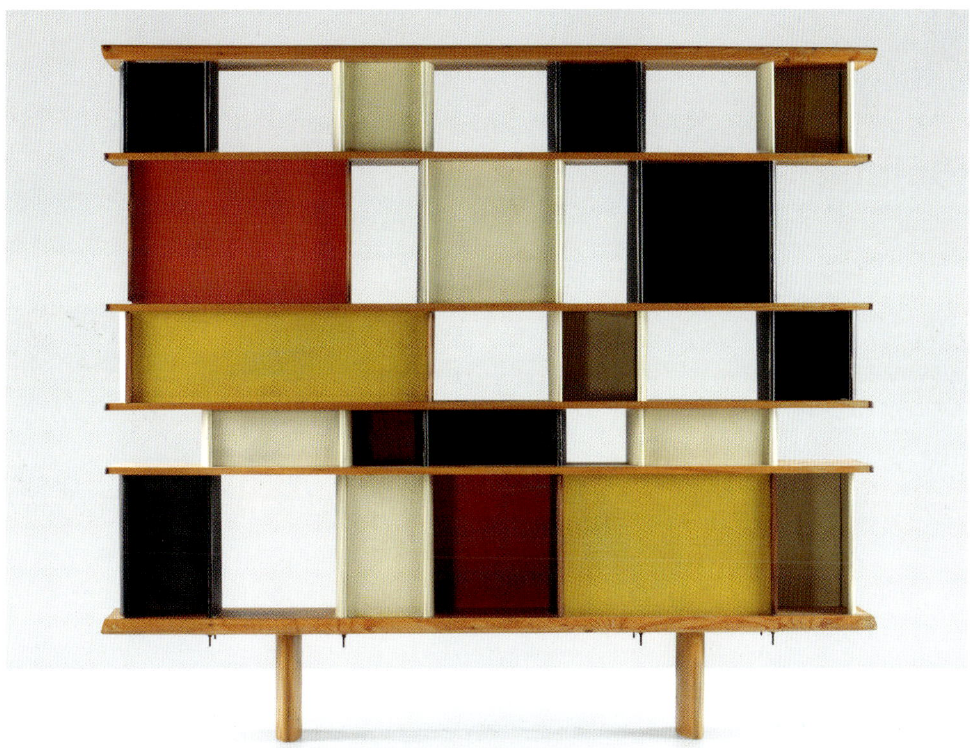

ABOVE:
Bibliothèque shelving unit from the Maison du Mexique for Ateliers Jean Prouvé and André Chetaille, 1952

a daybed and the LC1 Grand Confort armchair and matching LC3 sofa (1928) designed "for relaxation". Perriand controversially posed for a photograph on the chaise longue wearing a calf-length skirt that exposed her shapely legs. In 1929, the trio exhibited these revolutionary designs in their L'équipement d'une Habitation (Equipment for the Home) model apartment installation at the 1929 *Salon d'Automne*. This installation, with its lit-glass floor, dividing screens and a glass-topped table incorporating biplane wing-stays, was a deluxe vision of modish modernity. At a stroke Perriand, along with Le Corbusier and Jenneret, had made Modernism fashionable and as such helped to promote its wider acceptance.

Perriand continued to work with Le Corbusier until 1937, when she left his studio in order to briefly collaborate with the artist Fernand Léger. When the Second War World broke out, however, she collaborated with Pierre Jeanneret and Jean Prouvé on the creation of prefabricated buildings made of pressed aluminium. At the instigation of the Japanese architect Junzo Sakakura, she was invited to Japan in 1940 to become an official advisor on industrial design to the Trade and Promotion department of the Imperial Ministry of Commerce and Industry with a view to raising design standards and increasing Japanese exports to the West. During this first trip to Japan (1940–42), she travelled throughout the country with the designer Sori Yanagi, whose father had founded the Mingei (Folk Craft) movement that advocated active support of traditional craft skills. When Japan entered the Second World War, Perriand was forced to leave the country, but because of a naval blockade became effectively trapped in Vietnam from 1942 to 1946. During this enforced exile, she took the opportunity to study local craft techniques, which had a major influence on her subsequent design work. After the war, Perriand resumed her design career and continued to be guided by the ideals of Modernism; as she would note towards the end of her life, "The Modern Movement is a spirit of enquiry, it's a process of analysis and not a style."

P

Pininfarina

Italian, founded 1930

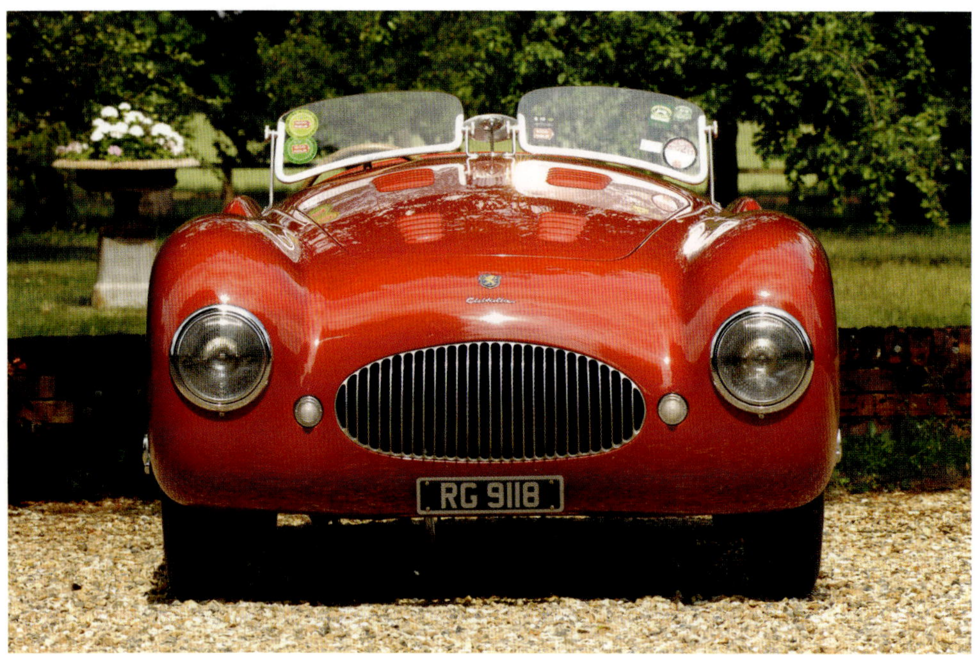

ABOVE:
Cisitalia 202
1947

Pininfarina is known throughout the world for having been at the forefront of automotive design for decades. Founded in 1930 by Battista "Pinin" Farina, the Carozzeria Pinin Farina, as it was then known, was a coach-building company based in Turin that initially created bespoke car bodies for individual customers or as small production runs for various Italian marques. One of the company's earliest triumphs was the sublimely beautiful Cisitalia 202 (1947), which became the first car to be permanently exhibited at the Museum of Modern Art, New York, and was described by the museum's design curator Arthur Drexler as "a sculpture in motion".

It was, however, Farina's sleek yet curvaceous Ferrari 375 MM Spider of 1953, one of the earliest examples of a pontoon-fender sports racer, which arguably paved the way for many of the most iconic Ferrari models. Another of Farina's designs that turned heads during the 1950s was the Lancia Aurelia B24 (1954), which, with its wrap-around windscreen and lack of side windows, became the star of Dino Risi's Italian cult film *Il Sorpasso* (The Easy Life) starring Italian heartthrob Vittorio Gassman. Five years later, Farina designed the even more outstanding Ferrari 250GT Coupé (1958), which was the first significant volume-produced road model manufactured by Ferrari.

In 1961, Pinin Farina handed over the day-to-day running of the family firm to his son, Sergio, and his son-in-law, Renzo Carli. That same year the Farina surname was officially changed to Pininfarina thanks to an Italian presidential decree. After Pinin's death in 1966, his successors continued to nurture his legacy for design innovation and opened an 8,000sq-m (86,000sq-ft) study and research centre in Grugliasco so that the firm could help clients with the design of a car's every aspect, rather that just its styling.

In the same year, 1966, the company began the related construction of a full-sized wind tunnel which, when finally completed in 1972, was the first facility of its kind in Italy, and one of the earliest anywhere in the world. In 1967, they also set up a centre of calculation and design, equipped with advanced precision-measuring machines developed by the Turin-based company DEA (Digital Electronic Automation) – an extremely early example of digital technology being used in the design process.

During the 1970s and 1980s, Pininfarina continued to design production and concept cars for Ferrari, including the widely acclaimed, mid-engined Ferrari 512 BB (1973). The 1980s also saw the company diversify into other areas of transportation design, notably taking responsibility for the aerodynamic research and styling of Italy's first high-speed train, the ETR 500 (1988). The 2000s saw Pininfarina building on its reputation for creating sublimely beautiful cars, with the introduction of the Maserati GranTurismo (2007) and the exceptional Ferrari 458 Italia (2009), while more recently the firm has been involved in the design of the external livery and interior for the new e320 train (2015) for Eurostar. For over eighty-five years, Pininfarina has been at the apotheosis of Italian design and engineering excellence and, as such, has helped define the extraordinary elegance of the famed Italian Line.

BELOW:
Ferrari 375 MM Spider
1953

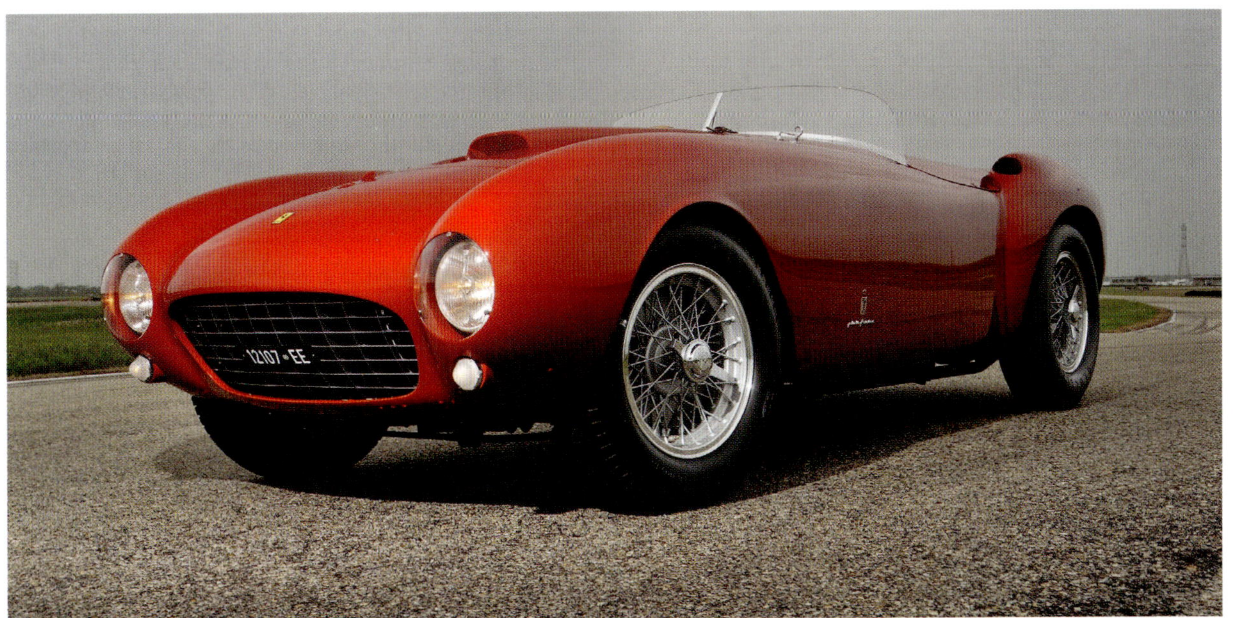

Gio Ponti

Italian, 1891–1979

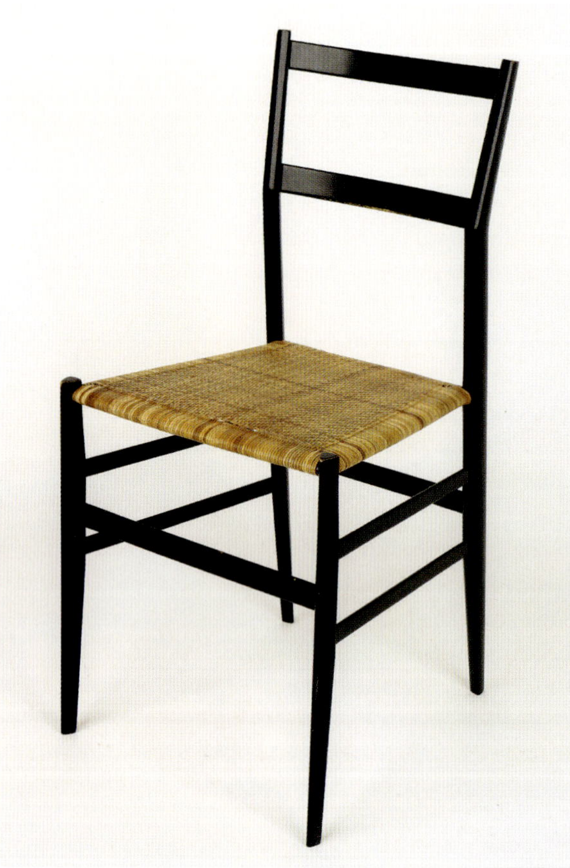

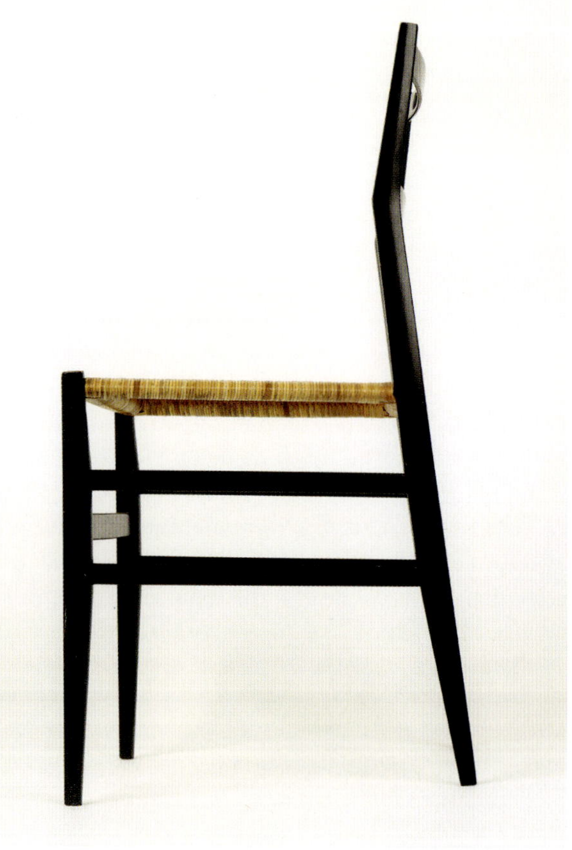

ABOVE:
Superleggera chair
for Cassina, 1957

The Milanese architect-designer Gio Ponti was one of the greatest champions of Modern Italian design, not only through his creation of innovative buildings, furniture, lighting, textiles and homewares but also through his longstanding editorship of *Domus* magazine. Having studied architecture at the Politecnico di Milano, Ponti became the art director of the ceramics manufacturer Richard Ginori in 1923. While there, he created simple ceramic forms that were decorated with Art Deco motifs, which epitomized the fashionable Novecento style – a style that reinterpreted Neo-Classicism within a Modern idiom.

In 1928, Ponti founded *Domus*, soon to be joined by the publisher Gianni Mazzocchi, as a means to publicize the work of designers similarly aligned to the Novecento style. Although initially produced as a lifestyle, architecture and decorating magazine, under Ponti's editorship it soon became the most authoritative voice on architecture and design in Italy. It was so strident in championing the cause of Italian design that it eventually became known as the "Mediterranean megaphone". The magazine also functioned as Ponti's "living diary" by

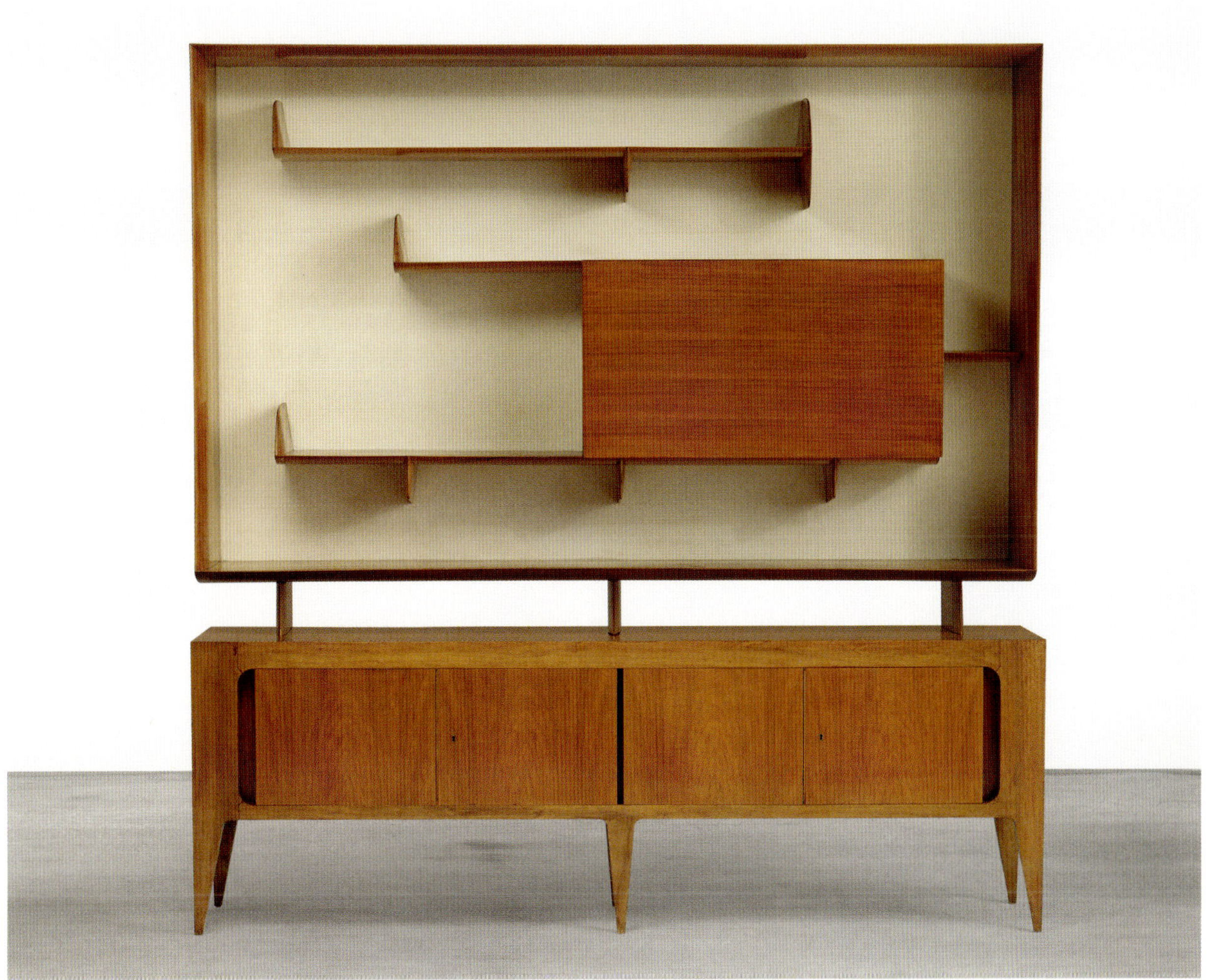

ABOVE:
Model 2140 display cabinet
for Singer & Sons, 1951

documenting his work and that of other designers he admired, at the same time serving as a forum in which to debate and raise awareness of the design issues that concerned him. In 1941, Ponti left *Domus* and founded another magazine, *Stile*, which was similarly an influential showcase for new design and architecture. Returning to *Domus* in 1947, he continued to promote his design agenda and the same year designed his well-known La Pavoni espresso coffee machine, which reflected the influence of American streamlining and symbolized a new post-war sculptural confidence in Italian design.

During the early 1950s, Ponti collaborated with the great Milanese maestro of Surrealistic decoration Piero Fornasetti, creating interiors for the San Remo Casino and exhibiting their Architettura range of furniture at the *IX Triennale* in Milan in 1951. As a way to publicize Italian design to the wider world and to thereby grow export markets, Ponti was instrumental in the establishment of the Compasso D'Oro awards in 1954. Above all else, he believed in quality over quantity and rejected the Rationalists' rallying cry for utilitarianism in preference of a more pragmatic approach to Modern design that was evolutionary rather than revolutionary and was often inspired by historical paradigms. A three-dimensional realization of this approach was his Superleggera chair designed for Cassina in 1957, which was a modern interpretation of a traditional fisherman's chair. Ponti praised such vernacular designs as being "without adjectives", meaning that they were not slaves to a particular style. He developed his own unique style, however, which was characterized by the use of diamond forms, seen not only in his designs for furniture, lighting and cutlery but also in the decorative motifs he employed in his interior design schemes – such as those for his cliff-hugging Parco dei Principi hotel in Sorrento.

While this project was the very architectural embodiment of the *dolce vita* era, Ponti's faceted Pirelli Tower (1950–56) in Milan was an even more progressive project, being among the first skyscrapers to have a non-blocklike form. Elegantly tapering skywards, the Pirelli Tower is rightly considered Ponti's architectural masterwork, with its structural skeleton of reinforced concrete supporting curtain-wall façades of glass. Constructed with the engineering assistance of Pier Luigi Nervi and Arturo Danusso, the structure's visual lightness was achieved with narrow gaps running up the two sides of the building and also between the top floor and the roof – making the roof look as though it was floating. A similar roofline separation gap was used to dramatic effect by Ponti for his exquisite Villa Planchart in Caracas (1955). Other notable buildings by Ponti include the Cathedral of Taranto (1970), with its perforated sail-like façade, and the Denver Art Museum (1971), a Brutalist fortress-like structure. The success of Ponti's designs rested not only on his desire for transcendent beauty in everyday things, but in his belief in solutions that intelligently address the needs of the user.

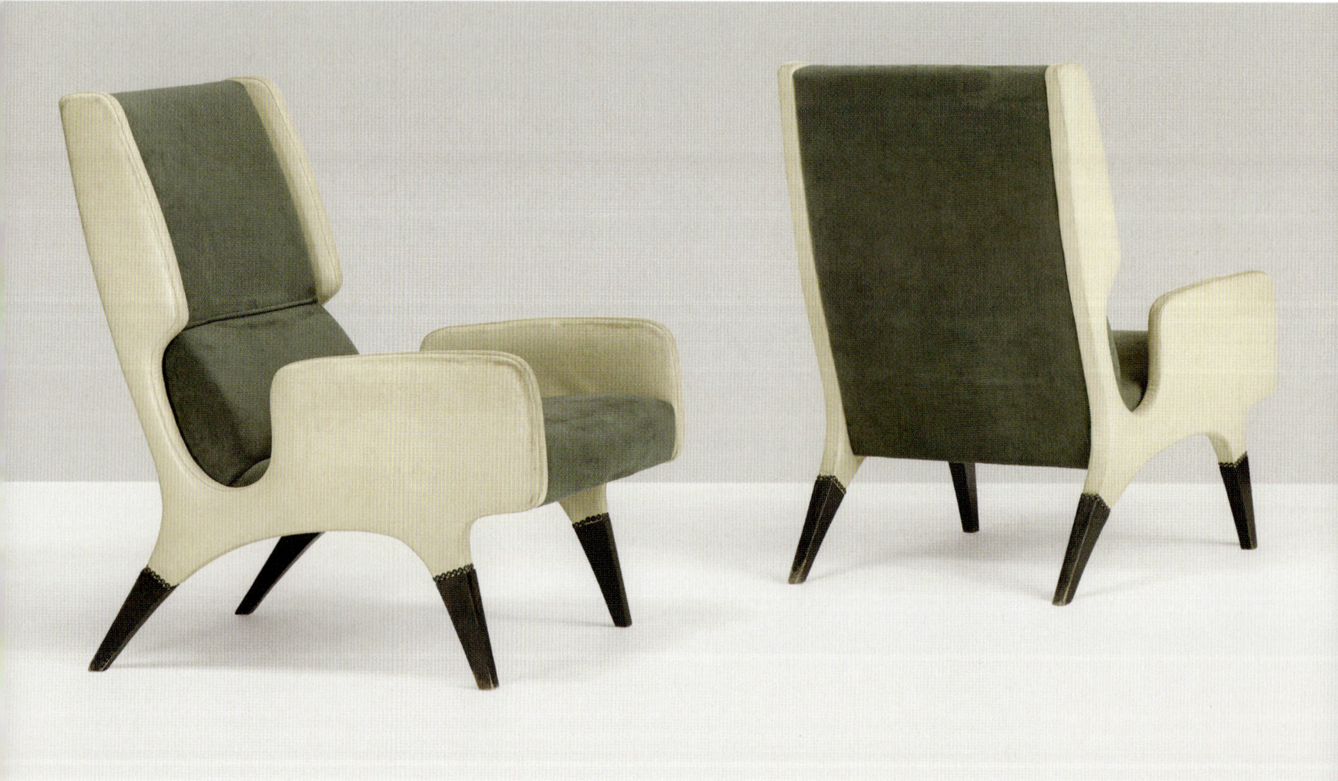

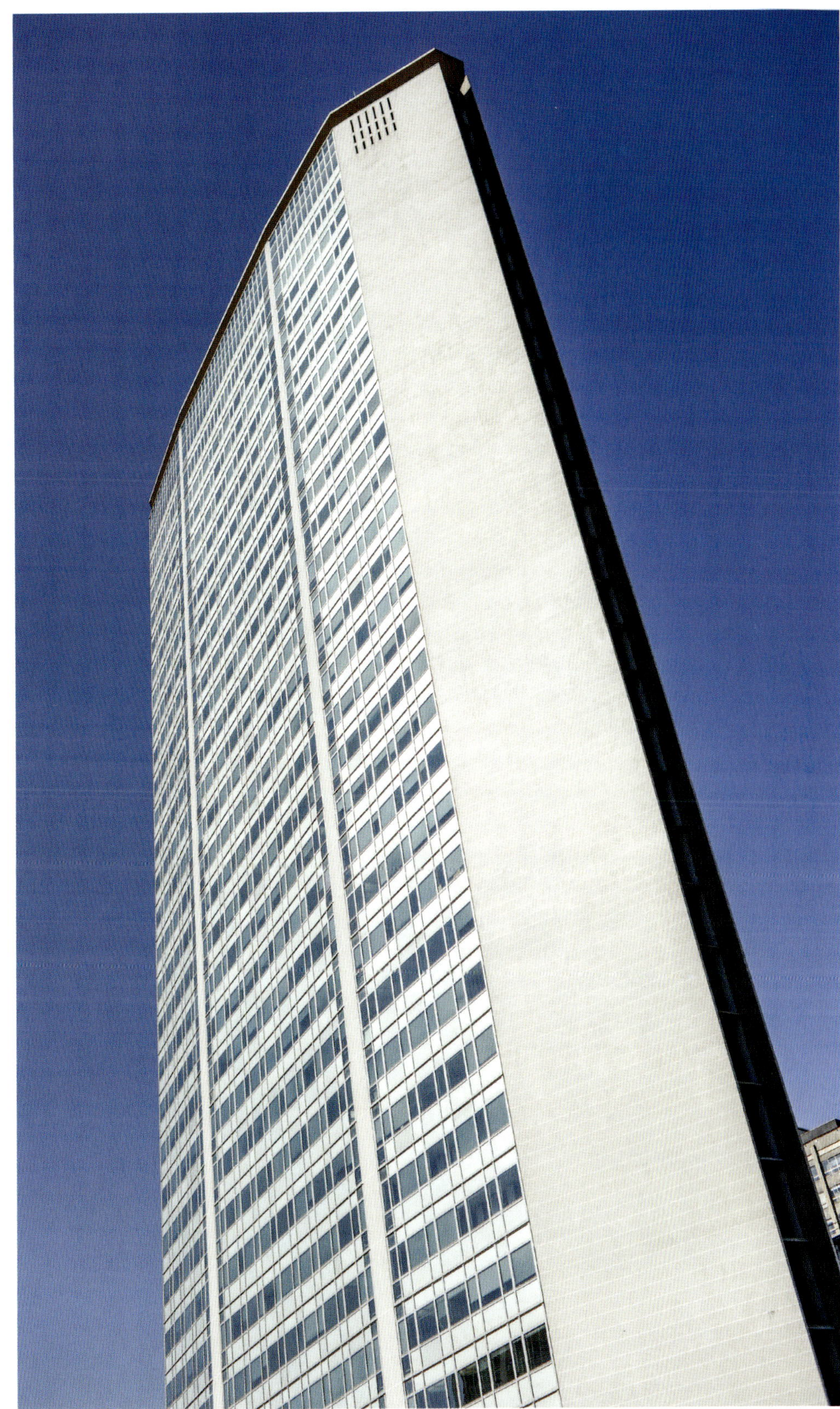

OPPOSITE:
Lounge chairs
from the Hotel Parco dei Principi, Rome, 1964

RIGHT:
Pirelli Tower
in Milan, 1950–56

Jean Prouvé

French, 1901–1984

Jean Prouvé came from an extremely well-connected artistic background, with his father Victor being not only an accomplished painter and sculptor but also a co-founder of the influential École de Nancy and a designer of Art Nouveau glassware and furniture for, among others, Émile Gallé and Daum. Between the ages of fifteen and eighteen, Jean Prouvé apprenticed with Émile Robert, a *ferronier d'art* (art-metalworker) based in Nancy, who produced extraordinarily beautiful Art Nouveau pieces in wrought iron.

Prouvé subsequently spent a further three years training in the metal workshop of A.G. Szabo in Paris, before eventually establishing his own art-metal studio in Nancy in 1923. He started by working on commissions for ornamental architectural ironwork – doors, grilles, balconies, railings and such like. He quickly realized the creative and manufacturing limitations of hand-forging, however, and began exploring new materials such as steel and aluminium and also new metalworking techniques, most notably arc welding. This resulted in a range of thin-sheet-metal furniture (1924), which caught the attention of various prominent Modernists including Pierre Jeanneret, Le Corbusier and Robert Mallet-Stevens – all of whom would later commission him to undertake work for them. Also in 1924, Prouvé developed the innovative *aplati* technique for the construction of seating, which involved flattening sections of tubular steel where there was the greatest amount of stress in order to strengthen the frame of a chair.

BELOW:
Cité desk and Standard chair no. 305
for Ateliers Jean Prouvé, *c.*1950

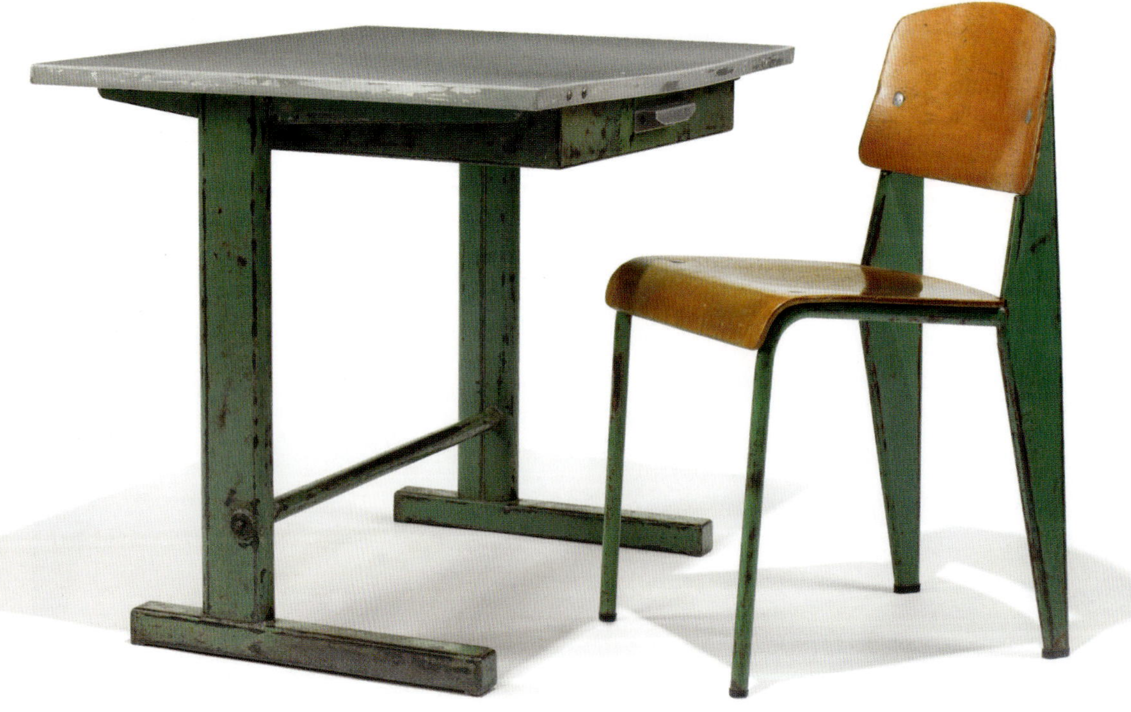

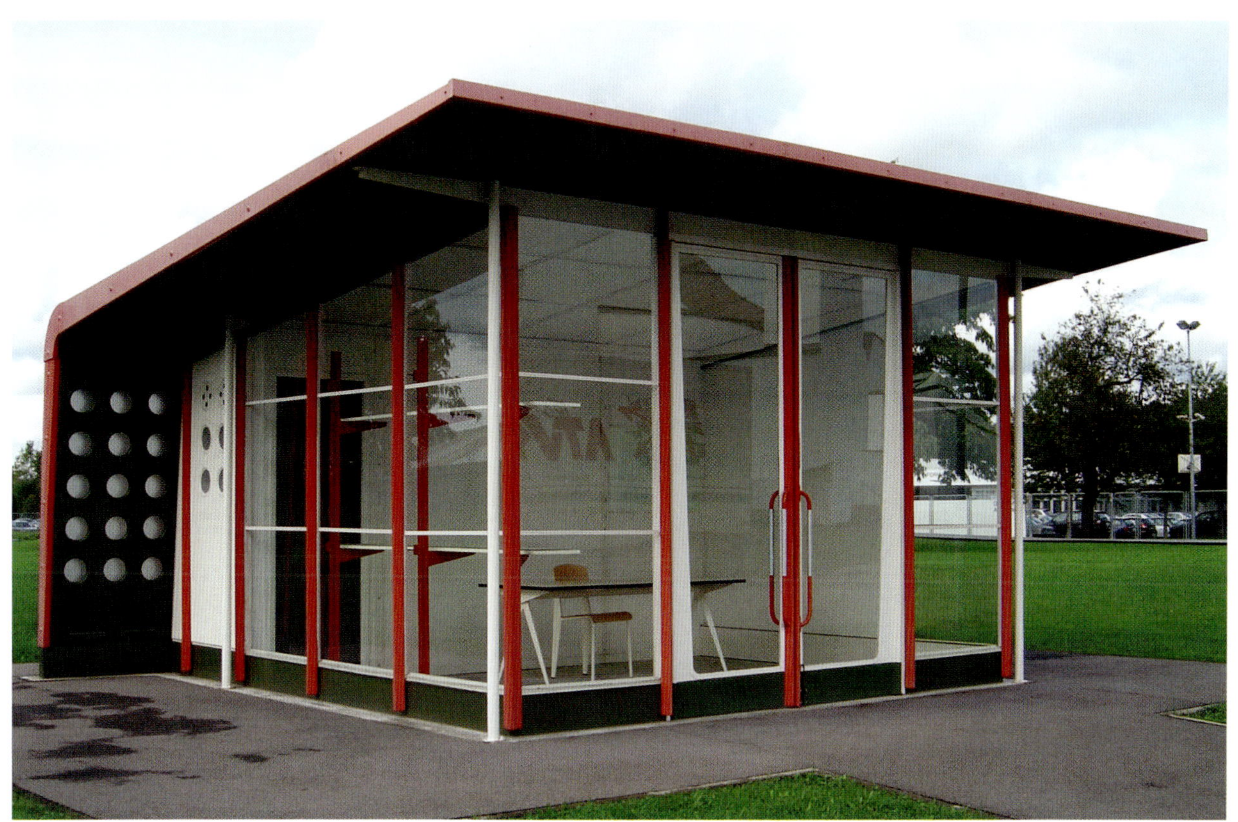

ABOVE:
Prefabricated petrol station by Jean Prouvé, 1953 – now sited at the Vitra Design Museum in Weil am Rhein

The following year he participated in the *Exposition Internationale des Arts Décoratifs et Industriels Modernes* in Paris, where he was awarded an honorary diploma for his utilitarian furniture designs that employed advanced manufacturing techniques. In 1929, Prouvé helped found the Union des Artistes Modernes (UAM) – the leading French association for promotion of the Modernist cause. In 1931, he also co-established, with his engineer brother-in-law A. Schotte, the Ateliers Jean Prouvé and opened a larger manufacturing facility equipped with cutting-edge stamping and folding machines in order to produce utilitarian furniture in high volumes, mostly intended for institutional usage. For instance, during the 1930s and 1940s, the workshop manufactured a comprehensive range of cheap, functional and highly durable school furniture.

During the Second World War, Prouvé was active in the Résistance, and after France's liberation he became mayor of Nancy in 1944. Three years later he opened the Ateliers Jean Prouvé factory in Maxéville, on the outskirts of Nancy. By 1950, this large-scale venture had around 250 employees, and made not only furniture but also architectural components. However, due to a disagreement with the company's majority shareholders, Prouvé left the firm in 1953. The following year he established his own design studio in Paris and around 1955 established Constructions Jean Prouvé, which under his direction went on to become the leading manufacturer of lightweight curtain-wall façades made of sheet-metal.

As an architectural cladding expert, he worked over the ensuing decades as an engineering consultant on various important architectural projects in Paris. As a foremost pioneer of Modern design and architecture, Prouvé's success lay in his systematic approach to problem-solving using trial-and-error technical experimentation, which ultimately resulted in him creating better design solutions that were first and foremost process-driven.

Jens Quistgaard

Danish, 1919–2008

Jens Quistgaard was a celebrated Danish industrial designer whose stylish yet practical tableware helped define Scandinavian Modernism during the post-war era, most notably in North America where his designs for Dansk were especially popular. Even at a very early age he had shown a remarkable talent for art and design, and set up his own workshop in his family's kitchen to produce all kinds of items from jewellery to hunting knives. During his childhood, he also frequented the forges of the local blacksmiths and the workshops of the village carpenters and joiners, and it was from these formative experiences and his youthful obsession with woodcarving that he acquired the necessary craft knowledge and skills to be able to make models from a variety of materials later in life. Quistgaard's father, Harald, was a well-known sculptor who taught at the Kongelige Danske Kunstakademi (Royal Danish Academy of Arts), Copenhagen, and it was from him that Jens received his only formal training.

Nevertheless, he became an accomplished self-taught carpenter, potter and draughtsman. As a young man, he also served an apprenticeship with the renowned silversmith Georg Jensen, and during the Second World War was an active member of the underground Danish resistance. After the war, he worked as an independent designer, creating a wide range of products, including an Oriental-style stoneware teapot (1949–50) and his teak-handled Fjord cutlery (1954). It was this latter design

BELOW LEFT:
Fjord flatware
for Dansk, 1954

BELOW RIGHT:
Teak ice bucket
for Dansk, 1958

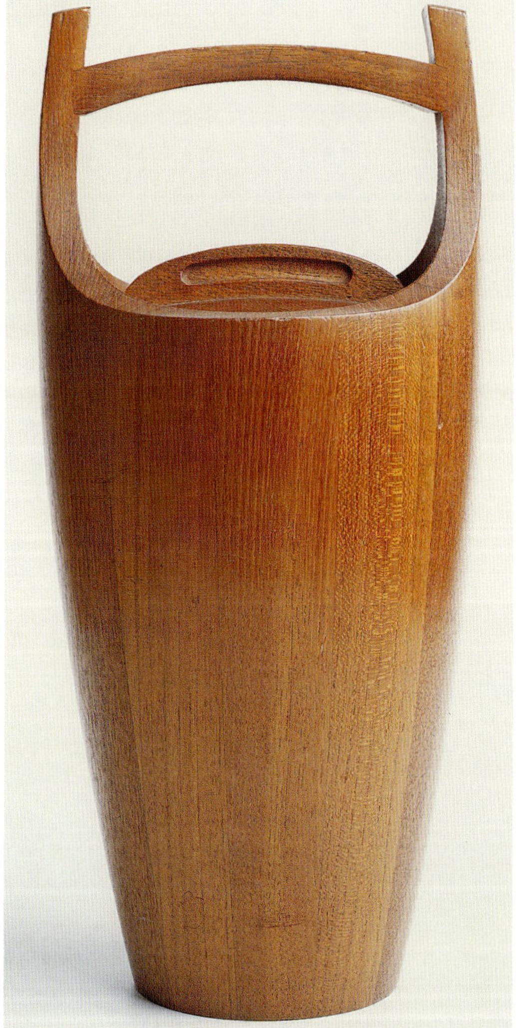

that would act as a springboard for his subsequent career – the American entrepreneur Ted Nierenberg saw this hand-forged flatware in an exhibition at a museum in Copenhagen in 1954 and was so taken with its unusual combination of materials that he sought Quistgaard out and persuaded him that designs such as these could be successfully mass-produced.

The same year, the pair founded their own manufacturing company, Dansk International Designs, and Quistgaard was awarded the prestigious Lunning Prize. Quistgaard designed for Dansk until 1984, and during this thirty-year tenure produced numerous homeware designs that employed a variety of materials, from staved teak to enamelled metal to cast iron. Among his best-known designs for the company are his enamelled Kobenstyle cookware range (1955) with its casseroles' distinctive X-shaped lid handles, and his iconic teak ice bucket (1958), inspired by the hulls of Viking ships and the handles of traditional Japanese wooden buckets. He also designed numerous cast-iron candleholders, glassware pieces, wooden trays and a plethora of teak peppermills that came in all shapes and sizes. In addition, he designed furniture, including a set of rosewood and leather/suede armchairs and tables for Richard Nissen (1966) that incorporated innovative constructions and epitomized the ever-cool yet homely warmth of the post-war Scandinavian look.

After leaving Dansk, Quistgaard continued to work as a designer for various European and American companies. It was his impressive body of work for Dansk, however, more than anything else, that popularized Scandinavian design in North America and helped define the Danish Modern style.

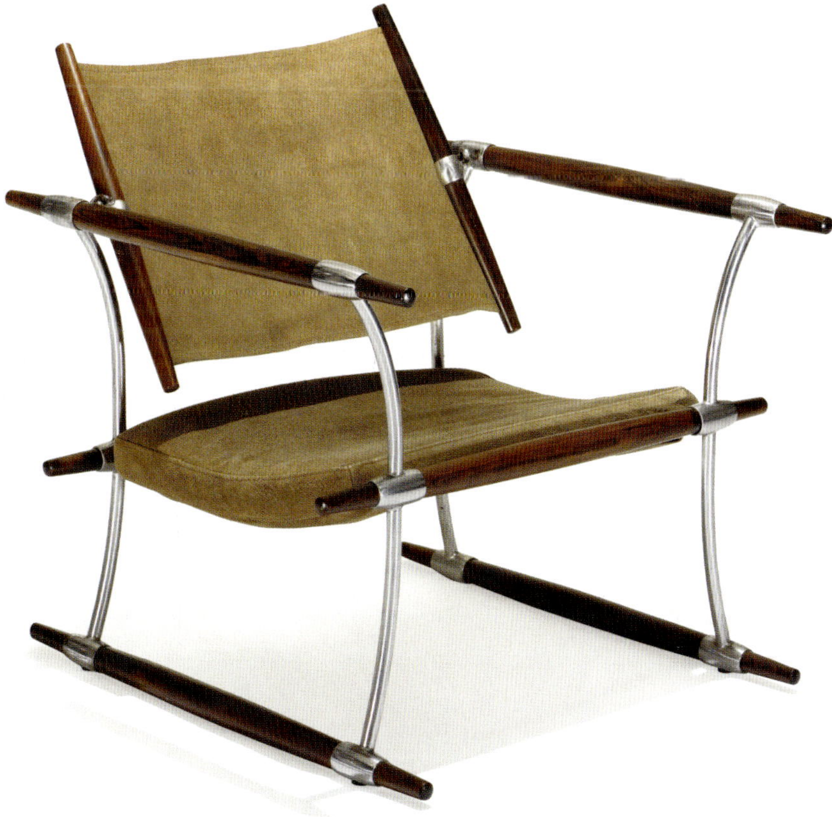

RIGHT:
Stick armchair
for Richard Nissen, 1966

R

Dieter Rams

German, 1932–

The German industrial designer Dieter Rams famously headed the design department at the Kronberg-based consumer electronics manufacturer Braun, where he instigated a highly rational in-house approach to design that was based on the concept of good design. Rams defined his ten principles for design in the clear, simple terms: "Good design is innovative. Good design makes a product useful. Good design is aesthetic. Good design makes a product understandable. Good design is unobtrusive. Good design is honest. Good design is long lasting. Good design is thorough down to the last detail. Good design is environmentally friendly. Good design is as little design as possible." By using these guiding principles, Rams and his colleagues created a programme of products for Braun that were remarkable for their clarity of layout, aesthetic elegance and practical functionality – indeed many of them went on to become regarded as icons of German Modernism thanks to their refined formal vocabulary and design excellence.

Born in Wiesbaden, Rams studied architecture and interior design at the local school of art, and also took a year's carpentry apprenticeship. After graduating in 1953, he joined the Frankfurt-based office of the architect Otto Apel, which at the time was collaborating on various US consulate buildings with the American architectural practice Skidmore Owings & Merrill. In 1955, Rams was hired by Braun to work as an in-house architect and interior designer, and the following year his remit was widened so that he worked with Hans Gugelot on the development of the Phonosuper SK4 record player. Nicknamed "Snow

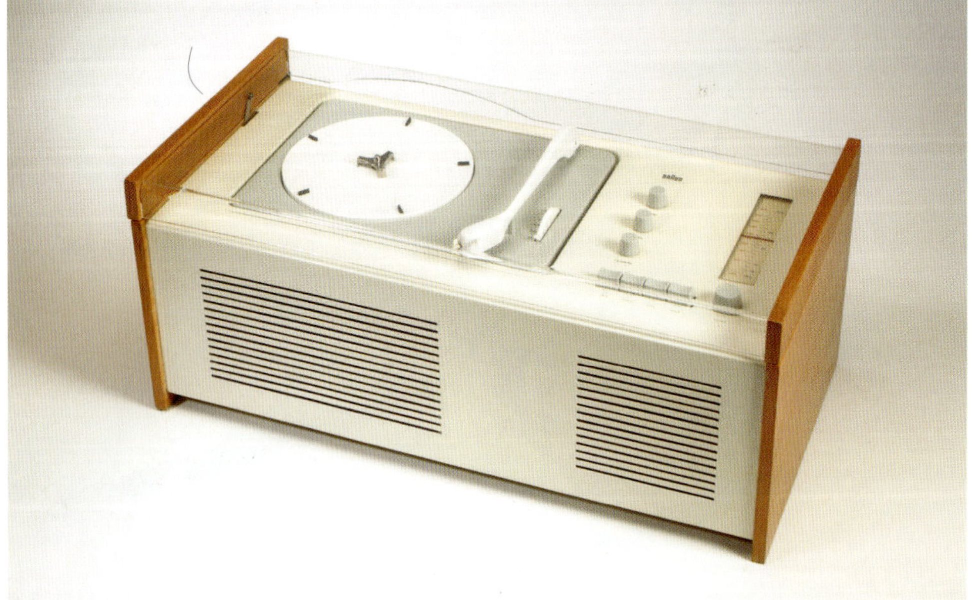

LEFT:
Phonosuper SK4 record player
for Braun, 1956 – co-designed with Hans Gugelot

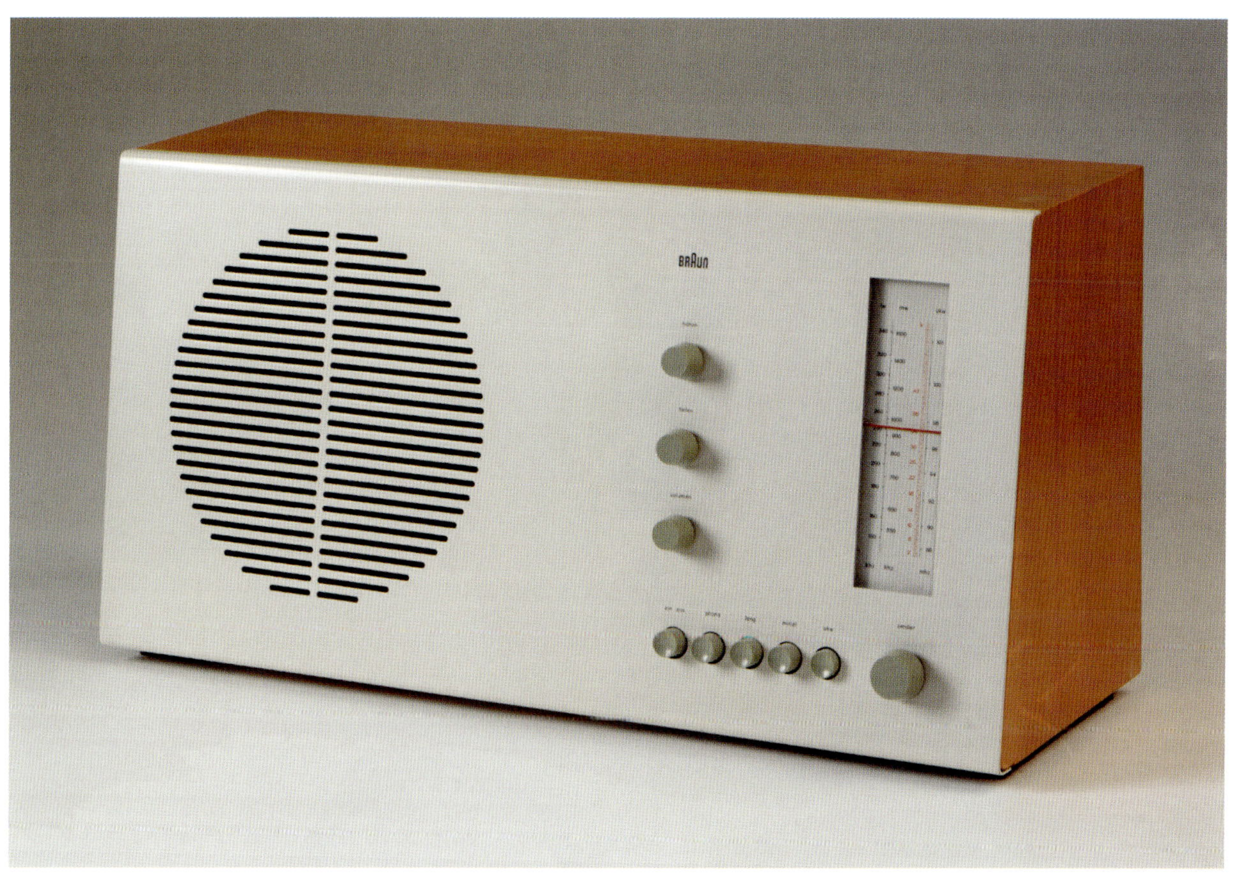

ABOVE:
RT20 radio
for Braun, 1963

White's Coffin" by Braun's competitors, the SK4 radically re-imagined products of its kind, featuring a white housing, a clear plastic top and a simple, functional layout. It was not an immediate commercial success, being too far ahead of popular taste, yet this revolutionary design was soon celebrated by design cognoscenti for introducing a new essentialist vocabulary of form, and it helped to establish Braun as one of the world's leading consumer electronic brands.

Rams also designed other audio products for Braun, such as the T41 pocket radio (1956) and the P1 portable record player (1959), which had a similar essentialism and clarity of layout, and embodied the practical, ordered approach to design that had been born at the Bauhaus Dessau and developed by the HfG or Hochschule für Gestaltung (School of Design) in Ulm. In 1961 Rams became head of Braun's design department, and during the decades that followed the firm produced much impressive work that echoed his legendary design philosophy, "Less, but Better."

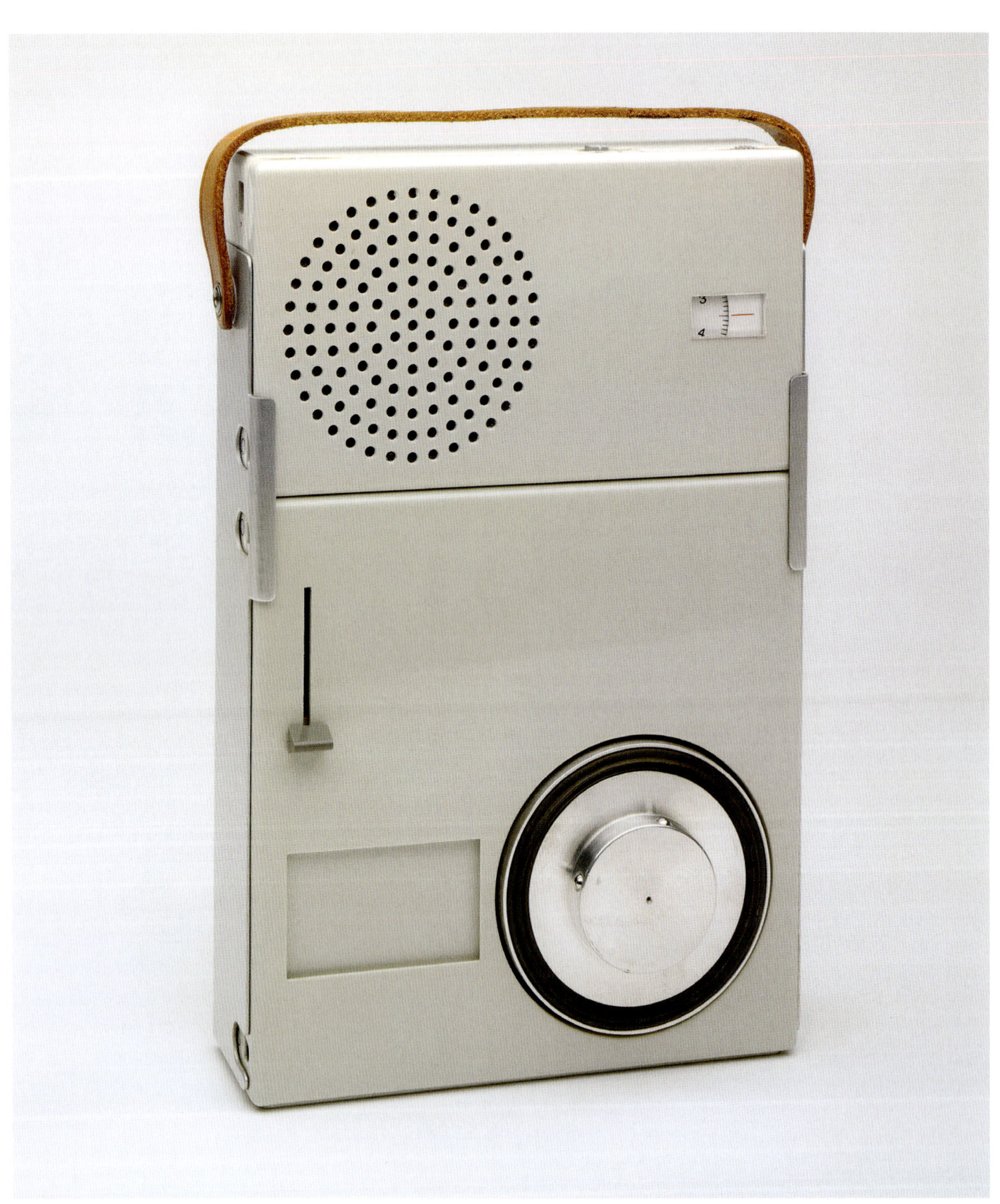

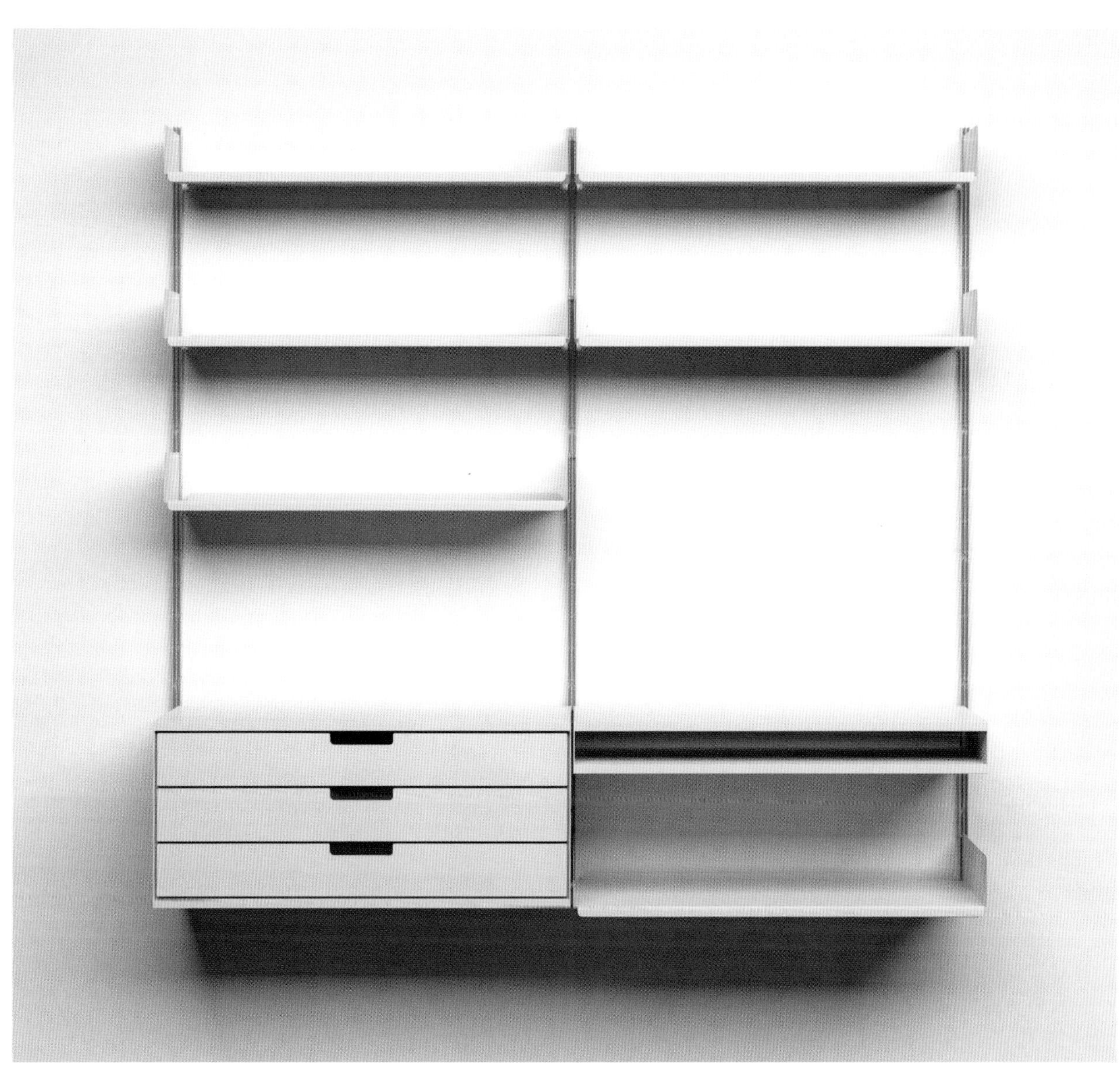

OPPOSITE:
TP1 portable transistor radio/record player
for Braun, 1959

ABOVE:
606 Universal Shelving System
for Vitsœ, 1960

Apart from his work for Braun, Rams also produced various furniture designs for Vitsœ including his highly successful 606 Universal Shelving System (1960), which continues to have a timeless appeal thanks to its impressive functionality, physical durability and aesthetic purity. Widely revered for his uncompromising belief in the morality of good design, Rams and his design vocabulary have profoundly influenced the approach taken by other designers, most notably Jonathan Ive in his development of products for Apple.

Paul Rand

American, 1914–1996

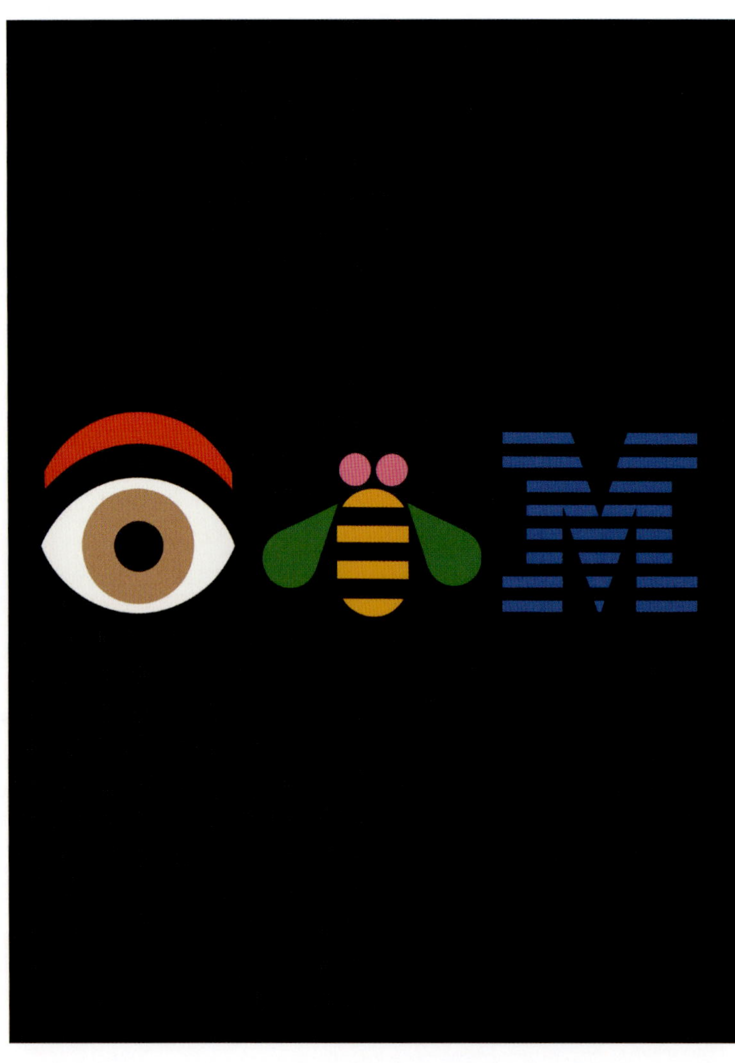

ABOVE:
Eye Bee M poster
for IBM, 1981

The legendary art director and graphic designer Paul Rand created a plethora of iconic corporate logos during his career, including those for IBM, UPS and ABC, and is generally credited with introducing the Modernist Swiss Style to American graphic design. Although he studied at the Pratt Institute, Parson's School of Design and the Art Students League – all in New York – Rand would later claim that he had largely taught himself, by reading imported European design journals such as *Gebrauchsgraphik*.

During the early years of his career Rand was influenced by the German advertising style known as *Sachplakat* (ornamental poster) where a striking representation of a product is given an artistic illustrative treatment, and by the work of the Danish-émigré designer Gustav Jensen, who was his mentor. It was around this time that he decided to change his name, from Peretz Rosenbaum to the more anglicized Paul Rand. With this new persona, he began to gain recognition for his bold eye-catching work, first as art director of *Esquire* and *Apparel Arts* magazines and then for his remarkable series of cover designs for *Direction* magazine, which incorporated photomontage and historical quotations.

Strongly influenced by the ideas he found in László Moholy-Nagy's book *The New Vision* (1932, originally published in German as *Neues Sehen*), Rand was among the first American designers to adopt a European avant-garde approach to the development of an authentically Modern style of graphic design in the United States. Discarding traditional symmetrical layouts and narrative-style illustration in favour of compositions that dynamically yet harmoniously merged typographic copy with bold photographic imagery, he pioneered a distinctive graphic language that was highly expressive and often engagingly humorous too.

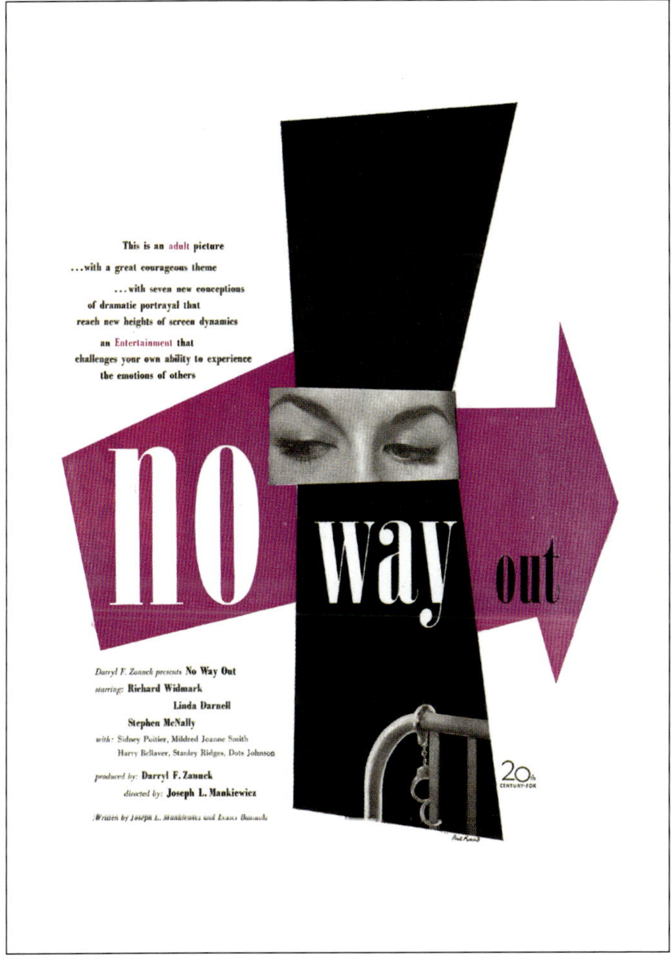

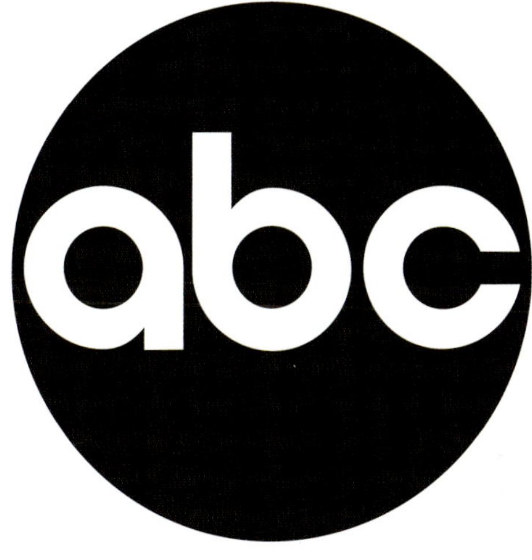

LEFT:
Movie poster
for *No Way Out*, 1950

ABOVE:
Logo
for American Broadcasting Corporation (ABC), 1962

By the 1950s and 1960s Rand was increasingly working in the realm of corporate identity development, having a gift for convincing corporations that commitment to design was a strategic investment. In so doing, he almost single-handedly helped raise the status of his chosen field from that of "commercial art" to that of graphic design. One of the reasons his logos and trademarks became so iconic was their bold underlying simplicity, which made them immediately impactful and universally understandable. An unquavering adherent to Modernist ideology, Rand rejected traditional narrative illustration in favour of dynamically combined typography and imagery that enabled him to produce work that was powerful, expressive and often visually witty.

Richard Riemerschmid

German, 1868–1957

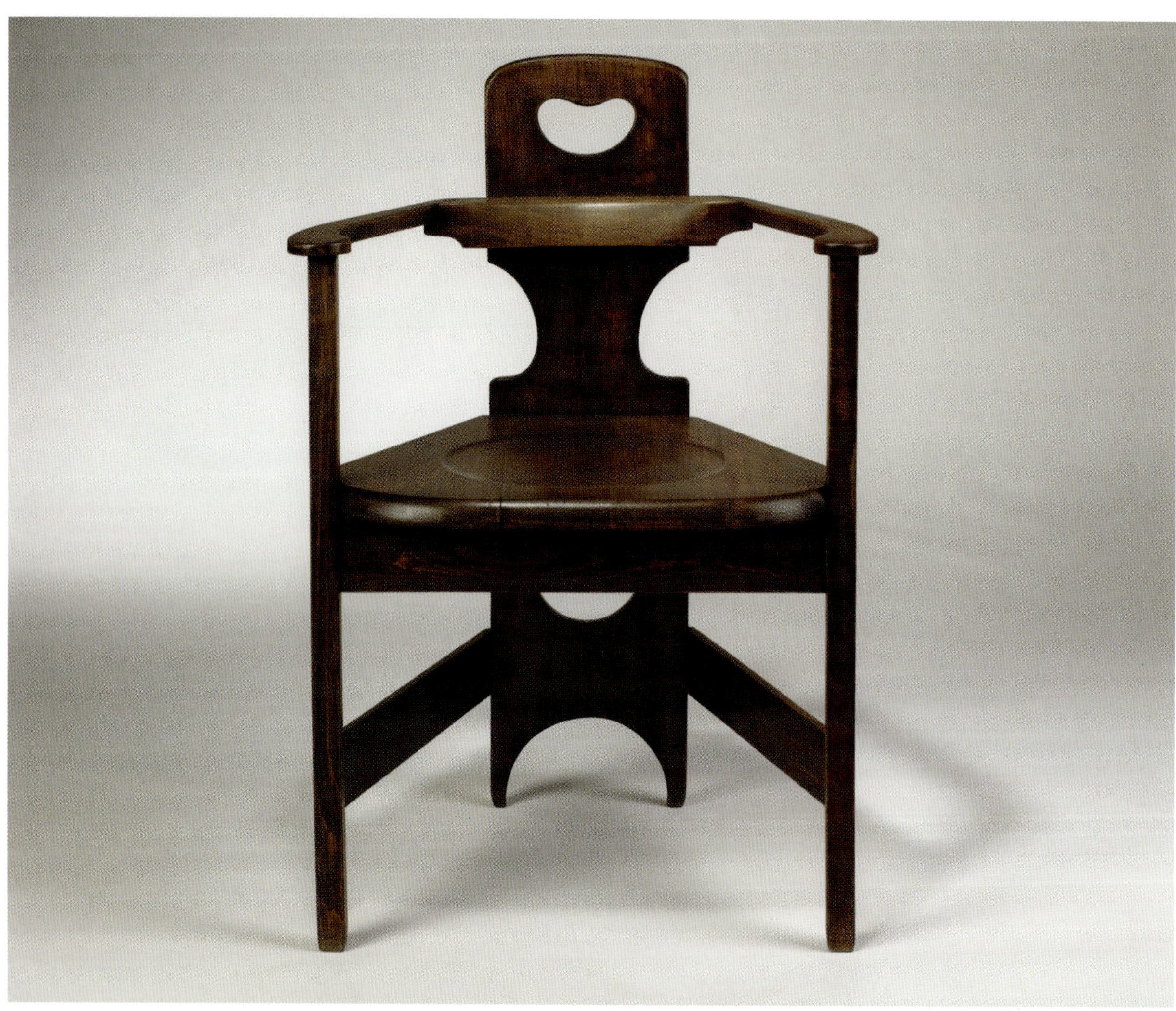

ABOVE:
Armchair
for Fleischauer Nuremberg, *c.*1900

OPPOSITE:
Copper candleholder
for Vereinigte Werkstätten, 1897

Richard Riemerschmid was a highly influential designer, architect, urban planner and design educator who, during the *fin-de-siècle* period, was also a leading proponent of Jugendstil – the Teutonic answer to the British Arts and Crafts Movement and the Franco-Belgian Art Nouveau style. Having later reconciled the ideals of handcraftsmanship with the industrial standardization and mechanized production of high-quality yet affordable products, he helped lay the foundations of the Modern Movement in Germany.

Riemerschmid initially studied painting at the Munich Akademie der Bildenden Künste (Academy of Fine Arts), and then worked as a freelance artist, producing paintings as well as posters and other graphic artworks, including some for *Jugend* magazine. In 1895 he turned his attention to the applied arts and designed his first pieces of furniture. Two years later, he exhibited his furniture and paintings at the *VII Internationalen Kunst-Ausstellung* (Seventh International Art Exhibition) held at the Glaspalast in Munich. The show's decorative arts section was such a critical success that afterwards Riemerschmid, along with other prominent Jugendstil designers – Hermann Obrist, Bernhard Pankok, Bruno Paul and Peter Behrens – founded the Vereinigte Werkstätten für Kunst im Handwerk (United Workshops for Art in Craft). Inspired by the guilds of the British Arts and Crafts Movement, this new design-reforming venture sought to establish a sound basis for the commercialization of "art manufactures" by promoting greater co-operation between designers and craftsmen. The workshop produced a large number of designs by Riemerschmid, including his Music Room chair, which had originally been designed as part of an interior installation for the *Deutsche Kunst-Ausstellung* (German Art Exhibition) in 1899.

The previous year, the Dresdner Werkstätten für Handwerkskunst (Dresden Workshops for Craftsmanship) had been founded by his brother-in-law, Karl Schmidt, and Riemerschmid subsequently designed suites of furniture for the venture that incorporated standardized "knockdown" items which could be made by machine and then assembled by hand. These simple and functional proto-modern *Typenmöbel* (type furniture) designs were exhibited as room installations at the third *Deutsche Kunstgewerbe-Ausstellung* (German Exhibition of Applied Arts) held in Dresden in 1906. The following year Riemerschmid helped found the Deutscher Werkbund (DWB), which sought to forge greater links between art and industry and raise the design-consciousness of designers, manufacturers and consumers alike through its promotion of Modern design using the conduits of exhibitions, workshops, lectures and publications. As a leading figure in the DWB, Riemerschmid produced a variety of designs for industrial manufacture, including lighting and other metalware pieces for Konrad Konig, furnishing textiles for the Dresdner Werkstätten, stoneware items for Reinhold Merkelbach, a coffee and dinner service for the Meissen porcelain factory, and glassware for Benedikt von Poschinger – all of which had a proto-Modern reductivist aesthetic while also retaining a vernacular sensibility.

Riemerschmid was also a pioneering architect who designed numerous villas, as well as a factory building and various exhibition pavilions. In addition, he was the leading planner for Germany's first garden city, in Hellerau, Dresden, (1907–13) and an early pioneer of prefabricated architecture, designing a complete industrially produced cabin-like kit house made from wood that was built for an exhibition in 1922.

Gerrit Rietveld

Dutch, 1888–1964

The Dutch architect-designer Gerrit Rietveld was a leading figure of the De Stijl movement, who created truly revolutionary furniture and interiors. Born in Utrecht, he had learnt carpentry skills while working in his father's workshop from the ages of eleven to fifteen. He then worked as a draughtsman for the goldsmith C.J.A. Begeer (1904–11) while taking architectural draughtsmanship courses given by Petrus Johannes Houtzagers at the Utrecht Museum van Kunstnijverhaid (Museum of Applied Arts). From 1906, Rietveld was a pupil of the architect Piet Klaarhamer, who was an associate of the artist Bart van der Leck, whom Rietveld met during this period. In 1917 Rietveld began working as a freelance furniture-maker in Utrecht and the same year designed a prototype of his famous slatted chair (1917–18), which would later become known as the Red/Blue chair.

The following year, Rietveld met Theo van Doesburg and became a founding member of De Stijl. In 1919, he opened his own architectural studio and exhibited for the first time with this progressive group of artists and designers. Four years later, at the suggestion of van der Leck, Rietveld painted his slatted chair in black, red, blue and yellow to enhance its rectilinearity, and it was subsequently included at the landmark exhibition held at the Weimar Bauhaus in 1923. The Red/Blue chair, as it now was, would go on to become one of the most famous chair designs of all time, and was a visually powerful three-dimensional realization of the De Stijl group's philosophy. More than just a chair, it was a dynamic composition of "scaffolding" with the transparency of its construction suggesting the dissolving of matter and giving a sense of spatial infinity. In this regard, the chair could be read as a piece of abstract sculpture and at the time must have seemed shockingly revolutionary.

The extraordinary spatial qualities achieved by this seating design were realized on a much larger scale in 1924 when Rietveld designed his first building, the Rietveld Schröder House in Utrecht. A completely unified *Gesamtkunstwerk* project, this revolutionary house was commissioned

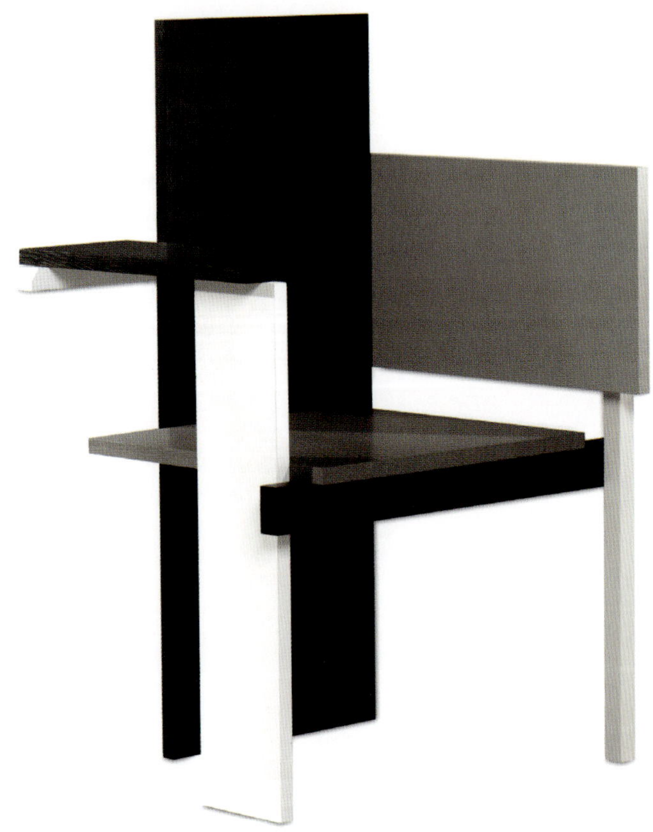

BELOW:
Berlin chair
1923 – originally designed as a scale model for the *Juryfreie Kunstschau* (Jury-free Art Exhibition) in Berlin and then later produced for the boardroom at the Rijksakademie of visual arts in Amsterdam in 1960

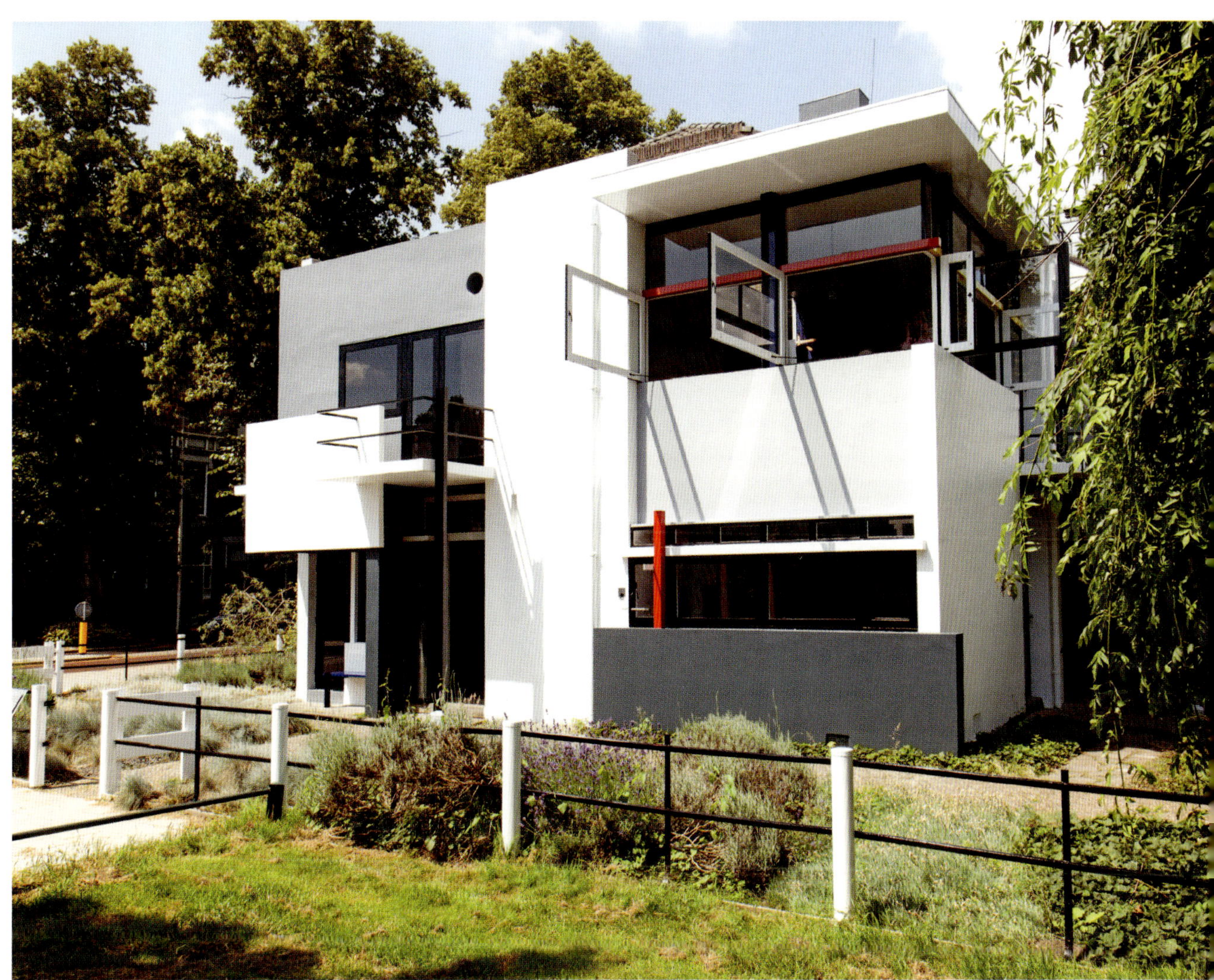

ABOVE:
Rietveld Schröder House
in Utrecht, 1924

by the recently widowed Truus Schröder-Schräder as a home for herself and her three children, and she liaised closely with Rietveld to ensure that its unconventional design would promote "active living". While the asymmetrical exterior of the house, with its geometric elements in grey, white and black, had a rather nautical air thanks to its protruding decklike balconies, inside, the light-filled interiors were notable for their bold primary-colour schemes and also for their interesting delineation of space using sliding partitions and folding doors. This stripped-down Modern villa was based on an uncompromising aesthetic and was essentially a statement of intent that offered an enticing glimpse of a utopian future.

Over the following years, Rietveld collaborated with Schröder, who became his partner, on a number of architectural projects, and created a large number of furniture designs characterized by a strong elemental quality and an uncompromising geometry – as seen in the Zig-Zag chair (1932–34), the Crate chair (1934) and the armchair designed for the UNESCO building in Paris (1958). One of the great design innovators of the twentieth century, Rietveld's championing of geometric reductivism had an enormous influence on designers at the Bauhaus, and ultimately through them helped shape the course of the Modern Movement.

Rockstar North & Rockstar Games

British/American, founded 1998

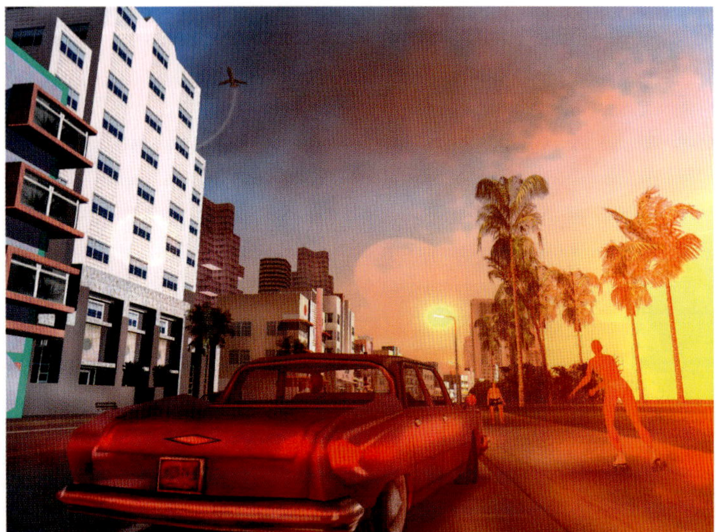

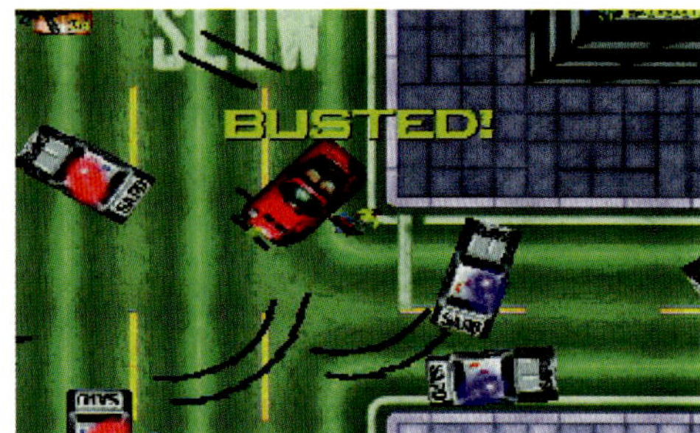

One of the most interesting areas of design practice to emerge over the last three decades has been that of computer games design. For most of this time, Rockstar Games has been at the vanguard of this fast-moving, technology-driven field. The company's Rockstar North studio is best known as the lead developer for Grand Theft Auto, the most successful gaming series of all time. The latest game, Grand Theft Auto V, broke seven Guinness World Records when it was released, including the fastest entertainment property to gross one billion dollars (a record achieved in just three days).

The two original Grand Theft Auto games were top-down personal computer games created by DMA Design. In 1998, Sam Houser, the British publishing producer for the series, convinced its American publisher, Take-Two Interactive, to purchase the DMA Design studio and the GTA series. Houser and his brother Dan subsequently founded the Rockstar Games subsidiary of Take Two to focus on progressive and innovative game design with high production values. DMA Design was renamed Rockstar North and became the primary development studio for the Grand Theft Auto series.

Rockstar Games transformed video game design with the release of Grand Theft Auto III, the first GTA game to use a street-level, third-person perspective in a 3-D environment. With its unique combination of open-world gameplay, gritty social satire and innovative use of narrative, Grand Theft Auto III helped usher in the PlayStation 2 era and propelled the medium of video games onto the cultural agenda.

Success continued in 2002 with Grand Theft Auto: Vice City, which won multiple Game of the Year awards and six BAFTAs. That same year, games design received long-overdue recognition as being an important emerging design discipline, when Rockstar Games was

OPPOSITE LEFT:
Street scene from Grand Theft Auto: Vice City, released 2002

OPPOSITE RIGHT :
Street scene from Grand Theft Auto, released 1997

BELOW:
Environment landscape from Grand Theft Auto V, released 2013

shortlisted for the Designer of the Year award by the Design Museum.

Grand Theft Auto: San Andreas, released in 2004, went on to become the highest-selling PlayStation 2 game to date, while Grand Theft Auto IV (2008) brought the series into high definition to rave reviews. Similarly Grand Theft Auto V (2013) pushed the series to new heights with a massive and incredibly detailed re-imagining of Southern California and a revolutionary approach to gameplay and story, allowing fans to simultaneously play three very different characters across one epic narrative, jumping between them at will. Meanwhile, the 2013 launch of Grand Theft Auto Online set the series on a new path as players were able to share in and create content for an ever-evolving version of the Grand Theft Auto V universe. One reviewer described GTAV as "Rockstar's definitive open-world masterpiece", claiming it was "quite simply perfect in every way".

As developer and publisher, Rockstar Games has released numerous other pioneering titles spanning various gaming genres, notably Manhunt, Bully, The Warriors, L.A. Noire, Max Payne 3 and Red Dead Redemption. It remains one of the most pre-eminent games developers in the world thanks to its unique combination of obsessive perfectionism, design-and-development teamwork and an abiding love for the medium of interactive entertainment, which enables it to take game-play to increasingly immersive levels.

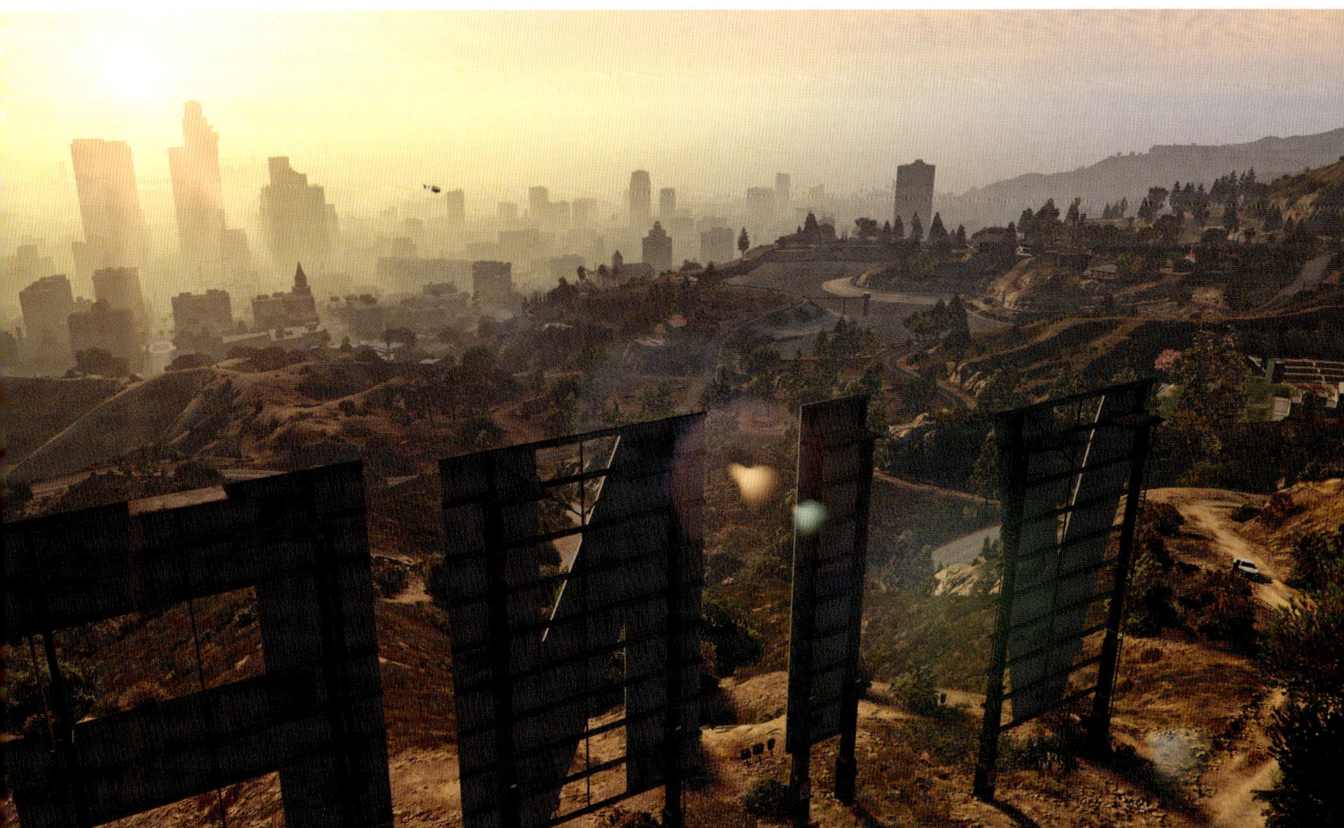

Aleksandr Rodchenko

Russian, 1891–1956

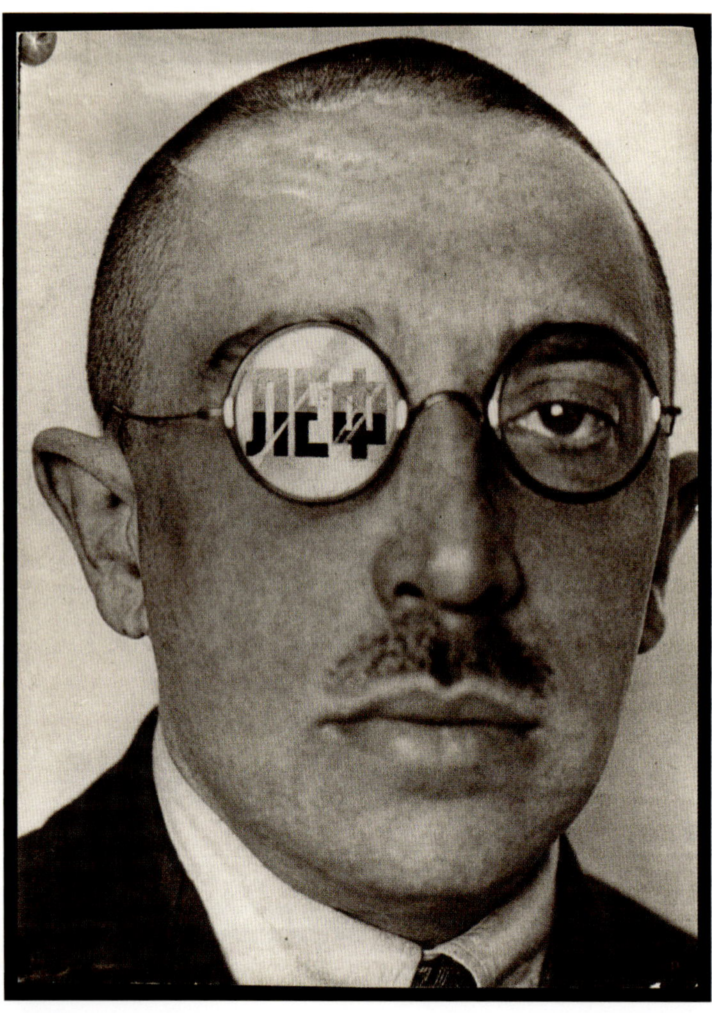

ABOVE:
Cover of *LEF* journal featuring a portrait of Osip Brik, 1924

A leading exponent of Russian Constructivism, Aleksandr Rodchenko produced propagandist work that captured the idealism and political zeal of the years immediately following the Russian Revolution in 1917. Indeed, his graphic design so powerfully embodied the Bolsheviks' sentiment that "the streets are our brushes, the squares are our palettes" that it has become forever identified with not only the utopian aspirations of Soviet ideology but also the idea of the artist as a revolutionary who can instigate meaningful social change through their work.

Having graduated from the Kazan School of Fine Arts in 1914, Rodchenko came under the influence of the Russian Futurists the same year, becoming a member of this new avant-garde art movement. He moved to Moscow in 1915 and enrolled in the graphic design department of the Stroganov School of Applied Arts. Around this period he participated in a number of exhibitions, including one entitled *The Store* that was organized by Vladimir Tatlin in 1916. After the Revolution in 1917, Rodchenko became increasingly politicized and was one of the first artists to actively support the Bolsheviks. To this end, he was appointed deputy head of the Art and Production Department at the newly established Fine Art Department (IZO) of the People's Commissariat of Enlightenment. In this capacity he helped to establish crucial links between the creative community and industry. Around this time there was a definite desire among the Russian avant-garde to redefine the role of the artist, bringing him or her closer to the position of an industrial worker – essentially an artist-constructor who would work within the realms of industrial production. In 1920, with his wife Varvara Stepanova and Alexei Gan, Rodchenko published the *First Programme of the Working Group of Constructivists* and became both a member of INKhUK (the Institute of Artistic Culture) and a professor at Vkhutemas (the state Higher Artistic-Technical

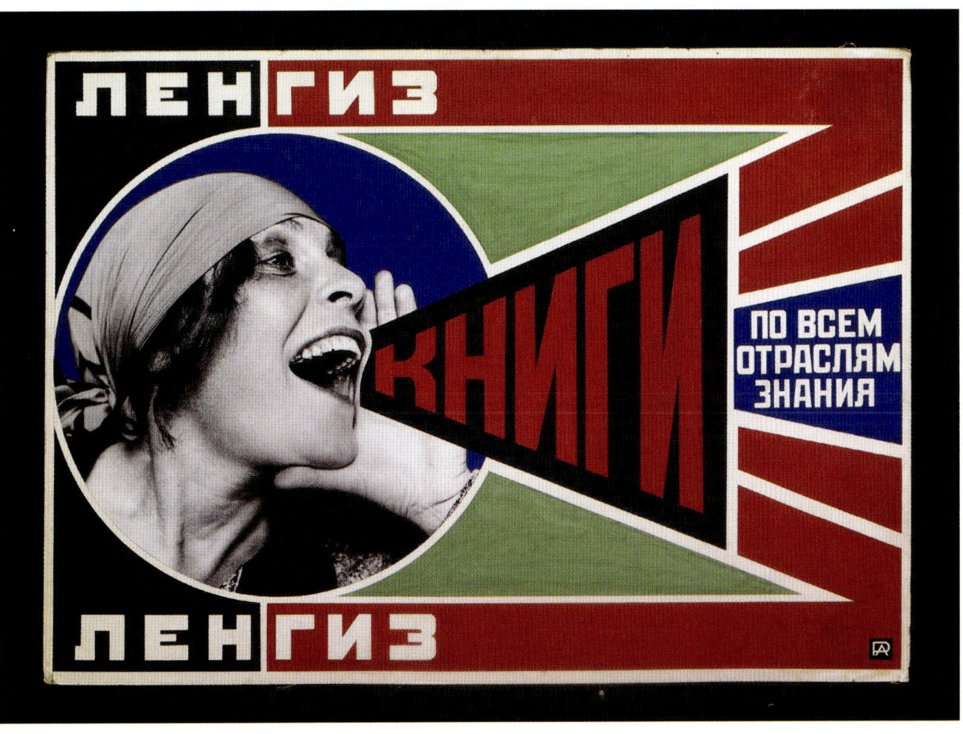

ABOVE:
Knigi (Books) poster
for Gosizdat, 1924

Workshops). He later denounced art for art's sake and abandoned his fine-art activities altogether in order to concentrate on Productivism – the production of functional art such as posters, furniture, photography and films.

During the 1920s, he mainly worked as a graphic designer for the journals *LEF* and *Novyi LEF* but also created many posters, which were often photomontages that exploited the expressive potential of typography. With his dynamic positioning of elements within a layout, often incorporating bold diagonals or triangulated configurations, Rodchenko created work that frequently glorified the worker as a hero of the new political order in the Soviet Union – for instance in his iconic Knigi (Books) poster of 1924, which featured a photograph of the Constructivist muse Lilya Brik wearing a proletarian headscarf and shouting out a typographic slogan. Rodchenko's graphic collages also often incorporated black-and-white photographs taken from unconventional angles that enhanced their sense of compositional dynamism. In addition to his graphic design work, he created a Workers' Club as an installation for the Soviet Pavilion at the *Exposition Internationale des Arts Décoratifs et Industriels Modernes* held in Paris in 1925, which again revealed his ability to create a dynamic composition of elements that reflected an optimistic forward-looking spirit of the early Soviet era that was an utter rejection of historicism. Through his eye-catching graphics with their layering of elements into complex compositions, Rodchenko's work came to typify the vehemently avant-garde aesthetic of Russian Constructivism, and by default defined "the Soviet look"; it has, as a result, had an enormous influence on the work of succeeding generations of graphic designers.

Gordon Russell

British, 1892–1980

Gordon Russell was a pioneering furniture designer and maker, as well as a successful design entrepreneur and one of Britain's most influential advocates of good design. During the Second World War, he led the UK government's Utility Furniture Scheme. In the post-war years he took a significant role in the organization of the landmark *Festival of Britain* in 1951. Through his directorship of the Council of Industrial Design (later renamed the Design Council) he profoundly influenced design policy and teaching in Britain during the 1950s and 1960s. Trained in the Arts and Crafts tradition of the Cotswold School, Russell tirelessly championed the idea of accessible, well-designed and beautifully crafted objects for everyday use, believing that good design was ultimately a question of teaching "the machine manners".

In 1904, when he was twelve years old, his father bought the Lygon Arms in Broadway, Worcestershire, and set about renovating it into one of the most celebrated country hotels in Britain. Russell encountered the Arts and Crafts Movement thanks to the Guild of Handicraft, which was located in nearby Chipping Campden, where he attended grammar school. At

BELOW:
Weston dining group
by Gordon Russell, 1929

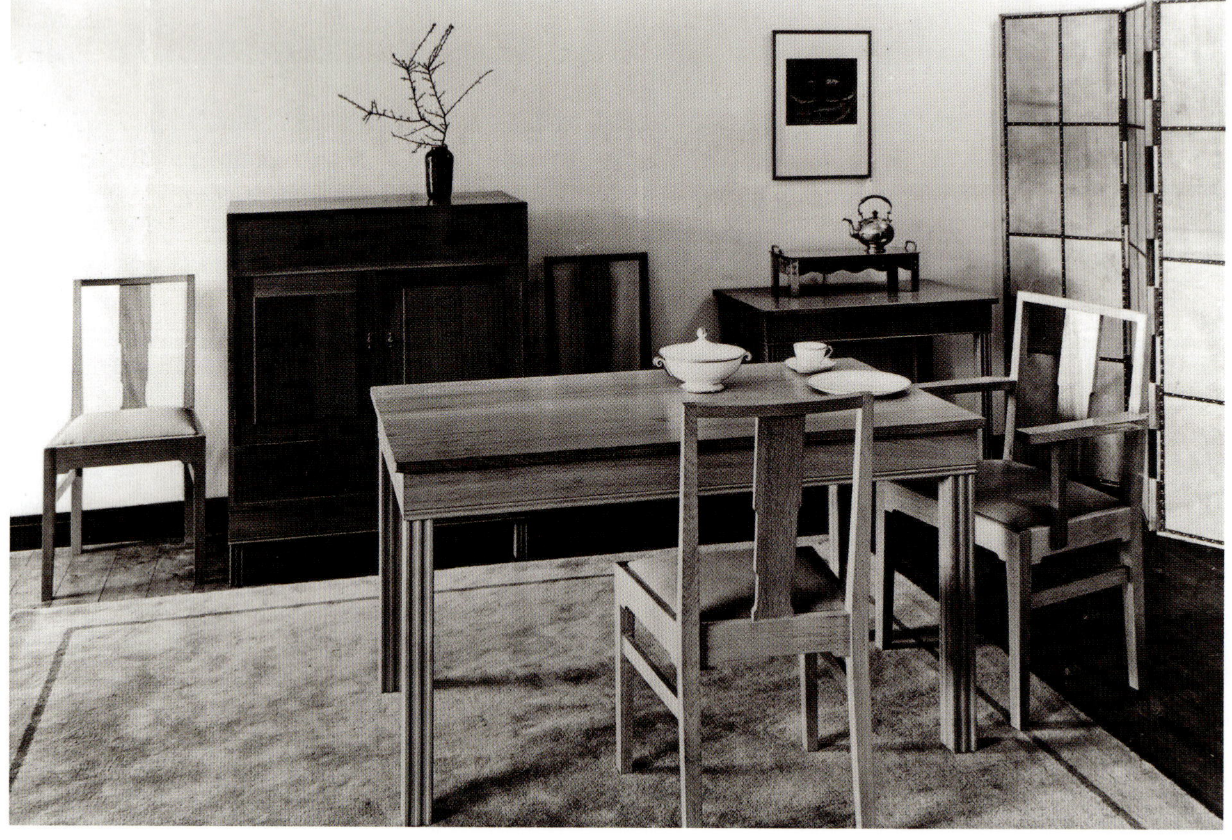

the age of fifteen he left and joined his family's furniture business, SB Russell, in Broadway, where he took charge of its repair workshop, which serviced the needs of his parents' hotel. Working alongside skilled craftsmen, he learnt the importance of knowing exactly how to make an object when trying to design it. He subsequently served in the army during the First World War and won a Military Cross. After the war, Russell and his brother Don returned to Broadway and the family business.

Russell exhibited his exquisitely detailed Lygon cabinet – a masterful expression of British craftsmanship and an exemplar of Cotswold School design – at the 1925 *Exposition Internationale des Arts Décoratifs et Industriels Modernes*. Around this time, he also began creating more affordable Modern-style furnishings that were plainer and therefore easier to produce, yet still of high quality. Unlike the Arts and Crafts Movement that scorned the machine, and the Modern Movement that regarded it as a saviour, Russell took a more ambivalent approach to its use. He judiciously controlled the use of mechanized production in his own workshops, employing it where it could save his workers unrewarding repetitive labour, yet making sure that they were still able to practise their craft skills.

BELOW:
Model 3a dining chair from the Chiltern Range
designed by Edwin Clinch and Herbert Cutler for the Board of Trade's Advisory Committee on Utility Furniture , 1943

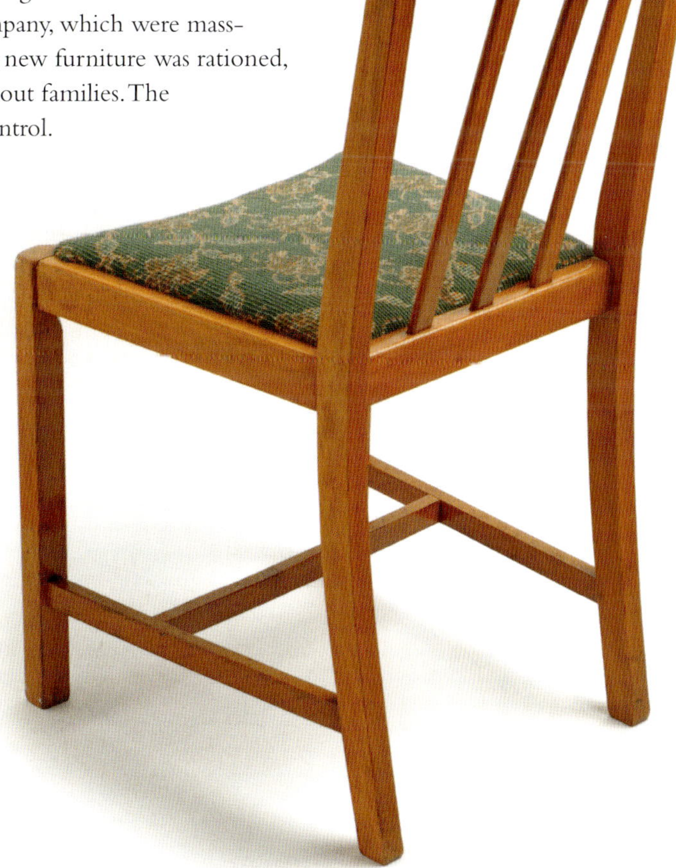

In the late 1920s, Russell decided to leave the designing of furniture to his other brother, Dick, and focus his skills on managing the growing manufacturing operation in Broadway. Around this time, the firm designed a series of moulded plywood radio-cabinets for the Murphy Radio Company, which were mass-produced in London. During the Second World War new furniture was rationed, and made available only to newlyweds and bombed-out families. The design of furniture was placed under government control. Russell joined the Utility Furniture Advisory Committee set up by the government to make the best use of scarce materials. He was responsible for helping to lay down its guidelines, which led to simple standardized furniture pieces in the Cotswold School idiom, such as the Model 3a dining chair that was produced in numerous workshops across the country.

In 1947 Russell became the second director of the Council of Industrial Design and during his tenure he oversaw the launch of *Design* magazine in 1949 and the opening of the Design Centre in London in 1956. Knighted in 1955, he was throughout his life a champion of good design, who understood the beneficial impact it could have on ordinary people's lives. As the Gordon Russell Design Museum notes, "He delivered this message to an international community of both manufacturers and the public alike," and as a result, "his legacy lives on in Britain's vibrant design industry."

S

Eero Saarinen

Finnish/American, 1910–1961

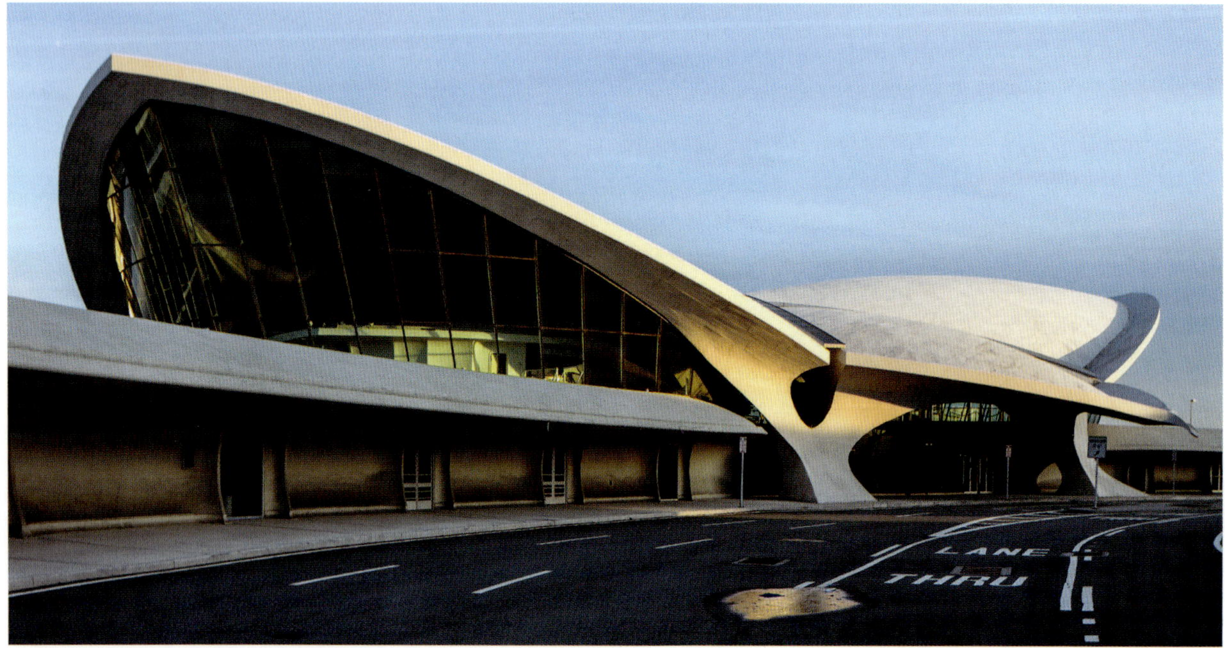

ABOVE:
TWA Flight Center at John F. Kennedy International Airport, 1956–62

OPPOSITE:
Pedestal Group Model No. 151 Tulip chair for Knoll, 1955–56

Born in Finland, Eero Saarinen was the son of the celebrated Finnish architect Eliel Saarinen, who had been a pioneer of Finnish National Romanticism in the early 1900s and later won second prize in the Chicago Tribune Tower design competition of 1922. Bolstered by this success, the Saarinen family, including Eero, emigrated to the United States the following year and two years later his father began designing the campus for the Cranbrook Educational Community in Bloomfield Hills, Michigan. This pioneering educational establishment would eventually include the Cranbrook Academy of Art, which opened in 1932 with Eliel Saarinen as its first director.

During this period, Eero studied sculpture at the Académie de la Grande Chaumière in Paris (1929–30) and then trained as an architect at Yale University in Connecticut (1931–34). After travelling through Europe on a scholarship, he returned to Cranbrook and began teaching there. In 1937, he began a fruitful collaboration with another staff member, Charles Eames, which would result in them jointly winning the 1940 *Organic Design in Home Furnishings* competition held at the Museum of Modern Art, New York. Their winning entry comprised a highly rational, modular system of case furniture, which included storage units and bench/bases that were put into production by the Red Lion Table Company.

It was, however, the duo's submission to the competition's seating section that would prove to be far more revolutionary – a group of sculptural chairs that used advanced technology to construct single-form, compound moulded plywood seat shells. These shapely, ergonomically refined forms not only testified to Saarinen's previous training as a sculptor but announced a completely new direction in furniture design: the concept of continuous contact and support. Although America's entry into the Second World War in December 1941 meant these designs were never put into volume production, they were among the most important furniture designs of the twentieth century and led directly to Saarinen's later highly successful furniture designs for Knoll International, for whom he began working in 1946. The resulting designs included: the spritely Grasshoppper chair (1946); the No. 70 Womb chair (1947–48), which was the result of Florence Knoll asking Saarinen to design a chair one could curl up in; the Saarinen Executive collection (1945–50) that set a new benchmark for office seating; and the groundbreaking Pedestal group of chairs and tables (1953–58). Hoping to counter the "ugly, confusing, unrestful world", Saarinen intended with the design of his Pedestal group to famously clean up "the slum of legs" that, as he saw it, so often marred interior spaces.

The pioneering Pedestal group was inspired by Eero Saarinen's quest for a total unity of design – materially, visually, structurally and functionally. Unfortunately, however, plastic moulding technology was not sufficiently advanced to allow this and instead he had to make do with sculpted fibreglass seat shells, and laminated or marble tabletops, joined to enamelled metal pedestal bases. Nevertheless, this collection with its famous Tulip chairs heralded a new sculptural confidence in design, as did various other projects Saarinen worked on, most notably his architectural masterwork, the TWA Terminal at John F. Kennedy Airport, New York (1956–62) and his soaring Gateway Arch in St Louis, Missouri (1947 – completed 1965).

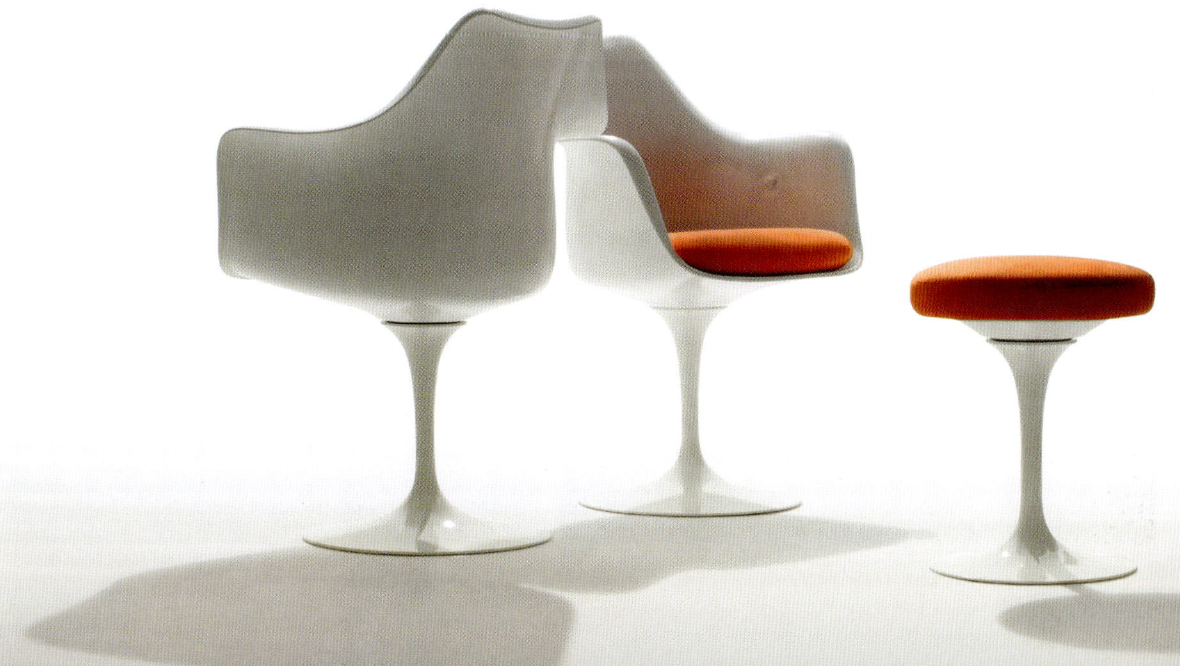

Stefan Sagmeister

Austrian/active USA, 1962–

One of today's most high-profile graphic designers, Stefan Sagmeister skilfully combines typography with imagery to create artwork that has a visual freshness and hooks viewers with its punchy element of surprise. He is especially well known for his numerous collaborations with AIGA (American Institute of Graphic Arts, the professional association for design) and for designing album covers for a host of musicians including The Rolling Stones, Talking Heads, Aerosmith, David Byrne, Lou Reed and Pat Matheny. Heading a small design consultancy based in New York, he creates identities, commercials, websites, apps, films, posters, magazines and books for both corporate clients and public institutions, while also making time for non-profit socially motivated work and experimental self-initiated projects.

Born in Austria, Sagmeister initially studied engineering before opting to train as a graphic designer at Die Angewandte Kunst (The University of Applied Arts) in Vienna. He subsequently won a Fulbright scholarship that enabled him to study at the Pratt Institute in

BELOW LEFT:
AIGA Detroit lecture poster
for AIGA Detroit, 1999 – art direction Stefan Sagmeister / photography Tom Schierlitz

BELOW RIGHT:
Play Hard poster
for Aïzone, 2013 – creative direction Stefan Sagmeister / art direction Jessica Walsh

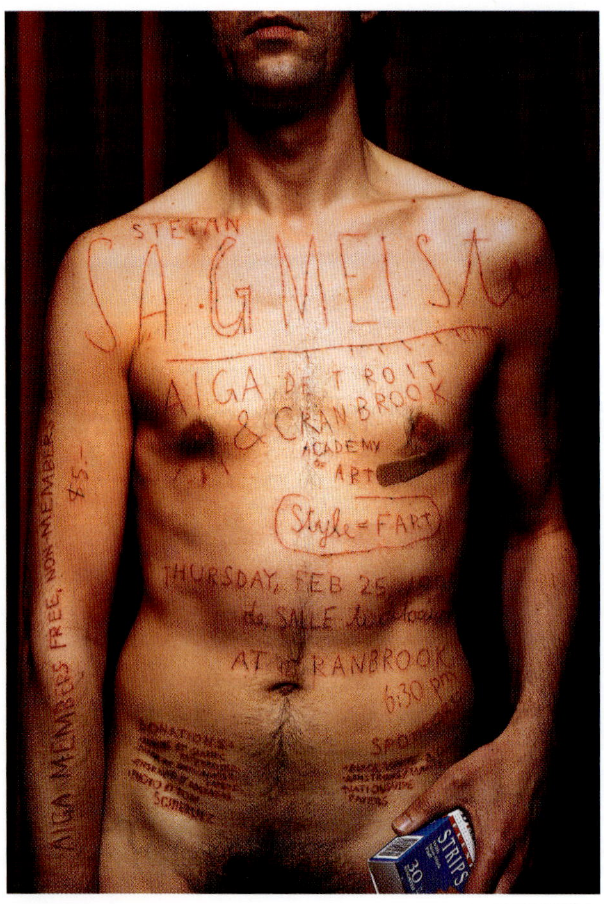

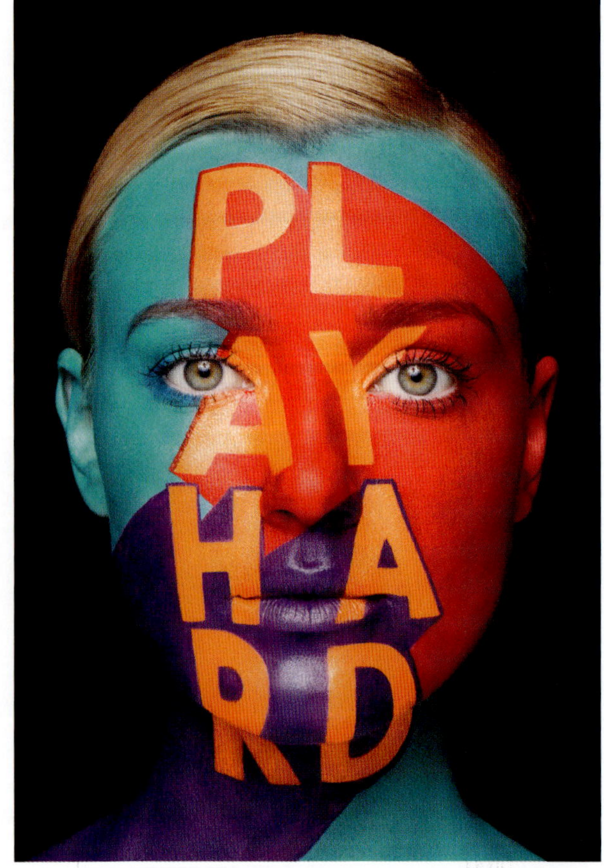

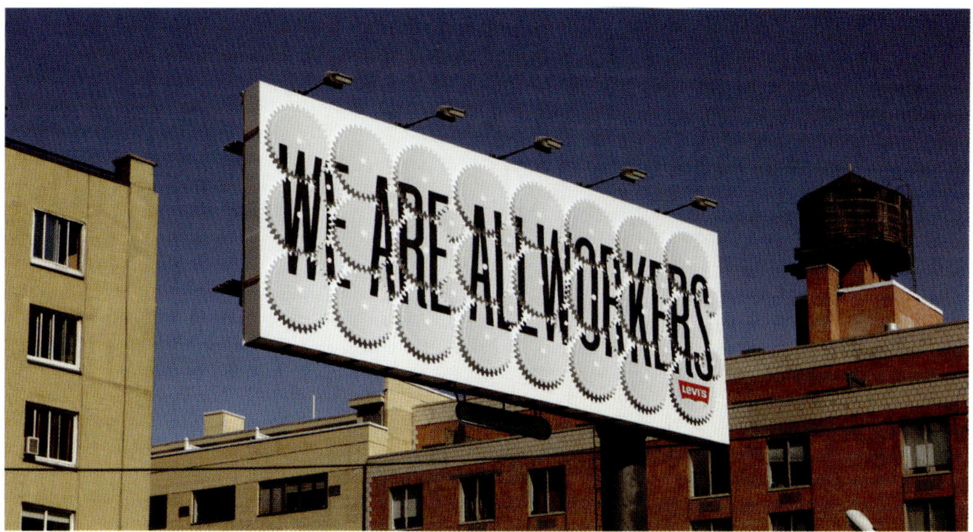

ABOVE:
We Are All Workers cog-wheel billboard
for Levi's, 2010 – art direction Stefan Sagmeister / design Jessica Walsh

New York. There, a girlfriend asked him to create some business cards for her that would cost no more than a dollar each and even at this early stage in his career Sagmeister came up with an ingenious attention-grabbing solution: he printed the cards on $1 bills.

After completing his studies, he returned briefly to Austria to do community work in a refugee centre as an alternative to national service, before landing a job in Hong Kong with the renowned advertising agency Leo Burnett in 1991. The following year, he courted controversy with his buttock-exposing Call for Entries poster designed for the 4As advertising awards in Hong Kong. He returned to New York in 1993 and briefly worked for the art director Tibor Kalman before founding his own studio, which initially worked mainly with music-industry clients. In 1994 he was nominated for a Grammy Award for his CD cover design of H.P. Zinker's *Mountains of Madness* album, which incorporated an optical illusion whereby the CD cover when in its red-tinted plastic case showed the musician with a benign expression, yet when removed his face appeared full of fury in a palette of disturbing red, white and green hues. In 1996, Sagmeister famously set a pair of phallic tongues on a rough hand-lettered background for an AIGA poster announcing its Fresh Dialogue talks. His use of hand-lettering intentionally countered the bland perfection of his graphics peers, who were increasingly relying on their Mac computers and digital fonts.

It was, however, the poster for his AIGA lecture held at Cranbrook Academy of Art in 1999 that brought him greatest notoriety: he had his assistant carve the poster's copy onto his naked torso with an X-Acto knife and then photographed the result – a self-harming (albeit via another person's hands) statement of self-sacrifice for art's sake that was as attention-grabbing as you can get. After taking a year's sabbatical in 2000, Sagmeister resumed working for clients and published *Sagmeister: Made You Look*, utilizing a transparent red slipcase which meant that when the paperback was removed the cover image optically transformed from a placid Alsatian dog into a rabid teeth-baring hound. In order to keep his ideas fresh, Sagmeister instituted a policy of regular sabbaticals – seven years of client work followed by one year of non-client experimentation – which seems to succeed as often the research undertaken in the "year off" goes on to inform his paid projects. Certainly, this was borne out by the Take It On subway posters for the School of Visual Arts (2013), where Sagmeister and his design partner Jessica Walsh both teach. Sagmeister's goal has been to "touch the viewer's heart" and this he manages to do with skilful consistency.

Richard Sapper

German/active Italy, 1932–2015

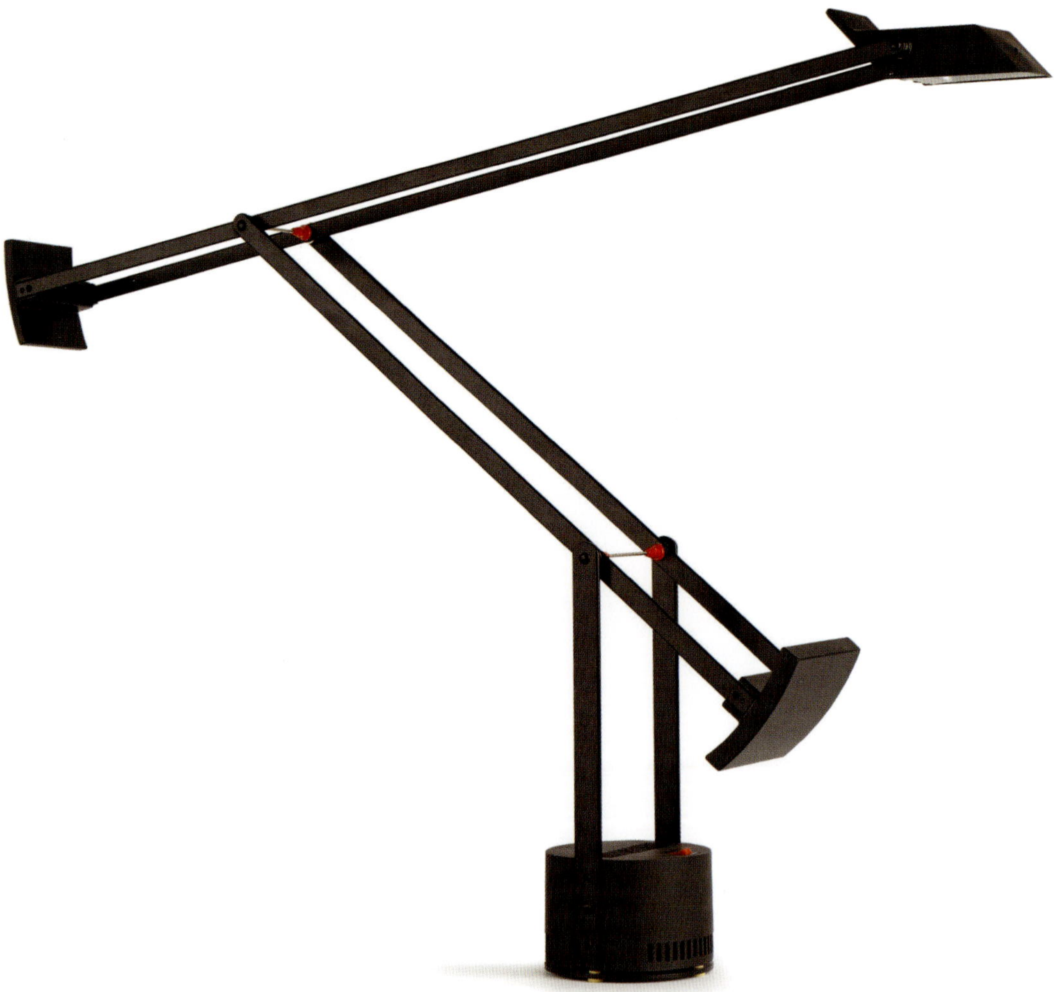

ABOVE:
Tizio task light
for Artemide, 1971–72

Over an illustrious career spanning nearly six decades, Richard Sapper designed a wide variety of products, ranging from furniture and lights to computers and kitchen appliances. His early studies of philosophy, anatomy and engineering made him an analytical problem-solver. Having obtained a business degree from the University of Munich, he also had an acute understanding of the economics of manufacturing.

After completing his studies, Sapper spent a year working in Daimler-Benz's styling department in Stuttgart before moving to Milan in 1957, where he worked in Gio Ponti's office for the next couple of years. In 1959, he joined the in-house design division of La Rinascente, a chain of Italian department stores, which at the time was renowned for its support of innovative design. That same year, Sapper began to work independently, designing clocks for Lorenz and radios for Telefunken – notably, his Static table clock (1960), which won a Compasso d'Oro award, and his elegantly leather-wrapped portable Match radio (1962). Both combined a high level of design logic with aesthetic sophistication. As Sapper would later remark, "I am totally against form simply for the sake of form itself."

Sapper had a fruitful creative partnership with the Italian architect-designer Marco Zanuso that produced four of the acknowledged masterpieces of Italian design: the TS 502 radio (1963) and Algol portable television set (1964) for Brionvega, the Lambda chair for Gavina (1959) and the Grillo telephone for Siemens Italtel (1966). It was, however, Sapper's Tizio light (1971–72) for Artemide that firmly established his reputation as an independent designer. This adjustable task lamp, incorporating a transformer and miniature bulb, used the design's structure to conduct the current and thereby dispense with excess wires.

In 1972, Sapper worked with Zanuso on a prototypical Mobile Housing Unit intended to be deployed in emergency situations, which was shown at the *Italy: The New Domestic Landscape* exhibition held at the Museum of Modern Art, New York. Tellingly, it was probably the most grounded item in the entire show. That same year, Sapper also formed a transportation systems study group with Gae Aulenti with a view to helping reduce inner-city congestion: the resulting research formed the basis of a display at the *XVI Milan Triennale* in 1979. From 1980, Sapper served as chief industrial design consultant to IBM, designing the ThinkPad laptop computer in 1992–95 as well as a host of other products for the company. He was one of many designers approached by Steve Jobs to design products for Apple, but with an exclusivity contract in place with IBM, he declined the offer.

One of Richard Sapper's most notable designs, the 9091 kettle (1982) for Alessi, is testament to his ability to create objects that go beyond the conventional idea of function. As Alberto Alessi recalls, Sapper did not just want to design a "beautiful kettle" but one that was "multi-sensorial" – for the ears as well as for the eyes. By chance, one of his sisters came across a craftsman located in the Black Forest who specialized in creating pipes for tuning musical instruments, known in Italian as *coristi*. Sapper adapted two of them for the whistle of his new design, tuned to the notes C and E, so that when the water boiled the kettle "sang" – a characteristically simple yet charming solution that reflects Sapper's unerringly pragmatic and engaging approach to design.

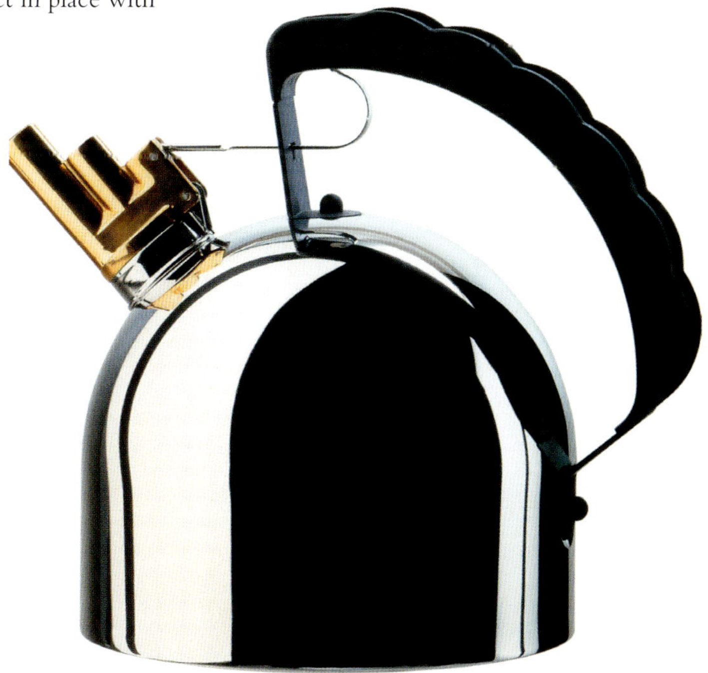

BELOW:
9091 kettle
for Alessi, 1982

Oki Sato / nendo

Japanese, 1977–

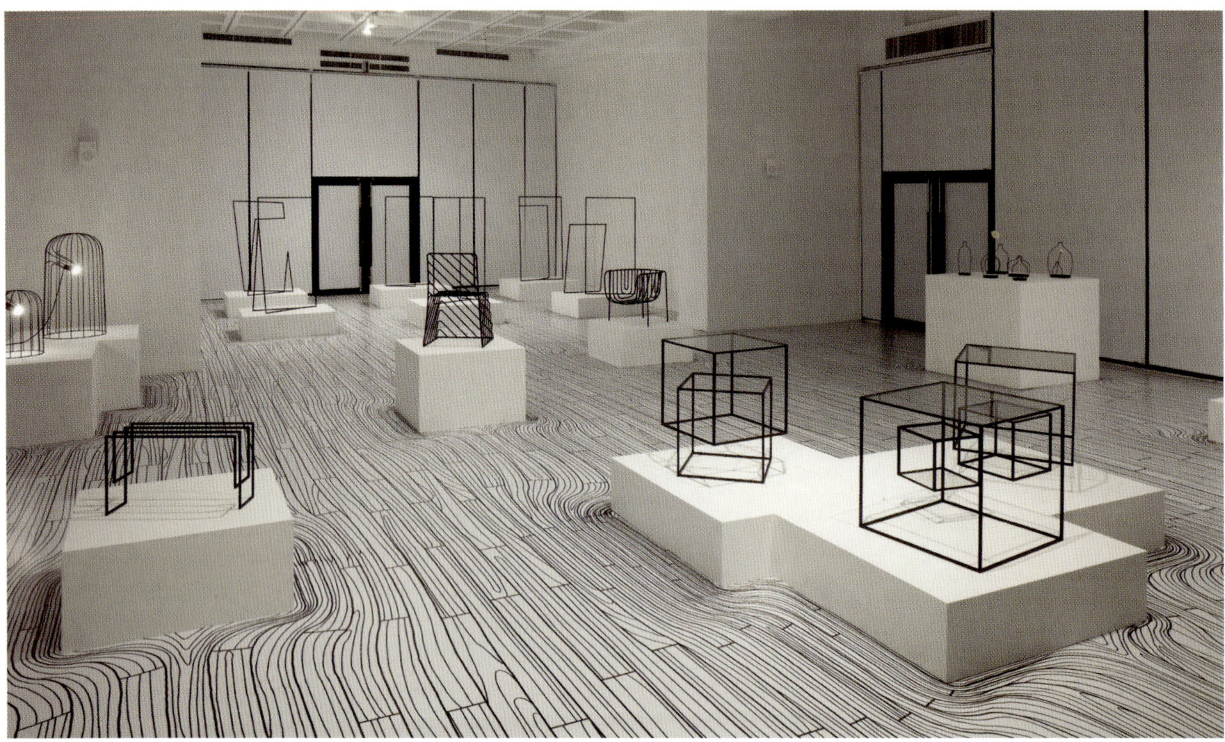

ABOVE:
Thin Black Lines exhibition held by Phillips de Pury at the Saatchi Gallery, London, 2010

OPPOSITE TOP:
Soft tables for Glas Italia, 2015

OPPOSITE BOTTOM:
Cabbage chair designed for XXIst Century Man exhibition curated by Issey Miyake, 2008

Oki Sato, who works under the name of his design studio, nendo, is one of the leading and most prolific Japanese designers active today. His productivity rate is highly impressive: at any one time he claims to be working on upwards of 400 design concepts, noting, "The more ideas I think of, the more ideas I come up with. It is like breathing or eating." Often, these ideas are turned into realities; for instance during a twelve-month period, spanning 2014 and 2015, Sato and his team of 30 designers and interns created over 100 products for nineteen different brands.

Sato's success lies in his left-field approach to design, whereby he follows the universally accepted goal of good design, a harmonious balance between form and function, but injects it with a "narrative" element. As he observes, "It's not the shape or colour, it's about what's behind the object," and certainly his designs, though possessing the harmony and simplicity generally associated with Japanese design, have a touch of playful irreverence too.

Born in Toronto, Sato was raised in Tokyo, where he later obtained a master's degree in architecture at Waseda University in 2002. The same year, he established his own Tokyo-based design office, which he christened *nendo*, the Japanese word for "modelling clay". The following year, nendo exhibited for the first time at the Milan Furniture Fair, participating in the *SaloneSatellite* event with its Streeterior range, which employed found street materials,

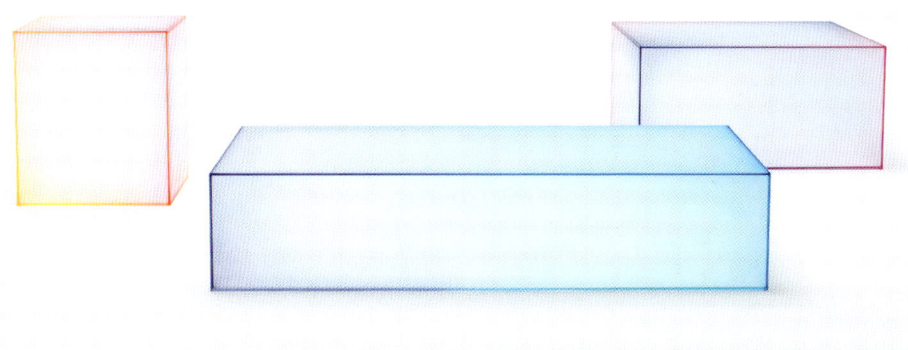

including manhole covers, and re-imagined them into furniture for the home.

In 2004, Sato again exhibited at the Milan event, and this time he was talent-spotted by Giulio Cappellini, whose furniture-manufacturing company began collaborating with him the following year. The first product resulting from this partnership was the Yuki screen (2006), which was innovatively made up of snowflake-shaped ABS plastic modules that interconnected. Other similarly inventive designs created by nendo for Cappellini have been the eye-catching Ribbon stool (2007), made from strips of laser-cut metal, lacquered and bent into the required shape, and the Thin Black Table (2010–11), which gives an Escher-like optical illusion of two transparent cubes intersecting each other. This latter design was originally created as at part of the *Thin Black Lines* exhibition held by Phillips de Pury at London's Saatchi Gallery in 2010.

It was, however, Sato's Diamond chair (2008), created for an installation at the Milan Furniture Fair and sponsored by Lexus, and his Cabbage chair (2008) designed for the *XXIst Century Man* exhibition in Tokyo curated by Issey Miyake that fully revealed his extraordinary ability to create poetic objects using unusual processes – the former being essentially grown from polyamide particles using what was then cutting-edge rapid prototyping technology, and the latter ingeniously constructed from rolled and precisely cut bales of waste-paper that is a by-product of Miyake's famous fabric-pleating process. In 2015, nendo was named Maison&Objet's Designer of the Year and also staged a solo show at the Museo della Permanente during the Milan Furniture Fair, reflecting just how respected Sato's inventive work is among the international design community.

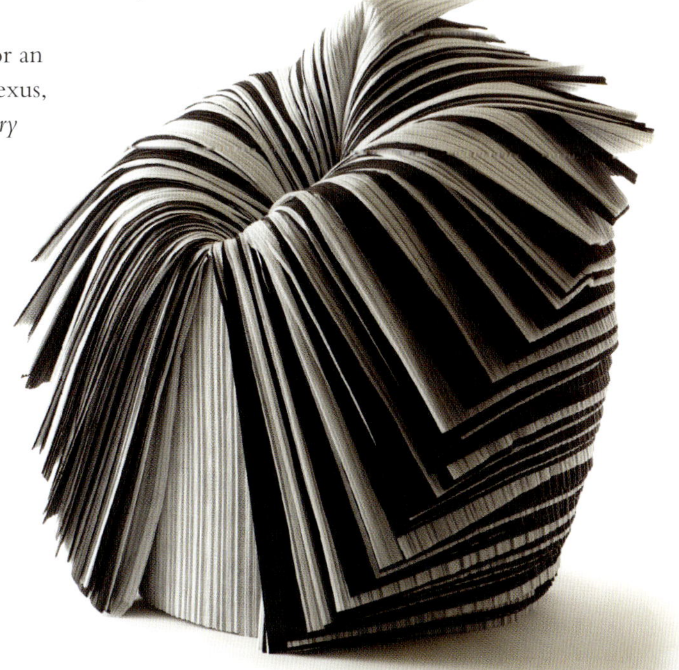

Peter Saville

British, 1955–

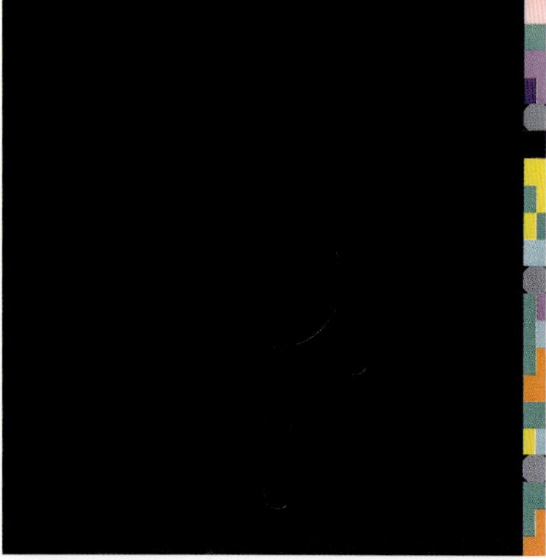

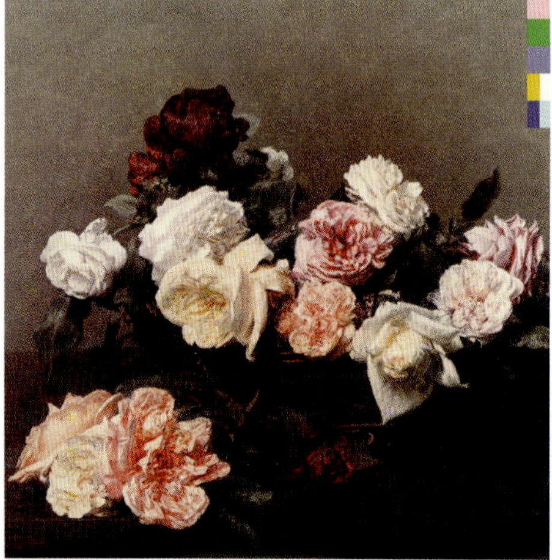

TOP:
Sleeve design for New Order's "Blue Monday" single
for Factory Records, 1983

ABOVE:
Sleeve design for New Order's *Power, Corruption & Lies* album
for Factory Records, 1983

Peter Saville is a gifted creative who continually blurs the boundaries of graphic design and fine art. During the late 1970s, he almost single-handedly put the art back into commercial art, and even to this day he is hugely respectful of what he calls the canon of Modernism, for it is from there he drew inspiration for his own groundbreaking work.

Saville studied graphic design at Manchester Polytechnic, graduating in 1978. The following year he co-founded the indie record label Factory Records and began working as its art director, creating artwork for the label's various bands including Joy Division and Orchestral Manoeuvres in the Dark (OMD). Instead of going the traditional record-sleeve route, Saville devised high-concept sleeves that were influenced by his self-initiated education into art and design history. This appreciation and understanding of the historical avant-garde allowed him successfully to translate the dynamic visual language of the Modern Movement – from Italian Futurism to the Bauhaus – into a thoroughly contemporary graphic language of his own, which perfectly captured the new zeitgeist that was emerging in the music scene. For instance, Saville's sleeve design for New Order's "Blue Monday" single (1983) did not feature the name of the band, nor the title of the single, but instead was designed to look like a floppy disk and featured an expensive-to-produce die-cut that revealed a silver inner sleeve. In fact, the band's name and title were actually coded as a series of coloured blocks – and the key to deciphering the code was printed on the back of the band's album *Power, Corruption & Lies* (1983), also designed by Saville, which itself features a detail of a painting in the National Gallery, London: Henri Fantin-Latour's *A Basket of Roses*. This remarkable sleeve design was later chosen by Royal Mail to feature on a set of "Classic Album Cover" postage stamps issued in 2010 – such is its iconic status.

In 1983, Saville established his own studio, Peter Saville Associates, in association with Brett Wickens. While he continued designing mainly for the music industry, he widened his remit by creating a new graphic identity for the Whitechapel Art Gallery (1985) and designing catalogues for the fashion label Yohji Yamamoto. In 1989, he designed the *Technique* album cover for New Order, which marked a new stylistic departure in his work. As he recalled, "I'd moved on from being interested in Eighties consumer products and had begun going to Pimlico Road to look at antique shops.

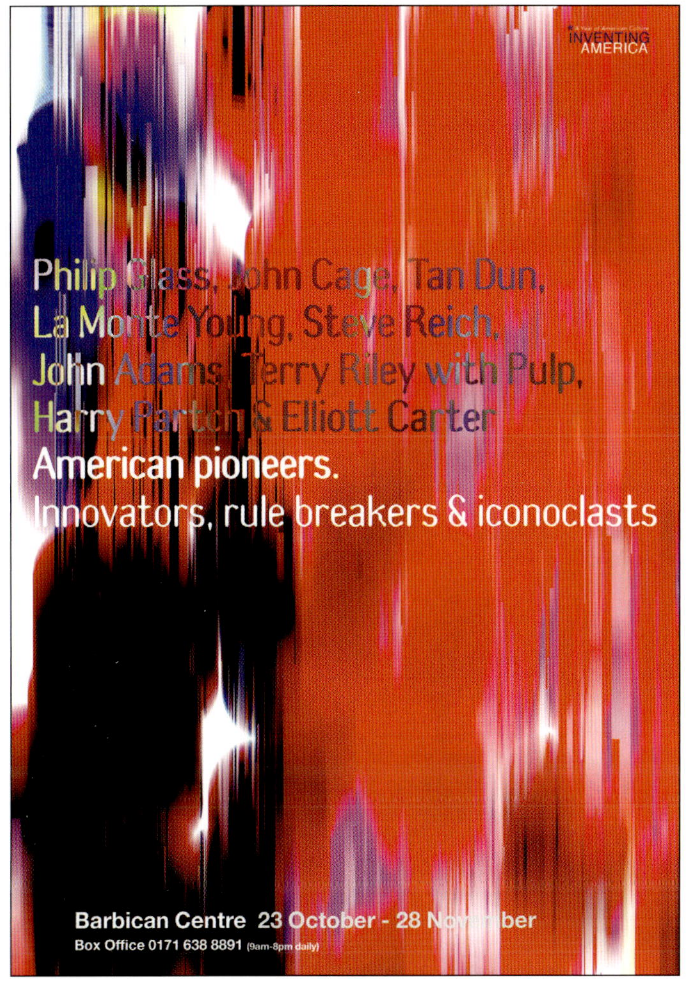

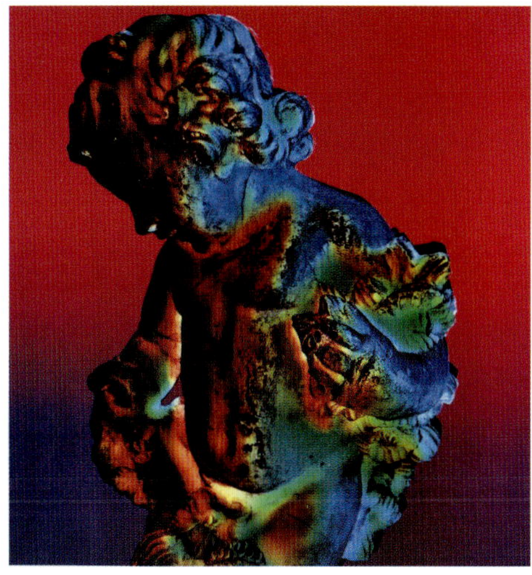

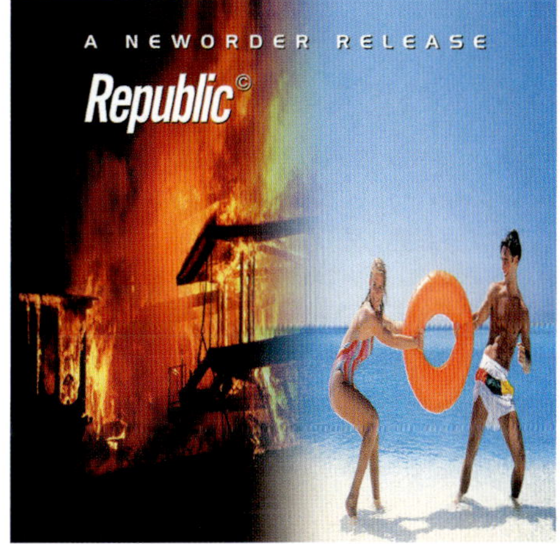

Which was where I saw the cherub statue.... It was a garden ornament and we rented it for the shoot. It's a very bacchanalian image, which fitted the moment just before the last financial crash and the new drug-fuelled hedonism involved in the music scene. It's also my first ironic work: all the previous sleeves were in some way idealistic and utopian."

From this point onwards, digital manipulation of imagery became an increasing feature of Saville's oeuvre, eventually evolving into a technique whereby his earlier artworks were digitally shredded and then reconstituted into beautiful abstract colour fields, such as the one used for his American Pioneers poster (1998) derived from the stars and stripes of the US flag, designed for the Barbican. In 2004, Saville was commissioned to create a new visual identity for the City of Manchester, and thanks to his creative direction the city now has a coherent civic look that has helped its cultural regeneration. A harsh critic of how graphic designers have pillaged the Modernist canon for flagrantly commercial ends, Saville now prefers to spend his time working as an artist, although he does art direct campaigns for select clients.

ABOVE LEFT
Poster for *American Pioneers* festival
for the Barbican Centre, 1998 – an early exercise in reconstituted digital shredding

ABOVE TOP RIGHT:
Sleeve design for New Order's *Technique* album
for Factory Records, 1989

ABOVE BOTTOM RIGHT:
Sleeve design for New Order's *Republic* album
for London Records, 1993

Margarete Schütte-Lihotzky

Austrian, 1897–2000

The Austrian-born architect Margarete Schütte-Lihotzky is famous for designing the Frankfurt Kitchen, a rational design exercise in household time-and-motion efficiency that was immensely influential in the development of the modern built-in kitchen. From a liberally minded bourgeois family, "Grete" was the first female student to train at the Kunstgewerbeschule (School of Arts and Crafts, later Die Angewandte, University of Applied Arts) in Vienna. A recommendation letter from the artist Gustav Klimt helped win her the place, in which she studied architecture under Oskar Strnad. She later recalled, "In 1916 no one would have conceived of a woman being commissioned to build a house – not even myself." Significantly, Strnad was a pioneer of social housing and planned living spaces and it was thanks to him that Schütte-Lihotzky, while still a student, came to realize that a functionalist user-centred approach to the design of buildings would become increasingly important in the years to come.

After graduating, she worked with Adolf Loos on various housing projects for the accommodation of post-war refugees. In 1926, the German architect and city planner Ernst May was so impressed with her work in this field that he invited her to join his team of architects working on the Neues Frankfurt (New Frankfurt) social housing project (1925–31). Also included in May's "brigade" were, among others, Walter Gropius, Adolf Meyer, Bruno Taut and Mart Stam. Initiated by the city's mayor, Ludwig Landmann, the project was intended to provide ten thousand new and affordable apartments in an effort to combat the city's dire housing shortage. When built, each one was equipped with a standardized kitchen that was highly functional and boasted various labour-saving features, such as a fold-down ironing board, a swivelling stool and labelled aluminium storage bins with handles that allowed their contents to be poured. The Frankfurt Kitchen, as it became known, was ingeniously designed and very compact, consolidating everything a housewife needed for her daily chores into a space measuring just 1.9m (6ft 3in) by 3.4m (11ft 2in).

The kitchen's design reflected the widespread concern for health and hygiene during the inter-war period and was inspired by earlier time-and-motion studies undertaken by the American mechanical engineer Frederick Winslow Taylor, who in 1911 had published his seminal book on the subject, entitled *The Principles of Scientific Management*. Schütte-Lihotzky's design was also influenced by the

BELOW
The original Frankfurt Kitchen
1926

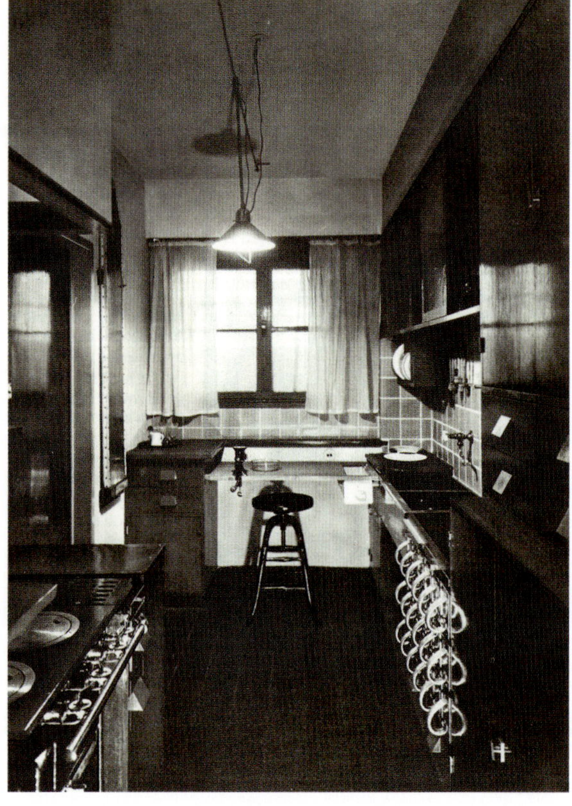

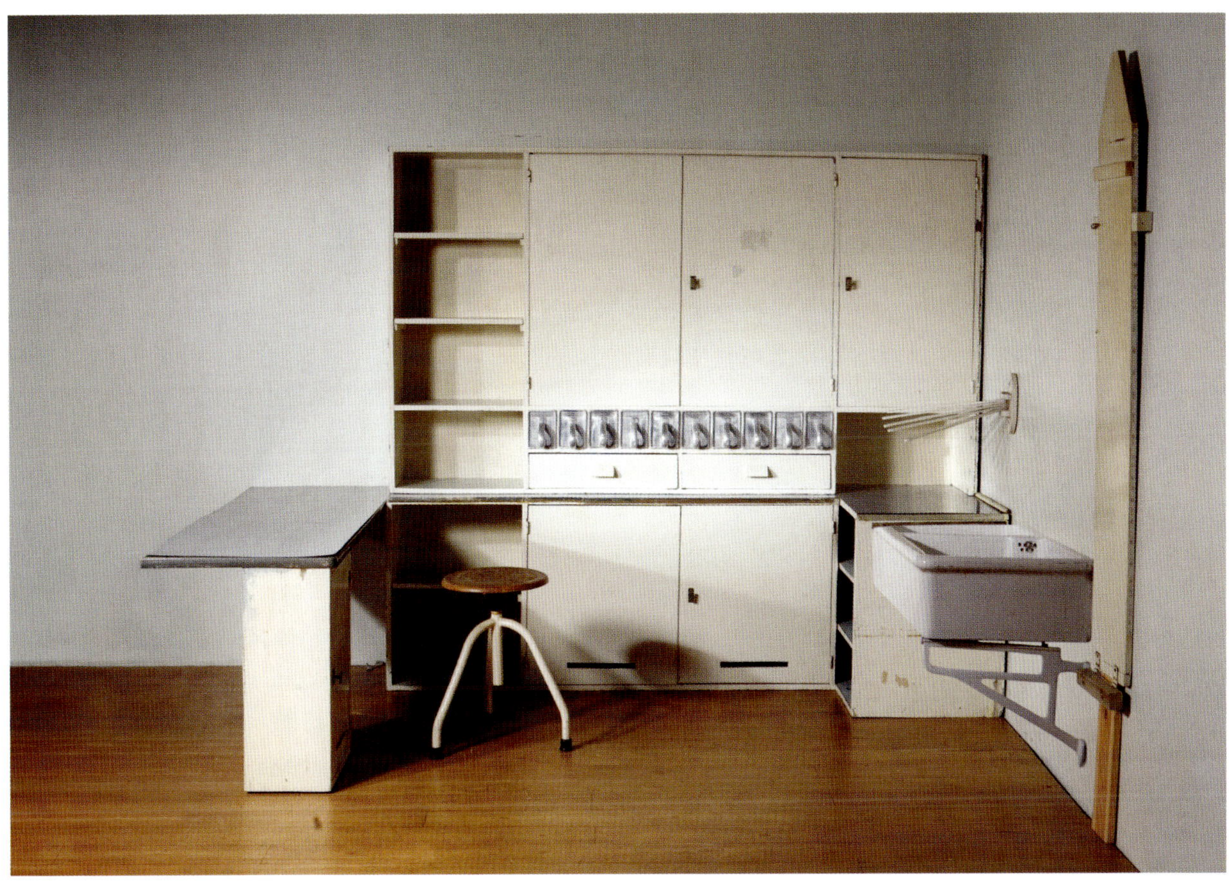

writings of the American journalist Christine Frederick, whose book *New Housekeeping: Efficiency Studies in Home Management* was translated into German in 1922. But over and above this, she also conducted research of her own using a railway dining car as a blueprint for her mass-produced and prefabricated "housewife's laboratory".

In 1930, Schütte-Lihotzky moved to the Soviet Union as part of a team of seventeen architects headed by Ernst May, to work on a far larger social housing project that included the planning of various new industrial towns, which were to be part of Stalin's Great Utopia. When the purges began, however, it became too difficult to live and work in the Soviet Union, so Schütte-Lihotzky moved to London, then Paris, and eventually Istanbul. A committed Communist and anti-Fascist during the war, she returned to Austria in 1940 to work with the anti-Nazi resistance movement; she was caught by the Gestapo and sentenced to fifteen years in a labour camp, but was liberated in 1945. After the war, she continued working as an architect, albeit mainly on private residential commissions, and acted as a planning consultant in China, Cuba and the German Democratic Republic. It was the Frankfurt Kitchen, however, that would be her greatest design legacy. Even so, in an interview when she was around 100 years of age, she declared, "If I had known that everyone would keep talking about nothing else, I would never have built that damned kitchen!"

ABOVE
Elements from a Frankfurt Kitchen
as used in the Professor's Lodgings, Niederrad Hospital, Frankfurt, *c.*1926

Smart Design

American, founded 1980

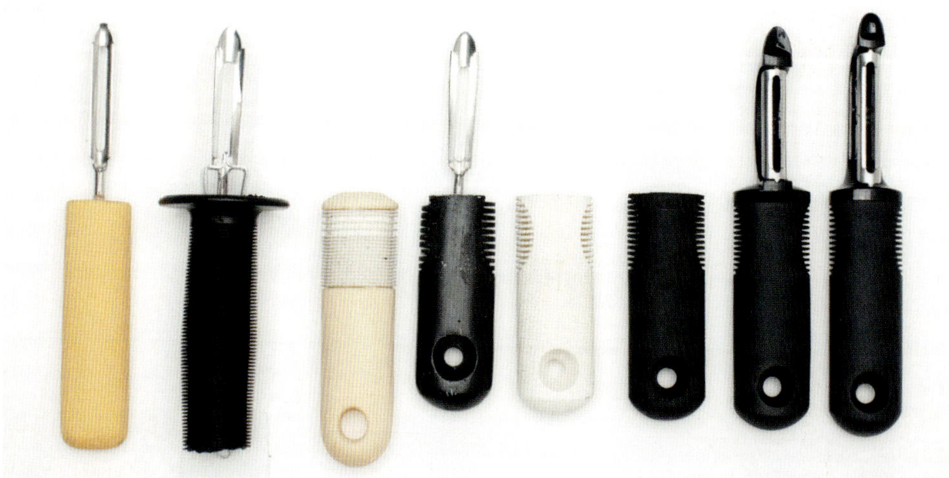

ABOVE:
Photograph charting development of Good Grips vegetable peeler
for OXO, 1990

Smart Design is a leading creative innovations consultancy, which has been at the forefront of inclusive human-centric design for over thirty-five years. During that time, its design team has been engaged as much with developing the innovative ideas behind products as with creating the actual products. As its founder and president Davin Stowel notes, "We interact with design on two levels: the physical and the emotional. We have a word for the physical part: ergonomics – what feels good to you. I call the emotional level 'psychonomics' – what makes you feel good. The baseline of good design is a perfect balance of the two." It is this research-led understanding of how people react to design that has made what Smart Design creates so compelling. There is, however, also a strong ethical dimension to Smart Design's work, for as a team they are interested in developing designs "with meaning" that will have a beneficial impact on people's lives. Fundamentally, the company believes that design is of paramount importance because if it is intelligently conceived then it is has the potential to bring about real improvements.

Smart Design's co-founders Davin Stowell and Dan Formosa both studied industrial design at Syracuse University in New York State. However, while still a design student, Formosa realized that design is ultimately all about people and therefore when it comes to designing one needs to put "people before products and technology". Armed with this insight, he went on to obtain a doctorate in ergonomics and biomechanics from New York University. After their respective studies, Stowell worked in Corning Glass's design department, gaining valuable hands-on experience, while Formosa worked in Eliot Noyes's design office as part of the team tasked with developing IBM's first personal computer. After founding Smart Design in New York City in 1980, their first commission was to design sunglasses for Corning Glass. For this project they undertook ergonomic studies to ensure correct physical fit, along with cognitive-psychology research into what people thought felt best. The result was that the sunglasses designed by Smart Design had double the comfortable-fit rate of those made by Corning's competitors.

During the 1980s Smart Design continued its mission of creating design that was about "people not objects", but it was not until 1990 that the consultancy really had its first big break, when OXO, a new start-up company founded by Sam Farber, commissioned them to create a range of kitchen tools that could be used by people suffering from arthritis. Rather than designing for disability, however, the brief was to instead design for inclusivity – creating products that could be used by a wide range of users with varying degrees of physical ability. The Good Grips range, featuring ergonomically contoured elastomer handles, was eventually introduced in 1989 and was subsequently extended by Smart Design to comprise a vast array of products.

Thanks to this one project, Smart Design became the go-to consultancy for clients wanting to create products or services with a social dimension – and their projects have since ranged from devising a SmartGauge with EcoGuide for Ford that allows drivers easily to see how the way they drive affects their fuel consumption, to award-winning, research-led sports bras for Under Armour, to the Nudge concept app to help people at risk of Type II diabetes to make healthier food choices. The underlying humanist ethos of all these projects is born of a baby-boomer 1960s spirit that both Stowel and Formosa amply possess, and it is their optimistic belief in the power of design to change the lives of real people for the better that ultimately makes Smart Design so smart.

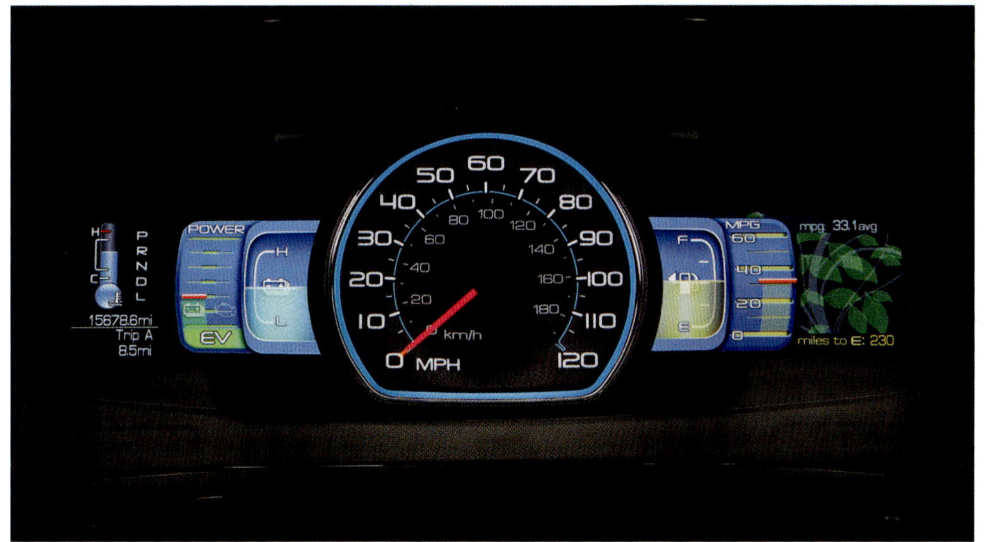

ABOVE:
Good Grips pastry brushes
for OXO, 2006

LEFT:
SmartGauge with EcoGuide
for Ford, 2008

Sony

Japanese, founded 1946

In the chaos of a Tokyo in ruins after the Second World War, Masaru Ibuka and Akio Morita, two scientists who had met in the Japanese navy's research laboratories, opened a small workshop in a burnt-out department store and struggled to find a way to survive by making products that used black-market components. One unsuccessful project was a primitive rice boiler. They adapted censored wartime radios that had been limited to Japanese stations so that they could receive international stations, and in 1946 founded Tokyo Tsushin Kogyo (Tokyo Telecommunications Engineering) corporation with a view to developing more advanced telecommunications equipment. It would eventually become the Sony Corporation, which for two decades was the world's most innovative, design-led consumer electronics company.

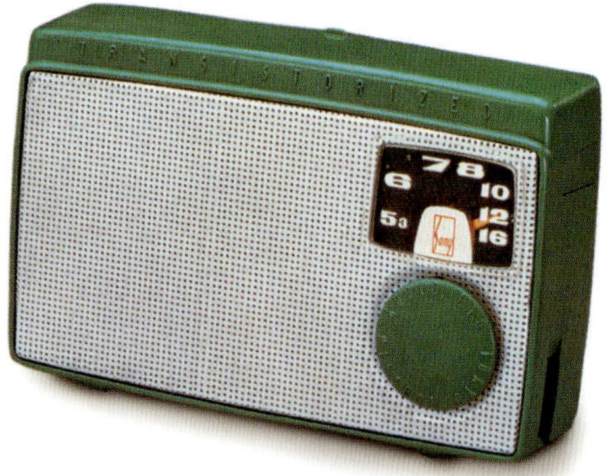

The company launched the first Japanese reel-to-reel tape recorder in 1950, based on US technology. Known as the G Type, it was intended for government use, hence its name. The firm's prospects were transformed four years later when it signed a licensing agreement with Bell Laboratories, allowing it to manufacture designs incorporating the American company's innovative transistor technology. At this stage transistors had limited use because of their low frequencies, but Ibuka realized that if their range could be increased then this new technology would offer enormous potential in the field of radio manufacturing. Within a year, his company introduced the first Japanese transistor radio – the futuristic-looking TR-55 (1955), which was remarkably compact, measuring only 8.9 x 14 x 3.8cm (3½ x 5½ x 1½in). This trend towards miniaturization was even more emphatic with the follow-on design of the TR-63 radio (1957), which was the first-ever pocket-sized radio. This diminutive design was also the first Sony-branded product to be imported into the US and became an instant success there despite its premium price.

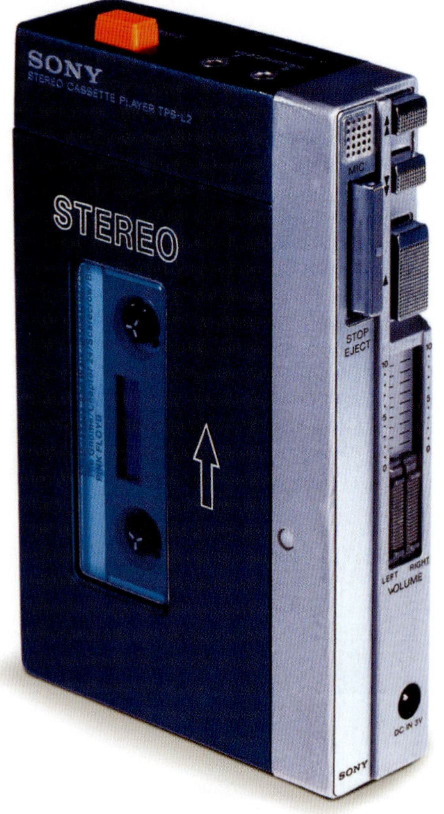

From then on, the company never looked back, and over subsequent decades pioneered numerous firsts in the consumer electronics industry, including the world's first portable television, the TV8-301 in 1960. Sony's impressive track record of miniaturizing technology led eventually to the introduction of the first Walkman in 1979, which would over the coming years be evolved and refined into numerous models. Sony also made waves in the gaming world with its launch of the PlayStation PS1 console in 1994, which

OPPOSITE TOP:
TR-55 Transistor radio
1955

OPPOSITE BOTTOM:
First Sony Walkman (TPS-L2)
launched in 1979

RIGHT:
PlayStation 4 (PS4) video games console
introduced 2013

went on to sell over 100 million units. The company has also been highly involved in the development of entertainment robots since the turn of the twenty-first century, with its cute AIBO robotic dog being launched to much fanfare in 1999.

Sony was one of the upstart companies that transformed the world's view of Japan in the 1960s as the source of cheap generic products. In its heyday as an innovator, it was seen as the Apple of its time. As Japan became a high-wage economy and shifted its production lines to cheaper Asian economies, Sony gradually turned into an entertainment-based company, increasingly active in the realms of music, games and cinema, thereby shedding its reliance on hardware products.

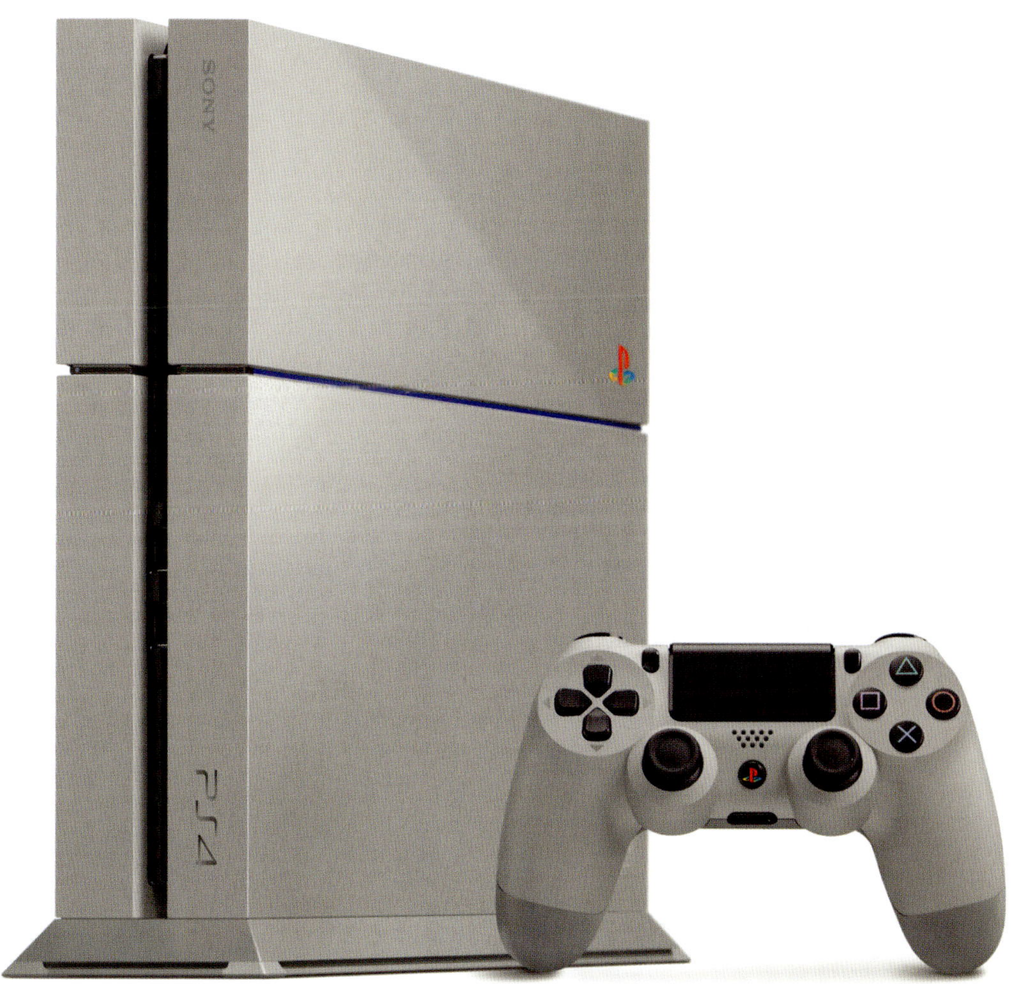

Ettore Sottsass Jr

Italian, 1917–2007

For fifty years Ettore Sottsass was a dominant figure in Italian design, his career having spanned over seven decades. Although best known as the founding impresario of the Memphis design collective in the 1980s, he was also an accomplished industrial designer who had previously created numerous landmark electronic products for Olivetti. He also designed an impressive number of sculptural ceramics and glassware pieces that employed traditional craft techniques to create thoroughly avant-garde forms.

Sottsass was born in Innsbruck, Austria to Italian-Austrian parents. His father, also called Ettore, was a prominent architect associated with the Italian Rationalist Movement. According to family legend, his father had so wanted him to follow in his professional footsteps that he put a pencil into Ettore's hands while he was still a baby. When Ettore was twelve, the Sottsass family moved to Turin for his father's work and also so he could obtain a better education than in the mountains. He would later study at the Politecnico di Torino (Turin Polytechnic), which at the time had the best architecture faculty in Italy, graduating in 1939. Soon afterwards he was conscripted into the Italian army and sent to Yugoslavia (then occupied by Italian and German forces) until in 1943 Italy signed an armistice with the Allies, and Sottsass was interned by the Germans.

After the war he exhibited his art in Milan and resumed his career as an architect, initially working in his father's office on post-war housing projects. In 1946, he moved to Milan to design a craft exhibition at the Triennale building. The same year he founded a design studio and began contributing articles to *Domus* magazine. Over the next decade or so, Sottsass built his reputation as a progressive artist-architect-designer by not only designing innovative furniture,

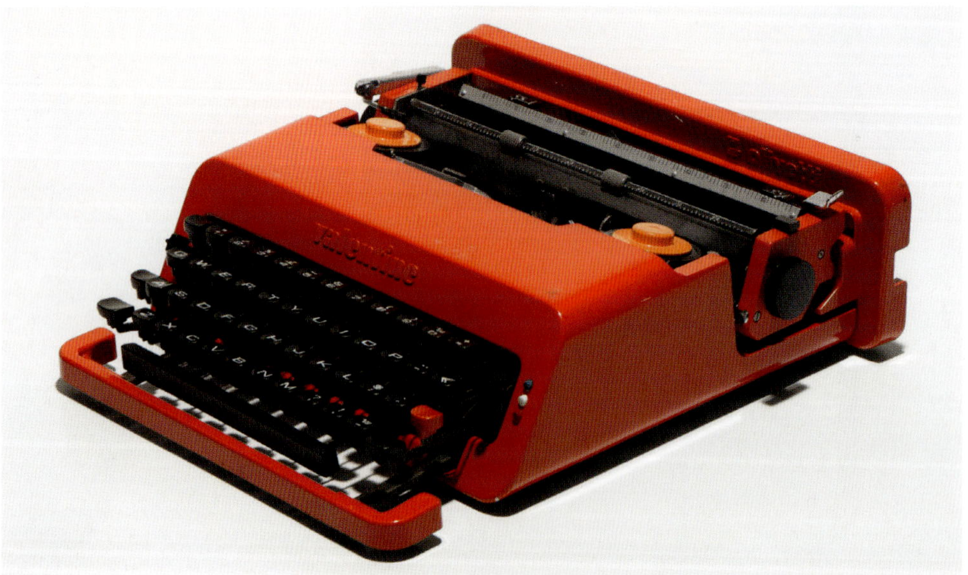

LEFT:
Valentine typewriter
for Olivetti, 1968–69 – co-designed with Perry King

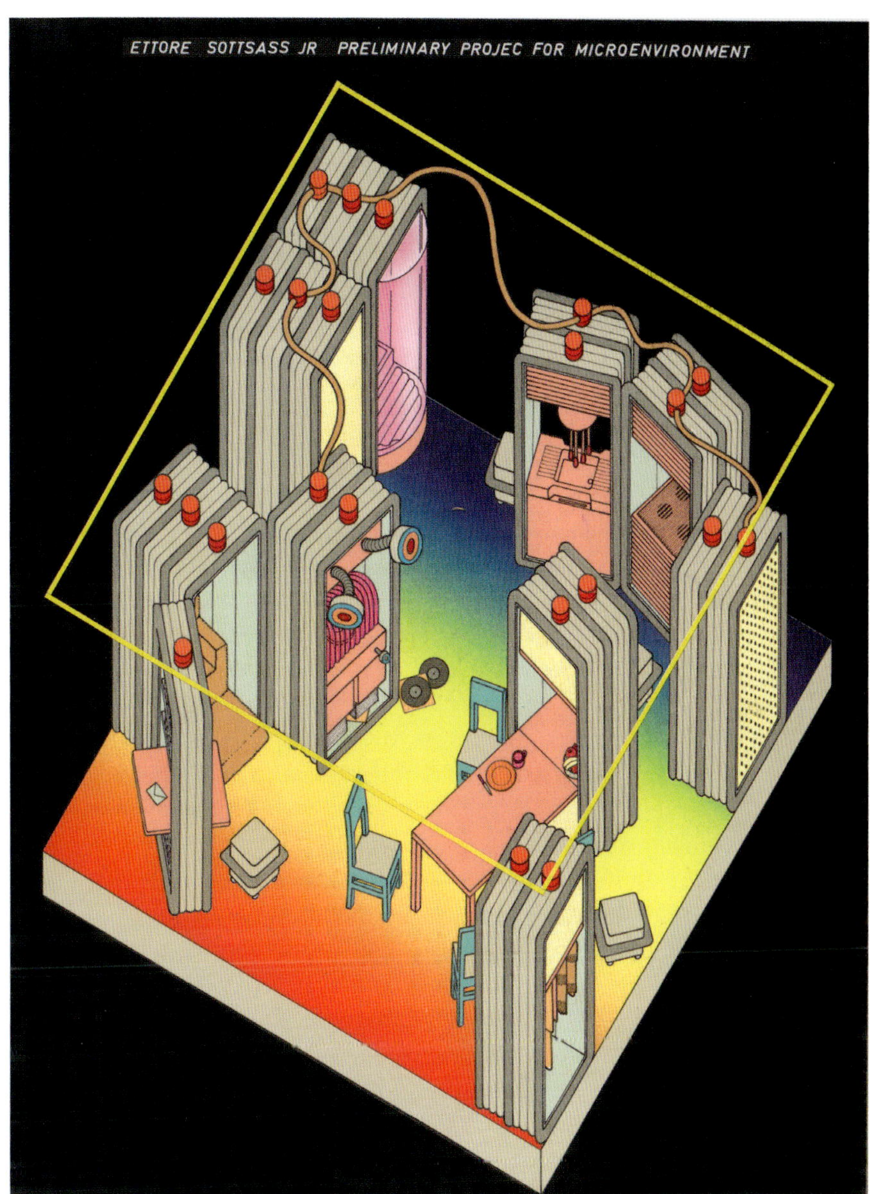

ABOVE:
Collage of Preliminary Project for Microenvironment
*c.*1971 – designed for the landmark *Italy: The New Domestic Landscape* exhibition held at the Museum of Modern Art, New York, 1972

lighting and interiors but also producing abstract sculptures – all featured on the pages of *Domus*.

In 1956, Sottsass travelled to the United States, and while there spent a month working in the design offices of George Nelson Associates. This trip was a transformative experience, with Sottsass later recalling that it had been "like Metropolis: everyone rushing around, and no-one caring a hoot" and with America's Pop Art and Beat culture making a lasting impression on him. On his return to Italy, he became a creative consultant to the pioneering furniture and lighting manufacturer Poltronova, and later was appointed design consultant to Olivetti's newly established electronics division. Working alongside Roberto Olivetti (grandson of the company's founder) and the talented engineer Mario Tchou, Sottsass devised a series of landmark products for Olivetti that were noted as much for their technical innovation as for their groundbreaking aesthetics, such as the angular-styled Tekne 3 electric typewriter (1958) and the Elea 9003 main-frame computer (1959) that won a Compasso d'Oro award in 1959.

BELOW:
Prototype of Mandarin Armchair
for Knoll, *c.*1986

OPPOSITE:
Carlton bookcase/room divider
for Memphis, 1981

During the 1960s, Sottsass took various trips to America and India and began exploring the Anti-Design tendencies of Pop through the creation of ceramics influenced by Eastern mysticism and the design of furniture for Poltronova that incorporated plastic laminates made by Abet Laminati. Significantly, these first explorations into "counter-design" can be seen to be one of the origins from which Italian Post-Modernism would evolve. His most famous design from this period was the Valentine typewriter (1968–69) for Olivetti, co-designed with Perry King. In bright red plastic, the Valentine possessed a distinctive, toy-like quality that spoke directly to a younger audience, and was a quintessential Pop design that celebrated the Sixties plastics age.

Ever in tune with the design zeitgeist, Sottsass became actively involved in the Italian Radical Design movement during the 1970s, first as a founding member of Global Tools (founded in 1973), and then later as an associate of Studio Alchimia (founded 1976). But Studio Alchimia's pessimistic premise that Modern design had ultimately reached a dead end was not in tune with Sottsass's zest for creativity. His founding of Memphis in 1980 was ultimately an attempt to find a new creative approach to design that was less intellectualized and rhetorically laden. Brightly coloured with bold shapes formed out of patterned plastic laminates, Sottsass's designs for Memphis, such as the Carlton bookcase/room divider (1981) and the Casablanca cabinet (1981), represented what was then termed "New Wave" design. Having an attention-grabbing presence, such designs intentionally countered perceived notions of good design, and thereby good taste. Ultimately they were totems of Post-Modernism, and Sottsass more than any other designer was the foremost protagonist moving towards this new international style in design and architecture. He was to later note, "It is important to realize that whatever we do or design has iconographic references, it comes from somewhere; any form is always metaphorical, never totally metaphysical; it is never a 'destiny' but always a fact with some kind of historical reference."

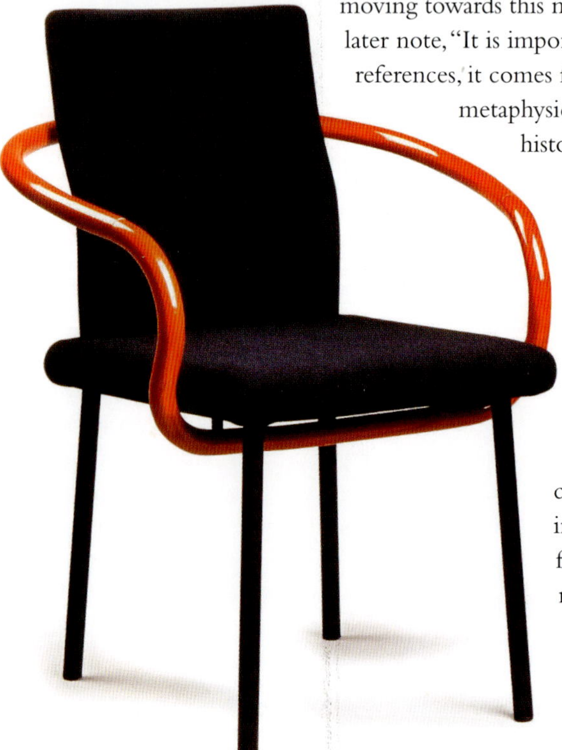

In 1980, he also founded the consultancy Sottsass Associati, which designed numerous products for various manufacturers, from the Enorme telephone for Brondi Telefonia (1986) to the Mandarin chair for Knoll (1986). The office, however, mainly worked on architectural projects, most notably stores and showrooms for Esprit and Malpensa Airport in Milan (2000). A prodigiously talented design iconoclast who never grew tired of courting controversy, Sottsass remained a revered and active member of the international design community well into his eighties, while his influential designs irreverently shook up the design world and remained influential for what they stood for – that design is not about function, but rather about creating emotional engagement.

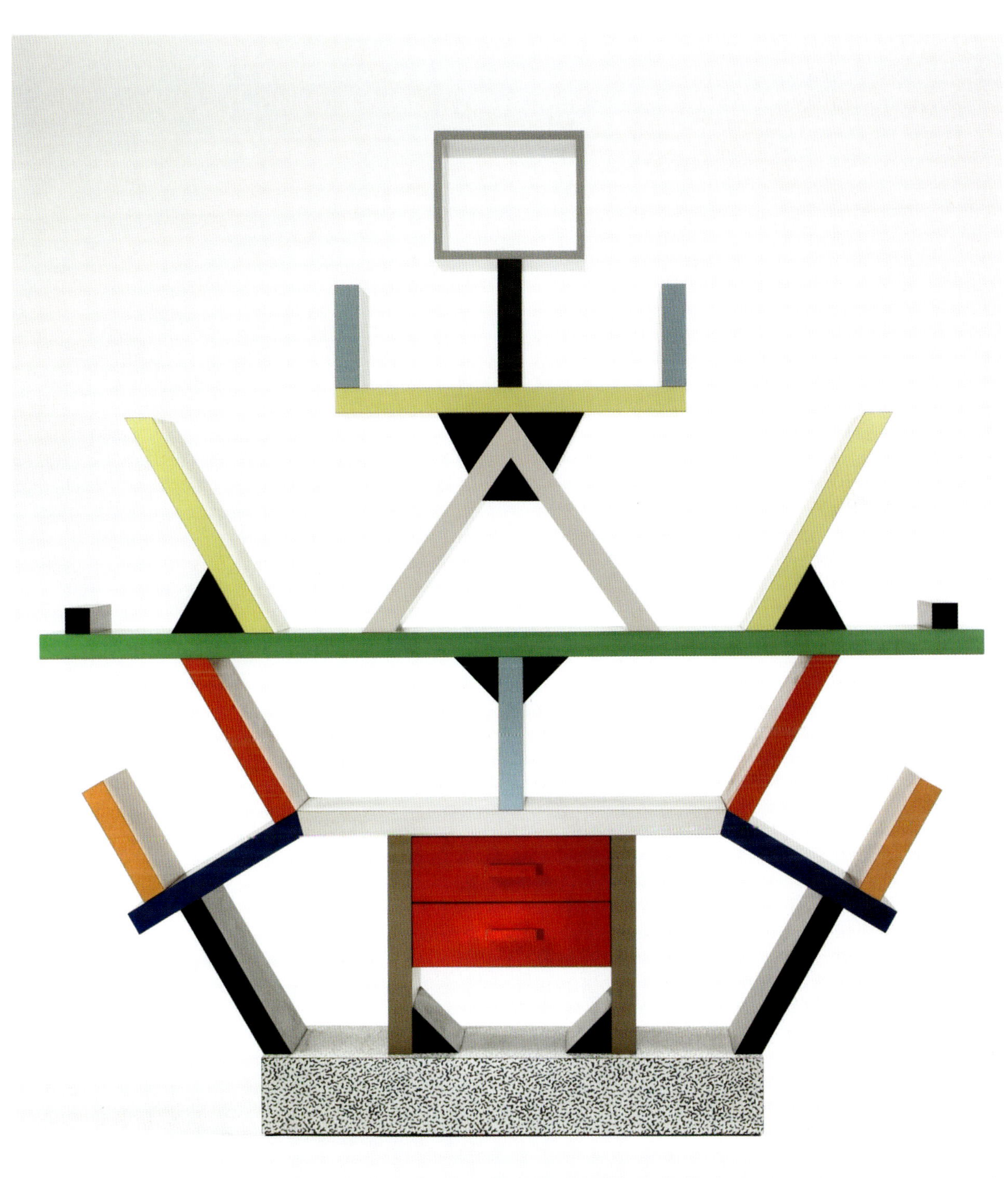

Philippe Starck

French, 1949–

Among the greatest of design showmen, Philippe Starck is a prodigiously talented creative who turns raw materials into seductive products. More than most designers, he truly understands the desires of the marketplace and has catered to them by designing thousands of products, from toothbrushes to micro-yachts. His success lies in being able to infuse products with character, thereby enabling them to provoke an all-important emotional engagement with the user.

The son of an aeronautical engineer, Starck spent hours in his father's office as a child, sitting under his drawing table. This proved to be a formative experience, for he grew up feeling "it was a duty to invent" and to this end he went on to study industrial and interior

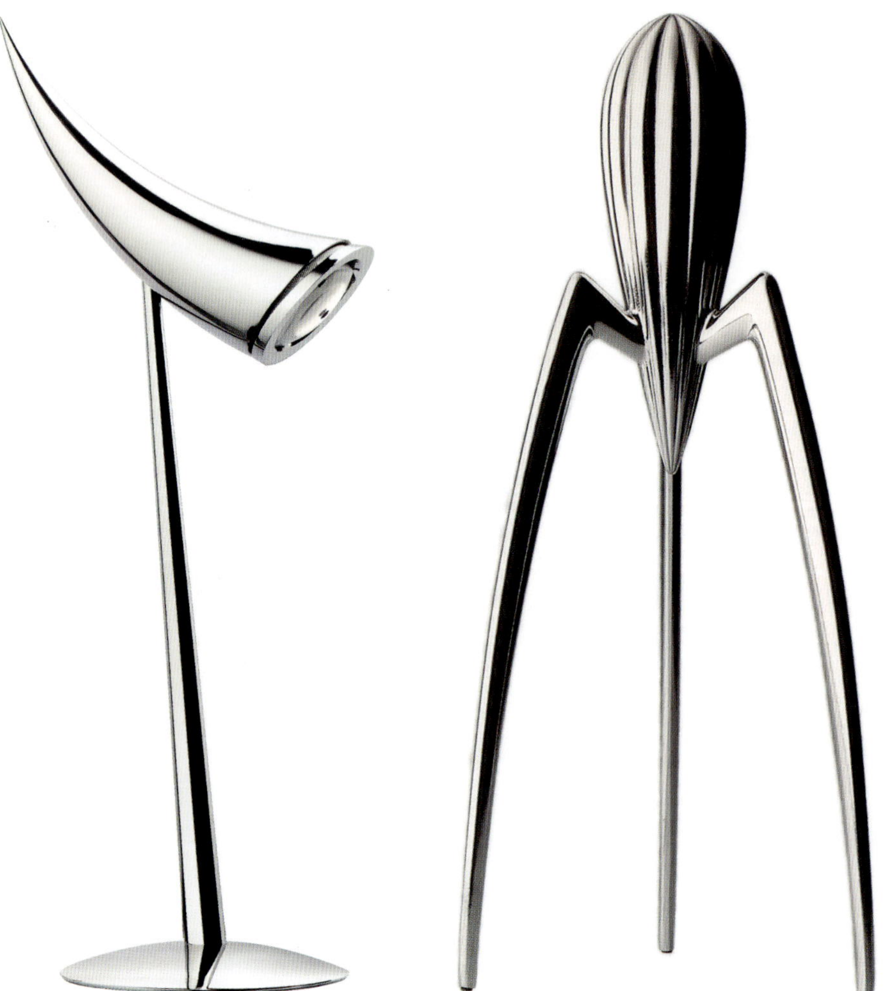

FAR LEFT:
Ara light
for Flos, 1988

LEFT:
Juicy Salif citrus press
for Alessi, 1990

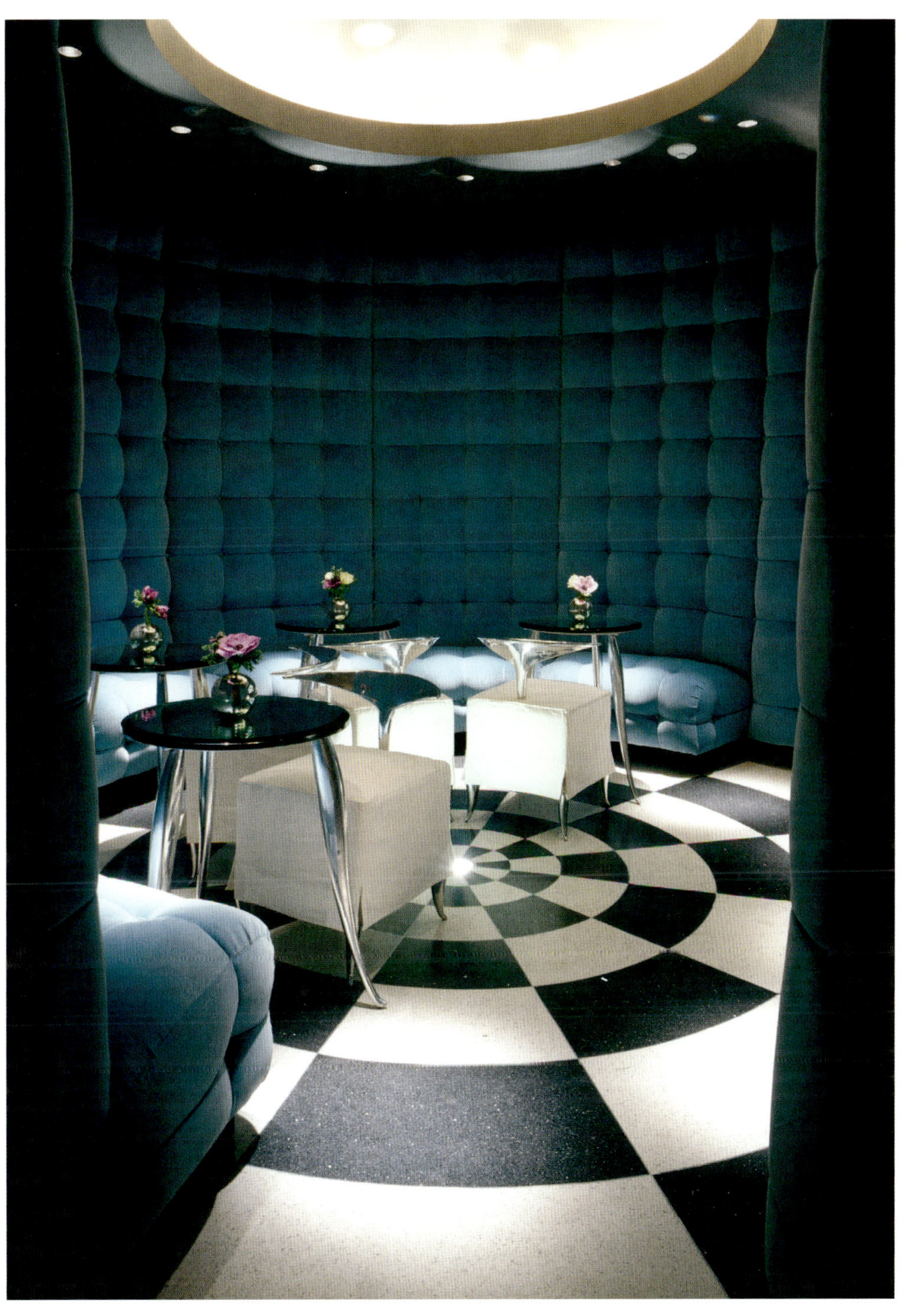

ABOVE:
Interior of Royalton Hotel
New York, 1988

design at the École Nissin de Camondo in Paris. In 1968, while still a student, he set up his own company to manufacture inflatable objects and the following year designed an inflatable house. Shown at the *Salon de l'Enfance* (Fair of Childhood), it was Starck's first design success and importantly attracted the attention of Pierre Cardin, who subsequently hired him as art director for the Pierre Cardin studio, for which he designed sixty-five furniture items.

In the 1970s, Starck created interiors for the nightclubs La Main Bleue in Montreuil,

BELOW:
Jim Nature television
for Saba, 1994 – made from resin-impregnated sawdust

OPPOSITE:
Louis Ghost armchair
for Kartell, 2002

Paris (1976) and Les Bains Douches, also in Paris (1978), which brought him widespread recognition. In 1980, he established Starck Product (later renamed Ubik), to commercialize his own creations such as the Mac Gee bookshelf (1979). At this stage his designs, for instance the Sarapis bar stool (1983), were in the Matte Black style – a short-lived Neo-Modernistic style – but his work soon morphed into a playful Late Modern style that was characterized by the skilful reinterpretation of past styles or forms taken out of context. Starck ingeniously used the names of his designs to inject a sense of personality, as for example with his Doctor Sonderbar chair (1983) and Lola Mundo chair (1986). Working with an array of manufacturers, including XO, Driade and Alessi, he wove his magic on all kinds of objects, most famously with the humble lemon squeezer in 1990. He became the first truly international design superstar and manufacturers were soon clamouring to collaborate with him, thanks to his commercial track record – the label "Designed by Starck" almost guaranteed commercial success. Throughout this prolific period, Starck consistently produced designs that were functionally innovative and had a poetic quality, for example the Ara light for Flos (1988) and the Jim Nature television for Saba (1994).

In the late 1980s and early 1990s, he also began creating innovative landmark buildings in Japan – each with a distinctive form. The copper-clad rampart-like Nani Nani office building in Tokyo (1989) was the first, and the Asahi Breweries headquarters (also in Tokyo) probably the best known, with its visually striking rooftop golden flame sculpture. These buildings were just the first of many such projects that Starck would create for a diversity of clients. Apart from his buildings, products, furniture and lighting, Starck also proved himself to be a skilful impresario of interior design, with his theatrical Royalton Hotel in New York (1988) igniting the designer-hotel phenomenon. This over-the-top interior was an exercise in architectural space being designed as a dramatic stage for experience rather than around functional concerns, and helped to popularize the concept of design as lifestyle.

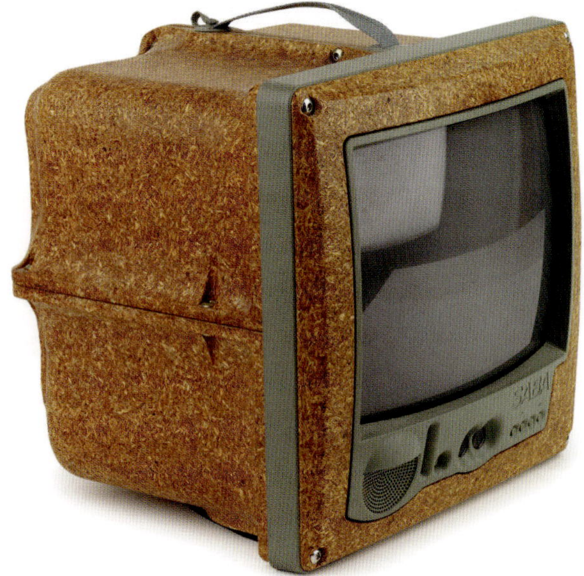

By the early 2000s, Starck was at the height of his creative powers, with designs such as the Louis Ghost armchair (2002) for Kartell, which translated an antique chair form into a dematerialist *tour-de-force*. Today, he continues to work on projects that are impressively diverse, yet are all born of the same design DNA, characterized by sleek refinement and innovative function, such as his prefabricated P.A.T.H. house (2014) that can be configured into thirty-four different permutations and has been designed for the potential integration of various eco-technologies. Having a comprehensive understanding of how the worlds of design and marketing work, Starck believes that ultimately honesty is the most important goal for design: it is all about creating things for people, and to do this properly one has to do it honestly.

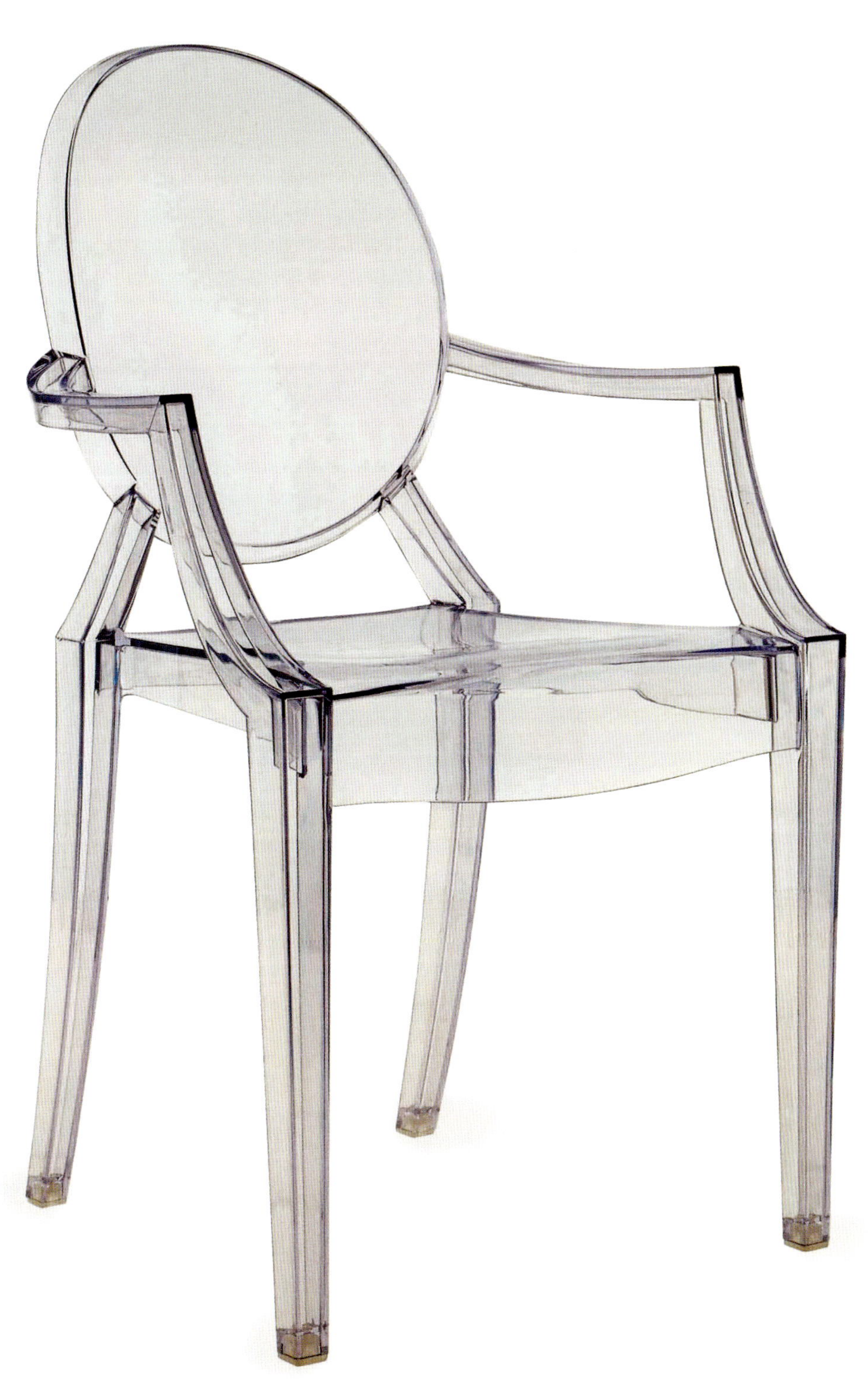

Superstudio

Italian, 1966–1978

Superstudio was at the very heart of the Italian Radical Design movement in the late 1960s and early 1970s, and was a highly influential force in the design world. Through its quirky furniture and "negative utopia" architectural proposals (or "projections" as they were sometimes known), it critiqued the Modernist dogma that had come to so dominate design practice during the twentieth century. Crucially, the designers associated with Superstudio realized that design was not just about making objects, but could also be used to transmit ideas. The group's conceptual designs – work that incorporated political rhetoric – radically questioned the status quo and vitally sowed the seeds for the emergence of Post-Modernism.

Superstudio was founded in Florence by Adolfo Natalini and Cristiano Toraldo di Francia in the year of that city's great flood, 1966. In many ways the submergence of the Renaissance city's historic centre was symbolic of the new wave of design thinking propagated by Superstudio that would similarly sweep away traditional notions as to what design and architecture was really all about. That same year, the group co-organized with Archizoom the first *Superarchitettura* exhibition, held at the Jolly 2 gallery in Pistoia, near Florence, which functioned as an installation manifesto; it comprised a series of rooms that were a riot of bright colours and sculptural forms, intentionally setting out to question the precepts of Modernism.

Through its challenging designs, Superstudio questioned the validity of the Modern Movement's adherence to Rationalism, while criticizing consumerism and promoting instead a "design of evasion", involving objects that were industrially produced, yet poetic. One such design was their futuristic-looking Gherpe table light created for Poltronova in *c.*1967,

BELOW:
Quaderna desk/table
for Zanotta, 1970

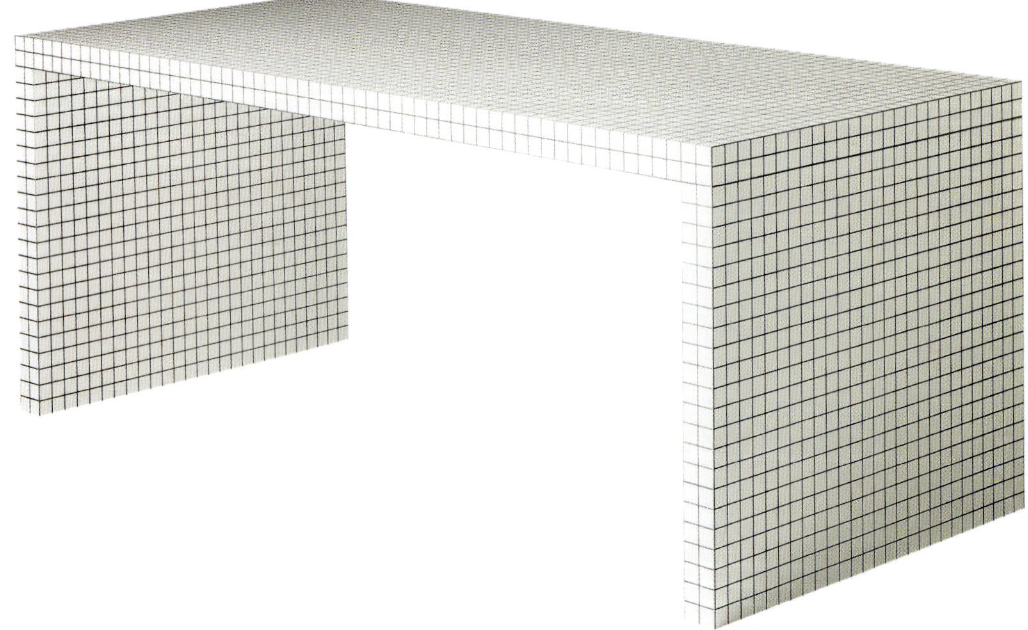

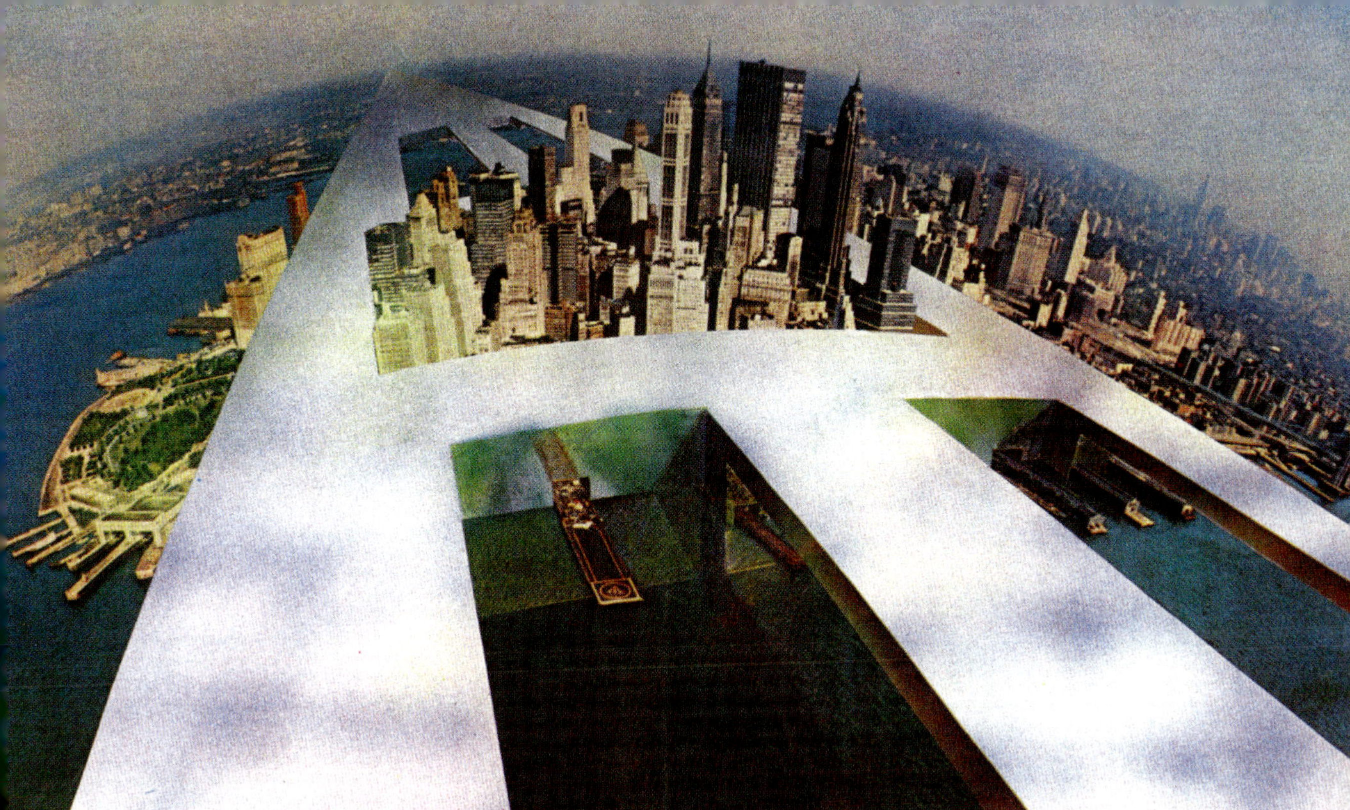

which was constructed from an arching fan of looped and glowing bands of fluorescent pink or yellow or milky-white acrylic. Though relatively low-tech in its construction, this experimental design took full advantage of the extraordinary optical qualities offered by new synthetic materials, and diffused the light in an otherworldly manner – functioning more as a light-sculpture than as an everyday lamp – yet its construction was entirely rational.

The same year, Natalini identified three specific areas of design research the group would focus on: "architecture of the monument", "architecture of the image" and "technomorphic architecture". By 1968, Superstudio had, however, rejected the belief that architecture and design could be a positive force for social change as being too improbably optimistic. The following year, it created its most influential project, Il Monumento Continuo (The Continuous Monument), an architectural projection made up of a series of photo-collages in which an endless grid-like monument, spanning landscapes and cityscapes, stretched across the world in order to "put cosmic order on Earth". This utopian vision, whereby the planet was united by a single monolithic architectural structure, pointed to a dream-like egalitarian state without consumer products.

In 1970, Superstudio designed the Quaderna range of furniture for Zanotta, which was made from plastic laminate screen-printed with the same grid-like "neutral surface" motif. This furniture collection was later shown at the landmark *Italy: The New Domestic Landscape* exhibition held in 1972 at the Museum of Modern Art, New York, where Superstudio also advanced the idea of controlled micro-climates beneath invisible domes – a visionary concept that has since become reality. Despite operating for a mere dozen years, Superstudio's intellectually challenging work had a lasting legacy, as it drew attention to the ecological impact of our built environment, the negative consequences of unfettered technological progress and the inability of politics to solve complex social issues – key matters that continue to concern many of today's leading architects and designers.

ABOVE:
Il Monumento Continuo (The Continuous Monument)
negative utopia
architectural projection, 1969

Roger Tallon

French, 1929–2011

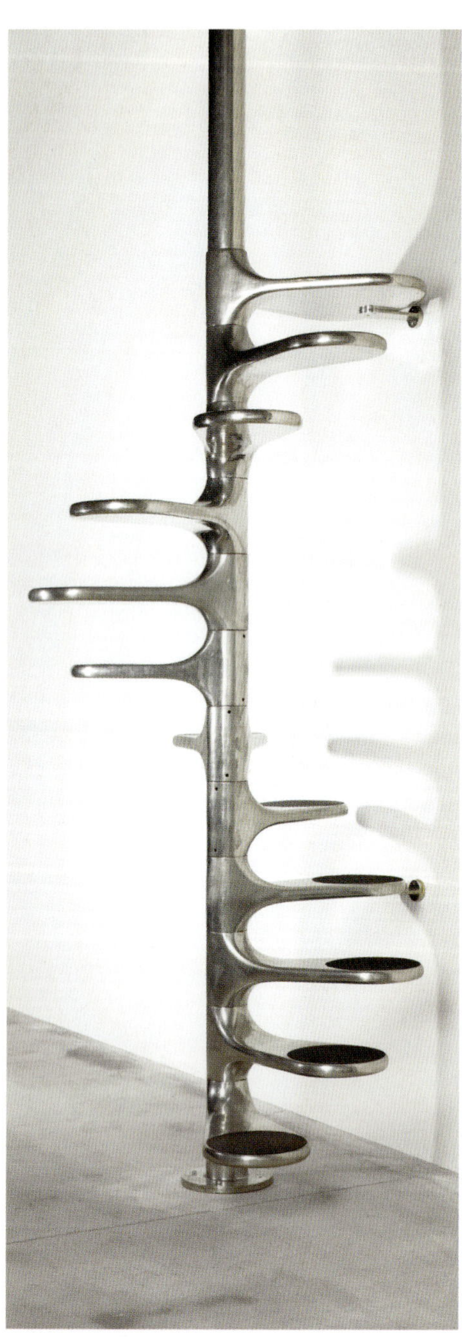

The French industrial designer Roger Tallon originally trained as an electrical engineer (1944–50) before working as a designer for Studio Avas (1951–53). While there, he met the French industrial designer Jacques Viénot in 1953, who was a prominent member of the *ésthétique industrielle* (industrial aesthetics) movement in France, which sought to bring greater artistry to the development of industrially produced goods. The same year, Tallon joined Viénot's pioneering design consultancy Technès, where he became head of research and was responsible for the development of numerous innovative and stylish industrial products. These included: the sculptural black and white PA 573 portable television set for Téléavia (1963); the Module 400 furniture range (1964), which innovatively incorporated sheets of grey noise-baffling polyester foam; the Helicoid spiral staircase for Galerie Lacloche (*c.*1966) made of polished-aluminium modules; and his Mach 2000 range of high-tech wristwatches for Lip (1973). During this period, he also designed the diminutive Micro 3

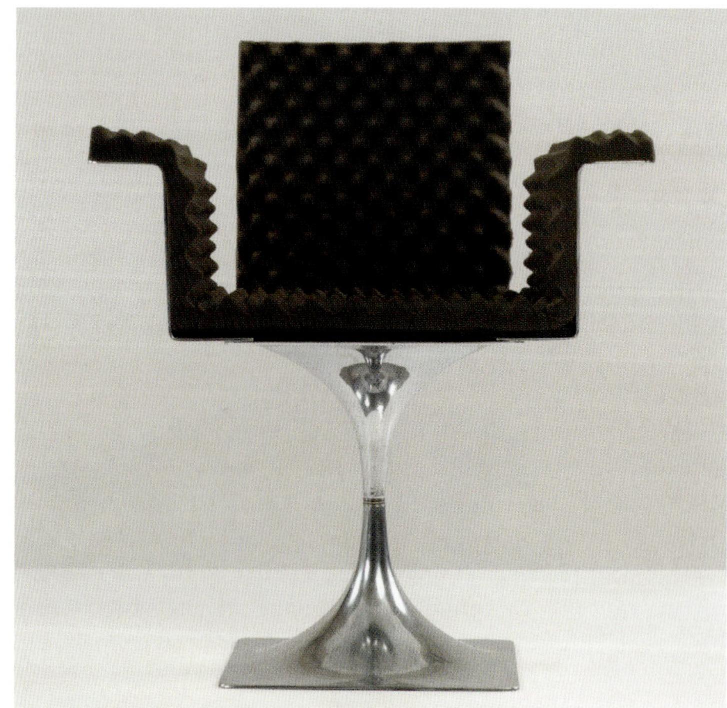

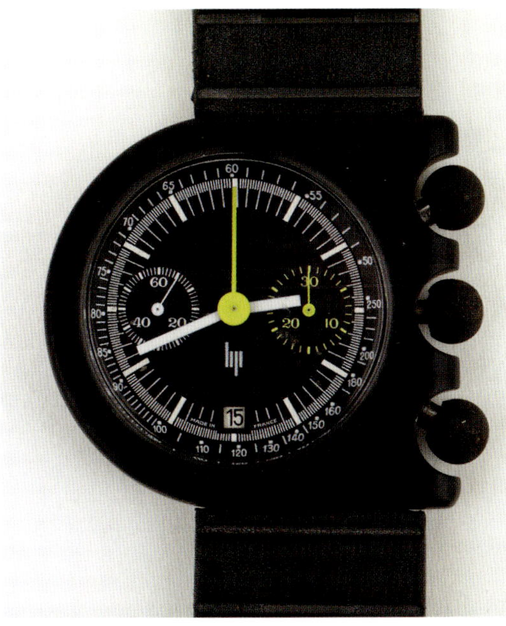

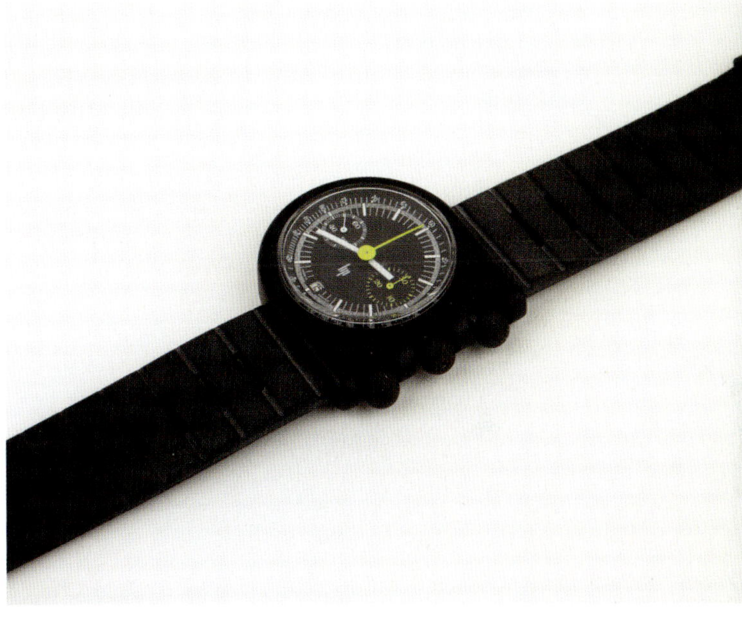

OPPOSITE LEFT:
Helicoid staircase
for Galerie Lacloche, *c.*1966

OPPOSITE RIGHT:
Module 400 armchair
for Galerie Lacloche, 1964

ABOVE:
NOS watch
for Lip, 1975

super-compact car for Peugeot (1955), and was awarded a prestigious Compasso d'Oro prize in 1958 for his sculptural Style typewriter for Japy (1953).

From 1967 onwards, he consulted under the auspices of Technès to France's national state-owned railway company, SNCF, and consequently gained increasing international respect for his transportation designs, which led to him working as a design consultant on Mexico City's metro system (1969). In 1973, he established his own multidisciplinary consultancy, Design Programmes, and the following year designed stylish yet comfortable carriages for SNCF's groundbreaking new-generation Corail train. This project, like so many others designed by Tallon, was successful because it was designed from a user-centric perspective; as he observed, when it came to designing the train's compartments, he tried "to put myself in the place of those who will use it". In 1983, Tallon co-founded ADSA + Partners consultancy with fellow French designers Pierre Paulin and Michel Schreiber, and continued designing interiors for trains, including those for the landmark high-speed TGV-Atlantique (1988) and the sleek Eurostar shuttle for Eurotunnel (1987).

During the early 1980s, Tallon also created the SX series of rear-entry ski boots for Salomon, which similarly combined his understanding of engineering with a distinctive Gallic flair for design innovation. Becoming known as "The Father of SNCF Design", Roger Tallon was a true pioneer of French industrial design, whose work spanned an impressive creative breadth, from car bodies and train interiors to furniture, lighting and electronic products.

Walter Dorwin Teague

American, 1883–1960

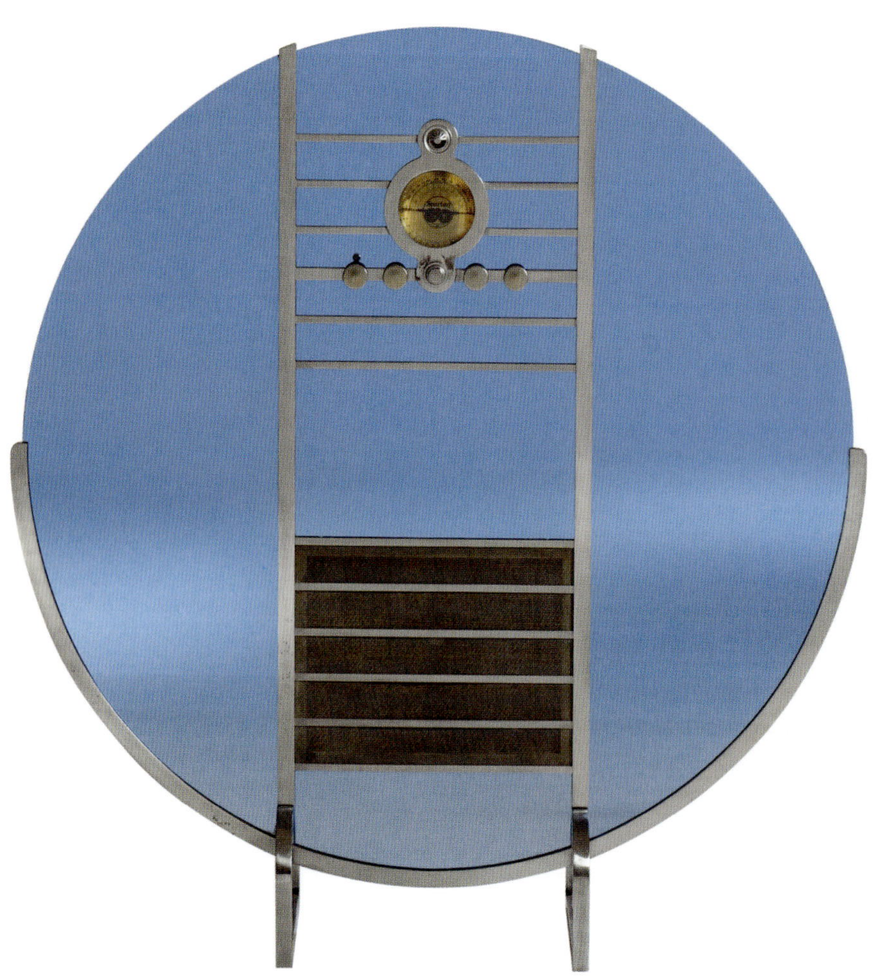

ABOVE:
Nocturne radio (Model No. 1186)
for Sparton Corporation, 1935

Walter Dorwin Teague was the original pioneer of industrial design consulting in America. Crucial to his success was his understanding that, as he put it, "no maker of things today works alone", and throughout his career combining art with industry he worked closely with companies to create forward-looking innovative design solutions.

Having moved from Indiana to New York in 1903, he attended evening classes at the renowned Art Students League, later working as an illustrator for a mail-order catalogue and also for the Hampton Advertising Agency. In 1912, Teague established his own studio in New York, working as a typographer and graphic designer, and in the mid-1920s he also began to design packaging. In 1926, he founded Walter Dorwin Teague Associates, which was the first professional industrial design consultancy to be established in the United States. Although Teague happily embraced new technologies, he also understood the importance of craft and often employed advanced materials using a thoughtful craft sensibility. Teague's first client was Eastman Kodak, for which he created a comprehensive design programme that included design research and product development. His first camera design, the Vanity Kodak (1928), was devised specifically for the female market and produced in various fashionable colours, with matching silk-lined cases. Teague later received widespread acclaim for his Baby Brownie camera (1934), one of the first consumer products made of plastic. His best-known camera, however, was the distinctively styled Bantam Special (1936), which was more compact and user-friendly than earlier Kodak models. In the early 1930s, he also designed pieces of furniture that exemplified the Art Deco Moderne style, including a stylish cabinet made of lacquered wood and nickel-plated steel.

BELOW:
Polaroid Model 114 lamp
for Polaroid Corporation, 1939

In 1931–33, Teague designed the streamlined body of the Marmon Model 16 car, which was among the most aerodynamically efficient automobiles of its time. This streamlined design was soon followed by other products, including glassware for Corning, kitchenware for Pyrex, pens and lighters for Scripto, mimeographs for AB Dick, radios for Sparton, and the Centennial piano for Steinway. Besides consumer products, Teague designed interiors for the Boeing 707 airliner; United States pavilions at various international trade fairs; exhibition interiors for Ford; service stations for Texaco; and various exhibits at the 1939 *New York World's Fair*, including a gigantic cash register based on his earlier design for the National Cash Register Company, which recorded visitor numbers. The same year he also produced one of his best-known designs, the Polaroid Model 114 table lamp with its streamlined Bakelite shade. He also wrote *Design This Day – The Technique of Order in The Machine Age* (1940), which celebrated the potential of mechanization and the "new and thrilling style" of the Modern era.

Importantly, among the various design consultancies founded in America during the 1920s and 1930s, Walter Dorwin Teague Associates has, along with Loewy Associates, fared the best. Indeed, one could say it has flourished over the decades thanks to the prevailing research-led design approach of its founder, with today a staff of over 200 professionals specializing in the development of innovative transportation design, systems engineering, human factors and corporate identity solutions.

T

Giuseppe Terragni

Italian, 1904–1943

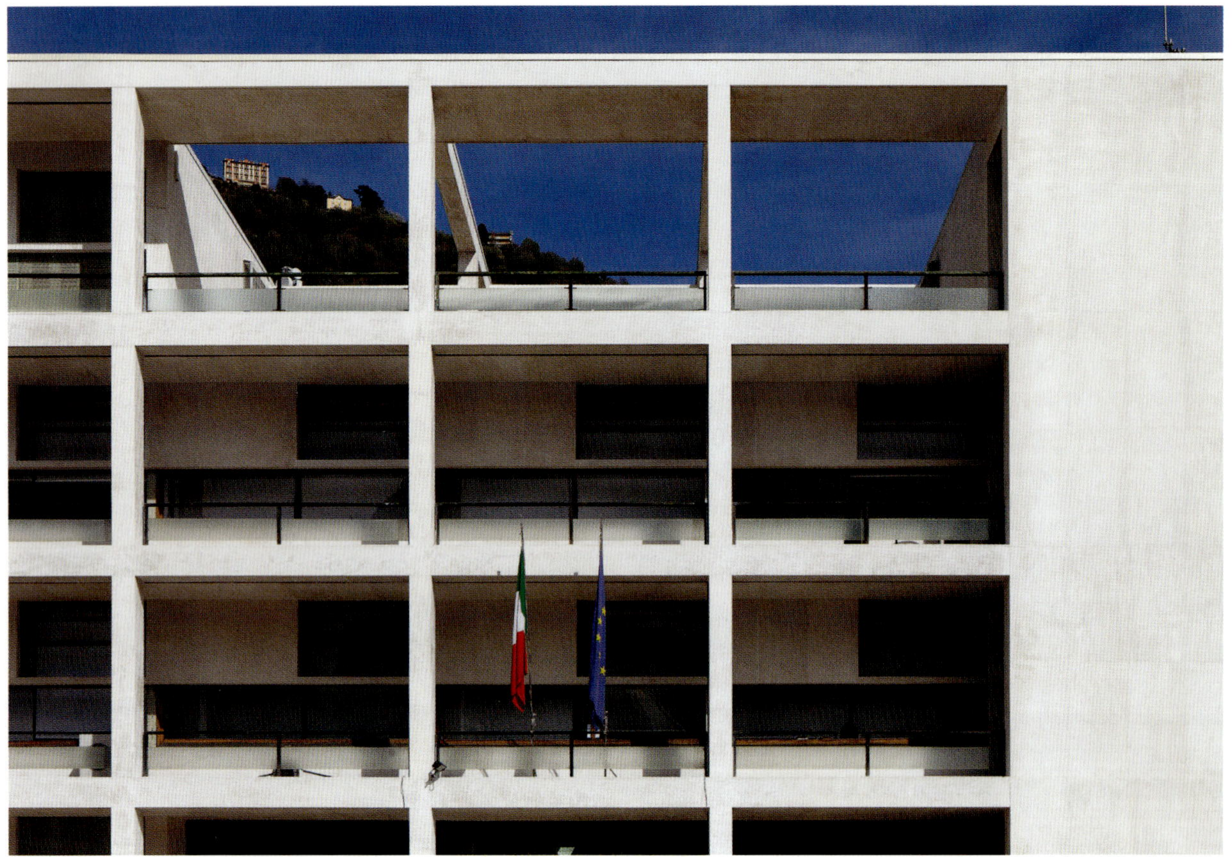

ABOVE:
Detail of façade, Casa del Fascio (Fascist headquarters) in Como, constructed 1932–36

The highly gifted architect-designer Giuseppe Terragni was at the forefront of the Italian Rationalist movement, which during the 1920s and 1930s effectively merged the utilitarian functionalism of the European avant-garde with Italy's Classical tradition to create a new yet thoroughly Classical expression of Modernism. The result was that Terragni's designs and buildings, while extremely forward-looking, also had a remarkable refined elegance thanks to their use of Classical proportions.

Having trained at the technical college in Como, Terragni later studied architecture at the Politecnico di Milano, graduating in 1926. That same year he founded, with other like-minded young architects including Luigi Figini and Giuseppe Pagano, Gruppo 7 – an architectural group that promoted the Rationalist cause. The following year Terragni established his own Como-based architecture practice (with his engineer brother Attilio) and subsequently designed the radically Modern Novocomum apartment block. When the building was unveiled in 1929 it caused quite a scandal, as the Neo-Classical plans that had been submitted to the municipality for approval were not the ones Terragani had handed over to the builders – in fact he had given them something far more radical. Such was the controversy generated by this stridently Modern apartment complex that its demolition was even considered. Members of the Italian avant-garde, however, came to its rescue, with Giuseppe Pagano lauding it for its daring Modernity in the pages of *La Casa Bella*.

It was, however, Terragni's Casa del Fascio (1932-36) – the Fascist Party's headquarters in Como – that was his architectural masterwork. Its visually airy, grid-like façade employed a similarly strict system of fenestration and was mathematically proportioned according to the Classical golden ratio. For this landmark edifice, which was fundamentally a Classical *palazzo* within the Modern idiom, Terragani also created some suitably Modern furniture, including a number of avant-garde chairs. Of these, it is the Follia chair (1934) that is the most striking – both in terms of its innovative construction, which utilized two sprung bands of chrome-plated steel to connect the seat to the back sections, and its resulting pared-down, essentialist aesthetic. A Rationalist *Gesamtkunstwerk*, the Casa del Fascio (later renamed Casa del Popolo) unified progressive architecture and avant-garde design into a harmonious whole that had a breathtaking spatial purity.

Terragni subsequently designed the light-filled Asilo Sant'Elia nursery school in Como (1935–37), as well as several private residences including the Casa Bianca, Seveso (1936–37) and the Casa Giuliani Frigerio, Como (1939–40). He also designed the Casa del Fascio in Lissone (1938–39), which today is known as the Palazzo Terragni and was, like his earlier project, conceived using precise mathematical proportions. Terragni's Rationalism was embraced by the Fascist regime, for it was seen to reflect a new world order, and even today his buildings and designs project a powerful sense of the contemporary due to his skilful translation of Classical proportions into a Modern formal vocabulary.

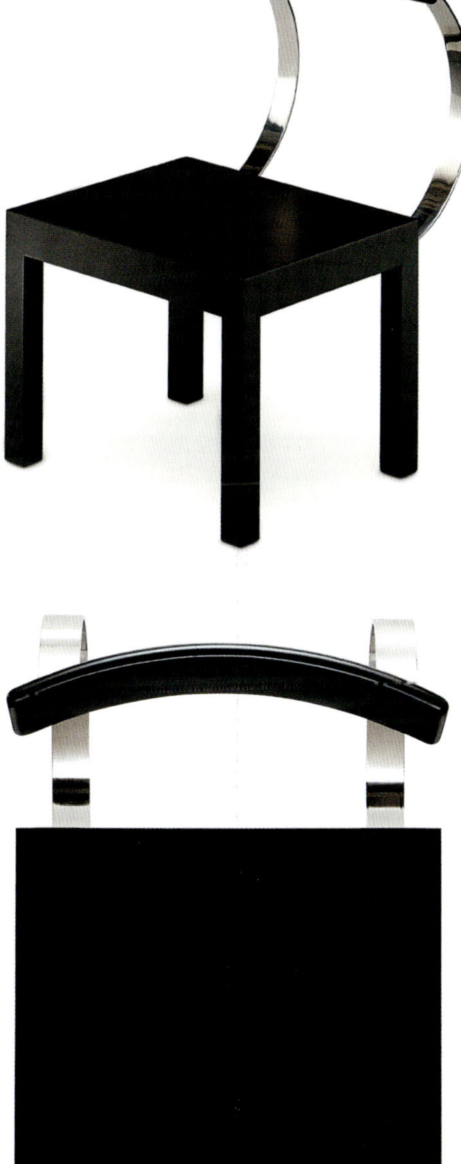

RIGHT:
Follia chair
1934 (reissued by Zanotta)

Michael Thonet

German/Austrian, 1796–1862

BELOW:
Model No. 14 chair
for Gebrüder Thonet,
introduced 1859

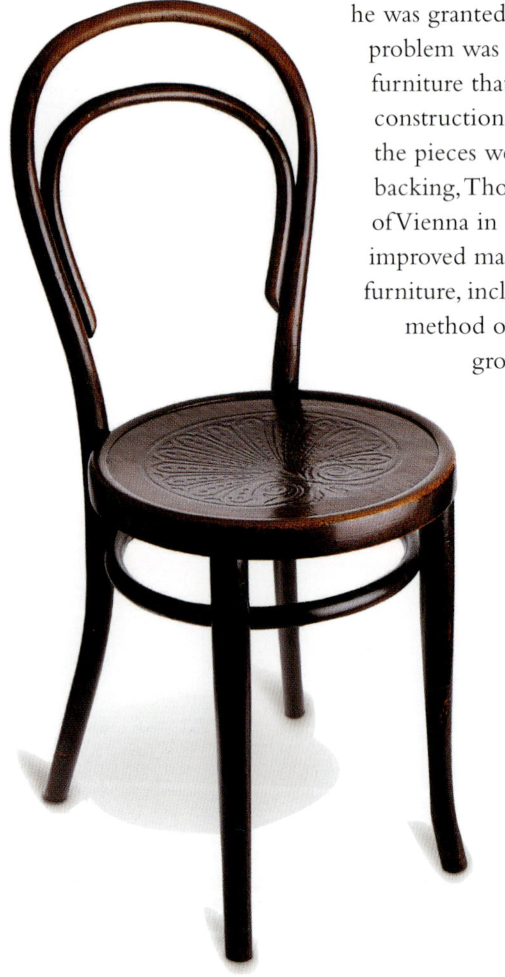

The German-born but mainly Austria-based designer Michael Thonet was one of the most significant manufacturing innovators of the nineteenth century, whose work presaged the advent of truly Modern design. Initially working within the fashionable Biedermeier style, which was itself characterized by a simplification of form and construction, Thonet pioneered an even greater degree of design reductivism that would have a huge bearing on his ability to successfully mass-produce furniture.

Around 1830, in his workshop in Boppard am Rhein, his German birthplace, Thonet began developing new methods of laminating wood whereby thin veneers were glued together and then placed in metal moulds to cure into the required shapes. These individual elements were then joined together to create a number of innovative bentwood Biedermeier-style chairs. These highly original designs came to the attention of the Austrian chancellor Prince Metternich, who invited Thonet to Vienna, where he was granted a patent for his new furniture-making process in 1842. The only problem was that, although the laminating process allowed Thonet to produce furniture that was both lightweight and elegantly formed with graceful looping constructions, it was relatively time-consuming and laborious – which meant the pieces were expensive to produce. After securing the necessary financial backing, Thonet established a furniture workshop with his sons in the suburbs of Vienna in 1849, and for the next two years he concentrated on developing improved manufacturing techniques that would enable the mass-production of furniture, including the steam-bending of solid wood. He perfected an inventive method of shaping wood using heat and pressure, and in 1851 exhibited his groundbreaking bentwood furniture designs at *The Great Exhibition* in London, where they were awarded a gold medal.

Among Thonet's chair designs, it was the Model No. 14 café chair (1859) and the Model No. 10 rocking chair (*c.*1866) that were to become the two "classic" Thonet models. The Model No. 14 was stripped of all superfluous ornamentation – every element of its steam-bent frame and its cane or moulded plywood seat was essential for its function. By reducing the chair into the most elemental components he could, Thonet significantly drove down both material and labour costs of its construction, thereby making the pared-down design utterly suited to high-volume production. Sold cheaply, Thonet's mass-produced, lightweight yet strong designs heralded a new economic democracy in design – for the first time, high-end cutting-edge furniture was affordable to the masses, with the firm's best-known Model No. 14 chair costing less than a bottle of wine in 1860. Thonet's ingenious reduction of elements and elimination of extraneous ornament also meant that his designs, such as

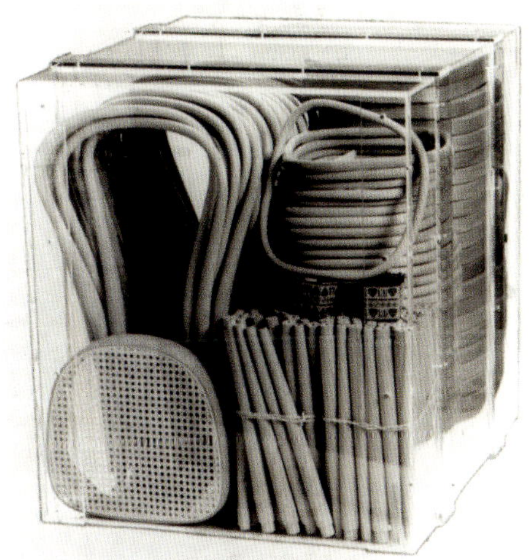

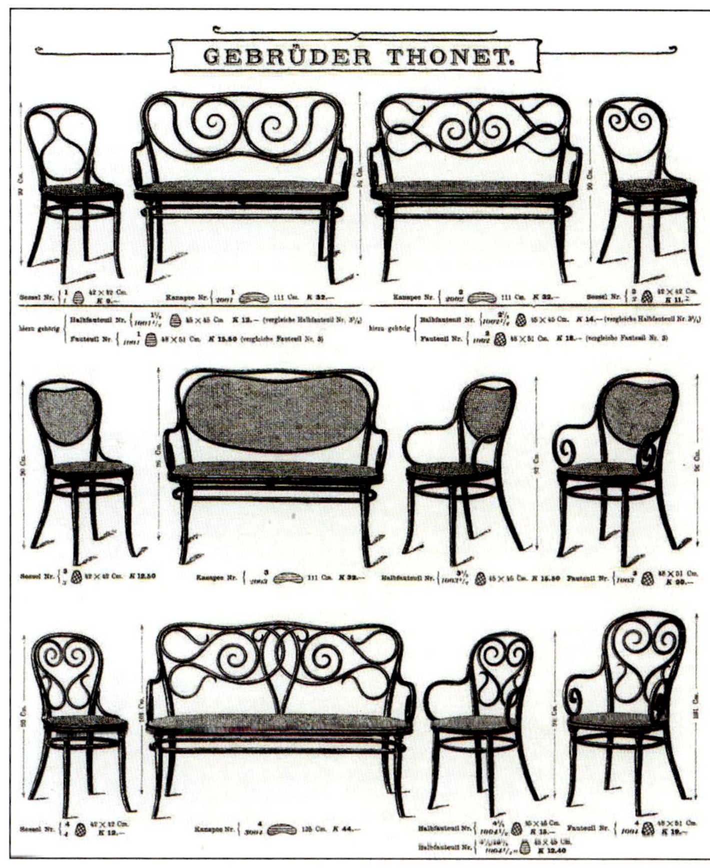

ABOVE LEFT:
Components for thirty-six Model No. 14 chairs
stacked into a single cubic metre

ABOVE RIGHT:
Page from Gebrüder Thonet catalogue
1904

the Model No. 10 rocking chair, were eminently suited for export, as they could be space-efficiently crated in their unassembled state and then simply reassembled with a few turns of a screwdriver once they had reached their destination.

Thonet's chairs demonstrated how factory system production could be successfully exploited for commercial gain. While this radically new way of making products facilitated the provision of democratic design, it also promoted a new kind of design thinking whereby items were conceived from a rational standpoint specifically for volume industrial production. After Michael Thonet's death, his company continued to thrive, based on his innovative design principles. In 1929, a sibling company, Thonet-Frères, was founded in Paris, which manufactured Modernist tubular metal furniture (including designs by Marcel Breuer) that was similarly rationally conceived. Above all else, Michael Thonet showed through example that if one's goal was large-scale industrial manufacture then the best design approach was from an analytical process-driven perspective.

Jan Tschichold

German/Swiss, 1902–1974

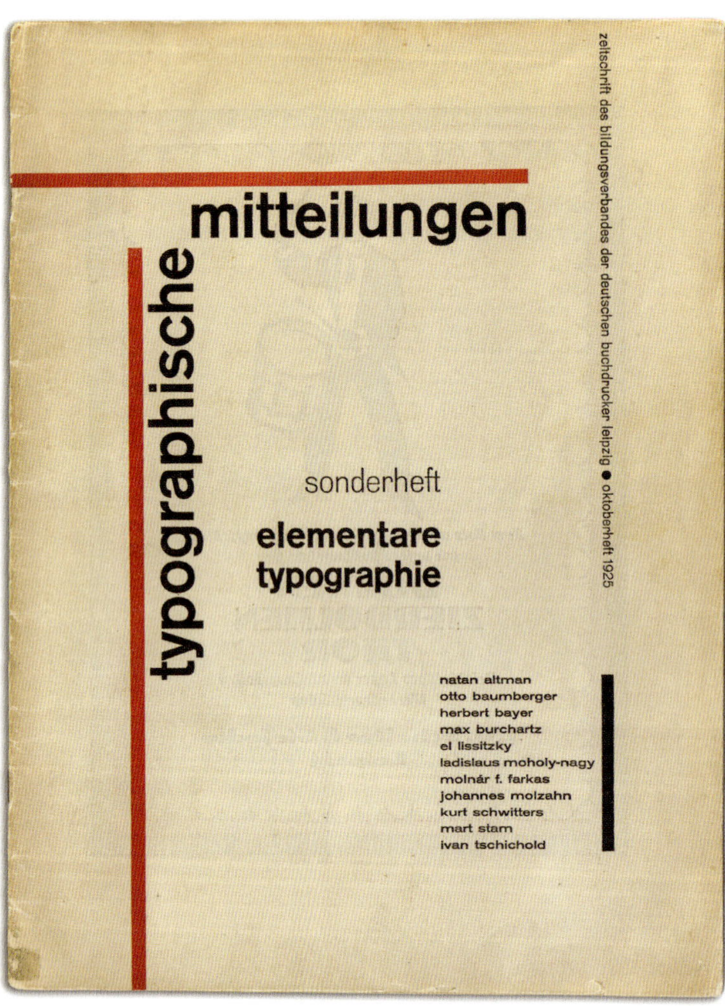

ABOVE:
***Typographische Mitteilungen: elementare typographie* (Typographic Messages: elementary typography)**
in which Tschichold's article appeared, 1925

Among the most influential typographers and book designers of the twentieth century, Jan Tschichold was largely responsible for introducing Modernist sans serif typography to the graphic design lexicon. He was also an influential educator and writer, who authored a number of important books on type design, book layout and lettering. Throughout his life, his quest was for typographic purity, and he would famously note: "Perfect typography is certainly the most elusive of all arts. Sculpture in stone alone comes near it in obstinacy."

The son of a signwriter, Tschichold studied calligraphy and graphic design at the Hochschule für Grafik und Buchkunst (Institute for Graphic Arts and Book Design) in Leipzig. Throughout his career, his calligraphic training would set him apart from other Modernist typographers, who mostly came from architecture and fine-art backgrounds. Tschichold's knowledge of calligraphy also gave him an eye for the subtle nuances of type creation. After his studies he regularly received commissions to design calligraphic advertisements, but his interest became increasingly focused on typefaces – both their form and their setting – and in 1923 he became a typographic designer for the Leipzig-based book printer Fischer & Wittig.

That same year his eyes were opened by a visit to the landmark Bauhaus exhibition in nearby Weimar, which as he would later recall left him "in a state of great agitation". The event had been staged ostensibly to introduce to the world the school's new Rational direction, which had been recently instigated by Walter Gropius with the appointment of László Moholy-Nagy and Josef Albers. Nothing conveyed this New Objectivity better than the exhibition's posters by Joost Schmidt and Fritz Schleifer and its eye-catching catalogue designed by László Moholy-Nagy and Herbert Bayer. Tschichold was intrigued by what was happening at the Bauhaus and its potential influence on future typography.

Around this time, he also became strongly inspired by the work of the Russian Constructivists – to such an extent that he began calling himself Iwan Tschichold. For him, the future of typography lay in breaking the rules of traditional typography, and he did this by adopting asymmetrical layouts and using exclusively sans serif typefaces. He first expounded his revolutionary views in an article in *Elementare Typographie* (Elementary Typography) in 1925, and then three years later published his influential book *Die Neue Typographie* (The New Typography) – a treatise on book design and graphic design for the modern industrial age. Becoming an indispensable reference source of working principles for graphic designers during the inter-war period, it is still regarded as a seminal publication. However, the political climate in Germany was not receptive to progressive ideas; Modernism was seen as "un-German" and eventually Tschichold was arrested and imprisoned for four weeks. He subsequently moved to Switzerland in 1933, where he taught at the Kunstgewerbeschule (School of Arts and Crafts) in Basel, and later published *Typographische Gestaltung* (Essential Typography, 1935), which reflected a softening towards more traditional typographic approaches, including the use of the golden mean.

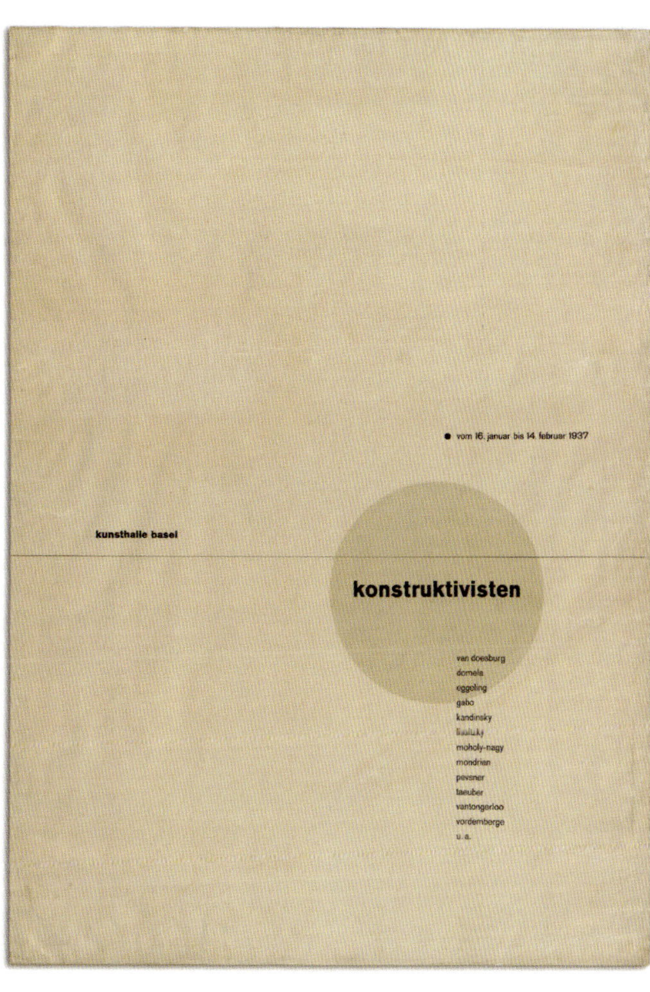

ABOVE:
Konstruktivisten (Constructivists) exhibition poster
for Kunsthalle Basel, 1937

After the Second World War, Tschichold moved to England and in 1947 joined Penguin Books, where he set about redesigning Edward Young's cover-design system into its more honed "classic" form, complete with the use of Gill Sans typeface. During his two-year tenure at the publishing house, Tschichold standardized the house design style by creating a set of layout and typographic guidelines, known as the Penguin Composition Rules.

Returning to Switzerland in 1949, he subsequently designed many notable typefaces, including Sabon (1964–67), which was inspired by a serif typeface designed by Claude Garamond in the sixteenth century. And while Sabon might have appeared the antithesis of New Typography, it would prove to be a very functional typeface, which even to this day is still widely used.

UsTwo

British, founded 2004

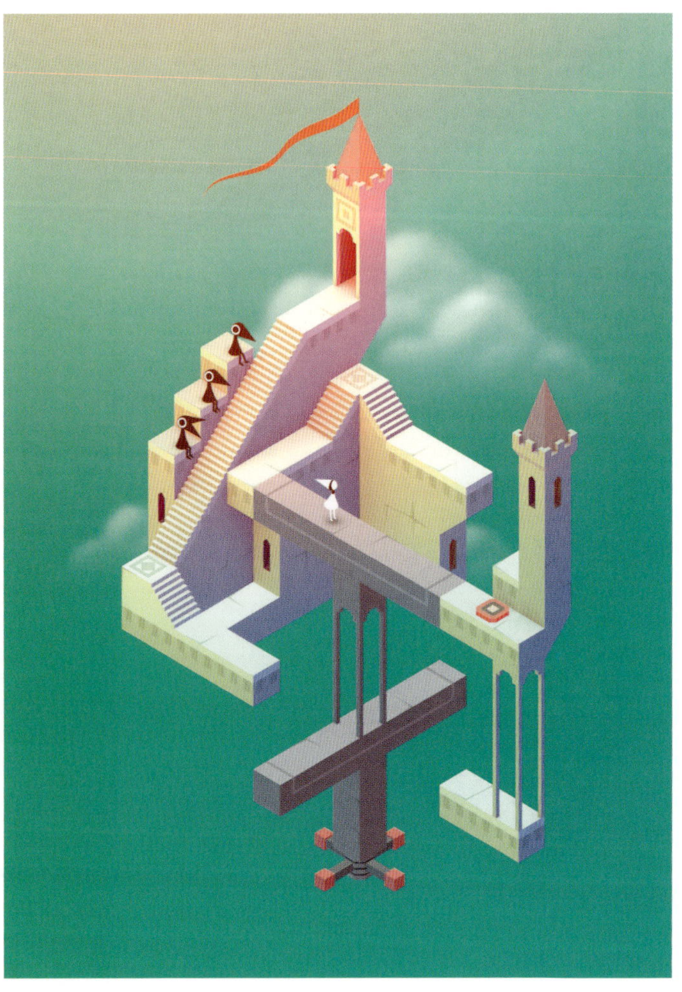

ABOVE:
Artwork for Monument Vallery computer game
Rookery environment, 2014

The twenty-first century has seen a huge shift in the practice of design, as digital products have increasingly replaced physical ones. The massive financial rewards that can be reaped from developing a best-selling game, app or piece of software has meant that it is these areas of design that have become the most competitive and are now attracting the best talent. While furniture, lighting and products might have been where the most skilled design creatives plied their trade in the twentieth century, in this century the most exciting design action is clearly in the digital realm.

This has already changed irrevocably the nature of design practice, for the development of a digital product requires a collaborative team effort involving software engineers alongside specialist designers, as generally such products are just too technically complex for one person to develop by themselves. The swing from physical to digital is quite difficult for design commentators to document successfully, as it is almost impossible to describe in words or static screen-shot imagery how an app interface or game-play system works, plus the design studios that undertake this type of work are notoriously secretive about what they are working on and for whom – the stakes are just too high.

While Silicon Valley has long been the epicentre of the computer industry, London's Shoreditch has since the early 2000s taken on the role of younger upstart brother, being home to a synergetic cluster of digital creative companies, all with smart new ideas. One such venture is UsTwo, which was founded in 2004 by two childhood friends, John "Sinx" Sinclair and Matt "Mills" Miller – both of whom had previously worked at Big Animal Design and Animation Studio on advertising projects.

Describing UsTwo, their global digital product studio, as a "fampany" of "dreamers and doers", the pair oversee the development of "transformative" products for a wide range of clients including American Express, Barclays, BT, eBay, Google, Nokia, Sony, Spotify, Tesco and Toyota. At the same time, each year they plough back a sizable percentage of their profits into the development of their own products, and work with other like-minded developers on speculative joint-venture projects.

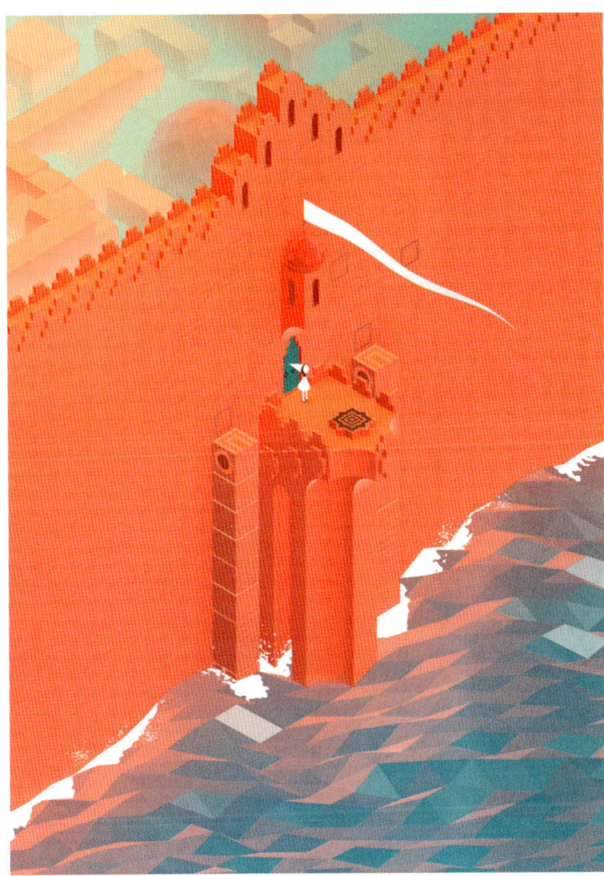

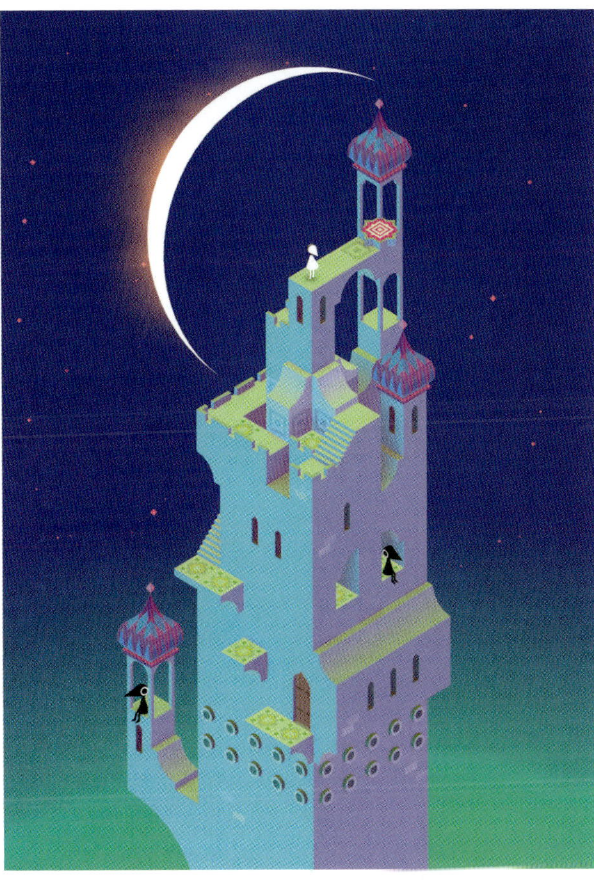

ABOVE LEFT:
Artwork for Monument Vallery computer game
Labyrinth environment, 2014

ABOVE RIGHT:
Artwork for Monument Vallery computer game
Moon environment, 2014

One of UsTwo's most successful in-house projects is Monument Valley – a game that took Apple's App Store by storm when it was released in 2014. It is a beautifully designed digital experience that takes the player on an exploratory journey of fantastical Escher-like monuments and hidden pathways. This is a game that is the very antithesis of franchises like Call of Duty or Grand Theft Auto or the bubblegum plethora of garish freemium games. Instead, it is a quiet cerebral game that is not only stunningly beautiful but ingenious in its weird spatial-physics gameplay. As UsTwo's lead artist and designer of Monument Valley, Ken Wong, noted before its release, "What [the game] brings to the table is an exploration of how to bring an interactive, emotionally engaging experience to a wide audience through a set of simple mechanics and a world that feels at once familiar and fantastical.... A few high-quality premium experiences have popped up to disrupt the system and prove that there really is a market for players with absolute quality in mind. We're aiming for Monument Valley to become the 'coffee table book' of iOS games – one you just have to show your friends." That is exactly what this multi-award-winning game has become, demonstrating that good design still matters, whether a product is physical or digital, and as UsTwo's founders note, it's the culture of design excellence that is becoming "increasingly the differentiator between a good company and a bad company".

Jop van Bennekom

Dutch, 1970–

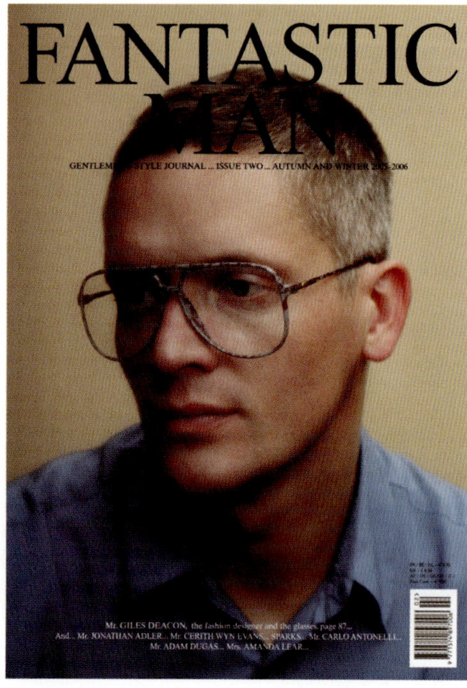

ABOVE:
Fantastic Man **cover**
Issue 2, 2005

The Dutch editor, art director, publisher and designer Jop van Bennekom began his career by studying graphic design at the Arnhem Hogeschool voor de Kunsten (Arnhem School of Arts) for five years. He cites his teacher there, Karel Martens, as a major influence in his development as a designer. Van Bennekom subsequently trained at the Jan Van Eyck Academie in Maastricht, but found the teaching there was too heavily focused on academic theories when all he really wanted to do was devise a new visual language that had contemporary cultural relevance and was, as he puts it, "about the everyday".

It was during his time as a student that he became increasingly influenced by the work of the BNO (Association of Dutch Designers) which was championing a more avant-garde design agenda through its publications and initiatives, and also by the covers and layouts of various British music magazines, most notably *The Face* – which was then under the inspired art direction of Neville Brody. He was also hugely galvanized by the work of Peter Saville, although, as he would later note, "I knew his designs for (the bands) Joy Division and New Order, but it never occurred to me that there was a person behind them," which in many ways reflects just how good Saville's groundbreaking high-concept artwork for the music industry was.

Van Bennekom was also influenced by the pioneering work of an older generation of Dutch graphic designers, such as Wim Crouwel and Jan van Toorn. Following his graduation, he launched his own magazine in 1997 with the aim of developing a new form of highly personalized communication. Catchily entitled *Re-Magazine*, this new journal was quite different from any that had gone before, with each issue being dedicated to a single theme or personality. Van Bennekom's concept of a single storyline influenced not only the overall concept of the magazine but its typographic detailing too. This very personalized approach to graphic design was the antithesis of the "one size fits all" language of universal communication. In 2001, van Bennekom launched a second magazine, *BUTT*, an influential and humorous pocket-sized "fagazine" quarterly that focuses on gay culture and carries the memorable by-line "The magazine for homos that doesn't suck".

Entering the world of fashion magazines was a natural progression for van Bennekom – he launched the bi-annual *Fantastic Man* magazine with Gert Jonkers in 2005, which has subsequently been lauded for its elegant design and its thoughtful editorial content that focuses on interesting personalities. Four years later the duo, along with editor Penny Martin, launched a sister publication aimed at women, *The Gentlewoman*, which, with its simple and direct covers, runs completely counter to the usual notion of the glossy women's

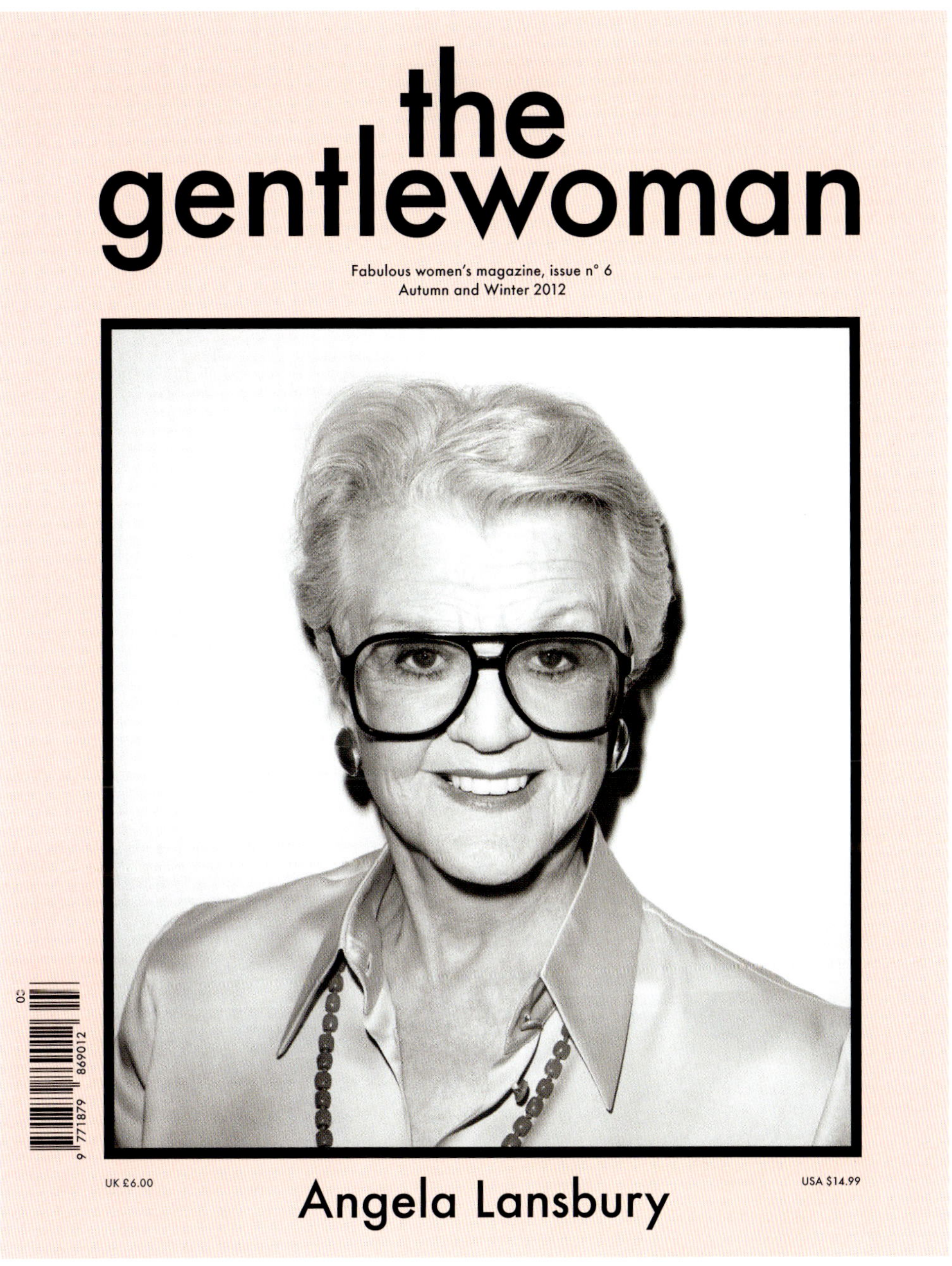

ABOVE:
***The Gentlewoman* cover**
Autumn/Winter issue, 2012

magazine. Beautifully designed, this groundbreaking anti-fashion fashion magazine is more about culture than the latest trends, or as the super-low-key van Bennekom notes, "it is not so much about handbags and so on, more on global understanding". Under his perceptive creative direction, *The Gentlewoman* perfectly reflects this all-too-rare sentiment in the world of women's magazines.

Henry van de Velde

Belgian, 1863–1957

The Antwerp-born architect and designer Henry van de Velde had a fundamental impact on the evolution of modern design, being not only an originator of the Art Nouveau style during the *fin-de-siècle* era but also an influential champion of Modernism during the early twentieth century. Indeed, more than any other designer, he acted as a crucial bridge, both intellectually and creatively, between the Art Nouveau movement and the later Modern Movement.

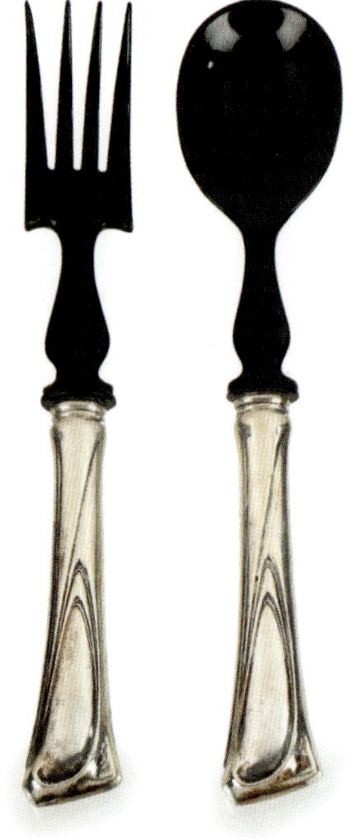

Van de Velde began his career as an artist, having studied painting at the Académie des Beaux-Arts, Antwerp, between 1881 and 1884. He then moved to Paris to train under the portraitist Carolus-Duran. In 1892, van de Velde decided to abandon art in favour of design after reading the design-reforming writings of John Ruskin and William Morris. The following year, he exhibited embroidery at the salon of the Les XX art society and began working as a graphic designer on books and journals. Apart from this, he lectured at the Université Nouvelle in Brussels from 1894 to 1896. In 1894, he published an influential essay entitled *Déblaiement d'Art* (Clearing Art) in which he called for a unification of the artistic disciplines. The next year, he started teaching industrial design – then known as *arts d'industrie et d'ornamentation* – at the University of Brussels.

During this period, van de Velde put his theories into practice with the construction of his own residence, Bloemenwerf (1895). With this house in the Brussels suburb of Uccle, he created a *Gesamtkunstwerk*, whereby not only the building but also all of the furniture, fixtures and fittings were designed by him to create a totally unified work of art. The progressive building was visited by Julius Meier-Graefe, founder of the *Dekorative Kunst* journal, and also by Siegfried Bing, a renowned art dealer. The latter subsequently asked van de Velde to create four rooms for his fashionable Maison L'Art Nouveau gallery in Paris. Importantly, the Bloemenwerf house was a physical

ABOVE:
Servers
for Koch & Bergfeld, *c.*1905

LEFT:
Bloemenwerf dining chair
1895

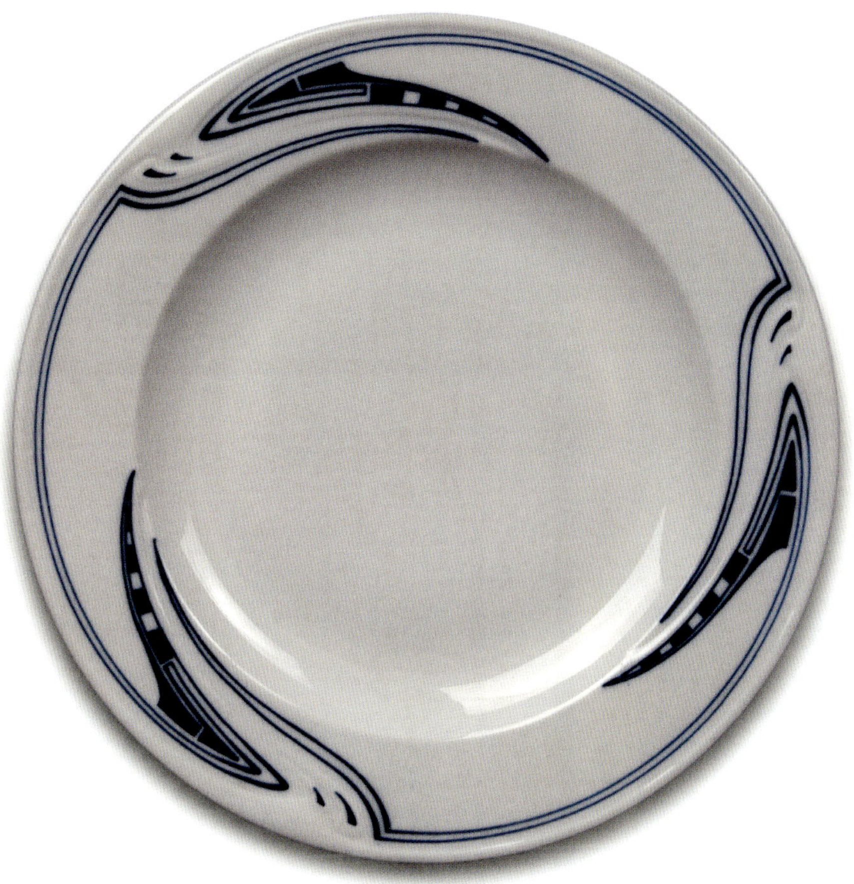

ABOVE:
Peitschenhieb plate
for Meissen, *c.*1903

expression of van de Velde's belief that decoration should always be informed by a design's construction rather than applied as surface ornamentation. In 1901, he noted, "No ornament can be permitted that is not organically absorbed.... Ornament has no life of its own but depends on the forms and lines of the object itself." Unlike earlier British design-reformers, van de Velde saw the machine as a means to achieve a new kind of logical engineered beauty.

His rallying cry for design honesty and fitness for purpose was later taken up by the Deutscher Werkbund, which was founded in 1907 and of which van de Velde – having moved to Germany in 1900 – was a prominent member. There was, however, a disagreement among members of this association on how best to reform design, with Hermann Muthesius calling for standardization and more industrialized production, and van de Velde continuing to stress the important contribution that individual creative endeavour could make to modern design practice. Eventually, he left the Werkbund in 1914 and three years later moved to Switzerland to work as an architect. In 1926, he returned to work in Brussels and established the Insitut Supérieur d'Architecture (ISAD).

Retiring to Switzerland in 1946, he published his autobiography a decade later. A hugely versatile and talented designer, van de Velde throughout his career managed skilfully to balance the demands of practical utility with a uniquely elegant style in order to create work that had a distinctive beauty born of a thoughtful approach to functionality.

Lella Vignelli & Massimo Vignelli

Italian/active America, 1934–2014 / Italian/active America,1931–2014

Husband and wife team Lella and Massimo Vignelli introduced an elegantly modern Milanese design sensibility to the American creative landscape through their stylish furniture and product designs as well as eye-catching graphic solutions and corporate identity work. As New York's pre-eminent design power couple, they collaborated throughout their careers, and their personal lives and design activities were totally intertwined – they lived and breathed design for more than fifty years. Even to this day, in the United States their legacy endures: their designs have a presence, albeit often unnoticed, in the everyday lives of millions of people, whether it is their design of the New York Subway map (1970–72) or the numerous logos they conceived which have come to symbolize corporate America from Bloomingdales to Ford.

Working within the Modernist canon, the Vignellis sought to create purposeful designs that were, as Massimo put it, "visually powerful, intellectually elegant, and above all timeless". Time and time again, they did just this, with stylish Italian panache. As Deyan Sudjic has observed, Massimo's greatest achievement was giving "America a modern look".

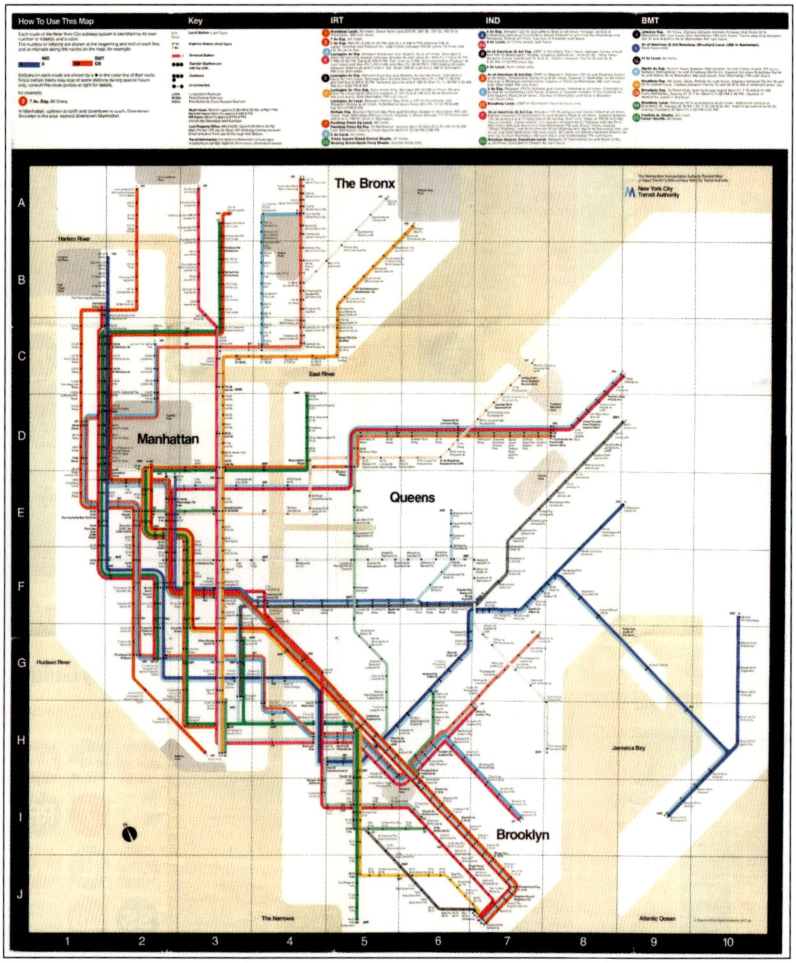

ABOVE:
New York Subway map
1970–72

Elena "Lella" Valle was born into a family of Italian architects. Her father, Provino Valle, designed buildings in the Novecento style, while her brothers, Gino and Nani, ran a respected architecture partnership in Udine. Following in the family's tradition, Lella trained as an architect at the Istituto Universario di Architettura (Higher Institute of Architecture, now Iuav University) in Venice. Born in Milan, Massimo, on the other hand, had become obsessed with design during his teenage years after a visit to the home of an interior designer who was a friend of his mother. So much so that at the age of sixteen he went to work as a draughtsman in Achille Castiglioni's office, and two years later enrolled to study architecture at the

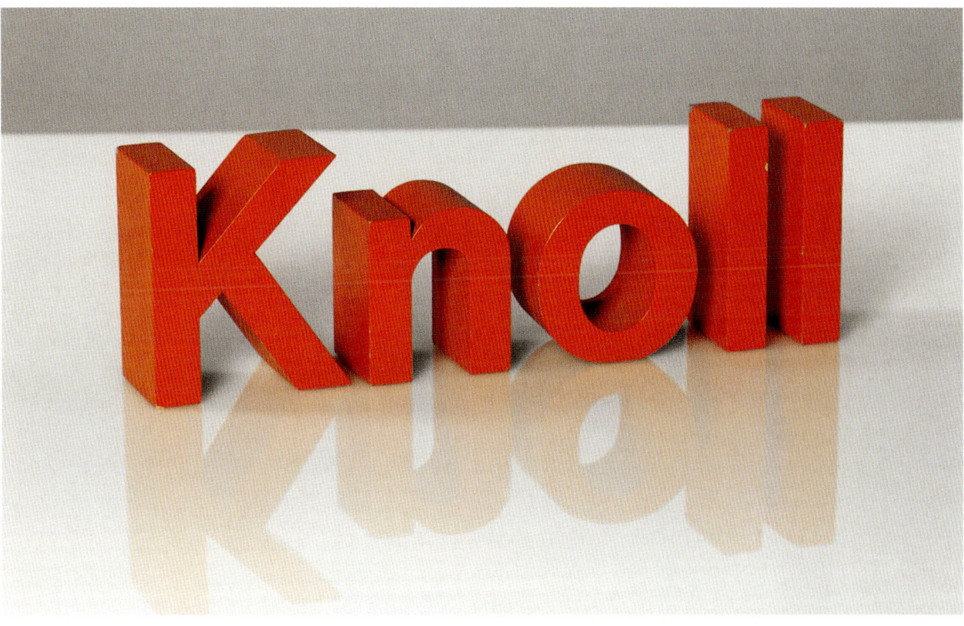

ABOVE:
Identity design (logo in lacquered wood)
for Knoll, early 1960s

Politecnico di Milano. Later he too trained at the Istituto Universario di Architettura in Venice and, while still a student, began designing lighting for the local Venini glassworks, notably his Fungo table lamp (1955).

In 1957, Massimo met Lella at an architectural conference, and the same year they were married. They both obtained fellowships to study in the United States – Massimo at the Institute of Design at the Illinois Institute of Technology and Lella at the School of Architecture at the Massachusetts Institute of Technology (MIT). In 1960 the couple established Vignelli Office for Design in Milan, and in 1965 Massimo co-founded, with five other partners, the Unimark International design consultancy in Milan, with Lella heading up its interior design department. The following year the couple moved permanently to New York and Unimark established a sister office there, specializing in pioneering corporate-identity work.

In 1971, they founded their own multidisciplinary consultancy, Vignelli Associates, which over the succeeding decades produced an exemplary high standard of work, whether graphic artwork for Knoll or COSMIT, packaging for IBM or Bloomingdale's, transportation graphics for the New York Subway or the Washington Metro, plastic tableware for Heller or ceramic dinnerware for Sasaki. Above all, the Vignellis' work was distinguished by an intelligent creativity and a purposeful clarity, in accord with Massimo's observation that he liked "design to be semantically correct, syntactically consistent and pragmatically understandable".

Charles Voysey

British, 1857–1941

A leading member of the Arts and Crafts Movement, Charles Francis Annesley Voysey created buildings, furniture, textiles and metalware with a strong emotionally engaging quality that was a direct result of his upbringing in a deeply religious family. His father had been a highly controversial Anglican clergyman who was eventually accused of heresy for effectively starting a new religion when he established the Theist Church in 1880. Dubbed "the Religion of Common Sense", theism embraced the theory of evolution and was an essentially humanist theology. Charles Voysey's work reflected this philosophy in his deployment of organic forms inspired by nature, or folk-influenced motifs.

After studying with the architect John Pollard Seddon, and later working in the architecture offices of Henry Saxon Snell and George Devey, Voysey established his own practice in 1882. As well as undertaking building commissions, he turned his hand to design, working in an Arts and Crafts style that was much influenced by William Morris and Arthur Heygate Mackmurdo. Voysey's earliest recorded furniture design was the Swan chair (*c.*1883–85), which took the form of two abstracted swans. With its gently undulating lines, flowing in accord with the human body, this anthropomorphic chair was an exceedingly progressive design that not only predicted the sculptural sensuality of the Art Nouveau style, but was also an extremely early example of ergonomically informed design.

Another piece of furniture that exemplified his pared-down vernacular style was an oak writing desk (1896) created for the home of William and Haydee Ward-Higgs in Bayswater, London. This beautiful design has a simplified proto-Modern form, stripped of any extraneous detailing apart from a pierced copper hinge plate depicting a shepherd with his wife and child walking in the English countryside with a sheep. The vignette of rural domesticity is framed with an arrangement of symbolic heart motifs, a favoured emblem of the Arts and Crafts Movement that is especially identified with Voysey's work. Apart from his furniture, Voysey also designed various metalwares and architectural fittings as well as a large number of textiles, both printed and woven, which were characterized by a strong stylization of natural forms and a flowing rhythmic patterning – a good example of this being his wonderful Let Us Prey textile pattern of 1909.

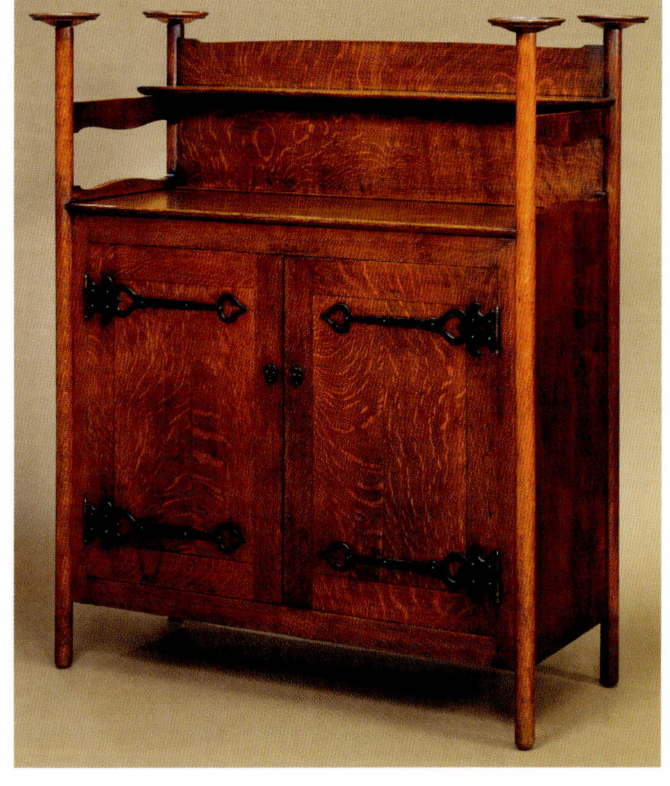

BELOW:
Sideboard
for Hurtmore (New Place) in Surrey, *c.*1897

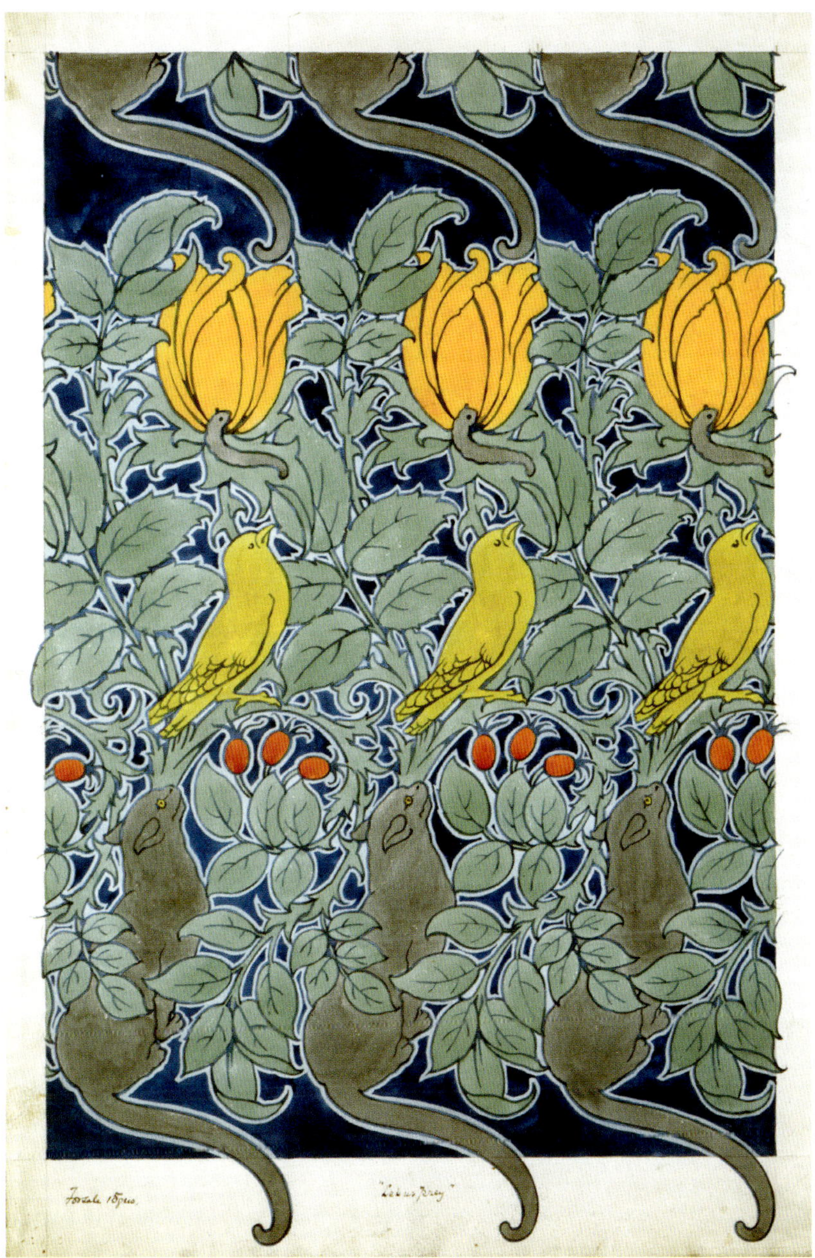

ABOVE:
Design for Let Us Prey textile
1909

Throughout his life, Voysey's work echoed his humanist philosophy and was motivated by an ethical imperative, as encapsulated in his declaration that "Simplicity, sincerity, repose, directness and frankness are moral qualities as essential to good architecture as to good men". For him this credo applied equally to architecture and to design – with his many holistically designed buildings attesting to this fact. Voysey's promotion of a simple yet modern vernacular architectural style was not only highly influential in Britain, spawning endless suburbs of cottage-style semis, but also abroad, both in North America and in Continental Europe. As the German cultural attaché Hermann Muthesius was to note, Voysey was "the first to achieve a complete synthesis" between the work of the designer and that of the architect, with many of his buildings being unified *Gesamtkunstwerk* (total works of art).

Wilhelm Wagenfeld

German, 1900–1990

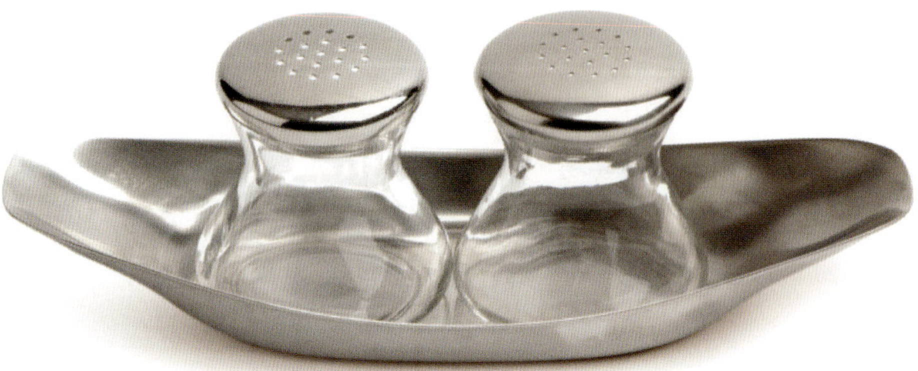

ABOVE:
Max & Moritz salt and pepper shakers
for WMF (Württembergische Metallwarenfabrik), 1952

Wilhem Wagenfeld was one of the few designers trained at the Bauhaus who successfully went on to design for large-scale industrial production. Indeed, many of his products are now seen as exemplars of German Modernism.

Wagenfeld began his career as an apprentice in the draughting department of the Koch & Bergfeld silverware factory, before studying drawing and typography in Bremen and Hanau. He then studied at the Staatliches Bauhaus in Weimar in 1923, undertaking the preliminary course before training in the school's metal workshop. It was there, in response to an assignment set by László Moholy-Nagy, that in 1923–24 he created his glass and metal MT9/ME1 table light (later also known as the Bauhaus Lamp), co-designed with Carl Jakob Jucker. In 1924, Wagenfeld obtained his journeyman's certificate as a silversmith and engraver, and when the Bauhaus moved to Dessau the following year, he remained in Weimar working alongside Christian Dell in the existing workshop of the school, which now became known as the Staatliche Bauhochschule. Between 1926 and 1930 he worked at the college, first as an assistant to Richard Winkelmayer and later as head of the school's metal workshop. From 1927, he also worked as a designer for the Walter & Wagner metalware factory in Schleiz, notably creating a tea caddy (1927) and a kettle (1929–30), which were remarkable for their clean Modernist lines. In 1928, he designed the WD28 door handle and matching window latch for the S.A. Loevy foundry in Berlin, which were astonishingly minimalistic for the time, being pared down to their most essential form.

Although he had specialized in metalwork, Wagenfeld was also able to apply his design skills to the creation of products in other materials, most notably heat-resistant glass. Between 1931 and 1935, he produced a number of designs for Jenaer Glaswerk Schott & Gen. Among these were his Sintrax coffee maker (*c.*1925) and his glass tea set (*c.*1932), which was a forward-looking dematerialist *tour-de-force*. He was subsequently the art director of the Vereinigte Lausitzer glassworks in Weisswasser from 1935 to 1942, and during this tenure he

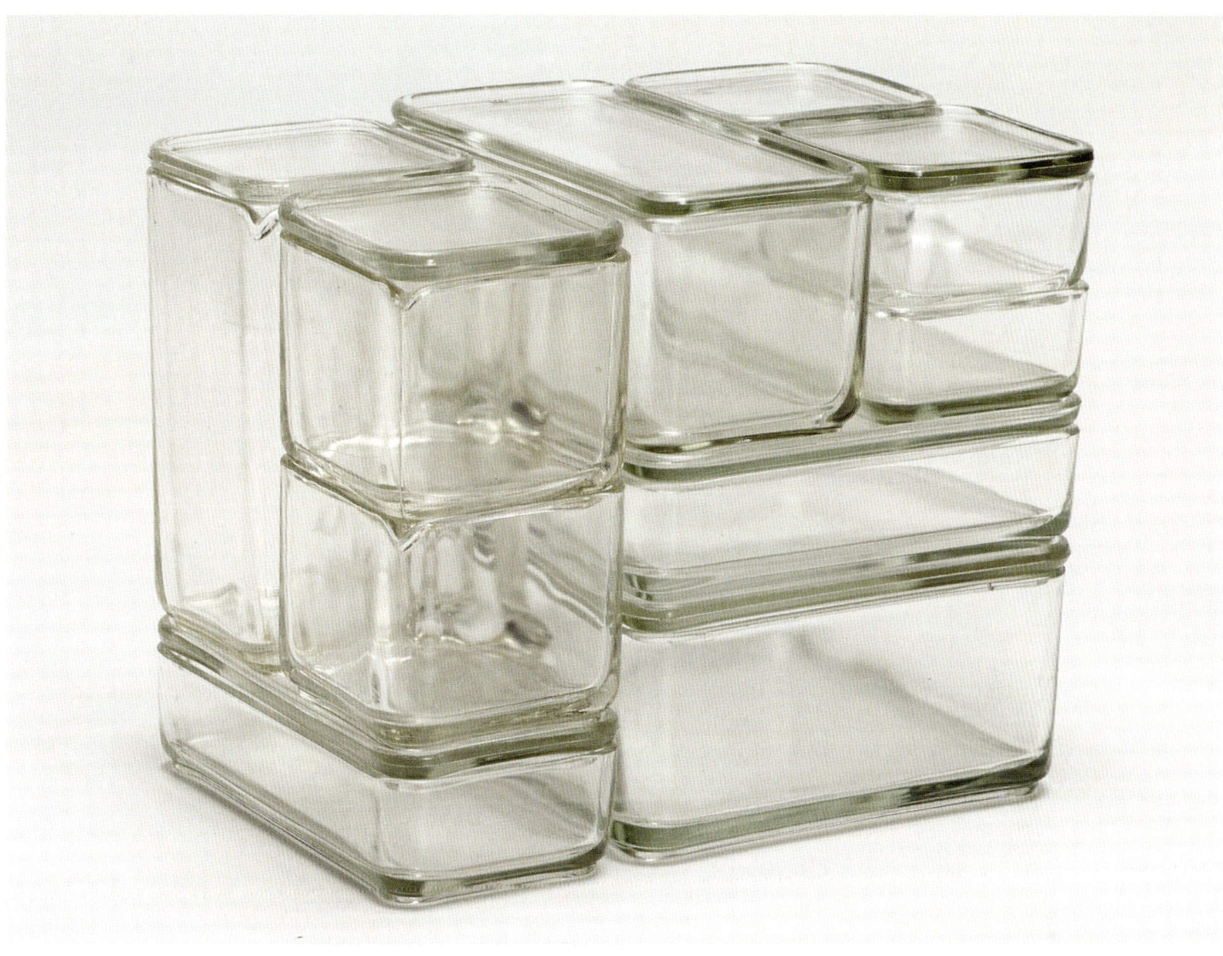

ABOVE:
Kubus stacking containers
for Vereinigte Lausitzer Glasswerke, 1938

created his iconic Kubus stacking storage containers (1938) made of thick moulded glass.

After the Second World War, Wagenfeld worked for a number of metalware factories, including Württembergische Metallwarenfabrik (WMF), for which he developed a number of well-known designs, including his Max & Moritz salt and pepper shakers (1952), named after two cheeky boys in a German children's book by Wilhelm Busch. This diminutive set, made of glass and stainless steel, reflected Wagenfeld's move towards a more sculptural approach, which was in stark contrast to the hard-edged geometric style he had pioneered during the 1920s and 1930s. Certainly this notable softening of line in his work accorded with the post-war tendency towards more fluid organic forms. As a highly trained and skilled metalworker, Wagenfeld was able to translate craft values into his designs intended for industrial production, thereby allowing them to transcend run-of-the-mill utilitarianism. Because of their perfectly considered proportions, refinement of form and practical function, many of his designs possess an enduring appeal that has kept them in production to the present day.

Marcel Wanders

Dutch, 1963–

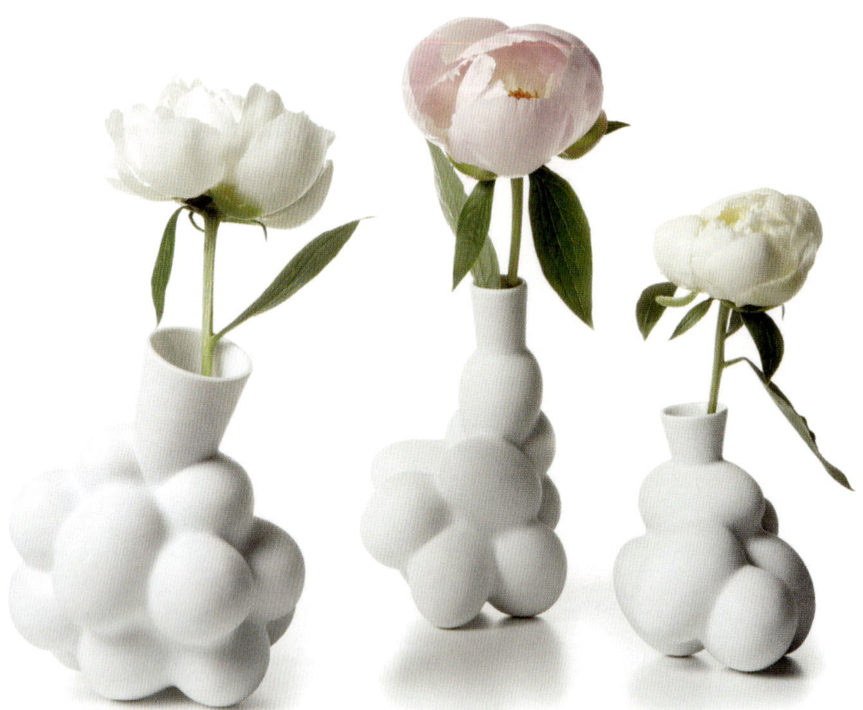

ABOVE:
Egg vase
for Droog/Rosenthal (later by Moooi), 1997

The highly successful yet controversial Dutch designer Marcel Wanders is known for his outré design work, typified by a theatrical exuberance and quirky surrealism. Unlike many of his contemporaries in the design world who follow an essentialist credo – such as Jasper Morrison, Jonathan Ive and Ross Lovegrove – Wanders in contrast is a celebrant of what is best described as maximalism. His work, however, is far more than just mere decoration, for at its heart it has an experimental playfulness that mixes the handcrafted with the high-tech. And it is this sense of hybrid synergy that gives his designs such an engaging neo-Post-Modern conceptualism, which in turn has defined the very essence of New Dutch Design.

Wanders initially trained at the Eindhoven Design Academy; then, after being expelled, he enrolled at the ArtEZ Hogeschool voor de Kunsten (ArtEZ Institute of the Arts) in Arnhem, where he completed his design studies. One of his earliest designs was his Set Up Shades floor light (1989), which comprised a stack of "found" lampshades. This design was later included in Droog Design's first collection, shown at the Milan Furniture Fair in 1993. Two years later, Wanders opened his own studio in Amsterdam, and the following year designed the Knotted chair (1996) for Droog, which combined high-tech materials with low-tech production methods. This design was ingeniously formed from a loose cat's-cradle of roped nylon and carbon-fibre

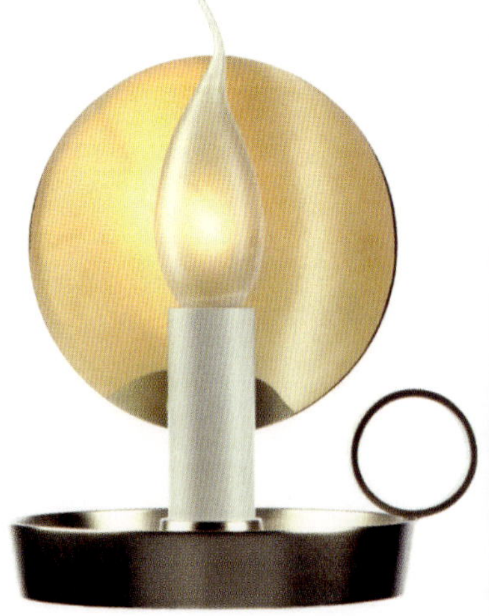

that was hung over a chair-shaped frame and then impregnated with liquid epoxy resin. Once dried, the woven mesh supported itself, appearing to defy the laws of gravity. Refreshingly different in its craft-meets-technology approach, this chair brought Wanders international acclaim and firmly established him as an emerging young star designer, a role he more than happily played up to.

Other designs that were widely publicized and helped build his reputation included his Egg vase (1997), the mould of which was created by stuffing a condom with hard-boiled eggs, and his Sponge vase (2002), made by taking a natural sponge and dipping it in liquid porcelain slip and then firing it at a high temperature in a ceramic kiln so that the sponge burnt away completely leaving a delicate form made of fine porcelain, which would have been impossible to achieve using traditional moulding techniques.

In order to commercialize his designs, in 2001 Wanders set up, with Casper Vissers, his own design-led manufacturing company, called Moooi – the word *mooi* means "beautiful" in Dutch. Over the next decade, Moooi became the driving force behind the ascendency of New Dutch Design, producing not only designs by Wanders but also work by other young designers from the Netherlands. Today, Wanders runs a large design office of some fifty members, creating designs for Moooi and a plethora of other design-led companies.

His studio also works extensively in the interior design field, mainly producing schemes for private residences and the hospitality sector. It has also designed extraordinary retail spaces for Cosme Decorte, Mandarina Duck and Villa Moda that have an over-the-top deluxe quality about them. According to Wanders's mission statement, he is "here to create an environment of love… live with passion and make our most exciting dreams come true" – and in many ways he does just that.

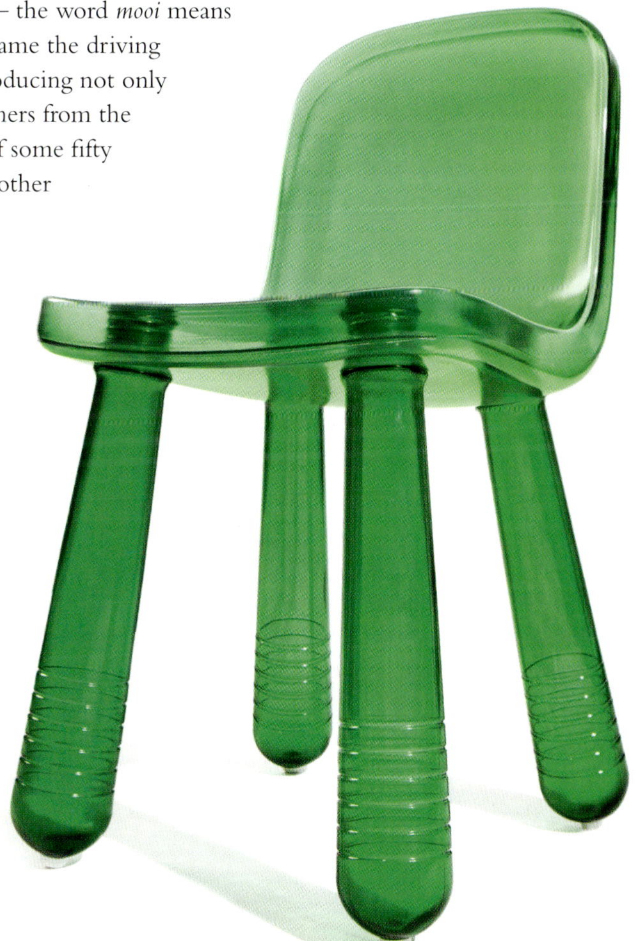

OPPOSITE:
Blo lamp
for Flos, 2001

RIGHT:
Sparkling chair
for Magis, 2010

Hans Wegner

Danish, 1914–2007

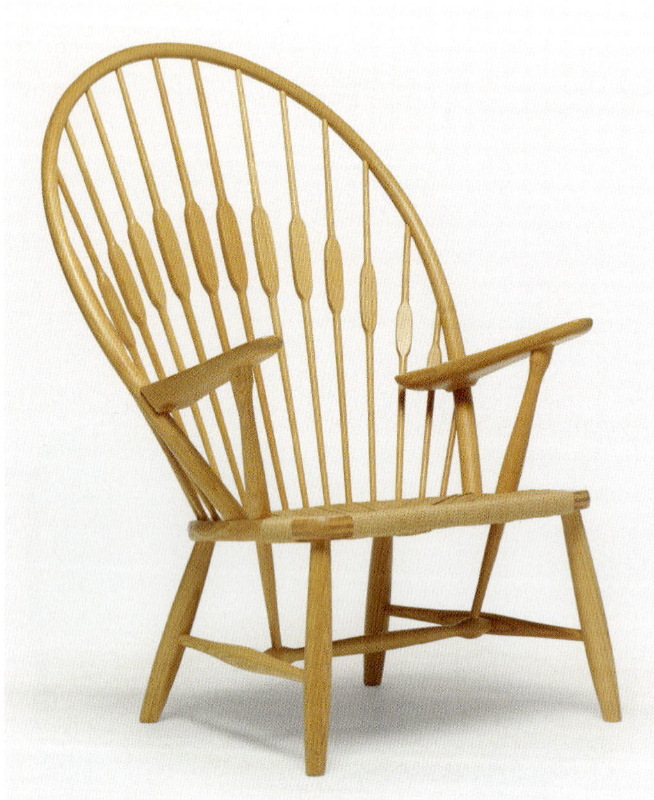

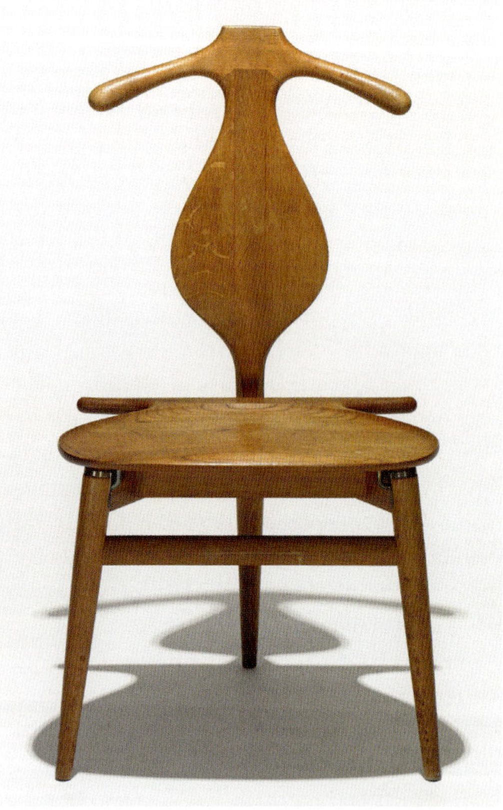

ABOVE LEFT:
Peacock chair
for Johannes Hansen, 1947

ABOVE RIGHT:
Valet chair
for Johannes Hansen, 1953

OPPOSITE TOP:
Shell chair
for Fritz Hansen, 1963

OPPOSITE BOTTOM:
Model 50 Swivel chair
for Johannes Hansen, 1955

The Danish furniture designer Hans Wegner was a renowned specialist in the design of chairs. Throughout his long and illustrious career he painstakingly explored historical seating antecedents and evolved them into modern form, resulting in a host of chair designs that epitomize Scandinavian Modernism. Wegner's evolutionary approach to design is actually a very Danish one, which can be traced back to Kaare Klint's quest for "ideal forms" based on the careful and precise study of earlier successful furniture designs.

The son of a cobbler, Wegner's genius was ultimately grounded in his brilliant cabinet-making skills, which he learnt as an apprentice from the cabinet-maker H.F. Stahlberg in his native Jutland. He also became well versed in the design teaching methods of Kaare Klint when he trained under Orla Mølegaard-Nielsen at what was then the Kunsthandvaerkerskolen (School of Arts and Crafts) in Copenhagen. It was here that he learnt an analytical approach to design through the study of human proportions and historical furniture precedents, which would act as a springboard for later designs such as his Peacock chair (1947) based on a traditional Windsor chair and his Chinese chairs (1943–45) inspired by an early-eighteenth-century model. Wegner was obsessive when it came to the detailing of his designs, believing that "there is never one damn thing that cannot be made better". Indeed, it was this conviction that led him to become one of the most prolific furniture designers of all time – creating over 3,500 designs, of which an astonishing 500 made it into manufacture. And with these he spanned the whole spectrum of seating design, from bespoke furniture pieces to simple mass-produced models.

Yet whether he was designing a one-off "throne" or a humble kitchen chair, Wegner was able to imbue his designs with, as he put it, "a touch of spirit" that helped engender an emotional engagement and endowed them with a naturalness that meant "they could only be what they were and nothing else". Wegner's focus on the design of chairs was spurred by his lifelong obsession with creating "just one good chair". Actually, he produced many outstanding chairs, but he was always mindful that there was no such thing as the definitive chair. Nevertheless, his Round chair of 1949 gained the moniker "The Chair" in the United States (much to his dismay), thanks to it being selected for the world's first televised presidential election debate, broadcast in 1960. Ultimately, Wegner gained the reputation of being "the chairmakers' chairmaker" and he continued designing them well into his eighties, by then a venerable design maestro. Certainly his designs were very much of their own era, with each chair reflecting the decade in which it was designed – perfect sculptural expressions of mid-to-late-twentieth-century Organic Modernism – and it is this inherent timeliness that, rather paradoxically, makes their appeal so timeless.

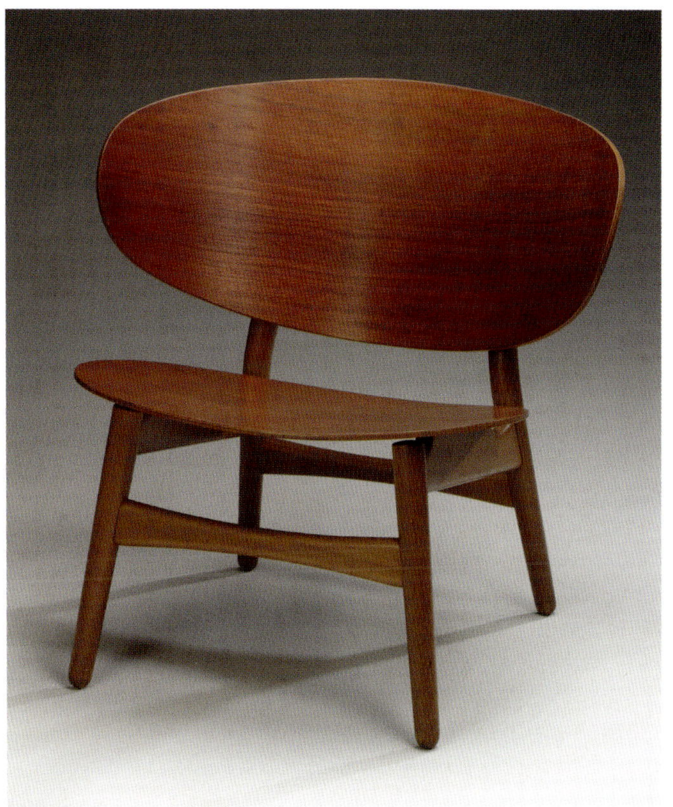

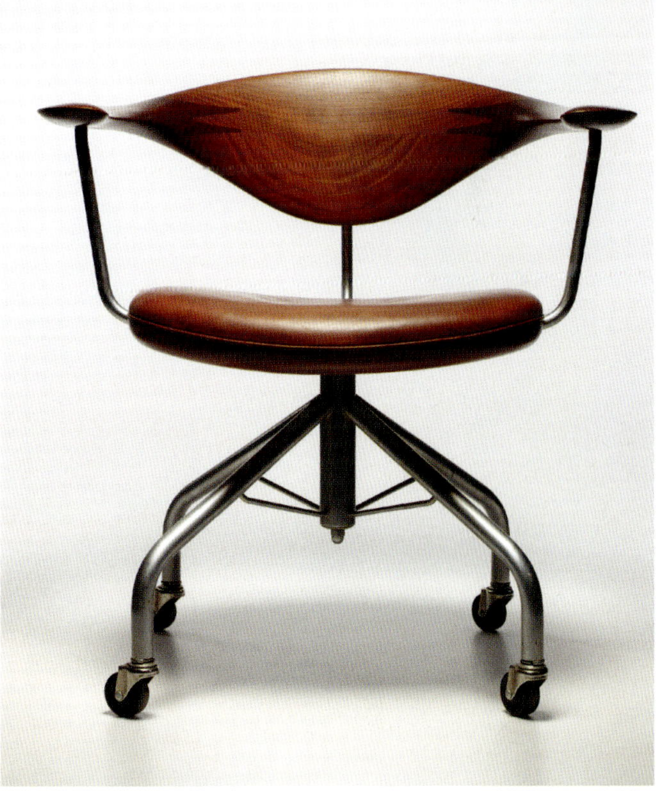

Robert Welch

British, 1929–2000

Robert Welch was a leading designer-maker who skilfully balanced his work as a silversmith creating bespoke commissions with his career as one of Britain's foremost industrial designers. Crucially, he was able to infuse his designs for industrial production with a craft sensibility, while at the same time industrial techniques often informed his creation of handcrafted pieces – for him hand and machine were equally important, with each continually informing the other.

Welch initially trained at Malvern School of Art, before transferring to Birmingham College of Art, where he studied silversmithing. He subsequently enrolled at the Royal College of Art, London in 1952, where he was the only silversmithing student in his year. While at the RCA, in 1953, he took a summer design course in Sweden, which would help determine his future career. For while there, he encountered a window display of modern stainless steel wares by Sigurd Persson and immediately realized that this was where the future of metalwork lay – so much so that he decided he had to focus on stainless steel design during his final year at the RCA, knowing that this then ultramodern material offered exciting formal possibilities in the realm of metalworking. This decision was further bolstered the following year by another student trip, this time to Norway, when Welch undertook work

BELOW:
Hobart/CD25 candlesticks
for Campden Designs (later Victor Cast Iron), 1961

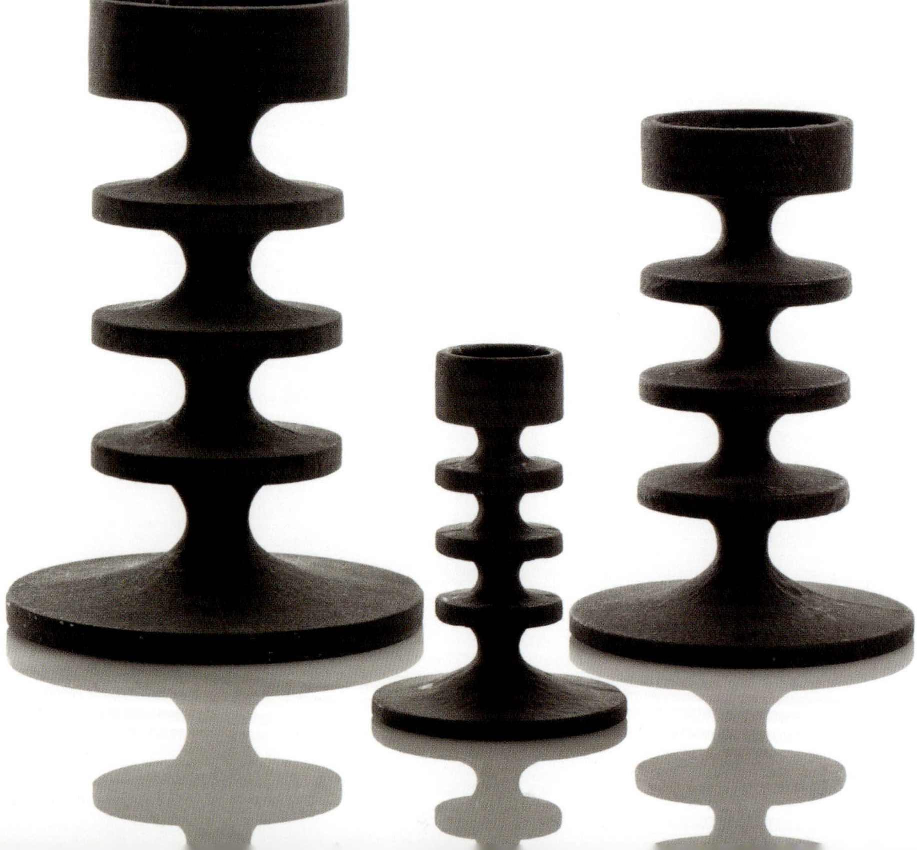

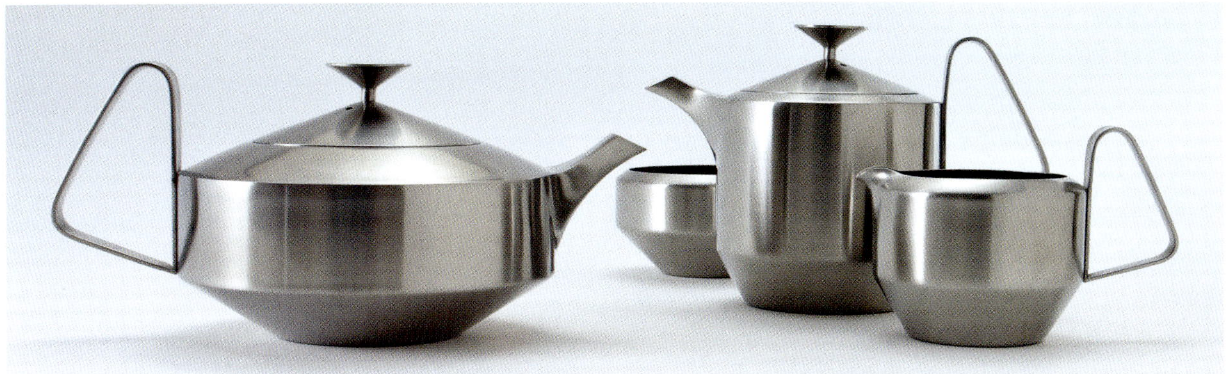

experience in the Bergen workshop of the silversmith Theodor Olsen and again came across examples of modern stainless steel wares being produced by various Scandinavian companies. Around this time, he began an association with J. & J. Wiggin, then the only British manufacturer of stainless steel tableware, and started designing for the firm under its Olde Hall (later Old Hall) brand.

ABOVE:
Alveston tea set
for Old Hall, 1961–62

BELOW:
Campden toast rack
for Olde Hall (later Old Hall), 1956

On graduating, he became the company's design consultant and set up his own studio-cum-workshop in the Old Silk Mill in Chipping Campden, Gloucestershire, which had previously been the headquarters of Charles Robert Ashbee's influential Guild of Handicraft. One of Welch's earliest successes was the Campden toast rack (1956), a design simplified to its barest functional bones that subsequently won a Design Centre Award and placed Welch firmly in the vanguard of the stainless steel revolution. It was, however, his later Alveston tea set (1961–62) with its precise crisp lines that was his most masterful design for Old Hall.

Welch also created some exquisite silverware pieces, most notably a seven-branch candelabra, inspired by the Abstract Expressionism of Jackson Pollock, that was commissioned by Goldsmiths' Hall and included in the Smithsonian Institution's *British Artist Craftsmen* travelling exhibition of 1959. He worked extensively in cast iron, too, creating a number of iconic designs – such as his Hobart candlesticks (1961).

During his career spanning over four decades he designed dozens of different cutlery patterns – including the groundbreaking Alveston (1961), which, although thoroughly contemporary, was based on historic cutlery precedents. In 1969, Welch opened his own studio shop in Chipping Campden to sell his silverware pieces alongside his designs for industrial production. This innovative venture into design-led retailing importantly allowed him to interact with customers, which gave him valuable feedback that helped inform his design work. A talented craftsman and skilful designer, Welch was guided by an unwavering belief in good design, and his numerous timeless products, many of which are still in production, attest to this principle.

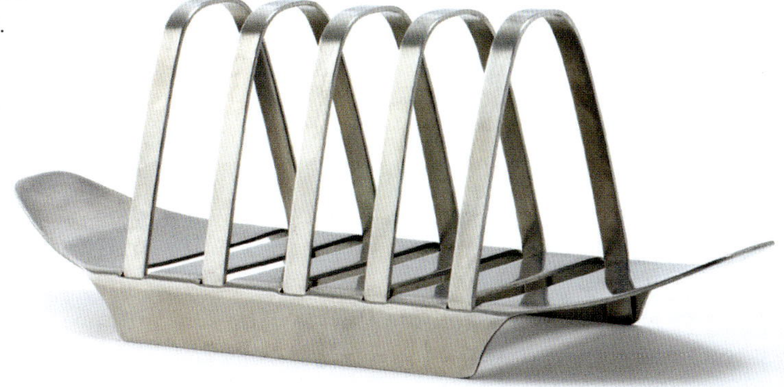

Wiener Werkstätte

Austrian, 1903–1932

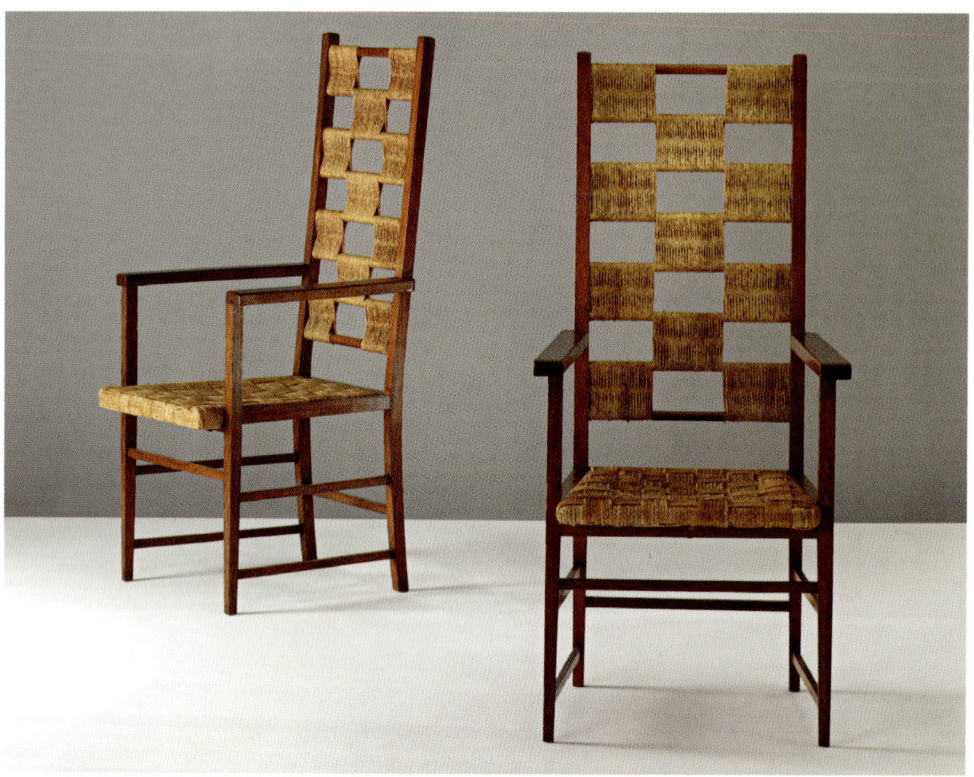

ABOVE:
Pair of armchairs
by Koloman Moser for Prag-Rudniker Korbwaren-fabrik, *c.*1903

Around 1900, Vienna was the most culturally exciting city in the world, home to forward-looking philosophers, scientists, political intellectuals, musicians, artists and architects, all of whom were attempting to express through their various endeavours the new spirit of the age. It was also the city where the Art Nouveau movement – called Jugendstil (youth style) in German – ultimately found its most fertile ground, with a group of like-minded artists and architects rejecting the overly academic conservativism of the Association of Austrian Artists housed in the Künstlerhaus and forming their own breakaway movement, the Vereinigung Bildender Künstler Österreichs (Union of Austrian Artists), which became better known as the Wiener Sezession or Vienna Secession.

Founded in 1897, the Secession counted among its members from the fine-art world Gustav Klimt, Carl Moll, Max Kurzweil and Josef Engelhart, and from the field of architecture and design Joseph Maria Olbrich, Koloman Moser and Josef Hoffmann. Young and talented, they together forged a highly progressive Viennese interpretation of the Art Nouveau/ Jugendstil movement, as evidenced by one of its architectural masterworks, the landmark Secession Building designed by Joseph Maria Olbrich with its large gilded dome of laurel leaves. Completed in 1898, this glittering building was the permanent exhibition centre for

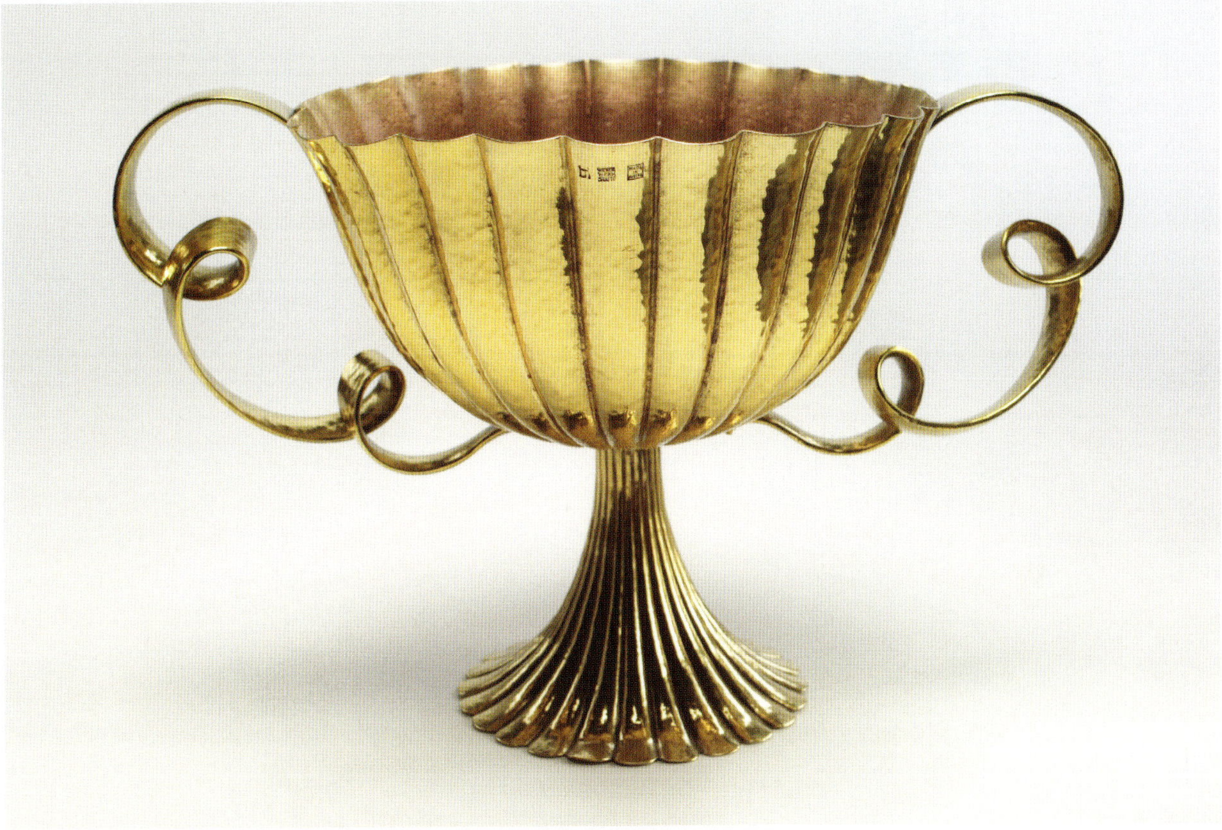

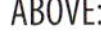

ABOVE:
Centrepiece
by Josef Hoffmann for the Wiener Werkstätte, 1924–25

RIGHT:
Table lamp
by Dagobert Peche for the Wiener Werkstätte, *c.*1922

FAR RIGHT:
Etched opaque and brown flashed glass vase
by Josef Hoffmann for the Wiener Werkstätte, *c.*1911

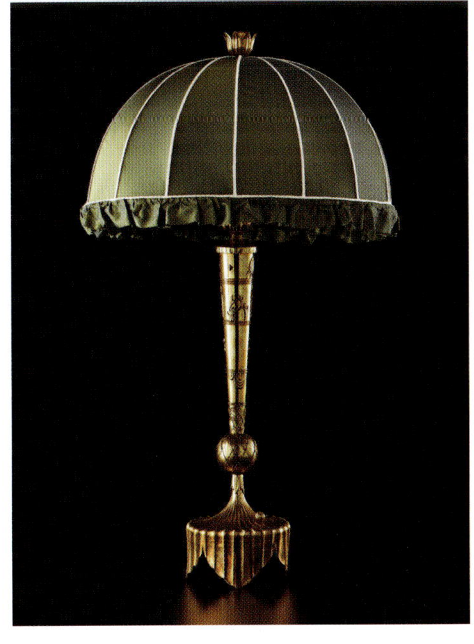

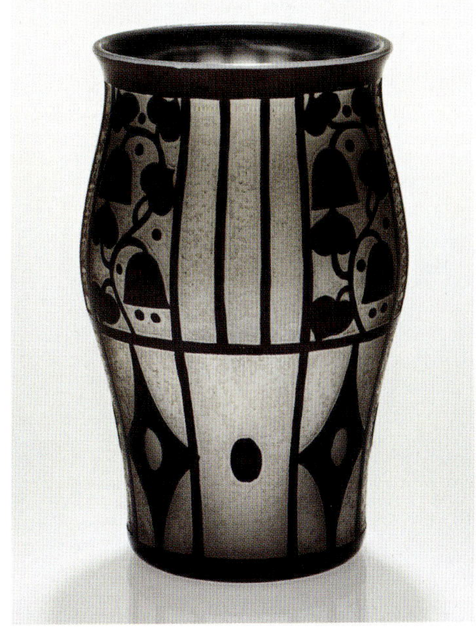

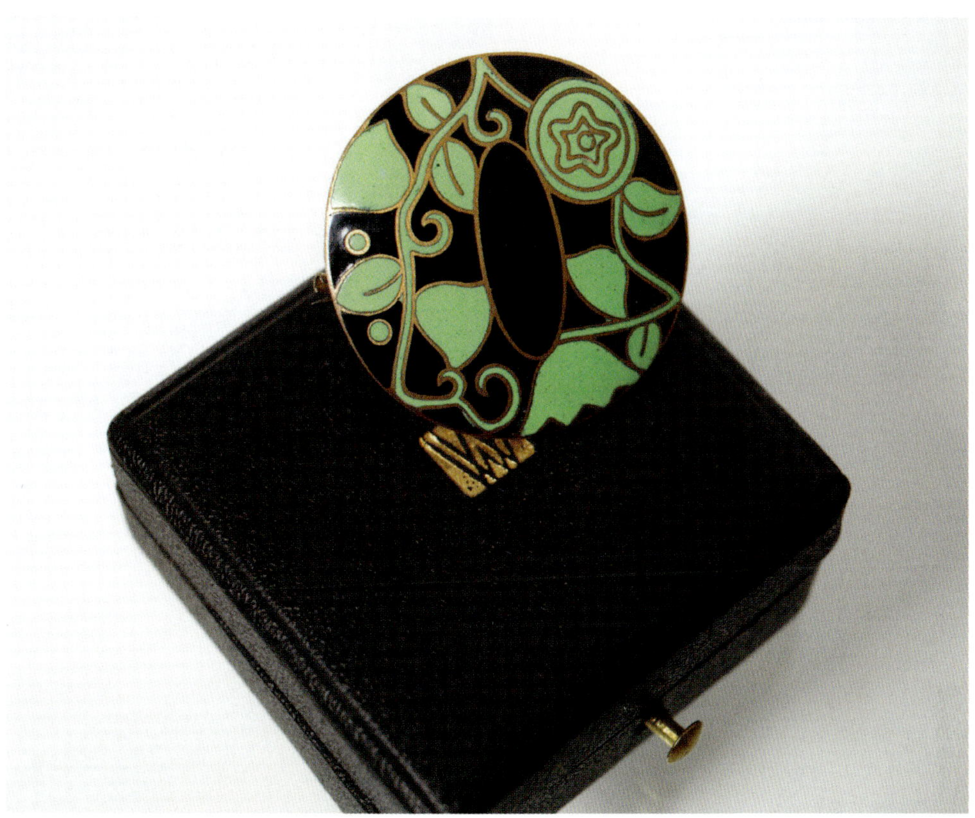

OPPOSITE:
Playing cards
by Editha Moser for A. Glanz and A. Berger, *c.*1905–09

ABOVE:
Brooch
by Josef Hofmann for the Wiener Werkstätte, *c.*1904

the Secession and above its entrance was boldly inscribed the group's motto: "To every age its art. To art its freedom." Although the building was not completed for the *Wiener Sezession I* exhibition held in 1898, it was the venue for all the group's subsequent exhibitions including the landmark *Wiener Sezession VIII* exhibition of 1900, which incorporated installations by foreign design luminaries including Charles Rennie Mackintosh, Charles Robert Ashbee and Henry van de Velde.

Inspired by Mackinstosh's geometric abstraction of form, and also by Ashbee's design-as-social-experiment activities at the Guild of Handicraft, Hoffmann and Moser subsequently established the Wiener Werkstätte (Vienna Workshops) in 1903, with the financial backing of Fritz Wärndorfer. The Werkstätte had a number of dedicated workshops that manufactured silverware, jewellery, metalware, leatherwork and furniture, which was typified by a distinctive rectilinearity, the use of luxury materials and an excellence of craftsmanship. There was also a bookbindery, as well as an architecture office and a design studio. Werkstätte members were notable for providing better-than-average working conditions and, like the Guild of Handicraft, they employed only the best available materials and refused to compromise on quality, even if this affected affordability.

By 1905 the Wiener Werkstätte had effectively taken over from the Vienna Secession as the leading Arts and Crafts force in Austria, the latter having suffered dissension among its ranks that led to several, including Hoffmann, leaving the group. The Werkstätte remained a going concern until 1932, and during its twenty-nine years of operation some 200 designers created projects that were executed by highly skilled craftspeople in its workshops. It was, however, the work produced prior to the First World War that was the most innovative and influential in that it predicted the stripped-down geometric formalism of the Modern Movement.

Tapio Wirkkala

Finnish, 1915–1985

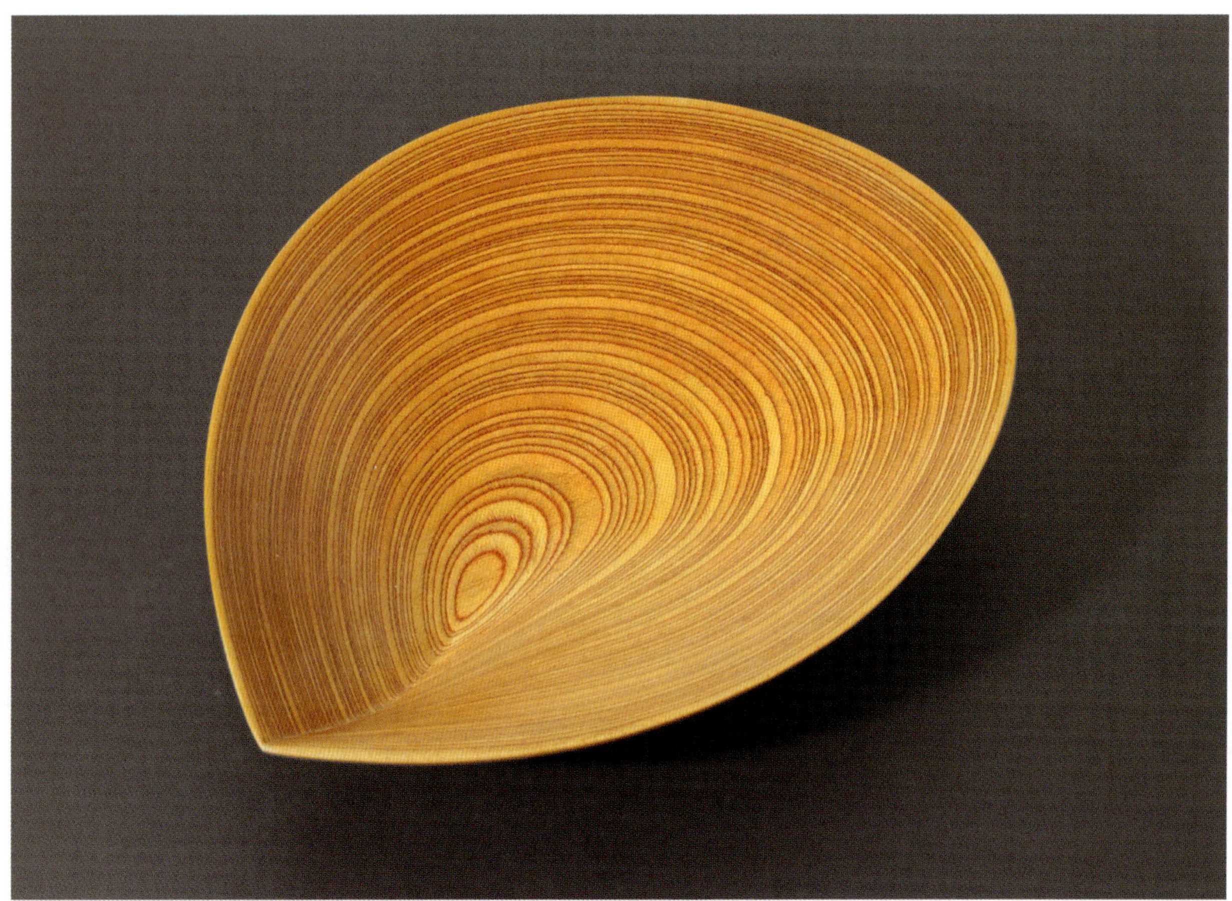

Tapio Wirkkala was among the most accomplished of all the Scandinavian form givers, working across a wide range of disciplines. Throughout the 1950s, 1960s and 1970s he was a prominent figure in Finnish design and his work came to be internationally recognized for its sculptural bravado and underlying human-centric logic.

Wirkkala's extraordinary versatility as a designer enabled him to work successfully in various design disciplines, be it art glassware, studio ceramics, metalware, jewellery, furniture, lighting or even exhibition graphics, packaging and industrial design. Whether his designs were intended for large-scale mass-production or created as limited-edition pieces, they possessed an engaging national identity. This was the result of him embracing the materials and processes associated with the handcraft traditions of Finland, along with the plethora of forms found in nature – the delicate veining of a leaf, the asymmetric patterns formed by ice, or the roughly gnarled bark of a tree.

ABOVE:
Leaf dish
for Soinne et Kni, *c.*1951 – made from laminted birch and teak

RIGHT:
Vases and bowl
for Iittala, *c.*1946 – the vase on the right is the Kantarelli (chanterelle) from 1946

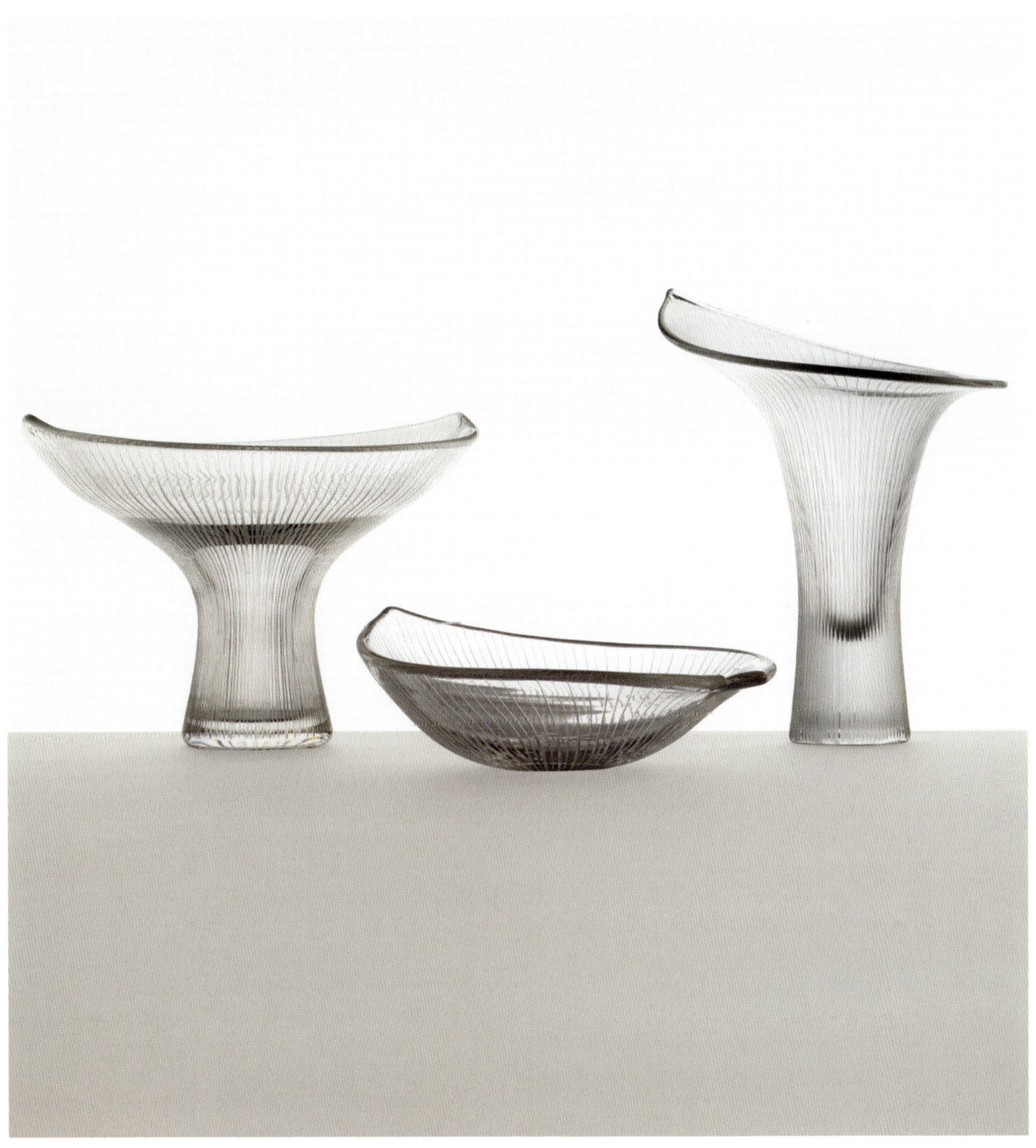

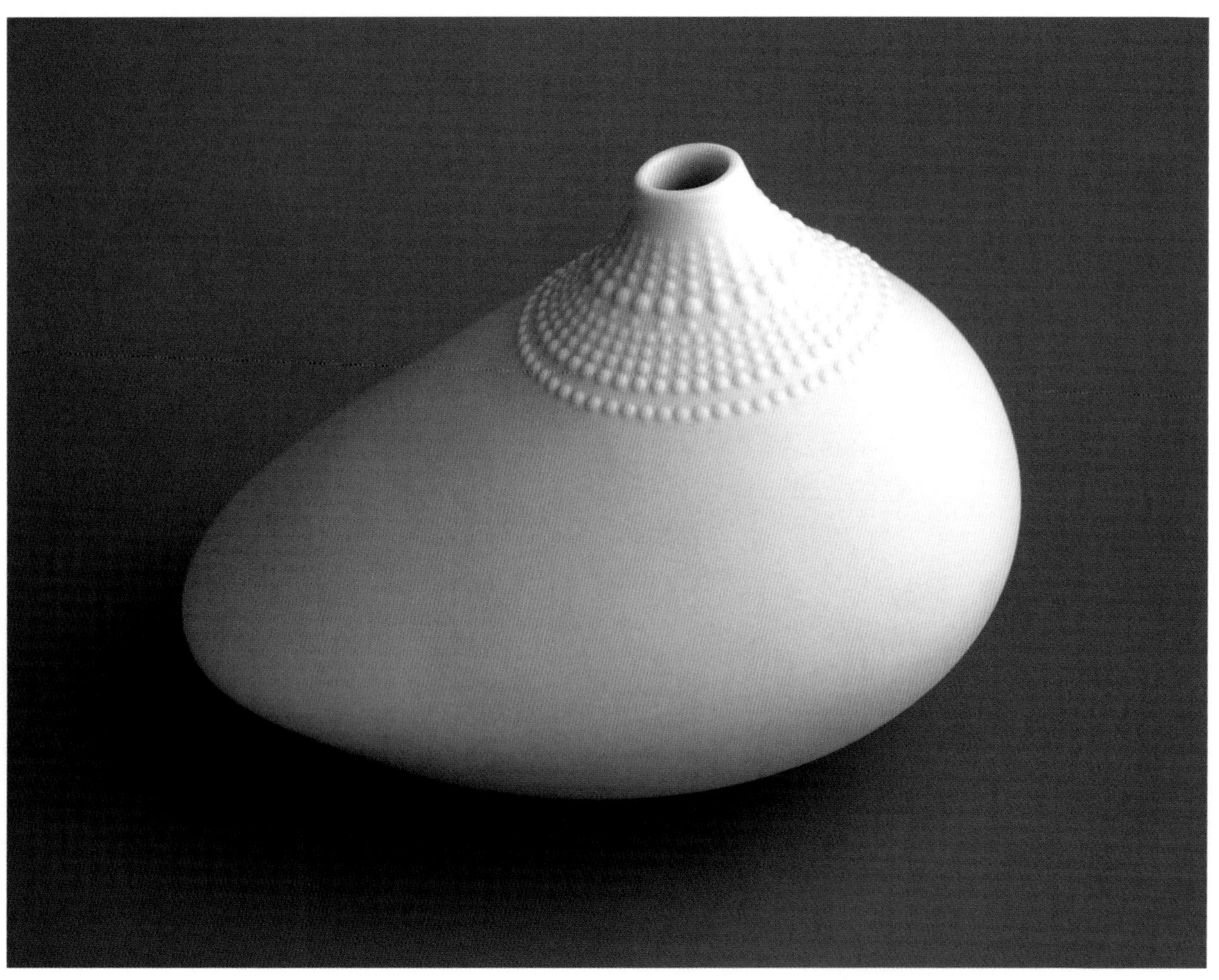

ABOVE:
Pollo vase
for Rosenthal Studio-Line, 1970

Having studied sculpture at the University of Art and Design in Helsinki, Wirkkala's first successful foray into the world of design was a winning entry for a competition to design a postage stamp to commemorate the planned 1940 Helsinki Olympic Games (later cancelled due to the Second World War). After the war, he created his series of Leaf platters using aircraft plywood, which were described by *House Beautiful* magazine in 1951 as "the most beautiful object of the year". The same year he won three Grand Prix awards at the Milan Triennale, for his exhibition design as well as his work in wood and glass.

From 1955 to 1956 he worked in the New York office of Raymond Loewy, which gave him a crucial insight into designing for industrial mass-production. Loewy also introduced him to Philip Rosenthal, who subsequently invited him to design a number of sculptural ceramic pieces for the successful Rosenthal Studio-Line.

Wirkkala had a profound empathy for the intrinsic properties of materials. Indeed, it could be said that he channelled the spiritual essence of the raw materials he employed into the

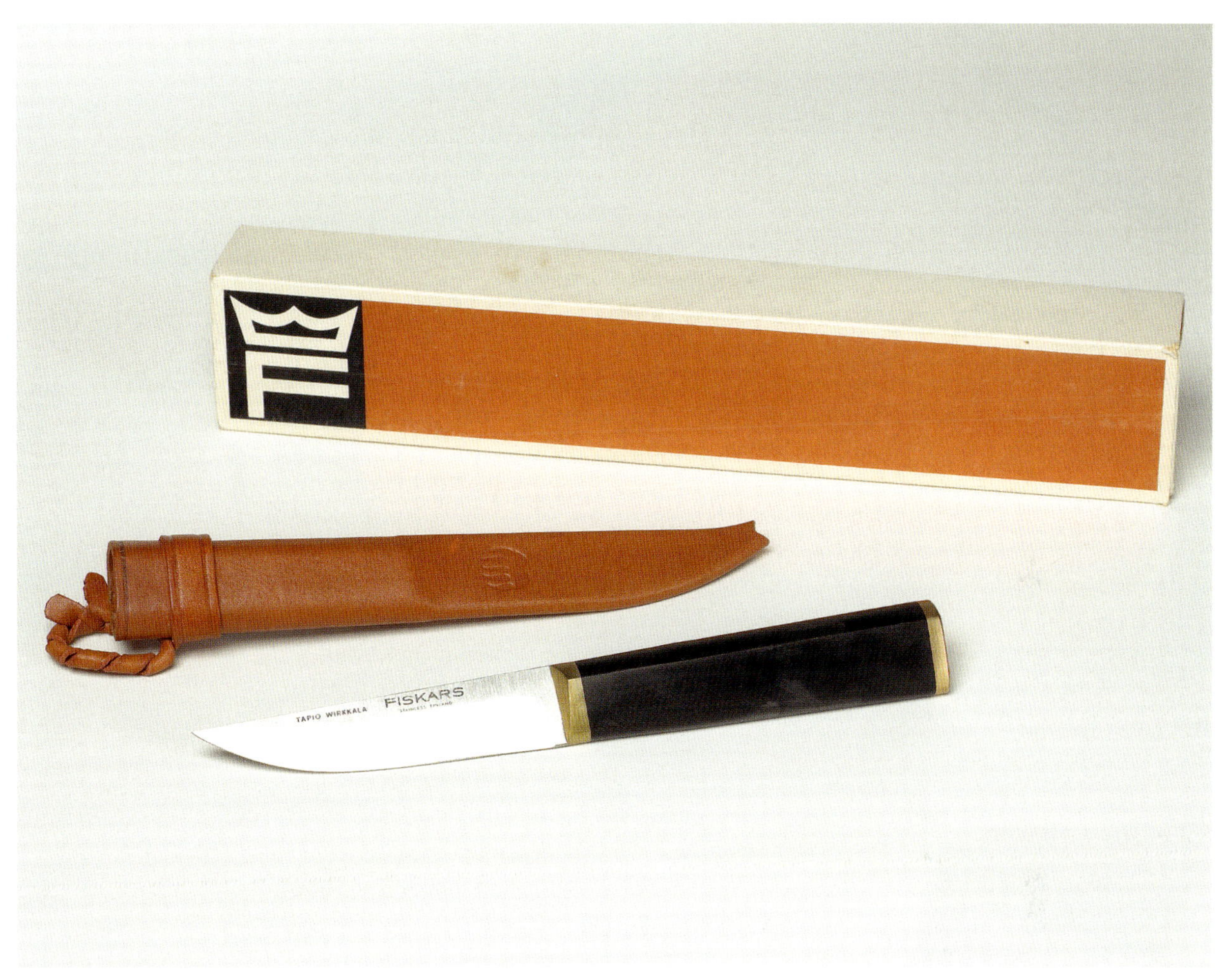

designs he created. Like the work of other Finnish designers, Wirkkala's designs also possessed a strong graphic quality, which revealed his mastery of form guided by a rare understanding of function – for example his cutlery designs were based on careful ergonomic studies so that their forms comfortably echoed the contours of the human hand. Among his best-known designs are the Puukko hunting knife for Hackman (1961), the mushroom-shaped Kantarelli (chanterelle) vase for Iittala (1946), the frosted Ultima Thule glassware range for Iittala (1968), the bird-like Pollo vase for Rosenthal (1970), various innovative lighting designs for Airam (1959) and a vodka bottle for Finlandia (1970). Guided by a dialogue between "eye, hand and thought", Wirkkala produced a truly impressive body of work that powerfully demonstrated the possibly of creating emotionally compelling objects which have functional intelligence, a rare sculptural beauty and an engaging tactility.

ABOVE:
Puukko knife
for Hackman/Fiskars, 1961

Frank Lloyd Wright

American, 1867–1959

The most celebrated American architect of the twentieth century, Frank Lloyd Wright pioneered a consicously holistic approach to architecture and design. He believed that form and function needed to be harmoniously unified, as did a building to its furnishings and to its environmental surroundings. Indeed, Wright went on to coin the term "organic architecture", which he believed needed to be guided as much by the laws of common sense as by the nature of materials. He was also influenced by forms found in the natural world, once stating, "Study nature, love nature, stay close to nature. It will never fail you." His subsequent Prairie Style houses with their low sloping roofs came to define an authentic national architectural identity in North America, while his later buildings such as the sculptural Guggenheim Museum in New York City epitomized a new and expressive interpretation of Modernism.

As a child he had been bought by his mother a set of toy bricks devised by the pioneering educationalist Friedrich Froebel, which promoted creative play. Using these geometric blocks of wood in different combinations allowed a multitude of different assemblages to be constructed, and playing with them had a formative influence on the young Wright, who would later use similar elemental forms to create real buildings. He initially trained as an engineer at the University of Wisconsin, but abandoned these studies and moved to Chicago, where he began working for the architectural firm of Joseph Lyman Silsbee. He then worked for the architect Louis Sullivan, who became his mentor and loaned him money to build his own house in the leafy Chicago suburb of Oak Park.

While still working for Adler & Sullivan, Wright began undertaking private commissions of his own and this conflict of interest eventually led to his dismissal in 1893. Following this, he founded his own architecture practice and over the next sixteen years designed around fifty Prairie Style homes in the Chicago area, most notably in Oak Park. These residences were mainly built from natural materials, such as stone, brick and wood, and were designed to accentuate the natural beauty of the surrounding Midwest prairie, with their low elevations and gently sloping rooflines that exaggerated the sense of horizontal perspectives.

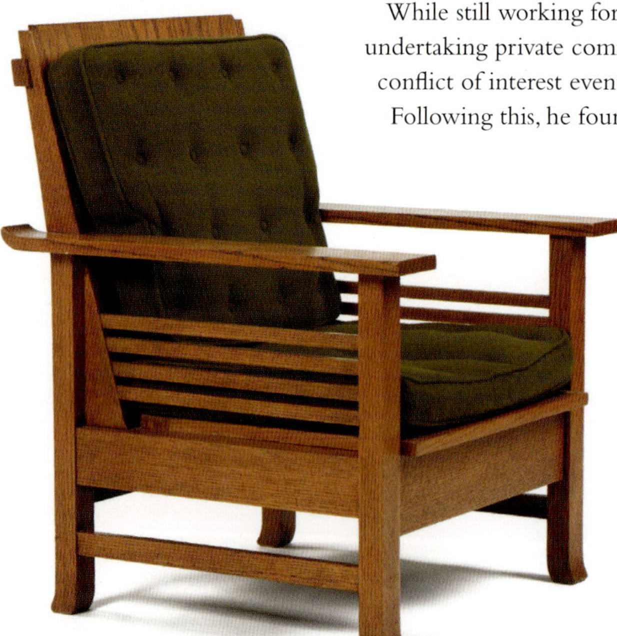

LEFT:
Armchair
for the Gilmore House in Madison, Wisconsin, 1909 – designed in collaboration with George Mann Niedecken and executed by Neidecken-Walbridge

OPPOSITE:
Children's playroom
in Frank Lloyd Wright's own house in Oak Park, Illinois, c.1900

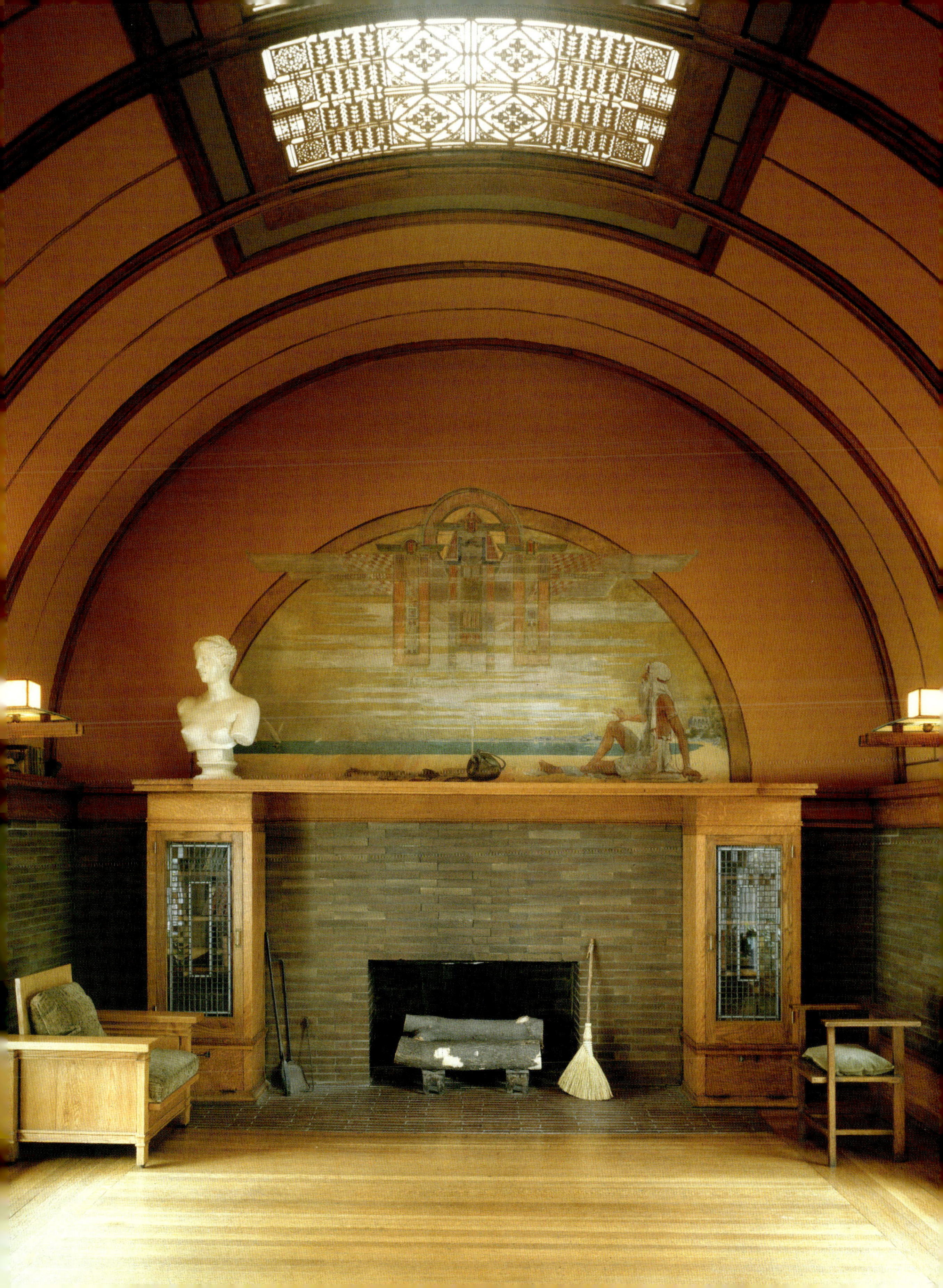

Their innovative, open-plan interiors were similarly thoughtfully conceived, with screen-like walls and soft-toned colours maximizing the sense of light and space. Many of these houses were conceived as *Gesamtkunstwerk* (total works of art), incorporating site-specific fittings and furniture, some of which was built-in. These unified projects were intended to give a sense of naturalness and spiritual transcendence.

Wright's later office and public buildings, such as the Larkin Company Administration Building in Buffalo (1903–04), were also designed as integrated schemes so as to provide as pleasant a working environment as possible. The revolutionary open-plan layout of the Larkin Building, for example, was not only functionally efficient but also helped promote a sense of shared community with all the employees working alongside each other. His Unity Temple in Oak Park (1905–09) had a similar bold external massing that belied the remarkable sense of space and light found within. With its innovative cantilevered construction, this building marked a turning point in Wright's career towards, as he put it, the "destruction of the box".

In 1914, Wright suffered a terrible personal tragedy when his then partner Mamah Cheney, together with her two children and four others, was murdered at Wright's home Taliesin by a servant, who then set fire to the beloved property. Around this time his work became increasingly distanced from the Arts and Crafts idiom; instead he began exploring the structural and ornamental potential of "industrial" concrete blocks, as in his extraordinary Hollyhock House (1919–21) in East Hollywood and his now sadly demolished Imperial Hotel in Tokyo, Japan (1915–23).

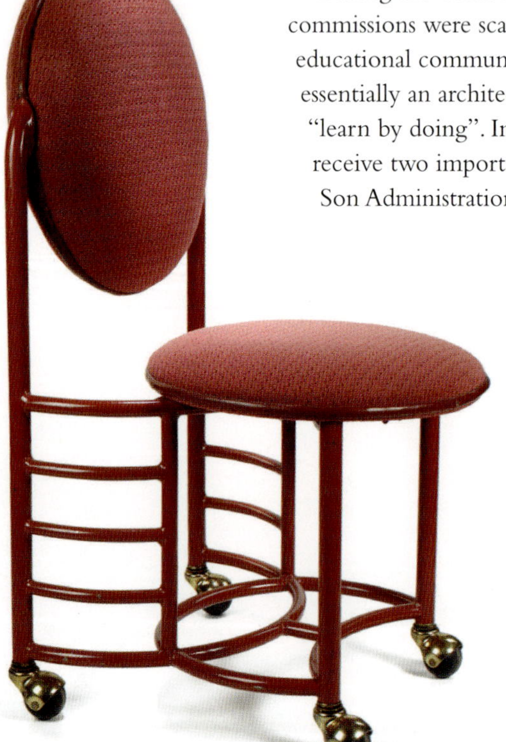

During the Great Depression of the 1930s architectural commissions were scarce, so in 1932 Wright founded an educational community, the Taliesen Fellowship, which was essentially an architectural school, governed by the credo "learn by doing". In the later 1930s, he did, however, receive two important commissions, the S.C. Johnson & Son Administration Building in Wisconsin (1936–39) and Fallingwater (1935–37), the cantilevered house in Pennsylvania built for Edgar J. Kaufmann. Both these projects, together with later buildings such as the Guggenheim Museum (1943–59) cemented Wright's reputation as the originator of a new liberated style of Modern architecture. He was fundamentally a design humanist whose work revealed an extraordinary breadth of creative vision, underpinned by a reverence for nature and an unshakable belief in humanity – values that still have an enormous relevance to the practice of design today.

LEFT:
Chair
for the S.C. Johnson & Son Administration Building, produced by Metal Office Furniture Company (later Steelcase), c.1936–39

OPPOSITE TOP:
Darwin D. Martin House
in Buffalo, New York State, 1903–05

OPPOSITE BOTTOM:
Fallingwater (Kaufmann residence)
overlooking Bear Run in south-western Pennsylvania, 1935–37

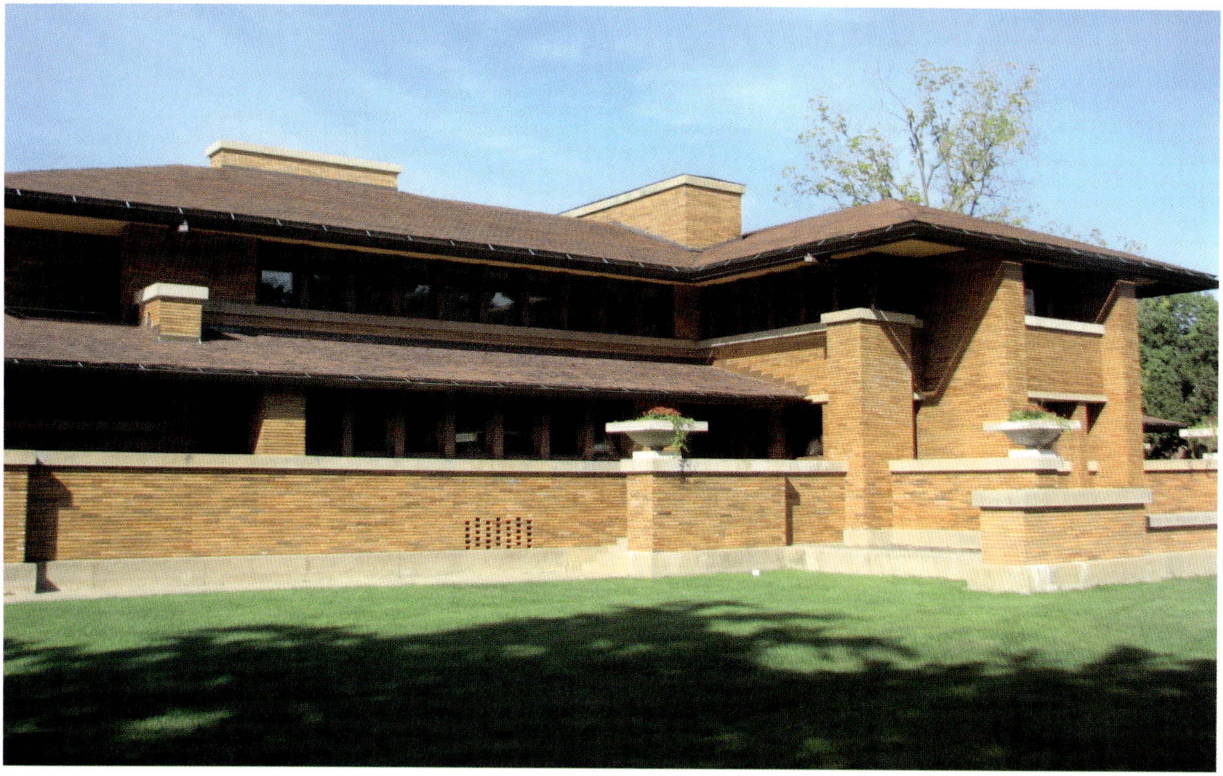

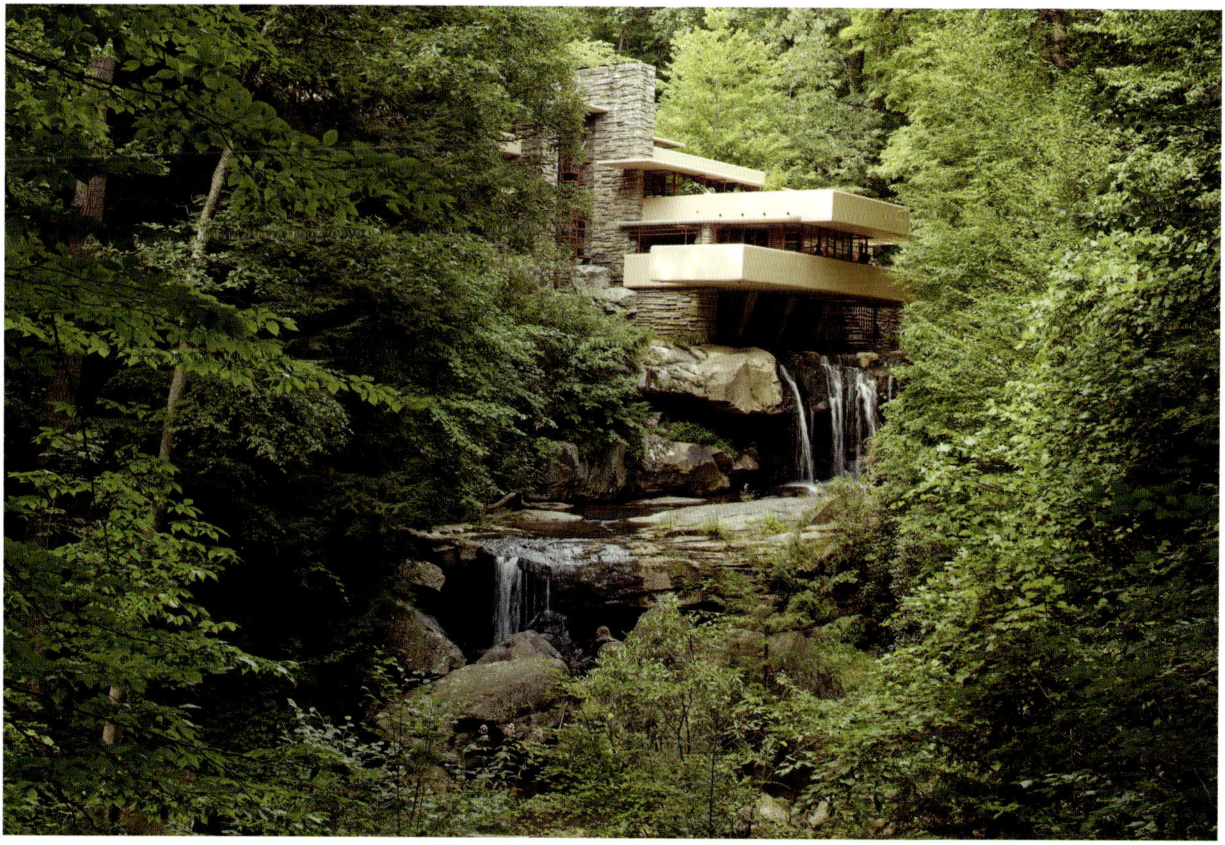

Tokujin Yoshioka

Japanese, 1967–

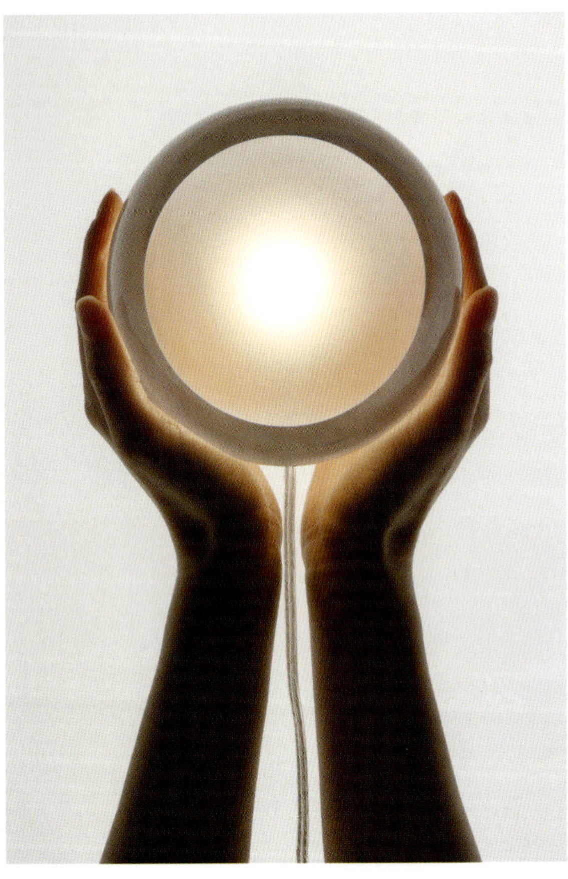

ABOVE:
Tear Drop light
for Yamagiwa, 2007

Japanese designer and artist Tokujin Yoshioka creates work that transcends the normal parameters of product design, exhibition design and architecture. The results have a refreshingly experimental nature, often incorporating new technologies and materials, and are also frequently characterized by interesting optical or spatial qualities. Like his mentor, Shiro Kuramata, Yoshioka creates beautiful things and extraordinary spaces – from consumer products to furniture and lighting to exhibition installations and interior schemes – with a precious alchemic quality. It is this rare ability to seemingly conjure up design magic that has ensured his place in the competitive ranks of international designer-superstardom.

Yoshioka studied at the Kuwasawa Design School in Tokyo, graduating in 1986. The following year he briefly joined the design office of Shiro Kuramata, before moving on to become an in-house designer for Issey Miyake in 1988. In 1992, he began working as a freelance designer and eventually in 2000 established his own design practice, Tokujin Yoshioka Inc. That same year he created his first notable "named" design, the ToFU light for Yamagiwa, which was inspired by the precise cutting of bean curd (tofu) into blocks. This minimalistic light was made from a block of transparent crystal-clear acrylic, which when illuminated by an internal bulb gave an otherworldly glow, especially along its sides – a phenomenon known as "live edge". This was a design that was not so much about a practical lighting solution but rather an aesthetic exercise in how to transmit light using minimum means to maximum effect.

Soon afterwards, Yoshioka created another widely publicized design, the Honey-Pop chair (2001), which was similarly innovative. Made from a layered wad of glassine paper, it had been carefully glued and cut in such a way that when it was opened out, it formed a curious self-supporting honeycomb chair structure, seemingly delicate but in fact able to support the full weight of an adult. Another seating design created by Yoshioka that was conceptually equally innovative was the Pane chair (2003–06), made from flexible polyester-elastomer fibres inserted into a paper tube and then kiln-baked, much like a loaf of bread – hence its name (bread being *pane* in Italian and *pan* in Japanese). After being cooked this way, the fibres form a loosely knitted self-supporting chair structure that is both lightweight and flexible, and has shape-memory so it returns to its original shape after being sat on.

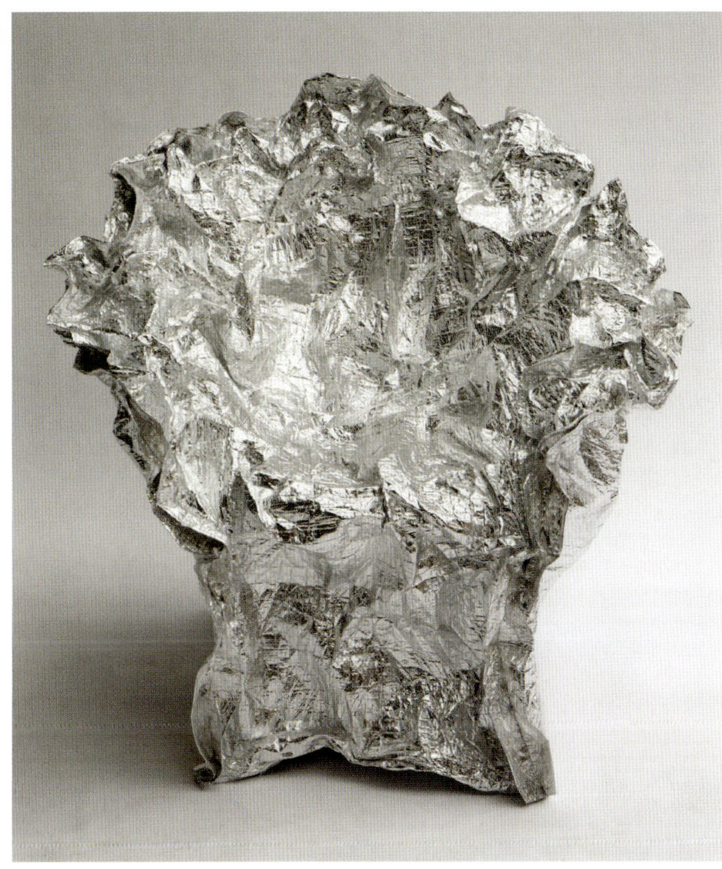

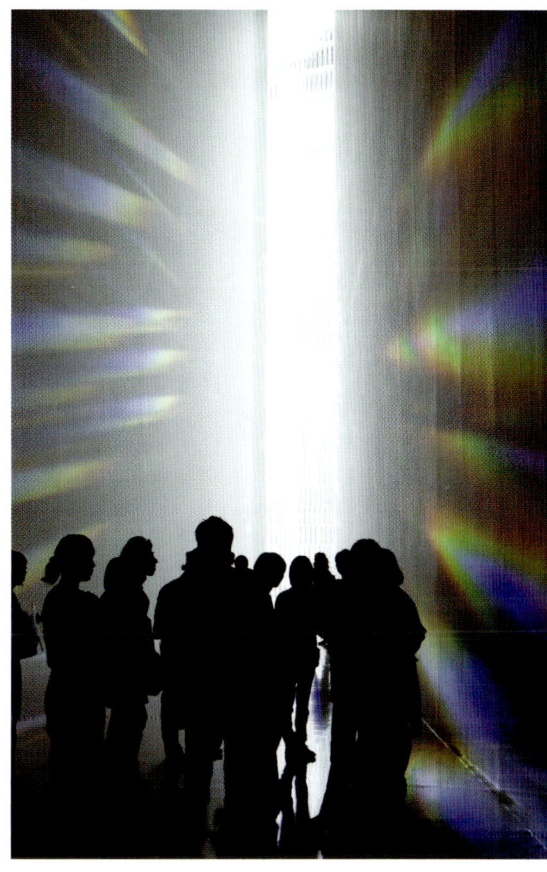

ABOVE LEFT:
Memory chair
for Moroso, 2010

ABOVE RIGHT:
Rainbow Church
2010

Apart from furniture, Yoshioka has also designed consumer electronics, watches and packaging – from his elastomer-coated Media Skin cellphone (2004–05) to his acrylic O bangle-watch (2011). But it is really his installations that reveal his artistry and have been responsible for bringing him international acclaim as one of the most influential artist-designers of his generation. These include the Rainbow Church (2010), adorned with an eight-metre-high (twenty-six-foot) glass window made up of 500 prisms that scatter a multitude of rainbows across its walls, and the all-glass Kou-An Glass Tea House (2015) set in the precincts of a historic temple in Kyoto. As Yoshioka once noted, "Sometimes my work is a bit artistic and other times it's design. I think my concept lies in between the boundaries" – and ultimately that is what makes it so interesting.

Marco Zanuso

Italian, 1916–2001

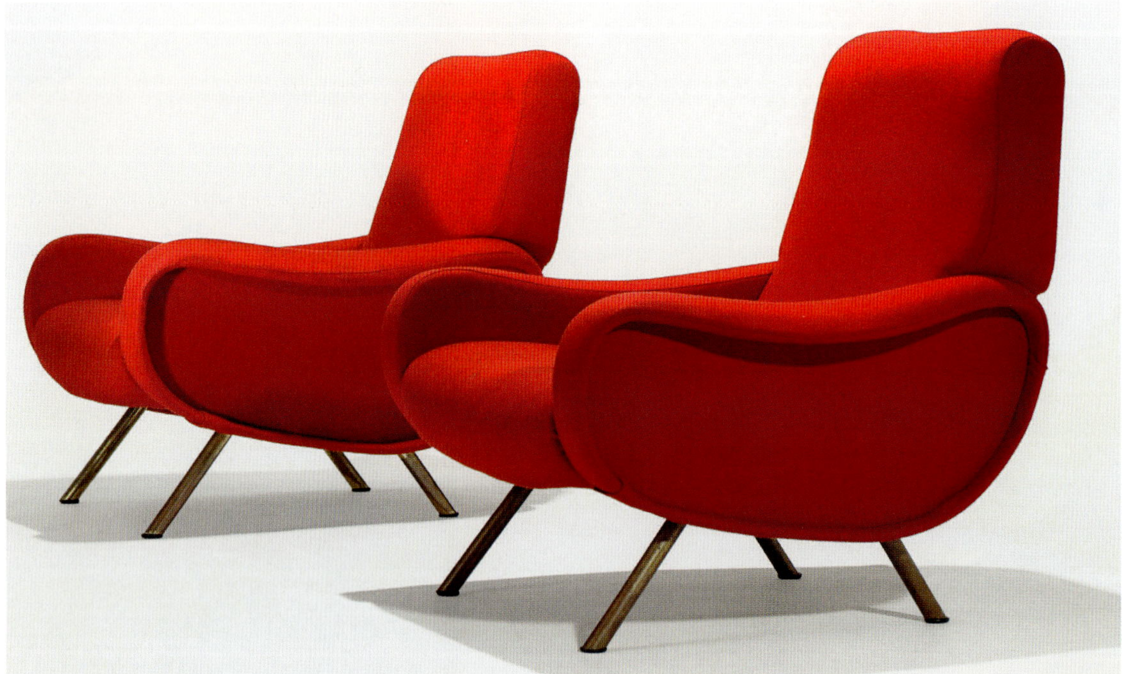

ABOVE:
Lady armchair
for Arflex, 1951

From the 1950s to 1970s, Marco Zanuso was one of the most prominent figures in Italian design with an almost unmatched track record for creating innovative products that exploited brilliantly new materials and technology. From furniture and lighting to telephones, televisions and electronic calculators, he created designs that were groundbreaking in terms of both their seductive sculptural forms and their underlying functional logic.

Zanuso was part of that talented post-war generation of Italian designers who drew their country out of economic crisis by creating objects that were so stylishly functional that everybody wanted them, which helped generate the export revenues needed to build Italy into a modern industrialized nation. Having studied architecture at the Politecnico di Milano (graduating in 1939), Zanuso established his own Milan-based office in 1945, which undertook architectural commissions and urban-planning projects as well as working in the areas of furniture design and product design.

In the late 1940s, Zanuso embarked on a period of particular creativity in relation to chairs when he was commissioned by the Pirelli rubber company to explore the potential of latex foam as a new kind of upholstery material. The resulting Antropus chair (1949) was the first seating design to be produced by Arflex – a sister company specifically set up by Pirelli to exploit the use of its new *gommapiuma* material. This early chair was soon followed by other latex-foam-upholstered seat furniture designed by Zanuso, including the Lady armchair (1951), which was awarded a gold medal at the *IX Milan Triennale* of 1951. Elegant and stylish, the Lady with its feminine rounded curves was a masterpiece of sculptural form. By fully upholstering its wooden frame in different thicknesses of foam to provide the maximum comfort, Zanuso was also able to create a chair that was far more ergonomically refined than earlier traditionally constructed seating designs, with its contours comfortably echoing the shape of the human body.

In 1958 Zanuso began working with the German-born industrial designer Richard Sapper and over the next nineteen years they created numerous notable products together. Their designs reflected Zanuso's ability to develop innovative forms and applications from newly developed materials, along with Sapper's innate understanding of how to create purposeful solutions through highly resolved engineering. The Model No. 4999 child's chair (1960–64) was one of their most noteworthy designs, being the first chair to be entirely made of injection-moulded plastic. Although not made in a single form, its designers conceived the assembled chair almost as a lightweight building block, so that a number of them could be stacked one on top of another. These elements could then be used by children to construct play forts, dens and the like, thereby adding a degree of multifunction and interactive fun to the design. Produced in gleaming red, bright yellow, royal blue or white plastic, the Model No. 4999 chair was a radical departure from the way children's seating had previously been conceived, and demonstrated Zanuso's creative ability to mould new polymeric materials into super-stylish products that were both functionally innovative and aesthetically progressive.

Other landmark designs that were the result of Zanuso and Sapper's collaboration included several created for Brionvega,

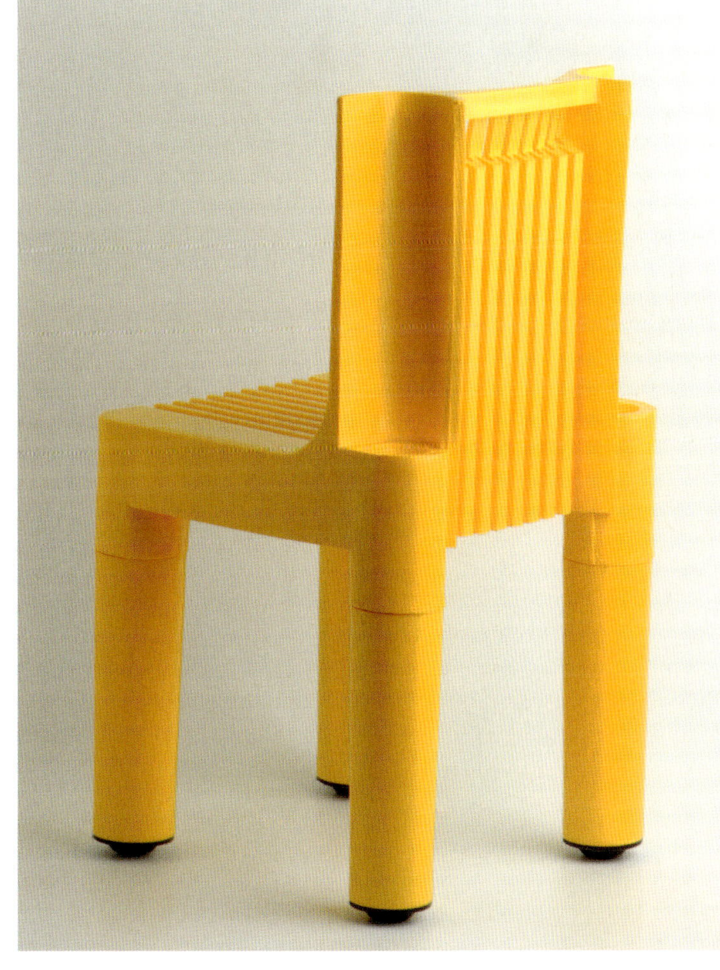

BELOW:
Model No.4999 stacking child's chair
for Kartell, co-designed with Richard Sapper, 1960

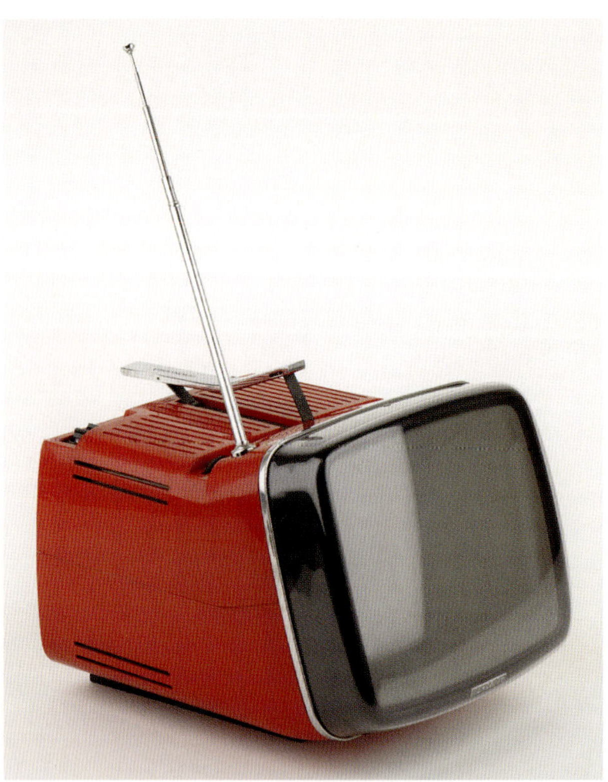

ABOVE LEFT:
Algol 11 television
for Brionvega, co-designed with Richard Sapper, 1964

ABOVE RIGHT:
Black ST201 television
for Brionvega, co-designed with Richard Sapper, 1969

which as a result became the most progressive consumer electronics company in Italy, consistently throughout the 1960s introducing cutting-edge design-led products such as the Doney television (1962), the Algol television (1964), the Model No. TS 502 portable radio (1963–64) and minimalist Black ST201 portable television (1969) – all of which helped redefine the design parameters of electronic products through the sleek forms of their casings and their miniaturization of technology. Another revolutionary contemporary design from the partnership was the Grillo telephone (1965–66), which folded in on itself to create a compact sculptural form. Its name, meaning "cricket" in Italian, referred to its unusual springing action when picked up and its curious chirping ringtone. In addition, the Grillo had a rotary dial integrated into its main body – an innovative feature that was to prove highly influential on the design of subsequent telephones.

The year following his design of the Grillo, Zanuso was appointed a professor of materials applications at the Politecnico di Milano and subsequently became the college's professor of industrial design in 1976 – thereby helping to inspire the next generation of Italian designers. Today, many of Zanuso's products are seen as exemplars of Italian design, for they perfectly encapsulate its two main attributes: stylish good looks and functional innovation.

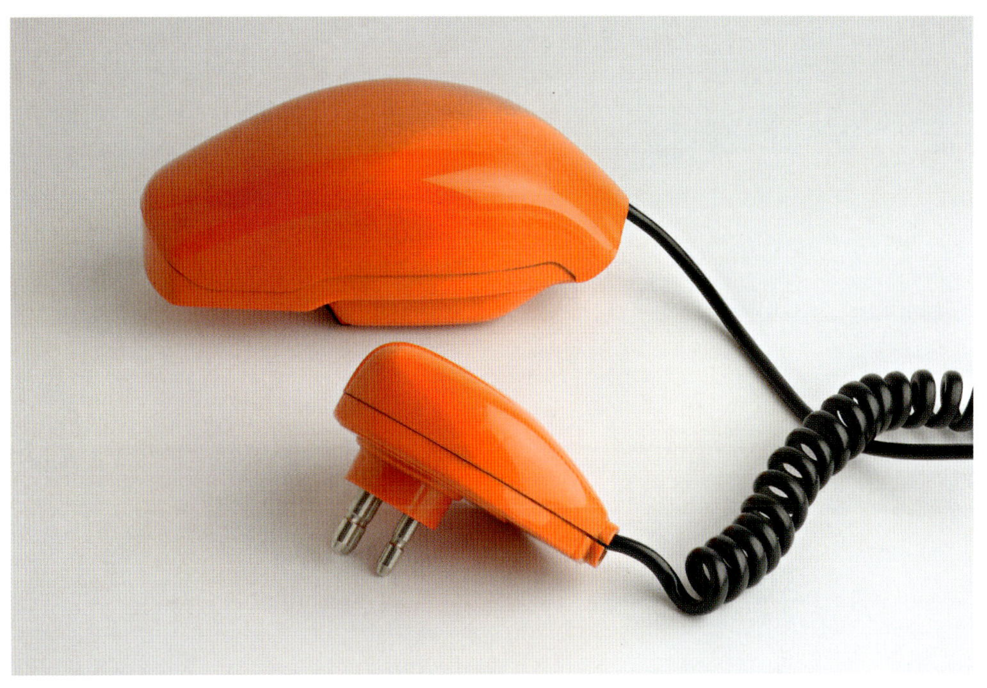

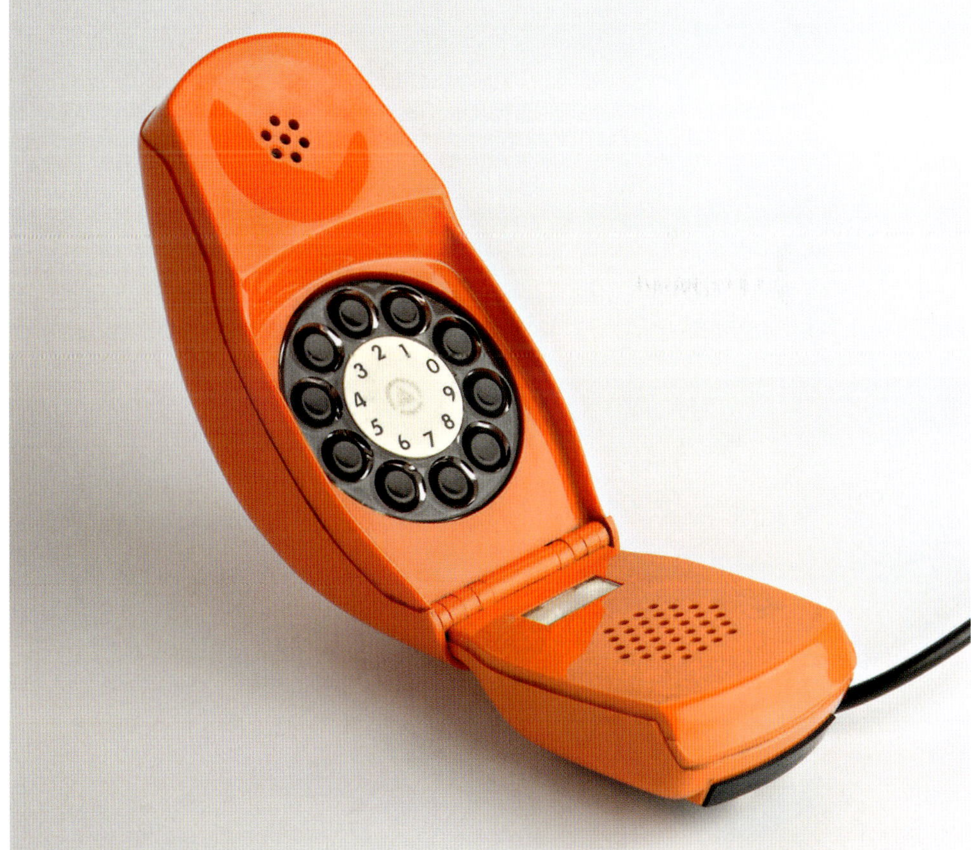

RIGHT:
Grillo telephone
for Società Italiana Telecommunicazioni Siemens, co-designed with Richard Sapper, 1965–66

Styles & Movements

Arts and Crafts Movement

Britain, America, Continental Europe and Japan, 1860s–1930s

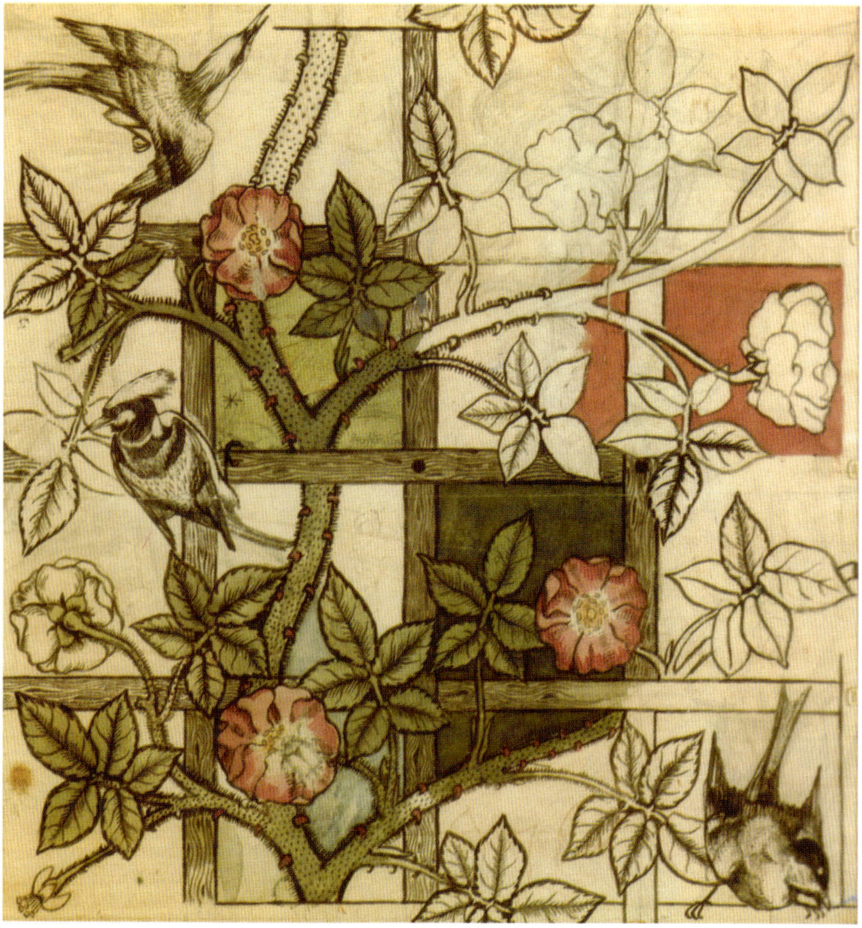

The Arts and Crafts Movement was a profoundly influential design-reform movement born of deeply held moral conviction. It emerged in the 1860s, inspired by the teachings of John Ruskin and first realized in the work of William Morris, but it was not until the 1880s that it became a prominent force in British design, spreading then to America and Continental Europe, and eventually emerging as the Mingei (Folk Crafts) movement in Japan.

The socialist ideals that guided the Arts and Crafts Movement originated from a deep concern about the negative effects rampant industrialization was having on ordinary working people's lives and in particular on the crafts skills that they historically relied upon to support themselves. Since the advent of mechanized production and the subsequent introduction of the division of labour, the acts of designing and making had become increasingly separated. Used in factories to increase productivity, this divisive organization of labour meant age-old artisanal skills were in jeopardy of being lost forever, as workers became mere machine-minders. The "joy in labour" that skilled craftsmen had traditionally understood in a job well done had been largely replaced by unskilled "wage slavery". Proponents of the Movement, therefore, advocated fundamental social reform through a wholesale revival of arts and crafts production, which, they argued, would result in not only more beautiful and better-made products but also improved social conditions for the skilled craft-workers who made them.

ABOVE:
Design for Trellis wallpaper
by William Morris, 1862

RIGHT:
Morris adjustable chair
by Philip Webb for Morris & Co., *c.*1870 – upholstered in Bird woven textile

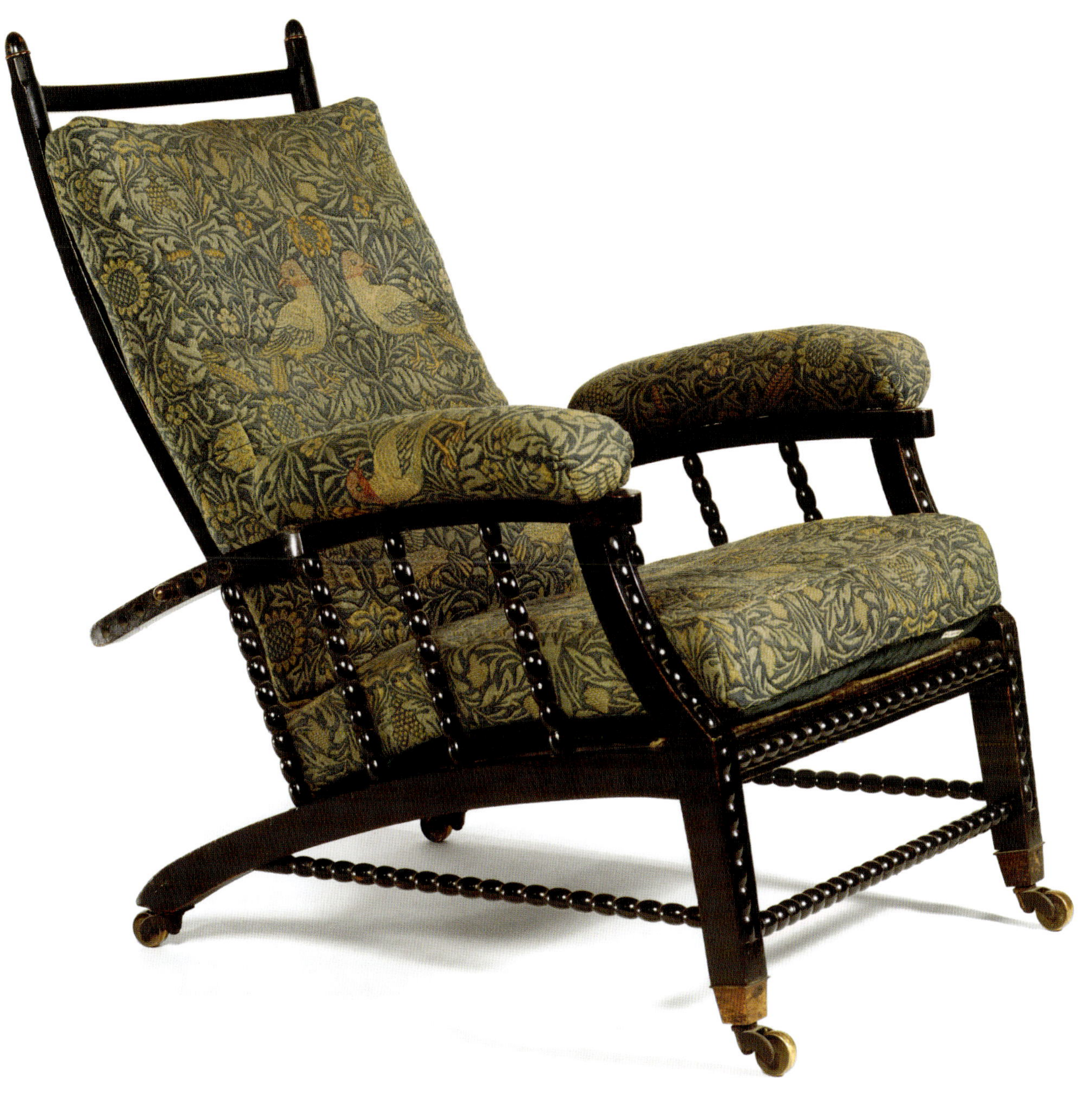

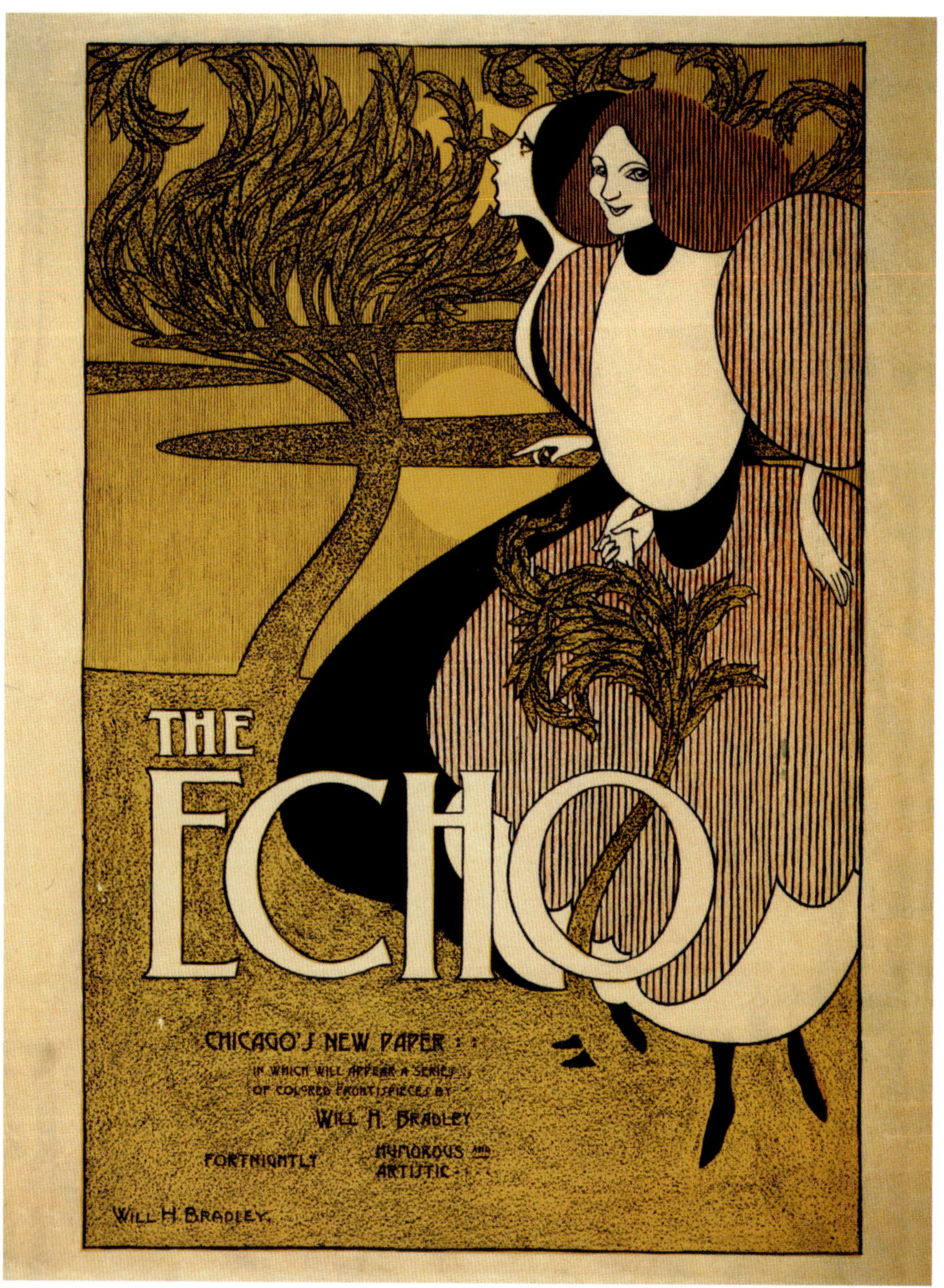

ABOVE:
Advertising poster
for *The Echo* by Will H. Bradley, 1895

The Movement was also strongly focused on the idea of fellowship and community, and looked to the way medieval guilds had been structured for inspiration as to how to teach the necessary skills to workers. The Movement took its name from the Arts and Crafts Exhibition Society, which was established in 1887 to promote the ideals of handcraftsmanship and to oppose the increasing industrialization of production.

The younger generation of Arts and Crafts designers who were associated with the Exhibition Society quickly came to understand the underlying paradox of the Movement: that handcraft could not be reconciled with affordability. Because of this, they were generally

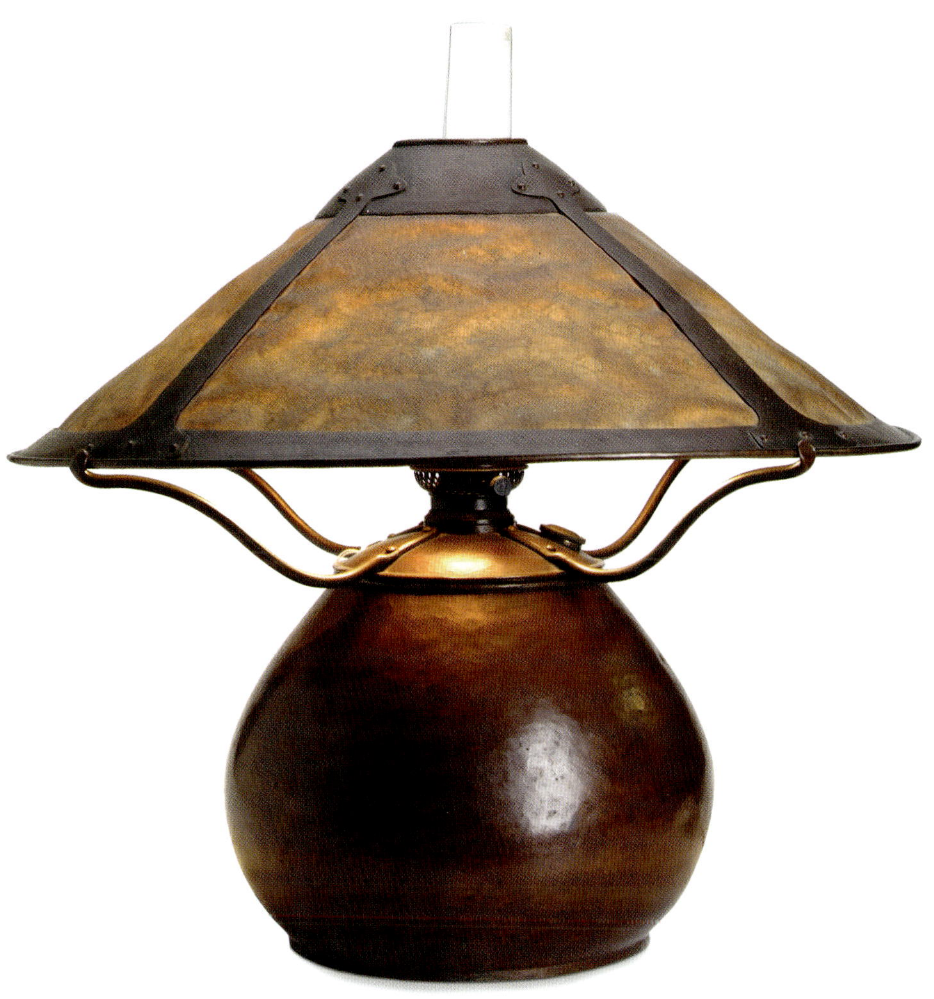

ABOVE:
Copper table lamp
by Dirk van Erp for the Copper Shop, *c.*1910

more ambivalent towards machine-production, yet they retained a belief in the physical and moral superiority of handcraftsmanship. This was the generation that came of professional age during the Edwardian era and took Morris's ideas into the new century. In so doing, they developed a coherent New Art aesthetic that was based on Morris's idea of "the art of everyday life" – practical yet beautiful designs that were intended to remake daily domestic living and thereby transform society.

In the United States, designers took inspiration not only from the social mission of the British Arts and Crafts Movement but also from their country's "can-do" pioneering roots and its colonial past, to create furniture and other homewares that had a distinctive no-nonsense character. American designers' more purposeful approach to design ensured that their work was generally more muscular and elemental than that created by their European counterparts. American Arts and Crafts design and architecture was typified by straightforward constructions and minimal decoration, which in many ways presaged the reductivist tendency of the Modern Movement. By placing value on the quality of design, materials and production, as well as on the lives of those employed in the production of things, the Arts and Crafts Movement was highly inspirational to later design-reforming movements, and even to this day continues to have a valid message: that design needs to be conceived holistically and guided by morality.

Art Nouveau

Europe and America, 1890s–1910s

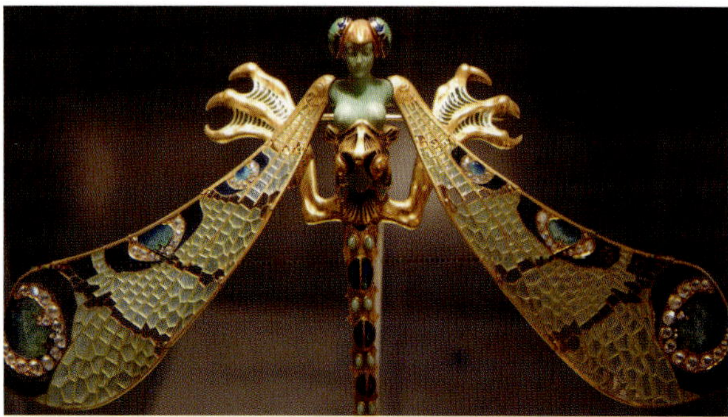

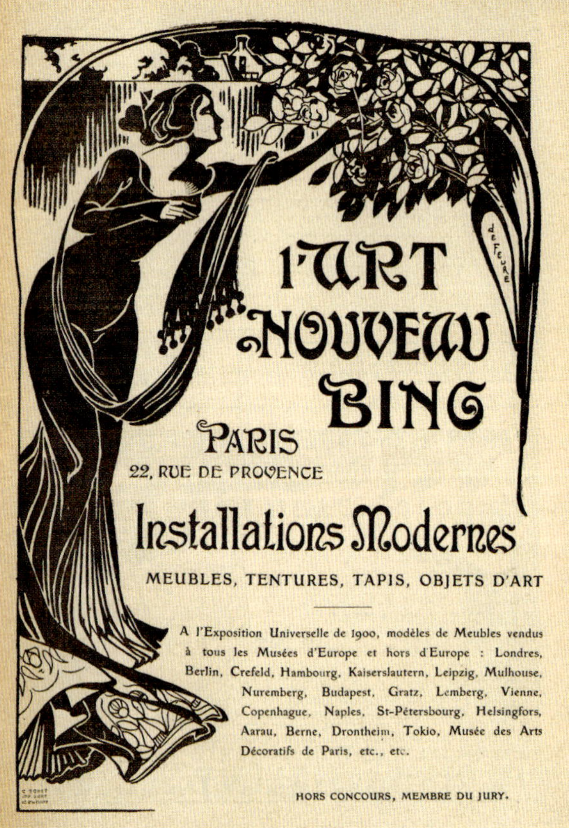

ABOVE TOP:
Dragonfly brooch
by René Lalique , *c.*1897–98

ABOVE BOTTOM:
Advertisement
for Siegfried Bing's Maison l'Art Nouveau, *c.*1900

The *Belle Époque* years, spanning 1890 to 1914, witnessed a new international style emerge that rejected the prevailing historical revivalism of the preceding decades and instead took inspiration from the natural world. It became known as Art Nouveau (New Art), and was the world's first modern style because, rather than stylistically borrowing from the past, it was guided by a forward-looking naturalism. Its adherents appropriated forms directly from nature – an unfurling leaf, a peacock feather, a blossoming rose – and dramatically stylized them in designs that invoked dynamic, swirling growth. Among its leading proponents in Britain were Charles Rennie Mackintosh and his wife Margaret, who created designs with an otherworldly, ethereal quality which also reflected the increasing interest in symbolism and spiritualism during the period. In fact, the Art Nouveau style was a direct descendant of both the Aesthetic Movement and the Symbolist movement.

But it was in France and Belgium that the Art Nouveau style found its most sublime architectural expression, with the buildings of Victor Horta and Hector Guimard. One of the greatest influences on Art Nouveau designers was the publication of Ernst Haeckel's *Kunstformen der Natur* (Art Forms of Nature) lithographic plates between 1899 and 1904. These prints of sea anemones, jellyfish, protozoa and the like bridged the gap between art and science, and revealed the natural world in all its phenomenal organic diversity. Likewise Haeckel's "ecology" theory, which proposed that everything in the natural world was interconnected, also acted as a strong impetus on architects and designers to create wholly unified *Gesamtkunstwerk* projects. One such building was Horta's Hôtel Tassel (1893–94), which is regarded as the first true example of Art Nouveau architecture, with its extraordinary interiors incorporating writhing decorative floral motifs throughout, from its sweeping staircase, site-specific furniture and light fixtures to its wall decorations, door handles and floor tiles.

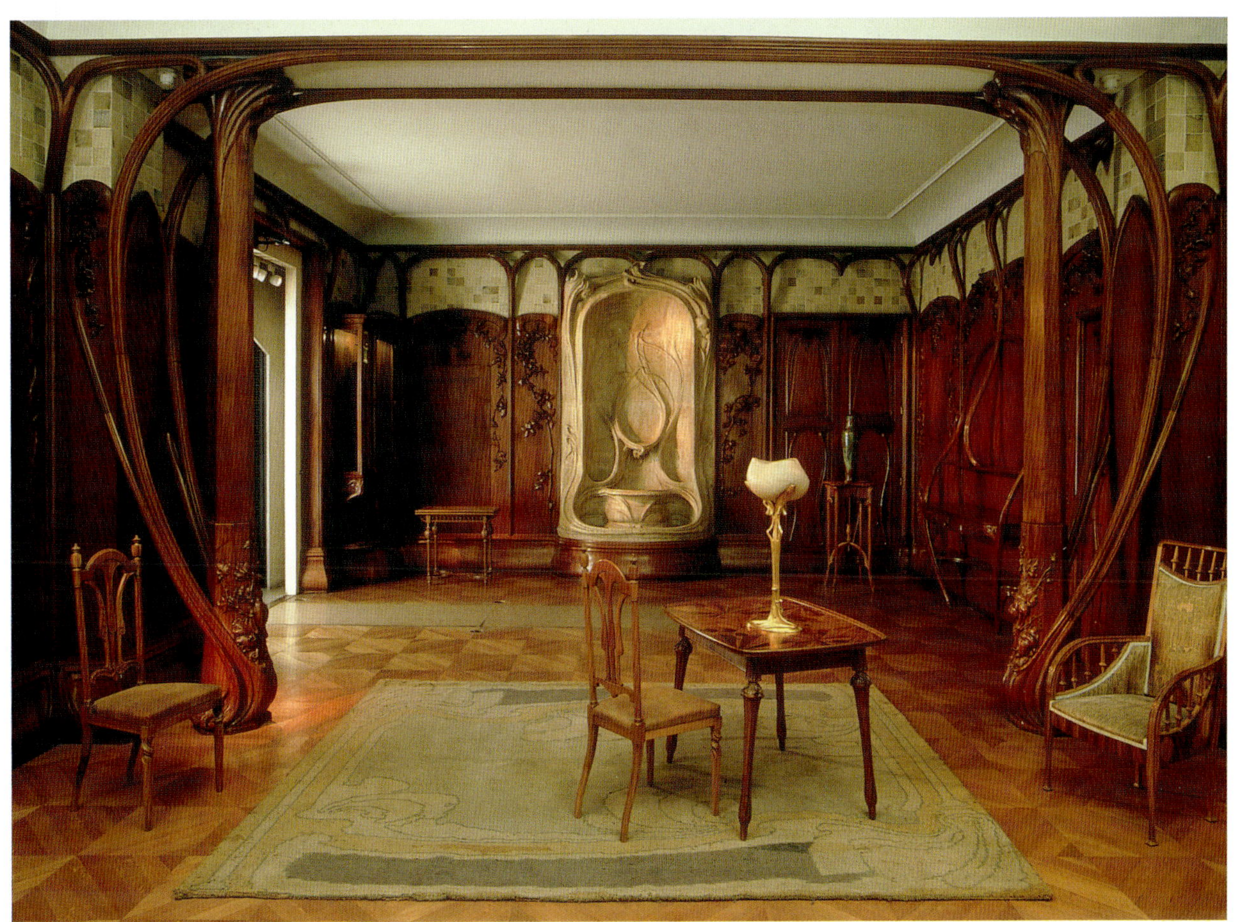

ABOVE:
Salle Charpentier dining room
by Alexandre Charpentier, 1900–01

The term Art Nouveau was actually derived from the name of Siegfried Bing's fashionable gallery in Paris, Maison l'Art Nouveau, which showcased not only avant-garde European design in the Art Nouveau idiom but also the work of Louis Comfort Tiffany – its most prominent American exponent. Similarly, the École de Nancy, founded in 1901, was an influential conduit of this new organic style, counting among its founding members Émile Gallé, Louis Majorelle and Antonin Daum – all of whom ran successful workshops that supplied an international clientele. It was, however, Guimard's cast-iron Paris Métro entrances with their gigantic stylized flowering stalks that were the most memorable expression of this new swirling tendril style.

The Art Nouveau style also emerged elsewhere in Europe: in Italy it was referred to as Stile Liberty (after the textiles created by the London department store Liberty), with Carlo Bugatti its most high-profile advocate, while in Spain it was known as Modernisme or Modernista – and best expressed in the fantastical designs of Antoni Gaudí. In Germany it was called Jugendstil (Youth Style) and was typified by a pared-down biomorphism that reflected the aesthetic and ideological influence of Haeckel's biological studies, for instance in the work of August Endell and Hermann Obrist. The Austrian variant was Sezession or Secession, exemplified by Josef Hoffmann. Although the Art Nouveau movement's initial agenda for design reform morphed over the years into a full-blown decorative style, its ahistorical approach was decidedly forward-looking. By rejecting the past, its protagonists stylistically unburdened the next generation of designers and architects, allowing them to seek the *Neue Sachlichkeit* – new objectivity – of Modernism.

Constructivism

Russia, 1910s–1920s

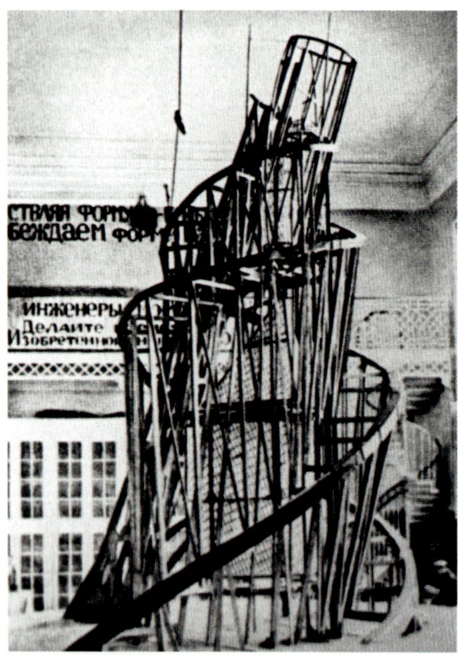

ABOVE:
The Monument to the Third International
architectural model by Vladimir Tatlin, 1919–20

OPPOSITE:
Cover for *Veshch* (Object) magazine, issue 3
designed by El Lissitzky, 1922

During the 1910s the Russian avant-garde became increasingly influenced by French Cubism and Italian Futurism, especially the latter's glorification of the machine. Prior to the First World War, many Russian artists had travelled to or worked in Western Europe and so were aware of the latest artistic developments there. Forced to return home by the war, they formed their own movement in fine art, architecture and design, which was based on non-figurative representation and geometric abstraction. Kazimir Malevich's Black Square painting (*c.*1915) exemplified the group's reductivist aesthetic, although, rather than being a culmination, it was the first of a series of abstract paintings that Malevich termed "Suprematist".

Like their De Stijl contemporaries, the Russian avant-garde juxtaposed geometric forms to create spatial compositions; however, they favoured a more dynamic placement of elements and a greater sense of layering. Around 1915 the Russian artist/architect Vladimir Tatlin began creating non-representational constructions from found objects or industrial materials, which paved the way for a new art and design movement that would become known as Constructivism.

As with De Stijl, Constructivism had utopian goals and sought to bring about a new social order by introducing a new formal language in art and design. After the Russian Revolution in 1917, Constructivism became the focus of the Russian avant-garde, who were searching for a way to make the production and distribution of goods more democratic. To this end, they began actively promoting a new approach to design that was more linked to industrial production. In the early 1920s the group issued two publications heralding the emergence of Constructivism: *Realistic Manifesto* (1920) by Antoine Pevsner and Naum Gabo and *Konstruktivizm* (1922) by Alexei Gan. Believing that the reform of the applied arts could bring about a new social order, the Constructivists began to make utilitarian "production art" and architecture, but the political and economic instability following the Revolution meant that their output was mainly confined to exhibitions, ceramics and graphics.

The most famous design created by the Constructivists was actually never built: Vladimir Tatlin's Monument to the Third International (1919–20). This massive, spiralling tower structure of iron, steel and glass, of which only a large-scale model was ever made, was intended to be both a monument and the headquarters building of the Communist International organization or Comintern

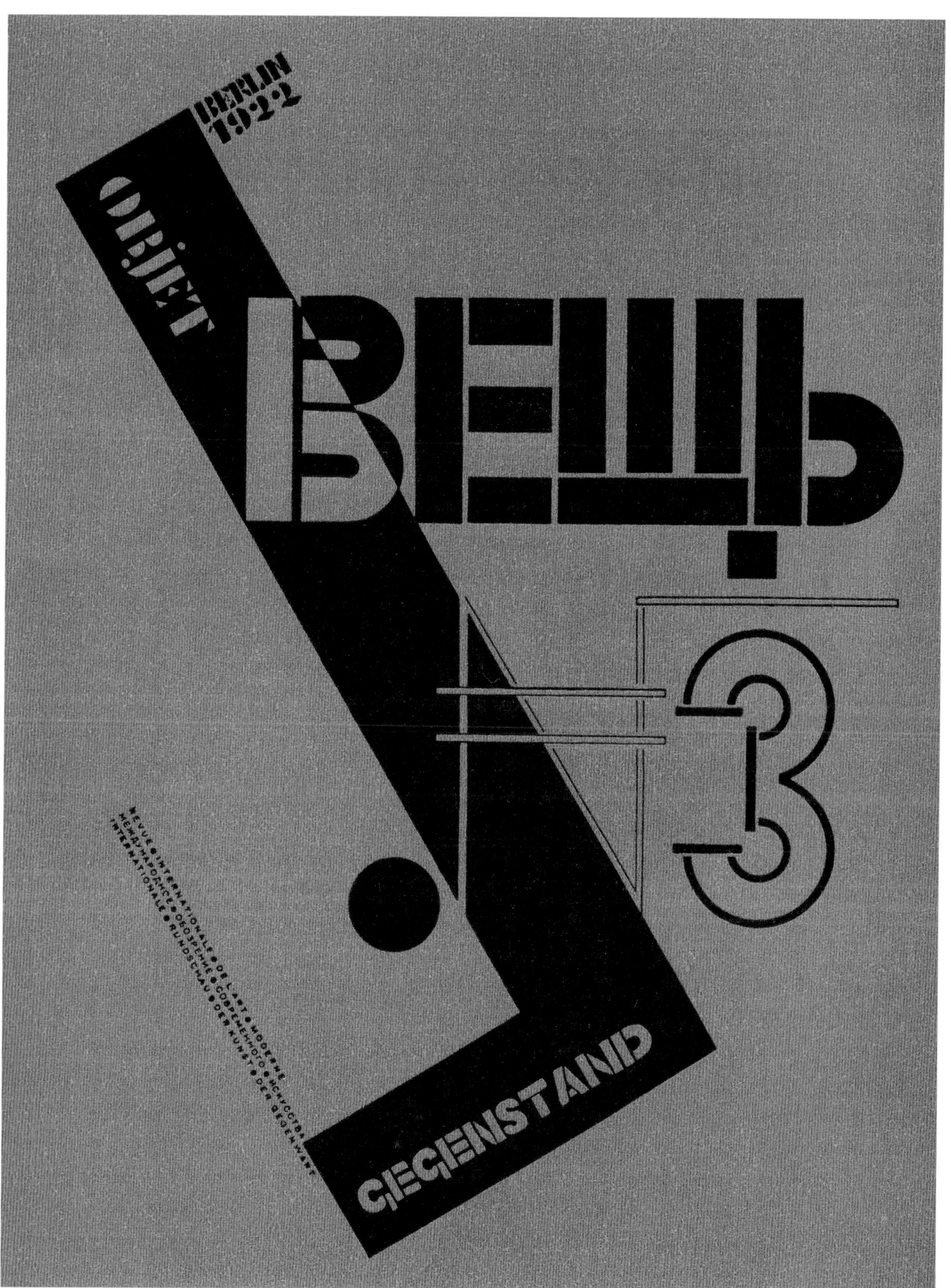
BERLIN
1922
OBJET
ВЕЩЬ
№ 3
REVUE • INTERNATIONALE • DE L'ART • MODERNE
МЕЖДУНАРОДНОЕ • ОБОЗРЕНИЕ • СОВРЕМЕННОГО • ИСКУССТВА
INTERNATIONALE • RUNDSCHAU • DER KUNST • DER GEGENWART
GEGENSTAND

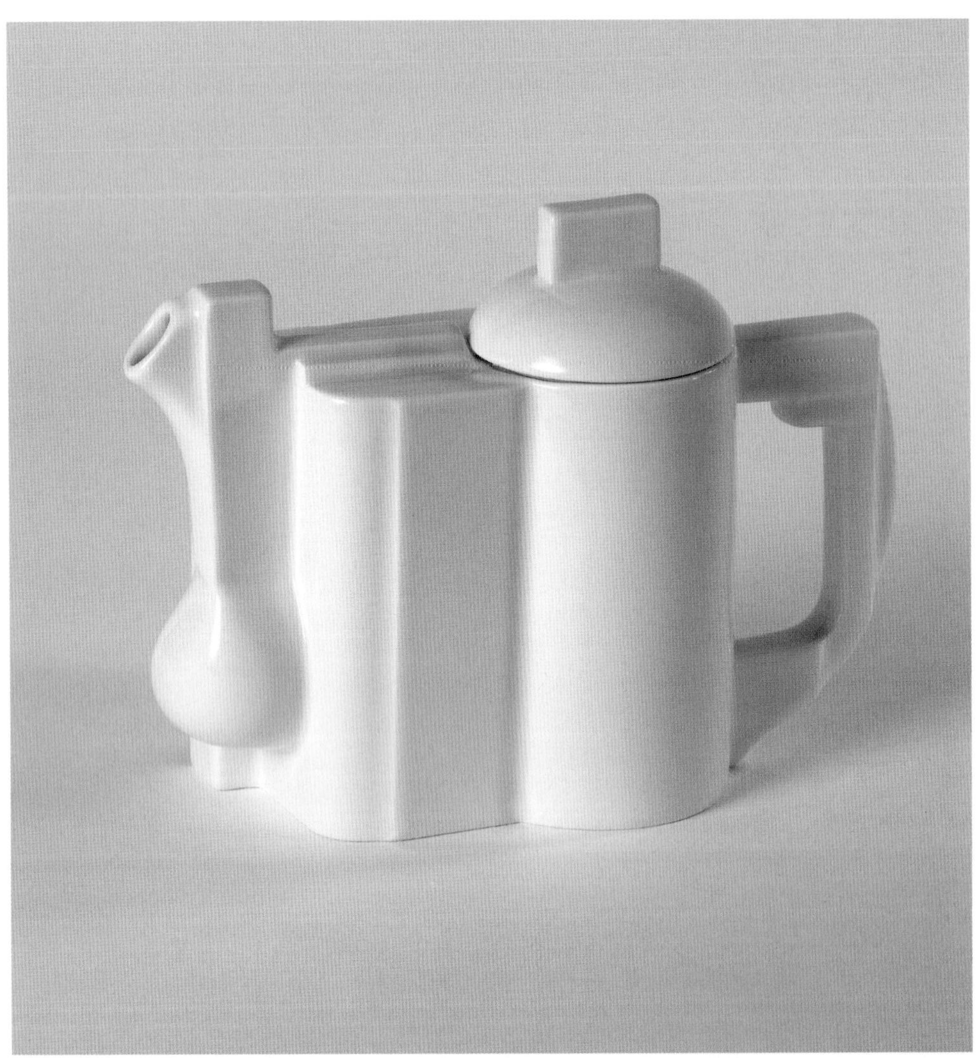

(also known as the Third International). Apart from this extraordinary architectural proposal, the most notable designs by the Constructivists were in the fields of ceramics and graphics – with the work of Aleksandr Rodchenko exemplifying the bold forthright aesthetic of Constructivists' posters and publications.

The Constructivists also established a state school of design known as Vkhutemas (Higher Artistic-Technical Workshops) in Moscow in 1920 – which was the Soviet answer to the Bauhaus, albeit actually a far larger enterprise. This progressive art and technical school promoted "production art" and established contacts with industry with the aim of merging art and craft traditions with modern industrial technology. Although Vkhutemas played a crucial role in forging a modern art-and-design ideology in Soviet Russia, the designers associated with it soon fell foul of the Soviet Regime, and it was closed in 1930 – effectively marking the end of Constructivism.

ABOVE:
Glazed porcelain teapot
by Kazimir Malevich, 1923 (later manufactured by Lomonosov Porcelain Factory in 2001)

OPPOSITE:
Lithographic poster
advertising *Chelovek s Kino-Apparatom* (Man with a Movie Camera) film by Vladimir and Georgi Stenberg, 1929

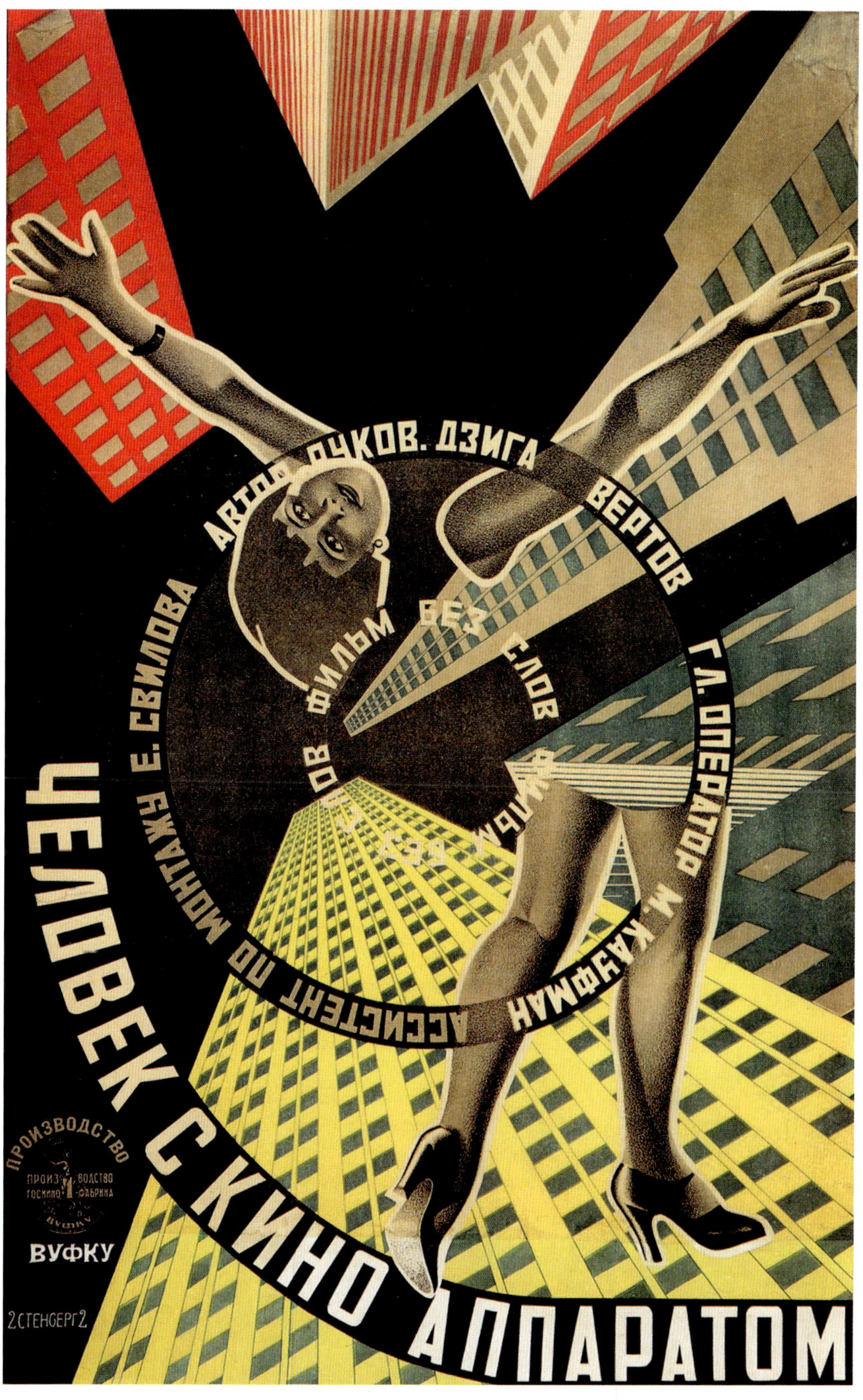
ЧЕЛОВЕК С КИНО АППАРАТОМ
РУКОВ. ДЗИГА ВЕРТОВ
ГЛ. ОПЕРАТОР М. КАУФМАН
АССИСТЕНТ ПО МОНТАЖУ Е. СВИЛОВА
ФИЛЬМ БЕЗ СЛОВ
ПРОИЗВОДСТВО
ВУФКУ
2СТЕНБЕРГ2

Art Deco / Moderne

Europe and America, 1920s–1930s

BELOW LEFT:
Inlaid corner cabinet
by Émile-Jacques Ruhlmann, *c.*1923

BELOW RIGHT:
FADA 1000 radio
manufactured by FADA Radio & Electric Company, 1941–46

The bold, often flamboyant Art Deco style first emerged during the 1910s, but did not reach its international zenith or stylistic maturity until the early 1920s. Booming economic conditions spawned the development of this new international style, which, with its connotations of luxury, flourished during the heady get-rich-quick years of the early Roaring Twenties.

Although an international phenomenon, the epicentre of the Art Deco style was Paris. There, numerous talented architects and decorating firms were able to call upon the skills of small specialist workshops to execute their unashamedly luxurious designs for furniture, metalwork, glassware, lighting, textiles and wallpapers. Thanks to the stock-market-fuelled prosperity of the 1920s, there were also a sufficient number of wealthy clients both in Paris and overseas who could afford to lavish seemingly limitless amounts of money on creating homes that were the height of fashionable luxury. Unlike the preceding Art Nouveau style, which was consciously anti-historical in its preference for sinuous motifs drawn from the natural world, Art Deco drew its references from an eclectic range of historic sources, from African tribal art to ancient Egypt. It was also influenced by contemporary artistic developments, most notably rectilinear French Cubism and Italian Futurism. The results were confident, varied and often geometric.

The term "Art Deco" was coined from the title of the landmark *Exposition Internationale des Arts Décoratifs et Industriels Modernes* held in Paris in 1925. As its name suggests, this well-received and highly influential event showcased Art Deco interiors alongside a few more progressive Modernist room schemes. The event's most notable Art Deco exhibit was Émile-Jacques Ruhlmann's interiors for the Pavillon du Collectionneur, designed by the architect Pierre Patout. This sumptuous "house for a collector" with its suite of theatrical-like room sets epitomized the Art Deco love of opulence and applied decoration.

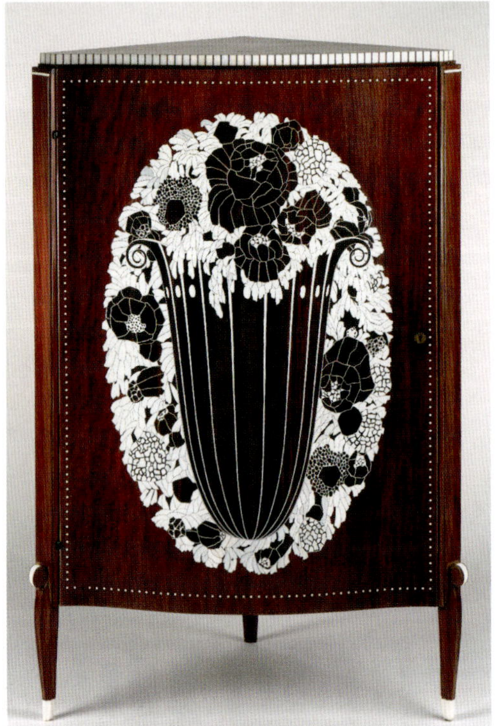

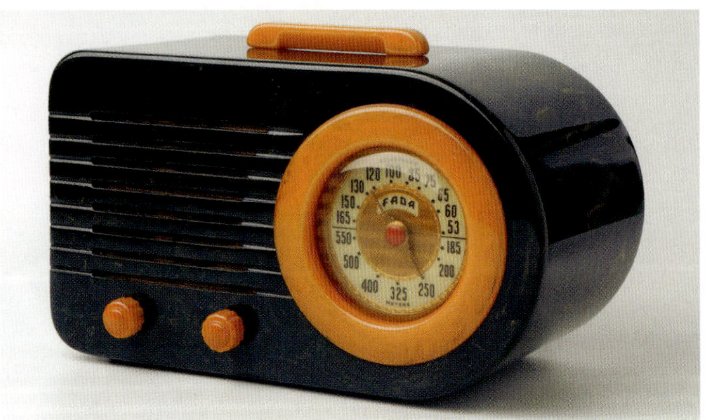

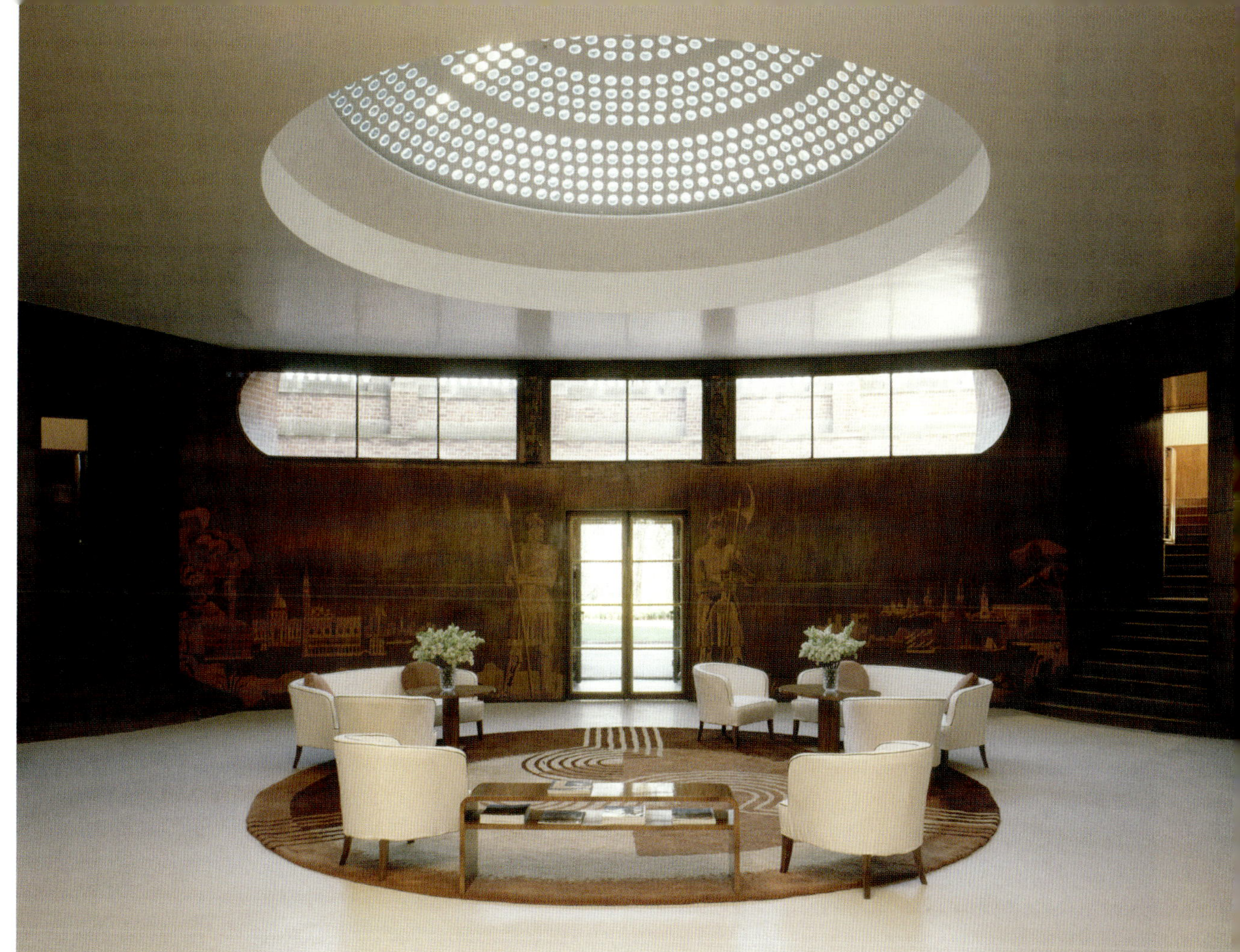

ABOVE:
Art Deco entrance hall of Eltham Palace, Greenwich, south-east London, created by the Swedish designer Rolf Engströmer for Stephen and Virginia Courtauld, 1930s

In North America, the Art Deco style also gained a substantial foothold, for as the stock market went ever skywards, so did American cities' skylines – with skyscrapers such as William Van Alen's Chrysler Building (1928–30) in New York being the most sublime expression of the American Art Deco style. American consumers during this period of rampant consumerism were captivated by the idea of affordable luxury and as a result homewares were frequently given a modish Art Deco styling treatment.

After the Wall Street Crash in 1929 and during the ensuing years of the Great Depression, things changed dramatically as manufacturers found themselves hard pressed to find any buyers for their wares. Struggling for market share, they eventually sought professional advice from a new breed of industrial design consultants, including Raymond Loewy, Walter Dorwin Teague and Henry Dreyfuss, who pioneered an interpretation of the Art Deco style based on streamlining, which would become known as Moderne.

Heavy on "eye appeal", the Moderne style was, as its name suggests, modernistic rather than Modern, and became closely associated with the glamorous lifestyles portrayed on Hollywood's silver screens. Essentially these industrial design professionals gave products an "artistic treatment" that made them look fashionably contemporary, yet they should never be dismissed as mere stylists, for often they were also able to reduce production costs significantly by using Moderne forms, which were usually ideally suited for moulding in early plastics such as Bakelite and Catalin.

Rationalism

Italy, 1920s–1950s

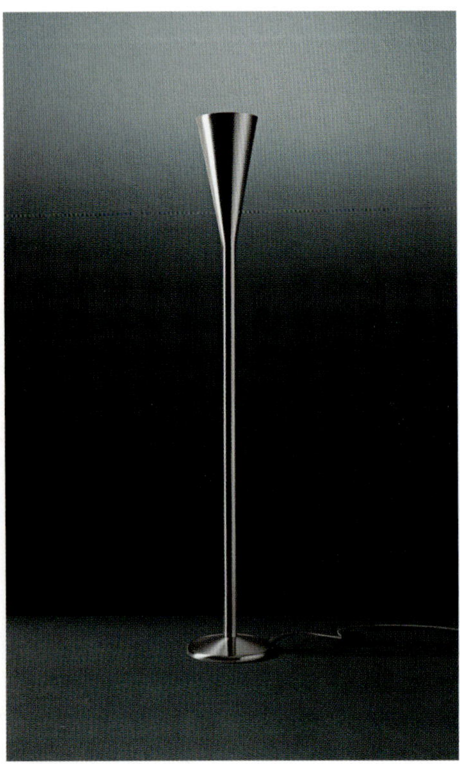

During the mid-1920s a new design and architecture movement emerged in Italy that sought to reconcile the strict functionalism of the European avant-garde with Italy's proud Classical tradition. It became known as Rationalism.

During this period in Italy there was an ongoing battle of styles. On one side, there were the Futurists, who lauded industrial progress through an aggressive machine-age aesthetic and sought to create order through radicalism. On the other, there were the protagonists of the Novecento style, a sort of Neo-Classical Art Deco. Occupying the middle ground between these two design factions were the Rationalists, who sought Modern order but based on Classical ideals.

The birth of Rationalism can be traced to 1926 when the Gruppo 7 (Group 7) was founded by seven like-minded architects intent on finding what was effectively a third way, a balance between Classicism and industrial-inspired architecture and design. This influential group's founding members were Luigi Figini, Guido Frette, Sebastiano Larco, Guiseppe Pagano, Gino Pollini, Carlo Enrico Rava, Giuseppe Terragni and Ubaldo Castagnoli (the latter being replaced by Adalberto Libera the following year). While the Novecento movement vocally promoted its cause through the pages of *Domus* magazine, the Rationalists used *La Casa Bella*, a rival architecture and design journal, as their mouthpiece. Later to become *Casabella*, the magazine was founded in 1928 and from 1933 was under the editorship of Pagano, who famously designed the forward-looking Icarus Room at the landmark *Esposizione Aeronautica Italiana* (Italian Aeronautical Exhibition) held at the Palazzo dell'Arte in Milan in 1934.

One of the purest and most notable manifestations of the Rationalist style, which was distinguished by a severe geometric formal vocabulary and the use of modern industrial materials, was Giuseppe Terragni's Casa del Fascio (Fascist Party headquarters building) in the lakeside town of Como, north of Milan. This totally unified *Gesamtkunstwerk* scheme was furnished with suitably progressive Modernist designs, such as Terragni's Follia chair from 1934. Rationalism was initially embraced by the Fascists, who regarded themselves as champions of a new world order, which they believed was symbolically represented by

LEFT:
Model No. 0556 Luminator floor light
designed by Pietro Chiesa for Fontana Arte, *c.*1933

OPPOSITE:
Detail of the Icarus Room
by Giuseppe Pagano, part of the *Esposizione Aeronautica Italiana* (Italian Aeronautical Exhibition) held in Milan, 1934

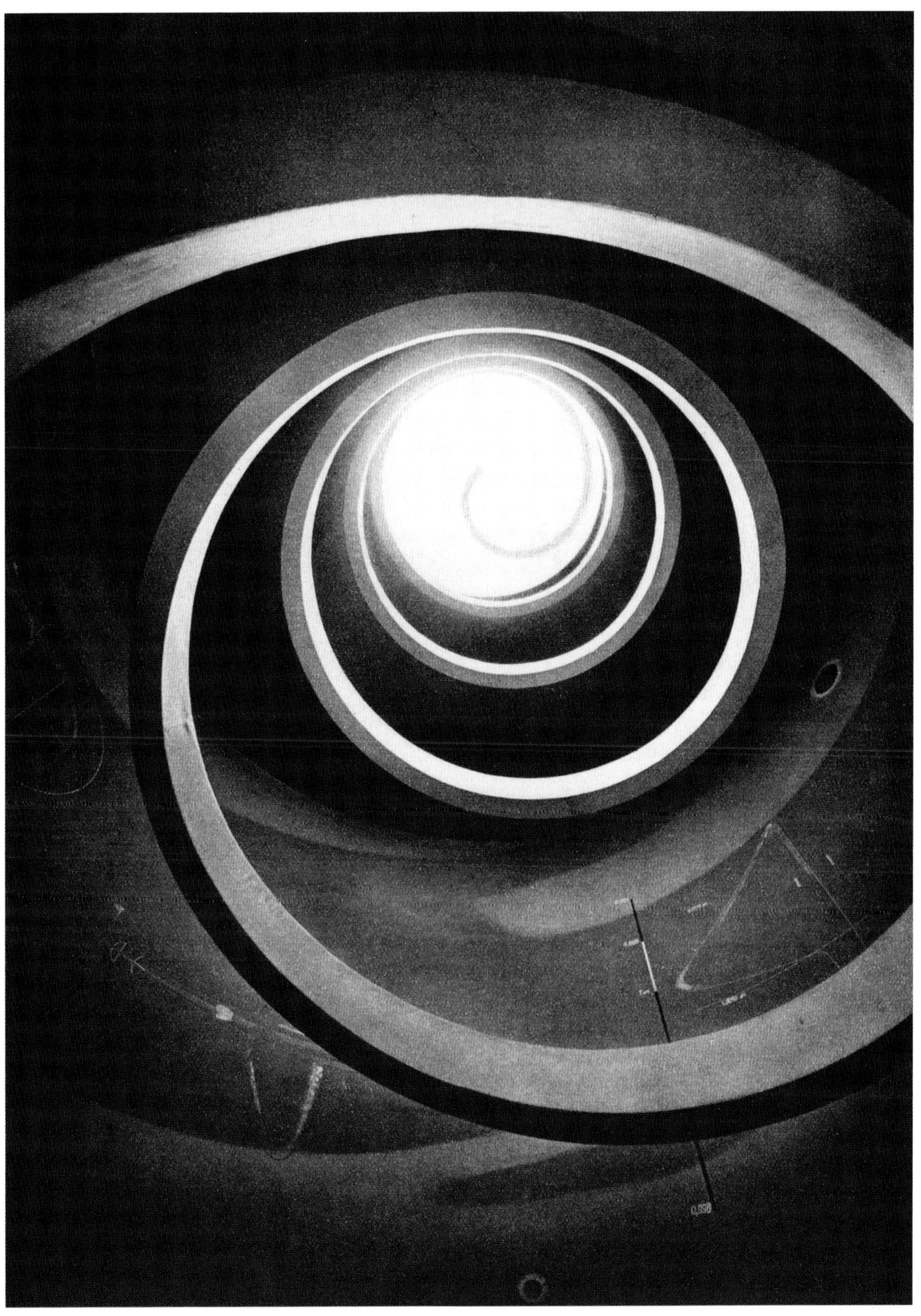

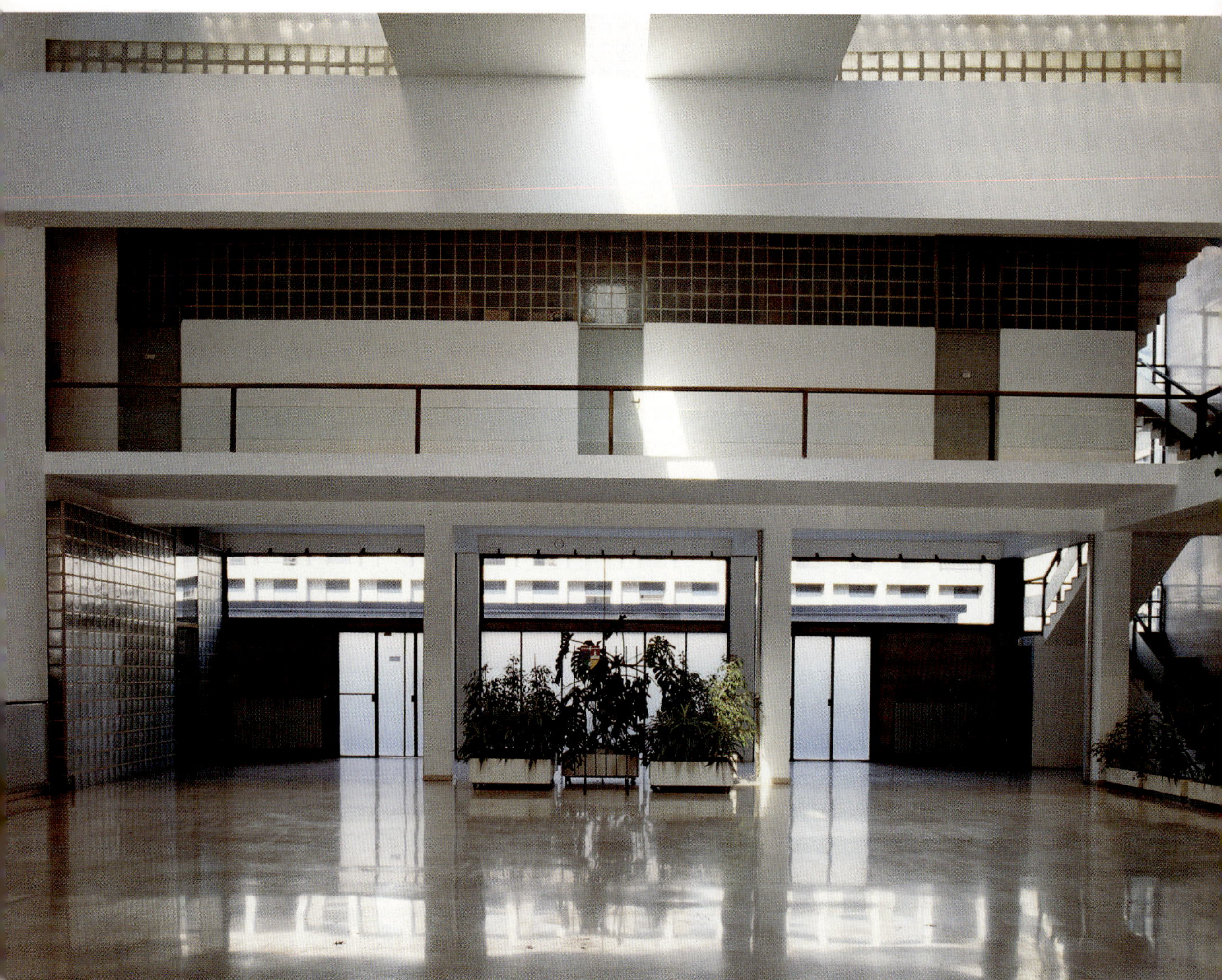

ABOVE:
Interior of Casa del Fascio, Como
by Giuseppe Terragni 1932–36

Rationalist designs. However, eventually the Fascists opted instead for the Novecento style, with its more overtly Classical and imperialistic connotations.

Another building that is regarded as a Rationalist masterpiece and was likewise built on Fascist dictator Benito Mussolini's orders was the Palazzo della Civiltà del Lavoro or Palace of Labour (1938), in Rome. Designed by the architects Giovanni Guerrini, Ernesto Lapadula and Mario Romano, this remarkable edifice, which is often referred to as the Colosseo Quadrato (Square Coliseum), was intended to be the centrepiece of a world exposition planned by Mussolini to take place in Rome in 1942 but, because of the Second World War, never staged.

Growing disillusioned with the political situation in Italy, the most vocal champion of Rationalism, Pagano, left the Fascist Party in 1942 and the following year joined the resistance, but was captured and ended his days in Mauthausen concentration camp in Austria. Yet despite this, the spirit of Rationalism lived on even after the war in the work of Studio BBPR (based in Milan) and that of the supremely gifted engineer Pier Luigi Nervi, whose extraordinary buildings reflected the Rationalist credo of Classical proportions following contemporary function.

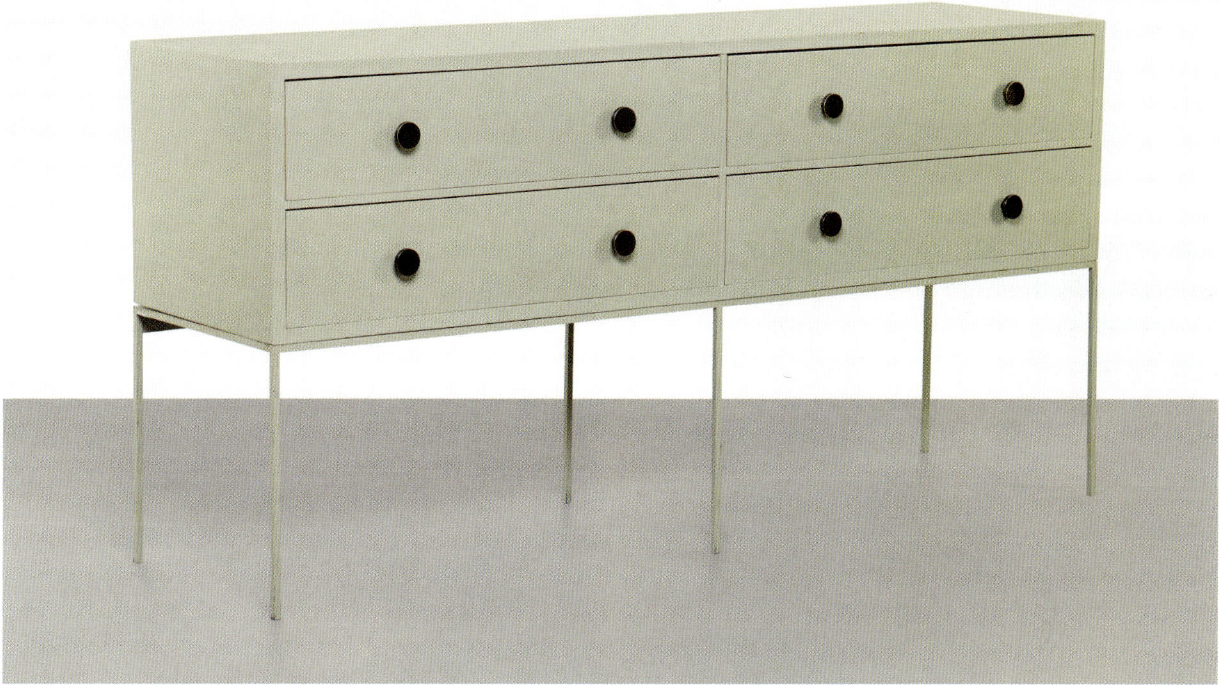

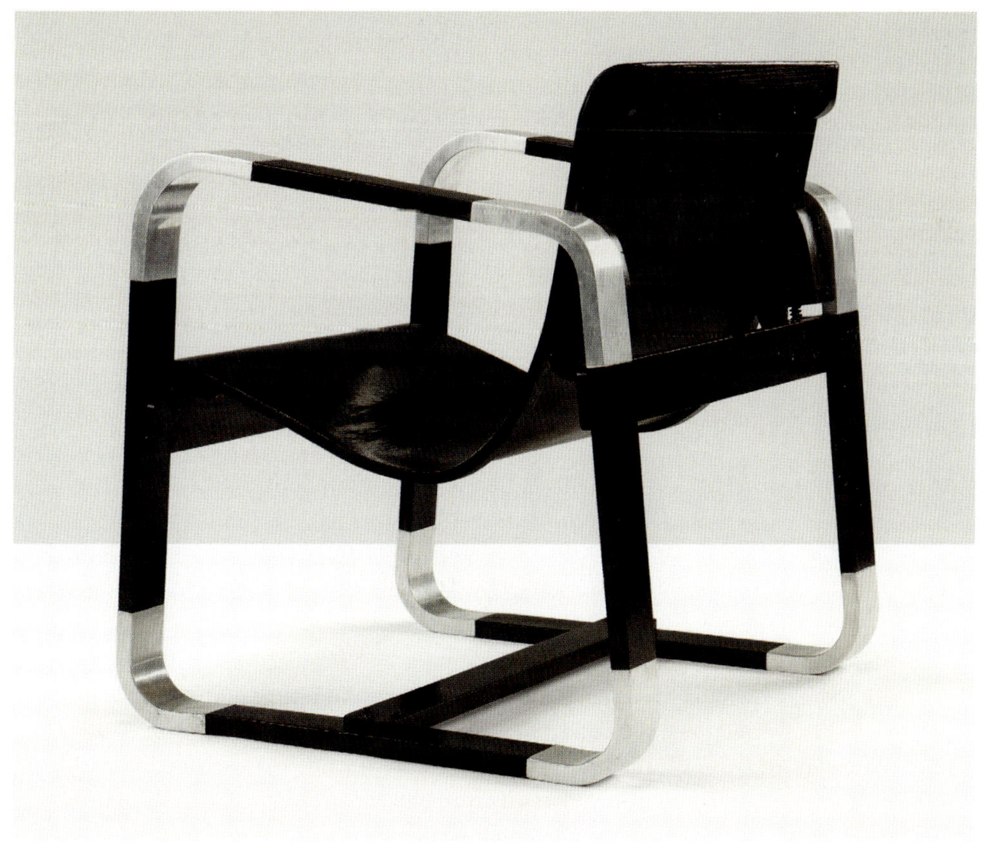

ABOVE:
Sideboard
by Studio BBPR, *c.*1935

LEFT:
Armchair
by Giuseppe Pagano, *c.*1942

Modernism

International, 1920s–1950s

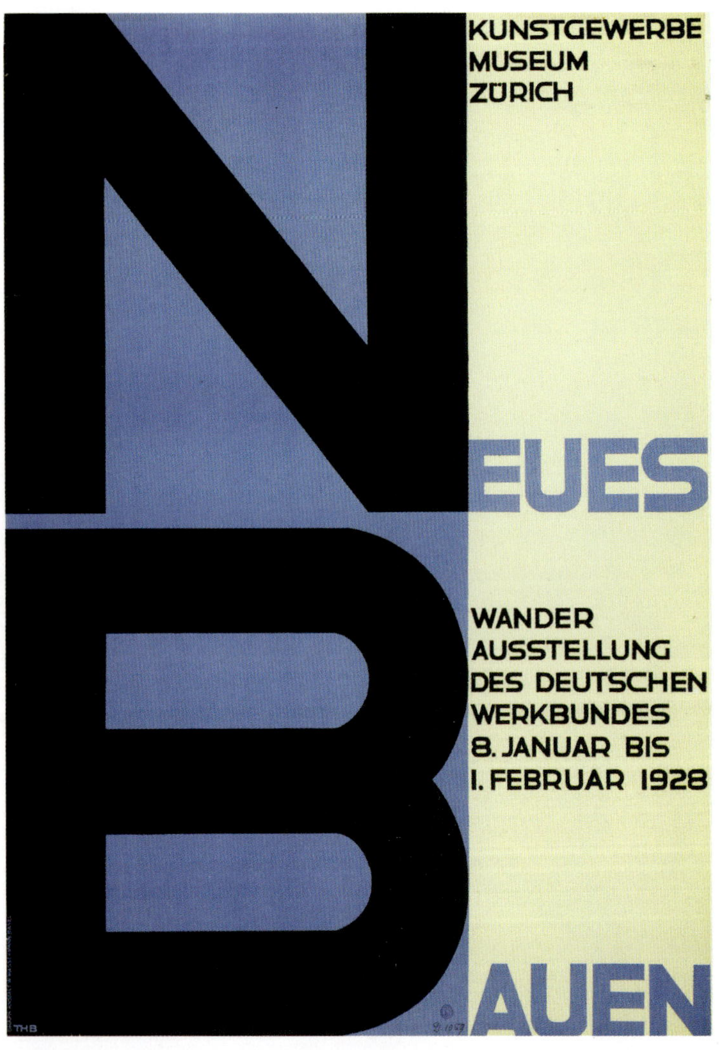

ABOVE:
Poster for Deutscher Werkbund's *Neues Bauen* (New Building) exhibition
by Theo Ballmer, 1928

During the opening years of the twentieth century there was a widespread desire for a more progressive and forward-looking style of architecture and design that would express the new spirit of the dawning industrial age. Yet at the same time, Modernism, as it became known, was also driven by a socially motivated ideology based on the conviction that design could be used as a powerful tool for social change.

The origins of these sentiments can be traced to nineteenth-century design reformers such as John Ruskin and William Morris, who had concluded that the highly decorative High Victorian Style was a reflection of a decadent society, driven by commercial greed and worker oppression. Striving to reform society's ills through the creation of simpler yet beautifully crafted wares, Morris advocated utility and appropriateness in design, although at the same time he passionately believed in the supremacy of handicraft, and by and large rejected factory production. His ideas inspired the foundation of various design-reforming workshops, guilds and associations that were more ambivalent to the machine, having accepted that a degree of mechanization was an irrefutable fact of modern life. And through their attempts at design reform, it was eventually realized that, for economic reasons, the goal of well-designed products for the masses would only be achievable if industrial production was fully embraced.

One such enterprise was the Deutscher Werkbund, which was founded in 1907 with the aim of forging closer links between designers and manufacturers in order to elevate the quality of produced goods. The Werkbund also held exhibitions and workshops to educate designers and craftsmen as well as the general public about the need for well-designed objects that were informed by practical utility rather than by decorative fashionability. Various architect-designers associated with the Deutscher Werkbund developed a purposeful approach

RIGHT ABOVE AND BELOW:
Interiors of the Farnsworth House
in Plano, Illinois, by Ludwig Mies van der Rohe, 1951 – an open-plan, one-roomed "glass house" intended as a weekend retreat

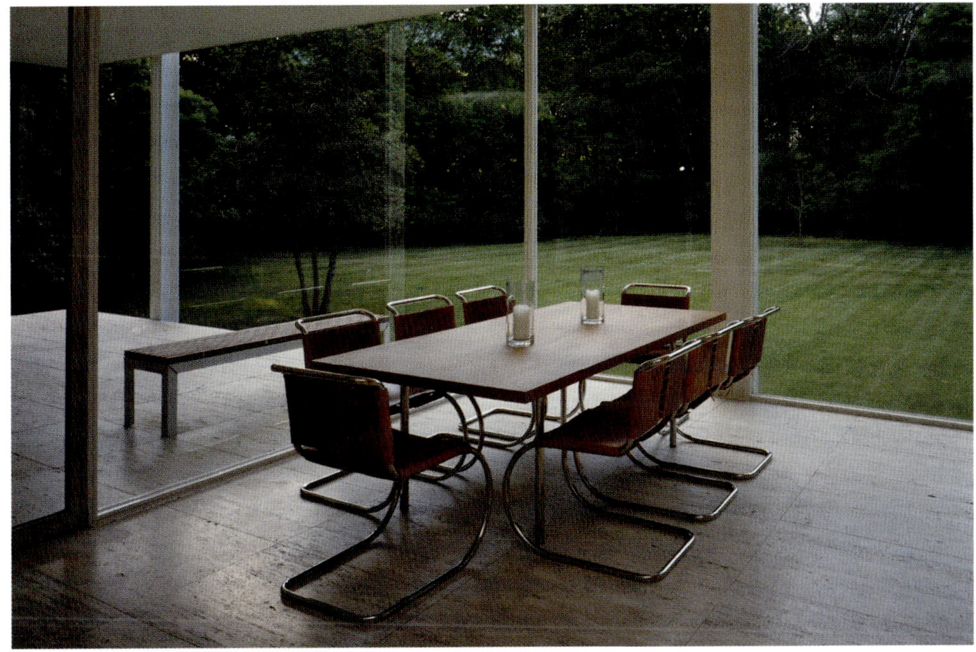

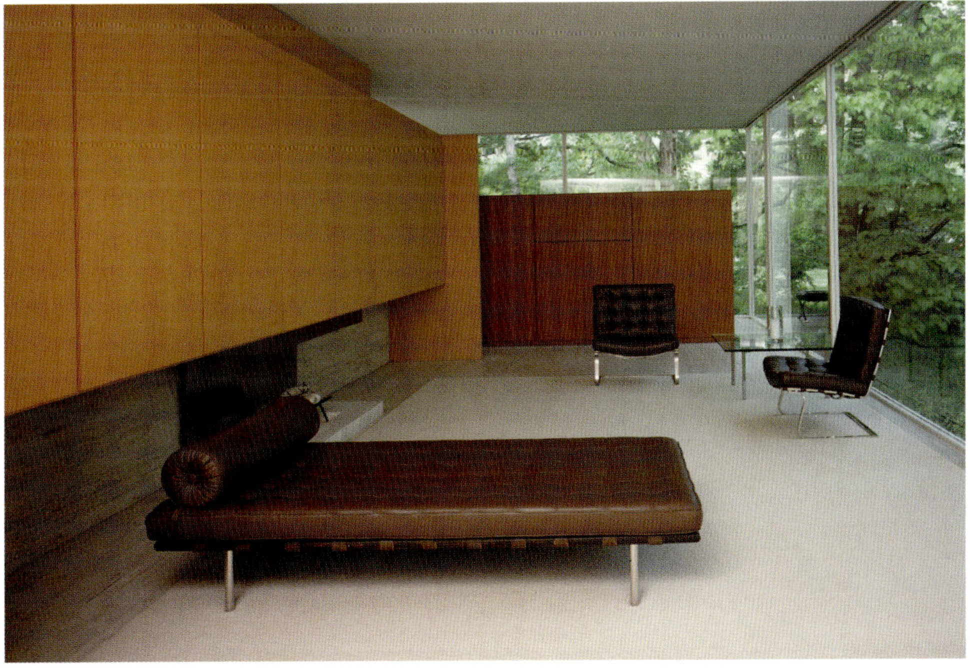

to design that more or less eliminated ornament and stressed functional simplicity. By following this rational approach, better standardization of elements could be attained, which resulted in increased manufacturing efficiency. In consequence, well-designed goods became more affordable, and thereby democratic.

In a similar vein, the Viennese architect Adolf Loos argued for the cleansing of form in his seminal essay *Ornament and Crime* of 1908, arguing that the superfluous decoration of an object was morally repugnant. He observed, "Ornament is wasted manpower and therefore wasted health. It has always been like this. But today it also means wasted material, and both mean wasted capital."

During the 1910s, the De Stijl movement in Holland also promoted aesthetic and functional purity, but as a means of affecting a new universalism in art, design and architecture. At the same time, the Futurists in Italy and the Constructivists in Russia celebrated new industrial materials and the new machine age. It was not until after the First World War, however, that Modernism properly coalesced into a definable international movement, mainly thanks to the foundation of the Staatliches Bauhaus in Weimar in 1919, which forged crucial links with the Constructivists and De Stijl.

After the move to Dessau in 1925, teaching at the Bauhaus became increasingly geared towards designing for large-scale and highly standardized industrial production. This new rational approach to design was referred to in Germany as the *Neue Sachlichkeit* (new objectivity), or sometimes *Neues Bauen* (new building), and was showcased emphatically at the landmark *Die Wohnung* (The Dwelling) exhibition organized by the Deutscher Werkbund in Stuttgart in 1927, where architect-designers from across Europe created thoroughly Modern model dwellings in line with this new pared-down approach. (After a further international exhibition, in New York in 1932, it would become known as the International Style.) The stark utilitarian machine-aesthetic so beloved by Modernists in France and Germany, such as Le Corbusier and Ludwig Mies van der Rohe, was not so well received in Scandinavia, however, where Alvar Aalto, among others, pioneered an organic approach to Modernism that relied on the use of more "humane" materials, such as plywood and laminated wood, rather than "cold" industrial materials like glass, aluminium and tubular steel.

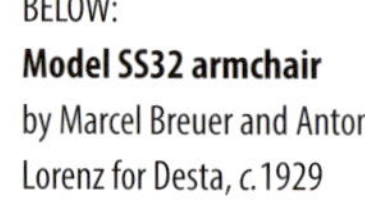

BELOW:
Model SS32 armchair
by Marcel Breuer and Anton Lorenz for Desta, *c.*1929

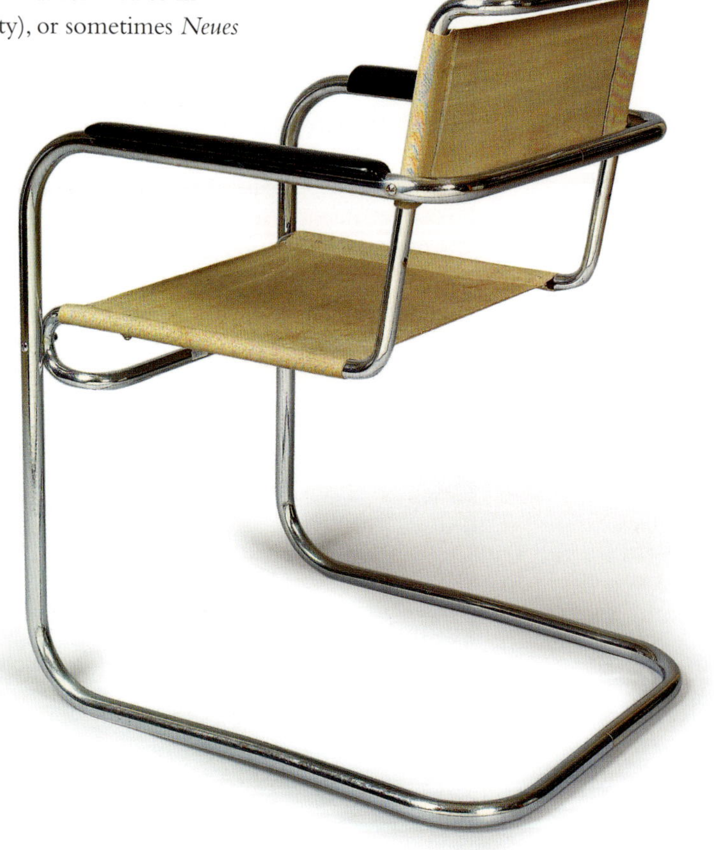

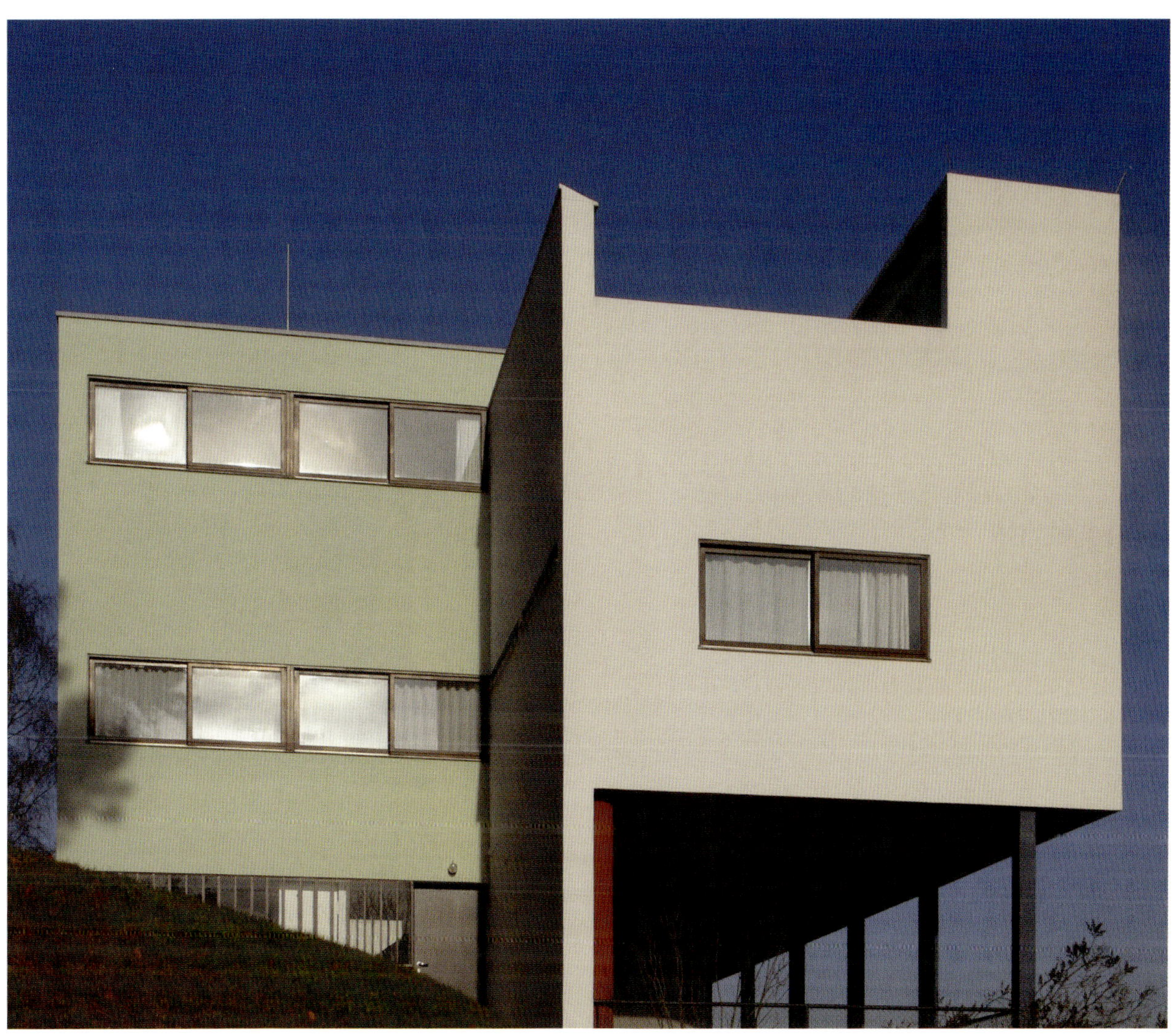

ABOVE:
Haus Le Corbusier
(now Weissenhof Museum) designed by Le Corbusier and Pierre Jeanneret as part of the Weissenhof-Siedlung (a model housing estate) for the Deutscher Werkbund's *Die Wohnung* (The Dwelling) exhibition, Stuttgart, 1927

Following the Second World War, this less hard-edged style of Modernism was taken up by designers in the United States, most notably Charles and Ray Eames, who perpetuated the Modern Movement's cause with their democratic well-designed furniture that epitomized the notion of good design. As the British-based Modernist architect Berthold Lubetkin noted in 1947, the Modern Movement, rather than being a definable group, was "a statement of the social aims of the age" that was a conscious attempt to bring to architecture and design a "universal, and purposeful order and clarity". Today, the underlying aims of Modernism remain more relevant than ever, for with natural resources being finite it makes complete sense for design to be guided by structural, functional and material efficiency together with a moral purposefulness.

Anti-Design / Pop Design

Europe and America, late 1950s–late 1970s

From the late 1920s onwards, Modernism ruled within the avant-garde, and inside architectural and design circles its guiding principle of form following function was taken as an irrefutable truth. Indeed, anyone who dared criticize the Modernist doctrine was dismissed as an intellectual Luddite, such was the zealous conviction of its devotees. Modernism celebrated the advance of the industrial age, but its adherents in their quest for social progress often lost sight of what it was actually all for, as untold numbers of alienating tower blocks littering skylines across the world still attest.

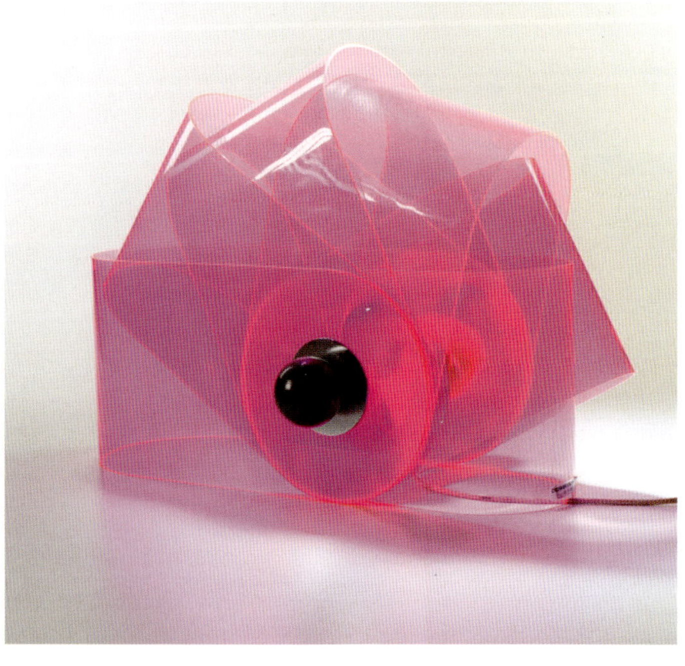

ABOVE:
Gherpe lamp
designed by Cristiano Toraldo di Francia/Superstudio for Poltronova, 1967

OPPOSITE:
Cactus coat rack
designed by Guido Drucco and Franco Mello for Gufram, 1972

Even by the early 1950s, the precepts of Modernism were being questioned by a new generation – most notably by the Independent Group, which held its first meeting at the Institute of Contemporary Arts (ICA) in London in 1952. The group, which included the artist Richard Hamilton, the sculptor Eduardo Paolozzi, the architecture critic Reyner Banham and the architects Peter and Alison Smithson, examined the achievements of American industrial production and its by-product, popular consumerist culture. Questioning Modernist doctrine, the Independent Group controversially drew inspiration from the "low art" of advertising, packaging and comics – although paradoxically Hamilton also created a series of prints featuring a toaster designed by Dieter Rams, an exemplar of Modern consumerist product design, which he claimed occupied his "heart and conciousness" in much the same way that Mont Saint-Victoire had inspired Cézanne. The term "Pop" was coined to describe this new tendency in the creative arts which lauded popular consumerism; in 1957 Hamilton wrote a letter to the Smithsons defining Pop Art as: "popular [designed for a mass audience], transient [short-term solution], expendable [easily forgotten], low-cost, mass-produced, young [aimed at youth], witty, sexy, gimmicky, glamorous and Big Business".

From the early 1960s to the early 1970s, a playful Pop aesthetic that was in tune with the counter-culture movement washed away the cultural dominance of Modernism, with the general precept for design now being "form follows fun" – whether it was Peter Murdoch's cardboard Spotty chair (1963–64) or De Pas, D'Urbino and Lomazzi's inflatable Blow chair (1967). Many parallels existed between Pop Art and Pop Design, especially in France and Italy, where designs were often produced as limited edition "multiples" and sold in a gallery context. Likewise, these Anti-Design pieces were far more akin to sculpture than to industrially produced mainstream design and, as with Pop Art, there was a noticeable trend for outsized, out-of-context creations, such as Studio 65's Capitello chair (1971). While Pop Design had initially expressed an optimistic Space Age look, from the late 1960s onwards a more psychedelic hippy-inspired aesthetic came to the fore, especially in the realm of graphic design, as evinced in Milton Glaser's Bob Dylan poster (1967) or the Art Nouveau-on-acid music posters created by Wes Wilson.

The hedonistic party of the Pop movement effectively came to an abrupt end with the global Oil Crisis of 1973, but the questioning spirit of Anti-Design lived on, especially in Italy with the work of Global Tools and Studio Alchimia. These Radical Design trailblazers, however, replaced the carefree creative fun of Pop with a sense of politicized cynicism. Studio Alchimia's explorations into "banal design" and "redesign" were fuelled by Anti-Design sentiments, which rejected unequivocally the Modern Movement's doctrinal mindset of "less is more". By the late 1970s and early 1980s, Anti-Design had grown into its own important international style, Post-Modernism, which was guided by the belief that in fact "less is a bore" – at least according to the American architect Robert Venturi, who coined the telling phrase.

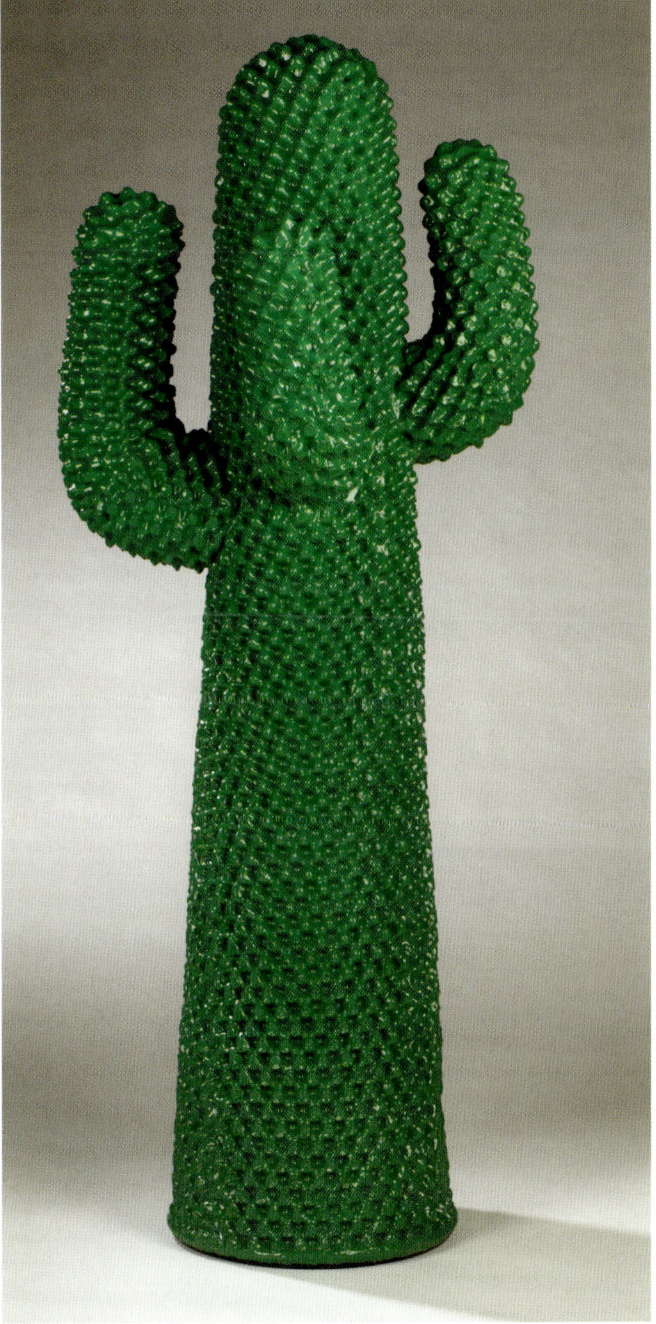

Radical Design

Europe, 1970s–1980s

The term Radical Design refers principally to a movement in architecture and design that emerged in Italy during the late 1960s, following in the wake of Pop Design and its promotion of Anti-Design.

The artist-designer Riccardo Dalisi was one of the foremost progenitors of the Italian Radical Design movement. In 1973, while working as a professor at the faculty of architecture at the University of Naples, he conducted an influential research project into the creative potential of the general public. This involved arranging workshops for underprivileged children in the Traiano district of Naples, which got the youngsters to use so-called *tecnologia povera* (poor technology) – in this case, planks of wood roughly nailed together – to create pieces of rough-and-ready furniture and other constructions. The resulting designs showed a remarkable level of personal and spontaneous creativity, as well as the possibility of cultural engagement among those who were the most economically and socially distanced from high culture.

Dalisi's project eventually inspired the establishment of a "school" of counter-architecture and counter-design in the editorial offices of *Casabella* magazine in Milan in January 1973. This new venture, known as Global Tools, was founded by a roster of Italy's most avant-garde design practitioners: Archizoom Associati, Remo Buti, Riccardo Dalisi, Ugo La Pietra, Gruppo 9999, Gaetano Pesce, Gianni Pettena, Ettore Sottsass, Superstudio, Gruppo UFO and Zziggurat. The central aim of Global Tools was to kick against the pervasive blandness of mainstream design culture, and "to stimulate the free development of individual creativity". With a do-it-yourself ethos and a left-leaning political agenda, Global Tools sought to creatively connect ordinary people with the design process. For the two years of its brief operation, it was the central forum of Radical Design, and the project's disbandment in 1975 signified the end of Radical Design's first phase in Italy.

Despite the eventual break-up of Global Tools, new mutating shoots of Radical Design had appeared a year earlier when the designer Alessandro Mendini set fire to two identical

BELOW:
Wassily Chair "redesigned" by Alessandro Mendini for Studio Alchimia, 1978/83

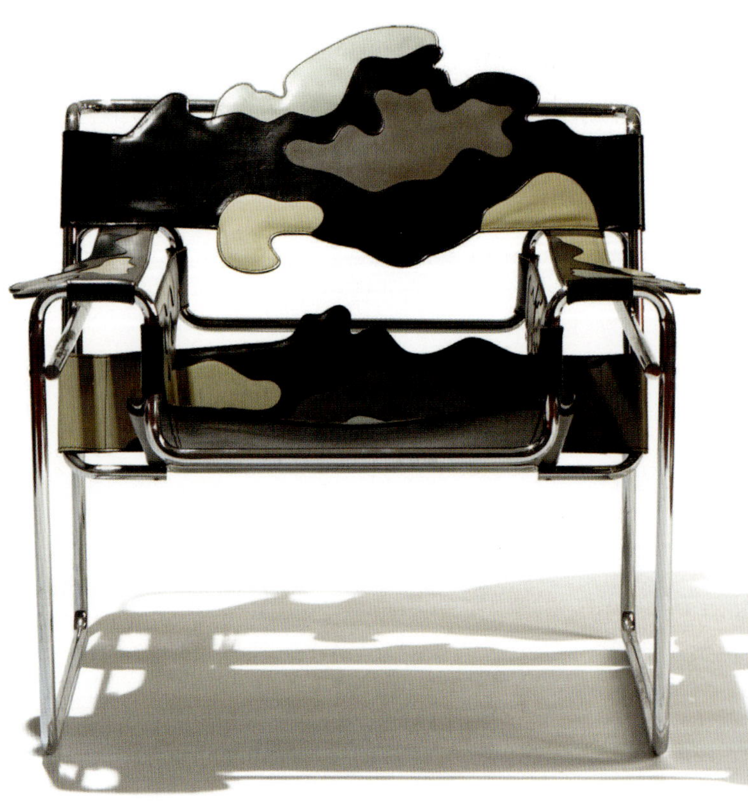

archetypal chairs outside the offices of *Casabella*, where he was editor-in-chief. Both chairs bore the name Lassù (Up There). This incendiary act was followed by another symbolic chair-burning later that same year.

Two years later, in 1976, the architect Alessandro Guerriero founded Studio Alchimia, which would become the main champion of this provocative new form of intellectually challenging counter-design, best described as the second phase of Radical Design. Although intended as a gallery space in which to exhibit work, not constrained by industrial production, Studio Alchimia soon became an influential design studio that produced avant-garde work by, among others, Alessandro Mendini, Andrea Branzi, Ettore Sottsass and Michele De Lucchi. The studio's name, which alluded to chemistry's pseudo-scientific predecessor, alchemy, was a jibe at the scientific rationale underlying Modernism. Highly intellectualized and politicized, Studio Alchimia's subversive work laid the foundations of the Memphis Design Group and ultimately Post-Modernism in the applied arts.

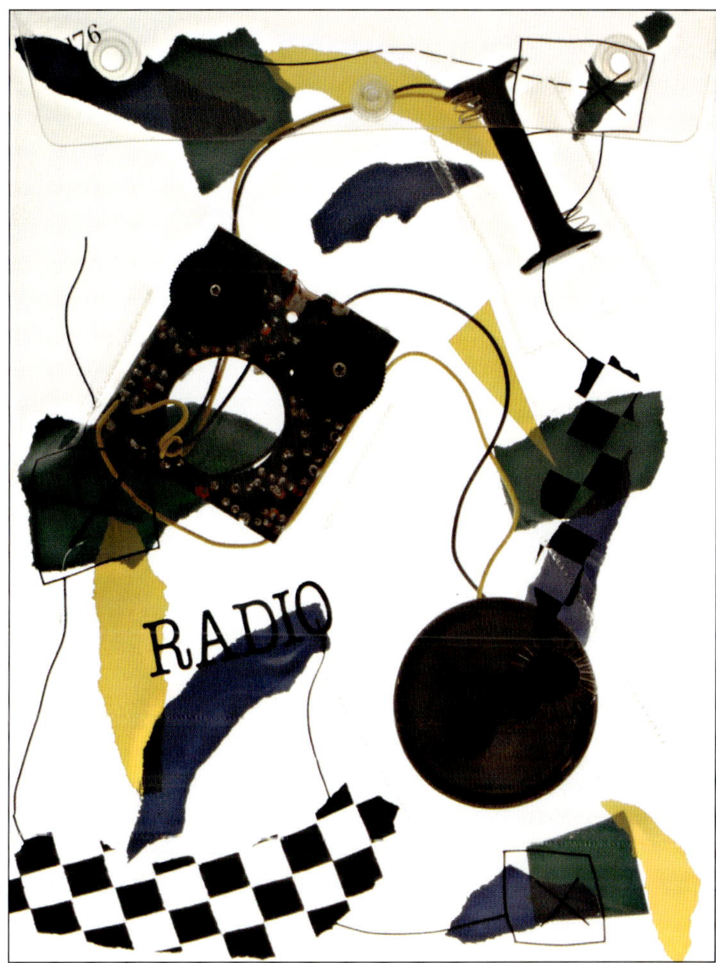

ABOVE:
Bag Radio
by Daniel Weil for Parenthesis, 1981

During the 1970s, a comparable Radical Design culture materialized in Britain, where a deep recession and high unemployment rates produced a disenfranchised generation that was deeply sceptical of the establishment. Punk was the natural expression of this disaffection, emerging first in fashion and music around 1974, then soon making inroads into graphic and product design, with Jamie Reid's anarchic 1977 cover for the Sex Pistols' single "God Save the Queen" and Daniel Weil's Bag Radio (1981) being the best-known examples of this new Radical spirit. Like Dalisi's earlier experiments with poor technology, the post-Punk Creative Salvage Movement that emerged in the early 1980s had a similarly Radical agenda, with designers such as Tom Dixon and Ron Arad also seeking to bring hands-on creativity back into the design arena, although perhaps in a less intellectualized way.

Post-Modernism

International, late 1970s–1990s

Post-Modernism emerged in the late twentieth century as a movement in the arts, literature, architecture, design and cultural discourse. It marked a complete disillusionment with Modernism and was predicated on a deep questioning of its principles. While Modernism centred on empiricism and rationality, and lauded "high culture", Post-Modernism in contrast was characterized by an intellectual relativism that viewed traditional cultural hierarchies as artificial constructs.

The origins of Post-Modernism in design can be traced back to the Anti-Design tendencies expressed in Pop Design during the 1960s. But while Pop had been playful in its counter-culture questioning of Modernism, Post-Modernism was (and still is) far more intellectualized and knowingly cynical in its rejection of Modernity. The first distinct stirrings of Post-Modern thought in architecture and design circles also occurred during the mid-Sixties, a decade of huge cultural upheaval that saw the long-held supremacy of Modernism being questioned. Did form have to follow function? What did function really mean anyway? Was less really more? And why did people living in Modernist social-housing tower blocks trash them? One of the most influential critiques of Modernism from this period was Robert Venturi's *Complexity and Contradiction in Architecture* (1966), in which he argued that Modern architecture was fundamentally banal since it lacked the rich symbolism of historic buildings.

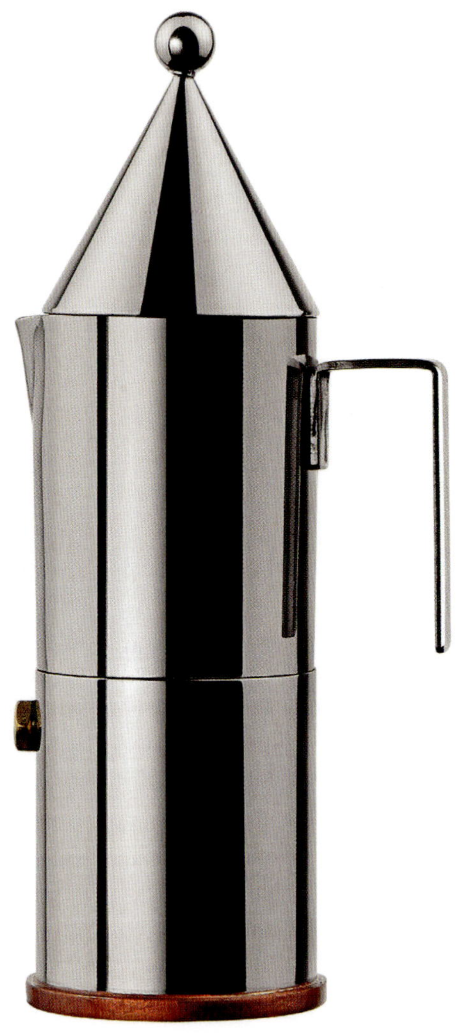

Venturi subsequently co-authored with Denise Scott Brown and Steven Izenour another hugely influential book, *Learning from Las Vegas* (1972), which celebrated the cultural honesty of Nevada's gambling nirvana with its garish billboards and over-the-top neon displays. Also published in 1972 was an English translation of the French writer Roland Barthes's *Mythologies* (1957), which likewise helped to disseminate Post-Modern semiotic theories to a far wider audience. Barthes's conjecture was that society had a tendency to mythologize socially constructed ideas and assumptions so that they became "naturalized", by which he meant they were taken unquestioningly. Just as this idea was gaining currency, so too was there a growing sense that Modern architecture had failed and that the main reason for its failure had been its adherents' ideological devotion to functionalism and their disregard of the important role that symbols play in culture. As if to prove this, 1972 also witnessed the famous demolition of the Modernist Pruitt-Igoe social-housing complex in St Louis, Missouri. Comprising thirty-three housing blocks, this Modernist urban-renewal project had been completed in 1954, but

ABOVE:
La Conica espresso coffee maker
by Aldo Rossi for Alessi, 1984

OPPOSITE:
Summer Room interior
in The Thematic House, London, by Charles Jencks, 1979–84

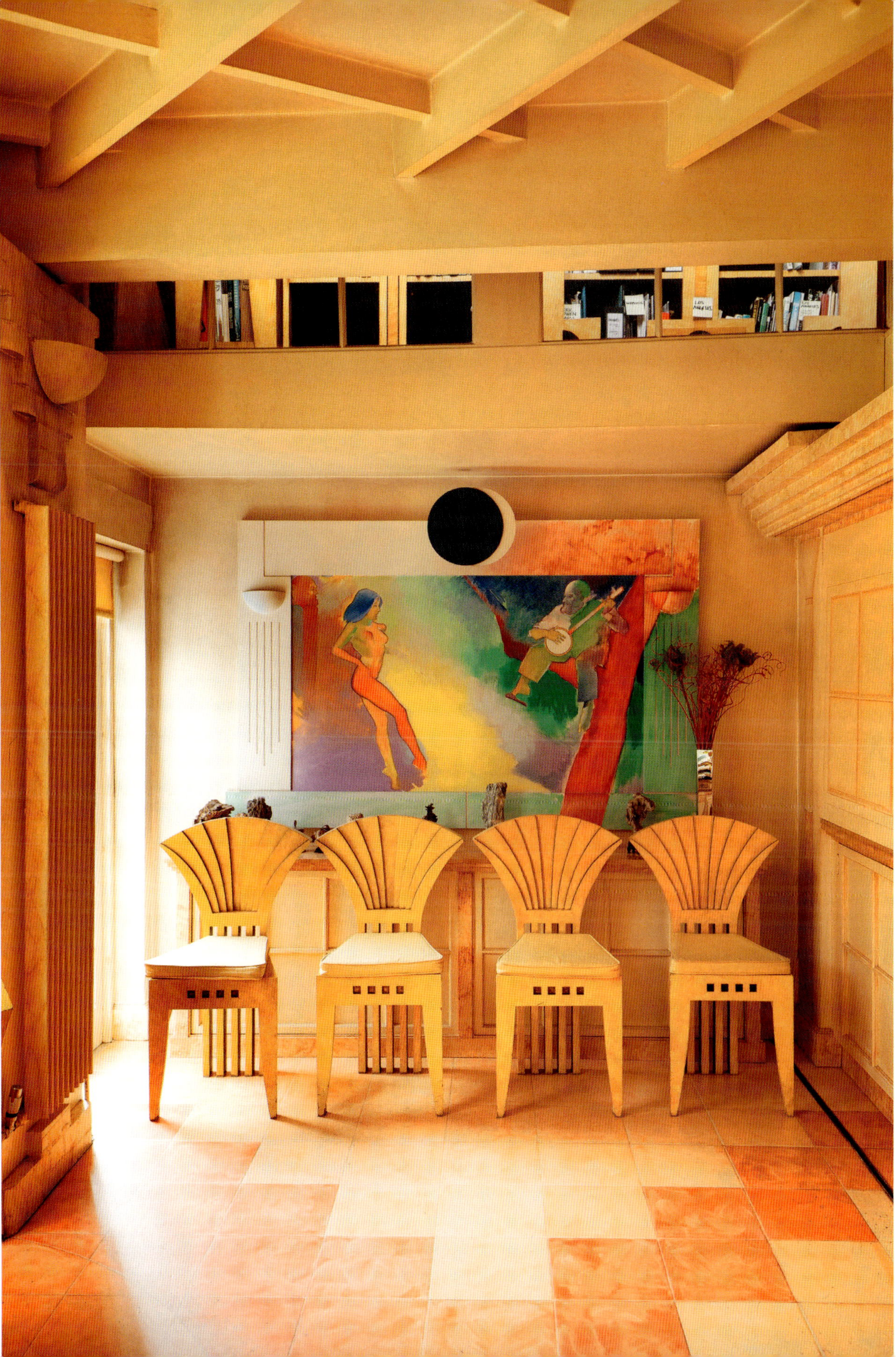

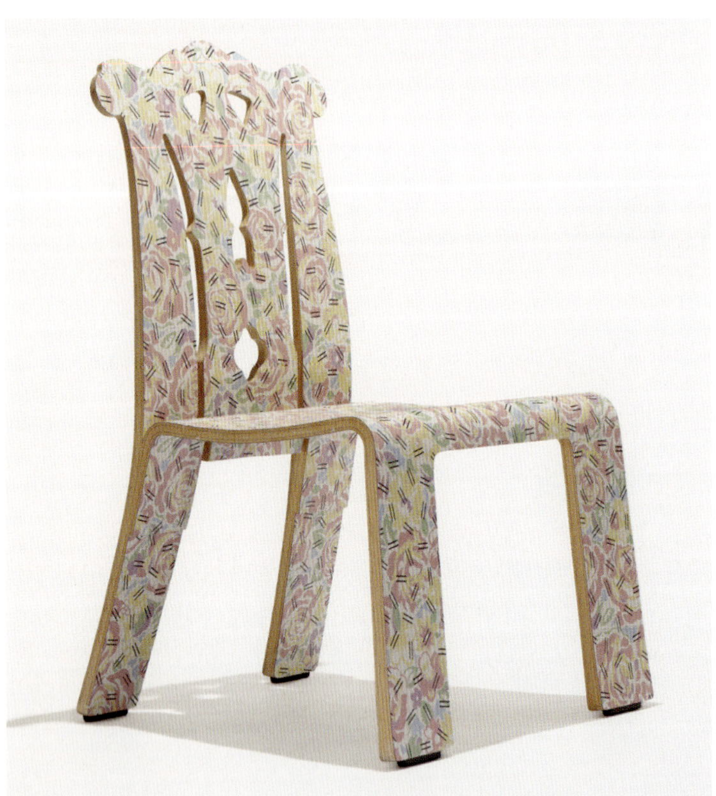

LEFT:
Chippendale chair
by Robert Venturi for Knoll, 1984

BELOW:
Vanna Venturi House
in Chestnut Hill, Philadelphia, 1964 – an early Post-Modern residence designed by Robert Venturi for his mother, Vanna Venturi

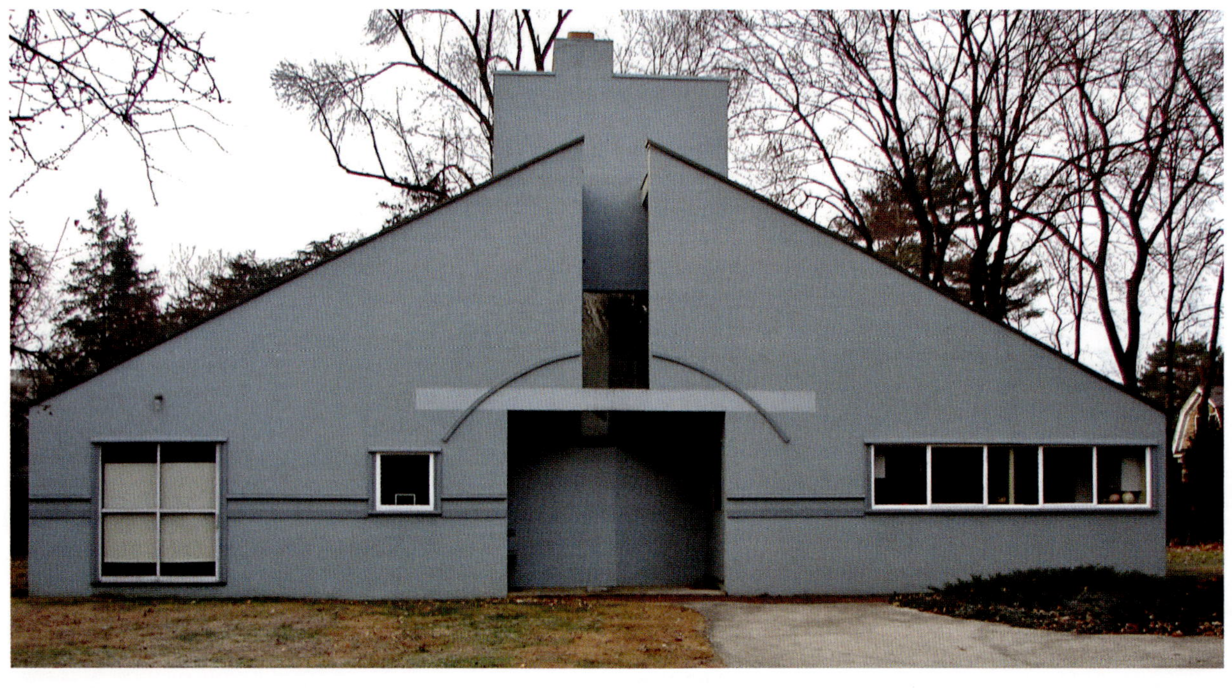

within just a few short years had turned into a dangerous, decaying high-rise slum with broken windows and crime-infested public spaces.

Given this background, a new generation of architects and designers felt that the answer to the ills of Modernism was to imbue their buildings and designs with meaning, and so they began incorporating decorative motifs that made tongue-in-cheek references to past historic styles and had an eclectic "double-coded" irony. Double-coding, which involved combining contemporary techniques and materials with historic stylistic "quotations", was a way of countering the malaise of what the architectural critic Charles Jencks called "dumb boxes", by which he meant the poorly designed and badly constructed tower blocks inspired by Le Corbusier and Ludwig Mies van der Rohe that were now blighting most major cities. From the mid-1970s, Jencks and Robert Venturi begun playfully subverting Classicism in America, while in Europe, the late 1970s saw designers associated with Studio Alchimia, most notably Alessandro Mendini, creating what were then termed "New Wave" designs that mockingly transformed, or redesigned, acknowledged icons of Modernism with the application of ironic decoration. For instance, Mendini decorated Marcel Breuer's Wassily Chair with cloud-like motifs, attached little nautical flags to Gio Ponti's Superleggera chair (making reference to its fisherman's-chair origins) and gave Joe Colombo's plastic Universale chair a faux-marble finish.

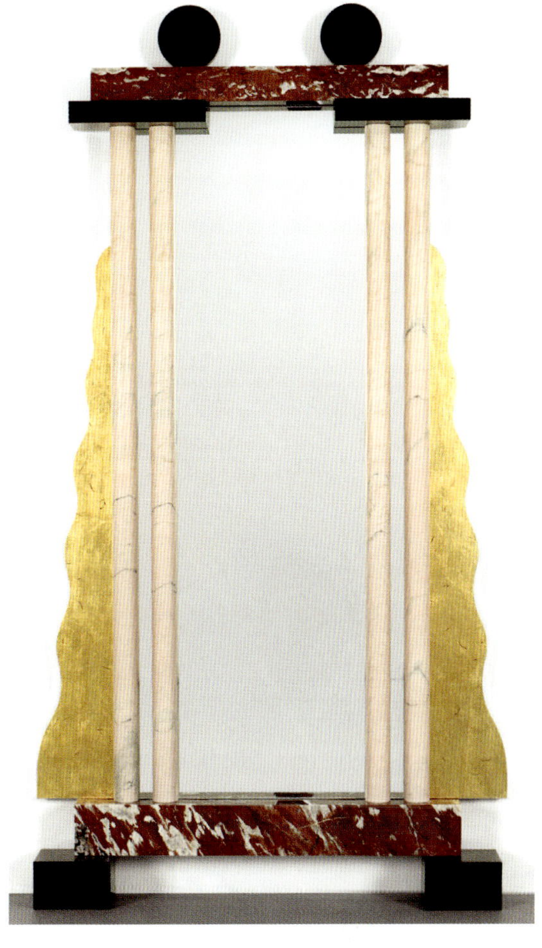

ABOVE:
Del Diavolo mirror
by Ettore Sottsass for Ultima Edizione, c.1980

Later, Ettore Sottsass and his Memphis design group created bold and colourful Neo-Pop furniture and lighting that similarly helped to popularize Post-Modernism. Launched at the Milan Furniture Fair in 1981, Memphis rocked the design world with its attention-grabbing totemic designs that were infused with double-coded symbolic meaning. Its designs drew eclectic references from not only past decorative styles but also kitsch, Surrealism and emerging digital imagery. Memphis heralded a new era of design, one that rejected the bland universality of Modernism and marked the ascendency of creative individualism.

During the 1980s Post-Modernism became a mainstream international style, making inroads into many areas of design practice, most notably graphic design with the work of Neville Brody, April Greiman and David Carson. By the mid-1990s, however, ennui with Post-Modernism could already be detected, for, like other ornamental styles, it was subject to fashionable obsolescence. Nevertheless, the intellectual underpinnings of Post-Modernism would have a lasting effect: today we live in a Late Modern age (also referred to as Post-Post-Modernity or Metamodernity) that is both an evolution of Post-Modernism and a reaction against it. While there has been a return to Modernist functionalist values, this has been tempered by an understanding of Post-Modern philosophy.

Late Modern

International, late 1980s–present

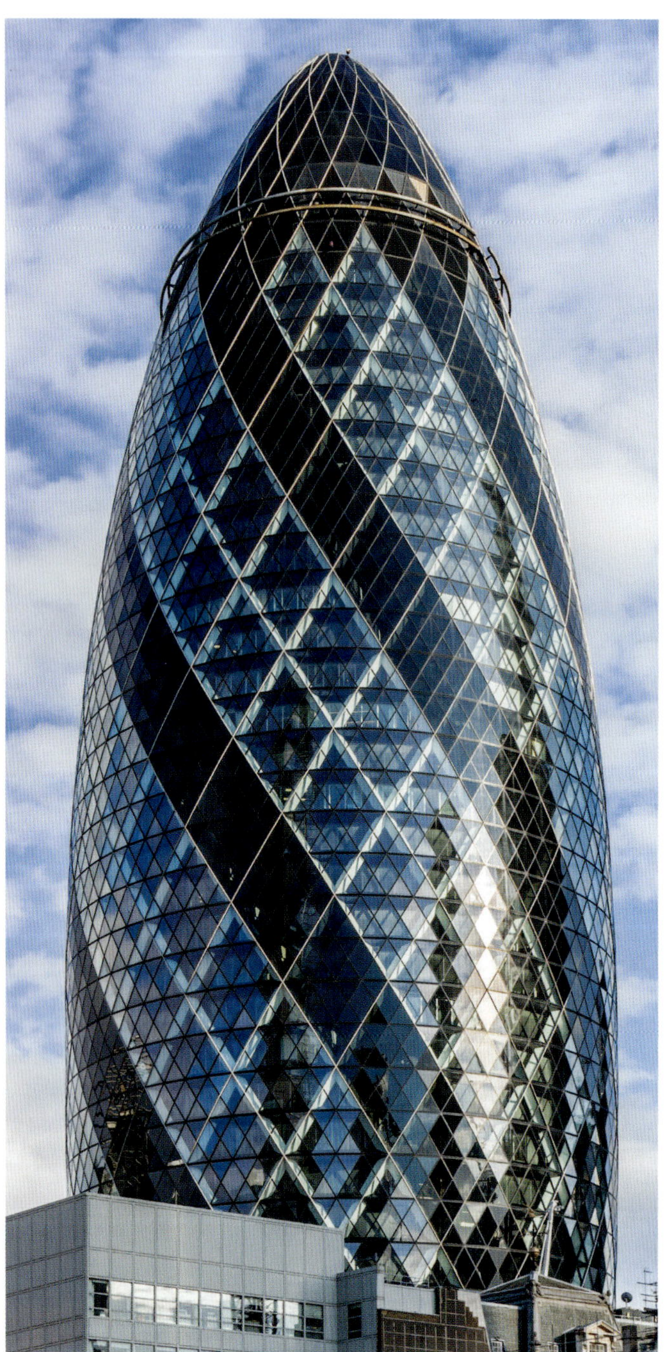

Late Modern – also sometimes referred to as Neo-Modern – emerged in design and architecture during the 1980s as a rejection to the eclectic mix-and-match decorative tendencies of Post-Modernism. As its name suggests, it is a Post-Post-Modern movement that is based on the precepts of the Modern Movement, yet cognizant also of its failings. In essence Late Modernism is Modernism 2.0 – a direct continuation of Modernity, but with a knowing Post-Modern critical edge.

Indeed, most designers who create products for large-scale production today fall within the Late Modern category, because successful industrial manufacture by necessity calls for a rational, i.e. Modern, process-driven approach to problem-solving. Among the many designers who can be placed in this categorization, Jonathan Ive, Jasper Morrison and Naoto Fukasawa are perhaps the most prominent, with their beautifully designed and executed products being the outcome of a thoughtful essentialist ethos based on function, but not dictated by it. A Late Modern approach is also found in the architecture of Norman Foster and Richard Rogers, both of whom create buildings by effectively skinning functional need with steel and glass, while at the same time being mindful of the users' psychological needs.

Importantly, practitioners of Late Modernism have a more nuanced understanding of design and architecture than their forebears. They understand that often the

LEFT:
30 St Mary Axe building
London, by Foster + Partners, 1997–2004

OPPOSITE:
Z-chair
by Zaha Hadid and Patrik Schumacher for Sawaya & Moroni, 2011

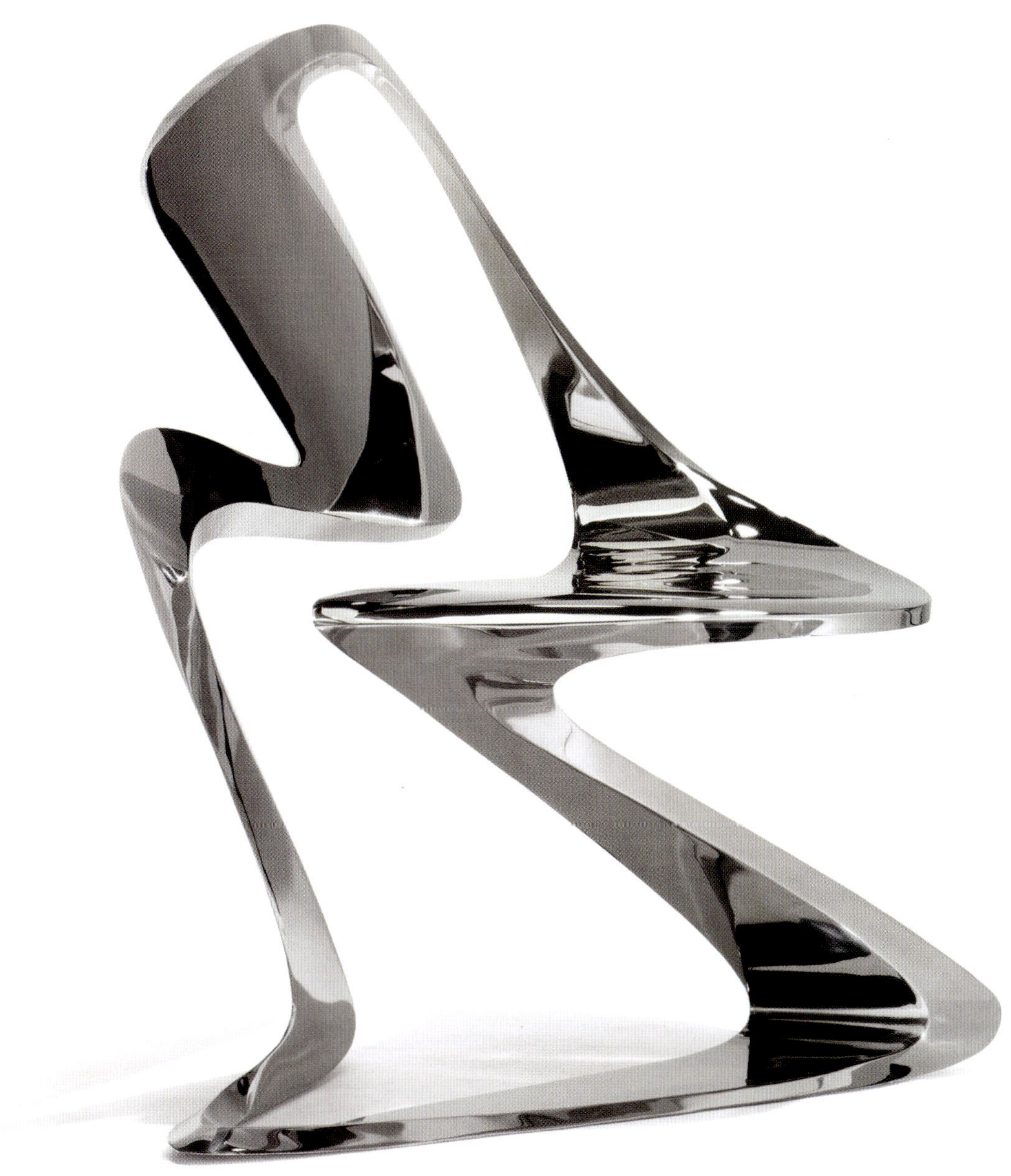

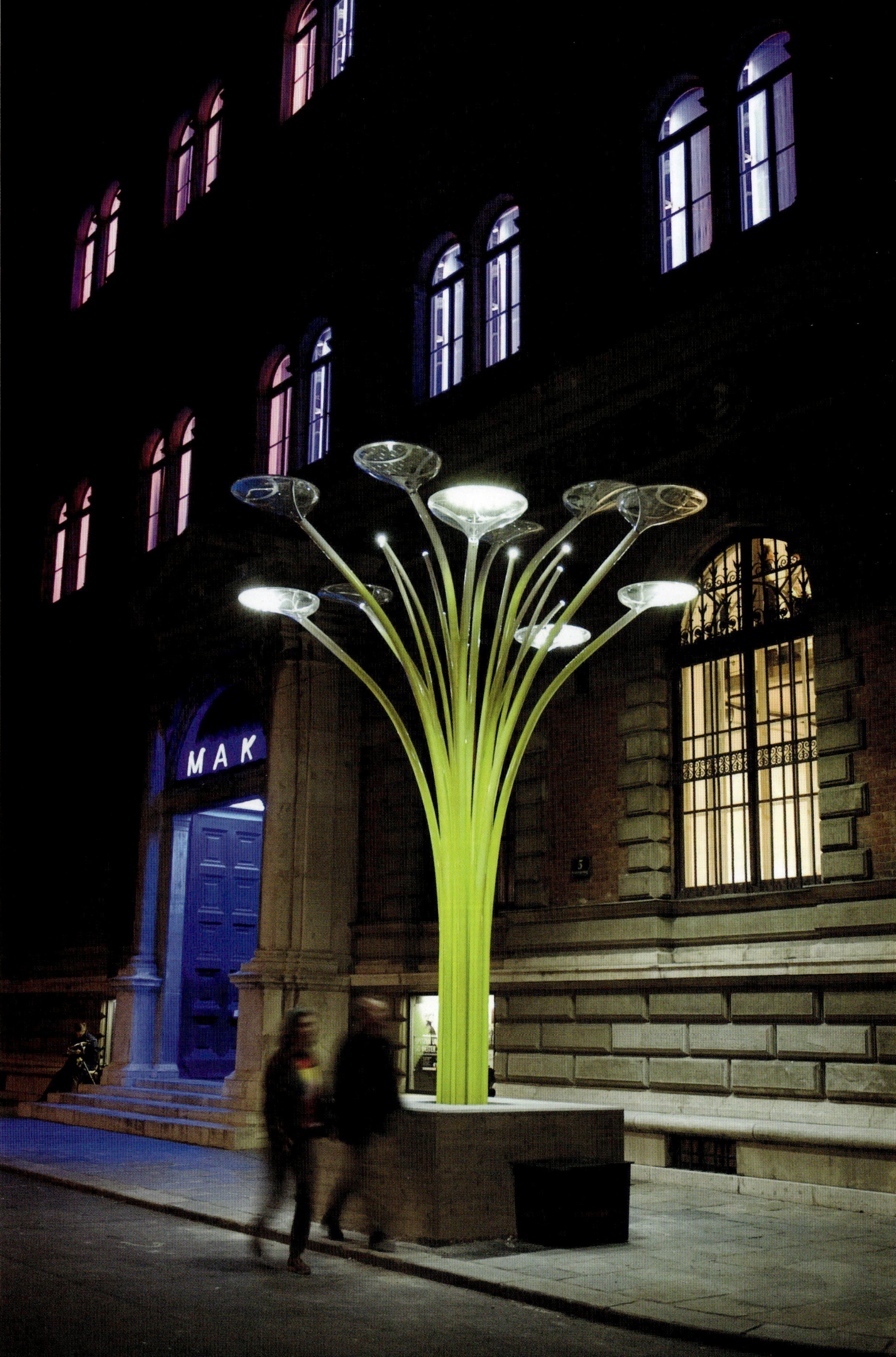
MAK

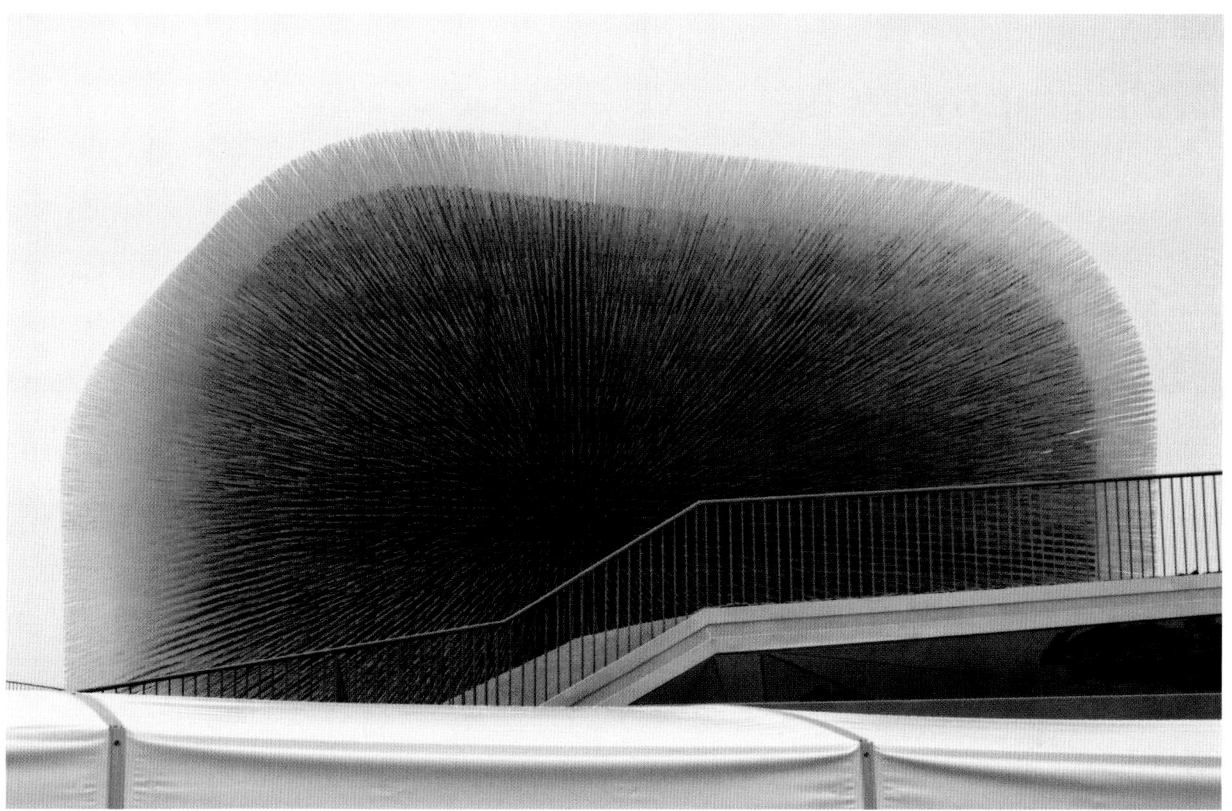

ABOVE:
UK Pavilion
at *Shanghai Expo 2010* by Thomas Heatherwick, 2010

OPPOSITE:
Solar Tree street light
by Ross Lovegrove for Artemide, 2006–10

crucial differentiating factor between two products, or indeed two buildings, is the way people emotionally connect with them. Although there are categories of products where engineered purpose is the most important factor, as in the design of scientific equipment or industrial machinery, most designs – whether a phone or a poster – need to function beyond just physical needs; they must also ideally connect with the user on an emotional level. Knowing this, the majority of Late Modern designers have become adept design-psychologists, thoroughly aware of how important psychological comfort and feel-good tactility are to the success of a design.

Smart Design's Good Grips kitchen tools are another example of the Late Modern emphasis on creating the best possible product experience for the end-user. While Modernism's focus was on one-size-fits-all universal solutions intended for the "average" user, Late Modernism's goal is for more adaptable solutions that can be tailored to individual needs or that have a broader and more diverse reach, thereby allowing the end-user to connect better on a personal level with the products they use or the buildings they are living or working in. This is the great difference between Modernism and its younger, arguably smarter brother Late Modernism – the understanding that design needs to be emotionally compelling and ultimately inclusive.

Bibliography

Banham, J., *Theory and Design in the First Machine Age*, Architectural Press, London/New York 1960

Bayley, S., *In Good Shape: Style in Industrial Products 1900–1960*, Design Council, London 1979

Bayley, S. & Conran, T., *Design: Intelligence Made Visible*, Conran Octopus, London 2007

Benton, T., *The New Objectivity*, Open University Press, Milton Keynes 1975

Benton, T., Benton, C. & Sharp, D., *Form and Function: A Source Book for the History of Architecture and Design 1890–1939*, Open University Press, Milton Keynes 1975

Brown, T., *Change by Design,* Harper Business, New York 2009

Buchanan, R. & Margolin, V. (eds.), *Discovering Design,* University of Chicago Press, Chicago 1995

Dormer, P., *Design Since 1945*, Thames & Hudson, London 1993

– *The Meanings of Modern Design: Towards the Twenty-First Century*, Thames & Hudson, London 1990

Dreyfuss, H., *Designing for People*, Simon & Schuster, New York 1955

Fiell, C. & P., *Design of the 20th Century*, Taschen, Cologne 1999

– *Industrial Design*, Taschen, Cologne 2000

– *Scandinavian Design*, Taschen, Cologne 2002

– *The Story of Design*, Goodman Fiell, London 2013

Forty, A., *Objects of Desire, Design & Society 1750–1980*, Thames & Hudson, London 1986

Giedion, S., *Mechanization Takes Command: A contribution to anonymous history*, Oxford University Press, New York 1948

Greenhalgh, P., *Modernism in Design*, Reaktion Books, London 1990

Heskett, J., *Industrial Design*, Thames & Hudson, London 1980

Heisinger, K. & Marcus, G., *Design Since 1945*, Thames & Hudson, London 1983

– *Landmarks of Twentieth-Century Design*, Abbeville Press, New York 1993

Kaplan, W. (ed.), *Designing Modernity, The Arts of Reform & Persuasion, 1985–1945*, Thames & Hudson/Wolfsonian, London/Miami 1995

Loewy, R., *Industrial Design*, Fourth Estate, London 1980

– *Never Leave Well Enough Alone*, Simon & Schuster, New York 1951

Lucie-Smith, E., *A History of Industrial Design*, Phaidon, Oxford 1983

Margolin, V., *Design Discourse, History, Theory, Criticism*, University of Chicago Press, Chicago 1989

Margolin, V. & Buchanan, R., *The Idea of Design*, MIT Press, Cambridge, Mass. 1995

McDonough, W. & Braungart, M., *Cradle to Cradle: Remaking the Way We Make Things*, North Point Press, New York 2002

– *The Upcycle: Beyond Sustainability – Designing for Abundance*, North Point Press, New York 2013

Molotch, H., *Where Stuff Comes From*, Routledge, New York 2003

Packard, V., *The Hidden Persuaders*, D. McKay Co., New York 1957

– *The Waste Makers*, D. McKay Co., New York 1960

Papanek, V., *Design for the Real World: Human Ecology and Social Change*, Pantheon Books, New York 1971

– *The Green Imperative: Natural Design for the Real World*, Thames & Hudson, London 1995

Pevsner, N., *Pioneers of Modern Design: From William Morris to Walter Gropius* (originally published as *Pioneers of the Modern Movement* in 1936; 2nd edition, New York: Museum of Modern Art, 1949; revised and partly rewritten, Penguin Books, 1960), Penguin, London, New Edition 1991

– *The Sources of Modern Architecture and Design*, Thames & Hudson, London 1968

Rams, D., *Less But Better*, Jo Klatt + Design Verlag, Hamburg 1995

Schaefer, H., *The Roots of Modern Design*, Studio Vista, London 1970

Schwartz, F., *The Werkbund: Design Theory and Mass Culture Before the First World War*, Yale University Press, New Haven 1996

Sudjic, D., *B is for Bauhaus*, Penguin Group, London 2014

– *Design in Britain: Big ideas (small island)*, Conran Octopus, London 2009

– *The Language of Things*, Allen Lane, London 2008

Triggs, T., *Communicating Design, Essays in Visual Communication*, B.T. Batsford, London 1995

Twitchell, J.B., *Lead Us into Temptation: The Triumph of American Materialism*, Columbia University Press, New York 2000

Verganti, R., *Design-Driven Innovation*, Harvard Business Press, Boston 2009

Whiteley, N., *Design for Society*, Reaktion Books, London 1993

Woodhamn, J., *Twentieth Century Design*, Oxford University Press, Oxford 1997

Exhibition Catalogues

American Modern 1925–1940: Design for a New Age, Metropolitan Museum of Art and the American Federation of Arts/Harry N. Abrams, New York 2000

Brani di Storia dell'Arredo (1880–1980), Museo dell'Arredo contemporaneo/Edizioni Essegi, Ravenna 1988

British Design from 1948: Innovation in the Modern Age, Victoria and Albert Museum/V&A Publishing, London 2012

Design 1935–1960: What Modern Was, Musée des Arts Décoratifs de Montréal/Harry N. Abrams, New York 1991

Design in America: The Cranbrook Vision 1925–1950, Detroit Institute of Arts and Metropolitan Museum of Art, New York 1983

Industrial Design: Reflection of a Century (published in conjunction with the exhibition *Design, Miroir du Siècle*) Grand Palais/Flammarion, Paris 1993

The Machine Age in America 1918–1941, Brooklyn Museum of Art/Harry N. Abrams, New York 1986

Modernism 1914–1939: Designing a New World, Victoria and Albert Museum/V&A Publishing, London 2006

Index

(italic page numbers refer to images; names in parentheses are those of designers, design houses, authors)

E

F

G

H

I

J

K

Acknowledgements & Credits

We would like to offer enormous thanks to Deyan Sudjic for undertaking this project with us on behalf of the Design Museum, and for his many excellent suggestions and insights along the way. Thanks must also go to Anna Marx and Gemma MacLagan Ram for their editorial management of the project, and to Emma Copestake and Paul Langan for their picture sourcing. We would also like to thank Lucy Palmer and Katie Baxendale for their beautiful graphic design work on this project, and Catherine Rubinstein for her careful proofreading. Last, but by no means least, we offer many thanks to all the designers, design studios, museums, auction houses, manufacturers, design dealers and picture libraries who have so kindly lent images for inclusion in the book.

The publishers would like to thank the following sources for their kind permission to reproduce the pictures in this book.

Alamy: /Arcaid Images: 67T, 86R, 309; /The Art Archive: 247; /Will Daniel: 138B; /Interfoto: 38, 302T; /Motoring Picture Library: 129; /John Peter Photography: 212; /Andreas von Einsiedel: 387; /Tom Wood: 262. **Alessi S.p.A., Crusinallo, Italy:** 5, 75T, 150, 226, 293, 308R, 386. **Anglepoise:** 79L, 79R, 149. **Apple:** 16. **Archivio Superstudio:** 313. **Artemide:** 217L. **Barber Osgerby:** 24, 25T, 25B. **Barnbrook:** 27. **Bonhams:** 161. **Irma Boom:** 54, 55T, 55B. **Manuel Bougot:** 153. **Bridgeman Images:** /Christie's Images: 236; /The Israel Museum, Jerusalem: 292, 370; /The Sherwin Collection: 106. **Neville Brody:** 68, 69. **Daniel Brown:** 70, 71. **Bukowskis Market:** 32R, 45T, 45B, 63, 93B. **Steve Cadman:** 90. **David Carson:** 76, 77. **Design Museum Image Bank:** 65T, 83T, 83B, 85L, 85R, 93T, 98, 116, 117T, 132BL, 132BR, 180L, 180R, 184, 190, 200, 205, 216T, 216B, 251, 264L, 264R, 287, 310, 315L, 315R, 358L, 358R. **Tom Dixon:** 117B. **Dorotheum:** 168, 170T, 344. **Dyson:** 122, 123L, 123R. **Patrick Ernzen:** 49. **Estudio Campana:** 74. **Fiell Archive:** 12, 13, 14, 18, 32L, 39, 40T, 40B, 41, 43, 44, 47, 53, 75B, 78, 82, 89, 92, 94, 95, 102, 104, 108, 112T, 112B, 113, 114, 115, 118, 121T, 121B, 124L, 124R, 146, 169B, 174, 176T, 177, 182, 183, 194, 197, 204, 214T, 214B, 215, 220, 232, 237, 242, 246, 252, 254TR, 254L, 254BR, 257, 270R, 319T, 319B, 320, 321L, 331, 334, 340, 341T, 341B, 348, 357, 359T, 359B, 366B, 367, 372R, 374, 380, 385, 391. **Courtesy of Paola Fletcher & Raffaella Fletcher:** 134L, 134R, 135. **Flos s.p.a.:** 84, 308L. **Naoto Fukasawa Design Ltd:** 140, 141L, 141R. **Courtesy of fuseproject:** 37. **The Gentlewoman:** 327. **Getty Images:** 181; /Jonathan Bailey/English Heritage/Arcaid: 373; /Fabrizio Carraro/Mondadori Portfolio: 376; /Christie's Images: 107; /The Gallery Collection: 238; /Thomas A. Heinz: 213; /Imagno: 206, 207T; /Kim Kyung-Hoon/Reuters: 253; /Sigrid Schütze-Rodemann/Arcaid: 31B; /Science & Society Picture Library: 250; /Sovfoto: 368; /Stapleton Collection: 239, 333; /Universal Images Group: 369. **Milton Glaser:** 145. **Yo Gomi:** 198. **Fabrice Gousset:** 244. **Courtesy of Oscar Graf, Paris:** 42. **David Grandorge:** 164. **Konstantin Grcic:** 155B. **April Greiman:** 156; /Jayme Odgers: 157. **Guus Gugelot, Hamburg:** 162, 163. **Walter Gumiero:** 241. **Horm.it:** 178. **Iittala:** 88. **iStockphoto:** 144, 203T, 267, 318. **Georg Jensen:** 185. **Källemo:** 23. **Kamm Teapot Foundation:** 33T. **Susan Kare:** 188, 189T, 189B. **Kartell:** 4, 19R, 311. **Knoll:** 289. **Morgane la Gall:** 58. **Library of Congress:** 364; /Arthur H. Fisher: 219; /Carol M. Highsmith: 127T, 351, 379T, 379B. **Frederik Lieberath:** 245B. **Ross Lovegrove:** 208T, 208B, 209; /Gerhard Koller: 392. **M/M (Paris):** 210L, 210R, 211L, 211R. **Magis Design:** 166. **Maharam:** 187. **Marimekko:** 175. **David Mellor Design:** 221L, 221R. **MidCenturyDesign:** 147. **Herman Miller:** 36T, 36B. **Alex Morris Visualisation:** 9, 10. **Lars Müller Publishers:** 229. **NCSU Libraries:** /Hazel Larsen: 73. **Nendo:** /Daici Ano: 294; /Masayuki Hayashi: 295B; /Kenichi Sonehara: 295T. **David Newhardt, courtesy of Mecum Auctions:** 263. **Lena Paaske:** 245T. **Pentagram:** 258TL, 258TR, 258L, 258BL, 259. **Image courtesy of Phillips:** 227, 342, 343BL, 343BR. **Plank Collection:** 154, 155T. **Private Collection:** 35, 48T, 96T, 96B, 97, 201, 202, 260. **Gavin Proud:** 240. **Quittenbaum Kunstauktionen GmbH:** 50, 234, 235, 279, 329. **Rago Arts:** 365. **Paul Rand:** 276. 277L, 277R. **Rietveld Originals for Spectrum Design:** 280. **Rockstar Games:** 282L, 282R, 283. **Rosenthal GmbH:** 159. **Gordon Russell Museum:** 286. **Sagmeister & Walsh:** 290L, 290R, 291. **Viviane Sassen:** 326. **Design by Peter Saville:** 296T, 296B, 297TR; /Paul Hetherington: 297L; /Brett Wickens: 297BR. **Scala:** 285; /Digital Image Museum Associates/LACMA/Art Resource NY: 225; /The Museum of Modern Art, New York: 62, 109T, 119, 218, 305, 322, 323, 378. **Gerrit Schreurs:** 186. **Science & Society Picture Library:** /Science Museum: 172. **Shutterstock:** 15, 17, 67B, 148B, 176B, 191, 281, 390. **Smart Design:** 300, 301T, 301B. **Juhan Sonin:** 173. **Sony Computer Entertainment Europe:** 302B, 303. **Sothebys:** 299. **Studio Andrea Branzi:** 20. **Studio Bouroullec:** 61. **Studio Tord Boontje:** 56, 57. **Tahon & Bouroullec:** 59. **Tecta:** 158. **Treadway Gallery:** 127B. **Twentytwentyone:** /Mark Whitfield: 103. **University of Applied Arts Vienna, Victor J. Papanek Foundation:** 256. **ustwo studio Ltd:** 324, 325L, 325R. **Victoria and Albert Museum, London:** 160, 273, 274, 363. **VirusFonts:** 26L, 26R. **Vitra:** 60. **Marcel Wanders:** 336T, 336B, 337. **Wikimedia Commons:** 7, 19L, 22, 28, 29T, 29B, 30, 31T, 33BL, 33BR, 34, 46, 48B, 52, 65B, 66, 72, 80, 81, 86L, 87, 92, 109B, 120, 128, 130, 131T, 131B, 132T, 133, 136, 137, 138TL, 138TR, 139, 142, 143T, 143B, 148T, 151, 152, 167, 169T, 170B, 171, 199, 203B, 228, 231, 233, 269, 275, 284, 288, 298, 306, 321R, 328B, 330, 332, 353T, 353B, 362, 366T, 371, 372L, 375, 381, 388B, 393. **Ray Williams:** 99. **Collection of Jill A. Wiltse & H. Kirk Brown III, Denver:** 100, 101. **Image courtesy of Wright, Chicago:** 21, 51, 64, 105, 110, 111, 125, 126, 192, 193, 195T, 195B, 207B, 217R, 222, 223, 224, 230, 243, 248, 249T, 249B, 255, 261, 265, 266, 268, 270L, 271, 272, 278, 304, 307, 314L, 314R, 316, 317, 328T, 335, 338L, 338R, 339T, 339B, 343T, 345, 346, 347, 349, 350, 352, 356, 377T, 377B, 382, 383, 384, 388T, 389. **Yamagiwa:** 179. **Tokujin Yoshioka:** 355L; /Masayuki Hayashi: 354; /Nacása & Partners Inc: 355R. **Zanotta:** 312. **Courtesy of Zumtobel Lighting:** 165.

Every effort has been made to acknowledge correctly and contact the source and/or copyright holder of each picture and Carlton Books Limited apologizes for any unintentional errors or omissions, which will be corrected in future editions of this book.